Islamic Thought Through Protestant Eyes

Early modern Protestant scholars closely engaged with Islamic thought in more ways than is usually recognized. Among Protestants, Lutheran scholars distinguished themselves as the most invested in the study of Islam and Muslim culture. Mehmet Karabela brings the neglected voices of post-Reformation theologians, primarily German Lutherans, into focus and reveals their rigorous engagement with Islamic thought. Inspired by a global history approach to religious thought, *Islamic Thought Through Protestant Eyes* offers new sources to broaden the conventional interpretation of the Reformation beyond a solely European Christian phenomenon.

Based on previously unstudied dissertations, disputations, and academic works written in Latin in the seventeenth and eighteenth centuries, Karabela analyzes three themes: Islam as theology and religion; Islamic philosophy and liberal arts; and Muslim sects (Sunni and Shi'a). This book provides analyses and translations of the Latin texts as well as brief biographies of the authors.

These texts offer insight into the Protestant perception of Islamic thought for scholars of religious studies and Islamic studies as well as for general readers. Examining the influence of Islamic thought on the construction of the Protestant identity after the Reformation helps us to understand the role of Islam in the evolution of Christianity.

Mehmet Karabela is an internationally recognized writer and scholar of religion. He teaches at Queen's University in Canada.

Routledge Research in Early Modern History

Manila, 1645
Pedro Luengo

The Polish-Lithuanian Commonwealth
History, Memory, Legacy
Edited by Andrzej Chwalba and Krzysztof Zamorski

German Imperial Knights
Noble Misfits Between Princely Authority and the Crown, 1479–1648
Richard J. Ninness

The Scramble for Italy
Continuity and Change in the Italian Wars, 1494–1559
Idan Sherer

Artistic and Political Patronage in Early Stuart England
The Career of William Herbert, Third Earl of Pembroke, 1580–1630
Brian O'Farrell

Bringing the People Back In
State Building from Below in the Nordic Countries ca. 1500–1800
Edited by Knut Dørum, Mats Hallenberg and Kimmo Katajala

Negotiating Exclusion in Early Modern England, 1550–1800
Edited by Naomi Pullin and Kathryn Woods

Islamic Thought Through Protestant Eyes
Mehmet Karabela

For more information about this series, please visit: *https://www. routledge.com/Routledge-Research-in-Early-Modern-History/ book-series/RREMH*

Islamic Thought Through Protestant Eyes

Mehmet Karabela

Routledge
Taylor & Francis Group

NEW YORK AND LONDON

First published 2021
by Routledge
52 Vanderbilt Avenue, New York, NY 10017

and by Routledge
2 Park Square, Milton Park, Abingdon, Oxon, OX14 4RN

Routledge is an imprint of the Taylor & Francis Group, an informa business

© 2021 Mehmet Karabela

Library of Congress Cataloging-in-Publication Data
A catalog record for this title has been requested

ISBN: 978-0-367-54954-1 (hbk)
ISBN: 978-0-367-54959-6 (pbk)
ISBN: 978-1-003-09134-9 (ebk)

Typeset in Sabon
by codeMantra

Dedicated to the memory of Prof. Fuat Sezgin (1924–2018)
- Memento mori -

Contents

Figures

Map

Acknowledgments

This book has been in the making for some time. In this endeavor, I have been supported and inspired by many colleagues, students, and scholars whose comments and critiques have greatly enriched my work. My Queen's colleagues were instrumental in providing valuable feedback and support; I must especially express my gratitude to Howard Adelman, Ariel Salzmann, Adnan Husain, and Richard S. Ascough. Howard Adelman, the former Director of the Jewish Studies Program, read earlier drafts of this book and made significant recommendations for the contents and structure of the book. I am also grateful to him for inviting me to co-teach a seminar course on the European perception of Jews and Muslims during the Enlightenment. The course we taught together was a great stimulus in shaping this book and an opportunity to refine my ideas. I must gratefully acknowledge my appreciation for Ariel Salzmann's generosity in sharing her knowledge and insight on rethinking Ottoman and Islamic intellectual history in a transregional context. While re-writing and revising, I received invaluable feedback from Adnan Husain, who was crucial in clarifying my initial foggy ideas concerning my theoretical framework. Richard S. Ascough offered practical suggestions, which improved the flow of my argument. I also benefited from my discussion with Bill Morrow, a biblical scholar at Queen's, on Protestant theologians' interpretation of the Old Testament and the patriarchal age. I want to record my gratitude to Rebecca Manley, a historian of Russia and the Soviet Union, for contacting the National Library of Russia in Saint Petersburg on my behalf to obtain an eighteenth-century Latin dissertation on the Ottoman educational system. I would also like to thank Daryn Lehoux of the Department of Classics at Queen's for directing me to excellent research assistants, Ryland James Patterson and Laura R. Bevilacqua, for this project. I must also acknowledge my appreciation for Ahmet Şeyhun of the University of Winnipeg, who shared his incisive comments on the Protestant perception of Turkish politics and Ottoman political thought.

No amount of thanks could possibly convey my debt of gratitude to my research assistants as well as the individuals who helped me with some parts of the translations, and nuancing my understanding of early modern Latin, German, Persian, and French. I have been especially fortunate to work with the one of a kind Ryland James Patterson, an organized, sincere, and hard-working true scholar of classical studies. Ryland and I worked many hours, days, weeks, and months to solve intricacies in the Latin texts and provide a more straightforward syntax for the modern reader. Heartfelt thanks must be extended to Shawn Daniel, who also assisted me with translations and gave me the benefit of his expertise in the neo-Latin style; I cannot express enough my appreciation for his meticulous attention to details and generosity with his time. My research assistant Laura R. Bevilacqua, a native of Italy and a PhD candidate at the University of Chicago, enlightened me on the cultural context for some of the Latin usages that no other could have. Also, I extend my special thanks to my long-time friend in Germany, Ferhat Ayaz, a software engineer and stand-up comedian, who was always a source of intellectual lucidity when I struggled with seventeenth- and eighteenth-century German texts. I cannot forget our *Darmbstadii Nächte* in the State of Hesse and our drive to Mönchengladbach in North Rhine-Westphalia. For the Persian text, my graduate student Hasan Doagoo was kind enough to share not only his knowledge of the Persian language, but also his profound knowledge of Shiʿite history and theology. I owe a special thanks to my Québécoise friend, Alexandra Courchesne, for her review of my French translations. I was also lucky enough to have my gifted and efficient research assistants, Ben Simms, Ruth Chitiz, and Tim Robinson for this project.

I wish to acknowledge the scholars whose works influenced and inspired my own. I have benefited from Alastair Hamilton's and Martin Mulsow's contribution to early modern religious thought as well as the transregional aspect of European intellectual history. From the beginning, Alastair Hamilton has been kind enough to send some of his excellent articles from England, which were not available as interlibrary loans in 2015. He further helped me with certain aspect of the authors' biographies and the proper transliteration of Latinized versions of Arabic names and terms. I first met Martin Mulsow in an international workshop held at the American University in Cairo that we participated in before the Arab Spring in 2010. Since then, I have been reading and following his work on early modern German intellectual history, which has stimulated my research. I want to express my appreciation to Andrew Colin Gow for sharing his vision on the significance of global history as well as the relationship between the post-Reformation perception of non-Christian religions and Orientalism. My appreciation also goes to Jeremy Fradkin for sharing his book chapter in *The Oxford Handbook of the Protestant Reformations*, in chaotic Covid-19 days when the university libraries were closed and interlibrary loan services were not reliable. I am also grateful to the Persian scholar Mehdi Estakhr, who sent me his chapter on the role of Zoroaster in the post-Reformation religious controversies from his book *The Place of Zoroaster in History*.

The librarian Evgeniya L. Naydina of the Russian National Library in St. Petersburg has been most helpful in providing the Swedish Lutheran Matthias Norberg's dissertation from their collection. I would also like to thank the following librarians: Martina Albrecht, Sophie Schrader, Stefan Philipp, Milena Fein, and Susanne Greßirer of Bayerische Staatsbibliothek München; Eva Rothkirch of Staatsbibliothek zu Berlin; Annika-Valeska Walzel of Staats- und Universitätsbibliothek Dresden; Rolf B. Röper of Niedersächsische Staats- und Universitätsbibliothek Göttingen; and Dr. Gertrud Oswald of Österreichische Nationalbibliothek in Vienna for permission to use the images in my book.

I am indebted to Max Novick, my editor at Routledge, for his belief in my work and his commitment to excellence. I would also like to thank the anonymous reviewer for their detailed and extensive comments, which motivated me to rethink the organization and argument of the book and deepen my analysis. Thanks to Jennifer Morrow and Isabel Voice at Routledge for their assistance during the production process and also Aswini Kumar for overseeing the final formatting of the book. My appreciation goes to Susan Karpuk for sharing her professional experience with cataloguing Latin manuscripts at Yale University library, which clarified the most fundamental issue in determining the authorship in the early modern German dissertations. Also, my thanks to Michael Warford for designing and preparing the map of Protestant universities.

This book would not have seen the light of day without the immense intellectual contribution and emotional support of my partner Janet Louise Darlington. Many individuals have been generous in terms of offering their feedback, however, Janet, as a brilliant editor, has been there from the first page until the last to offer the modern reader the most accessible text. I owe an enormous debt of gratitude to her for making my arguments in this book more precise.

Writing a book is never an individual effort. Working on this project with a team of highly motivated and talented people made a Herculean task a pleasure. This book is theirs as much as mine. However, I am solely responsible for any mistakes or imperfections in this work: *nemo sine vitio est*.

Although this book took its final shape through the indispensable contribution of the above wonderful people, there is one person who deserves special acknowledgment. When I was working on early modern Islamic dialectic and argumentation theory (*ādāb al-baḥth*) for my PhD, the late Fuat Sezgin suggested I should also study *dissertationes*, *disputationes*, and *orationes* of German Lutherans in order to reframe Islamic thought in a global intellectual context. Sezgin kindly gave me copies of two

Latin works that were invaluable for the direction of my scholarship. As a younger scholar, I was humbled by his contagious enthusiasm and encouragement. He listened to my ideas as if he had something to learn from me, although the exact opposite was the case. Unfortunately, he passed away in 2018 and did not live long enough to see my book. It is to Fuat Sezgin that I dedicate this work.

Part I

Post-Reformation Protestant Uses of Islam

When Martin Luther wrote his ninety-five theses in 1517, he unintentionally set off the chain of events that led to the Reformation. His original aim was not to establish a new religion; rather, he expected to spark an intellectual debate with his fellow Wittenberg scholars on issues he was having with the Catholic Church. As a devout Catholic, Luther did not expect to divide Christianity or to be branded a heretic; he hoped to reform the Church from within. However, due to the intransigent response from the Pope and Luther's excommunication by the Church of Rome, he and his followers developed a separate religious identity over time. This religion came to be called Protestantism, with new churches emerging, such as the Evangelical in Germany and the Reformed (Calvinist) in Switzerland. After Luther's death, Lutheran theologians further struggled to differentiate their new identity from Catholicism and intra-Protestant movements.[1]

These developments did not, however, take place in isolation from other religious traditions, especially Islam. In the seventeenth and eighteenth centuries, this new Protestant identity was further defined by Lutheran scholars' engagement with Islamic thought. Despite this, many previous commentators on cultural and intellectual history interpret the Reformation and post-Reformation[2] as a uniquely Protestant-Catholic schism and intra-Christian confessional divisions.[3] There has been little emphasis on how post-Reformation Protestant thinkers engaged with Islam and used it as a foil to differentiate themselves from Catholics.[4]

On the following page (Figure 0.1),[5] the seventeenth-century anti-Catholic and anti-Muslim illustration in Lutheran theologian Johann Ulrich Wallich's book shows the mirrored imagery of both: the papal crown hovering above an altar, encircled by two fire-breathing serpents that are covered in frogs, lizards, insects, and scorpions. Over the heads of the two serpents is a large object resembling a turban, meant to be that of the Ottoman Sultan. Between the turban and the crown are the words "They are joined into a circle," implying an equivalency between Islam and Catholicism. On the altar are the words "Lest [they come] too close," and on either side are tall trees with banners draped around them. The banner on the left reads "unequal agreement in matters of fate," while the other reads "each of you either kill or shun!" When the phrases are considered together, they warn about the pernicious influence of Islam and Catholicism: "They are joined into a circle. Lest

Figure 0.1 The Papal Crown and the Turban of the Ottoman Sultan, "They [Pope and Sultan] are joined into a circle" (Courtesy of the Bavarian State Library, Munich).

unequal agreement in matters of fate [i.e., religion] come too close, every one of you either kill or shun [the infidel]!" The satanic depiction of the headdresses of the Sultan and Pope draws an equivalency between Islam and Catholicism, the serpents symbolizing both as evil. The Protestant reader, as he or she delves into an account of the exotic heresy of the Turks,[6] is thereby encouraged to draw parallels with the superstitions and heresies of the Catholic Church.

Although Protestant theologians and scholars of the seventeenth and eighteenth centuries closely engaged with Islamic thought, modern historians of religion have primarily focused on the Protestant-Catholic divide as the critical chapter in the history of Christianity.[7] This approach resulted in their seeing the Reformation and its aftermath as a European Christian phenomenon, isolated from other religious thought, including Islam.[8] Therefore, this book addresses this gap by exploring the engagement of post-Reformation scholars with Islamic thought, as well as Protestant disruptions with Catholicism and Judaism, using unpublished dissertations and academic works of Protestant scholars— primarily Lutheran theologians—from the seventeenth and eighteenth centuries.

During the seventeenth and eighteenth centuries, Islam and the life of Muhammad played a crucial role in the evolution of Christianity and religious thought in Europe.[9] While some Catholic theologians denigrated religious movements inspired by the Reformation, such as Socinianism and Unitarianism,[10] by comparing them with Islam, some Protestant theologians asserted the superiority of Islam over Catholicism. If Muhammad was the anti-Christ, then so was the Pope in the eyes of Protestants. To a lesser extent, Catholics also used Muhammad and Islam to denigrate Protestants, likening Luther to Muhammad and Calvinism to Muslim heresy. Furthermore, Protestant scholars also compared Islam to Judaism in order to strengthen their new religious identity.[11] Conversely, some Jews also used Islam against Christianity. For example, in his critique of Christianity, Venetian Rabbi Leon Modena (d.1648) presented Islam in a positive light by using a translation of the Qur'an and likened Islam to Rabbinic Judaism.[12]

Framing the Post-Reformation Study of Islam

The institutional and social shifts of the Reformation from Catholicism as well as encounters with non-Christian communities, especially Muslims and Jews,[13] provided the context for redefining the nature of religion by Protestant theologians and academics in European universities.[14] Among Protestants, Lutheran scholars distinguished themselves as the most invested in the study of Islam and Muslim culture. However, all Lutheran institutions were not the same in terms of their focus on Islam. For example, at University of Wittenberg, the center of Lutheran orthodoxy, scholars, influenced by their belief in *Sola Scriptura*, focused on the Qur'an as the basis of Islamic theology, and were not particularly interested in converting Muslims to Christianity. At the University of Halle, the center of Lutheran Pietism, the focus was on Islamic morality and religious conversion because they valued the individual experience with God. Theologians at Helmstedt, the center of ecumenism, as exemplified by Georg Calixt and the Syncretic Controversy, were interested in converting Muslims using universally accepted Christian beliefs, rather than confusing the catechumen with Protestant doctrinal differences.[15] Although there are exceptions, the Protestant denomination that prevailed at the university influenced the way scholars approached Islamic thought in their works. The map of Protestant universities in the seventeenth century shows the three major Protestant faith communities (Map 0.1).

Protestant academic works, specifically *dissertationes, disputationes, exercitationes, orationes,* and *disquisitiones,* give us an overview of the research and teaching in early modern Protestant academies and universities. These sources are a window into the ways Protestant scholars reinterpreted Islamic sources for their university students and teaching candidates in theology, philosophy, and literature. There are many unstudied dissertations on Islam, the Qur'an, and Muhammad in European university archives.[16] In German universities alone, there are more than a hundred thousand *dissertationes* and *disputationes* on almost all aspects of social sciences and the humanities.[17] A considerable number of these Lutheran works are concerned with Qur'anic studies, Islamic theology, the concept of predestination, the Sunni and Shi'ite schism, Islamic morality, Turkish politics, Arabic literature, and the state of learning among the Arabs.

This is not to suggest that only Lutheran theologians and academics contributed to this new study of Islam, but rather that they produced more in-depth works on Islam and gave it more attention than other Christians (i.e., Roman Catholics, Socinians,[18] Church of England scholars, [19] Calvinists,[20] Anabaptists,[21] and Quakers[22]). As Alastair Hamilton shows, German Lutherans in the early modern period studied Arabic and Islam, and produced more work in both quantity and quality on Islamic studies than their Catholic counterparts.[23] A possible explanation for German Lutheran interest in Islam lies in the expansion of the Ottoman Empire into Europe as well as the collapse of the relative religious unity of Christianity that occurred during the Reformation and after the Thirty Years' War. The dispute between Catholics and Protestants in a religiously divided Europe opened the way for Islam to become a field of battle.[24] Lutherans, in particular, seized on Islam as a weapon against Catholicism. To a lesser extent, they also used Islam to critique intra-Protestant divisions, such as the Pietist movement, the Syncretic movement, and the Reformed Church.

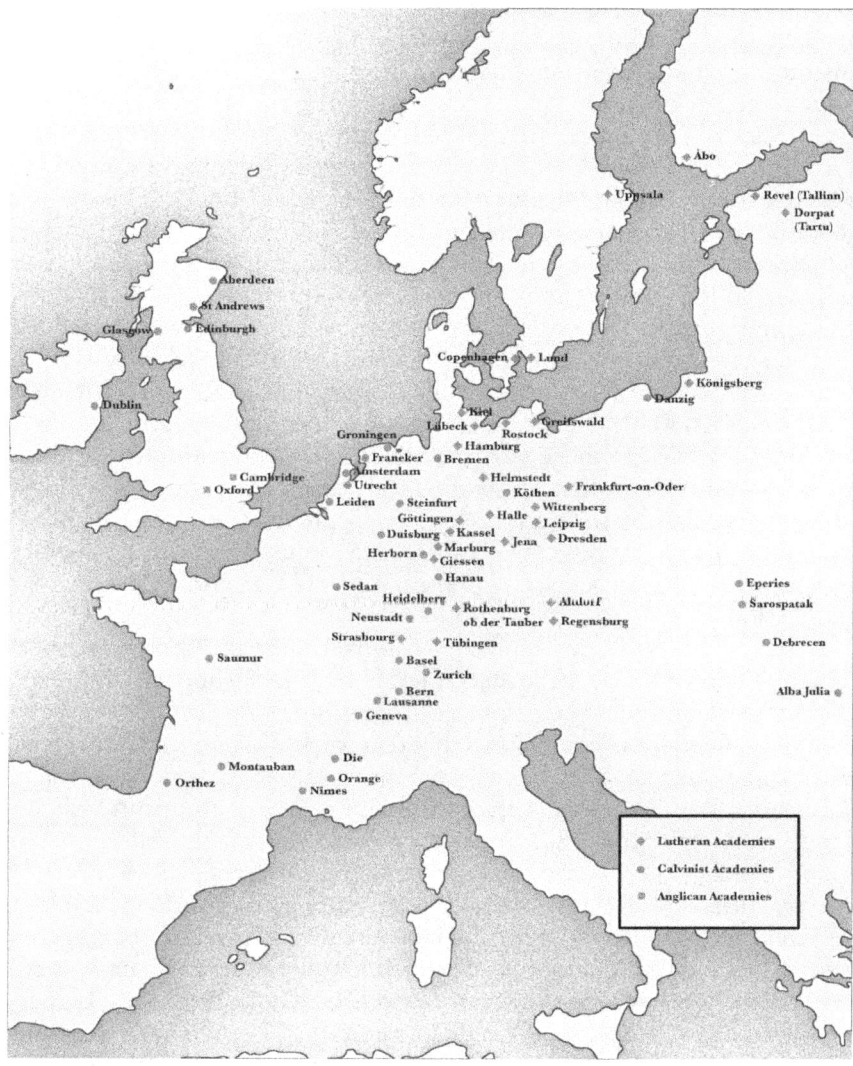

Map 0.1 Protestant Universities in the Seventeenth and Eighteenth Centuries.

The majority of Protestant authors selected for this work are German-speaking Lutherans who wrote their academic works (*dissertationes* or *disputationes*) and delivered their speeches (*orationes*) in Latin at major Protestant universities, such as Wittenberg, Leipzig, Helmstedt, Halle, Jena, and Danzig. However, these scholars should not be seen as homogenously Lutheran as the Reformation had neither a straightforward nor a consistent trajectory. For example, after Luther's death, Lutheran theologians became divided between Philipists, who were followers of Philipp Melanchthon (d.1560), and Gnesio-Lutherans, who opposed the Philipists on a number of theological matters, including justification, human participation in salvation, and problem solving that which was not prescribed in the scripture. Furthermore, after this short-lived initial split, Lutheran theologians divided into further groups: Orthodox Lutherans, Calixtinians, and Pietists. Orthodox Lutherans focused on understanding the true faith based on the scripture alone (*Sola Scriptura*), which resulted in an overly intellectualized form of Christianity.[25] Orthodox Lutherans defended their faith against not only Catholics, but also non-Lutheran intra-Protestant groups. This was the context for the beginning of Syncretism, a Lutheran pro-ecumenical movement started by Georg Calixt (d.1656) and his followers (Calixtinians) calling for unification between Orthodox Lutherans and Calvinists (Reformed Church).[26] Calixt also hoped to pacify the Catholics. This certainly appealed to those who were tired of the competition over "true faith" between Catholics, Lutherans, Calvinists, Arminians, Socinians, and others. This Syncretic Controversy inspired Orthodox Lutherans' interest in the Muslim Sunni-Shi'a divide to justify the lack of unity among the Lutheran sects, in opposition to the Calixtinians' desire for unification.

A further internal development within Lutheranism was the emergence of Pietism under the leadership of Philipp Jacob Spener (d.1705).[27] Pietism arose in the seventeenth century within both the Reformed and Lutheran Churches, originating in areas such as Bremen, Frankfurt, Halle, and Leipzig. Pietism was not only successful among German Lutherans, but also spread rapidly among Protestant groups in Switzerland, the Netherlands, Scandinavia, and the Baltics as well as in England where it played a prominent role in the emergence of Methodism. Pietism introduced a new paradigm by emphasizing individual piety, personal religious rebirth with Bible study, mysticism, and social activism. While Pietism did not break away from the Lutheran Church, it did lead to the development of new circles *within*. Unlike Orthodox Lutherans, Pietists tended to locate religious certainty in individual religious experience as opposed to Orthodox Lutherans' emphasis on adherence to their doctrine. As Lutheran emphasis on doctrine dominated the curriculum of Lutheran theological academies, Spener became critical of the use of the scholastic dialectical methodology in Lutheran theological education. He condemned it with his forceful statement: "The scholastic theology which Luther had thrown out the front door had been introduced again by others through the back door."[28]

Both the Pietist and Syncretic movements show that there were multiple perspectives within Lutheranism and that Lutherans studied Islam partially to understand their own intra-denominational developments and shifting beliefs. These scholars' perceptions of Islam and the competing ideologies within Protestantism provide an opportunity to further explore the impact of their ideas on the construction of modern Islamic studies.[29]

Global History and Post-Reformation Thought

Inspired by a global history approach to intellectual history, this book, therefore, provides new sources to challenge the received interpretation of the Reformation as a solely European and Christian phenomenon. Such an approach, recently propounded by German intellectual historian Sebastian Conrad, aims to incorporate regional units, such as Europe and the Ottoman Empire, into an integrated transregional narrative of history that acknowledges their interaction rather than viewing them as separate entities.[30] This book intends to show that the European Reformation and its evolution cannot be understood in isolation from Islamic thought. Conversely, Kecia Ali, an Islamic studies scholar, raised an interesting interpretation of modern Islam as part of the Protestant tradition.[31] Until recently, one core element of Reformation textual practice, *Sola Scriptura*, reading the scripture in isolation from their commentarial traditions (*sharḥ* and *ḥāshiya*), enjoyed wide acceptance among Islamic scholars. To support her view, Ali gives as an example Salafism, which prioritized the conduct of Muhammad and the first Muslim community rather than the opinions or interpretations of later scholars. Salafism was an influential intellectual movement that transformed into Islamic modernism and puritanical Wahhabism. Ali says that both reform movements owe a debt to Protestantism, including Protestant assumptions about clerical and textual authority.[32] Modernist Islamic movements, which prioritize the Qur'an over other religious texts (*ḥadīth* and *tafsīr*, or Qur'anic commentaries), show the influence of this Protestant understanding of *Sola Scriptura*. This was alien to pre-modern Islamic thought as the Sunni Islamic legal theory is largely based on extra-Qur'anic sources such as the Prophet Muhammad's sayings (*ḥadīth*) and the consensus of Muslim legal scholars (*ijmā'*). For these modernist thinkers, Islam means purely "Qur'anic Islam,"[33] based on values established in the Qur'an alone, independent of the traditions or customs.[34]

Therefore, the global nature of intellectual influences on modern Islam cannot be studied without considering other transregional actors, particularly Protestant scholars.[35] What is less acknowledged is the influence Islam had on Protestantism. From this perspective, Islam, as a theological utility, became a part of Protestant development as Lutherans used Islam for self-criticism against their Catholic origins. In this sense, history is dialectical as shown in the formulation and reformulation of religious ideas and concepts.[36] For example, Adam Neuser (d.1576), a German Lutheran pastor from Heidelberg, converted to

Islam and ended up living in Istanbul as a Muslim loyal to the Ottoman court and Sultan Selim II. Neuser was baptized as a Lutheran and became a Calvinist, before becoming a Muslim. Neuser was a Muslim convert working on a Latin translation of the Qur'an in Istanbul, who used his Christian background to translate and explain Islamic doctrine for his Lutheran and Calvinist friends and colleagues in Europe.[37] In this respect, a global intellectual history approach to religious thought proves to be an important tool for understanding history and society rather than the traditional divisions of regional and triumphalist Whig history that portray history as the product of internal events and agents alone.[38]

Earlier works by John V. Tolan and Suzanne Conklin Akbari examined the European perception of Islam in the medieval period. Norman Daniel not only addressed the medieval period, but also provided a broader survey of the Western perception of Islam up until the twentieth century.[39] However, recent studies by Alastair Hamilton, Martin Mulsow, Frederick Quinn, Asaph Ben-Tov, Humberto Garcia, Jan Loop, Gregory J. Miller, David Grafton, Gary Waite, Daniel Cyranka, and Alexander Bevilacqua, have studied some aspect of the perception of Islam by early modern scholars.[40] Among them, Alastair Hamilton produced several pioneering articles demonstrating the significance of the German Lutheran study of Islam in the seventeenth and eighteenth centuries. Martin Mulsow's scholarship further highlights the transregional aspect of Islamic thought and intellectual exchanges between Islam and Protestantism, especially Lutherans in the seventeenth and eighteenth centuries. Ian Almond's *History of Islam in German Thought* analyzes the understanding of Islam by focusing on the well-known eighteenth- and nineteenth-century German thinkers such as Leibniz, Kant, Goethe, Hegel, Marx, and Nietzsche.[41] John V. Tolan's recent work, *Faces of Muhammad*, traces the evolution of Western perceptions of Muhammad from the Middle Ages to the present without a specific focus on the seventeenth- and eighteenth-century Lutherans.[42] Additionally, Noel Malcolm's *Useful Enemies* examines Islam and the Ottoman Empire in Western political thought from 1450 to 1750, but without a focus on German Lutherans.[43]

Within this scholarly genealogy, my book contributes in three ways to these studies. First, it engages with unstudied post-Reformation theologians by providing translations and analysis of their works on Islamic thought (theology, philosophy, and sects). Second, it shows how Lutheran scholars used Islamic thought to further define their new religious identity in the context of intra-Christian (Protestants versus Catholics) and intra-denominational disputes (Lutheran versus the Reformed, Pietist, and Syncretic movements). Third, my book provides resources to challenge the subsequent evaluation of seventeenth- and eighteenth-century European thinkers as the seeds of a later Orientalism.[44] Up until now, Orientalism was largely seen as part of the history of colonialism or empire-building in the wake of Edward Said's influential work *Orientalism*. However, the sources I analyze in this book complicate this picture. In his book, Said did not include a study of the seventeenth- and eighteenth-century Lutheran theologians, who were not involved with colonialism or empire-building.[45] On the contrary, these Lutheran scholars felt extremely threatened by the Ottoman Empire's expansion into the heart of Europe.[46] As the threat of the Ottoman Turks continued until the end of seventeenth century, Lutherans became more interested in eschatology. Some Lutherans interpreted the Turkish advance as a manifestation of Gog and Magog; they considered this to be the proof that the prophesized final battle between the faithful and the Antichrist was at hand. Furthermore, these theologians had serious concerns about Christian conversions to Islam[47] since the conversion to Islam was central to the articulation of Ottoman imperial identity and the creation of Sunni Muslim orthodoxy against the Shi'ite Safavids.[48] Therefore, while I acknowledge the significance of Orientalist scholarship as part of the colonial enterprise in the nineteenth century, the Protestant works in this book were not written from a colonial perspective. Rather, these Lutherans used Islam to solidify their own Protestant identity, and their engagement with Islamic thought helped to expand the Christian canon beyond Catholicism.

Within this historical and theoretical framework, this book provides translations and analyses of dissertations, disputations, and excerpts from academic works to show the new perception of Islam by seventeenth and eighteenth-century Lutheran scholars. By new, I mean the re-evaluation of Islam giving rise to two distinct, and contradictory, points of view. On the one hand, Islam was seen as a relatively tolerant religion compared to Catholicism. On the other hand, it was a false and hollow religion, stained by empty rituals, also like Catholicism. In addition to the historical and political context, this new Protestant entangled perception was also the result of newly translated material from Arabic into either Latin or German, which became increasingly available to Lutheran scholars at that time as well as firsthand accounts from European travelers to the Ottoman Empire and Persia. Because they quoted extensively from the Qur'an and other classical Islamic sources, such as theological manuals and other historical works, they provided greater detail and depth in their analysis, which enabled them to be more knowledgeable and to appear more neutral in dealing with the origin and rise of Islam, while still presenting Muhammad as an impostor—albeit a smart political operator. They did, however, give more credit to Muhammad than earlier writers had, acknowledging Islam as a religion containing legitimate moral and theological principles of its own.[49]

To show this new perception of Islam, *Islamic Thought Through Protestant Eyes* is designed around three themes that are fundamental to understanding the perception of Islamic thought within Lutheran academic circles from 1650 to the 1800s: Islam as religion and theology; Islamic philosophy and liberal arts; and Muslim sects: Sunni and Shi'a. There is no section on Islamic mysticism (Sufism) or law (*Sharī'a*) in these works, because Lutheran authors seemed interested in neither. This omission says something about post-Reformation Lutheranism and its focus,[50] but the absence of Islamic mysticism may be an Orthodox Lutheran reaction against Pietism. This also explains why the first academic study on Sufism, *Sufismus sive Theosophia Persarum Pantheistica* (Sufism, or, the Pantheistic Theosophy of the Persians), was written by a Pietist Lutheran, August Tholuck (d.1877), published in 1821.[51] Although there are comments here and there in Lutheran works about Islamic law during this period, it seemed Lutherans were not particularly interested in law.[52] The answer for why early Lutherans as well as almost all post-Reformation Protestant scholars were not interested in Islamic law can be related to the nature of the Reformation itself.[53] As legal historian John Witte Jr. points out, Luther himself had more pressing theological questions rather than pondering on legal questions,[54] as expressed in one of Luther's most famous aphorisms, "Jurists are bad Christians."[55] Although Luther was not interested in law, Lutheranism and Calvinism had far-reaching influences on the evolution of legal philosophy, criminal law, civil, and economic law in Germany and England, and on the Western legal tradition as a whole.[56]

In the following pages, I analyze the above-mentioned three themes in these texts. Although I will provide each author's biography as well as a summary and analysis of each text in Parts II, III, and IV, the following analyses will consider all authors and texts, regardless of where the author's text is thematically located. These texts show the ways in which post-Reformation Protestants used Islam for their own purposes. This book serves as a starting point for sparking a conversation between modern religious studies scholars and Islamic studies scholars about the interconnected nature of post-Reformation Protestantism and Islamic thought as part of global intellectual history.[57]

Analysis of Themes

Religion and Theology

This section focuses on Islam as religious thought, a system of theology and morality viewed through the eyes of Lutheran scholars. I analyzed the texts using five sub-categories: Islam as a patchwork religion; rationality versus coercion; religious text and authority; faith, good works, salvation, and conversion; and moral laxity in Islam. All of the scholars considered here wrote at a time when European Christianity was fragmented and Islam and its theologies were caught in the maelstrom.

Protestant theologians used Islam to support the claim that Protestantism was not only 'true,' but also the only 'true religion' as it challenges each individual to have faith rather than focusing on good works.

Islam as a Patchwork Religion

One key characteristic of Islam, according to August Pfeiffer (d.1698), a well-known German Orthodox Lutheran theologian at the University of Leipzig, is that it is not original, but rather an uninspired patchwork of borrowed ideas.[58] Pfeiffer describes this religious tapestry as "poor" since evidence of the original sources is manifest throughout the Qur'an.[59] Created from both Judaic and Christian sources, the Qur'an, according to the Protestant narrative, was the handiwork of Muhammad, who learned all he needed to know about religion from a Nestorian monk named Sergius.[60] The narrative runs like this: Sergius had grievously sinned and was banished from his monastery. Later, he met Muhammad and tried to convert him to please the monks. Muhammad became his student and used the Old and New Testaments to fashion the Qur'an, a borrowed patchwork, which, in Pfeiffer's words, "was poorly implemented."[61] It is important to note that this understanding of a poorly implemented religion implies that Muhammad had neither the skill nor the knowledge to fully understand Jewish and Christian doctrine. It also meant that Sergius, who helped Muhammad craft the Qur'an, knew only an imperfect form of Christianity, being himself an exiled heretic and sinner. This is why Friedrich Ulrich Calixt (d.1701), a German Lutheran theologian at the University of Helmstedt, said that while Muslims do not reject canonical scripture, they are challenged by many Christian ideas and neglect key biblical passages.[62]

Calixt accepts that there were, of course, similarities between Islam and Christianity as the Qur'an acknowledges that Christ was born of the Virgin Mary and that he was a great prophet. What the Qur'an did not accept was Christ being "like the Father and consubstantial with Him."[63] Indeed, Islamic theology claims that passages relating to the coming of the final Prophet, Muhammad, in the Old and New Testaments were erased by Christians, so that the early biblical texts were corrupted. Conversely, since the Islamic theological view of Jesus did not incorporate all of the New Testament's elements, which Christians saw as testifying to Jesus being the Son of God, then, for Calixt, the Islamic view of the Bible was defective.[64]

Lutheran scholars saw Islam as a religious patchwork because they disparaged any religion that did not align with their own, including Judaism. For example, Pfeiffer claimed that the Jews "whisper against the terrible mystery of the Trinity," just as Muslims, using similar logic, call Christians *al-mushrikūn* (polytheists) due to their belief in a Triune God. A further example, again from Pfeiffer, is of Jesus criticizing the Jewish practice of animal sacrifice, which he says Muslims copied. Furthermore, Jews and Muslims emphasized regular fasting times,[65] unlike Luther who emphasized individual fasting over collective fasting and disliked the use of fasting by Catholics to try to win God's approval. Thus, by exposing the suspect Jewish practices that Muslims shared, the Protestant scholars could accuse Islam of being a patchwork religion, taking many of its worst ideas from the 'wrong religion' (i.e., Judaism), and by differentiating Protestantism from both Judaism and Catholicism, they could claim the theological high ground for their religion.

Rationality versus Coercion

Although Protestant scholars tried to show Christian thought as superior, they battled other Christians, chiefly Roman Catholics, for the title of the true faith. For Protestants, the criticism that Islam does not always follow the canonical scriptures was a failing for which Catholicism was also guilty. What we see here is the beginning of many commonalities found between Islam and Catholicism, and the use of these faiths to differentiate Protestantism from both. One of the more interesting commonalities is the idea that Catholicism, like Islam, spread by the sword. The "violent converters" in Islam, the Saracens, are equated to the "Catholic converters," the Inquisitors, who used violence against fellow Christians.[66] In fact, Catholics were worse than Turks, as Calixt said, since the latter at least attempted to initiate public peace with Christians, while the Roman Pope attacked non-Catholic Christians with sword and fire. What is interesting here is not the sword in itself, but rather that Calixt associated it with irrationality.[67] The sword represents irrationality, or to be more precise, losing one's head.[68] In Lutheran eyes, Muslims and Catholics were not able to convert other people through rational arguments, but used coercion.[69] Therefore, for Lutherans, Protestant faith represents the most rational religion as Christ Himself was represented by *Logos*, which they equated with rationality.[70]

Similarly, Johann Michael Lange (d.1731), a Lutheran theologian and lecturer at the University of Altdorf, criticized Catholics directly due to their suppression of the Qur'an by fire,[71] when it was first introduced to Europe.[72] Lange presents the Roman Curia as being so studious in doing away with all copies of the Qur'an published in Venice in 1530 that it seemed as if the Qur'an had only recently found its way to Europe in the 1690s.[73] Lange cites several sources to show how the Qur'an had, in fact, existed in Europe for some time and explains that the Roman Church was afraid for their Catholic community's well-being, believing that the Qur'an would lead to conversions and thus had the copies burned.[74] For Lange, however, this fear of conversion is disproven by reading the Qur'an since, he argues, it contains falsehoods and contradictions that would not impress any rational person. Furthermore, he declares that the Qur'an is no less dangerous than other pagan texts which the Church hypocritically permits. He calls for the burning of the Qur'an to stop unless the Church is willing to burn other pagan books as well.[75] By tracing the history of the publication of the Qur'an in Europe,[76] Lange was able to use Islam to separate the Protestant identity from the Catholic. Lange believes that, while Protestants can study different religious texts critically and reveal their flaws in the light of 'rational' Protestant dogma, Catholics are illogical and hesitant about their own doctrines, so they burn books instead of exposing their doctrinal fallacies. In this respect, Lutherans are convinced that theirs is the more rational religion.

Religious Text and Authority

The defining foundational principle of the Reformation is its scripture-based belief (*Sola Scriptura*). This requires no extra-scriptural authorities to understand the text. As a result, Pfeiffer tends to categorize Islamic and Jewish thought into two camps: scripturalists and traditionists—Shi'ites and Sunnis, and Karaites and Rabbanites, respectively.[77] Further, Calixt emphasizes that Christians feel the internal force of the Holy Spirit when they ponder both Testaments since the Holy Spirit is revealed through the scripture.[78] This means that the doctrine extracted from the Bible gains its own authority through scripture without papal or institutional approval. For this reason, Calixt accuses Catholics and Muslims of not properly following canonical scriptures, even though they believe in them.[79] For Lutheran scholars, Muslim's refusal to acknowledge Christ as the Son of God meant that they misinterpreted the scriptures,[80] while Catholics, believing in Christ's divinity, introduced their own interpretations rather than basing their belief on the scripture itself.[81]

Consequently, this scripturalist view affected the way Lutheran scholars perceived not only Islamic and Catholic, but also Jewish thought. In Pfeiffer's text, for example, he refers to two schools of thought in Judaism and also in Islam.[82] For Pfeiffer, Karaites, a minor Jewish sect content with their sacred scriptures, do not accept extra-textual oral traditions that were codified in the Talmud and Midrash as binding. However, the major Jewish sect, the Rabbanites, accept these oral traditions, which they embrace with the same veneration and piety as they do scripture. Similarly, the Persian Muslims (Shi'ites) are a smaller sect that accepts the Qur'an as the only written religious authority, while the Turkish Muslims (Sunnis) accept the Qur'an and also the *Sunna* or *ḥadīth*, written texts, which act, according to Pfeiffer, as an oral law or tradition.[83] This is a crucial point for the post-Reformation scholars—although it reveals a key Protestant preconception. By projecting their own understanding of the scripture onto Judaic and Islamic religious authorities and using this as evidence that Islam and Judaism had split into sects due to different understandings of the relationship between the text and religious authority, these scholars criticized Catholics, who also ignored the authority of the scripture only (*Sola Scriptura*) and valued their own commentaries on the scripture.

Faith, Good Works, Salvation, and Conversion

The Islamic acceptance of both faith and good works as paths to salvation is emphasized by several Lutheran authors, allowing them to implicitly criticize Catholics who hold a similar view while Protestants believe faith alone can save. In the spirit of Luther's doctrine of *Sola Fide*, Hieronymus Kromayer (d.1670), a German Lutheran theologian and the Dean of the Theological Faculty at Leipzig, sees Muslims as those who, like Catholics, mistakenly believe in both faith and good works as paths to salvation. He argues that Muhammad promised Muslims would be saved through faith in one God and through good works, especially fasting, alms, prayers, and pilgrimage.[84] Kromayer outlines his understanding of the Islamic path to salvation: "Muhammad often says that the sins of a generous person who does not expect a reward will be forgiven. If a man feeds ten paupers, or clothes them, or redeems captives, he can obtain forgiveness for his sins…"[85] Also, Kromayer tries to find a parallel Muslim position on the Christian doctrine of atonement: "But Muhammad says nothing about the free forgiveness of sins through and according to Christ's merit."[86] He also emphasizes that Muhammad believed even a Christian or Jew who has lived uprightly can obtain salvation.[87] To Orthodox Lutherans like Kromayer, the belief in a path to salvation other than through faith in the one true religion, Lutheranism, is a pernicious false doctrine.[88]

Kromayer blames several Christian heresies for propagating false teachings, such as the Arian idea of pursuing their enemy with the sword, which he believes made their way into Islam.[89] Kromayer's statement implies that these heresies have influenced Islam to hold a false view of salvation, similar to that held by the Catholic Church. Pfeiffer goes beyond Kromayer and draws a comparison between Islam and Judaism, critiquing both religions for promising salvation through good works.[90] Likewise, Johann Karl Valentin Bauer, an eighteenth-century Lutheran theologian who wrote his dissertation on Turkish Muslim theology, notes that Muslims believe in both faith and good works, although Bauer acknowledges that Muslims place greater importance on faith.[91] Pfeiffer is less charitable, as he argues that Muhammad contradicts himself in the Qur'an by stating that salvation is gained by grace, not good works alone; to a Lutheran theologian, only faith is a valid means to salvation.[92]

Unlike many other Lutheran authors, Calixt is concerned with the conversion of Muslims to Christianity. He echoes the Pietist emphasis on the issue of conversion of others and oneself through the constant renewal of faith.[93] As a Calixtinian, Muslims are not just a foil with which to criticize Catholicism, but represent an opportunity to save souls through the adoption of universal Christian teachings. Calixt states that religious dogma that is unanimously agreed upon by Christian sects is what should be presented to Muslims for their conversion; otherwise, one would run the risk of confusing Muslim catechumens with conflicting dogmas. The key to the salvation of Muslim souls lies in this presentation of non-ambiguous sacred texts. According to Calixt, the unclear verses in the scripture are never related to salvation. Since Muslims believe that the Christian scripture is divinely revealed, it should be possible to convince them of the divinity of Jesus by pointing to relevant passages in the Bible, and pointing out the false dogmas of Islam, Catholicism, and Christian heresies.[94] Calixt says that potential Muslim converts to Christianity should not be troubled by complex logical reasoning. He insists that the focus should be on essential dogma and self-evident foundational teachings from a reading of the scripture rather than the use of syllogisms to understand complex issues.[95] Otherwise, the potential convert could be turned away from Christianity by the multiplicity of sects, or choose the wrong sect to convert to. This danger can be avoided by focusing on those teachings upon which Christians universally agree.[96] This ecumenical form of Christianity looks suspiciously like Lutheranism, as he thinks other sects of Christianity, especially Catholicism, are deficient in their doctrines for various reasons. Thus, Calixt advocates for a stripped down basic form of Christianity as ideal for converts, while simultaneously portraying Lutheranism as closest to this ideal.

Moral Laxity in Islam

Focusing on the dissertation by Christian Benedikt Michaelis (d.1764), a German Pietist professor at the University of Halle, this section looks at the claim that Muhammad consciously and strategically created a morally lax faith system to win converts.[97] Other post-Reformation Protestant scholars provided reasons for the rapid spread of Islam, such as the sword, internal factions in Christianity, and God's curse.[98] Although Michaelis believes that all of these explanations are valid, he has a particular theory for why Islam spread so quickly: moral laxity, appealing to man's basic corruptibility and love of ease.[99]

Michaelis argues that the prime example of Islam's moral laxity lies in Muhammad's emphasis on 'easiness' in the Qur'an (Q. 2:181): "God wants easiness for you and does not want difficulty for you." According to Michaelis, this is used as a clever cover for all types of immorality, since any moral precept involving the exercise of self-restraint or denial is negated in Islam by God's permissive and indulgent nature. Michaelis contrasts this with quotations from the New Testament warning that the path to salvation is hard. Also, for Christians, self-control is to be exercised and revenge abjured in all circumstances, while for Muslims revenge is permitted. Michaelis disregards the Old Testament's "eye for an eye" approach to personal or public enemies; he only considers the New Testament's approach of "turning the other cheek." In analyzing the issue of revenge in Islam, it is as if the Old Testament is not a part of his scripture. He believes Muhammad willingly caters to humanity's baser instincts.[100]

For Michaelis, Islam's attitude toward sexual immorality is similarly lax; while forbidding acts such as adultery, Islam does not sufficiently shame and suppress lustful thoughts. Nor is its acceptance of polygamy and divorce moral to the Protestant sensibility of that time. He contrasts a verse in the Qur'an, whereby a woman who converts to Islam may leave her nonbelieving husband, with a teaching from St. Paul, which says that a Christian convert should not leave her nonbelieving husband.[101] This reveals Islam's laxity toward divorce. Michaelis concludes that Muhammad's emphasis on easiness and his unwillingness to restrain baser instincts, such as lust and vengeance, makes Islam an attractive, but less moral, religion. Bauer, Pfeiffer, and Schelwig also consider sexuality as one of the most important aspects of Islam, saying that Muhammad's populistic approach to sexuality goes beyond this life and promises good Muslims a sensuous heaven, transforming Paradise into a *lupanar* (brothel).[102]

Michaelis gives other examples of Islam's moral laxity. While martyrdom in the face of persecution is celebrated in Christianity, Muhammad encourages Muslims to lie or even to deny their faith to save their lives, signaling a lack of principle among its adherents. He also criticizes Islam's non-retroactive enforcement of laws, particularly those concerning the prohibition of incest and usury (*ribā*). Muhammad recognized pre-existing incestuous marriages and said that no restitution was necessary from those who profited from usury. Michaelis contrasts this with a quote from Saint Augustine—a sin is not forgiven unless recompensed.[103] Furthermore, according to Michaelis, Muhammad swore oaths on frivolous things and granted a four-month window of grace during which Muslims could renege after taking an oath.[104]

According to Michaelis, Islam takes advantage of the corruption that dwells in all mortals to attract followers and creates a religion around it. For him, since Arabs were a race accustomed to living by the sword, the promise of great spoils and a ticket to Paradise through death in battle would appeal to many.[105] In short, for Michaelis, Islam was a religion crafted to take advantage of weak people who could not resist man's corrupt ways, especially as he thought Arabs were a rapine people. When Michaelis says that he hopes God illuminates the "light of the Gospel" upon the nations that Muhammad had deceived by creating a morally lax religion,[106] he means to create an identity for the Protestant religion as the one true faith that challenges people to be morally upright. Like a medieval alchemist, Michaelis turns the criticism of one religion into a theological narrative to validate another, his own.

Philosophy and Liberal Arts

This section introduces Lutheran views on the origins and development of Islamic philosophy in the context of Aristotelianism and Scholasticism. According to these authors, early Muslims learned a corrupted version of Aristotle, while later Muslims, especially the Turks, used philosophy and science for practical purposes such as building naval ships and producing military equipment. This utilitarian approach to philosophy presented a serious threat to Europe in the eyes of Lutheran authors. Two significant ideas permeate these texts: first, that Islam is a barrier to philosophical thinking because it is antithetical to reason; and second, that the highest truth is revealed in true ancient Greek philosophy, not in the corrupted Scholastic form as advanced by Catholics and Muslims.

I also included an important text on political philosophy, *Disputatio politica de republica Turcica (Politics of the Turkish Republic)*.[107] This particular writing demonstrates how Lutherans draw a parallel between the tyrannical Turkish monarchy and the Catholic Church, represented by the untrustworthy Pope and the 'satanic writings' of the Catholic Machiavelli. The final two texts discuss Muslim philosophical education and liberal arts among the Arabs and Turks. These illustrate the Lutheran argument that Muhammad feared the study of philosophy and argumentation would challenge his religious authority, much like Luther's argumentation challenged the authority of the Pope. Despite Muhammad's perceived prohibition of these sciences, these texts also reveal Lutheran academics' awareness of the continuing study of philosophy and liberal arts among the Turks, Persians, and Arabs.

Origins of Islamic Philosophy

According to these Lutheran scholars, the origins of Islamic philosophy had less to do with religion than with its cultural context; that is to say, with the people among whom it arose: pre-Islamic Arabs. Johann Peter von Ludewig (d.1743), a German Lutheran lawyer and historian, maintains that pre-Islamic Arabs, eager to learn and share such things as language, speech, poetry, and knowledge of the stars, influenced Greek philosophy as much as the Greeks influenced the pre-Islamic Arabs.[108] For his part, Johannes Steuchius (d.1742), a prominent Swedish Lutheran academic and theologian, claims that philosophy originated in the East and that Greek philosophers drew many of their ideas from the East— key Arab contributions being in astronomy and logic.[109] These Lutheran

scholars emphasized pre-Islamic Arab contributions to Greek philosophy and liberal arts prior to the arrival of Islam.

Although there is general agreement that Arabs had some semblance
of philosophical thinking, Lutheran scholars saw a lull in the development of philosophy among the Arabs with the arrival of Muhammad.
There it slumbered until re-awakened by Christian philosophers, such
as the Nestorian Abū Bishr Mattā b. Yūnus, the Jacobite Yaḥyā ibn
'Adī, and Ḥunayn ibn Isḥāq.[110] In other words, Christians saved Muslims from their dormancy by introducing modes of rational thinking
into their culture and delivering scientific and philosophical thinking to
Islam. Steuchius notes, for example, that during the reign of the Abbasid
caliph al-Ma'mūn (r.813–33), a Christian physician was appointed as
head of a group of learned men because al-Ma'mūn believed that Christians were the most learned men of their day. Although philosophy and
literature were taught in mosques during al-Ma'mūn's reign, Steuchius
claims that Muslims could not have restored their lost learning were it
not for the influence of Christian thinkers.[111] These scholars considered
Islamic philosophers irrational, particularly compared to the Enlightenment thinkers with whom they identified. Moreover, they believed in a
victim-savior complex, where Muslims were intellectual captives of their
faith, dependent on Christians to deliver them to a place of reason.

Aristotelianism, Islamic Philosophy, and Scholasticism

While Muslim societies had contributed to philosophy, physics,
mathematics, and metaphysics, these scholars thought that Islamic
thinking was inherently flawed. According to the Lutheran theologian
and philosopher Johann Weitenkampf (d.1758), the lack of logic in
Islamic physics, metaphysics, and mathematics accounted for the absurd
principles that Muslims held, such as a belief in fate.[112] Steuchius claims
philosophy re-emerged among Muslims when Christians introduced
Greek literature to the Arabs, leading many to travel to Greece to study
philosophy and the liberal arts.[113] Ludewig theorizes that it might have
been trade between Christians and Arab Muslims that introduced
Muslims to Greek philosophy.[114]

Even though Martin Luther and early Reformers criticized Aristotelianism as the dominant paradigm in theology due to its extensive use by
Catholic Scholastics,[115] most post-Reformation Lutheran scholars saw
Greek thought as the pinnacle of philosophy.[116] For his part, Ludewig
believes that Christianity (or, more specifically, Protestantism) was
wholly compatible with philosophical thinking due to its logical or
enlightened nature, since the Christian idea of God as *Logos*, in his eyes,
represents reason and rationality.[117] Through a Protestant reading of the
history of philosophy, many scholars gave specific historical examples of
Christians providing scientific and philosophical assistance to Muslims

through Greek learning. For instance, when the Arab physicians were baffled by the illness of caliph Hārūn al-Rashīd's wife, the caliph sent a Christian physician to save her.[118] For Johann Jakob Brucker (d.1770),[119] the well-known Lutheran historian of philosophy, this reduced the caliph's bigotry toward Christians, and he repaid by returning confiscated Christian lands in Egypt. Ḥunayn ibn Isḥāq, another Christian physician, translated many Greek works for al-Ma'mūn, making himself one of the fathers of Arabic philosophy.[120]

Even so, some Protestants, such as Christian Friedrich Rudolph Vetterlein (d.1842), a Reformed theologian and philosopher, claims that the translations from Greek into Arabic possessed by Muslims were very poor and led to a misunderstanding of Aristotelian logic.[121] In the opinion of post-Reformation Protestants, philosophy reached its zenith during the Reformation, which implied that pre-Reformation Christians— and Catholics specifically—had not grasped the true nature of Aristotelian philosophy. The reason I use the word "true" is because Johann Georg Walch (d.1775), a Lutheran theologian and professor of philosophy, uses it deliberately.[122] The Protestant call for a return to "true Aristotle" is similar to the Reformation call for a return to the correct text and true teachings of the scripture. Walch argues that Jews and Muslims were incapable of fully understanding the fundamentals of Aristotelian truths. However, he believes this led to Islam spreading Arab-Aristotelian philosophy to Spain and ultimately to the creation of Scholasticism.[123] He also explains that only Christian logicians preserved Aristotelian truths within their system of theology. On the one hand, Walch maintains that the system of theology taught at the medieval European universities (Scholasticism) was created through the introduction of Arab-Aristotelian philosophy into Spain and Africa. However, he thinks, both Muslims and Jews corrupted Aristotelian philosophy by combining it with their "weak theology."[124] On the other hand, he contradicts himself by praising Christian Scholastics for being the ones—and the only ones—who use their philosophical understanding to defend their theology.[125]

Walch's theory that Islamic theology was the source of Scholasticism discredited the logic of Catholic theologians as many of them were Scholastics. These post-Reformation scholars tended to see the history of philosophy divided by the Reformation.[126] In this sense, Lutheran theologian and polymath Christoph August Heumann (d.1764) argues that the Reformation is not merely about Church reform; it is a wholesale rejection of the Catholic interpretation, or to be more precise, the Catholic corruption of Greek philosophy.[127] Luther himself forcefully declared that the Church of Thomas (referring to Thomas Aquinas) was nothing other than the Church of Aristotle,[128] which, according to Heumann, makes Thomas simply a "commentator (*Auslegern des Aristotelis*)."[129] Therefore, a considerable number of Protestant scholars condemned

Catholic Scholasticism as corrupt, so that they could establish a "true Aristotelian" philosophy to save Reason (*Logos*), which they equated with Christ Himself.[130] Even though Luther and early Lutherans were critical of the use of Aristotelian philosophy and the Scholastic method in theology, there are diverse opinions toward Aristotelianism and Scholasticism among Protestants, even among some Lutherans themselves, such as Gnesio-Lutherans and Philipists.[131] After Luther's death, Lutheran theologians became divided for a time between Philipists, who were followers of Philipp Melanchthon, and Gnesio-Lutherans, who opposed the Philipists. Some Lutherans used Aristotelian logic and disputation methods in their own curriculum in their academies and universities. There was also a widespread acceptance within the Calvinist circles of Scholastic approaches to theology using Aristotelian logic as a method. Therefore, dialectic as outlined in Aristotle's *Organon* played a big role as an educational tool of theology and Biblical exegesis out of which Reformed Scholasticism grew.[132] Although there were diverse opinions on Scholasticism and Aristotelianism, prominent eighteenth-century Lutheran theologians and historians of philosophy such as Christoph August Heumann, Johann Franz Buddeus, and Johann Jakob Brucker thought Scholasticism was an exclusively Catholic methodology and that the Reformation freed Protestants from both the authority of the Pope and of Aristotle.[133]

Islam as an Anti-Intellectual, Anti-Rational, and Enthusiastic Religion

Lutheran scholars, such as Ludewig and Koch, believed that Muhammad declared war on the liberal arts (*belles-lettres* or *ars liberalis*), which had grave consequences for those who studied them.[134] However, the reason they gave for Muhammad declaring war on liberal arts was personal: he was an illiterate man and feared that philosophy and the liberal arts would cause him to lose power.[135] Indeed, the perception of Islam being anti-intellectual began with the idea that Muhammad could neither read nor write (*ummī* or illiterate person),[136] which, to some like Steuchius, rendered him ignorant.[137] As a Pietist, under the influence of Enlightenment culture,[138] Michaelis also called Muhammad an enthusiastic man,[139] echoing the Lutheran concept of enthusiasm (*Schwärmerei*) as irrational tendencies in religion, such as miraculous revelations, inspired ecstasies, prophetic trances, and excessive sexual fantasies.[140]

Therefore, Lutheran scholars believed to hide the Qur'an's many inconsistencies and to remain in control Muhammad suppressed philosophical logic and reasoned argument. This led his followers to undervalue ancient philosophy and Arabian literature. However, due to Muhammad's illiteracy and disregard of ancient philosophy and literature, Christians and Jews in the Arabian Peninsula were called upon to assist in framing

Muhammad's new religion as expressed in the Qur'an. From a Protestant perspective, this anti-intellectual, illiterate, and enthusiastic root explains why, after Muhammad's death, only 'sober' Christians living in the region continued to study Greek and to introduce their Islamic neighbors to philosophy.[141]

This re-introduction narrative, propounded by Lutheran scholars, accounts for how Eastern nations contributed to philosophy and yet were saved by learned Christians. It explains why, left unchecked, Islam would corrupt philosophy with its religious dogmas and enthusiasm, and also, why the proponents of Arab-Aristotelian philosophy did not fully understand Greek thinking or recognize the irrationality of their own theology. In fact, these scholars claimed philosophy heightened tensions among Muslims themselves since their religion was built on superstition and not rational explanation.[142] The critique of Islamic philosophy was not only a Lutheran criticism, but was also based on the Enlightenment idea of "rational philosophy (*philosophia rationalis*)."[143] Islam, with its repudiation of philosophy and the liberal arts, was flawed and irrational, which cemented Protestantism's place as the most rational of all religions.[144]

However, this Lutheran critique should not be interpreted as a pure critique or simplistic polemic against Islamic philosophy. The critique of Muhammad being illiterate, anti-rational, and enthusiastic reveals the intellectual environment of the late seventeenth and early eighteenth centuries. Here, their critique serves an important purpose: to defend Lutheranism as the most rational faith in the wake of radical Enlightenment using the relationship between revelation and reason in order to restore the place of reason in religion.[145]

Philosophy as a Practical Instrument and Physical Threat

Lutheran philosophers recognized that Islam and its philosophy were a real and imminent threat to Europe. Samuel Schelwig (d.1715), a philosopher and a proponent of Lutheran orthodoxy, claimed that Turks used mathematics predominantly in such areas as sailing, naval warfare, and the fortification of buildings and cities, knowledge of which they learned from Christians.[146] He thought that the forms of philosophical thinking beloved of Islam and the Ottoman Turks were militaristic, which rendered philosophy as a practical instrument. Schelwig said that rather than studying philosophy as abstract thought, the Turkish Muslims were interested only in the apprehended 'table and cup' and not in a philosophical discussion on 'tableness' and 'cupness' that they did not even see.[147] His exposes Islam and Turkish Muslims as a threat to Christian Europe because he praises the European King John III for pushing the Turkish Hannibal before the gates of Christendom. He declares he too will attack Islam with whatever skill he has; evidently, Schelwig's war would be fought with philosophy.[148]

The Lutheran perception of Ottoman philosophy as strictly milita-ristic and practical is the result of the perceived idea of Turks' inabil-ity to understand theoretical philosophy. Schelwig sums up this idea by referencing a debate between Diogenes and Plato on the latter's concept of ideas. He compares the mentality of the Turks to that of Diogenes the Cynic, saying that "he [the Turk] has eyes, with which the table and cup are seen but he does not have a mind, with which the 'tableness' and 'cupness' are seen."[149] He argues that Ottoman schol-ars lack the theoretical capacity that Europeans possess, and because of this, Islamic philosophy was limited to a stunted form of metaphys-ics which cannot see beyond the basics of reality into the realm of ideas. To show the traces of this type of metaphysics, Schelwig cites a Latin translation of 'Azīz Nasafī's most popular treatise *Maqṣad-i Aqṣā (The Furthest Goal)*[150] on the difference between God's essence and existence.[151]

Weitenkampf uses the example of the Turkish concept of fate to further contribute to the notion that Turkish philosophy is practical rather than theoretical.[152] He argues that the Turkish concept of fate is foolish and illogical as Weitenkampf believes all events in the world are mutable and contingent. The Turkish belief in predestination encourages them to stay in their plague-ridden cities and, most importantly, bolster their martial resilience. Turks were formidable enemies as they believed they could not change the date they were predestined to die so were unlikely to quit the field of battle.[153] Eric Ormsby, a scholar of Islamic studies, sees this type of fatalism, which "causes the Turks not to shun places ravaged by plague," as a reassertion of Ash'arite theology in Islamic thought—a uniquely Muslim response to the problem of theodicy.[154] Muslim fatalism, or *Fatum Mahometanum* as the eighteenth-century German Lutheran philosopher Gottfried Wilhelm Leibniz called it,[155] was based on the reasoning that everything in life good or evil, including death, was written by Allāh, so there was no escape. This is why Leibniz criticized the Muslim idea of fate as the "sophism of lazy reason" and asserted the superiority of the more rational and sophisticated Protes-tant understanding of fate, which he called *Fatum Christianum*.[156]

Many Protestant scholars held negative views about Islam's historical encounters with philosophy. Although they recognized the historical significance of philosophical thought within the ancient Eastern na-tions, they, nevertheless, believed that Islam created an intellectual barrier that held Muslims back, and any positive semblance of phil-osophical thinking after the era of Muhammad was due to Christian intervention. This supported their view that Muslims could not develop their own philosophical thought and that Islam, left alone with philoso-phy, was a danger to Christian Europe as they were considered reckless fatalists.

Political Religion and Islamic Governance

In the late sixteenth century, a distinctive academic discipline dealing with politics (*politica*) as a science was established at Protestant universities in Germany. Although politics claimed its relative independence as a discipline by dissociating from other sciences, its closest rival disciplines remained ethics, theology, and law. In this context, a subdiscipline emerged as political theology (*theologia politica*). German historian Martin Mulsow argues that Lutheran scholars, such as Johann Heinrich Boeckler (d.1672), Daniel Clasen (d.1678), and Daniel Georg Morhof (d.1691), believed one had to maintain the force of Protestant Christianity, spirituality, and religiosity against the Catholic Machiavellians and political elites.[157] They understood the concept of political religion not as a component of reason of state, but as the political function of religion as political elites were using religion for domination. Many seventeenth-century Lutherans saw this development as a dangerous form of politics. They believed religion should never be used to achieve political ends, but should only contribute to the spiritual good. Based on this political theology, Lutherans found themselves in a challenging position. Either one could interpret divine rule as a way to understand and legitimize rulers or states; or one could use the concept of political idolatry, seeing rulers as idols, to criticize and discredit Catholics.[158]

Mostly, the Lutheran scholars in this volume chose to take the second option and to separate religion from the political sphere. The German Lutheran biblical scholarship, under the influence of Lutheran doctrine of the two kingdoms, highlighted the non-political character of the Christian Gospel, from the early seventeenth century onwards. This Lutheran interpretation has contributed to the view that earlier Christianity was non-political but rather spiritual, dominated by the eschatological expectation of the end of the world; this view emphasized that the Christian religion is separate from politics.[159] Therefore, Lutherans saw both Catholicism and Islam as political religions by nature.[160] In his comparison of the Sunni and Shi'a Muslim sects, Pfeiffer compares the religious leaders of both sects to the Catholic Pope.[161] In his opinion, the mixing of the political and religious spheres was responsible for the schism that split Islam in the first place; Shi'ites performed political and religious acts in the name of 'Alī, a religious figure, against the Sunni sect.[162] Schelwig also draws a negative comparison between Turkish Sufi dervishes and Catholic Jesuits, as both groups inserted themselves into politics where they do not belong.[163]

Michael Wendeler (d.1671), a Lutheran professor of theology at the University of Wittenberg, sees a negative political-religious parallel between Islam and Catholicism. He opens his disputation with the image of the little horn from the book of Daniel, which he associates with the Turkish Monarch.[164] In his eyes, Turkish Muslims had a monarch, not a king, since their leader was a tyrant, ruled with violence, and was only able to gain territory due to the divisions between his Christian neighbors. In explaining the nature of this tyranny, Wendeler bases his arguments on Aristotle's *Politics*, in which the ruler was a tyrant who was unaccountably acting in his own interest, but not in the interest of his subjects.[165] Wendeler also critiques Catholics who believe in a tyrannical way of governing, and surprisingly praises the Turkish Sultan as more trustworthy than the Pope.[166] For him, the Catholic Church is on the same playing field as Islam, but as the losers. Therefore, in Wendeler's eyes, both Catholics' and Muslims' politics and their way of governance have corrupted their religions.

Muslim Sects: Sunni and Shi'a

This section examines Lutheran uses of the Sunni-Shi'a schism by focusing on four sub-themes: pre-Islamic religion and the introduction of Islam; the perception of 'Alī and Ṣafī al-Dīn al-Ardabīlī; the authority of the scripture and oral tradition; and saints and miracles. When Lutheran scholars looked at the Sunni-Shi'a divide, they saw two nations—the Sunni Ottoman Turks and the Shi'ite Safavid Persians—but their interest in that divide was related to the Protestant-Catholic schism after the Reformation. Although these scholars tackled the questions "What is religion?" and "What can be considered a religion?," they were not primarily interested in the inner workings of Islam or its sects. Instead, they used the political-theological split within Islam to justify the Protestant-Catholic divide in Christianity and to establish Protestantism as the true religion.

While it is safe to say that these Lutheran scholars did not hold Muslims in high regard, especially Muhammad, believing him to be an impostor with mad teachings, what is more significant is that they recognized Islam was not a single entity and they differentiated Safavid Persians (Shi'a) from Ottoman Turks (Sunni).[167] This shows an increased awareness and knowledge of Islam compared to their Reformation predecessors. However, these Lutheran authors held Persian Shi'ites in higher regard than Turkish Sunnis. For example, Sebastian Kirchmaier (d.1700), a Lutheran professor of theology at the University of Wittenberg, wrote his *Oratio Persica* in Persian about the Sunni-Shi'a divide (see Figure 0.2). All of Kirchmaier's other works were written in either German or Latin; one wonders why he wrote specifically in Persian. In introducing Kirchmaier's work, Johann Erich Ostermann (d.1668), the Rector of the Academy of Wittenberg, refers to Persians as an "ancient and exceptionally noble nation" whereas, for him, the Turks are "foul and four-day-old swill."[168] Luther himself also wrote extensively against the Turks, but not the Persians. Ostermann would have been strongly influenced by Luther, but he was also born into an anti-Turk milieu.[169]

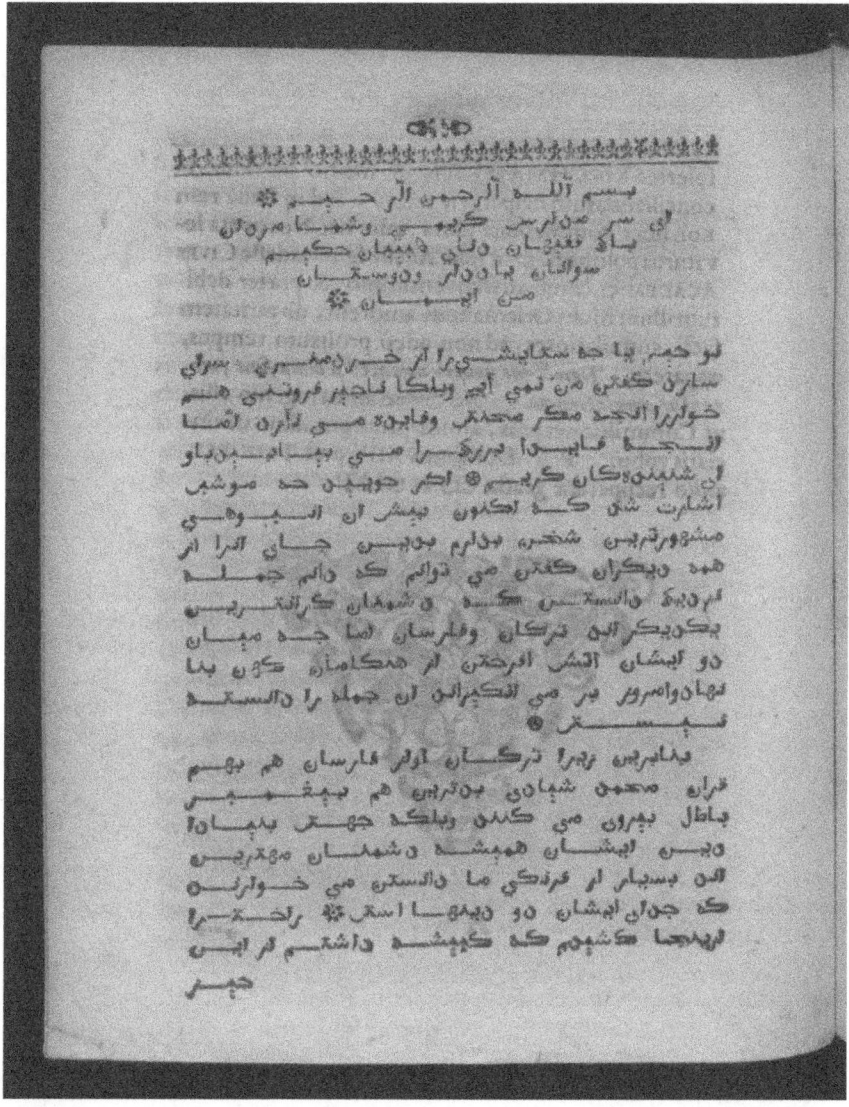

Figure 0.2 Sebastian Kirchmaier, *Oratio Persica* in Persian, 1662. Kirchmaier wrote his speech in Persian as the script for a lecture delivered in September 1662, the year he received his degree at the University of Wittenberg; it was simultaneously published with a Latin text. (Courtesy of the Staatsbibliothek zu Berlin, Preußischer Kulturbesitz).

Lutheran scholars did not sympathize with Persians because they valued the Shi'ite faith, but rather because they could use it to weave a specific historical narrative that supported their own theological preconceptions, especially *Sola Scriptura*. Moreover, the German Lutherans had not suffered from recent military defeat by the Persians, but the expansion of the Ottoman Empire in Europe was a present danger that influenced their judgment of the Sunnis.[170]

Pre-Islamic Religion and the Introduction of Islam

Prior to considering any inherent differences between Persians and Turks, the Lutheran scholar Pfeiffer began with an explanation of the pre-Islamic backgrounds of these Muslim nations. He says that in the distant past Persians worshipped the sun, which developed into a cult of Venus and then into a cult of Fire, both early forms of worship similar to that of the ancient Romans who worshiped Vesta.[171] For him, none of the past Persian gods and deities is the God of Abraham. Pfeiffer describes Persians as polytheistic; however, he sees them as an ancient nation more relatable to European Christianity than the Sunni Turks. His equation of Persia's final beliefs before the introduction of Islam to the ancient Roman worship of Vesta is especially pertinent; after all, the Romans had persecuted Christians, but they were also a major reason for Christianity's success—hence the name Roman Catholics. However, according to Pfeiffer, the Turks lived in a time of ignorance, steeped in savage idolatry with numerous gods and goddesses, worshipped many gods; and, hence, they were polytheistic pagans.[172] This leaves an image of the Persians being relatable, but flawed, and the Turks being ignorant and cruel.

As for the introduction of Islam to both nations, Pfeiffer explains that the Turks absorbed Muhammad's teachings from the beginning, becoming the most passionate champions of Islam, while the Persians, in contrast, adopted Islam and Muhammad's teaching because of Arab military expansion. During the conquest of Persia, the Prophet Muhammad's second successor, the caliph 'Umar, extinguished the fire of Gaures—the fire cult and belief system—before Islam's introduction into Persia. Pfeiffer believed that Persia (the Sassanid Empire) embraced Islam because of Islamic military domination, while the Turks naturally accepted Islam as the final incarnation of the Abrahamic religions.[173] In other words, the Turks were religious zealots bent on expansionism, whereas Persians were forced to accept Islam. The Turks were presented as harsh and cruel like the Arabs and Muhammad while Persians were perceived as noble and non-threatening. This view was the result of seventeenth-century real-world events as the Ottoman expansion caused Lutherans to fear the Turks as a growing menace to Christendom. Similarly, Kromayer had seen Islam's threat to Christianity firsthand in the captive Christians held in the Ottoman Empire. Since many Christians had witnessed Turkish violence, he believed Christian Europe had more in common with the peaceful Shi'ite Persians than with the militaristic Sunni Turks.[174]

The Perception of 'Alī and Ṣafī al-Dīn al-Ardabīlī

One of the most important reasons for the separation of the two Islamic sects was their perception of 'Alī, whom the Shi'ites expected to assume the mantle of a religious leader (*imām*) after Muhammad's death. According to Kirchmaier, the Sunni Turks accepted Muhammad's four consecutive successors: Abū Bakr, 'Umar, 'Uthmān, and 'Alī. They considered them all outstanding men, companions of Muhammad, and all legitimate successors to him. However, the Safavid Persians believed that 'Alī, Muhammad's cousin and son-in-law, was his rightful successor, a position wickedly usurped by others greater in power.[175] Therefore, to use Kirchmaier's words, "an unworthy exile and banishment came to 'Alī and his sons."[176] Although this was not the root of the schism in Islam, it became the dominant belief for the Safavid Persians after Ṣafī al-Dīn al-Ardabīlī (d.1334) claimed to be a descendant of 'Alī and imposed himself and this version of events on his followers.[177] For post-Reformation Protestants, the image was of a squabbling family fighting among themselves over trivialities, not too distant from the trifling debates about Rome's holy relics.

While the Lutheran scholars may not have fully understood or agreed with Shi'ite theology, they sympathized with its cause far more than they did with the Sunni Turks. Kirchmaier was inclined to support the notion that the succession was unjustly taken from 'Alī, lending legitimacy to the Shi'ite claim for the foundation of their sect. As a Lutheran, Kirchmaier could look at al-Ardabīlī and see Luther—which is not to say that he gives legitimacy to Islam's religious claims, but rather that he identifies with a fellow religious renegade. Surprisingly, though, he also demonized al-Ardabīlī, seeing him more as an impostor than a reformer. It may seem contradictory, but once again we must recognize Kirchmaier's intent behind his exploration of Islam. On the one hand, he uses al-Ardabīlī to underscore similarities between Protestantism and Shi'ite Islam. On the other hand, by presenting al-Ardabīlī as a false prophet, Kirchmaier presents the Persians as coerced into adopting al-Ardabīlī's version of Islam.

Kirchmaier and Pfeiffer acknowledged the importance of al-Ardabīlī for Shi'ite history and also the Safavid rulers' use of his spiritual authority as a source of legitimacy for a type of new Shi'ism in the early sixteenth century. However, Lutheran scholars did not seem to be aware that it was the sixteenth-century émigré scholars (*'ulamā'*) to Persia, who first provided sources of legitimacy for Safavid rulers as an ideological defense against the Sunni Ottoman Turks. Rula Abisaab shows how this process of converting Persia to Shi'ism took place through the leading Arab scholars from Ottoman Syria, Iraq, Bahrain, and Jabal 'Amil (present day Lebanon), resulting in a distinct, urban, and legalistic type of Shi'ism.[178]

Lutheran scholars' analysis of 'Alī reveals a Protestant theological viewpoint in their interpretation of the Sunni-Shi'a divide. Kirchmaier, for example, describes the veneration of 'Alī as excessive, claiming that "the Persians profess that if 'Alī did not reach God's divinity, he at least came close to it."[179] Likewise, Pfeiffer also argues that the Persians "following their 'Alī, make him semi-divine."[180] Pfeiffer, based on al-Shahrastānī's analysis, claims that a branch of Shi'a believes in 'Alī as the one "in whose form God appeared, and by whose hands He made the world, and by whose tongue He gave his teachings."[181] Some of these statements sound similar to those Christians say about the divinity of Christ. This similarity—the conflation of 'Alī with Christ—helped Lutheran theologians identify more with the Shi'ite sect than with the Sunnis.[182]

Authority of the Scripture and Oral Tradition

In the eyes of Lutherans, one of the key religious differences separating Sunni Turks from Shi'ite Persians is their interpretation of scripture and oral tradition. Both groups accept the Qur'an as the canon of their faith, with Turks also following the *Sunna*, which Pfeiffer calls "oral law." For him, the *Sunna* or *ḥadīth* collections were the product of seven men who diligently compiled Muhammad's sayings, deeds, and actions and passed them down through their descendants. Since Turks follow these separate *ḥadīth* traditions along with the Qur'an, they were often referred to as traditionists.[183] Pfeiffer presents Persians, on the other hand, as scripturalists, decrying anything not in the Qur'an, which aligns with the Protestant doctrine of *Sola Scriptura*.

In describing the scriptural differences between Turks and Persians, Pfeiffer compares Jewish traditions and sects with both. For example, he compares the Persians to the Sadducees since they both rejected unwritten traditions, and the Turks to the Pharisees who followed not only the written texts, but also unwritten laws and ancient traditions. Pfeiffer makes clear that Islam, like Christianity, has been divided into different and opposing sects, based on their understanding of scripture, oral history, and tradition. He emphasizes a similar split in Judaism when he compares the mutual enmity of Persians and Turks to the way in which the Karaite Jews were despised, because they rejected the Talmudic traditions of the Rabbanites.[184]

Protestant theology is similarly scripture-based, its adherents believing that all one needs for faith can be found in the Bible. One can see, therefore, why the Protestants would sympathize with the Shi'ites, who take scripture as the sole canon—while Catholics, like the Sunnis, believe in traditions and beliefs that developed outside the scripture. Although a modern reader may see the description of the two sects' interpretation of the Qur'an as quite straightforward, a Catholic reader at the time would be appalled to see their traditional ways being compared to the Turks. By incorporating Jewish sects into his argument, Pfeiffer is commenting on traditionists as intolerant toward other scriptural-based sects. By discussing the Karaites and how they were hated, Pfeiffer is not only highlighting the Turks as being intolerant toward the Shi'ites, but is also commenting on the Catholic Church and their intolerance of Protestants. Furthermore, highlighting the idea that the other two major religions had schisms based on scripture versus tradition justifies the Reformation.

Saints and Miracles

According to Pfeiffer, while Turks and Persians venerated ancient saints and visit their tombs, the Turks also believed in more modern (living) saints and their miracles. As he does not give credence to their marvels, Pfeiffer refers to these miracle workers as impostors. In Kromayer's account, the Persians elevated 'Alī to sainthood as he was someone to "whom they attribute many miracles, and nearly extoll above Muhammad himself."[185] While 'Alī's miracles and his marvelous sword are venerated,[186] along with his lineage and successors, whose tombs the Persians visit annually, the Turks, as noted by Kirchmaier, considered this contemptible—although they do elevate Muhammad's other successors to 'Alī's level in a religious quid pro quo.[187]

Even though the Lutheran scholars distinguished between the saints of the Persians and Turks, they were looking not to elevate one above the other, but rather to criticize the concept of sainthood. Unlike Catholics, Lutherans do not pray to saints or call upon them for guidance. Furthermore, the description given of Islamic saints, their deeds and who they protect, resembles the Catholic veneration of saints. Thus, the Lutheran analysis of Turkish and Persian saints was not to support one Islamic sect against the other, but rather to highlight the fundamental problem of sainthood itself. Luther himself asserted that all believers are saints, not a few select persons the Catholic Church declares to be saints, and that no believer could save another as only Christ can intercede for human salvation.[188]

We have seen how Lutherans used similarities between themselves and the Persians to validate their own religion. Now, with miracles and sainthood, we see how they use both sects to undermine Catholicism and to strengthen their own theological claims. If one considers the critique of two important Catholic concepts, sainthood and miracle, by Protestants after the Reformation, one can see these as defining differences. Protestants drew a boundary between natural and supernatural by rejecting miracles as they believed the age of miracles had passed and that miraculous intervention by God was strictly limited to biblical times. Therefore, they denied the possibility of mystical visions, revelations, and all other supernatural events; they were all things of the past or Catholic hocus-pocus.[189] As for sainthood, Protestants also defined the relationship between life on earth and the hereafter, resulting in a sharp distinction between the living and the dead. This interpretation meant the living and the dead could no longer communicate or experience miracles. In other words, the Reformation not only removed the bodies of the dead, the saints, from the churches, it also made their souls inaccessible: there were no longer any saints to pray to for help or favors. These Protestant theological underpinnings on miracle and sainthood had immense ramifications for the reinterpretation of the sacred and the profane, ultimately leading to a secular view of human life (*Entzauberung der Welt*).[190]

Epilogue: A Note on the Texts

Though many modern intellectual historians trace the secularization of the world to the Enlightenment philosophers with their focus on rationality,[191] they tend to overlook the earlier contribution of post-Reformation Protestant theologians who removed some of the miraculous and mystical elements from the Christian religion, by their dismissal of saints and miracles.[192] These theologians contributed to the evolution of Enlightenment ideas such as rationality; these ideas did not originate strictly from the philosophers or freethinkers of the eighteenth century. Like Luther, who was unaware he was creating the Protestant religion when he published his ninety-five theses, these post-Reformation scholars were unintentionally contributing to a secularized world view in which religion has been marginalized.[193]

Intellectual historians tend to study famous thinkers, such as Leibniz, Kant, Hegel, and Marx, to understand the trajectories and changes in early modern European thought. However, the Protestant scholars in this book helped create the intellectual milieu in which these famous philosophers thrived. Some of these theologians were also well known in their time, but have slipped into obscurity in ours. Weitenkampf, one of the Lutheran theologians and philosophers included in this book, was the schoolmate and peer of well-known German philosopher Kant. In today's undergraduate class, students who are familiar with Kant have never heard of Weitenkampf. Kant's 1784 famous essay "Was ist Aufklärung? (What is Enlightenment?)" is often featured in the syllabus of undergraduate philosophy and religion classes. What is not commonly known today is that Kant and Weitenkampf studied philosophy and metaphysics together in Königsberg under the direction of

Professor Martin Knutzen, a follower of the Enlightenment philosopher and Lutheran theologian Christian Wolff. At University, the young Kant debated the question of the spatio-temporal finitude of the Universe with Weitenkampf. Kant had a rivalry with him as Knutzen favored Weitenkampf and did not consider Kant one of his better students.[194] Nevertheless, Kant's rivalry with Weitenkampf inspired Kant to write his thesis on the first antinomy in his famous *Critique of Pure Reason*.[195] Unfortunately, the early death of Weitenkampf at age thirty-two prevented him from developing his ideas and publishing, whereas Kant survived to the age of seventy-nine, publishing important works and thus ensuring his place among Enlightenment thinkers.

Likewise, Pfeiffer influenced the faith, thought, and, possibly, job opportunities of the famous German composer Johann Sebastian Bach, who had many of Pfeiffer's theological works in his library.[196] There are two theories for Bach's interest in Pfeiffer's work, *Anti-Calvinismus*, a study of the differences between Lutheranism and Calvinism. Either, Bach was recommending them to his young wife, or he was studying them to ensure he sounded appropriately Orthodox Lutheran as opposed to Calvinist when he wanted to move from his position as Capellmeister at Calvinist Köthen to a position as cantor and director of music in Lutheran Leipzig.[197]

One of the Lutheran authors, Cornelius Dietrich Koch wrote an influential work on the method of studying the history of logic, which was encouraged by the famous German Lutheran Enlightenment philosopher Leibniz.[198] The latter discussed his metaphysical work with his seniors, including Hobbes, Spinoza, and Locke, but he also consulted with the younger Koch.[199] Therefore, these unstudied but influential Lutheran authors' texts will not only shed light on the post-Reformation uses of Islamic thought, but also help understand these theologians' influence on Enlightenment thinkers.[200]

A Note on the Translations

The Question of Authorship

The title pages of most of these works list a *praeses*, which in this context may be translated as supervisor, and a *respondens* as defender. The modern reader would be forgiven for thinking that the thesis supervisor/defender system worked as it does in a modern university.[201] This would mean that the *praeses* acted as a modern thesis advisor, providing guidance and critiquing early drafts, whereas the defender is the actual author of the dissertation. However, unlike in modern times, it seems that usually the *praeses* was the actual author of the dissertation, which was then publicly presented and defended by someone else. Susan Karpuk agrees with Kevin Chang's convention that authorship should be assigned to the *praeses*, unless the defender is specifically named the *auctor* or author of the dissertation.[202] Therefore, according to this convention, I have assumed that the *praeses* is the author of a work unless it is explicitly stated otherwise. For each author, I have compiled a short biography. If you would like to see a full list of the authors' works, you can consult the sources provided in the endnotes of each text.

Latin Texts, Readability, and Flow

The archival information about the original texts used for translations are provided in the bibliography. Most of the original texts are located in German libraries (Augsburg, Berlin, Dresden, Göttingen, Halle, Jena, Munich, and Regensburg); however, some texts were found in libraries in France (Paris), Austria (Vienna), and Russia (St. Petersburg). The translations are intended to be accessible to modern readers, but also to encourage researchers' further study of these Protestant academic works. Therefore, scholars who want to compare the translations with the Latin texts are recommended to review the sources in the bibliography.

The Latin in which these authors composed their texts is often a tangle of lists, digressions, and clauses within clauses. As a general principle, my main concern was to produce readable translations in modern English that remain faithful in meaning to the original text. I have, therefore, attempted to strike a balance between a literal translation of the Latin texts and a more reader-friendly idiomatic modern English translation. Although I am primarily concerned with readability, I also want to transmit to the modern reader some of the literary flavor of the Latin texts, which tend toward floridity, prolixity, and even pomposity at times.

In the Latin texts, the authors often use first person plural pronouns, "we" and "our," to refer to themselves; I have converted these to "I" or "my" for the most part. Oftentimes, an ambiguous pronoun or verb form has been replaced with a proper noun to ease readability. For example, an ambiguous "he" referring to Muhammad is replaced with "Muhammad." I have changed passive-voice sentences to the active voice as much as possible. For clarity in modern English, I have eliminated certain instances of repetition, excessive verbiage, and unnecessary details to provide a more concise and smooth text for the reader. To this end, I have sometimes altered or eliminated overly prolix passages or clauses, without giving up any fundamental points in the text.

In several cases, authors make factual errors about Islamic theological concepts. For example, a *jinn* is interpreted as a "family spirit" of a dead infant as opposed to the Islamic notion of the *jinn* as a supernatural creature that has nothing to do with a dead infant or the family.[203] Needless to say, authors' conceptual or terminological errors have not been corrected in order to remain faithful to the original text.

Technical Issues

I have replaced the original Latin form of names as they appeared in the text with the modern or transliterated version of the Arabic, Turkish, and Persian names giving the Latin original in the index. For instance, I use Yaʻqūb al-Kindī instead of the Latin Jacobus Alcendius; al-Mutawakkil and not al-Motawacelus; ʻAzīz Nasafī and not Aziz Nesephaeus; Abū al-Barakāt al-Baghdādī and not Baruch ben Malka; Henry of Ghent and not Henricus Gandavensis; Otto of Freising and not Otto Frisingensis; René Rapin and not Renatus Rapinus; Hıdırellez and not Chiridelles; Hızır İlyas and not Chederle; al-Shahrastānī and not Sharastanius; al-Ṭūsī and not Ettosius; al-Qazwīnī and not Kazuinensis; Sunna and not Sunnaton; Sunni and not Sunita; and Mongols and not Mogulenses. If there is no accepted modern transliteration for a term, I kept the author's original Latin expression of the word or term. However, frequently used names and terms that have become a part of the English language such as Muhammad, Ramadan, Abbasid, Sunni and Shiʻa have not been transliterated. Also, birth and death dates of Muslim thinkers are given where appropriate, according to the Islamic (*hijrī*) and Christian (Julian/Gregorian) calendars; thus, (d.864/1459) corresponds to 864 *anno hegirae* and 1459 *anno domini*.

Most Latin book titles have been translated to English to make them more accessible to the reader. Scholars who want to see the original Latin titles of book of the texts can easily consult the original text. In all texts except Text 4, I have removed the authors' footnotes due to the length of the book. In instances in the translated texts where I inserted my opinion or provided the reader with additional information, I identified these endnotes with my initials [MK]. All sources I used for the authors' biographies are given in the endnotes of the translations.

For Bible quotations, I have used the New American Standard Bible for numeration. In some cases, I have also altered my own initial translation of the biblical verses to conform in whole or in part to that from New American Standard Bible. Qur'anic references are expressed in this format: Q.13:24; the first number refers to the *sūra* (chapter) and the second the *āyah* (verse). Many of the Qur'anic references in the original texts do not correspond with the modern numeration of the Qur'an as these scholars often used the editions of the Qur'an published in the seventeenth century by German Lutheran theologians Salomon Schweigger (d.1622) and Abraham Hinckelmann (d.1695). Therefore, in all instances I have corrected the authors' *sūra* and *āyah* numbers, conforming to Yusuf Ali's numeration so that the modern reader may consult these passages.[204]

If I needed to provide the Arabic, Turkish, or Persian equivalent of a Latin word, I have provided them in parentheses. However, if I thought it was necessary to insert a word or short expression in the text, I used brackets to clarify the meaning in English. Italics were used to identify the book titles as is the standard in modern English; however, in some cases, I also retained the original authors' use of italics for emphasis. I use an ellipsis [...] to indicate an omission in the text. I eliminated sentences or paragraphs where there were unnecessary or lengthy explanations, which would divert the reader from the main discussion or topic.

In the appendix, I have compiled a selected bibliography of additional works by Protestant scholars on Islamic thought to aid further study and research. I have also included a map illustrating the geographical regions relevant to the authors of these texts and the academies and universities they are affiliated with, including Lutheran, Calvinist, and Anglican universities in the seventeenth and eighteenth centuries.

Like most translations, finding the right or the best possible word in another language, especially considering the three-to-four century gap between these authors and twenty-first-century readers, is a challenging task. Therefore, in cases where there was a need to explain something, I have drawn upon my expertise in Islamic studies to provide the reader a more accurate and accessible translation.

Notes

1 On the emergence and evolution of the Protestant identity and narrative in Europe, see Christopher Ocker, *Luther, Conflict, and Christendom: Reformation Europe and Christianity in the West* (Cambridge: Cambridge University Press, 2018); Peter Marshall, *1517: Martin Luther and the Invention of the Reformation* (Oxford: Oxford University Press, 2017); Eamon Duffy, *Reformation Divided: Catholics, Protestants and the Conversion of England* (London: Bloomsbury, 2017); Thomas F. Mayer (ed.), *Reforming Reformation: Catholic Christendom, 1300–1700* (Burlington: Ashgate, 2012); Heinz Schilling, *Martin Luther: Rebell in einer Zeit des Umbruchs* (Munich: C. H. Beck, 2012); John M. Frymire, *The Primacy of the Postils: Catholics, Protestants, and the Dissemination of Ideas in Early Modern Germany* (Leiden: Brill, 2010); Ulinka Rublack, *Reformation Europe* (Cambridge: Cambridge University Press, 2005); Michael A. Mullett, *Martin Luther* (London: Routledge, 2004); Ronald K. Rittgers, *The Reformation of the Keys: Confession, Conscience, and Authority in Sixteenth-Century Germany* (Cambridge: Harvard University Press, 2004); Heiko A. Oberman, *The Two Reformations* (New Haven: Yale University Press, 2003); C. Scott Dixon, *The Reformation in Germany* (Oxford: Blackwell, 2002); Hans R. Guggisberg and Gottfried G. Krodel (eds.), *Die Reformation in Deutschland und Europa: Interpretationen und Debatten* (Gütersloh: Gütersloher Verlagshaus, 1993). Also, for the importance of Luther's colleagues in Wittenberg in the creation of the movement, see Jens-Martin Kruse, *Universitätstheologie und Kirchenreform: Die Anfänge der Reformation in Wittenberg, 1516–1522* (Mainz-am-Rhein: Philipp von Zabern, 2002).

2 As most of the authors in this book wrote their works between 1650 and 1750 following the Reformation, I use the term "post-Reformation" to define the historical period from the 1600s to the early 1800s.

3 On this scholarship, see A. G. Dickens and John M. Tonkin, *The Reformation in Historical Thought* (Cambridge: Harvard University Press, 1985);

John Bossy, *Christianity in the West 1400–1700* (Oxford: OUP, 1985); Geoffrey R. Elton, *Reformation Europe: 1517–1559* (Oxford: Blackwell, 1985); Alister E. McGrath, *The Intellectual Origins of the European Reformation* (Oxford: Blackwell, 1987); Euan Cameron, *The European Reformation* (Oxford: Oxford University Press, 1991); Andrew Pettegree, *The Early Reformation in Europe* (Cambridge: Cambridge University Press, 1992); Luise Schorn-Schütte, *Die Reformation: Vorgeschichte, Verlauf, Wirkung* (Munich: Verlag, 1996); Carter Lindberg, *The European Reformations* (Oxford: Blackwell, 1996); Mark Greengrass, *The European Reformation c.1500–1618* (London: Longman, 1998); Bernd Moeller, *Deutschland im Zeitalter der Reformation* (Göttingen: Vandenhoeck & Ruprecht, 1981); James D. Tracy, *Europe's Reformations, 1450–1650: Doctrine, Politics, and Community* (Oxford: Rowman and Littlefield, 1999); Ernst Koch, *Das konfessionelle Zeitalter-Katholizismus, Luthertum, Calvinismus (1563–1675)* (Evangelische Verlagsanstalt: Leipzig, 2000); Owen Chadwick, *The Early Reformation on the Continent* (Oxford: Oxford University Press, 2001); Diarmaid MacCulloch, *Reformation: Europe's House Divided 1490–1700* (London: Penguin, 2003); Helga Schnabel-Schüle, *Die Reformation 1495–1555: Politik mit Theologie und Religion* (Stuttgart: Reclam, 2006); Thomas Kaufmann, *Geschichte der Reformation* (Frankfurt: Suhrkamp, 2009); Martin H. Jung, *Reformation und Konfessionelles Zeitalter, 1517–1648* (Göttingen: Vandenhoeck & Ruprecht, 2012); C. Scott Dixon, *Contesting the Reformation* (Oxford: Wiley-Blackwell, 2012); Mark Greengrass, *Christendom Destroyed: Europe 1517–1648* (New York: Penguin, 2015); Rolf Decot, *Geschichte der Reformation in Deutschland* (Freiburg: Herder, 2015); Diarmaid MacCulloch, *All Things Made New: The Reformation and Its Legacy* (Oxford: Oxford University Press, 2016) and Michael W. Bruening, *A Reformation Sourcebook: Documents from an Age of Debate* (Toronto: University of Toronto Press, 2017).

4 There were some studies on Protestant views of Islam done by German scholars. For example, Christoph Bochinger examined the Hallenian Pietist perception of Islam. In his *Habilitation*, he has a section on Arabic and Islamic works known to eighteenth-century Lutherans and a list of all Arabic books published by the *Institutum Judaicum et Orientale* in Halle. See Christoph Bochinger, *Abenteuer Islam: Zur Wahrnehmung fremder Religion im Hallenser Pietismus des 18. Jahrhunderts, Habilitationsschrift* (Munich: LMU, 1996). However, these works were sporadic and did not reflect a widespread scholarly interest in the post-Reformation engagement with Islam. In this context, one notable exception is Alastair Hamilton, who wrote several pioneering articles highlighting the importance of the Lutheran study of Islam in the seventeenth and eighteenth centuries. See Alastair Hamilton, "A Lutheran Translator for the Quran: A Late Seventeenth-Century Quest," in *The Republic of Letters and the Levant*, eds. Alastair Hamilton, et al. (Leiden: Brill, 2005), 197–221; idem, "'To Rescue the Honour of the Germans': Qur'an Translations by Eighteenth-and Early Nineteenth-Century German Protestants," *Journal of the Warburg and Courtauld Institutes* 77 (2014): 173–209; and idem, "Lutheran Islamophiles in Eighteenth-Century Germany," in *For the Sake of Learning: Essays in Honor of Anthony Grafton*, eds. Ann Blair and Anja-Silvia Goeing (Leiden: Brill, 2016), 327–43. Another notable work, a multivolume bibliographical project on Christian-Muslim engagements from the seventh century to the early twentieth century, is edited by David Thomas and John A. Chesworth; see *Christian-Muslim Relations: A Bibliographical History* (Leiden: Brill, 2009–present).

5 Johann Ulrich Wallich, *Religio Turcica, Mahometis vita, et orientalis cum occidentali antichristo comparatio*, Bayerische Staatsbibliothek München, 4 Turc. 73u (Stade, 1659), folio 140b. On the biography of Johann Ulrich Wallich (d.1673) and the significance of his book, see Gábor Kármán, "Johann Ulrich Wallich," in *Christian-Muslim Relations: A Bibliographical History, Volume 9, Western and Southern Europe (1600–1700)*, eds. David Thomas and John A. Chesworth (Leiden: Brill, 2017), 901–5.

6 The "Turk" was the prototype of the Muslim during the sixteenth and seventeenth centuries in Lutheran texts. The term was interchangeably used for "Muslim," although less used expressions like Saracen, Persian, and Moor also existed. After the eighteenth-century Protestant fascination with Wahhabis and European interest in the Middle East, "Arab" replaced "Turk" in this geopolitical role. See Ivan Kalmar, *Early Orientalism: Imagined Islam and the Notion of Sublime Power* (New York: Routledge, 2011), 23.

7 For one influential example among others, see Daphne Hampson, *Christian Contradictions: The Structures of Lutheran and Catholic Thought* (Cambridge: Cambridge University Press, 2001).

8 Notably, two recent works by German historian Heinz Schilling should be mentioned as he sees the Reformation in the context of global history. However, his works highlight the Protestant Reformation's contribution to global redefinitions of faiths, such as Islam, Judaism, Buddhism, Sikhism, and Confucianism, rather than the impact of these religions on Protestantism. The risk with this approach, however well-intentioned, is that it could establish the Reformation as a focal point of comparison; therefore, maintaining, rather than breaking down, a normative Eurocentric and Protestant perspective. Schilling is, nevertheless, well-aware of this problem as he cautions his readers and reiterates his objective of examining the Reformation as a comparative religion endeavor rather than using it as a normative tool or a criterion. See Heinz Schilling, *1517: Weltgeschichte eines Jahres* (Munich: C. H. Beck, 2017), and Heinz Schilling and Silvana Siedel Menchi (eds.), *The Protestant Reformation in a Context of Global History: Religious Reforms and World Civilizations* (Bologna: Società editrice il Mulino/Berlin: Duncker & Humblot, 2017). See also the recent volume edited by Nicholas Terpstra, *Global Reformations: Transforming Early Modern Religions, Societies, and Cultures* (New York: Routledge, 2019).

9 For examples of how Islam played a crucial role in the evolution of Christianity, see John Tolan, *Faces of Muhammad: Western Perceptions of the Prophet of Islam from the Middle Ages to Today* (Princeton: Princeton University Press, 2019); Kecia Ali, *The Lives of Muhammad* (Cambridge: Harvard University Press, 2014); Laura Lisy-Wagner, *Islam, Christianity and the Making of Czech Identity, 1453–1683* (Burlington: Ashgate, 2013); Noel Malcolm, "The Study of Islam in Early Modern Europe: Obstacles and Missed Opportunities," in *Antiquarianism and Intellectual Life in Europe and China, 1500–1800*, eds. Peter N. Miller and Francois Louis (Ann Arbor: The University of Michigan Press, 2012), 265–88; Adnan Husain and Katherine Elizabeth Fleming (eds.), *A Faithful Sea: The Religious Cultures of the Mediterranean, 1200–1700* (Oxford: Oneworld, 2007); Nabil Matar, *Islam in Britain, 1558–1685* (Cambridge: Cambridge University Press, 1998); and David A. Pailin, *Attitudes to Other Religions: Comparative Religion in Seventeenth- and Eighteenth-Century Britain* (Manchester: Manchester University Press, 1984).

10 On Socinianism and Unitarianism, see Earl Morse Wilbur, *A History of Unitarianism: Socinianism and its Antecedents* (Cambridge: Harvard

University Press, 1945); Martin Mulsow and Jan Rohls (eds.), *Socinianism and Arminianism: Antitrinitarians, Calvinists and Cultural Exchange in Seventeenth-Century Europe* (Leiden: Brill, 2005); and Sarah Mortimer, "Early Modern Socinianism and Unitarianism," in *The Oxford Handbook of Early Modern Theology, 1600–1800*, eds. Ulrich L. Lehner, Richard A. Muller, and A. G. Roeber (Oxford: Oxford University Press, 2016).

11 On the Reformation and post-Reformation uses of Judaism, see Kenneth Austin, *The Jews and the Reformation* (New Haven: Yale University Press, 2020); Irene Aue-Ben David, Aya Elyada, Moshe Sluhovsky, and Christian Wiese (eds.), *Jews and Protestants: From the Reformation to the Present* (Berlin: De Gruyter, 2020); Stephen G. Burnett, *Christian Hebraism in the Reformation Era (1500–1660): Authors, Books, and the Transmission of Jewish Learning* (Leiden: Brill, 2012); Yaacov Deutsch, *Judaism in Christian Eyes: Ethnographic Description of Jews and Judaism in Early Modern Europe* (Oxford: Oxford University Press, 2012); Achsah A. Guibbory, *Christian Identity, Jews, and Israel in Seventeenth-Century England* (Oxford: Oxford University Press, 2010); Anders Gerdmar, *Roots of Theological Anti-Semitism: German Biblical Interpretation and the Jews, from Herder and Semler to Kittel and Bultmann* (Leiden: Brill, 2009); Aya Elyada, "Protestant Scholars and Yiddish Studies in Early Modern Europe," *Past & Present* 203 (2009): 69–98; Dean Phillip Bell and Stephen G. Burnett (eds.), *Jews, Judaism and the Reformation in Sixteenth-Century Germany* (Leiden: Brill, 2006); Maria Diemling, "Jewish-Christian Relations in Early Modern Germany," *European Association for Jewish Studies Newsletter* 17 (2005): 34–47; Andrew Gow, *The Red Jews: Antisemitism in an Apocalyptic Age 1200–1600* (Leiden: Brill, 1995); and Frank E. Manuel, *The Broken Staff: Judaism Through Christian Eyes* (Cambridge: Harvard University Press, 1992). For an earlier work in the nineteenth century about the influence of Judaism on the Reformation, see Heinrich Graetz, *Influence of Judaism on the Protestant Reformation*, trans. Simon Tuska (Cincinnati: Bloch & Co, 1867).

12 Howard Tzvi Adelman, "A Rabbi Reads the Qur'an in the Venetian Ghetto," *Jewish History* 26 (2012): 125–37.

13 For Luther's views of Jews and Turks (Muslims), see Thomas Kaufmann, *Luther's Jews: A Journey into Anti-Semitism*, trans. Lesley Sharpe and Jeremy Noakes (Oxford: Oxford University Press, 2017); idem, "Luthers Sicht auf Judentum und Islam," in *Der Reformator Martin Luther 2017: Eine wissenschaftliche und gedenkpolitische Bestandsaufnahme*, ed. Heinz Schilling (Munich: De Gruyter, 2015), 53–83; Gregory Miller, "Luther's Views of the Jews and Turks," in *The Oxford Handbook of Martin Luther's Theology*, eds. Robert Kolb, Irene Dingel, and L'ubomír Batka (Oxford: Oxford University Press, 2014), 427–34; Andreas Pangritz, "Martin Luthers Stellung zu Judentum und Islam," in *Arbeitsbuch Religion und Geschichte: Das Christentum im interkulturellen Gedächtnis*, ed. Harry Noormann (Stuttgart: Verlag, 2013), 15–48; Brooks Schramm and Kirsi I. Stjerna (eds.), *Martin Luther, The Bible, and The Jewish People: A Reader* (Minneapolis: Fortress Press, 2012); and Johannes Ehmann, *Luther, Türken und Islam: Eine Untersuchung zum Türken- und Islambild Martin Luthers (1515–1546)* (Gütersloh: Gütersloher Verlagshaus, 2008). For a case study of Lutheran academic interest in Jews and Jewish studies at Wittenberg, see Giuseppe Veltri, "Academic Debates on the Jews in Wittenberg: The Protestant Literature on Rituals, the *Dissertationes* and the Writings of the Hebraists Theodor Dassow and Andreas Sennert," *European Journal of Jewish Studies* 6/1 (2012): 123–46.

14 For a concise overview of the Protestant study of non-Christian religions, see Andrew Gow and Jeremy Fradkin, "Protestantism and Non-Christian Religions," in *The Oxford Handbook of the Protestant Reformations*, ed. Ulinka Rublack (Oxford: Oxford University Press, 2016), 274–300; and Emanuele Colombo, "Western Theologies and Islam," in *The Oxford Handbook of Early Modern Theology, 1600–1800*, eds. Ulrich L. Lehner, Richard A. Muller, and A. G. Roeber (Oxford: Oxford University Press, 2016), 482–98.

15 On Protestant academic life and universities as instruments of intra-Protestant identity, see Kenneth G. Appold, "Academic Life and Teaching in Post-Reformation Lutheranism," in *Lutheran Ecclesiastical Culture: 1550–1675*, ed. Robert Kolb (Leiden: Brill, 2008), 65–116.

16 For a number of these works, please see the selected bibliography in the appendix.

17 On early modern dissertations in Germany, see Manfred Komorowski, "Research on Early German Dissertations: A Report on Work in Progress," in *The German Book 1450–1750: Studies Presented to David L. Paisey in His Retirement*, eds. John L. Flood and William A. Kelly (London: British Library, 1995), 259–68; and Hanspeter Marti, *Philosophische Dissertationen deutscher Universitäten, 1660–1750: Eine Auswahlbibliographie* (Munich: K.G. Saur, 1982).

18 Martin Mulsow, "Socinianism, Islam, and the Origins of Radical Enlightenment," in *Religious Obedience and Political Resistance in the Early Modern World: Jewish, Christian and Islamic Philosophers Addressing the Bible*, ed. Luisa Simonutti (Turnhout: Brepols, 2014), 435–57.

19 For a study of Islam and Church of England scholars, see Nabil Matar, *Henry Stubbe and the Beginnings of Islam* (New York: Columbia University Press, 2014); Humberto Garcia, *Islam and the English Enlightenment, 1670–1840* (Baltimore: Johns Hopkins University Press, 2012); Matar, *Islam in Britain*, 73–119; Justin Champion, *The Pillars of Priestcraft Shaken: The Church of England and Its Enemies, 1660–1730* (Cambridge: Cambridge University Press, 1992), 99–169; and Pailin, *Attitudes to Other Religions*, 81–104 and 121–36.

20 For a few examples of the Reformed (Calvin and Calvinists) perception of Islam, see William Emilsen, "Calvin on Islam," *Uniting Church Studies* 17/1 (2011): 69–85; Emidio Campi, "Early Reformed Attitudes towards Islam," *Theological Review of the Near East School of Theology* 31 (2010): 131–51; Jan Slomp, "Calvin and the Turks," *Studies in Interreligious Dialogue* 19/1 (2009): 50–65; Dietrich Klein, "Hugo Grotius' Position on Islam as Described in *De veritate religionis Christianae, Liber VI*," in *Socinianism and Arminianism: Antitrinitarians, Calvinists and Cultural Exchange in Seventeenth-Century Europe*, eds. Martin Mulsow and Jan Rohls (Leiden: Brill, 2005), 149–76; and Jacques Pannier, "Calvin et les Turcs," *Revue historique* 180 (1937): 268–86. Also, for the Reformed study of Arabic and Islam, see Arnoud Vrolijk and Richard van Leeuwen, *Arabic Studies in the Netherlands: A Short History in Portraits, 1580–1950*, trans. Alastair Hamilton (Leiden: Brill, 2014).

21 See Gary Waite, "'Turning Turke the Anabaptist Way': Muslims, Jews, Christian Spiritualists, and Polemical Discourse in the Dutch Republic, c. 1570 to c. 1630," in *Global Reformations: Transforming Early Modern Religions, Societies, and Cultures*, ed. Nicholas Terpstra (New York: Routledge, 2019), 73–94; and idem, "Menno and Muhammad: Anabaptists and Mennonites Reconsider Islam, 1570–1650," *Sixteenth Century Journal* 41 (2010): 995–1016.

22 On Quaker encounters with Muslims in the seventeenth century, see Justin J. Meggitt, *Early Quakers and Islam: Slavery, Apocalyptic and Christian-Muslim Encounters in the Seventeenth Century* (Eugene: Wipf and Stock Publishers, 2016).

23 Hamilton, "To Rescue the Honour of the Germans," 173–209.

24 For how Islam became a field of battle in the post-Reformation period among different stakeholders (Socinians, Trinitarians, Reformed Church, Catholic Jesuits, and Lutherans), see Maria Rosa Antognazza, *Leibniz on the Trinity and the Incarnation: Reason and Revelation in the Seventeenth Century*, trans. Gerald Parks (New Haven: Yale University Press, 2007), 137–49.

25 For the trajectories of the post-Reformation Lutheran theology, see Robert Preus, *The Theology of Post-Reformation Lutheranism: A Study of Theological Prolegomena* (St. Louis: Concordia Publishing House, 1970); idem, *The Inspiration of Scripture: A Study of the Theology of the 17th Century Lutheran Dogmatics* (St. Louis: Concordia Publishing House, 1955).

26 On the historical background of the term syncretism, see A. M. Leopold and J. S. Jensen (eds.), *Syncretism in Religion: A Reader* (New York: Routledge, 2004), 14–28. Also, on the Calixtinian idea of syncretism, see E. W. Gritsch, *A History of Lutheranism* (Minneapolis: Fortress Press, 2010), 129–39.

27 On Pietism, see Douglas H. Shantz (ed.), *A Companion to German Pietism 1660–1800* (Leiden: Brill, 2014), idem, *An Introduction to German Pietism: Protestant Renewal at the Dawn of Modern Europe* (Baltimore: The Johns Hopkins University Press, 2013); Hans Schneider, *German Radical Pietism*, trans. Gerald T. MacDonald (Lanham and Toronto: The Scarecrow Press, 2007); Richard L. Gawthrop, *Pietism and the Making of Eighteenth-Century Prussia* (Cambridge: Cambridge University Press, 1993); and Fred Ernest Stoeffler, *German Pietism During the Eighteenth Century* (Leiden: Brill, 1973).

28 P. Jacob Spener, *Pia Desideria*, trans. and ed. Theodore G. Tappert (Minneapolis: Fortress Press, 1964), 54. Although Pietism started as the critique of orthodox Lutheranism later Pietists created their own orthodoxy. On this issue, see Richard A. Muller, "J. J. Rambach and the Dogmatics of Scholastic Pietism," *Consensus* 16/2 (1990): 7–27. On the relationship between Pietism and Protestant orthodoxy, see Markus Matthias, "Pietism and Protestant Orthodoxy," in *A Companion to German Pietism, 1660–1800*, ed. Douglas Shantz (Leiden: Brill, 2014), 17–49.

29 On the impact of Protestant biblical criticism on the modern study of Islam, see Dietrich Jung, "Islamic Studies and Religious Reform: Ignaz Goldziher—A Crossroads of Judaism, Christianity, and Islam," *Der Islam* 90/1 (2013): 106–26.

30 Sebastian Conrad, *What is Global History?* (Princeton: Princeton University Press, 2016), 62–114.

31 Kecia Ali, *The Lives of Muhammad* (Cambridge: Harvard University Press, 2014), 239–40.

32 Giovanni Bonacina shows how Europeans thought Wahhabis challenged the established political and religious authority of the Ottoman Empire as well as Muslim devotional and mystical traditions. In this way, Europeans thought Wahhabis were similar to Protestants who challenged the political and religious authority of the Catholic Church. For an in-depth view of Wahhabism as seen by Europeans, see Giovanni Bonacina, *The Wahhabis Seen Through European Eyes (1772–1830): Deists and Puritans of Islam* (Leiden: Brill, 2015), 81–83, 158–76, and 184–95.

33 In the eyes of modernists, the Qur'an was the main source of salvation, whereas traditions or customs were the obstacle to attaining it. For the views of modernist Islamic intellectuals and the ideas of "the Qur'anists," popularly known as *Ahl al-Qur'ān* or *Qur'āniyyūn*, see Aisha Y. Musa, "The Qur'anists," *Religion Compass* 4/1 (2010): 12–21; Charles Kurzman and Michaelle Browers (eds.), *An Islamic Reformation?* (Lanham: Lexington, 2004); Suha Taji-Farouki (ed.), *Modern Muslim Intellectuals and the Qur'an* (Oxford: Oxford University Press, 2004); Nazir Ahmad, *Qur'anic and Non-Qur'anic Islam* (Lahore: Vanguard, 1997); Yaşar Nuri Öztürk, *Kur'andaki Islam* (Istanbul: Yeni Boyut, 1999); and Bayraktar Bayraklı, *Kuran Müslümanlığı* (Düşün Yayıncılık: Istanbul, 2019). For Muslim scholars who are against the idea of the Qur'an as a sole scriptural authority in the modern period, see Aisha Y. Musa's book, *Ḥadīth as Scripture: Discussions on the Authority of Prophetic Traditions in Islam* (New York: Palgrave Macmillan, 2008), 83–112.

34 By "traditions or customs," I refer to the idea of using any extra-Qur'anic sources as authoritative on religious matters or law. The concept of "tradition" in Islam requires more careful theoretical attention as Sunni and Shi'a, the two major sects of Islam, have different understandings of religious and legal authority as well as tradition. This issue is important in itself and deserves another monograph; however, I am not able to delve into this here as it is beyond the scope of this book.

35 Inspired by Luther's Reformation and various Protestant movements such as Lutheranism, Pietism, and Calvinism, there is also literature on different expressions of "Islamic Reformation," "Islamic Protestantism," and "Protestant Islam." See the following works: Abdullahi Ahmed An-Na'im, *Toward an Islamic Reformation: Civil Liberties, Human Rights, and International Law* (Syracuse: Syracuse University Press, 1990); Dale Eickelman, "Inside the Islamic Reformation," *The Wilson Quarterly* 22/1 (1998): 80–89; B. A. Roberson (ed.), *Shaping the Current Islamic Reformation* (London: Frank Cass, 2003); Charles Kurzman and Michaelle Browers (eds.), *An Islamic Reformation?* (Lanham: Lexington, 2004); Rachid Benzine, *Les nouveaux penseurs de l'islam* (Paris: Albin Michel, 2004); Roman Loimeier, "Is There Something like 'Protestant Islam'?" *Die Welt des Islams* 45/2 (2005): 216–54; Sukidi, "The Traveling Idea of Islamic Protestantism: A Study of Iranian Luthers," *Islam and Christian-Muslim Relations* 16/4 (2005): 401–12; idem, "Max Weber's Remarks on Islam: The Protestant Ethics among Muslim Puritans," *Islam and Christian-Muslim Relations* 17/2 (2006): 195–205; Nasr Abu Zayd, *Reformation of Islamic Thought: A Critical Historical Analysis* (Amsterdam: Amsterdam University Press, 2006); Syed Farid Alatas, "Contemporary Muslim Revival: The Case of 'Protestant Islam'," *The Muslim World* 97 (2007): 508–20; Richard W. Bulliet, "Islamic Reformation or "Big Crunch"? A Review Essay," *Harvard Middle Eastern and Islamic Review* 8 (2009): 7–18; Filippo Osella and Caroline Osella (eds.), *Islamic Reform in South Asia* (Cambridge: Cambridge University Press, 2013); Marc David Baer, "Protestant Islam in Weimar Germany: Hugo Marcus and "The Message of the Holy Prophet Muhammad to Europe," *New German Critique* 44/2 (2017): 163–200.

36 A valuable contribution to the scholarship appeared recently which shows this dialectical unfolding of history. Initially, Muhammad saw Islam as a reformulation of Judaism and Christianity, not a separate religion. Similarly, Luther was not trying to establish Protestantism when he published his 95 theses, but to reform Catholicism. The title of a recent book, *The Qur'an's Reformation of Judaism and Christianity: Return to the Origins*

(Routledge, 2019) edited by Holger M. Zellentin, refers to the main argument of the Qur'an as a reformation of Judaism and Christianity, rather than a replacement of the religion of the Jews and the Christians.

37 Martin Mulsow, "Antitrinitarians and Conversion to Islam: Adam Neuser reads Murad b. Abdullah in Ottoman Istanbul," in *Conversion and Islam in the Early Modern Mediterranean: The Lure of the Other*, ed. Claire Norton (New York: Routledge, 2017), 181–93. Also, for the story of Johannes Heyman, a Dutch Protestant pastor in the Ottoman Empire, see Maurits H. van den Boogert, "Learning Oriental Languages in the Ottoman Empire: Johannes Heyman (1667–1737) between Izmir and Damascus," in *Teaching and Learning of Arabic in Early Modern Europe*, eds. Jan Loop et al. (Leiden: Brill, 2017), 294–309. On interactions between Catholics and Protestants in the Ottoman Empire, see Felicita Tramontana, "An Unusual Setting: Interaction between Protestants and Catholics in the Ottoman Empire," in *Protestant Majorities and Minorities in Early Modern Europe: Confessional Boundaries and Contested Identities*, eds. Simon J.G. Burton, Michal Choptiany, and Piotr Wilczek (Göttingen: Vandenhoeck & Ruprecht, 2019), 189–212.

38 Dipesh Chakrabarty questioned the imagined Europe that has often been considered exceptional and the origin of the modern world, independent of other parts of the globe; see his *Provincializing Europe: Postcolonial Thought and Historical Difference* (Princeton: Princeton University Press, 2000), 3–26. Historiographical contributions, notably recent works by Simon Mills, Sanjay Subrahmanyam, Nelly Hanna, Nabil Matar, Karen Barkey, and Margaret Meserve, and earlier works by Peter Gran, Rifa'at 'Ali Abou-El-Haj, Ariel Salzmann, Nancy Bisaha, and Daniel Goffman have supported the view that Europe and the Islamic world were far more interconnected during the early modern period than once assumed. For these works, see Simon Mills, *A Commerce of Knowledge: Trade, Religion, and Scholarship between England and the Ottoman Empire, 1600–1760* (Oxford: Oxford University Press, 2020); Sanjay Subrahmanyam, *Empires between Islam and Christianity, 1500–1800* (New York: SUNY Press, 2019); Nelly Hanna, *Ottoman Egypt and the Emergence of the Modern World 1500–1800* (The American University in Cairo Press: Cairo, 2014); Nabil Matar, *Europe Through Arab Eyes, 1578–1727* (New York: Columbia University Press, 2008); Karen Barkey, *Empire of Difference: The Ottomans in Comparative Perspective* (New York: Cambridge University Press, 2008); Margaret Meserve, *Empires of Islam in Renaissance Historical Thought* (Cambridge: Harvard University Press, 2008); Ariel Salzmann, *Tocqueville in the Ottoman Empire: Rival Paths to the Modern State* (Leiden: Brill, 2004); Nancy Bisaha, *Creating East and West: Renaissance Humanists and the Ottoman Turks* (Philadelphia: University of Pennsylvania Press, 2004); Daniel Goffman, *The Ottoman Empire and Early Modern Europe* (Cambridge: Cambridge University Press, 2002); Rifa'at 'Ali Abou-El-Haj, *Formation of the Modern State: The Ottoman Empire, Sixteenth to Eighteenth Centuries* (Albany: SUNY Press, 1991); and Peter Gran, *Islamic Roots of Capitalism: Egypt, 1760–1840* (Texas: University of Texas Press, 1979). A recent article that examines how Arabs saw the Protestant Reformation illustrates the importance of global history; see Nabil Matar, "The 2018 Josephine Waters Bennett Lecture: The Protestant Reformation through Arab Eyes, 1517–1698," *Renaissance Quarterly* 72 (2019): 771–815.

39 See Norman Daniel, *Islam and the West: The Making of an Image* (Edinburgh: The Edinburgh University Press, 1960); John V. Tolan, *Saracens:*

Islam in the Medieval European Imagination (Columbia: Columbia University Press, 2002); and Suzanne Conklin Akbari, *Idols in the East: European Representations of Islam and the Orient, 1100–1450* (Ithaca: Cornell University Press, 2009).

40 For full references to Alastair Hamilton's works, see footnote 3. For the other scholars, see Martin Mulsow, *Moderne aus dem Untergrund: Radikale Frühaufklärung in Deutschland 1680–1720* (Göttingen: Wallstein Verlag, 2018); idem, *Enlightenment Underground: Radical Germany, 1680–1720* (Charlottesville: University of Virginia Press, 2015); idem, "Socinianism, Islam and the Radical Uses of Arabic Scholarship," *Al-Qanṭara* 31/2 (2010): 549–86; Frederick Quinn, *The Sum of All Heresies: The Image of Islam in Western Thought* (Oxford: Oxford University Press, 2008); David Grafton, *Piety, Politics, and Power: Lutherans Encountering Islam in the Middle East* (Eugene: Pickwick Publications, 2009); Asaph Ben-Tov, "Historia Literaria Alcorani: Two Lutheran Scholars Chronicling Oriental Scholarship at the Turn of the Eighteenth Century," in *Scholarship between Europe and the Levant: Essays in Honour of Alastair Hamilton*, eds. Jan Loop and Jill Kraye (Leiden: Brill, 2020), 195–216; idem, "Hellenism in the Context of Oriental Studies: The Case of Johann Gottfried Lakemacher (1695–1736)," *International Journal of the Classical Tradition* 25 (2018): 297–314; Humberto Garcia, *Islam and the English Enlightenment, 1670–1840* (Baltimore: Johns Hopkins University Press, 2012); Jan Loop, *Johann Heinrich Hottinger: Arabic and Islamic Studies in the Seventeenth Century* (Oxford: Oxford University Press, 2013); Gregory J. Miller, *The Turks and Islam in Reformation Germany* (New York: Routledge, 2017); Gary Waite, *Jews and Muslims in Seventeenth-Century Discourse: From Religious Enemies to Allies and Friends* (New York: Routledge, 2018); Daniel Cyranka, *Mahomet: Repräsentationen des Propheten in deutschsprachigen Texten des 18. Jahrhunderts* (Göttingen: Vandenhoeck & Ruprecht, 2018); and Alexander Bevilacqua, *The Republic of Arabic Letters: Islam and the European Enlightenment* (Cambridge: Harvard University Press, 2018).

41 Ian Almond, *History of Islam in German Thought: From Leibniz to Nietzsche* (London: Routledge, 2009).

42 John V. Tolan, *Faces of Muhammad: Western Perceptions of the Prophet of Islam from the Middle Ages to Today* (Princeton: Princeton University Press, 2019).

43 Noel Malcolm, *Useful Enemies: Islam and The Ottoman Empire in Western Political Thought, 1450–1750* (Oxford: Oxford University Press, 2019).

44 For the interpretations of seventeenth- and eighteenth-century Europe as "early modern Orientalism," see Marcus Keller and Javier Irigoyen-García (eds.), *The Dialectics of Orientalism in Early Modern Europe* (London: Palgrave Macmillan, 2018) and Daniel J. Vitkus, "Early Modern Orientalism: Representations of Islam in Sixteenth- and Seventeenth-Century Europe," in *Western Views of Islam in Medieval and Early Modern Europe*, eds. David Blanks and Michael Frassetto (New York: St. Martin's Press, 1999), 207–30.

45 Edward Said, *Orientalism* (New York: Vintage Book, 1978). Said's omission of German scholars from his discussion has been recently challenged by Suzanne L. Marchand, Gregory J. Miller, and Noel Malcolm. See Suzanne L. Marchand, *German Orientalism in the Age of Empire: Religion, Race, and Scholarship* (Cambridge: Cambridge University Press, 2009), 1–52; Miller, *The Turks and Islam in Reformation Germany*, 1–28 and 177–90; and Malcolm, *Useful Enemies: Islam and The Ottoman Empire in Western Political Thought*, 415–17. Said's *Orientalism*, with its large number of

defenders and detractors, has a long history since its publication in 1978. I am not in a position to engage in a lengthy discussion on Orientalism due to the scope of my book; however, my forthcoming study will deal with the legacy of Reformation in the modern study of Islam.

46 There is much literature on the expansion of the Ottoman Empire into Europe and the indelible impact of the Turks on European and Lutheran historical memory. For these works, see Gregory J. Miller, *The Turks and Islam in Reformation Germany* (New York: Routledge, 2017); Damaris Grimmsmann, *Krieg mit dem Wort: Türkenpredigten des 16. Jahrhunderts im Alten Reich* (Berlin: De Gruyter, 2016); Charlotte Colding Smith, *Images of Islam, 1453–1600: Turks in Germany and Central Europe* (London: Pickering and Chatto, 2014); Nina Berman, *German Literature on the Middle East: Discourses and Practices, 1000–1989* (Ann Arbor: The University of Michigan Press, 2011); Johannes Ehmann, *Luther, Türken und Islam: eine Untersuchung zum Türken- und Islambild Martin Luthers (1515–1546)* (Göttingen: Gütersloher Verlagshaus, 2008); Gábor Ágoston, "Information, Ideology, and Limits of Imperial Policy: Ottoman Grand Strategy in the Context of Ottoman-Habsburg Rivalry," in *The Early Modern Ottomans: Remapping the Empire*, eds. Virginia H. Aksan and Daniel Goffman (Cambridge: Cambridge University Press, 2007), 75–103; Matthew Dimmock, "'Machomet dyd before as Luther doth nowe': Islam, the Ottomans, and the English Reformation," *Reformation* 9 (2004): 99–130; Almut Höfert, *Den Feind beschreiben: "Türkengefahr" und europäisches Wissen über das Osmanische Reich 1450–1600* (Frankfurt: Campus Verlag, 2003); Daniel Goffman, *The Ottoman Empire and Early Modern Europe* (Cambridge: Cambridge University Press, 2002); Christine Isom-Verhaaren, "An Ottoman Report about Martin Luther and the Emperor: New Evidence of the Ottoman Interest in the Protestant Challenge to the Power of Charles V," *Turcica* 28 (1996): 299–317; Charles A. Frazee, *Catholic and Sultans: The Church and the Ottoman Empire, 1453–1923* (Cambridge: Cambridge University Press, 1983); Stephen Fischer-Galati, *Ottoman Imperialism and German Protestantism, 1521–1555* (Cambridge: Harvard University Press, 1972); and John W. Bohnstedt, *The Infidel Scourge of God: The Turkish Menace As Seen by German Pamphleteers of the Reformation Era* (Philadelphia: American Philosophical Society, 1968).

47 For this serious Lutheran concern, see Hieronymus Kromayer, *Scrutinii religionum disputatio III, de Muhammetismo tum Turcarum tum Persarum*, Niedersächsische Staats- und Universitätsbibliothek Göttingen, Th. Polem. 124/3 (Leipzig, 1668), fols. 2v–3r.

48 On the conversion to Islam and the stages of the Islamization process by the Ottomans in the post-Reformation period, see Anton Minkov, *Conversion to Islam in the Balkans: Kisve bahası Petitions and Ottoman Social Life: 1670–1730* (Leiden: Brill, 2004); Marc David Baer, *Honored by the Glory of Islam: Conversion and Conquest in Ottoman Europe* (Oxford: Oxford University Press, 2007); and Tijana Krstić, *Contested Conversions to Islam Narratives of Religious Change in the Early Modern Ottoman Empire* (Stanford: Stanford University Press, 2011). On the significance of the Sunni Ottoman Empire for Safavid Iran, see Rudi Matthee, "Safavid Iran and the "Turkish Question" or How to Avoid a War on Multiple Fronts," *Iranian Studies* 52/3–4 (2019): 513–42.

49 For Reformation polemical views of Islam, see Adam S. Francisco, *Martin Luther and Islam: A Study in Sixteenth-Century Polemics and Apologetics* (Leiden: Brill, 2007).

50 The relationship between Protestantism and mysticism has been a contentious issue among historians and scholars. See the following works: Ronald K. Rittgers and Vincent Evener (eds.), *Protestants and Mysticism in Reformation Europe* (Leiden: Brill, 2019); Dennis E. Tamburello, "The Protestant Reformers on Mysticism," in *The Wiley-Blackwell Companion to Christian Mysticism*, ed. Julia Lamm (Malden: Wiley-Blackwell, 2013), 407–21; Markus Wriedt, "Mystik und Protestantismus—ein Widerspruch?" in *Mystik: Religion der Zukunft—Zukunft der Religion?*, ed. Johannes Schilling (Leipzig: Evangelische Verlagsanstalt, 2003), 67–87; Paul Rorem, "Martin Luther's Christocentric Critique of Pseudo-Dionysian Spirituality," *Lutheran Quarterly* 11/3 (1997): 291–307; Dennis Tamburello, *Union with Christ: John Calvin and the Mysticism of St. Bernard* (Louisville: Westminster John Knox, 1994); Werner O. Packull, "Luther and Medieval Mysticism in the Context of Recent Historiography," *Renaissance and Reformation* 6/2 (1982): 79–93; David Steinmetz, *Luther and Staupitz: An Essay in the Intellectual Origins of the Protestant Reformation* (Durham: Duke University Press, 1980); Steven Ozment, *Mysticism and Dissent: Religious Ideology and Social Protest in the Sixteenth Century* (New Haven: Yale University Press, 1973); Horst Weigelt, *Spiritualistische Tradition im Protestantismus* (Berlin: Walter de Gruyter, 1973); and Heiko Oberman, "Simul Gemitus et Raptus: Luther and Mysticism," in *The Reformation in Medieval Perspective*, ed. Steven Ozment (Chicago: Quadrangle Books, 1971), 219–52.

51 However, the twentieth-century Western study of Islam, especially after the creation of Islamic studies in North America by Wilfred Cantwell Smith, focused on Indo-Persian Sufism in order to combat the idea of political Islam or fundamentalist Islam, as Sufism represented the "peaceful version" of Islam or "liberal Islamic modernity" during the Cold War. See Rosemary R. Hicks, "Comparative Religion and the Cold War Transformation of Indo-Persian 'Mysticism' into Liberal Islamic Modernity," in *Secularism and Religion-Making*, eds. Markus Dressler and Arvind-Pal S. Mandair (Oxford: Oxford University Press, 2011), 141–69. Also, for the State Department's efforts in creating a modern liberal Islam, see Saba Mahmood, "Secularism, Hermeneutics and Empire: The Politics of Islamic Reformation," *Public Culture* 18/2 (2006): 323–47.

52 One notable exception is a work by Johann Heinrich Callenberg (d.1760), a Pietist theologian and missionary, who published his *Iuris circa Christianos Muhammedici particulae* (*Particulars of the Islamic Law on Christians*) in 1729 in Halle an der Saale. His work focused on the legal issues concerning Christians in Islamic law, based on *Khizānat al-Fiqh* (*A Treasury of Islamic Law*) by Ḥanafī legal theorist Naṣr ibn Muḥammad Abū al-Layth al-Samarqandī (d.373/983). On Callenberg, see Fuat Sezgin, *Geschichte Des Arabischen Schrifttums: Qurʾānwissenschaften, Ḥadīṯ Geschichte, Fiqh, Dogmatik, Mystik. Bis ca. 430 H.* (Leiden: Brill, 1967), 447.

53 On the relationship between the Reformation and law, see Virpi Mäkinen (ed.), *Lutheran Reformation and the Law* (Leiden: Brill, 2006).

54 John Witte, Jr., *Law and Protestantism: The Legal Teachings of the Lutheran Reformation* (Cambridge: Cambridge University Press, 2002), 33–55.

55 John Witte, Jr., "'The Law Written on the Heart': Natural Law and Equity in Early Lutheran Thought," in *Law and Religion: The Legal Teachings of the Protestant and Catholic*, eds. Wim Decock, Jordan J. Ballor, Michael Germann, and Laurent Waelkens (Göttingen: Vandenhoeck & Ruprecht, 2014), 231–65.

56 Harold Joseph Berman, *Law and Revolution, II: The Impact of the Protestant Reformations on the Western Legal Tradition* (Cambridge: Harvard University Press, 2003).

57 A recent collection of conversations between intellectual historians, who specialize in the study of the early modern period (1400–1800), urges us to consider intellectual history in a global context; therefore, the study of any culture or intellectual tradition on their own terms is no longer tenable. See Alexander Bevilacqua and Frederic Clark, *Thinking in the Past Tense: Eight Conversations* (Chicago: The University of Chicago Press, 2019).

58 August Pfeiffer, *Theologiae, sive potius Ματαιολογίας Judaicae atque Mohammedicae seu Turcico-Persicae principia sublesta et fructus pestilentes,* Bayerische Staatsbibliothek München, Exeg. 856 (Leipzig, 1687), folio i.

59 Pfeiffer, *Theologiae,* folio i.

60 On Sergius, Friedrich Ulrich Calixt, *De religione muhammedana dissertatio,* Bayerische Staatsbibliothek München, 4 Diss. 632/9 (Helmstedt, 1687), fols. 14–18 and Hieronymus Kromayer, *Scrutinii religionum disputatio III, de Muhammetismo tum Turcarum tum Persarum,* Niedersächsische Staats- und Universitätsbibliothek Göttingen, Th. Polem. 124/3 (Leipzig, 1668), fols. 1v-2r and 3v.

61 Pfeiffer, *Theologiae,* folio i.

62 Calixt, *De religione muhammedana,* folio 3.

63 Calixt, *De religione muhammedana,* fols. 4–5.

64 Calixt, *De religione muhammedana,* fols. 3–4 and 14–15.

65 Pfeiffer, *Theologiae,* folio viii.

66 Calixt, *De religione muhammedana,* fols. 11–12.

67 Calixt, *De religione muhammedana,* fols. 10–12.

68 On the peculiar relation between the sword and the cross, see Charles A. Truxillo, *By the Sword and The Cross: The Historical Evolution of the Catholic World Monarchy in Spain and the New World 1492–1825* (Westport: Greenwood Press, 2001). See also the relationship between the sword and the Catholic idea of good works in English literature: Joseph Pearce, *Through Shakespeare's Eyes: Seeing the Catholic Presence in the Plays* (San Francisco: Ignatius Press, 2010).

69 Calixt, *De religione muhammedana,* fols. 11–12 and Kromayer, *De Muhammetismo tum Turcarum,* fols. 7r–7v.

70 Johann Peter von Ludewig, *Disputatione inaugurali historiam rationalis philosophiae apud Arabes et Turcas,* Sächsische Landesbibliothek—Staats- und Universitätsbibliothek Dresden, Coll. Diss. A 71/49 (Halle, 1699), fols. 43–44.

71 Johann Michael Lange, *Dissertatio historico-philologico-theologica de Alcorani prima inter Europaeos editione Arabica,* Bibliothèque nationale de France, BNF Gallica 4 O2G 195 (Altdorf, 1703), fols. 5–6.

72 See Asaph Ben-Tov's recent study on Lange and the eighteenth-century Lutheran theologian Zacharias Grapius in the context of *historia literaria,* a scholarly practice in the eighteenth-century German academia; "Historia Literaria Alcorani: Two Lutheran Scholars Chronicling Oriental Scholarship at the Turn of the Eighteenth Century," 195–216.

73 On the Latin translations of the Qur'an before and during the Reformation, see Thomas E. Burman, *Reading the Qur'an in Latin Christendom 1140–1560* (Philadelphia: University of Pennsylvania Press, 2007).

74 Lange, *Dissertatio,* fols. 22–23.

75 Lange, *Dissertatio,* fols. 21–22.

76 On the history of translation of the Qur'an and the Qur'an in early modern Europe, see Pier Mattia Tommasino, *The Venetian Qur'an: A Renaissance*

Companion to Islam, trans. Sylvia Notini (Pennsylvania: University of Pennsylvania Press, 2018), 15–18; Jan Loop, "Introduction: The Qur'an in Europe—The European Qur'an," *Journal of Qur'anic Studies* 20/3 (2018): 1–20; Alexander Bevilacqua and Jan Loop, "The Qur'an in Comparison and the Birth of 'scriptures'," *Journal of Qur'anic Studies* 20/3 (2018): 149–74; and Alastair Hamilton, "After Marracci: The Reception of Ludovico Marracci's Edition of the Qur'an in Northern Europe from the Late Seventeenth to the Early Nineteenth Centuries," *Journal of Qur'anic Studies* 20/3 (2018): 175–92.

77 For the use of the Karaites in another context in the Catholic-Protestant controversy in the seventeenth century, see Johannes van den Berg, *Religious Currents and Cross-Currents: Essays on Early Modern Protestantism and the Protestant Enlightenment* (Leiden: Brill, 1999), 43–56.

78 Calixt, *De religione muhammedana*, folio 29.

79 Calixt, *De religione muhammedana*, fols. 3–5.

80 Johann Karl Valentin Bauer, *Conspectum theologia Turcarum Mochammedicae, von der Religion der Türcken*, Augsburg Staats- und Stadtbibliothek, Diss. Phil. 1101 (Jena, 1720), fols. 17–19 and Calixt, *De religione muhammedana*, fols. 3–4.

81 Calixt, *De religione muhammedana*, folio 3.

82 Pfeiffer, *Theologiae,* fols. ii–iii and August Pfeiffer, *Dissertatio philologica quinta de Alishiis et Sunnitis, sive de praecipuis Persarum et Turcarum circa religionem dissidiis*, Universitäts- und Landesbibliothek Sachsen-Anhalt, Bb 282 (Wittenberg, 1670), fols. 113–14.

83 Pfeiffer, *Theologiae,* folio iii, and idem, *De Alishiis et Sunnitis*, fols. 113–14.

84 Kromayer, *De Muhammetismo tum Turcarum*, folio 5v.

85 Kromayer, *De Muhammetismo tum Turcarum*, folio 5v.

86 Kromayer, *De Muhammetismo tum Turcarum*, folio 5v.

87 Kromayer, *De Muhammetismo tum Turcarum*, folio 6r.

88 In his work *Scrutinium religionum tum falsarum, Paganismi, Muhammetismi, Iudaismi, Catabaptismi & Quakerismi, Weigelianismi & Rosae-Crucianismi, Socinianismi, Arminianismi, Calvinismi, Abyssinismi, Anatolicismi, Papismi, Tum unice verae & orthodoxae Lutheranismi*, Kromayer presents each religion's arguments and refutes their validity, including Paganism, Judaism, Islam, and various non-Lutheran Christian sects, such as Quakerism, Calvinism, Weigelianism, Arminianism, Socinianism, and Catholicism, in order to demonstrate that orthodox Lutheranism is the only true religion.

89 Kromayer, *De Muhammetismo tum Turcarum*, fols. 7r–7v.

90 Pfeiffer, *Theologiae,* folio vi.

91 Bauer, *Conspectum theologia Turcarum*, fols. 28–29 and 39–40.

92 Pfeiffer, *Theologiae,* folio vi.

93 On the issue of Pietist emphasis on conversion, see David William Kling, *A History of Christian Conversion* (Oxford: Oxford University Press, 2020), 289–324; and Jonathan Strom, *German Pietism and the Problem of Conversion* (Pennsylvania: The Pennsylvania State University Press, 2018).

94 Calixt, *De religione muhammedana*, fols. 32–42.

95 Calixt, *De religione muhammedana*, fols. 40–41.

96 Calixt, *De religione muhammedana*, folio 50.

97 Christian Benedikt Michaelis, *Disputatio academica de Muhammedismi laxitate morali*, Universitäts- und Landesbibliothek Sachsen-Anhalt, D Hb 870 (Halle, 1708), fols. 5 and 13–14.

98 Pailin, *Attitudes to Other Religions*, 81–104.

99 Michaelis, *Disputatio academica*, folio 4.

100 Michaelis, *Disputatio academica*, fols. 5–6.

101 Michaelis, *Disputatio academica*, folio 13.

102 Pfeiffer, *Theologiae*, folio ix; Bauer, *Conspectum theologia Turcarum*, fols. 30–31; and Samuel Schelwig, *De philosophia Turcica, oratio inauguralis*, Sächsische Landesbibliothek—Staats- und Universitätsbibliothek Dresden, Hist. Turc. 495 (Danzig, 1686), fols. 23–25.

103 Michaelis, *Disputatio academica*, fols. 15–16.

104 Michaelis, *Disputatio academica*, fols. 16–17.

105 Michaelis, *Disputatio academica*, folio 24.

106 Michaelis, *Disputatio academica*, folio 28.

107 Michael Wendeler, *Disputatio politica de republica Turcica*, Staatsbibliothek zu Berlin—Preußischer Kulturbesitz, Bibl. Diez Qu. 2537 (Wittenberg, 1655).

108 Ludewig, *Disputatione inaugurali*, fols. 5–6 and 12–13.

109 Johannes Steuchius, *Disputatio gradualis historiam logicae Arabum*, Bayerische Staatsbibliothek München, Diss. 55/2 (Uppsala, 1721), fols. 1–13.

110 Ludewig, *Disputatione inaugurali*, fols. 24–32.

111 Steuchius, *Disputatio gradualis historiam logicae Arabum*, fols. 24–29.

112 Johann Friedrich Weitenkampf, *Disputatio historico-metaphysica de fato Turcico*, Österreichische Nationalbibliothek, 131348-B (Helmstedt, 1751), fols. 14–15 and 18.

113 Steuchius, *Disputatio gradualis historiam logicae Arabum*, fols. 24–27.

114 Ludewig, *Disputatione inaugurali*, fols. 18–19.

115 On Martin Luther's critique of Aristotle and Aristotelianism, see Martin Luther, *De captivitate babylonica ecclesiae*, Bayerische Staatsbibliothek München 4 A. gr. b. 969 (Wittenberg, 1520), fols. B3v–C1r.

116 Steuchius, *Disputatio gradualis historiam logicae Arabum*, fols. 1–3; Ludewig, *Disputatione inaugurali*, fols. 24–29; Johann Georg Walch, "Libri II: De progressu ac fatis logicae," in *Parerga Academica*, Universitäts- und Landesbibliothek Sachsen-Anhalt, TM0848 (Leipzig, 1721), fols. 570–74; and Christian Friedrich Rudolph Vetterlein, *De philosophia Turcarum*, Universitäts- und Landesbibliothek Sachsen-Anhalt, AB 155562/8 (Köthen 1790), folio 9. For a positive appraisal of not only Greek philosophy but also Greek antiquity by one of the most important figures of the Reformation, Philipp Melanchthon, see Ben-Tov, *Lutheran Humanists and Greek Antiquity*, 35–131.

117 Ludewig, *Disputatione inaugurali*, fols. 43–44.

118 William Enfield, *The History of Philosophy from the Earliest Period: Drawn up from Brucker's Historia Critica Philosophiae* (Balne: London, 1791), 421.

119 Johann Jakob Brucker, a German Lutheran historian of philosophy, was born in 1696 in Augsburg and graduated from the University of Jena in 1718. Brucker became the parish minister of Kaufbeuren in 1723 and was elected as a member of the Academy of Sciences in Berlin in 1731. He was invited to return to Augsburg as a pastor and senior minister of the Church of St. Urlich and served there until his death in 1770. His chief work, *Historia critica philosophiae* (*Critical History of Philosophy*), was a five-volume historical compendium of philosophical development. It was the modern era's first complete history of the different philosophical schools. Since Brucker's work was translated into English by British Unitarian minister William Enfield in 1837, I did not include the excerpt entitled "Book V: Of the Philosophy of Saracens" in this book. For that section, see Enfield, *The History of Philosophy*, 418–41.

120 Enfield, *The History of Philosophy*, 422. On the Graeco-Arabic translation movement, see Dimitri Gutas, *Greek Thought, Arabic Culture: The Graeco-Arabic Translation Movement in Baghdad and Early 'Abbāsid Society (2th–4th/8th–10th centuries)* (London: Routledge, 1999).
121 Vetterlein, *De philosophia Turcarum*, folio 8.
122 Walch, "Libri II: De progressu ac fatis logicae," fols. 572–3.
123 Walch, "Libri II: De progressu ac fatis logicae," fols. 574 and 581–2.
124 For my review of the account of medieval Islamic, Jewish and Christian philosophies by French intellectual historian Rémi Brague, see Mehmet Karabela, "Review of the Legend of the Middle Ages: Philosophical Explorations of Medieval Christianity, Judaism, and Islam," *Philosophy East and West* 62/4 (2012): 605–8.
125 Walch, "Libri II: De progressu ac fatis logicae," fols. 581–5.
126 Walch, "Libri II: De progressu ac fatis logicae," fols. 581–2.
127 Christoph August Heumann, *Acta philosophorum, das ist: Gründliche Nachrichten aus der Historia philosophica*, vol. 1 (Halle: Rengerischen Buchhandl, 1715), 462–72. On Heumann's method of periodization and writing the history of philosophy, see Leo Catana, *The Historiographical Concept 'System of Philosophy': Its Origin, Nature, Influence and Legitimacy* (Leiden: Brill, 2008), 169–76.
128 Luther, *De captivitate babylonica ecclesiae*, folio B III v. For Luther's critique of Scholasticism, see Martin Luther, *Disputatio contra Scholasticam Theologiam* (Wittenberg, 1517). Also, for studies on Luther's critique of scholastic theology and scholasticism, see Michael Allen, "Disputation for Scholastic Theology: Engaging Luther's 97 Theses," *Themelios* 44/1 (2019): 105–19; and Theodor Dieter, "Luther as Late Medieval Theologian: His Positive and Negative use of Nominalism and Realism," in *The Oxford Handbook of Martin Luther's Theology*, eds. Robert Kolb, Irene Dingel, and L'ubomír Batka (Oxford: Oxford University Press, 2014), 31–48.
129 Heumann, *Acta philosophorum*, vol 1, 470.
130 Ludewig, *Disputatione inaugurali*, fols. 43–44.
131 Lutherans also used Aristotelian logic and disputation methods in their own curriculum in their academies and universities. Lutheran critique of the Catholic use of "corrupt Aristotelian" philosophy oscillated between Scholasticism (dialectic as the method) and Aristotelian philosophy (ethics, metaphysics, and politics as content). Aristotelianism and Scholasticism among Protestant academic circles is a contentious subject, and there is a vast amount of literature on the relationship between Protestantism, Scholasticism, and Aristotelianism in the wake of Richard A. Muller's groundbreaking scholarship. See the following works: Danilo Facca, *Early Modern Aristotelianism and the Making of Philosophical Disciplines* (London: Bloomsbury, 2020); Alice Ragni, "Johannes Clauberg and the Search for the Initium Philosophiae: The Recovery of (Cartesian) Metaphysics," in *The Oxford Handbook of Descartes and Cartesianism*, eds. Steven Nadler, Tad M. Schmaltz, and Delphine Antoine-Mahut (Oxford: Oxford University Press, 2019), 465–80; Guido Bartolucci, "Jewish Thought vs. Lutheran Aristotelism: Johann Frischmuth (1619–87) and Jewish Scepticism," in *Yearbook of the Maimonides Centre for Advanced Studies*, ed. Bill Rebiger (Berlin: Walter de Gruyter, 2017); Dolf te Velde, "Reformed Theology and Scholasticism," in *The Cambridge Companion to Reformed Theology*, eds. Paul T. Nimmo and David A. S. Fergusson (Cambridge: Cambridge University Press, 2016), 215–29; Irena Backus, "G.W. Leibniz and Protestant Scholasticism in the Years 1698–1704," in *Church and School in Early*

Modern Protestantism: Studies in Honor of Richard A. Muller on the Maturation of a Theological Tradition, eds. Jordan J. Ballor, David Sytsma, and Jason Zuidema (Leiden: Brill, 2013), 679–98; Francesco Valerio Tommasi, "Zwischen radikalem Aristotelismus und lutherischer Orthodoxie: Die These der doppelten Wahrheit in der Altdorfer Schule," *Archiv für Begriffsgeschichte* 55 (2013): 61–74; Carl R. Trueman and R. Scott Clark (eds.), *Protestant Scholasticism: Essays in Reassessment* (Eugene: Wipf & Stock, 2006); Brian Armstrong, *Calvinism and the Amyraut Heresy: Protestant Scholasticism and Humanism in Seventeenth-Century France* (Eugene: Wipf & Stock, 2004); Richard A. Muller, *Post-Reformation Reformed Dogmatics: The Rise and Development of Reformed Orthodoxy, ca. 1520–1725* (Grand Rapids: Baker Academic, 2003); idem, "The Problem of Protestant Scholasticism: A Review and Definition," in *Reformation and Scholasticism: An Ecumenical Enterprise*, eds. W. J. van Asselt and Eef Dekker (Grand Rapids: Baker Academic, 2001), 45–64; idem, "Reformation, Orthodoxy, "Christian Aristotelianism," and the Eclecticism of Early Modern Philosophy," *Dutch Review of Church History* 81/3 (2001): 306–25; W. J. van Asselt and Eef Dekker (eds.), *Reformation and Scholasticism: An Ecumenical Enterprise* (Grand Rapids: Baker Academic, 2001); Willem J. van Asselt, "Protestant Scholasticism: Some Methodological Considerations in the Study of its Development," *Dutch Review of Church History* 81/3 (2001): 265–74; Volker Leppin, *Antichrist und Jüngster Tag: Das Profil apokalyptischer Flugschriftenpublizistik im deutschen Luthertum 1548–1618* (Gütersloh: Gütersloher Verlagshaus, 1999); Constance Blackwell, "The Case of Honoré Fabri and the Historiography of Sixteenth and Seventeenth Century Jesuit Aristotelianism in the Protestant History of Philosophy: Sturm, Morhof and Brucker," *Nouvelles de la Republique des Letters* 15 (1995): 49–77; Erika Rummel, *The Humanist-Scholastic Debate in the Renaissance and Reformation* (Cambridge: Harvard University Press, 1995); John Platt, *Reformed Thought and Scholasticism: The Arguments for the Existence of God in Dutch Theology, 1575–1650* (Leiden: Brill, 1982); and John Patrick Donnelly, *Calvinism and Scholasticism in Vermigli's Doctrine of Man and Grace* (Leiden: Brill, 1976); and Hans Emil Weber, *Der Einfluss der protestantischen Schulphilosophie auf die orthodox-lutherische Dogmatik* (Darmstadt: Wissenschaftliche Buchgesellschaft, 1969).

132 On the use of dialectic in Calvinist educational curriculum, see Amy Nelson Burnett, "The Educational Roots of Reformed Scholasticism: Dialectic and Scriptural Exegesis in the Sixteenth Century," *Dutch Review of Church History* 84 (2004): 299–317. For my review of the use of Aristotelian dialectical tradition for the later development in the history of philosophy, see Mehmet Karabela, "Review of the Art of Dialectic between Dialogue and Rhetoric," *Journal of the History of Philosophy* 52/4 (2014): 841–42.

133 Heumann, *Acta philosophorum*, vol. 1, 462–72; Johann Jakob Brucker, *Historia critica philosophiae*, 5 vols. (Leipzig: C. Breitkopf, 1742–44), vol. 3: 554–58, 709–21, 872–74; vol. 5: 6–38; and Johann Franz Buddeus, *Elementa philosophiae instrumentalis, seu institutionum philosophiae eclecticae*, vol. 1 (Hale, 1722), 66–98. For an in-depth study of Buddeus, see Friederike Nüssel, *Bund und Versöhnung: zur Begründung der Dogmatik bei Johann Franz Buddeus* (Göttingen: Vandenhoeck & Ruprecht, 1996). For a discussion of scholasticism and Reformation, see Catana, *The Historiographical Concept 'System of Philosophy,'* 168–90.

134 Ludewig, *Disputatione inaugurali*, fols. 16–17; and Cornelius Dietrich Koch, *Dissertatio inauguralis historico-litteraria de fatis studiorum apud*

Arabes, Thüringer Universitäts- und Landesbibliothek Jena, 4 Bud. Hist. Lit. 6/18 (Helmstedt, 1719), fols. 10–11.

135 Ludewig, *Disputatione inaugurali*, fols. 17–18.

136 On the term *ummī*, or illiterate, see Isaiah Goldfeld, "The Illiterate Prophet (*nabī al-ummī*): An Inquiry into the Development of a Dogma in Islamic Tradition," *Der Islam* 57 (1980): 58–67.

137 Steuchius, *Disputatio gradualis historiam logicae Arabum*, fols. 22–23.

138 Enlightenment culture defined itself as rational against irrational religious enthusiasm. Critics of enthusiasm described the beliefs and actions of religious enthusiasts as mental illness. Many writers used the terms 'fanatic' and 'enthusiast' interchangeably. Enthusiasm, a key term, was used in a pejorative sense by various Protestant denominations to exert their authority and retained pejorative connotations until the nineteenth century. On the meaning attached to enthusiasm during the Enlightenment and its importance in the post-Reformation period, see Lawrence Eliot Klein and Anthony J. La Vopa (eds.), *Enthusiasm and Enlightenment Europe, 1650–1850* (San Marino: Huntington Library, 1998); Timothy Clark, *The Theory of Inspiration* (Manchester: Manchester University Press, 1997), 61–91; David S. Lovejoy, *Religious Enthusiasm in the New World: Heresy to Revolution* (Cambridge: Harvard University Press, 1985); Susie I. Tucker, *Enthusiasm: A Study in Semantic Change* (Cambridge: Cambridge University Press, 1972); and Ronald Arbuthnott Knox, *Enthusiasm: A Chapter in the History of Religion, with Special Reference to the XVII and XVIII Centuries* (Oxford: Oxford University Press, 1950).

139 Michaelis, *Disputatio academica*, folio 4.

140 On the origins and Luther's uses of the *Schwärmer*, see Amy Nelson Burnett, "Luther and the *Schwärmer*," in *The Oxford Handbook of Martin Luther's Theology*, eds. Robert Kolb, Irene Dingel, and L'ubomír Batka (Oxford: Oxford University Press, 2014), 511–24. On the transformation of the Lutheran concept of *Schwärmerei* to fanaticism in modern politics and the liberal state, see Alberto Toscano, *Fanaticism: On the Uses of an Idea* (London: Verso, 2017).

141 Ludewig, *Disputatione inaugurali*, fols. 16–19.

142 Ludewig, *Disputatione inaugurali*, fols. 16–18.

143 For French Calvinist Pierre Bayle's and radical Enlightenment *philosophes'* perception of Islamic philosophy, see Jonathan Israel, *Enlightenment Contested: Philosophy, Modernity, and the Emancipation of Man 1670–1752* (Oxford: Oxford University Press, 2006), 615–39.

144 It must be noted that not all Protestants thought Islam was an irrational religion. Indeed, a considerable number of post-Reformation Protestants (even some deists and freethinkers) thought the exact opposite: Islam was the most rational of all religions. Regardless of their stance on Islam's rationality, the competing Protestant sects used Islam in a utilitarian fashion in their religious polemics against each other. Therefore, Islam was of primary importance in the development of various Protestant identities, including Lutheranism, Calvinism, Pietism, Unitarianism, Socinianism, and Anglicanism. For an in-depth analysis of this alternative view of Islam as a rational religion, see Noel Malcolm, "Islam as a 'Rational' Religion: Early Modern European Views," in *Scholarship between Europe and the Levant: Essays in Honour of Alastair Hamilton*, eds. Jan Loop and Jill Kraye (Leiden: Brill, 2020), 15–33. Also, see Jan Loop, "Islam and European Enlightenment," in *Christian-Muslim Relations: A Bibliographical History*, eds. David Thomas and John Chesworth with al., vol. 13 (Leiden: Brill, 2019), 16–34.

145 For Lutheran theologian and philosopher Christian Wolff's effort us-
ing reason to defend religion, see his *Philosophia rationalis sive logica,
methodo scientifica* (Leipzig: Rengeriana, 1740), 692–706. For a critique
of "religious enthusiasm," see Jon Mee, *Dangerous Enthusiasm: William
Blake and the Culture of Radicalism in the 1790s* (Oxford: Clarendon
Press, 1992); Michael Heyd, *"Be Sober and Reasonable": The Critique of
Enthusiasm in the Seventeenth and Early Eighteenth Centuries* (Leiden:
Brill, 1995), 165–90; Frederick C. Beiser, *The Sovereignty of Reason: The
Defense of Rationality in the Early English Enlightenment* (Princeton:
Princeton University Press, 1996), 184–219; J. G. A. Pocock, "Enthusiasm:
The Anti-Self of Enlightenment," *Huntington Library Quarterly* 60/1–2
(1998): 7–28; Gregory R. Johnson, "The Tree of Melancholy: Kant on Philosophy and Enthusiasm," in *Kant and the New Philosophy of Religion*,
eds. Chris L. Firestone and Stephen Palmquist (Bloomington: Indiana University Press, 2006), 43–61; Alasdair Raffe, *The Culture of Controversy:
Religious Arguments in Scotland, 1660–1714* (Woodbridge: Boydell Press,
2012), 121–48.
146 Schelwig, *De philosophia Turcica*, fols. 22–23.
147 Schelwig, *De philosophia Turcica*, folio 16.
148 Schelwig, *De philosophia Turcica*, folio 3.
149 Schelwig, *De philosophia Turcica*, folio 16.
150 'Azīz Nasafī's work *Maqṣad-i Aqṣā* exists in numerous manuscripts and in
various versions of the original Persian, as well as in several Turkish translations. The Turkish translation of the *Maqṣad* was the basis for the Latin
translation by the Lutheran pastor Andreas Müller (d.1694), published in
1665. This translation eventually found its way into the Pietist German
theologian August Tholuck's *Sufismus sive Theosophia Persarum Pantheistica* in the nineteenth century.
151 Schelwig, *De philosophia Turcica*, fols. 16–18. For a study of 'Azīz Nasafī on the differences between God's essence and existence, see Hermann
Landolt, "Azīz-i Nasafī and the Essence-Existence Debate," in *Consciousness and Reality: Studies in Memory of Toshihiko Izutsu*, eds. Sayyid Jalāl
al-Dīn Āshtiyānī et al. (Leiden: Brill, 2000), 387–95. On Nasafī's life and
works, see Llyod Ridgeon, *Persian Metaphysics and Mysticism: Selected
Works of 'Azīz Nasafī* (Richmond: Curzon Press, 2002).
152 On the history of the concept of fate in German thought in the seventeenth
and eighteenth centuries with references to Lutheran authors, including
Weitenkampf, see Franziska Rehlinghaus, "Der Grenzbereich zwischen
Wissen und Glauben: Zur Geschichte des deutschen Schicksalsbegriffs,"
Archiv für Begriffsgeschichte 55 (2013): 111–43.
153 Weitenkampf, *Disputatio historico-metaphysica de fato Turcico*, fols.
11–14.
154 Eric Ormsby, *Theodicy in Islamic Thought: The Dispute Over Al-Ghazālī's
Best of All Possible Worlds* (Princeton: Princeton University Press, 1984),
3–31.
155 Maria Rosa Antognazza, "Ecclesiology, Ecumenism, and Toleration," in
The Oxford Handbook of Leibniz, ed. Maria Rosa Antognazza (Oxford:
Oxford University Press, 2018), 756–69; Paul R. Hinlicky, "A Leibnizian
Transformation? Reclaiming the Theodicy of Faith" in *Transformations
in Luther's Reformation Theology: Historical and Contemporary Reflections*, eds. C. Helmer and B. K. Holm (Leipzig: Evangelische Verlagsanstalt, 2011), 85–103; and Ursula Goldenbaum, "Leibniz as a Lutheran,"
in *Leibniz, Mysticism, and Religion*, eds. Allison Courdert, Richard H.
Popkin, and Gordon M. Weiner (Dordrecht: Kluwer, 1998), 169–92. For

a study on Leibniz as a Protestant theologian, see Irena Backus, *Leibniz: Protestant Theologian* (Oxford: Oxford University Press, 2016).

156 On Leibniz's concept of *Fatum Christianum* and his critique of *Fatum Mahometanum*, see Andrea Poma, *The Impossibility and Necessity of Theodicy: The "Essais" of Leibniz*, trans. Alice Spencer (Dordrecht: Springer, 2013), 45–56. For a further study on Muslim fate, see Josef van Ess, "Fatum Mahumetanum. Schicksal und Freiheit im Islam," in *Kleine Schriften by Josef van Ess*, ed. Hinrich Biesterfeldt, vol. 3 (Leiden: Brill, 2018), 1988–2010.

157 Mulsow, *Radikale Frühaufklärung*, 256–66. For Daniel Clasen's work on political religion and his definition of political religion, see *De religione politica liber unus*, Niedersächsische Staats- und Universitätsbibliothek Göttingen, 8 Pol IV, 9359-b (Magdeburg, 1681), fols. 50–64.

158 On the Lutheran understanding of political religion, political theology, and political idolatry, see Mulsow, *Radikale Frühaufklärung*, 195–307.

159 For a detailed examination of the Christian political thinking in the Bible, see Christopher Rowland, "Scripture," in *The Cambridge Companion to Christian Political Theology*, eds. Craig Hovey and Elizabeth Phillips (Cambridge: Cambridge University Press, 2015), 157–75.

160 The twentieth-century controversial Catholic jurist and political theorist Carl Schmitt affirms this Lutheran position of Catholicism being a political religion. In his *Roman Catholicism and Political Form*, Schmitt discusses political consequences of Protestant inwardness, spirituality and asceticism for which he finds a cure in the political idea of Catholicism. See Carl Schmitt, *Römischer Katholizismus und Politische Form* (Munich: Theatiner-Verlag, 1925).

161 Pfeiffer, *De Alishiis et Sunnitis*, fols. 97–99.

162 Pfeiffer, *De Alishiis et Sunnitis*, fols. 116–18.

163 Schelwig, *Inaugural Speech on Turkish Philosophy*, 155. On the significance of Sufi dervish groups in the Ottoman Empire, see Halil İnalcık, "Dervish and Sultan: An Analysis of the Otman Baba Vilayetnamesi," in *The Middle East and the Balkans under the Ottoman Empire: Essays on Economy and Society*, ed. Halil İnalcık (Bloomington: Indiana University Turkish Studies, 1999), 19–36; Ahmet Yaşar Ocak, "Kalenderi Dervishes and Ottoman Administration from the Fourteenth to the Sixteenth Centuries," in *Manifestations of Sainthood in Islam*, eds. Grace M. Smith and Carl Ernst (Istanbul: Isis Press, 1993), 239–56; Ahmet Karamustafa, *God's Unruly Friends: Dervish Groups in the Islamic Middle Period 1200–1550* (Salt Lake City: University of Utah Press, 1994); John J. Curry, *Transformation of Muslim Mystical Thought in the Ottoman Empire: The Rise of the Halveti Order, 1350–1650* (Edinburgh: Edinburgh University Press, 2010); and Rıza Yıldırım, "The Safavid-Qizilbash Ecumene and the Formation of the Qizilbash-Alevi Community in the Ottoman Empire, c. 1500–c. 1700," *Iranian Studies* 52 (2019): 449–83.

164 Wendeler, *Disputatio politica de republica Turcica*, fols. 1r–8v.

165 Wendeler, *Disputatio politica de republica Turcica*, fols. 8v–10r. Ottoman historian Linda Darling argues that the influential seventeenth-century British writer Paul Rycaut's reference to Ottoman style of absolutism and sultanic tyranny is an indication of the religious and political anxieties of the seventeenth century, rather than a pure critique of the Ottoman political system. According to Darling, Rycaut used the Ottoman example to comment on the English monarchial Restoration of 1660; he was concerned that this could be a step toward the absolutist tendencies of the French monarchy. See, Linda Darling, "Ottoman Politics through British

Eyes: Paul Rycaut's *The Present State of the Ottoman Empire*," *Journal of World History* 5/1 (1994): 71–97.

166 Wendeler, *Disputatio politica de republica Turcica*, folio 14r.

167 A recently edited volume by Vefa Erginbaş contains several important articles toward not only understanding the contested nature of Ottoman Sunnism, but also the study of religion in early modern Islamic history; see *Ottoman Sunnism: New Perspectives* (Edinburgh: Edinburgh University Press, 2019).

168 Sebastian Kirchmaier, *Oratio Persica de differentia religionis Turcicae & Persicae*, Staatliche Bibliothek Regensburg, 999/4 Theol. syst. 284 angeb. 17 (Wittenberg, 1662), folio 2r.

169 On Luther's view of the Turks, see Gregory J. Miller, "The Turks," in *Martin Luther in Context*, ed. David M. Whitford (Cambridge: Cambridge University Press, 2018), 152–9; idem, "Islam," in *The Dictionary of Luther and the Lutheran Traditions*, ed. Timothy J. Wengert (Grand Rapids: Baker Academic, 2017), 370–5; and David D. Grafton, "Martin Luther's Sources on the Turk and Islam in the Midst of the Fear of Ottoman Imperialism," *The Muslim World* 107/4 (2017): 665–83.

170 A recent study suggested that the Protestant Reformation actually benefited politically and economically from the Ottoman advances in Europe. For this interpretation, see Murat Iyigun, "Luther and Suleyman," *The Quarterly Journal of Economics* 123/4 (2008): 1465–94.

171 Pfeiffer, *De Alishiis et Sunnitis*, fols. 91–93. Zoroaster was also used by the post-Reformation scholars to bolster Protestant identity. See Mehdi Estakhr, *The Place of Zoroaster in History: Using the Cult Personality as a Literary Source of Authority in the Western Tradition* (Queenston: Edwin Mellen Press, 2012), book 2, chapter 11. Monica M. Ringer further studied the history of the interactions between Zoroastrianism (in Iran and India) and Protestantism from the nineteenth century to early twentieth century. Her work demonstrates how Protestant missionaries redefined and used Zoroastrianism in the nineteenth century to create modern "pious citizens." See Monica M. Ringer, *Pious Citizens: Reforming Zoroastrianism in India and Iran* (Syracuse: Syracuse University Press 2011), 47–90.

172 Pfeiffer, *De Alishiis et Sunnitis*, fols. 93–94. Pfeiffer uses Turks and Saracens interchangeably as he sees Turks as Arabs at this stage. This Lutheran perception of race and religion could be an important study for future researchers.

173 Pfeiffer, *De Alishiis et Sunnitis*, fols. 90–94.

174 Kromayer, *De Muhammetismo tum Turcarum*, fols. 2v–3r.

175 Kirchmaier, *Oratio Persica*, fols. 8v–9v.

176 Kirchmaier, *Oratio Persica*, folio 8v.

177 Kirchmaier, *Oratio Persica*, folio 9v.

178 Rula Abisaab, *Converting Persia: Religion and Power in the Safavid Empire* (London: I.B. Tauris, 2004). See also Abisaab's article, "The Ulama of Jabal 'Amil in Safavid Iran, 1501–1736: Marginality, Migration and Social Change," *Iranian Studies* 27 (1994): 103–22.

179 Kirchmaier, *Oratio Persica*, folio 10v.

180 Pfeiffer, *De Alishiis et Sunnitis*, fols. 115–16.

181 Pfeiffer, *De Alishiis et Sunnitis*, fols. 116–17.

182 In fact, the extremist Shi'ite (*ghulat*) sects maintained that *imām* 'Alī's soul transmigrated (*tanāsukh*) into the body of chosen Shi'ite *imāms*. This meant that 'Alī was the incarnation of God as they believed in the doctrine of *ḥulūl*, which stated that God could pass into human form. On these sects

and their beliefs, see Matti Moosa, *Extremist Shiites: The Ghulat Sects* (Syracuse: Syracuse University Press, 1988), 50–76 and 185–93.

183 Pfeiffer, *De Alishiis et Sunnitis*, fols. 113–14.

184 Pfeiffer, *Theologiae*, folio iii, and idem, *De Alishiis et Sunnitis*, fols. 113–14.

185 Kromayer, *De Muhammetismo tum Turcarum*, folio 9a.

186 'Alī's sword, called *Zulfiqār*, is said to have been given to him by Muhammad to replace the broken sword of 'Alī on a battlefield. Although there are variant legends and narratives around the sword of 'Alī, the main point here for us is that the Shi'ites attribute miracles to 'Alī's sword.

187 Kirchmaier, *Oratio Persica*, fols. 11r–12v.

188 On the Lutheran concept of sainthood, see Robert Kolb, *For All the Saints: Changing Perceptions of Martyrdom and Sainthood in the Lutheran Reformation* (Macon: Mercer University Press, 1987).

189 Alexandra Walsham, "Miracles in Post-Reformation England," *Studies in Church History* 41 (2005): 273–306.

190 In his *The Protestant Ethic and the Spirit of Capitalism* (1905), it was the German Calvinist Max Weber who first proposed the idea of *Entzauberung der Welt*, or the elimination of magic from the world, which was usually translated as disenchantment in English and has become known as "secularization thesis" in religious studies. For Weber's concept of *Entzauberung der Welt*, see *Die protestantische Ethik und der Geist des Kapitalismus*, 3rd ed. (Munich: Verlag, 2010), 146–78. Also, see Richard L. Gawthrop, "Lutheran Pietism and the Weber Thesis," *German Studies Review* 12/2 (1989): 237–47.

191 For a historiographical critique of the Eurocentric Enlightenment narrative, see Sebastian Conrad, "Enlightenment in Global History: A Historiographical Critique," *American Historical Review* 117/4 (2012): 997–1027.

192 On the early modern Protestant theologians' critique of saints and miracles, see D. P. Walker, "The Cessation of Miracles," in *Hermeticism and the Renaissance: Intellectual History and the Occult in Early Modern Europe*, eds. Ingrid Merkel and Allen G. Debus (London: Associated University Press, 1988), 111–24; Philip M. Soergel, *Wondrous in His Saints: Counter-Reformation Propaganda in Bavaria* (Berkeley: University of California Press, 1993), 15–74; and idem, "Miracle, Magic, and Disenchantment in Early Modern Germany," in *Envisioning Magic: Princeton Seminar and Symposium*, eds. Peter Schäfer and Hans Kippenberg (Leiden: Brill, 1997), 215–34.

193 On the consequences of the Reformation in secularizing modern society, see Brad S. Gregory, *The Unintended Reformation: How a Religious Revolution Secularized Society* (Cambridge: Harvard University Press, 2015).

194 On the relationship between Knutzen and his students, see Manfred Kuehn, *Kant: A Biography* (Cambridge: Cambridge University Press, 2001), 88–105; idem, "Kant's Teachers in the Exact Sciences," in *Kant and the Sciences*, ed. Eric Watkins (Oxford: Oxford University Press, 2001), 11–30; and Martin Schönfeld, "Kant's Early Dynamics," in *A Companion to Kant*, ed. Graham Bird (Oxford: Wiley-Blackwell, 2006), 33–46.

195 On the relationship between Kant and Weitenkampf, see Riccardo Pozzo, "Kant e Weitenkampf: Una fonte ignorata della Allgemeine Naturgeschichte und Theorie des Himmels e della Prima Antinomia della ragion pura," *Rivista Di Storia Della Filosofia* 48/2 (1993): 283–323.

196 Bach is also considered a theological musician. See Eric Chafe, *Tears into Wine: J. S. Bach's Cantata 21 in its Musical and Theological Contexts* (Oxford: Oxford University Press, 2015), 64–75; David P. Scaer, "Johann

Sebastian Bach as Lutheran Theologian," *Concordia Theological Quarterly* 68 (2004): 319–40; Robin A. Leaver, "Johann Sebastian Bach and the Lutheran Understanding of Music," *Lutheran Quarterly* 16/1 (2002): 21–47; and idem, *Bachs Theologische Bibliothek: Eine kritische Bibliographie* (Stuttgart: Hänssler, 1983).

197 Robin A. Leaver, "Churches," in *The Routledge Research Companion to Johann Sebastian Bach*, ed. Robin A. Leaver (New York: Routledge, 2017), 173–84; Peter Williams, *Bach: A Musical Biography* (Cambridge: Cambridge University Press, 2016), 179–255; Robin A. Leaver, "Bach's Mass: 'Catholic' or 'Lutheran'?" in *Exploring Bach's B-minor Mass*, eds. Yo Tomita, Robin A. Leaver, and Jan Smaczny (Cambridge: Cambridge University Press, 2013), 21–38; and Philipp Spitta, *Johann Sebastian Bach: His Work and Influence on the Music of Germany, 1685–1750*, vol. 2 (London: Novello and Company, 1899), 148–9.

198 Marcelo Dascal, *Gottfried Wilhelm Leibniz: The Art of Controversies* (Dordrecht, Springer, 2008), 429–34; Gonzalo Rodriguez-Pereyra, *Leibniz's Principle of Identity of Indiscernibles* (Oxford: Oxford University Press, 2014), 56–67; and Massimo Mugnai, Han van Ruler, and Martin Wilson (eds.), *Leibniz: Dissertation on Combinatorial Art* (Oxford: Oxford University Press, 2020), 35.

199 Leibniz also corresponded with Ludewig, one of the Lutheran authors included in this book; for these correspondences, see Gottfried Wilhelm Leibniz, *Sämtliche Schriften und Briefe* (Berlin: Akademie Verlag, 2005), 609–14.

200 In this direction, a recent study by Mario Biagioni shows that some radical reformers of the sixteenth century played a pivotal role in the development of Enlightenment and the rise of modern Europe. See Mario Biagioni, *The Radical Reformation and the Making of Modern Europe: A Lasting Heritage* (Leiden: Brill, 2016). Also, see David Jan Sorkin, *The Religious Enlightenment: Protestants, Jews, and Catholics from London to Vienna* (Princeton: Princeton University Press, 2008), 1–22.

201 On the uses of early modern dissertations and disputations, see Robert Seidel, "Debating the Use of Academic Travel: Early Modern Disputations *De arte peregrinandi*," in *Artes Apodemicae and Early Modern Travel Culture, 1550–1700*, eds. Karl A. E. Enenkel and Jan de Jon (Leiden: Brill, 2019), 114–47; Marion Gindhart and Ursula Kundert (eds), *Disputatio 1200–1800: Form, Funktion und Wirkung eines Leitmediums Universitärer Wissenskultur* (Berlin: De Gruyter, 2010); Ku-ming (Kevin) Chang, "From Oral Disputation to Written Text: Transformation of the Dissertation in Early Modern Europe," *History of Universities* 19/2 (2004): 129–87.

202 See Susan Karpuk, "Cataloging Seventeenth- and Eighteenth-Century German Dissertations: Guidelines and Observations," *Cataloguing and Classification Quarterly* 48/4 (2010): 303–14; and Kevin Chang, "Kant's Disputation of 1770: The Dissertation and the Communication of Knowledge in Early Modern Europe," *Endeavour* 31/2 (2007): 45–49. Also, on early modern academic writings and protocols, see Gerhard Wiesenfeldt, "Academic Writings and the Rituals of Early Modern Universities," *Intellectual History Review* 26:4 (2016): 447–60.

203 On the *jinn* in the Qur'an and Islamic culture, see Amira El-Zein, *Islam, Arabs, and the Intelligent World of the Jinn* (Syracuse: Syracuse University Press, 2009).

204 Abdullah Yusuf Ali, *The Holy Qur'an* (London: Wordsworth, 2000).

Part II
Religion and Theology

1 Moral Laxity of Islam

Christian Benedikt Michaelis

Christian Benedikt Michaelis was born in 1680 in Ellrich in modern Thuringia, where he attended school. In 1694, Michaelis' uncle Johann Heinrich Michaelis (d.1738) brought him to Halle, a Lutheran university and center for Pietism in the late seventeenth and early eighteenth centuries. In 1697, he went to the Gymnasium in Gotha and, in 1699, Michaelis moved to Halle to study theology and oriental languages, acquiring a Master's degree in 1706. He was first appointed as an adjunct faculty of philosophy at Halle in 1708, then, as an associate professor in 1713, and finally, a full professor of Greek and Oriental languages in 1714. In 1731, he became a professor of theology and taught at Halle's Collegium Orientale Theologicum, which had been founded in 1702 by his uncle, Johann Heinrich Michaelis. At the Collegium, there was a strong focus on Eastern languages and the Hebrew Bible, and many of the professors there were Jewish converts to Christianity. Michaelis contributed to the text, *Biblia Hebraica,* of the Old Testament edited by his uncle. He also wrote on philological topics, especially concerning Hebrew and other Semitic languages. He encouraged the study of the Syriac language, publishing a Syriac grammar in 1741, and he promoted the usefulness of the Ethiopian Ge'ez translation of the Gospels as a tool for New Testament textual criticism. He died in Halle in 1764.[1]

Variant Names: Christian Benedict Michel, Christian Benedikt Michael, Christianus Benedictus Michaelis, Christian Benedickt Michaelis, and Chr. B. Michaelis

Summary and Analysis

In his academic disputation, Michaelis argues that Muhammad deliberately and cunningly created a morally lax religion to win converts. He begins by remarking on Islam's astonishing progress in the Arabian Peninsula and beyond, for which he outlines various reasons, including the warlike nature of Muslims, their enemies' internal weaknesses and divisions, and God's wrath. While he says that all these explanations are widely known, he has a specific reason in mind for Islam's success: its moral laxity.

Michaelis claims that Islam is light and easy on the question of penitence, requiring believers only to keep faith in their hearts. Muhammad, he says, goes further, stating that forced blasphemy is not sinful and that God will be merciful. To deny God because of fear is not a sin, but prudent. In Islam, there is no need to fear sin since God forgives all. This idea, Michaelis claims, deepens with the Qur'an's abuse of God's indulgences and kindness as expressed in Q. 2:185: "God wants easiness for you and does not want difficulty for you," because man was created weak. For Michaelis, Muhammad's insistence that religion should be 'easy' and his permissive attitude toward venial sins can only lead to immorality, laziness, and moral deficiency, and even seemingly strict rules such as the prohibition of alcohol, pork, and adultery can be flouted with an appeal to 'easiness' under mitigating circumstances.

By giving several examples, Michaelis aims to show that Islam spread rapidly because it catered to men's debased tastes. For instance, Islam nurtured the sensuality of its adherents both in this world and the next. For Michaelis, Muhammad gratified the Arabs' passion and corrupt sexuality, which he claimed they were strongly addicted to. In this way, Muhammad made it 'easier' to draw people to his religion, which gave a full indulgence to the lusts of mankind. Michaelis brings lying and cheating in warfare or during the time of persecution as another example of moral laxity in Islam. The idea Michaelis refers to is known as *taqiyya* or *hud'a* in Islamic literature which allows and, in some cases, promotes a lie to non-Muslims to protect and promote Islam as well as to save oneself from persecution and death. Muslim believers under the authority of non-Muslims are allowed to lie or deceive infidels by bowing and worshipping idols and crosses and offering false testimony, including lying under oath before a court. This kind of religious deception during a time of persecution is what Michaelis calls hypocrisy and immorality since Christians must never lie under any circumstances and martyrdom is celebrated in Christianity, especially in the face of persecution, as shown through the vivid example of Christ's crucifixion.

Michaelis then outlines the laxity of the five pillars of Islam: professing God's unity (*shahāda*), almsgiving (*zakāt*), prayers (*ṣalāt*), fasting (*ṣawm*), and pilgrimage (*ḥajj*). Professing God's unity is meaningless, he says, since it can be denied in the face of danger; almsgiving can always be ignored by claiming that there is not enough for one's own needs; prescribed prayers are not as demanding as the continuous prayers ordered by Christ (Luke 18:1); Islamic fasting is insufficiently strict because it allows sexual intercourse and night-time gorging; and the pilgrimage to Mecca was a concession to the pagan sensibilities of those Arabs who already used it as a shrine. Michaelis ends his disputation by dismissing the ritual ablutions of Islam as mere outward cleanliness and contrasts such rituals with Protestant inner purity and piety. As a Pietist, he concludes that Islam is, like Catholicism, morally lax, superficial, and concerned only with external appearances. Reformation scholars claimed that Islam's rapid expansion was due to the sword, the political weaknesses of Islam's enemies, Christian divisions, and God's punishment. However, post-Reformation Pietist scholars' preferred reason

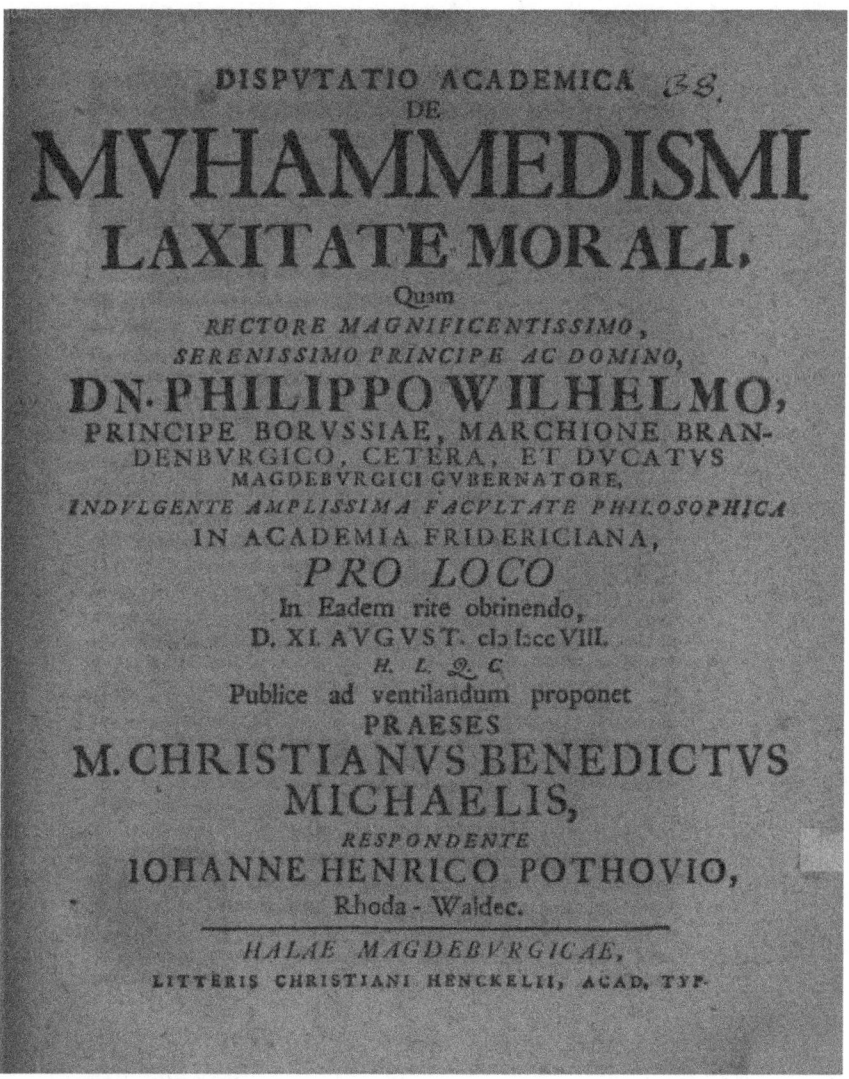

Figure 1.1 Christian Benedikt Michaelis, *Disputatio academica de Muhammedismi laxitate morali*, 1708 (Courtesy of the Bavarian State Library, Munich).

for Islam's popularity was moral laxity; this allowed them to assert the moral superiority of Protestantism.

Academic Disputation on the Moral Laxity of Islam (Halle, 1708)

I will begin by making some comments on Islam, the religion, which is spread today throughout most of the world. It was first born in a corner of Arabia, between Mecca and Medina, created by an enthusiast man, Muhammad. Muslim tradition says that he was illiterate [*ummī*]. Islam soon progressed outside Arabia, and swiftly spread through Asia, Africa, and a significant part of Europe itself. This progress was so rapid and widespread that in a short time—just as someone once said about the Arian heresy—the world was surprised that it became Muslim.

People provide various reasons for such an admirable expansion. Some assert that success of Islam is due to arms and the warlike Muslims, since it was through these agencies that their superstition poured into peaceful provinces. Others point to the misery of the Jews at that time, and the magnitude of weaknesses stemming from the Christians' quarrels, their depraved morals and their indolence. Others blame the ignorance and blindness of that age, especially among the Arab race; religion was new to them, and they were therefore prone to be deceived by an impostor. Finally, many saner men add the wrath of God to these reasons. Due to the world's steadfast contempt for divine truth, Islam lay heavily upon it. Islam gained influence by man's ignorance, so that they who were unwilling to obey the truth believed lies (2. Thess. 2:10–12). As there may be many causes for one thing, therefore, I think that all of the reasons that I have mentioned came together to promote Islam.

There is a distinguished man in Holland, Adriaan Reland, who attributes the growth of Islam to its own innate qualities. He thinks that Islam is closer to the truth than Christians generally believe. Reland says this in the preface of *De religione Mohammedica*:

> I have always thought that this religion, which diffused itself far and wide throughout Asia, Africa and Europe, can be praised for a powerful appearance of truth that persuades men, thus, it is not so worthless as many Christians think.

Reland examined some of the seemingly absurd practices of the Muslims and explained them using the Arabic works, so that they seem less absurd. However, it cannot be denied that there is a great abundance of teachings in the Qur'an, which contain much absurdity and gross error. These teachings should have aroused the suspicion of being false to the attentive reader. Even now, I find it difficult to persuade myself that Islam spread so quickly and widely due to the soundness of its doctrines.

I think that Islam spread because it was attractive and not because it appeared to be the truth; it attracted adherents rather than persuading them. I have observed that Islam accommodates itself to man's corruption: easy, lax, seductive, indulgent in nature, carnal, titillating, deceiving—to express it in one word: 'populist.' What is more likely to be adopted than a religion of this kind? And what has more capacity to attract the impulsive and imprudent multitude? For this corruption (alas!) dwells in mortals, so that the seductive is followed, and the pleasurable is easily seen as the truth, and Muslims are completely captivated with lies and promises of the fruit of pleasure, like birds with allurements of bait. This error seduces men's will with its own charm. It suspends the intellect's judgment, and slowly gains our assent, making it so that we approve of what is pleasing to the senses and the will. As the Comic said, a man "dreams of what he wants when awake" and believes what he wants to be true.

This reflection inspired me to sketch briefly the moral laxity of Islam, through which it infiltrated so many nations. I am so well versed that I assign nothing to Islam rashly; whatever I say has been taken from the Qur'an itself and other documents of the Arab Muslims and has been accurately translated into Latin. The defects in typography prevent me providing the Arabic text alongside.

First, let us see how Muhammad himself describes his religion in the Qur'an. In various places, he commends laxity under the specious name of 'easiness,' such as in Q. 2:185, "God wants easiness for you and does not want difficulty for you" (2:181 in Hinckelmann edition). Muhammad abuses this word 'easiness' often in the Qur'an, so that it ought to be admitted to the highest principles of Islam. Of course, this easiness is most popular among the Muslims; as indeed the nature of man shrinks from adversity and difficulty. There is a similar statement in Q. 4:28: "God wants to give you relief," that is to give you a lighter religion, "for man was created weak." What 'weakness' does Muhammad exactly accommodate with his religion? Jalāl al-Dīn, the most famous interpreter of the Qur'an among the Muslims, responds that "a man cannot restrain himself from women and pleasures." Hence it is clear, I think, that this 'easiness' of Muhammad is nothing other than licentious laxity. Likewise, Q. 22:78 says: "God chose you, Muslims, and did not impose on you anything arduous or anything restrictive in religion." Also in Q. 5:6 see: "God does not want to impose anything arduous on you; but wants to purify you" (be careful not to understand this as purification of the heart; here Muhammad is speaking about washing the body), "and to perfect His kindness towards you." An egregious religion! How very different it is from the doctrine and religion of Christ, which requires us arduous tasks for the flesh, limiting the path of salvation to a narrow and difficult track (Matthew 19:23 and Luke 13:24).

In Q. 73:5, the impostor imagines that Gabriel spoke to him in these words in the name of God: "We will certainly cast upon you a heavy word [*qawlan thaqīla*]," which Jalāl al-Dīn interprets as "the Qur'an is strict and harsh because of its difficult and troublesome requirements" in its precepts. Another Muslim interpreter al-Qatādah, in his commentary *Elkarae*, swears by this passage: "By God!" he says, "the statutes and rulings in the Qur'an are difficult, because of what it prohibits, commands and delineates." Muqātil agrees with al-Qatādah about this passage. But does Muhammad himself oppose the 'easiness' of his religion he praised before? First, in the same commentary, *Elkarae*, other interpreters understand the 'heavy word' as the 'strength and value,' rather than the 'difficulty' of the constitutions of the Qur'an. But, if you interpret it as 'difficulty,' Muhammad himself (what a marvel!) retracts this difficulty in the same chapter. If you examine the context, that 'difficult word' [*qawlan thaqīla*] related to verses 1–4 and verse 6, concerns "passing most parts of the night not with sleep, but with prayers and reading the Qur'an." But Muhammad is a hypocrite regarding his own precepts, because he established these things for mere show, as he soon tired of his own strictures and of the complaints of the Arabs (Q. 73:20). Thus, he makes his own words Gabriel's: "God knows that you will not count the night in any way," that is, you will not distinguish the hours of the night, so that you know how great a part you should spend in prayers, and a part in rest; "for which reason He is more lenient towards you. So, choose what is easy in the Qur'an," that is, as much as you can easily do. "For God knows that there will be sick people among you; others who wander the earth for the sake of seeking sustenance and others who fight in God's name against infidels, so they cannot be idle with prayers for much of the night." Here the testimony of Abū 'Ubayd b. al-Qāsim b. Sallām, a Muslim writer, is relevant, in his tract on abrogation [*Kitāb al-Nāsikh wa'l-Mansūkh*, Ar. or *de Abrogante & Abrogato*, Lat.]: "Whatever adversity and difficulty there is in the Qur'an, flavored with threats, was annulled through these words of God: 'God wants light and easy things from you, not heavy and difficult things'."

Let us see some examples of the religion departing from its own precepts so that we can judge more properly about Muhammad's 'easiness.' The law of Christ is holy: he abolishes private revenge and orders that enemies themselves be loved (Matthew 5:38). But there is nothing more troublesome to the mind than this law, since those who suffer injustice are most prone to taking revenge; they are roused as if with a goad, exchanging hatred for hatred, and injustice for injustice. But now Muhammad seems to have said in a similarly holy manner in Q. 23:96, "Drive out evil through what is best," almost like how Paul (Romans 12:21) says "Conquer evil by what is good." Likewise, in Q. 28:54, Muhammad praises those "who are patient, and repel the bad with the good." Indeed, it seems that hardly anyone can express the meaning of Proverbs 25:21 and Romans 12:20 concerning the hot coals to be piled up on the enemy's head better than Muhammad. For he says in Q. 41:34:

"Repel the evil with one which is good; then whenever enmity comes between you and him, he will become as if he were your close devoted friend." I think this is pious, heartfelt and serious enough! However, from the whole character of the Qur'an, I am persuaded that Muhammad, while he seems to speak truthfully and piously in some places, helps mortals to obtain serious piety and sincere holiness in vain, thus deceiving the imprudent under the guise of piety more easily.

Muhammad most intelligently debilitates the law against private revenge, which he had sanctified elsewhere so piously, as if it were not a requirement, but (to use the Pontific phrase) only counsel. For Q. 16:126 says: "If you decide to avenge an injustice, do it by the same measure after you have carefully weighed the injustices done to you," that is, do not exceed the limit, but only return like for like. "But if you are patient," refraining from revenge, "indeed it is better for those who are patient." Q. 2:191 not only allows for private revenge, but also orders it in these words: "Kill those who oppose you whenever you catch them, and cast them out from where they cast you." And in verse 194: "whoever does you wrong, do wrong to them," in turn, "just as he did wrong to you." Indeed, he decrees that a reward is to be expected from God if someone avenges an injustice done to them (Q. 42:36–41).

> Whatever is given to you is only the fruit of the present life; but what is with God is better and everlasting for those who believe and for those who, when some injury befalls them, avenge themselves. But let compensation for evil brought upon you be through a similar evil,

that is, let like be returned for like: "but also anyone who condones injustice, and brings harmony, his reward will be with God. And whoever avenges himself after receiving an injury does not merit punishment" and is not condemned to punishment by law. However, what Muhammad said about having to love enemies clearly goes against his own intentions. For in Q. 3:119 he says it is a most absurd thing that they love their enemies: "Look," he says, "you yourselves (poor confused men!) love them, although they do not love you." In Q. 9:23, he says: "O believers, oppose those who are unbelievers among you, and practice cruelty on you." Therefore, Abū al-Qāsim says:

> Whenever Muhammad says in the Qur'an, 'withdraw from those,' or 'depart from those', these mean that 'do not harm them because of the injury they have inflicted,' or anything of this kind, is understood to be annulled through the 'little line of the sword,' which orders the sword to be taken up against infidels. Whenever Qur'an orders patiently enduring Jews and Christians, and forgiving them, it is annulled through these words: 'Fight against those who do not believe in God and the last day.'

Therefore, let the reader judge whether Muhammad accommodated himself to his own and his people's inclination and strayed from Christ's doctrine. Indeed, this is so evident that it twisted a confession from someone among the Muslims themselves. This is a certain Muhammad, an Arab, who pretended to be Moldavian, and acted as a spy of the Turkish Sultan for forty-five years in Paris disguised as a monk. He sent copious letters to the elders of the Ottoman Kingdom, in which he wrote about deeds of great importance accomplished in all of Europe and France under Richelius, Mazarinus, and King Louis XIV. He wrote:

> Above all, let's observe with care this precept written in the Holy Book of the Christian people, a precept that is not always imprinted in their hearts. Do unto others, even your enemies, as you would have them do unto you. A Duke of Guise set the example for the entire French people, and this is what you shall preach throughout the vast Muslim empire.

Expounding upon this example, he continues thus:

> Sage Brededin! (this is the man to whom the letter was written) Muhammad never showed such generous sentiments when he made this precept into law against those Christians who never offended him. When you cross the path of infidels, kill them, cut their heads off, imprison them and keep them in shackles until they pay their ransom or until you decide it fit to free them. Persecute them all into submission, or until they are all lost.

Furthermore, how lax and licentious is Muhammad's teaching regarding chastity and modesty? Certainly, he condemns whoring and adultery, but only external acts: it is so far from him to reprehend the lusts lying within from which shameful acts sprout that he excuses and permits them as if they were indifferent. In Q. 2:235, Muhammad says

> You will not be guilty of a crime if you reveal your mind to women in some conversation, or if you hide anything of this kind in your soul. For God knows that you think of them, and that you cannot refrain from them.

It seems as if it is the Prophet's duty to act like a teacher and trainer of lovers. The good Muhammad, since he was himself most lascivious, divined that his followers could not have been charmed more easily than by being persuaded that God willingly tolerated lustful thoughts of men. Shame prevents me from saying how much he promotes promiscuous lust. In Q. 2:223, he says: "Your women are a place of sowing seed for you: so come to your field, however you want; but do also some good works for your souls." What superstition and nefarious hypocrisy! I think this defends lust so grossly that even the Muslim interpreters affirm that impious sex with women, that is, the Sodomitic sin, is allowed by this passage. Marracci quotes their words, but it is better to be damned to eternal darkness than to read them and offend one's modesty.

There are still two kinds of laxity with which the impostor promoted his religion as if with very strong arguments: one is polygamy, the other the licentious freedom of divorce. On the Muslim allowance of polygamy, the principle verse is Q. 4:3, "But if you are afraid that you do not treat orphans fairly," and on that account (Marracci supplies from his commentaries) you do not take care of them, fear also that you might not treat many wives fairly. Therefore, take as many women in marriage as seems good to you, two or three or four ex-slaves. Or if you are afraid that you will not treat them fairly as well, take only one; or whatever your right hand possesses—that is, slave girls—as many as you can and want. These words prove what the distinguished Reland denies, that Muhammad, the author of the Qur'an, allowed Muslims to take as many wives as they could maintain: for the words of the Qur'an had already long been used to allow no more than four [wives]. I gladly concede this concerning ex-slave and freeborn wives; especially since in Q. 33:50, it is called a peculiar 'privilege of Muhammad.' But Reland omitted, "or whatever your right hand possesses"; by which indeed slave girls are permitted for marriage without being limited to a fixed number.

However, when Muhammad writes about himself, he egregiously introduces his own Gabriel, who addresses him in Q. 33:50,

> O Prophet, just as I permitted you your wives, to whom you gave your wealth (although he had 21, or according to others 26, and, apart from his legitimate wives, four slave concubines as well). I permitted you whatever your right hand possesses concerning that which God assigned to you (that is, slave girls captured in war). And the daughters of your father's brother, and the daughters of your father's sister, and daughters of your mother's brother, and the daughters of your mother's sister, who fled with you from the city of Mecca, and any faithful woman, if she gave herself to the prophet, and the prophet wanted to marry her. This will be your privilege beyond other faithful men, so that you can marry as many wives as you please.

I have refrained from mentioning many other things on this matter.

The license of divorce, which the disgraceful man established in his religion, has no condition at all, except the willingness, or rather, the desire of the divorcer. In Q. 2:227, Muhammad says: "If spouses decree divorce, God indeed is listening and knows." And verse 229 says:

"Divorce is conceded in two turns, that is, divorce can be threatened twice by a husband to wives; then either the wives are to be kept, and he should treat them justly, or they should be sent away kindly." In Q. 4:20, he makes it permissible, "to exchange wives with others," which is not done except for the sake of lust. In Q. 60:10–12 he allows women who have embraced Islam to marry Muslims, after deserting their 'unbelieving' and 'unwilling husbands' as Muhammad calls them; yet Paul teaches the complete opposite (1 Corinthians 7:13). And to make it even more obvious, how Muhammad crafted Islam to serve either his or others' lust, behold a new license! The false prophet was desperately in love with Zaynab, the wife of his slave and adopted son Zayd. Zayd, more from fear than from willingness divorced his wife for Muhammad's sake. Nevertheless Muhammad, fearing Zayd's jealousy, was not willing to marry Zaynab until that impure Gabriel of Muhammad told him in Q. 33:37:

> Remember Muhammad! When you spoke to Zayd, to whom God was kind, and you also were kind to him: Keep your wife for yourself, and fear God. And you, Muhammad, hid in your soul what God had revealed, (i.e. Zaynab's love): and you feared a man, when, however, you should have feared God instead who made it free for you to marry her. For after Zayd had divorced Zaynab, I gave her to you as your wife.

From these words, it is easy enough to agree that Qur'anic law is so lax in restraining lust that there can be no doubt how any good and religious man could be a Muslim, and yet still be immersed in most unrestrained lusts. Muhammad made his religion more attractive with these allurements, especially to the Arabs, a lustful race which was long notorious for whoring and lasciviousness; the Talmudists in Kiddushin 49b preserved the saying: "If ten measures of whoring descended to the world, Arabia took nine, and the whole remainder of the world, one."

Islam is so light and easy in reproving sins that it is no wonder that Muhammad infused it so easily into the hearts of so many nations. The Qur'an praises his virtue often with magnificent words, for example: "he orders vices to be despised." Yet, there is almost no shameful deed or crime left unencouraged. What is holier than professing and worshipping true God? Yet Muslims are not concerned if they fear anything inconvenient or dangerous to deny God and pretend to some idolatry, however superstitious, as long as they keep the faith as they assume it to be in their hearts. For the flesh shrinks from martyrdom for the sake of God and the truth; and prefers to set its own comfort above professing the truth. You want to hear Muhammad's opinion on this matter? In Q. 5:3, he says: "I have confirmed the Islamic religion to you; but whoever was forced to do something blasphemous—still Muhammad speaking—as long as the believer did not deviate into sin intentionally, God certainly will be indulgent to him and merciful." In Q. 16:106, Muhammad speaking, "Whoever denies God after taking up the faith, having been forced to this while his heart remains firm in his faith is forgiven, but whoever denies God with a willing heart God's anger will be upon them." Muhammad is guilty of the sin of weakness; nor indeed (as they say) does he chide softly which once caused Peter to weep a store of tears. There is no mention of penitence since to deny God out of fear is no sin at all to Muhammad, but prudence. Indeed, in Q. 48:25, Muhammad praises some of his followers who remained in Mecca and did not separate themselves from the idol worshippers so that they could still secretly be Muslims even when Muhammad himself fled to Medina. The Arab whom I have mentioned above relied on this very indulgence and pretended to be a Christian in Paris for forty-five years.

Muhammad also softened the rigor of his law on not eating sacrifices to idols, and carrion, blood, and pork, which he had partially borrowed from Judaism, so that it would not be burdensome for anyone. For he says in Q. 2:173: "Whoever is forced by necessity to eat those things, and not transgressing, and not acting unjustly, there is no charge against him: for God is indulgent and merciful." And he repeats this in Q. 16:115. However, even if they care about the condition which Muhammad placed on the consumption of these things, most Muslims undoubtedly delude themselves that they meet this condition. For this is what Iahias and Jalāl al-Dīn say, "not transgressing and not acting unjustly," to paraphrase: "Not acting unfairly against others, and not making the roads unsafe, and not rebelling from obedience to the priests, and not going too far in disobedience to God." Marracci says that Saint Paul did not teach this and indeed, he did not permit that unlawful things be eaten, either from necessity, or to stave off death itself. And it is even less allowed to eat food if one is forced to do it in contempt of religion, as the example of the Maccabees shows.

Islam displayed another form of laxity when Muhammad allowed the continuation of certain disgraceful pagan practices. When in Q. 4:22–23 he prohibited incestuous marriages, in which he understood most of his race were still complicit, he made concessions to the Arabs. For he said:

> Do not marry women wedded to your fathers, excepting those marriages which have already occurred (e.g., if anyone now has stepmothers in matrimony, they can keep them). You are forbidden from your mothers and sisters and your father's sisters and your mother's sisters, excepting that which has already passed; for God is indulgent and merciful.

In Q. 2:275, he gravely forbids usury [*ribā*], but he still inserts this [clause]:

> This warning from his Lord comes for those who consume interest: if anyone abstains from usury in the future [after this admonition], they may keep what they gained from usury previously; but whoever returns to usury, they will be members of Hell.

With these words, Muhammad conceded that whatever anyone had acquired illicitly through usury could be kept, without paying back the debt. For this reason, he did not need to act according to his own principles, since he had decreed usury absolutely illegal, likening it to theft. For as Augustine says, "There is no remission from sins, unless what was taken away is restored."

Oath-swearing in religion is holy and not to be profaned by reckless abuse or perjury; but, Muhammad, as is his custom, also gave an example of laxity here. For he had no qualms about swearing in the Qur'an, without any sufficient reason, by things that were often frivolous, as a wicked example for his own followers, such as by dispersing winds, by pregnant women, by ships travelling swiftly, by distributing something, by the pen, by the sun and moon, by winds hurled like a mare's mane, by violently blowing winds, by dividing winds, by winds taking things away, by flowing winds, by passing winds, by governing winds, by Mount Sinai, by the book written on parchment, by shooting stars, by the reddening dawn, by the layered sky, and other silly things, which I do not have time to recount now. Muhammad treated the impulsive swearing of oaths indifferently. For in Q. 2:225, he says, "God does not refute you if you swear impulsively; but he punishes you because of that which is in your heart, (i.e. if you swear intentionally and knowingly and with foreknowledge): for God is indulgent and merciful." He repeats the same thing in Q. 5:89. In his gloss, Jalāl al-Dīn explains what is meant by "swearing impulsively": "If the tongue comes first, it is swearing without internal intention; as when someone says: 'No, by God! Yes, by God!'. In this, there is no iniquity or impiety." Finally, although someone might swear knowingly, Muhammad still gives the ability elsewhere in the Qur'an to retreat from their oath within four months, even if the oath is such that the swearer could fulfill its terms without harm to their conscience, according to Muhammad's principles. In Q. 2:226, he says: "Those who swear that they will not want to be involved with their wives in the future," that is, by divorcing them (because it is lawful and a matter of indifference to the Muslims), "a pause of four months" is allowed to them, within which, "if they change their mind, God will be indulgent and merciful." Muhammad brings in this license both for his own benefit and for the benefit of others. For, as Iahias himself says, "Ḥafṣa (Muhammad's wife) once set out to visit her father; and when she came back she caught the Messenger of God (Muhammad, a wonderful messenger of God, indeed!) with her slave girl Maria in her house. And so, after Maria had come out, Ḥafṣa came to the Messenger of God, saying: 'Did I not see what woman was with you in my house?.' To which God's Messenger says: 'By God, I swear, I will never lie down with her in the future'." Muhammad, although he felt that it was very painful for him, abstained from shameless meetings with Maria. But he soon remembered the privilege that he had heard in Gabriel's address, which he imagines in Q. 66:1–2,

> O Prophet! Why do you abstain from that which God has made lawful out of mere desire to please your wives (who because of their jealousy hardly put up with your license); although God is in favor and merciful? For He has already sanctified it for your sake, so that you can absolve yourself from your oaths.

I cannot give more examples of the unrestrained freedom and laxity of Islam if I am to be brief; nor is there any need, since I have already said enough. But we should touch on the preconceptions from which Muhammad deduced this laxity. These are almost the same things that pseudo-Christians tend to abuse on the pretext of impiety and carnal pleasures against 'the truth in Jesus Christ'; but these are more effective among the Muslims, since they are approved in Qur'anic law, and therefore have the authority of the divine word.

Evidently, the first [preconception] is that extraordinary *indulgence of God,* fashioned by the impostor; on which I have this to say in brief. Muhammad devises a religion which, by the great beneficence of God, progressively becomes more and more easy for humankind so that no cause can remain for mortals to complain about. Hence, he said that Judaism was grave and harsh, Christianity easier, and Islam the easiest. To this end, in Q. 3:50, he makes Jesus, our Messiah, speak accordingly: "I come to confirm that which was before me from the law of Moses, so that I can make lawful the part of that which was prohibited to you." Concerning himself in Q. 7:157, he says:

> Anyone who follows Muhammad the Messenger, the unlettered Prophet, whose description they find in their Torah and the Gospel, advising them about what is just, and prohibiting them from what is unjust, and allowing them what is good, and banning for them what is bad, he who takes away their heavy burden from them, and their chains that were on them; these men are blessed.

Also, in Q. 2:286, when he is speaking to his Muslims:

> Do not place a heavy burden on me, just as you placed one on those who were before me; and do not force me to carry, O Lord, for what [must be carried] I do not have enough strength for; but spare me, and pardon me, and pity me.

Indeed, these words do not seem to have such a disagreeable meaning, concerning the annulment of Jewish ceremonies; since Peter (Acts 15:10) asserted that they were "an unbearable yoke," but the reasoning of the times prevents us from interpreting Muhammad's statements in this way. For Muhammad generally decried "the burden of those who were before us" and chronology necessitates that both Christians and Jews are being referenced. Furthermore, the burden of the laws of the Levites, as Muslims themselves admit, had already been taken away beforehand by Christ, nor was it necessary for Muhammad to reintroduce them unless he wished to do so. But then it is a wonder if it had been decreed to Muhammad to make religion easier in this way. Nevertheless, the false prophet restored ceremonies that were already annulled by Christ, such as circumcision, the rite of washing sacred objects, forbidden foods, sacrifices, and the Nazirite vow. I pass over the rites of pilgrimage to Mecca, gargling, throwing stones near Ka'ba or the shrine at Mecca, and so on, which Muhammad added on top of the old rites. Therefore, I think, to use Marracci's words,

> that the Great Muhammad was lax, and a friend to license and sinful freedom. And that he was not speaking about the Jews, whose graver legal or ceremonial precepts Muhammad was aware that Christ had already absolved; but about Christians, and the weight of the Gospel law: which, since the whole is holy and immaculate, prohibits divorce, polygamy, revenge, retaliation, and other laxities of this kind. On the contrary, it orders indissoluble marriage to one wife, charity towards enemies, kindness, chastity, abstinence, humility, perpetual self-denial, contempt of all worldly things, and other perfect virtues of this kind. Gospel law seemed too burdensome and completely unbearable to Muhammad, who was totally addicted to sex, his stomach, murder, rapine and worldly glory.

The second preconception is Muhammad's opinion on God's indulgence and kindness, which the Qur'an abuses as if it were under the protection of a veil of piety. For the reader will remember that Muhammad, when he relaxed the reins of license either to lust, or to gross hypocrisy and denial of God, or to incest, or finally to perjury, added this tagline: "For God is lenient and merciful." He repeats this very sentence throughout the Qur'an so often that it almost turns into a sort of punctuation mark, although it is frequently irrelevant. Muhammad presumes to divine impunity with his profane reasoning, frequently and carelessly appealing to God's mercy.

The third preconception is the tolerance for human stupidity and impotence. Muhammad inculcates a recognition of stupidity in men not with the purpose of leading them to an internal affliction over their own inability, to be seriously recognized and detested, but only to foster laziness, petulance, and impudence. Let Q. 4:28, be an example, where, when he had permitted to his followers a crowd of wives, he knew of no refuge beyond this: "God wants to give you relief, since man was created weak"; as Jalāl al-Dīn's gloss explains, man cannot restrain himself from women and lusts. But, as if by divine grace, I have noticed that many Gentiles have abstained from these things, however blind and unknown they are to God, with only the strength of their character to abstain from gross lusts of this kind.

Yet it is a great wonder that Muhammad, although he knew that man's nature was so enormously weak, nevertheless "required nothing more from man than what he is capable of" and this is his fourth preconception. This can only increase Muslims' sense of security, giving a pretext for the most open intemperate behaviors. Muhammad says "I do not drive man beyond what he is capable of"; Q. 23:62, Q. 2:286, Q. 6:152, and often elsewhere. For this is as familiar a saying of Muhammad's, as is 'easiness' in 6 above. Therefore, Muhammad either abolishes "the heaviness in the law," as Christ calls it (Matthew 23:23), since it is set beyond our strength (and this indeed is Muhammad's opinion); or, if he does not abolish it, he at least accommodates the law to man's choice and natural ability. This is not far from popular flattery for it is pleasing to men that whatever they can manage is the true worship required by God.

The fifth preconception concerns downplaying sins of weakness as they call it or more venial sins; as if they did not offend God or impart guilt on man. On this matter Muhammad says in Q. 33:5, "A charge will not be upon you, if you are ever deluded, but only if your hearts show intention, (i.e., if you do it by design and with premeditation); for God favors you and is merciful." In Q. 53:32, he says, "Your Lord will certainly be more indulgent on you who avoid more serious vices and do not commit anything except venial sins." And finally, in Q. 4:31, "Avoid only more serious sins, which are prohibited to you, and I will expiate you of your evil (more venial) sins and give you the best introduction into Paradise"; the more serious sins are in Jalāl al-Dīn's opinion, upon which a warning of punishment falls from God, such as homicide, fornication, theft. Anyone, who is not a murderer, or fornicator, or thief, is thus capable of hoping for divine grace and salvation. But of course, if someone does not care about 'venial' sins they would not care greatly about 'more serious' sins.

Muhammad's sixth preconception is forgiveness of all sins, even more serious ones, with a declaration of faith in professing one God, that is orthodox Islam. For Muhammad says in Q. 4:48, "Certainly God will not forgive another god being associated with Himself; but He will forgive any other sin that He wishes." He repeats this in verse 116. But what Muhammad says about God showing remission for all sins, except idolatry and polytheism, cannot be understood, except in this sense: any sin, except idolatry and the worship of many gods, is presumed to be condoned by God, even if a sinner never repents nor ceases his sin. This is because (if Muhammad understood the sins to be forgiven after a serious renunciation and penitence for the future) not even polytheism should be called unforgivable, since Muhammad himself, along with his allies, clung to it until he was forty, and sought pardon nevertheless. But Muslim tradition agrees with this, and they heard it from Muhammad's mouth, in the thirtieth part of al-Bukhārī's *Ṣaḥīḥ al-Bukhārī*. For it says that their Prophet said: "Gabriel came to me, and brought me a happy message; because assuredly anyone who was dead, and did not associate with another god at all (i.e., worshipped no other God except Him) will go to Paradise. The narrator says, "I said to the Prophet: 'But, what if he was a thief, or an adulterer'? And the Prophet responded: Even if he was a thief, or an adulterer." I leave theologians to judge whether this is anal-ogous to the Trentines who dream about "the faithful being fornicators, adulterers, soft, lying with men, thieves, greedy, accursed, rapacious, and everyone else who commits fatal sins." See also al-Thaʿlabī's commen-tary which says this: "This verse shows the falsity of the proposition of the Kharijites—the word for Heretics among the Muslims—who think that a serious sinner is an infidel." On this agreement of Muhammad with Pontifical doctrine, Marracci, a man otherwise deserving merit against the Islamic sect, almost congratulates him.

While I am describing the indulgence and laxity of Islam, the bans and precepts of the Qur'an might also come to the reader's mind, of which there are indeed many serious ones. They appear more austere than in-dulgent, and therefore my words would seem not to retort against them enough. As far as the 'bans' are concerned, the prohibition of wine, the ban on usury, along with various kinds of forbidden food, and more of that kind, from which mortals abstain with difficulty will perhaps stands against my argument. But my concern is valid. For first, Mu-hammad could not be without bans of this kind since, if nothing had been totally prohibited, the deceit of his false religion would have been more easily exposed and would not have been so effective at enthrall-ing minds. It was enough for Muhammad and his undertaking if he promised a license to his followers that neither Jewish law nor Christ's Gospel had ever permitted, so long as the law [i.e., Muhammad's law] still seemed to be religious. But then I hardly see what stops any Muslim, if he thinks that the bans are too heavy for him, from temporarily remov-ing the difficulty by that canon of Abū al-Qāsim; whatever harshness is contained in the Qur'an was annulled through these words: "God wills light and easy things from you, and not heavy and difficult things." Cer-tainly, Muhammad himself relaxed the law about not eating pork and other foods. It is also notable that Muhammad in this very prohibition of unclean food showed an example of his populism. Marracci says that pork was rejected by Arabs as they thought it was harmful to the body's health. Muhammad knew that camel (prohibited by the law of Moses, permitted by Muhammad) was greatly in use among the Arabs; for this reason, he suited the laws to their inclination and taste. Nor should there be any fear that the prohibition of interest might be too harmful to Muslims, since he devised a method of abstaining from interest, and yet of loaning out money with the hope of profit from others. Finally, Muslims should more easily go without wine, since their own legislator indulged them with the best drinks, made with grapes and other fruits. As Marracci attests, Muslims freely and copiously drink even wine, nor, as I think, without legitimate credibility: since the two primary interpreters, Jalāl al-Dīn[2] and al-Zamakhsharī, decided that the prohibition in Q. 2:219 and 5:90 does not ban wine absolutely, but "an excessive enthusiasm and devotion to it"; and Muhammad himself, elsewhere in Q. 16:67, praises wine as the best drink and God's special favor.

But as far as the Qur'an's requirements are concerned, at first glance they indeed seem strict; but if one considers them in depth, they are such that both hypocrites and the openly shameless can meet them without difficulty. For the Qur'an's whole structure fosters a vain presumption of holiness; it has no relevance to true holiness or to a solid change of heart and all of man's faculties (which the divine law of the sacred Letters demands). Most of the laws are merely civil, such as on inheritance, debt, war, marriage, or they are ceremonial like prayers, washing and sacred pilgrimages, punishing sins, and other things of this kind, which are freely performed, as the way to Paradise is thought to be made shorter through rites and exterior acts rather than through an earnest renunciation of the self and the world.

Let us suppose that the fight against infidels, which is seriously inculcated in Muslims in all of Sura 9, is inconvenient to Muslims, yet what can be more popular and more pleasing than a promise of great spoils? In Q. 8:70, this finds favor, especially among the Arabs, a race accustomed to living by plunder. Or what can lighten their sense of inconvenience more than the promise that whoever dies in the war against infidels will cross immediately into Paradise, entitled to eternal joys? In Q. 2:154–5, Muhammad says:

> Do not say that those who fall (that is, in war for religion) in the path of God are dead; indeed, rather they live. You do not know the truth, upon them will be blessings from his Lord, and mercy; and they are obtained directly.

Again, in Q. 3:157–8,

> If you are killed in the war against infidels, or die, certainly the indulgence and mercy from God will be better than what others who stay at home get. And if you die or are killed, you will certainly be assembled before God.

Moreover, the precepts of Muhammad do not have one kind of value among the Muslims. For some precepts are 'of the law' and 'necessary,' others of 'tradition,' and finally others of 'addition.' Therefore, let us take up some of the fundamental requirements of the previous kind, which are called "the roots and pillars of the law" by Muslims, and treated as five in Marracci's definition in *Tractatus de legibus Islamiticis*: professing the unity of God, almsgiving, prayers, fasting, and pilgrimage to the shrine at Mecca, to which Abū al-Faraj adds "cleanliness in the body's extremities." None of these requirements are too heavy for the Muslims. For the first is discharged with that formula, which for the Muslims is symbolic: "There is no God except the one God." This profession of faith is also a source of salvation for thieves and brigands among the Muslims. However, it can be abnegated in times of peril if it is dangerous to profess it.

Muhammad advises alms to be given often. But Marracci says that there are two kinds of alms-giving among the Muslims, one *zakāt*, which is properly a kind of tribute or a tithe for the expense of wars against infidels, and the second *ṣadaqa*, or spontaneous alms for beggars and the poor. For the first, Q. 57:10 says,

> Hence you will not refrain from alms on the path of God for war against infidels, since God has the inheritance of heaven and earth. Anyone among you who pays out (*zakāt*) before victory and then fights has no equal; they will be greater in rank than those who fight and pay out afterwards. But God promised the best (i.e., paradise) to everyone.

Thus, it was greatly in Muhammad's interest to exact such alms-giving from his followers if he wanted to wage war on his neighbors. Concerning this, see Q. 2:215–6, where he says, "They will ask you, what or how much should they give to poor people? Respond: the leftover." Truly this is so generalized and ambiguous that I think that greedy Muslims will never have anything 'leftover': nor, if they give any alms, do they do it because of the rigor of the law, rather than for the sake of ostentation or merit.

Concerning prayers, Q. 4:103 says this: "Prayers are prescribed for the faithful, decreed at specified times." Muslims pray five times according to their legal precept: in the morning, at noon, in the afternoon, at sunset, and finally after sunset. Because of these five prayers (arduous command, certainly!) Muslims persuade themselves that they are the true worshippers, who Christ predicted would worship God in spirit and in truth (John 4:23). But if the matter is to be measured by number of prayers, they should certainly concede to David, since he says in Psalms 119:164 that "he praises God" not just five times, as the Muslims do, but "seven times a day," to say nothing of the unceasing prayers ordered by Christ (Luke 18:1).

But can fasting deter men from Islam? No, indeed it is not to be feared, since Muhammad's fasting was arranged so that is doubtful if even the fattest Epicurean could ever desire more profuse pleasures and lusts than Muhammad permitted in times of fasting. Let us hear the man himself preaching about this matter in Q. 2:187,

> At night during a fast you are permitted conjugal access to your wives, for they are your garment, and you are their garment. God knows, that (in the beginning of Islam) you defrauded your souls in this: He had mercy on you and indulged you. Therefore, enter into them, and seek what God prescribed for you, and eat and drink all night until you can distinctly discern a white thread from a black one in the dawn.

An outstanding fast, and against which it can be said from the most eminent law: "What is this fasting that I have chosen?" (Isaiah 58:5). And yet assuredly, whatever justice there was in such a burdensome fast, Muhammad indulged, or as I say, managed it, not only "for the sick and likewise travelers," so that it could be transferred to other days; but also for those "who could fast," so that they could completely omit fasting without any pretext, "as long as they redeem it by feeding one poor person." To which that trite phrase applies, "God wants easy things for you, and does not want hard things for you" in Q. 2:185.

Pilgrimage, or visiting the shrine of Mecca, which Marracci profusely explains, involves difficulties so small that I think it cannot dissuade any Arab from Islam since Muhammad did not introduce it as a new thing, but preserved [the shrine] already long frequented by pagan Arabs over the course of many centuries. Muhammad's desire to please the people of Arabia with this law is indeed well-known. During the same pilgrimage, he ordered the mountains of Mecca, Ṣafā and Marwa, once sacred idols, to be circled in the old rite of the pagans, in Q. 2:158. He had no cause for doing this except to soothe his Arabs, long accustomed to this thing. On top of that, many Muslims went on that pilgrimage for the sake of trade, which was greatest at that time at Mecca because it was the confluence of the whole Orient, and this was permitted by Muhammad, not without the precedent of this sacred ceremony, in Q. 2:196. Finally, whoever has only once set out on that account [to Mecca] in their whole life has done enough for this requirement. Also, if the route to [Mecca] was not safe, or if one could not afford to go on the pilgrimage, the religion did not oblige them.

Finally, on purification, or Muslim cleanliness, the Qur'an does not go farther than Abū al-Faraj's precise description as washing "a man's outermost parts, that is, the face, hands, elbows, head, feet, and ankles." Indeed, in Q. 5:6, Muhammad says:

> O faithful, when you stand to do prayers, first wash your face, and your hands up to the elbows, and scrub your head, and likewise your

feet up to your ankles, and if you are unclean because of sex, wash yourselves with water. Or, if you are ill or on a journey, (so that water is not available, or does not help), or if one of you comes from the toilet, or if you touch women, and cannot find water, take some good dust for purification (a ridiculous purification!) and rub your face and hands with it. God does not want to place any difficulty on you.

Thus, Q. 4:43 [says the same thing], however, there is no inner spiritual purification. Although more prudent Muslims portray it as allegorical, such as al-Ghazālī, who establishes four stages of purification: first, cleanliness of the body from excrement of the stomach, impurities, and excess; second, cleanliness of the limbs from wickedness and iniquity; third, cleanliness of the heart from vices and depraved habits; and fourth, cleanliness of the secret (i.e., heart) from everything except God. Al-Ghazālī greatly grieves since Muslims meanwhile have "internal desolation and are full of the vices of arrogance, pride, ignorance and hypocrisy." In truth, when Ismā'īl, the son of 'Alī Abū'l-Fidā, describes the difference between Christianity and Islam, he says: "Christians do not use purification before prayer, and they disapprove of the Jews' and Muslims' purification, asserting that the foundation should be placed in purity of the heart." Even a Muslim affirms this. Therefore, that alone teaches us that Islam is superficial, lax, easy, and only occupied with externals.

This is what I have undertaken to explain briefly with my study. I ask God to illuminate the many races poorly deceived by Muhammad's frauds with the light of His Gospel! May He preserve me and sanctify me in His truth since the Word is His Truth.

Notes

1 Michaelis' biography was compiled from the following sources: Heinrich Döring, *Die Gelehrten Theologen Deutschlands im achtzehnten und neunzehnten Jahrhundert. Nach ihrem Leben und Wirken dargestellt* (Neustadt an der Orla: Johann Karl Gottfried Wagner, 1832), 498–502; Carl Gustav Adolf Siegfried, "Michaelis, Christian Benedikt," in *Allgemeine Deutsche Biographie*, vol. 21 (Leipzig: Duncker & Humblot, 1885), 676–7; R. Kittel, "Christian Benedikt Michaelis, in *Real-Enyklopädie für protestantische Theologie und Kirche*, ed. Johann Herzog and Albert Hauck (Leipzig: Hinrichs, 1903), 53–54; Manfred Fleischhammer, "Die Orientalistik an der Universität Halle (1694–1937): Eine Skizze,"· *Wissenschaftliche Zeitschrift Martin-Luther-Universität Halle-Wittenberg* 7 (1958): 877–84; Christoph Bochinger, *Abenteuer Islam: Zur Wahrnehmung fremder Religion im Hallenser Pietismus des 18. Jahrhunderts*, Habilitationsschrift (München: LMU, 1996), 58–68; Christian Stephan, *Die stumme Fakultät: Biographische Beiträge zur Geschichte der theologischen Fakultät der Universität Halle* (Dössel: Stekovics, 2005), 49–50; Michael C. Legaspi, *The*

Death of Scripture and the Rise of Biblical Studies (Oxford: Oxford University Press, 2010), 84–85; Avi Lifschitz, *Language and Enlightenment: The Berlin Debates of the Eighteenth Century* (Oxford: Oxford University Press, 2012), 96–99.

2 [MK] The name refers to the author of *Tafsīr al-Jalālayn*, one of the most significant commentaries (*tafsīr*) of the Qur'an. Composed by the two "Jalāls" – Jalāl al-Dīn al-Maḥallī (d. 864/1459) and his pupil Jalāl al-Dīn al-Suyūtī (d. 911/1505), *Tafsīr al-Jalālayn* is generally regarded as one of the most easily accessible works of Qur'anic exegesis because of its simple style and length.

2 Muhammadan Religion

Friedrich Ulrich Calixt

Friedrich Ulrich Calixt was born in Helmstedt in 1622. His father, Georg Calixt, was a well-known theologian at the University of Helmstedt. Young Calixt studied philosophy and medicine at Helmstedt and Leipzig before turning to the study of theology. In 1650, he became professor of theology at Helmstedt and, in 1652, he became a Doctor of Theology. He upheld the theological opinions of his father, dubbed 'Calixtinian,' which argued against the claim to the theological and ecclesiastical exclusivity of Lutheran orthodoxy. It would not be an exaggeration to say that the whole seventeenth century of Helmstedt theology was dominated by the two Calixts: the younger Calixt and his more famous father. For his views, the elder Calixt had been accused of 'syncretism' and being a 'crypto-Catholic' during the Syncretic Controversy, which set the more extremist Lutheran theologians of Wittenberg, led by Abraham Calov, against the more liberal Lutheran theologians of Helmstedt. The Syncretic Controversy (1640–1686) was a theological debate provoked by the elder Calixt and his supporters; they wanted to provide a means to bridge the gap between Lutherans, Roman Catholics, and the Reformed churches. After the assumption of his professorship at Helmstedt, the younger Calixt renewed the Syncretic Controversy in 1662, arguing that all sects of Christianity contain some of the universal truths needed for salvation. He viewed the first five centuries of the Church as a pure and nearly uncorrupted age, with the worst heresies and corruption setting in afterwards. He believed the Roman Catholic Church was the most corrupt due to the papacy's claims to supremacy and superstitious additions to fundamental articles of the faith, but he was also critical of various aspects of Reformed and Lutheran theology. Calixt was, therefore, in favor of religious tolerance between sects, but he was hesitant about reunification with the Catholic Church. In 1684, Calixt was appointed Abbot of the monastery in Königslutter and he died in Helmstedt in 1701.[1]

Variant Names: Friderico Ulrico Calixto, Friderici Ulrici Calixti, Frid. Ulricus Calixtus, and Friedericus Ulricus Calixtus.

Summary and Analysis

Calixt begins his dissertation by saying that, while Muslims do not reject Christian scripture and nominally accept the Old and New Testaments, Muslim understanding of scripture is deficient since they give priority to the Qur'an. He maintains that many Christians, chiefly Catholics, are guilty of giving the same weight to oral traditions as to scripture as do Muslims, and this sets the stage for his critique of Islamic and Christian sects. He also analyzes the Qur'an for similarities and differences between the Qur'an and the Christian scripture, such as passages from the Qur'an that support the virgin birth and others that deny the divinity of Christ. He also cites Luther's unfavorable comparison of Muslims to Catholics, saying that Muslims are cruel and slaughter Christians, while Muhammad advocated conversion by force rather than persuasion, hence, Catholics are no better. In fact, Calixt maintains the Pope persecutes non-Catholic Christians more than the Turks.

According to Calixt, a religion that did not always exist cannot be true, and since Muhammad's religion began in the seventh century, then it must be false. However, he fails to say whether Christianity's origin lay in Creation. Furthermore, he says that Muhammad was an illiterate camel herder who came into wealth when he married a rich woman. With few followers, Muhammad could not establish himself as king as he wished to do, so instead used his wife's wealth and his cunning charisma to claim that he was a prophet of God. Calixt asserts that Muhammad used force instead of reason to make others accept his claims, just as Catholics compel non-believers to join the Holy Mother Church. Although the Turks, in an apparent contradiction of an earlier policy, allowed Christians to worship freely, this was to ensnare and entrap them. Calixt explains that Muhammad's sources for his religion, having much in common with Christianity, came from a heretical monk named Sergius, who converted Muhammad from paganism to Nestorian Christianity. It was the heretical Nestorian doctrine that Christ was not crucified that gave rise to that false teaching in Islam. Therefore, for Calixt, Islam is nothing other than a reformulation of a heretical sect of Christianity.

Following a brief aside into the etymology of Saracen and the Saracens' relationship to Muslims, Arabs, and Turks, Calixt considers the demise of Islam, citing the opinions of those who believed that Gog and Magog refer to the Turks. He also cites a Turkish prophecy in which Christians will be conquered—only to rise up and put the Turks to flight. Turks and Muslims, however, will not be defeated until Christians cease their evil ways and love one another as brothers. Calixt then discusses selected biblical passages that support the claim that Islam will disappear and all people, including Muslims, will convert to Christianity before Christ's final coming. This is followed by a detailed discussion of the etymology and possible identity of Gog and Magog, the man and land, respectively.

According to Calixt, although Muslims accept the divine provenance of Christian scripture, they believe that the Christians erased the future coming of Muhammad. Dismissing this as false, he says that many Muslims will need convincing by reasoned argument if they are to convert to Christianity. Neither Moses, nor the prophets, nor the Evangelists prophesized the coming of Muhammad, but Jesus is superior

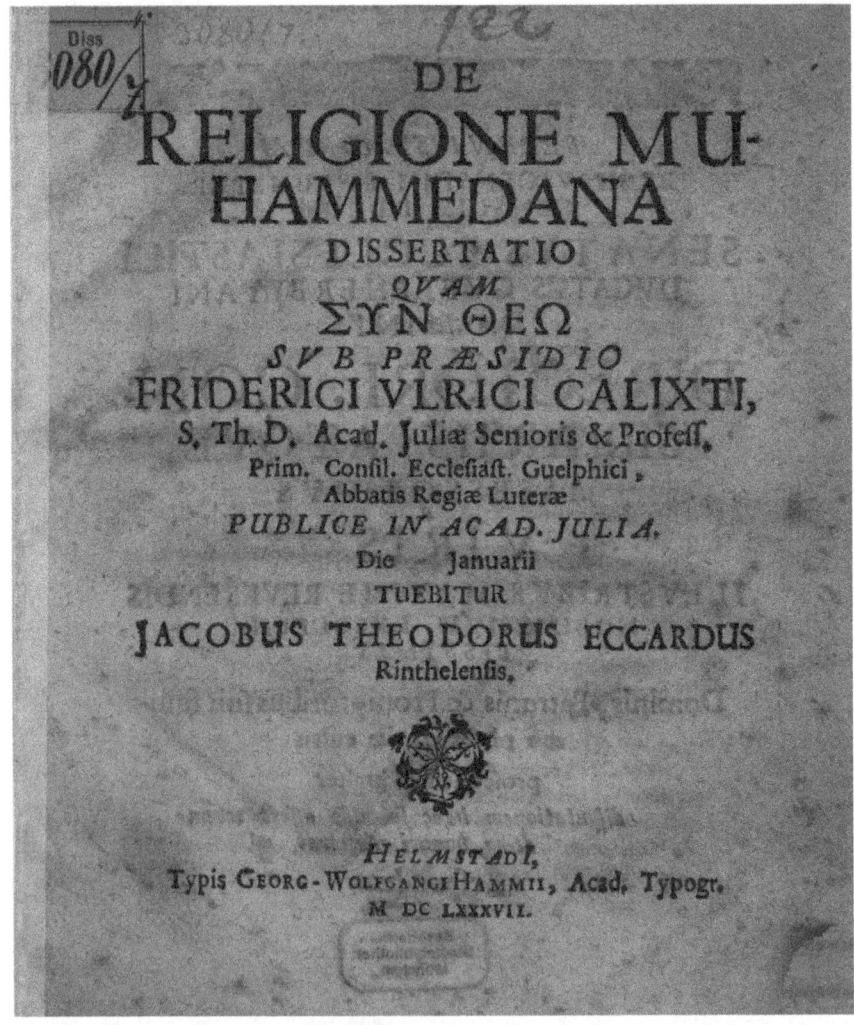

Figure 2.1 Friedrich Ulrich Calixt, *De religione Muhammedana dissertatio*, 1687 (Courtesy of the Bavarian State Library, Munich).

to him because he was born of a virgin while Muhammad was not and was resurrected while Muhammad was not. Even so, Muslims should be easier to convert than Jews, since the former, unlike the latter, recognize the truth of the New Testament.

At this point, Calixt presents a lengthy account of salvation and how Muslims might be converted using Christian scripture. He says that those who want to convert Muslims must focus on the fundamentals and not be distracted by arguments about issues that cause doctrinal differences in Christianity. These differences cause difficulties for the prospective convert to know which path leads to salvation. The answer, for Calixt, is to embrace all those teachings which are agreed upon by all Christian sects. Pernicious teachings can be identified when there is no such unanimity, and he gives examples of false teachings in Greek Orthodox, Reformed, and Lutheran Christianity—although he reserves most of his criticism for Catholicism, which emphasizes traditions not found in the Bible. Calixt concludes with an appeal for unity and consensus among the many Christian sects, for only in unity can Christians hope to convert unbelievers to their faith.

Unlike other Lutheran authors, Calixt's *dissertatio* is a clear indication of his close engagement with the Syncretic movement, which supported the idea of conversion and ecumenism. As the Calixtinians wanted to create a bridge between Lutherans and other Christian sects, including Roman Catholics and the Reformed Church, the struggle between the Orthodox Lutheran theologians of Wittenberg against the more liberal Calixtinian theologians of Helmstedt reached an impasse toward the end of the seventeenth century. Therefore, for Calixt, unlike Orthodox Lutherans, Muslims are not just a tool to criticize Catholicism, but present an opportunity to save souls through the adoption of universal basic Christian teachings, which are unanimously agreed upon. For him, only unity among Christian sects can accomplish this goal of conversion.

Dissertation on Muhammadan Religion (Helmstedt, 1687)

Muslims do not reject the canonical scripture completely, but nominally accept the books of the Old and New Testament. However, they do not read or pay attention to the passages they should: indeed, they claim that the Scriptures are deficient in many ways. Also, it is a serious discredit to the Christian religion that even Christians are guilty of treating divinely revealed scripture as no better than incomplete unwritten traditions; just as the Saracens and Persians do not so much add the traditions as believed and recorded in the wicked Muhammad's absurd Qur'an to both Testaments, but rather they greatly prefer the Qur'an.

Moreover, Muslims recognize that Christ was born from a virgin. They consider and value Jesus as a great prophet, in whom the very soul of almighty God was placed. Muhammad spoke in God's persona in Q. 2:253, "We raised some prophets in rank above others, and then some of them spoke with God. We gave Jesus Christ, the son of Mary, strength and virtue above others and blessed him with the Holy Spirit." Although the Qur'an seems to understand Christ sufficiently, yet it says that he was inferior to the grim and bloody Muhammad. But it is not too surprising that Muslims consecrate the mind of God to Christ, since they attribute another part of the divine soul to men formed from clay. This mystery is revealed in Q. 15:28–29 with these words: "I said to the angels that I will create a man formed of clay, and I breathed a portion of my spirit into him." The verse speaks again in God's persona. Since men have a portion or a part of God's spirit, Christ can have part of God's spirit while still being a man. But the viewpoint that Christ's soul is in communication with that of God in the same way as souls of other men is absurd. Every aspect of God's spirit is part of His divine essence. Therefore, if Muslims concede that an aspect of God lives in Christ, they should say that the whole essence of God is in Christ, and that the two are therefore one and the same, and Christ is the true God.

Muslims deny the divinity of Christ again and again. Since Christians constantly affirm what Muslims deny without any fear of opposition or falsehood, Muslims call Christians 'associaters' (*al-mushrikūn*) on the grounds that they associate and join Christ with God, the Creator of heaven and earth. On the associating with the other God, Sura 25 in the Qur'an can be consulted; in the beginning as in other places, the worship of one God is foisted:

> Can those who associate another god with God really know the truth? Those who do so are engaging in contradiction and harming their own minds. You all should worship one God, and may you not cease to call upon Him until death comes, by humbling and abasing yourselves and pouring out your prayers.

Sura 14 says: "The unbelievers (Christians) place Christ as identical and equal to God (made like Him and consubstantial to Him)." This is the chief disagreement between Muslims and Christians; however, there are many other disagreements which betray the vanity of the religion that Muslims argue for and treat as a divine oracle. They impudently peddle these and other such beliefs.

Therefore, Muslims attribute nothing to Christ—whom they neither recognize as the Father or consubstantial with Him—above and beyond the dignity of a prophet. They also associate many others with him, among whom they do not even grant Christ the honor of the highest position. 'Muslims only admit three prophets,' says Volaterranus, 'whom they call *rasūl*, or Messenger: Muhammad, Moses, and Christ, whom they yet do not consider God in any way.' To these three, Munsterus in his *Cosmography* adds a fourth, namely, David, prophet of kings, to whom the Psalms were given from heaven when the law of Moses had been weakened. In one way, Muhammad is the last and best and greatest of these men, the one who stands above them all, "just as the moon among the lesser stars"; however, that very man [Muhammad] is a false prophet and the worst impostor.

The Qur'an, dictated by Muhammad himself, shows this belief to his followers. For the sake of brevity, it would not be reasonable to give all possible examples of this. Just as Islam is a doctrine of faith, it is also a doctrine of morals. Instead of "the sanctimony without which no one will see God," Muslims show a different sort of sanctity, demonstrated by their religious ceremonies. The spectators of this sufficiently laborious ostentation observe many religious superstitions. Concerning this specious sanctity, which exceeds even that of the Christians, our B. Luther in his preface to the *History of the Saracens or Turks*, published in Basel in 1543, recounts: "We see from this book that the religion of the Turks and Muhammad is more specious by far in terms of its ceremonies than those of our own religious fanatics and clerics." After Luther tells about some of the practices in the Catholic Church, he mentions "specious ceremonies, shavings, hoods, pale complexions, fasting, feast days, canon hours, the whole appearance of the Roman Church throughout the world; in all of these the Turks far outstrip them." Meanwhile, they are so far removed from love and humanity to their neighbor that no human blood can sate their cruelty. Muslims are more rapacious than any vulture and they are always grasping at another's life and fortune. Undertaking a speech about war against barbarians, which provoked the Turks to slaughter Christians, the Byzantine emperor John VI Kantakouzenos expounded Muhammad's moral theology in these words:

> The teacher and leader of error, Muhammad, clearly persuaded his men, who have lived chastely here, that whoever fights against us or dies or kills as many of us as possible would enjoy the immortal prizes which have been set aside for them.

Muslims do not persuade people of their prophet's dogma through reason but propagate it by force. Indeed, Muhammad completely forbade that the truth of his dogmas should be disputed or questioned. Having conducted life most evilly in this age, Muslims hope it will continue more wickedly in the afterlife. Naturally, they place the highest blessedness of the next life in bodily pleasures: food, drink, and sex. However, with what little rationality remains to them, Muslims know that these things are inconsequential. Therefore, their reason does not reach perfection as their religion is naturally imperfect. Although Muslims teach that their religion follows the course of reason, it is in fact opposed to reason. In his refutation of al-Ghazālī's *The Incoherence of the Philoso-phers*, Averroes wrote that al-Ghazālī disagreed with philosophers, and with Muslim theologians, who are known to be loquacious. Indeed, it is not difficult to prove this with examples, and it was not long before Hieronymus [Girolamo] Savonarola alleviated me in this task, as he demonstrated in his short commentary, titled "Muhammadan sect lacks all reason," which was included in *Confutatio Legis Machumeticae* (*Refutation of the Muhammadan Law*). Avicenna explains the theology of Muhammad, which he condemns in no uncertain terms, and at the same time indicates something greater, of which there is not the slightest evidence in the Qur'an. Thus, he wrote in *Metaphysics* 7, Chapter 9:

> Our law, which Muhammad gave, relates to an ordering of hap-piness and misery which arises from the body. Wise theologians were much more desirous for true happiness rather than happiness of the body. If the happiness of the body is granted to them, it does not compare in value to the true happiness of intellectual union with the first truth, which is the blessed God. But since we wallow in this age and in this body in many wicked acts, we do not feel that spiritual delight, nor seek it, nor are we drawn to it, unless we first shake the yoke of pleasure, anger, and female lovers from our necks. When we do, then, the paralysis will be removed and we will look on true delight, which is with the King of Ages, who is the blessed God.

Every sound mind knows that a religion that did not exist from the beginning and whose inventor is known is not a true religion. Since the beginning of Muhammad's religion—or rather, superstition—is very well known, it cannot be a true religion. That grievous religion, with the permission of God angry with mortals, lay on the earth for a thousand years and more. The impostor and false prophet Muhammad appeared in the seventh century under Heraclius, around the year of Christ 622. In the manner usual to impostors, he did not immediately burst onto the world stage, but spread secretly for ten years like a virus in his native Mecca. As soon as he arrived with a new law, he began to attract follow-ers and divided the community. When his fellow Meccans rose against him, Muhammad was forced into exile and withdrew to Medina, where he spent his forty-fourth year. Medina was once called *Yathrib*, a small town ten-days distant from Mecca. After Medina gave sanctuary to Muhammad, it became known as *madīnat al-nabī*, which means 'the prophet's city.' Clearly, the false prophet located the seat of his power there.

   That flight of the false prophet is so venerated among Muslims that they began to count their years from it and took it as the beginning of their era. That is why the 'Epoch of the Saracens' comes from the name *hijra*, which means 'flight' in Arabic. Joseph Scaliger speaks well on this matter:

> Since Islam apes Christianity in many ways, it gives the beginning of its era the same name, which the Christians took from Diocletian. As the age of Diocletian was called 'the age of martyrs,' the Islamic era was called *hijra*, from the Arabic root *hajara*, that is, 'religious persecution'.

The time of this most auspicious flight was the sixteenth of July 622 A.D., on the fifth day, according to the average calculation, or the sixth according to the phase of the moon. Ulugh Beg [d.1449] states in *Epochs* that Muslims count the months of this epoch from the phase of the new moon to the phase of the following new moon, and this interval never exceeds thirty days nor is it less than twenty-nine, so that there are four months following alternately of thirty days, and three of twenty-nine. Thus, the years and months are truly lunar, according to their usage.

Muhammad's natural gifts and strength of character went far enough so that he did not lack instruments of malice, but he was a sly and shape-shifting man, ignorant of letters, since he could neither read nor write as he himself says in Q. 7:158: "Emulate the prophet and messenger, who is illiterate." And shortly after says: "Believe in Him (meaning God, of course), and me, His messenger, who is ignorant of reading and writing. So, believe Him and His precepts wholeheartedly." As Muhammad was sent into service for the business of Khadīja, the daughter of Hulert, he lacked the opportunity to learn to read and write. A most learned anonymous Christian disputer says that slavery 'made Muhammad a servant to Khadīja and the camels.' He recounts that

> after Muhammad became rich from the wealth of a woman he married, he tried to seize rule over his tribe and home country. When he attempted this, he was unable to do things as he liked, since he still had only a few followers. As he could not be a king, he used his great skill and character to pretend to be the prophet of God and a messenger.

Muhammad speaks of himself in the Qur'an, Q. 93:6–7: "Through dawn and dusk, God will never send you away, who found you as an orphan" (for he was a ward of his uncle, 'Abd al-Muṭṭalib) "and an unbeliever" (indeed in the beginning he was a worshipper of idols, and then became a Nestorian) "and taught you the correct path, and having found you a poor man made you rich."

Muhammad did not invite others to join the new worship or persuade them of the dogmas of his new religion with rational arguments but promoted his superstition with violence. Muhammad says that "anyone who does not obey his law should die, unless they give tribute." That Christian disputer cited above recounts Muhammad's behavior, rebuking, and berating him:

> You have never read in the divine scripture that some were turned to God violently with the sword, by pillage, and by being taken captive as your friend [Muhammad] had done. Muhammad ordered those he coerced to obey himself. He coerced his sect not with his shrewdness and ingenious talking alone, but with the sword, violence, oppression and pillaging. It was never heard before Muhammad: 'Whoever will not confess me as a prophet of the lord of ages, I will strike him with the sword. Everyone, whoever he is, even my progeny, if they act similarly I will both seize his house and throw all of his family into captivity'.

Muslim superstition was propagated and increased and became strong by the sacrilegious impostor's effort, through mere violence, wars, and theft. However, many who wanted to be considered Christians were not able to damn and execrate such violence of men in the name of religion. But is not the same tragedy played today with different characters? Certainly, I should have justly and rightly rebuked the 'friends of Loyola,' who inciting the same high treasons as the wicked and bloody 'friends of Muhammad,' which they did, with the same words as the 'anonymous Christian disputer.' I wish none of these things that have been said of 'Muhammad's violent convertors,' could be also said of the 'violent Catholic convertors,' who go to teach and preach the gospel surrounded by mounted soldiers! But this is equally true of these men. For what violence was not committed by the Saracens which the Christians do not also perpetrate against other Christians today? Are they forced today to superstitious acceptance by 'the sword, oppression, devastation, pillaging, and captivity' more gently than those whose necks are bent under the baneful Turkish yoke?

Although Muslims could compel anyone to deny their own religion by the law of the Qur'an, they noticed it was more profitable for their state to tolerate other religions, using the forceful collection of taxes [i.e., *jizya*, the collection of a tax that guarantees tolerance for Christians]; as a result, non-Muslims no longer had to observe Muslim dogma. Johann Wolf states: "The Turks force no one to deny their religion, although in the Qur'an it was ordered that they [Muslims] wipe out their [religious] opponents. Why, therefore, do Papists want to be worse than the Turks?." Again, Johann Wolf says

> The Turk indulges in public peace for Catholics in Greece and elsewhere, not indeed because the Turk wishes peace on any Christian,

but because, thereby, they draw more to the snare and entice them to obedience. The Turks see that the Roman Pontiff, whom Christians make a god, persecutes those who are of a different religion to his own, with monstrous violence. The Turks, more humanely and mercifully, leave the worship of whatever god to each man's conscience. In this, of course, they act kinder towards Christians than the Roman Pope, who murders them most monstrously with the sword, fire, and water. The Pope prefers to tolerate, foster, and love whoever is the most wicked idol worshipper, Sodomite, and Jew as his followers.

It is certainly most ignominious to the Christian name that some Christians are persecuted under Christian majesty like pagans, while others live more freely under Turkish rule with a pure and simple heart.

Otherwise, we would be surprised such firm foundations could be laid with such daily impiety and strong tyranny within a few years. For Muhammad himself did not survive long after his flight, but breathed his unhappy last in the eleventh year after he fled from Mecca, in the year 633 A.D. But just as he was always eager to imitate Christ and his miracles like an ape, so he did not fear to say that "he would return from the dead on the third day and rise again to the living." On Muhammad's prophecy, Volaterranus wrote:

> Before Muhammad died, he predicted that he would go to heaven. His followers, waiting long for this, were at last forced by the foul smell to consign him to a tomb in the city of Mecca, which they visit as we visit Jerusalem.

The Christian disputer cited earlier describes the same thing as Humbrem recounts: "That thing," he says,

> is so ridiculous to us, and so lamentable to them, when Muhammad ordered them not to bury his dead body, on the grounds that he would be taken to heaven on the third day. They themselves, observing this order, awaited it with great longing, and now tired from the long wait on the second day, realized that nothing rose up in him, except for a great stench, and at last buried him naked.

Muhammad's religion lasted for a thousand years and more through the will of a God angry with mortals. Even if it lasts until the end of the world, this would not prove the truth of this religion, but rather its falseness, since its origins are well-known. For Islam did not exist for as long as human beings have existed but owes its birth to a man's desperate malice. Muhammad, indeed, was converted to Christianity from idolatry through a Nestorian heresy, which usurped the name of Christianity.

He was converted by the efforts of a certain fugitive monk, whose name was Sergius. On this man the writer above says:

> Since the monk Sergius had sinned grievously in his monastery, he was excommunicated and expelled. He came to the region of Cuhenna, and from there he went down to Mecca where there were two peoples, one a worshipper of idols and the other Jewish. There he found Muhammad, who worshipped idols. Since Sergius wanted to please the monks who expelled him and merit reconciliation, he persuaded Muhammad to abandon idols and become a Nestorian Christian. Muhammad became his student, and he called himself Nestorius because of this. The monk taught Muhammad something about the Old and New Testament, and he weaved it into his Qur'an mendaciously and dishonestly.

From this, it should be obvious that Islam derives from Christianity, since from its very beginning it was nothing other than a certain sect and heresy. It is, therefore, not surprising that it has many similarities to Christianity, so much so that they should not be called 'half-Christians,' as Erasmus does, but, rather, to use Joseph Scaliger's words 'apes of the Christians.' Clearly, they seem to differ from us in the most important matters, but in the smallest, they seem the same. Although Muslims do not shrink in horror at Christ, as the Jews do, the principal intention of Muhammad is to persuade us that "Christ is neither God nor the son of God, but a certain holy and wise man; he was the greatest prophet and was born from a [biological] father and a virgin."

Christians never gloried in Muhammad's conversion, even for a short time. For it was more ignominious than honorable and glorious to produce such a vicious enemy and persecutor of men, a false prophet and impostor as Muhammad was. However, the monk Sergius chased after thanks from the men who expelled and proscribed him, on the grounds that he made a Christian similar to himself (i.e., a Nestorian heretic), from the idol worshipper Muhammad. Nor did he reflect much about the salvation of the man who turned away from worshipping idols and converted to Nestorian treachery. For just as the Nestorians perish, so he himself perished; and everyone bewitched by Muslim superstition perishes. Instead, Sergius caused the worst problems for Christianity by drawing [Muhammad] away from idol worship. If he had remained in idol worship, he would not have been condemned by Christians, as he was a false Christian after his conversion, and later, became a false prophet. If Muhammad had remained an idol worshipper, his descendants would not have acquired such great strength, by which the Christian world tragically lost a great part of itself. Since Muhammad became a Nestorian Christian, he left some obvious traces of Nestorianism in Islam.

One such alleges that "Christ was not killed by the Jews, or crucified, but another man like him was." Although [Franciscan Friar] Richard, in his *Refutation of the Law of the Saracens*, says that "Muhammad agrees in these matters with the Manicheans and Jacobites," he agrees in these matters more with Nestorius, who thus berates Christ's executioners, "Do not rejoice for Judea, since you crucified not God, but a man." In this at any rate he is worse than Nestorius, since he recognizes nothing divine in Christ. Nestorius did not deny Christ's divinity, although he falsely claims [two] distinct persons, one crucified and the other not, as there are two natures joining the divine and human in Christ. Nestorius said that "he does not want to worship one who was nourished with milk for two months, nor one who fled to Egypt, or to call them God." Nestorians do not fear to strike with anathema those who "say that Mary gave birth to God." Another eminent man, Anastasius Antiochenus said: "No one should call Mary one who gave birth to God as Mary was human. For God cannot be born from a human." Is it from this Nestorian root that all denial of Christ's divinity was sifted into Muhammad's corrupt brain like a pitchfork? But this is incidental to the obvious traces of Nestorianism in Islam.

The general name that Muhammad's descendants chose for themselves is 'Saracens,' although they should have derived their name from Ishmael, the son of the slave girl Hagar, rather than from Sara, after whom they are also commonly called Ishmaelites. In the words of the praiseworthy historian Sozomenus:

> Indeed this race of 'Muslim' Saracens drew its origin and took its name from Ishmael, the son of Abraham; and moreover, people used to call them Ishmaelites because of their ancestor. With this, they completely erased the stain of their spurious lineage, and the commonness of Hagar, the mother of Ishmael, for she was a slave, and called themselves Saracens, as if they were born from Sara the wife of Abraham.

The etymology of the Arabic word Saracens is derived from 'Sarac,' which means seized, plundered, or mad. Since the word Saracens means mad and pillagers, many people today use it for the Turks. As there were many races living by plunder, this word was applied to all plunderers, as well as specific pillagers or others of this same kind. Ammianus Marcellinus meaningfully describes the Saracens' ways in words worth quoting here. He says,

> the Saracens, never wanting either to be friends or enemies with us, roaming everywhere, devastated whatever they found like greedy kites who never delay. If they look down on their prey from on high they seize it in rapid flight.

The origins of the Muslim superstition are as certain as its ending is ambiguous and doubtful. We cannot know for certain whether or not Islam will endure to the end of the time or descend to Hell like Muhammad and Sergius. There are those who want to interpret Revelation 20:8–9 concerning the invasion of Gog and Magog, and the repression and killing to be about Turks. They believe with such certainty that the predicted disaster and ruin will befall the Turks, and think the killing [of the Turks] will be among the signs to come before the Last Day of Judgement. Josephus also supports this conjecture. He considers the Scythian race was derived from Magog, the son of Japheth. "Magog,' he says, 'was the originator of those called Magogi, who called themselves Scythians." Therefore, it is very probable that the cited passage of Revelation refers to the Scythians or the Turks, who after some centuries occupied the region of the Scythians and succeeded them. Theodoret and many others have read the works of Josephus. However, some interpreters, most notably Jerome, disagree. I am unsure that the interpretation of Revelation refers to the Turks, but I hope that this is the case, and that disaster quickly overtakes them. Perhaps, with God's kindness to Christians, this ruin will befall the Saracen race before long. Among all the prophecies of their fanatical prophets, the Turks hold none more certain than the prophecy, which foretells their numerous victories over our race and our ultimate destruction. Bartholomew Georgiewitz translated this prophecy from common Turkish to Latin and illustrated it with notes. The translation has this kind of tone:

> Our Sultan will come and take the kingdom of the pagan prince and its red apple, and bring it into his power; but if the sword of the Christians does not rise in rebellion in the seventh year, they will be ruled over until the twelfth year; they will build houses, they will plant vines, they will fortify the gardens with fences, they will produce children; after the twelfth year since the red apple was put in the Turks' power, the sword of the Christians will appear and put the Turks to flight, scattering them in all directions.

To the Christians' great ill, the Turks believe the first prophecy was fulfilled. They still fear this last threatening disaster, and fear that the rest of the prophecy will be fulfilled. This prophecy disheartens their minds. Ashamed of their iniquity and injustice, they devolve into wailing in public when they read the end of the prophecy, as if the future calamity was already at hand and was pressing down on their necks. Indeed, I know that such oracles deserve no credence, and therefore, I do not believe them. However, I would greatly like the destruction of that most wicked race to be predicted in a true prophecy. If only this prophecy, which was truthful enough against us, would also prove true against them! After so many calamities, most of that which has been lost would be restored, to solace the afflicted, for the glory of God, and for Christendom! When our merciful Father fulfills this prophecy, we will attribute nothing to the vanity of the Muslim oracle, but we will give thanks to divine benevolence for a received act of kindness. But we will not obtain what we hope and wish for unless we leave our evil ways for the straight path and walk according to the will of Him who wants to love us as brothers, since we are of the one heavenly Father.

Those who attack Christians and turn their victorious arms to Christians' own bowels will experience the disasters destined for them in place of victory, to their great cost and highest penalty of the Christian state. For God is just and sees the hidden thoughts of our hearts and our secret actions.

There is reference to the "coming unto the fullness of pagans" regarding the signs to appear before the last coming of our Lord and Redeemer Jesus Christ to judgement and the universal resurrection. In the Scripture's phrase, 'fullness' means the embrace of everyone and everything without exception. That phrase is widely used in the Scripture, especially in David's Psalms. "The land and the fullness of the land is the Lord's" (Psalm 24:1), which means whatever is on earth with no exception. And in the same sense, "The world is mine in its fullness" (Psalm 50:12) 'You have created the world and its fullness' (Psalm 89:12), which is a brief and elegant description of the whole universal creation both visible and invisible. That 'fullness' as applied to the pagans must mean the entirety of the pagans, so no one to whom the name applies is excepted. If no one is excluded, whether bewitched by Muhammad's superstition or any other, the Turks and others must not be excluded from the pagans.

However, the sacred scripture seems to attribute this 'fullness' to a certain race and a peculiar people, namely, the 'Israelites.' See Paul (Romans 11:25): "I would not want you to be ignorant, brothers, of this mystery, so that you are not arrogant among yourselves," holding in contempt the sensible, insolent, and Jews, as if they were shut out from the kingdom of Christ forever: the nation of Israel will remain obdurate in part, until the fullness of the pagans has entered [the new faith]. Or does this restriction to the Israelites mean that the words of the Apostle, promising entry to the Church, are concerned not with other pagans, but with Israel alone? I think this passage indicates that neither pagans nor Israelites will be excluded, but Paul took the conversion of both into account. Indeed, the meaning of "the fullness of pagans" is the multitude of Gentiles from all parts of the world, who will "lead the Jews, and enter into the Church of the faithful first." This means that after all the pagans have been received into the bosom of the Church, Israel, hitherto blinded and obdurate, will embrace the faith and enter into the Church. Therefore, the blindness and obduracy of Israel will persevere in part, not a small or middling part, but the greater part of it by far, until all pagans have entered. That 'entrance' should be understood as faith in

Christ, not only for the Jews and the Gentiles, but for everyone in the universe, whether or not they are outside the Church. But as the Turks are also outside the Church, that entrance must also be understood to pertain to them. But they will not accept Christ or enter into the Church, which is open to them, until they suffer for their impiety with repeated disasters. Therefore, the killing of Gog and Magog predicted in Revelation refers to the Turks.

Gog and Magog or the land of Magog is also mentioned in Ezekiel 38:2. Since this prophecy was fulfilled, the Turks cannot be understood as Gog or Magog. For those names must have the same meaning in Revelation as in Ezekiel. As Luis del Alcázar explains in *Vestigatio arcani sensus in Apocolypsi* (*An Investigation of the Hidden Sense of the Apocalypse*):

> From those words, it can easily be understood that in Ezekiel Gog signifies the pagan Roman emperors and the universal empire of idol worshippers, waging war against the Christian Church. In Revelation, the whole army of the Antichrist is denoted through the same name Gog, and whoever is deceived by him. But in either case, the race described as Magog is the same as Gog. Indeed, by 'Gog,' I mean the home of the demon; by 'Magog,' their rage against the Church, since they are the habitation of the demon.

Thus, "the whole army of the Antichrist" is understood as Gog in Revelation. Could one not refer to the Turkish horde as the Antichrist's army as well? For one who is not with Christ is against Christ.

The ancient interpreters of Revelation knew neither Muhammad nor the Turks. The modern interpreters believe that the prediction of John concerning Gog and Magog meant disaster for the Saracens and Turks. Most of the interpreters cling to the etymology of the words. Since they interpret Gog as covered, and Magog as uncovered, they think that the names Gog and Magog should be interpreted as hidden and open enemies of the Church, respectively. This could be true. Are there any more openly professed enemies of Christians than the Turks and Muslims? Are heretics who claim to be Christians not hidden enemies of the Church? Thus, the ancients' interpretation does not contradict the conjectures of modern interpreters; certainly, it does not cancel them out, nor disprove them.

Commenting on Ezekiel 38, Jerome says:

> Gog is called 'building' in Greek, and 'covering' in Latin. Furthermore, Magog is also interpreted as 'covering'. Therefore, all the false interpretations that conceal the meaning of these names are disproved. 'Covering' means the leaders of the heretics who have adopted their doctrines.

Muhammad, indeed, adopted the heterodox dogmas of Sergius the Nestorian heretic, and became a Nestorian instead of an idol worshipper. I have shown this previously. Also, Ambrose says, "those, who are interpreted as a 'covering' through 'Gog', are those who hide their malice in their hearts, and seem just to men though they are sinners." Covering certainly refers to heretics, since they conceal and hide in their heart their malice and hostility while they profess themselves as Christians. They seem just to some, or at least want to seem just. Ambrose continues, "those people interpreted as a 'covering' through 'Magog' are those who, from the covering of their heart, will burst into open malice, and prove that they are impious to all." Who will deny this, that those Ambrose predicted as Magog would be the future Muslims, especially the Turks, and that they fulfill all these predictions with their actions? It is obvious that the conjecture of the modern interpreters can be reconciled with the ancient interpreters of Revelation and Ezekiel, and do not contradict them.

After the above historical account, I will show the falsity and vanity of Muhammad, concerning the beginning, rise, and the tyranny of Turkish religion, so that the truth of Christian religion may be even more evident. I have already indicated that the Muslims recognize the divine revelations of both Testaments, the Old as much as the New. The Byzantine emperor John VI Kantakouzenos confirms this assertion in the preface to *Apology on Behalf of the Christians*: "the things written by Moses, the prophets, and the writers of the Gospel are considered sacrosanct even by the Saracens." Indeed, they place Christ among the prophets, though they believe him to be neither the greatest nor the last among the others. They assert and contend that Muhammad succeeded Christ, and there are even prophecies of Muhammad's coming in the Old and New Testaments which were erased by the Christians. Musulmannus Sampsates Isphachanes, a Persian, accuses Christians of this sacrilege. The Muslim priests are called *Musulmans*, the prophets are called *rasūl*, and theologians are called those who speak [*mutakallim*]. There was a certain Achenemides, who converted to Christianity after recognizing the vanity of Turkish religion; he withdrew to the court of the emperor Kantakouzenos. "And when God"—these are the words of the emperor himself—"called the more studious emperor to the life of Christian philosophy, with Achenemides among his companions, they were consecrated together into the monastic life, and Achenemides was renamed Miletius." Kantakouzenos abdicated from the empire and became a monk. Musulmannus tried to drag Miletius from the Christian faith back into Muslim faithlessness by sending him persuasive letters, full of lies. This one is especially conspicuous because it contains shameless words such as this: "The name of Muhammad himself was described in the Old Testament, and in the Gospel, even as it commended Christ, but the Christians removed it [the references to Muhammad]." The

Emperor Kantakouzenos greedily seized the opportunity to dispute the Musulmannus' objections to the truth of Christianity, to demonstrate the vanity of Islam, and to prove the truth of Christianity [...].

A Muslim tradition claims that the Old Testament and Gospel foretell Muhammad, although the Christians deny this. All of that is a fable; it is obvious that it was an obtrusive lie divulged by unbelievers and the father of lies. All this authority of Muhammad that depends on this lie also falls apart. Whatever he claimed about himself and his invented religion, and whatever semblance of truth it has, still cannot be defended; having been founded on known falsehoods, Muhammad's religion will collapse upon itself.

Although the falsity of the Qur'an's dogmas is known to all Christians, it may not be recognized by others, especially by those who believe in Islam. To make them recognize the falsity of their religion, Muslims must be persuaded with arguments and be introduced to the divine scripture, which will conquer Muhammad's dogma and reveal the truth. The way to convert Muslims is to choose a catechism, which is appropriately suited to the catechumen. I doubt that any Muslim is so barbarous that he would not recognize that Christian revelation predates Islamic revelation, meaning that anything revealed to Muslims was previously revealed to Christians. So, if Moses and the prophets were just as silent about Christ as they were about Muhammad, the Christian religion could not be considered greater than Muhammad's. This means that Christianity would not exist, and we would simply have to practice Judaism. As neither Moses nor the prophets nor even the Evangelists and Apostles made any prophecies about the coming of Muhammad, the new religion of Muhammad is empty and meaningless. Therefore, Muslims must accept either Judaism or Christianity. If Muslims were to compare the dogmas of the Qur'an against the scripture of either Testament intelligently, they could do nothing but blush and be confounded. How can Muhammad be considered greater than Christ, as even according to the Qur'an Christ was "born from a virgin." It says that Muhammad was born in the common way through a man joining with a woman. Christ, as the Qur'an teaches, is not dead, and still lives. He was in fact dead but rose on the third day, and ascended into heaven. Muhammad is also dead, but lied that he would come forth alive on the third day. He was buried in *madīnat al-nabī*, whose tomb the Muslims often visit.

It is universally agreed that Christians feel the internal force of the Holy Spirit when they ponder the scripture of either Testament with attention and fear of the Lord. For Christians, the revealed doctrines gain approval by virtue of the scripture, not as if they were written by men, but as if by God. Yet this argument is not so effective that Muslims can be convinced. But this argument must be made with the points mentioned above, so that the non-believers might be enticed to read the scripture, and therefore obtain the truth. If enthusiasm for the truth stimulates them into becoming Christians by calling on God's aid, they will not be barren of spiritual fruit. But the catechumen will strive and read the scripture by the grace of the Holy Spirit, through which they may agree with the truth revealed in scripture, as Christians do sincerely.

If the Turkish War continues (since God thinks it right to favor it for longer) and the unbelievers come under Christian rule, every effort for their salvation should be made, with the force of all our resources, so they are led to recognition of the truth and their souls become profitable to Christ. I have already indicated the way to act and proceed. Muslims are to be induced and invited to a careful reading of scripture, or they are to be faithfully preached to and inculcated with the cardinal and fundamental dogmas of scripture. No matter how it is achieved, it has to be beneficial whether it is by reading or preaching or some other appropriate ways suggested by the word of God and with the grace of the Divine Spirit to convert them to the Christian faith. Preaching the word of God is as efficient as reading the Holy Scripture to sow God's truth into the hearts of all readers and attentive listeners, both Christians and unbelievers. I will give you an example from the Thessalonians 2:13. Paul writes on unbelievers, in the letter addressed to them, that they "have accepted the word, which they heard from us, not as the word of a man but as the word of God." If the power of God is not less and if it is no less efficacious than it once was, there is ample hope that when we preach to the Muslims "they will accept the word of God, not as the word of a man but as the word of God."

The example of the Jew, Christianus Gerson, is well-known. He chanced upon a codex of the New Testament, reflected upon it, believed in it, and was converted [to Christianity] with nothing but the scripture alone (*Sola Scriptura*). Therefore, he was moved by authority of the scripture to convert. Conversion of the Muslims will be less difficult than the conversion of Jews. For the latter repudiate the scripture of the New Testament, while the former embrace it and treat the words of the Gospel writers as sacrosanct to quote Catacuzenus. Therefore, Muslims accept the New Testament, which the Jews reject. Since Muslims accept the New Testament, unlike the Jews, it can be used to convince them. The divinity of Christ is the basis and foundation of the Christian faith, which is denied by the Muslims and Jews. However, His divinity is revealed so clearly in the New Testament, so not even the Jews can deny what is taught in it, that Christ is the true God. If the Muslims recognize this Testament, and treat it as a divine revelation, they have to say either that Christ is the true God, or they are saying that the author of that Testament (who they recognize as God Himself) wanted to deceive us about the divinity of Christ. But Muslims cannot claim that God wants to deceive, and so they must claim faith in Christ's divinity, which is so clearly revealed in the New Testament.

Furthermore, if all necessary doctrines for salvation are divinely revealed and cannot be known other than through special divine revelation, then Christ was neither the last nor the greatest prophet. After his appearance, Muhammad came as the last and greatest of all to whom "God brought down the Qur'an from heaven to earth through the angel Gabriel." So, let them assert the faith by citing the clear testimonies and words of the Old or New Testament, both of whose divine revelations they recognize and embrace. But no commentary will back them up, because they talk nonsense and say with no appearance of truthfulness that the Christians excised the memory of Muhammad from both Testaments.

Since the Muslims believe that there is something important [i.e., Muhammad] in the scripture of the New Testament, they recognize it as divinely revealed; the Jews, however, do not. Therefore, it is obvious that the Muslims' conversion is easier than the Jews'. Therefore, the conversion of Muslims hinges on the scripture of both Testaments. By leading the Muslims to the scripture, they must be persuaded that the scripture alone—excluding their Qur'an—contains the principal truth of the religion. The scripture is therefore given and revealed in preference to all others so that men might be led with its goodness to the path of salvation and be taught the means to obtain it. For mortals who are left to themselves and the power of nature and are not helped by divine revelation do not grasp what comes from God. They do not know, nor can they understand why God should be acknowledged and worshipped, so that they might attain eternal life through the pleasing worship they owe to Him. Realizing that the divinely revealed scripture shows such things and that these things are learned through reading them; everything that leads to salvation should be expressed clearly, so that they can be understood by any reader—though I speak not about proof, but of the manner of expression. For clarity is the most important and primary virtue of speaking. But must not God, the best teacher of speaking and the author of the scripture, ignorant of how to deceive and be deceived, know how to speak clearly? Considering His infinite and eternal justice, how could He communicate obscurely in a matter of such great importance, since He wants to save all with eternal life and have none perish? Let us not suspect that God indulges in verbal obscurity, through which men might be led into error, and thus lose eternal life. To leave things doubtful, unknown, and hidden contradicts the infinite divine justice and providence. The scripture should reveal things that are not evident in themselves (doubtful, unknown, and hidden), but necessary to obtain salvation. Anyone who argues that the revelation was written in an obscure manner accuses God Himself. How could the proverb of 'the rich brothers' in the Gospel refer to 'Moses and the prophets' and mean 'listen to Moses and the prophets' if the scripture was so obscure that it could not be understood?

Muslims do not pretend there is scriptural obscurity in what is necessary to know and believe for salvation. However, the recognition of

Christ's divinity, denied by them, is such a necessity. Yet Christ's divinity in the scripture of the new covenant, which Muslims accept as a divine revelation while still denying the divinity of the Savior, is the most obvious thing. When the scripture affirms that Jesus is the true God who assumed a human nature as the hypostasis of the divine word; that God suffered in the flesh, died, and was crucified; that He is one in essence and three in person, it claims something that is inscrutable and foreign to their understanding. Therefore, rationality obligates obedience with "a reason that must be taken captive to obey God" (Corinthians 2:5). If nothing arcane was present but everything was understood clearly by reason, there would be no mysteries. Since unknown and abstruse dogmas are given to men in scripture, they must be presented with clear speech and be properly understood. The more obscurely a matter is written about, the more clearly it must be presented in speech, if what is unknown is to be made known so the revelation does not fail in its intended result.

Those who remain unconvinced by my arguments must realize that the knowledge necessary for salvation, without which they will perish, is found in the scripture and not in the other doctrines. Yet everything in the divinely revealed scripture is not of such great importance, but it tells many things that do not pertain to eternal life, and therefore are not necessary to follow. If this is the case, either God has revealed pointless things or the purpose of telling those things was not important. But His purpose is obvious. Many historical examples of remarkable piety, unbeatable perseverance, fervor in God's love, love toward one's neighbor, and other examples of virtue are not exactly necessary for salvation. Nevertheless, all things being equal, it is good to know as this knowledge goes some way toward forming a moral character through warnings and examples.

There are, moreover, some things in the scripture that are difficult to explain and understand, which Peter states in Paul's letters (Peter 3:16). But for which people's convenience and benefit did the scriptures relate such things? St. Augustine solved this long ago:

> To tame arrogance with effort and challenge the intellect of the man for whom most investigations easily become trivial. For the Holy Spirit set limits to the scriptures so wondrously and salubriously that in more open passages one's hunger is satisfied, and in more obscure passages contempt is driven away.

Pagan philosophers once exercised their genius and sharpened their intellect. Today, Christians and whoever stands outside the crowd, occupied with natural and civil matters, exercise and sharpen their intellect. They are justly celebrated, whose ability in understanding is of a higher caliber and transcends others' intellect. But it is not the Lord's will that the human intellect is concerned only with what pertains to civil and natural matters, but divine and spiritual affairs ought to receive special care and attention. Most importantly, we are ordered to "seek the kingdom of God" before all else. The author of the sacred scripture supplies abundant material, stimulating the mind to scrutinize it, so no occasion or opportunity is lacking. It occupies and exercises the intellect in natural matters, but also in supernatural ones. But no one should wonder that the author of the divinely revealed scripture wanted to create certain obscurities for this purpose. The revealed truth is not obvious everywhere in the scripture; but, is sometimes veiled. But this is not the case for those doctrines which are necessary to know to achieve salvation. Without the knowledge of these things, Christianity cannot endure unharmed, nor can eternal life be acquired. For if such necessary doctrines in scripture were put forth shrouded in darkness and bound in inextricable obscurities, how would the author be perceived except as one who wanted to seduce men into losing eternal happiness? But such a sinister suspicion cannot fall on Him who is infinitely good, just, and merciful. And so, let us be far from accusing Him of this.

However, it cannot be denied that some writings in the scripture pertaining to mysteries of great necessity are not so clear that they remove all doubt from the readers' minds, since obvious examples are not used. But as Augustine says, another "more open passage satisfying hunger" stands out elsewhere in the scriptures, and declares the doctrine of salvation so clearly, that everyone who grasps the meaning of the words, and fears to misinterpret it, through their grace, can be saved. Just as this proposition is true: 'Everything necessary to know for salvation is clearly set forth in the sacred scripture, and none of it is not given clearly at some point in the scripture'; this proposition is false: 'All the sayings of the sacred scripture that are about some dogma necessary to know for salvation are clear.'

Besides this, I have warned in the preceding sections that the sacred scripture abounds with dogmas and mysteries "concerning which nothing will ever be known by man, nor can be known." If they are known, it is because of the word of God revealed in the sacred scripture. Therefore, the reader of the scripture acquiesces to clear and obvious [passages] touching on and embracing such mysteries. The ability is not conceded to anyone's judgment to twist such things as they like, but they must be left with the meaning that common usage gives them, so a wise reader, skilled in the ways of speaking and endowed with the ability to judge, may understand clearly. If a man takes the words with which mysteries are set forth and transforms them from their common meaning to another peculiar and unusual meaning that suits his preconceived opinion, he will not be able to say that the mysteries were understood according to divine revelation, but rather they depend on arbitrary human interpretation.

I can illustrate this matter with an example from school. Let us imagine that a teacher is teaching a student a new subject which the student knows nothing about. The student certainly ought to accept the words of the teacher just as they are and as they sound in their simple, common, and usual meaning. It would not be right for him to twist and coerce those words into another meaning which opposes the teacher's opinion and fits with the student's preconceptions. When the student changes the meaning, he is not learning the discipline from his teacher but keeps his preconceived notions. Therefore, he trembles in thick darkness without his light being kindled, and he understands nothing that relates to the discipline. This example is not much different from what relates to God and divine mysteries. As we saw in the above example, if we assume that the student understands the secrets of his discipline before his teacher led the way we make the same assumption about understanding of the divine revelation. Therefore, it follows that divine revelations in scripture are to be understood for their intrinsic meaning and are not to be interpreted differently, as in the example of the unsophisticated student challenging his teacher's interpretation.

Therefore, it cannot be doubted or denied that in religion, matters concerning mysteries and salvation must be extracted and explained by preaching the intrinsic meaning of divinely revealed scripture. According to this primary principle, the errors of the Catholics and their carefully considered novelties are uprooted and overturned. Nor do I oppose the second principle of the universal consensus of the first and better 500 years after Christ's birth. Catholics introduced more dogmas, which they wanted to be considered as articles of faith, than was to the benefit of Christianity. It can be proved and demonstrated that no trace of them are in the sacred scripture, nor are they of any genuine antiquity. But if Catholic errors and novelties are uprooted and overturned by both principles, the primary as much as the secondary, why should not the most absurd errors and outlandish novelties of the Muslims, which they consider articles of faith, also be uprooted and overturned from the same principles? The mysteries and dogmas of the faith in the sacred scripture are to be understood by their intrinsic meaning. This in itself distresses the Arians, Remonstrators, and many other heretics. It also disturbs others who are not heretics, though they still live in a schism, such as the Reformed men with their errors. It is plainly pronounced in clear words that "Christ is the true God" (1 John 20:28, 1 Tim. 3:16, Tit. 2:13, 1 John 5:20). These words of scripture are potent against the Arians, and therefore, the same words should be strong against the Muslims. Indeed, the Arians as well as the Muslims recognize the Scripture as divinely revealed, which asserts the divinity of the Savior. That 'baptism' is necessary for salvation for every human being, including infants, conceived and born carnally through sex between a man and a woman, as clearly stated in the words of John 3:5 and elsewhere. That 'election' to eternal life is not made by an absolute decree, but according to prescience. This is observed in the pronouncements of scripture, Rom. 8:29,

11:2, and 1 Peter 1:2. Our Savior gave His flesh to be eaten and His blood to be drunk in the Holy Eucharist, as taught in Matthew 26:26 and by the other Apostles and Evangelists who describe the Eucharist. Scripture, left with its intrinsic meaning, strongly overcomes the heretical viewpoints which I spoke of earlier.

It is now clear that some doctrines in scripture are presented simply and clearly, others less clearly (obscurely and not self-evidently). The former concerns things necessary for salvation; the latter leads toward "taming arrogance with effort, and challenging the intellect of the man, for whom most investigations easily become trivial." There are also doctrines on which the Christian faith is founded for which scripture does not provide clear explanations. These doctrines can be understood using the [dialectic] skill which we call Scholasticism, or else their meaning can be deduced using syllogisms, which can be difficult.

In order to lead as many Muslims as possible to recognize the truth, do not tire them out with syllogisms and logical conclusions. Instead, teach them the essential dogmas and mysteries on which the Christian faith is founded.

However, I see a potential stumbling block for the Muslim who has become a seeker of Christianity and is still a catechumen, which could divert him from Christianity in the middle of being converted. Perhaps he might say that Christians disagree with each other, and are divided by schisms which damn one another. So, the question arises for him as to which faction is right. When he is about to choose one of them, he might make a mistake and not come to the orthodox faction but go to a heterodox faction. Thus, he will evade damnation no more than if he had persevered in his Muslim faithlessness. But I will solve this difficulty, and steady the catechumen's fluctuating mind. I will suggest that it is enough for his salvation if he believes and embraces those things which Christians, although torn apart by schisms, unanimously agree upon. The rest that they disagree on is not as important. Because, if one Christian faction keeps and defends a dogma which the other Christians disagree with, everyone contradicts it, saying that such a dogma is neither free from suspicion of falsehood, nor necessary to know and believe for salvation. There are truths universally agreed on by everyone; no error about these truths is so dangerous that it excludes the one who errs from eternal salvation. Error not only starts with an obstinate will, but with stupidity and lack of judgement.

What are these dogmas belonging to one faction or another, with which other Christians disagree? Before I explain them, I will examine the schisms of the whole Christian world. With the bonds of Christian charity mutually violated, the unity of the Church is broken and drawn apart by schisms. It has divided into four distinct factions. The mother of all Churches is the Greek Church, which occupies the whole East. The Western [Church] seceded from its mother in the seventh century after Christ in the reign of the parricide Phocas. But the Western Church was also torn into three large factions. The first of these is the "Roman-Catholic" or "Pontifical" Church. The second is the Church of "the friends of the Augustine Confession," which left the Roman-Catholic Church. They are called "Protestants" or "Evangelists" to distinguish them from the Catholics. This is not because the Catholics do not believe in the doctrine of the Gospel, but because they do not recognize its sufficiency. Catholics champion the necessity of unwritten human tradition, whereas our faction simply accepts the written Word. Finally, among the Protestants a new schism was born under an unlucky star, and two different Churches came forth. Each of these got their names from the primary authors of the attempted Reformation, which was necessary at the time, but not entirely successful. The Reformers of one faction were named after Luther, who was the first to rise against the sellers of Indulgences and their grossest abuses. They delight in being called 'Lutherans' and take this name as an honorific. Although the other faction follows in the footsteps of Calvin, they do not like to be called 'Calvinists,' because they do not recognize Calvin as the author of their doctrine. Nor do they all approve of his opinions, embrace them, or consider them articles of faith. Therefore, they prefer to be called the 'Reformed,' because they reformed their Church by purging it of Pontifical contamination. Indeed, I do not look down on their title of 'Reformed' and grant it to them, so long as our own Lutherans are not considered foreign to the Reformation. Indeed, we should not accuse the Calvinists of being lazy, or of being slow to spur the necessary reformation of the Church.

The Church today does not have the youthful splendor of earlier centuries. The age of doctrine exhausted the purity of the Church. Schisms grew powerful with God's permission like a weed that did not get plucked by the gardener. God's plans are arcane, and His judgments are inscrutable, but always just. This Iliad of evil, schisms, although it unfortunately tore the Church apart, did not destroy the religion and truth of the faith, which is necessary for each man's salvation, especially the uneducated. But truth of the faith was fortified by the defense of ecumenicalism. Therefore, the faith endured safe and sound among individuals who did not join schismatic factions. This is the reason that the Church, translating the Apostolic saying into vernacular verse, sings: *die ganze Christenheit auf Erden/hält (der helige Geist) in einem Sinn gar eben* (The whole of Christendom on earth affirms with one accord: Holy Spirit). Let the seeker of Christianity, or the newly converted but doubtful Christian, be directed to this one true faith. While each faction of Christians fights and debates the doctrine of faith, let him choose the proper path. This is the truly catholic faith [all-embracing faith], or as it is called, καθολικόν, which was *always* believed from the beginning of the Church to this day. This faith exists wherever Christians exist. In short, when the catechumen embraces what was always believed by Christians everywhere, let him follow it as a neophyte. Let him not trouble himself much in the beginning about the finer details of doctrine before he progresses further in the faith.

If something is not universally believed by Christians, it creates dissent and precedent for error within the Church, and should carry with it the suspicion of falsehood. There is hardly any Church in the whole world which does not nurture one or more of its own dogmas. Certain private opinions are boldly added to the doctrine of what must be believed without the authority of public and general opinion. This places the Church in danger of error, and it is openly condemned by the unanimous assent of all other Churches. I must demonstrate what I say about individual Churches. Let me start with the mother of the other Churches (i.e., the Greek Church), which is spread through the whole East, and groans miserably under the Turkish yoke. Oh, the pain! Truly, this Church has something unique apart from all others, in that they tenaciously defend that "the Holy Spirit proceeds only from the Father." This mother of Churches gave birth to daughters spread far and wide through the Eastern and Western branches, but none of them have anything to do with their mother. They all contradict it with one voice, and all condemn their mother for error.

If any other Church acts riddled with new dogmas unknown in antiquity and not recognized or approved of by any other Christians in the whole world, the 'Roman' or 'Catholic' Church certainly lies infected and prostrated by such things. I will give one [critical] example that will suffice as most other problems are bound to it. For example, Catholics teach that the Roman Pope was constituted by divine law and by Christ himself as the Head and Chief of the Church. He is considered to have the authority to determine and define matters of faith infallibly, so much so that what is decreed by him cannot be doubted without harm to their soul. Indeed, they say that there is no other certain and unquestionable rule of truth and faith in the Church today beyond that authority of the Pope. Hence, it follows that what Christians [Catholics] believe is ultimately resolved in and by the authority of the Pope, as if his authority was a first principle. Because of this, dogmas of Papal infallibility gained strength and became a principle among Catholics. The Pope's authority created their long-desired domination over the universal Church, or rather a certain universal empire over the whole world. Once one unsuitable dogma was in place many others followed. After this supposition, it follows that the Bishop of the Roman Church is the head of all others and is the infallible judge over controversies. They believe that he was appointed over this matter by Christ Himself and thus divinely. Such is all this luminary power transcending human abilities that he competes with the divine law. In the same way, it is necessary for salvation to recognize Christ as his head and that he is set below Christ. Thus, it is also necessary for everyone to recognize the Pope as their head and be subject to him. Boniface IX says this very thing eloquently, "I declare, say, define, and pronounce that it is necessary for every human creature's salvation to be set below the Roman Pope." But if everything that the Pope declares, decides, defines, and pronounces is infallibly true, it should be an infallible authority. But it is far from being the case that Papal authority is recognized by everyone, as the Roman seat quite ambitiously pretends. The Greek Church in the East, as well the majority of the Latin Church, spread from the West to the colder northern zone, severely contradicts the Pope with a large consensus. That unanimous contradiction ought to be acknowledged as an evident argument for error, of which no Christian can approve, and even less a foreigner converting to the Christian faith.

The contradiction of the Churches torn away from the Roman schism is abundantly sufficient to refute Papal infallibility and omnipotence. It is further proof that not even all Churches, which otherwise persevere in their communion with the Roman Church, defer everything to the Pope. Some, who are suspected of high treason, apply moderation. Others limit authority and power to Princes especially, and Kings, and their principalities and kingdoms. Others recognize no authority. Long ago, there were arguments in the University of Paris, calling into doubt the Pope's infallibility and pre-eminence. Only the Jesuits and those who study at the Roman Curia disagreed. This, however, is hardly sufficient to overturn the vote of all the Churches in the whole Christian world; especially since the Catholics believed untruthful interpreters who decided the bounds and limits of the Pope's immense and unlimited power.

Only the Reformed nurture a certain singular opinion concerning the Sacrament of the Sacred Eucharist. They do not recognize the Sacrament as "the true and physical presence of the body and blood of Christ." Although all the rest of the Christians profess the truth of this presence: some through more literal transubstantiation; others a true and physical presence that is beyond the senses and indeterminate. Therefore, the Reformed are divided from all the remaining universal Church occupying the East and West. They are obviously in error, nor is there anyone left who denies this; but rather all work to unveil and refute this error.

I have proven that the friends of the Augustine Confession are no more immune to contagion of private and public dogma than either the Greeks or the Catholics or the Reformed. Clearly a new dogma of ubiquity or of the omnipresence of Christ's flesh has insinuated itself among them. But this dogma has been constructed so that it offends all other Christians under heaven, with the exception of those Lutherans who seem to strive for puritanism. This is also not approved of by all the Churches devoted to the Augustine Confession. Therefore, what I said before about the Papal or Roman-Catholic Churches also applies to those who embrace the Augustine Confession. It is true that the French Churches disapprove the Pope's omnipotence. It is also true that the Augustine Churches disapprove the omnipotence of Christ's flesh. In the same way, all the Churches in the whole Christian world agree that the French Catholics as well as the friends of the Augustine Confession are in error.

These are the dogmas of the French Catholics and the friends of the Augustine Confession which are not universally believed. Let's set aside those dogmas and many other similar dogmas, which are followed by the French Catholics and the friends of the Augustine Confession. To be safe, let the catechumen, whether Muslim or Jewish, be bound only to those dogmas that all Christians unanimously agree on. The disagreements over the head of their religion among Christians and their doctrinal arguments should not disturb the seeker of Christianity, who is disposed to recognize the truth of the salvific religion of Christianity. Otherwise, the faction, to which doubtful seekers may turn, will make them more foreign to the Christian faith. Either they will slide back to their former faithlessness or continue to persevere in schismatic error.

It is now clear that the universal consensus of the whole Church will help in converting unbelievers. It should also be obvious that there is much weight and much importance in that consensus. Therefore, the consensus of everyone shows the heedlessness of the few and refutes their dissent.

Note

1 Calixt's biography was compiled from the following sources: "Syncretismus," in *Das Grosse vollständige Universal-Lexicon aller Wissenschafften und Künste*, ed. Johann Heinrich Zedler (Leipzig and Halle, 1744), 780–967; J. Baur, "Calixtus, Friedrich Ulrich," in *Allgemeine Encyclopädie der Wissenschaften und Künste*, ed. Johann Samuel Ersch (Leipzig: Verlag, 1825), 144–5; Ernst Ludwig Theodor Henke, *Georg Calixtus und Seine Zeit*, 2 vols. (Halle: Waisenhause, 1853–1860); Wilhelm Gass, "Calixt, Friedrich Ulrich," in *Allgemeine Deutsche Biographie*, vol. 3 (Leipzig: Duncker and Humblot, 1876), 704–6; B. Pick, "Calixt, Friedrich Ulrich," in *Cyclopædia of Biblical, Theological, and Ecclesiastical Literature*, vol. 1, ed. John M'Clintock and James Strong (New York: Harper and Brothers Publishers, 1890), 739; Johannes Wallmann, "Zwischen Reformation und Humanismus: Eigenart und Wirkungen Helmstedter Theologie unter besonderer Berücksichtigung Georg Calixts," *Zeitschrift für Theologie und Kirche* 74/3 (1977): 344–70; Hermann Schüssler, "Calixt, Friedrich Ulrich," in *Neue Deutsche Biographie*, vol. 3 (Berlin: Bürklein-Ditmar, 1957), 96–97; Giovanni Santinello and C. W. Blackwell (eds.), *Models of the History of Philosophy: From Its Origins in the Renaissance to the 'Historia Philosophica'* (Dordrecht: Kluwer Academic Publishers, 1993), 398–400; Benjamin T. G. Mayes, "Syncretism in the Theology of Georg Calixt, Abraham Calov and Johannes Musäus," *Concordia Theological Quarterly* 68 (2004): 291–318; Timothy R. Schmeling, "Lutheran Orthodoxy Under Fire: An Exploratory Study of the Syncretistic Controversy and the *Consensus Repetitus Fidei Vere Lutheranae*," *Synod Quarterly* 47 (2007): 316–55; and Quentin D. Stewart, *Lutheran Patristic Catholicity: The Vincentian Canon and the Consensus Patrum in Lutheran Orthodoxy* (Münster: Verlag, 2015), 143–71.

3 First Arabic Edition of the Qur'an among the Europeans

Johann Michael Lange

Son of a Nuremberg pastor, Johann Michael Lange was born in 1664 in Etzelwang in the Duchy of Sulzbach. Lange studied philosophy, medicine, and theology at the University of Altdorf beginning in 1682. In 1687, he received the title of poet laureate and also his Master's degree. In 1688, he began his advanced theological studies at Jena University with Johann Wilhelm Baier (d.1695), a disciple of the well-known Lutheran Johannes Musäus (d.1681), the representative of the middle party in the Syncretistic Controversy. In 1690, he became an adjunct in the Faculty of Philosophy at Jena. In 1692, he served as a pastor in Vohenstrauss in Sulzbach'schen, and studied theology at Halle in 1694. In 1697, Lange received his Doctor of Theology and was Professor of Theology at Altdorf until 1709. He also served as the rector of the university in 1704 and 1705. In 1709, he was involved in a dispute with his colleagues over his adherence to Pietism. Consequently, Lange was accused of open deviation from the confessions of the Orthodox Lutheran Church and he was forced to resign his position. He spent the rest of his career as an ecclesiastical inspector in Prenzlau in the Uckermark, where he died in 1731.[1]

Variant Names: Johannes Michael Lang, Johann Michael Lang, Johann Michael Langius, Iohannes Michael Lange, Joh. Mich. Langi, and Joh. Michaelis Langii

Summary and Analysis

Lange's dissertation considers the first Arabic edition of the Qur'an printed in Europe in the sixteenth century. He is not concerned with the Qur'an's contents or with Islam per se, but rather with proving the existence of this early edition, about which there was some doubt in Europe at the time. Lange wrote his dissertation, he says, because of false information passed down by philologists about certain editions of the Qur'an. He sets out to recount the history of the first printed edition, destroyed by the Catholic Church, laying out the evidence in the writings of several European scholars who refer to this first edition, known as

Alcorano di Macometto.[2] He then evaluates whether the Church was justified in suppressing it.

According to Lange, most European scholars believed that the first complete edition of the Qur'an in Arabic was printed at Hamburg in 1694 by Abraham Hinckelmann. He cites a 1692 publication, which included statements by other European scholars that the correspondence of Theseus Ambrosius, an Italian humanist and student of Semitic languages, mentions the Qur'an being printed in Arabic in Italy. The printer was a certain Paganino of Brescia, also known as Paganino Paganini, who produced the edition in Venice in 1530. Because no trace of this edition remained, many European scholars were unaware of its former existence. Lange names those who had affirmed its existence, citing their testimonies, each of whom asserts that the Qur'an was first printed in Venice and then burned by the Church. He says that he found the testimonies of Theseus Ambrosius and Guillaume Postel, a philosopher and linguist, in a little-known book on Eastern languages and, in his epilogue, presents their collected correspondence, which reveals that Postel, who wanted to use the presses to publish an Arabic grammar had asked Ambrosius to look into purchasing them from the person who had published the Arabic Qur'an. He replied that he would ask Alexander, the son of Paganini, to consider selling the Arabic character plates.

After presenting evidence of a printed edition of the Arabic Qur'an and its circulation in sixteenth-century Italy, Lange moves on to examine accounts by other scholars that the Catholic Church had suppressed that edition of the Qur'an. Through quotations from these scholars, he recounts the Church's suppression of Islamic writings in the recently conquered kingdom of Granada, which he takes as indicative of the Church's policy toward Islamic writings generally. Lange raises the question of whether the destruction of all copies of the Qur'an is morally justifiable, giving four arguments for burning the Qur'an and then contesting them: first, a biblical passage from the Book of Acts, which seems to support burning heretical books; second, the idea that careless men might be seduced by the Qur'an; third, that the Turks might be emboldened if their holy book is published in Europe; and finally, that Divine Will prevented the successful publication of the Qur'an for the past 160 years. Regarding the biblical passage (Acts 19:19) used to justify the burning of heretical books, he argues that the Qur'an is no worse than the majority of pagan texts. Therefore, for Lange, there is considerable hypocrisy in burning the Qur'an when pagan texts are printed in fine editions and studied in learned schools.

Lange dismisses the Catholic argument that the Qur'an should be suppressed lest it leads Christians astray as another hypocrisy because a Latin translation of the Qur'an was created at Cluny long before Paganini's Arabic edition and the Church did not destroy this. In a lengthy excursus, he discusses and discredits the myth that Martin

Luther had published a bilingual Latin-German edition of the Qur'an. He also dismisses the third argument that the Turks will think that Christian Europeans will admire their law or that they might be encouraged by the printing and dissemination of the Qur'an by pointing out that the Turks know that the European editors intend to refute, not to promulgate, Islam and that, in any case, Muslims dislike seeing their holy books in Christian hands. On the fourth argument, he equivocates,

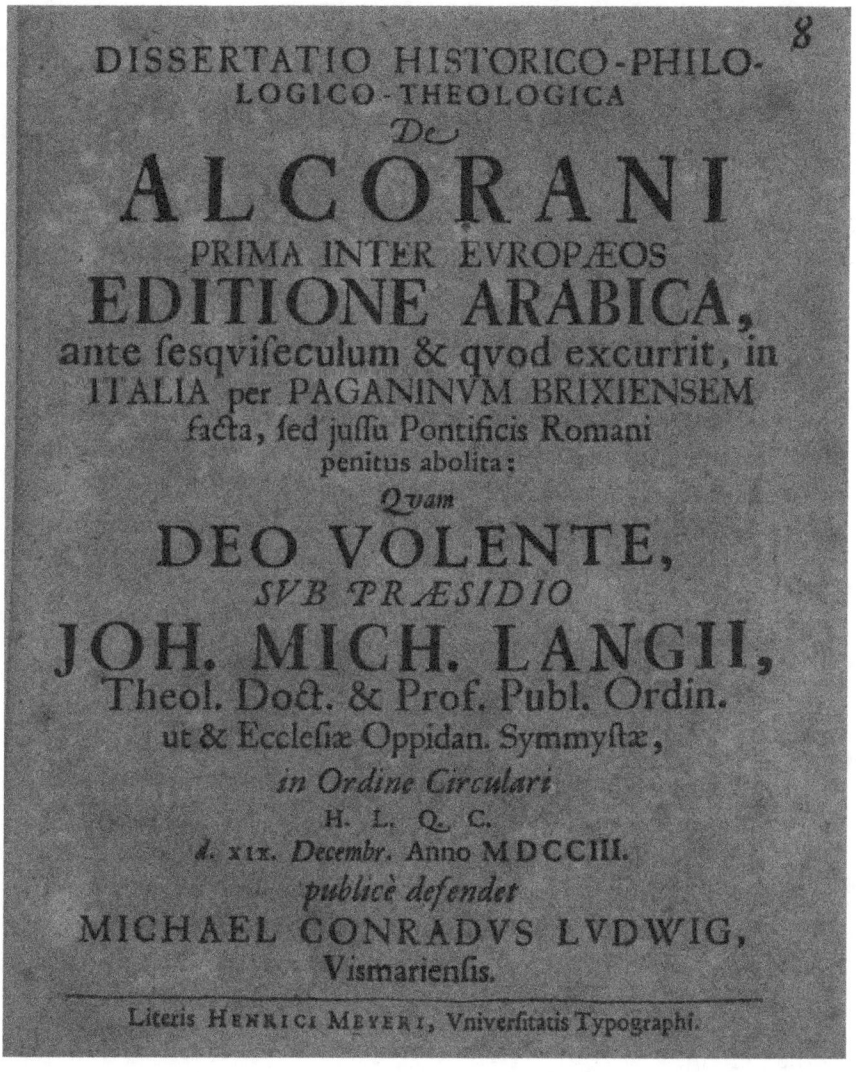

Figure 3.1 Johann Michael Lange, *Dissertatio historico-philologico-theologica de Alcorani prima inter Europaeos editione Arabica*, 1703 (Courtesy of the Bavarian State Library, Munich).

acknowledging that a lot of scholars have tried and failed to publish an Arabic Qur'an in the intervening 150 years and that many factors had hindered its publication. It was no wonder, he says, so many scholars failed in light of so many obstacles. Lange thus tries to prove not only that a sixteenth-century Arabic edition of the Qur'an existed, but also that its destruction by the Catholic Church could not be justified on religious or any other grounds.

Historical, Philological, and Theological Dissertation on the First Arabic Edition of the Qur'an among the Europeans (Altdorf, 1703)

As a Christian theologian, I have spent many years in diligent and earnest study, during which I have gathered literary documents that outline the history of the publication and editions of the Qur'an. I stumbled upon this subject almost by accident when I studied the Muslim religion. I applied myself to understanding the Qur'an, and during this exercise, I discovered a tremendous number of things concerning certain publications and editions of the Qur'an that were passed down incorrectly by the best philologists and accepted as truth. Fortune favored my plan when I decided to take up this small part of literary history in order to illustrate it. Indeed, in a short time, various scholars helped me so much with their kind assistance, giving me important tools to produce my desired outcome. As an example of my efforts, I will begin with the fate of the first edition of the Arabic Qur'an among the Europeans. This edition was quite a lot older than all known editions of the Qur'an that have been printed. Until recently, only a few men knew firsthand of this first edition; and very few today know its complete history. The Roman Curia was so diligent in destroying all copies of this Arabic edition that hardly a trace of it can be found in the literary texts of those times. Some information can be found in Theseus Ambrosius' *Introduction to Various Eastern Languages*, as well as in a certain Italian letter to Theseus Ambrosius' that was discovered by Guillaume Postel and included in the aforementioned *Introduction*. Also, there is a reference in Thomas Erpenius' *Catalogue of Books published in Arabic*, which was added to the *Rudiments of the Arabic Language*, published in the form that we call an *octavo* at Leiden in 1620. However, you would seek this *Catalogue* in vain in another edition of the same *Rudiments*, which was published in 1628. In this work, I will name recent authors who have referenced this edition. After giving the history of this edition, we shall explore how well or poorly the Roman Curia acted toward this edition of the Qur'an.

It is certain that a small number of scholars had a dim awareness of the first edition of the Arabic Qur'an, but their awareness was so weak that when documents were discovered only a few believed in its existence.

The majority agreed that the Qur'an was never published before Abraham Hinckelmann printed the entire Qur'an in Arabic at Hamburg in 1694. A few others who referenced the first edition, produced in the sixteenth century, spoke about it almost as though it were a myth. Therefore, those who are skeptical immediately doubted these tales and embraced the former idea firmly [that the first Qur'an was printed by Hinckelmann].

Let us examine famous scholars who believe that the Arabic Qur'an has never been printed before Hinckelmann's edition. Augustus Pfeiffer, an important philologist who previously ennobled Wittenberg and Leipzig, studied this matter. In his *Dissertation on the Qur'an*, he says:

> One would hope that an accurate version would be produced at some point, as promised for a long time by some well-known men, for the Qur'an has never been printed, but is written down by Turkish scribes, who scorn printing presses. Thus, copies of it do not go for sale except at great cost.

The same theologian and famous philologist repeated almost the same things in *Critique* (in the second edition, chapter 4): "The Qur'an has never been printed, but only a manuscript exists, which was produced by Turkish and Persian scribes." Scholars and others who have stumbled upon this topic seem to take Pfeiffer at his word. Our [Theodor] Hackspan says nothing about this Arabic edition of the Qur'an in his scholarly treatise, *On the Faith and Laws of Muhammad*. He speaks about the Arabic text of the Qur'an after he had complained about the rarity of the Latin version (which is the faulty version): "The Arabic manuscripts of the Qur'an are both rare and expensive, and I would bet that a very few scholars have seen the Arabic Qur'an with their own eyes." If other scholars disagreed with Pfeiffer's argument; Georg Calixt in his *Dissertation on the Truth of the Christian Religion*, and Johannes Hoornbeek in the *Summary of Religious Controversies,* they would have mentioned it.

Master Tenzelius [Wilhelm Ernst Tentzel], the most famous author of the *Dialogues in the German Language*, published in November 1692 under the title *Monthly Conversations between some Good Friends*, believes he must thoroughly prove his declaration, "that the entire Qur'an was already published in Arabic in the sixteenth century." He says, "I must prove this all the more clearly, since they are scholars who affirm both in words and in writing, that the Qur'an has never been printed in Arabic." He brings forward four witnesses, including Johann Heinrich Häner, who wrote in his *Philological-Critical Observations*:

> It is the consensus of scholars that the Qur'an has never been printed in Arabic. But this opinion is false; for a certain Italian gentleman

shows us in his correspondence that the Qur'an was already printed 150 years ago in Italy. Theseus Ambrosius' *Introduction to Various Eastern Languages* makes this clear by stating that the Arabic characters were used to print the Qur'an in Italy. If the Qur'an was printed in Italy, why has nobody seen a single copy of it? I answer: the Roman Pontifex eliminated all the printed copies but one, as trustworthy men relayed to the great Bosio [Giacomo Bosio], according to Häner.

Then, Master Tenzelius says on the same topic that the famous Bosio, the Jenensian polymath, stated in his *Dissertation III on the State of Europe* that the Qur'an exists only in manuscript form. However, it was printed at least 120 years ago by a certain Paganino of Brescia in Punic characters (that is, Arabic letters), on the authority of Theseus Ambrosius, in the Appendix to his *Introduction to Various Eastern Languages*, printed at Pavia in 1539, who also provides certain parts of folio 84 of the *Introduction* from the fourth quarto of his work.

The third witness Tenzelius names is Erpenius. I have already mentioned him above, but I will elaborate below on a few things related to this matter. Finally, the last is our Johann Saubert, who says the following in his *Theologico-Philological School*: "Theodore Biblaender produced an apology for his edition of the Qur'an, which, after being published in Arabic, was burned at Venice in 1530." These are the four witnesses by whom the laureate Polyhistor Tenzelius supports his assertion concerning the Arabic edition of the Qur'an, which was previously printed in Italy.

Tenzelius' observations are reinforced by those of Master Andreas Acoluthus, a most outstanding man in Arabic literature, a theologian and Professor of Eastern Language at Wrocław, and a celebrated orator.[3] In the *Example of the Qur'an in Four Languages*, published in Berlin in 1701, he says on page 40:

> From the lap of Italy an Arabic Qur'an was produced a century and a half ago. I would like to determine whether or not Hinckelmann had knowledge of its publication. Certainly, few philologists knew about this Arabic Qur'an, which has perhaps been consigned to obscurity or destroyed by some wicked fate. Indeed, I first learned about it at Wrocław, but how? I no longer remember. As I write these things while being out of the country and away from my library (a fate perhaps uncommon for writers), I cannot check the private resources of my mind. Maybe my friend from Berlin, whom I consulted, the Reverend and esteemed Master Andreas Rittner, the most faithful co-priest in the Temple of Mary, in his extraordinary kindness and readiness in giving thanks, will correct that mistake. He shared with me two dissertations, published at Rostock in 1696,

in which the famous author, Zachary Grapius, produced a scholarly literary history of the Babylonian Talmud, the first of which, in *Epimetron* 4, is as follows: 'Most scholars make a mistake in thinking that the Qur'an was not published before Hinckelmann's edition, but it was printed a century and a half before that'.

I have this on the authority of Acoluthus, who is very knowledgeable in these matters, and whom I frequently cite out of esteem and love.

In addition to the famous Acoluthus, we include the author Master Zachary Grapius whom Acoluthus praised for his *Epimetron*. At that time, Grapius was the Doctor of Holy Theology, Professor of Physics and Metaphysics by public ordination, as well as Archdeacon at the Cathedral of Lord Jacob at Rostock. In September 1701, the same year that the wonderful speech of Master Acoluthus was produced, Grapius brought his *Literary History of the Qur'an* to public light in the form of an academic dissertation. In it, he reaffirmed what he had said briefly in the aforementioned *Epimetron*, making it clear that he owed his opinion to the previously celebrated Master Tenzelius. According to the famous Grapius:

> If it is true that the Arabic edition of the Qur'an, by God's will, existed already in the previous century, I do not see why it would be controversial today. But it was overlooked, as was the evidence of those who knew that an Arabic Qur'an was printed before Hinckelmann's edition. But that evidence has now been confirmed most decisively by the famed Tenzelius, with the testimony of four exceedingly learned men: Häner, Bosio, Erpenius, and Saubert.

Grapius refers us to the authority of Häner, Bosio, Erpenius, and Saubert, well-regarded by Tenzelius. I have something to say about each of these authors.

Although the testimony of Master Häner is relevant, it is absolutely certain that all of his assertions depend on the authority of Master Bosio. Indeed, Bosio had a scholarly guild worthy of a polymath; his *Schediasma de comparanda notitia scriptorum ecclesiasticorum* was printed at Jena in 1673. Among the other discussions held at Bosio's scholarly guild, there is a speech about *Knowledge of Religions* (*Notitia Religionum*), which was written down by members of the audience. I possess a copy of this, thanks to a certain friend who suggested that I write about this Bosian scholarly guild almost twenty years ago.

In Bosio's account, two things should be noted: first, the history of the printing of the Qur'an; and second, an account of the destruction of all copies by fire. The first is known from the testimony of Guillaume Postel Barentonio-Norman (who is, no doubt, that "Italian" whom Häner speaks of in his Bosian speech) and from Theseus Ambrosius. Postel had given the *Italian Epistle* to Theseus Ambrosius concerning this matter, which Ambrosius then included in his own introduction. It is not clear from where Bosio learned the destruction of this Qur'an by fire. His words, as written, strongly suggest they are sourced from an oral account. But those who informed Bosio no doubt relayed the words of that outstanding gentleman, Thomas Erpenius. Erpenius told the scholarly community about the destruction and the year of printing of the Arabic Qur'an in a public speech—he alone is among the older witnesses who are yet known to me. But if someone brings my attention to any other witnesses, I will thank them.

Erpenius' testimony is extremely valuable although I make no pretense that nothing could undermine it. For the vast span of time which passed between Erpenius and that publication of the Qur'an requires proof, which Erpenius has not provided. But this great man laid out the entire affair so confidently in this text, using these words: "The Qur'an was printed around 1530, in Arabic script, at Venice; but all copies have been burnt." Hence, I do not want to doubt the truth of the matter and the secure foundation which Erpenius, the studious investigator of this literature, built. Perhaps, one may object that the aforementioned *Catalogue* which mentions the Arabic Qur'an is not in the second edition of the *Rudiments*. It is not clear why the Arabic Qur'an was not mentioned in this edition; it could be argued that Coddaeus tinkered with it. But this objection is not so important that it undermines Erpenius' account. At the least, it does not follow that one should not accept Erpenius' account of the destruction of the Qur'an by fire.

There remains the testimony of B. D. Saubert, who clearly owes a debt to Erpenius for his claims about the destruction of the Qur'an by fire. But let the reader beware lest he think that Theodore Bibliander published his defense for the Arabic edition of the Qur'an, as Saubert claims. Rather, it is certain that Theodore Bibliander wrote a defense for his publication of a Vulgar Latin translation of the Qur'an, which he had first published through a printing house in 1543, and then again in 1550, just as Peter, the Abbot of Cluny, once did. We will talk further about this matter in its proper place.

We shall move from streams to their sources, the testimonies of contemporary scholars such as Theseus Ambrosius, Guillaume Postel, and Thomas Erpenius. The first two left their own testimonies (which are exceedingly trustworthy) in a book that is known to few and is used today by even fewer, the title of which is: *Introduction to the Chaldean Language, Syriac, Armenian, and Ten other Languages.* The edition that I used (since I included this title, together with other excerpts, in my papers) is the Bosian edition, kindly shared with me fourteen years ago from the public Academic Library, under the care of my most worthy Teacher, Johann Wilhelm Baier, outstanding Doctor of Theology in Salana in that time. Coddaeus mentions this book in his expanded version of Erpenius' *Catalogue* under the title of *An Intro-duction to Thirteen Languages, together with the alphabets of many Languages.* Coddaeus accurately describes the Bosian edition, except that fairly often, in the copy which I have seen, one finds complete gaps, not even filled by handwritten Arabic letters. For instance, in folio 23b, where he deals with Arabic and Phoenician consonants, he includes only twenty-one Arabic characters, from *alif* to *qaf.* The remainder, from *qaf* to the end of the Arabic alphabet, are entirely absent. Thus, in Chapter 13, folio 142, fascicle a, only an empty space is found for a certain Arabic text that was to be inserted. Why? Bosio, in the end of his edition, included lengthy handwritten notes of the passages in this work where Arabic letters were entirely absent or were written by hand. It will help to provide his notes here:

> Letters are needed in folio 13b, 16b, 17, 18, 25a, 48b, 49, 50, 51, 52, 56a, 59a, 60b, 61b, 62a, 64b, 66b, 68a, 69b, 72a, 73, 74, 75, 76, 77, 83a, 84b. The letters are written and completed with a pen at folio 11, 12, 23b, 34.

We owe these to Bosio's diligence. Thus, scholars should conclude that Coddaeus' *Catalogue* includes this book of Theseus Ambrosius.

Lovers of literary history will not take it badly if I linger for some time on the edition of the work, upon which almost the entire history of the first Arabic printing of the Qur'an depends. The entire work consists of fifteen chapters, of which the first deals with Chaldean letters, those who inhabit Syria, those which are also called Syriac, and what the patriarchal Church of Antioch uses in its rites. The second chapter shows the connections of names from a straight and inverted alphabet; that is, two alphabets providing words that are conflated from letters combined first in one way and then another, which produce a mystical meaning. The third chapter contains names attributed to God based on the order of letters, so that He is called by the first letter, God; from the second letter, Creator; from the third letter, Powerful. The fourth chapter outlines the division of letters into vowels and consonants. He grants six vowels to Hebrew, Samaritan, and Chaldean: *Alef, He, Vav, Hhet, Jud,* and *Ayn*; seven vowels to Arabic, Phoenician, Turkish, Persian, and Tartar—*Eliph, Ha, Cha, Ayn, Wau, He,* and *Je*; not to mention the things that he says in the same chapter on the vowels of Latin, Greek, Jacobite, Coptic, Macedonian, and likewise of Dalmatians, Ethiopic, and Armenians. In the fifth chapter, he treats at length the consonants in Hebrew, Chaldean, Syriac, Samaritan, Arabic, Phoenician, Greek, Ethiopic, Macedonian, and Dalmatian. The sixth chapter is entitled "On letters which take diacritics within, below, and above." The seventh chapter is on the marks of Hebrew vowels, their names, and certain other points. The same chapter also deals with the names, shapes, and accents of vowels in Chaldean, Arabic, and likewise with the languages of certain other peoples. The eighth chapter is on the instruments with which letters are produced and what the letters are for each instrument. The ninth chapter deals with double letters in Hebrew, Chaldean, Phoenician, and others. The tenth chapter treats "radical and servile letters" at great length. The eleventh chapter contains many things on the numbers and means of counting, and the letters and names of numbers in Chaldean. The twelfth chapter is entitled "On Servile Syllables"; the thirteenth chapter is on Armenian Letters. The fourteenth chapter is on the division of Armenian letters. Finally, the fifteenth chapter is on the "Servile Syllables" among the Armenians [...]. Following the work's Conclusion, an Appendix contains correspondence between our Ambrosius and Guillaume Postel, which shows the rivalry these two men had in the field of Oriental literature. As we shall soon see, this correspondence wonderfully illustrates the history of the first edition of the Qur'an.

Yet before we see their words, it will be useful to describe the rivalry between Ambrosius and Postel. Ambrosius started the argument, and then Postel responded. But Postel won, as he was the first to place his *Introduction to Twelve Languages, Differing in Characters* (published in 1530 in Paris), if I remember correctly. Ambrosius, at last, published his *Introduction* some time later as we shall soon show. I myself saw the work of Postel twenty years ago. When I first opened the book, published in a larger four-volume set, as I recall, and not terribly difficult to read, I was still fairly unfamiliar with this type of literature—or rather, was fairly uncouth, and thus I neglected to extract those things that would now strongly support my endeavor. Yet I shall offer what I excerpted from Ambrosius [in the work that I have related thus far, in *An Introduction to thirteen languages, together with the alphabets of many Languages, Epilogue*], where he writes:

> My dear Postel heard my prayer; he spends his time kindly with me. He saw my printed characters for Chaldean and Armenian. He saw my engraver with me. He has known me in my old age, even now sixty-eight years old and hardly up for the task. As I understand, he kept my letters to him, as I did his. He heard in Ferrara that I had published many works on literature and languages. The young man, after he set out for France, wrote other letters to me, and he produced a *Booklet on Twelve Languages*, which I must respond to diligently.

Thus, the elder [Theseus Ambrosius] supported the youth; he gave Postel his worldly goods, without which perhaps Postel would have accomplished less, though he was an outstanding youth. But enough about Ambrosius and Postel, the leading authors in the history of this discussion; now for the history itself.

Let's speak about Postel first. Here, he will speak in Italian as he did when he exhorted our Ambrosius to look diligently into "whether or not the person who had published the Arabic Qur'an wanted to sell off his presses, so that Postel, who was going to publish an Arabic Grammar, might use them to create his work." Coddaeus, in the cited *Catalogue to the Rudiments of Arabic Grammar by Erpenius*, is a witness to the fact that Postel produced this *Grammar*. For among the Arabic books with which he had expanded *The Catalogue of Erpenius*, published in 1620, Coddaeus included Postel's *Introduction to Twelve languages in different characters*, and also Postel's *Arabic Grammar and Other Works*, published in Paris in 1538. Theodore Bibliander also references Postel' *Arabic Grammar* in his exceptional book, *On the Common Rationale behind all the Languages and Literature of Zurich*, published in four volumes, 1548. On page 4, he writes as follows: "I would not mention Guillaume Postel without honor—of course, he was the one who gave us our lessons in the Arabic language." Therefore, Postel's *Arabic Grammar* was published; but, as the Italian words of Postel plainly said, he wanted to produce it with those plates with which Paganino Paganini had published his Arabic Qur'an. This reference can be found in the Appendix to the *Operis Theseani*:

> I earnestly entreat you to ask whether or not the person who published the Arabic Qur'an wanted to sell his plates, or even a matrix. When you let me know the price, I will send you the money, since I have quite a need for them to print out an Arabic grammar and other books useful for doctors to read. If you do this, you will be praised in all languages.

After reading this, who can doubt that the Qur'an was in print in Arabic at that time?

Ambrosius will shed more light on the story, adding his own Latin words to the Italian words of Postel:

> In the meantime, with all passion, care, and diligence, I did not cease from asking Alexander, the son of Paganini, with all earnestness and the assistance of my friends, to consider selling at a fair price the plates and forms of the Eastern characters with which his father had previously printed his Qur'an. He was prepared to do it, but before I could inform Postel about the matter, I saw that he had already published a *Booklet on Twelve Languages and Their Different Letters*.

Ambrosius' splendid testimony tells us that the Qur'an was once printed in Arabic, and the man who printed that edition was Paganino Paganini.

After explaining these matters in detail, I can now prove with ease the consensus that exists between Erpenius, Bosio, and the other authors mentioned above, who claim that all the copies of this Qur'an were burnt and suppressed. Indeed, this is obvious, because no copies of that first edition exist today, nor has anyone seen them. Moreover, the historical context and the attitude of the Roman Curia support this assertion. Due to the upheaval of the Reformation, everything was in turmoil at that time, and those who were dedicated to the Roman Church were afraid for their well-being. They feared certain people would abuse their freedom, perhaps by spreading or preaching the religion of Muhammad. Was their fear justified? That is another question. Therefore, they would have considered it a most effective cure to oppose with fire anyone's attempt to publish the Qur'an in such tumultuous times. This is nothing new for the Roman Church according to my step-father Master D. Wagenseil. In the preface of his praiseworthy work, *Fiery Weapons of Satan*, he references *Book 2* of Alvarus Gomesius, which describes the actions that the Cardinal from Toledo, Franciscus Ximenius, took toward Saracen books. He says,

> Because the Cardinal was intent on stamping out Muslim perfidy in the kingdom of Granada, he also zealously ordered the books in which the superstitious believed to be destroyed. Therefore, the *fuqahā'* (as the Moors name their jurist), brought out the Qur'an, the most important book for that superstition, and all the other volumes of Muslim wickedness, whoever their authors and of whatever sort, without command or compulsion as they were eager to show obedience at that time. Five thousand volumes were piled in a heap, which—because they were decorated with various designs, Punic skill and effort, and gold and silver—seized not only the eyes but also the minds of those who beheld them. Many asked Ximenius to give them the volumes, but nothing was given to anyone; every last copy was burnt in a public fire, except some pertaining to medicine, in which the Arabs were very skilled. These were saved from that conflagration because of their value in that most salutary art and are now kept in the Complutense Library.

This will easily persuade anyone that the reason that no copy of the first edition of the Qur'an exists today is the fiery strictness of the Roman Curia. Their savagery was often brought against books of this sort—although we do not forget that the Roman Curia did not always have this mentality; a time existed when they acted differently. Anyone who is familiar with the history of Arabic literature has heard the most famed name of Master Louis [Ludovico] Marracci. He was the confessor to the Roman Pontiff Innocent XI, by whose diligence we have been able to publish not only the Arabic text, but also a Latin translation of the Qur'an. God willing, we shall say more about this edition at the appropriate time.

Paganini had already published the Arabic text of the Qur'an in Italy in the sixteenth century, around the beginning of the Lutheran Reformation, and specifically, as Erpenius says, at Venice in 1530. But all copies of it were destroyed by the authority of the Pontiff and the Roman Curia.

Not undeservedly, in this theological forum a question is raised about the theological morality of that Pontiff, whose passion burned the copies of that edition. Should we approve or disapprove of the Pontiff condemning those works to destruction? Let those who defend this fiery zeal bring forward Acts 19:19, where we read that "many of those who had practiced magic arts gathered and burnt their books in front of everyone, and when their prices were reckoned, they were valued at fifty thousand coins." Let those same people also realize that the souls of the faithful are more readily saved from the danger of seduction by annihilating those enticements, which can poison the careless. This is especially important in times when people hold sentiment against the received dogmas of the Church. Certain of Pontiff's men declare that those times undoubtedly contained anti-Church sentiments, and at times they hatefully compare the Augsburg (Augustan) Confession with the Qur'an. Others say that the Turks must not be encouraged by the publication of their books among the Christians, which might lead the Turks to sink even deeper into error. Finally, there is a noteworthy argument for Divine Will: for the past 160 years, all attempts by those men to print copies of the Arabic Qur'an had been thwarted. Apart from Paganini, all men have toiled in vain in this field: Thomas Erpenius, Louis de Dieu, Jacob Golius, Johann Zechendorf, Christian Ravis, August Pfeiffer, and others, about whose attempts and outcomes it will be possible to offer a full account at the appropriate time. But these arguments can readily be refuted.

As for the first argument from Acts 19:19, there is the greatest disparity between books of magic and the Qur'an. For magical processes were described in them, and deeds were taught that are not only in opposition to divine law, but also worthy of capital punishment (Exodus 22:18, Leviticus 20:27). The Qur'an is unlike these for although it teaches falsehoods, it contains trifles which contradict themselves, nor is the Qur'an worse than the majority of pagan texts, especially the Poets, which contain things likewise false, fictional, indecent, and even wicked. Therefore, if the Qur'an had been banished entirely according to Acts 19:19, the majority of other authors born outside the Church would also have to be condemned to the flames. Yet one could be easily persuaded that this was not the opinion of the Apostle Paul, based on the verses of Aratus, Menander, and Epimenides, which were also a part of the canonical scriptures. Hence, the Roman Church should not savage these books so terribly. It also seems good to cite here some parts from the *Apology of Theodore Bibliander on behalf of Publishing the Qur'an*, which says:

> Certain serious men did not hesitate to call licentious poets the 'flautists of the Demon', as if he were trying to insinuate deathly lies among men through those people whom he inspired. Tertullian as well, a theologian of the first order, calls philosophers the 'patriarchs of heretics.' Yet their books are published with engravings and read through and are set before the youth in schools in such a typical manner that if anyone rebukes them, he straight away hears the braying of the ass.

Certain men, burning with Catholic zeal (particularly Jacob Gretzer, the most renowned Jesuit) did not hesitate to publicly defend the idea that the Books of the Pagans, Jews, Turks, and others, should be allowed, or at least tolerated. But still, those same men felt that the books of Protestants should be destroyed and burnt up, as though they were threatening such damage to the Catholic Church and carrying such hidden poison within them that they would trouble the sacred flock more than the books of infidels. Disturbed at the unworthiness of this accusation, Jacob Laurentius, the minister of the holy word in Hoogkarspel, long ago published a *Theological Dissertation to Maximiliam Sandaeus, the Jesuit*, to challenge Jacob Gretzer (published in Amsterdam in 1619). Therefore, let the Pontiffs cease to defend the burning of the Qur'an, unless they want either to burn it with all the works of the Pagans which they still deal with and disseminate, or to challenge other Catholics who saved the books of Muslims from being burnt out of their hatred for Protestants.

There is a second less important argument. It was pointless to burn the Arabic Qur'an to prevent the souls of the faithful from being tainted by the teachings of Muhammad. How many Europeans existed at that time who had sufficient knowledge of even the Arabic alphabet? Thus, a fear of widespread reading—much less a fear of widespread conversion to Islam—could hardly accompany the printing of an Arabic book. But long ago there existed a Qur'an translated into Latin in the time of St. Bernhard, made by his dear friend Master Peter, the Abbot of Cluny. Afterwards, Theodore Bibliander issued his Latin edition, which was printed at a press. If the Roman Curia had for this reason wanted to protect its own Church, this copy should have been destroyed, not the Arabic book. Anyone who looks into the literary history of those times is rightly amazed that the 1530 edition of the Arabic Qur'an was entirely suppressed; but that nevertheless, shortly thereafter, in the year 1547, "with grace and privilege," an Italian translation of the Qur'an was duly printed in Venice. Not only did the editor Andrea Arrivabene boast that it was translated from Arabic to the vernacular Italian, *a commune utilità di molti*, that is, "for the use of the many," but it was also inscribed and dedicated by Gabriel de Luetz [Gabriel d'Aramon], Advisor to the Christian King and Ambassador to the Ottoman Throne. Therefore, that fear must have vanished in a short time that the Qur'an would obstruct the affairs of Christians. Unless you prefer to say that Luther, in the noteworthy Preface to the Transylvanian monk's book *On the Religion and Customs of the Turks*, made it so that the Pontiffs of the Roman Church, steeped with shame, ceased to suppress the religious writings of the Muslims, so that Luther would no longer have an opportunity to repeat what he had said in the aforementioned preface:

> Now I see what the rationale was for hiding the religion of the Turks from the Papists. It is because they sensed the truth of the matter—if it comes to arguing about religion, the entire Papacy would fall, nor would they be able to defend their faith and repress the faith of Muhammad.

None, however, can make themselves fouler than those who poisonously compare the Augsburg Confession with Islam and the Qur'an. They thought that the Qur'an printed in Arabic needed to be suppressed, lest it create an environment unacceptable to the Roman Church. The Church was threatened in the same way by the Augsburg Confession. The poisonous man who published documents in 1630 under the title *Scrupel über das Lutherische Jubel-Jahr (Scruple about the Lutheran Jubilee-Year)* dared to compare the Augsburg Confession with the Qur'an. In order to make the comparison between the Augsburg Confession and the Qur'an bitter, he fabricated the character of a certain Lutheran layperson, who was offended by the assemblies of the sycophants of the Augsburg Confession, which were held all through 1630. He made this third comparison:

> Our Jubilee Sermons rejoice that such a Confession has been brought to many kingdoms and Lords' countries. Thus, I want to know what we can send them for Jubilee? The books of the followers of Zwingli, the Calvinists, the Arians, and even the Turks have been carried to every country and kingdom. Our Holy Father Luther himself allowed the Turkish Qur'an to be produced in Latin and the German language with a fine preface, and sent throughout the world. […].

That author boldly mocks and throws foul bile—hardly befitting a man—into the face and fame of Luther. The author speaks boldly when he crudely states "that Luther published the Qur'an in Latin and German." Luther did not publish the Qur'an. But, there was a certain refutation of the Qur'an, authored by Father Richard. Luther translated it into German and added his own preface, which has thus been included in his works, *Wittenberg and the Eight Jenensians* (volume 2). Luther also published another book, which was written against Muslims, about which we have provided a few comments toward the end of the previous section. But Luther never published the Qur'an in Latin or German, which the aforementioned storyteller lied about, poorly. I am not ignoring the fact that Theodore Bibliander produced a Latin translation of the Qur'an at a printing press. In his own first edition, which was published in 1543, he offered at the beginning of the Qur'an a sort of preface, giving himself the name "B. Luther." It must be known that first, Luther himself did not publish that Qur'an, much less one in Latin and German, as the deviser of that lie said, but the publisher was Theodore Bibliander, as I mentioned. Second, the name "Luther" was without a doubt a mistake, since the author of the well-known *Premonition* to the Qur'an is far more likely to be Philipp Melanchthon than Luther; for which reason this error is corrected in another of Bibliander's editions of the Qur'an, published in 1550, which is in my hands, where this very same *Premonition* is clearly stated to have been written by Philipp Melanchthon.

Some light can be shed on the outstanding observations of Master Acoluthus from what he has said so far. This man, in the oft-praised *Specimen*, has prepared scholarly refutations for our fellows, especially for that assertion concerning Bibliander's Latin Qur'an. Acoluthus challenges the unjust accusations contained within Florimond de Raemond's *The Origin of Heresies*, where he lies in a similar manner to the aforementioned anonymous slanderer of Luther. Raymond treats only Melanchthon and Bibliander with terrible hatred, among the extremely studious editors of the Qur'an; but he also argues daringly alongside Anonymous, saying that "Luther did not hesitate to deck out the Qur'an with an illuminating preface." In either case, Raymond must be mistaken. For he supposes that the edition of the Qur'an that Bibliander published was either the first or the second edition. If the first, Raymond is properly reprimanded by my Master Acoluthus, because he considered Philipp Melanchthon one of the editors of the Qur'an; and yet, the first edition in no way resembles the work of Melanchthon. But if he means the second edition, and considers the preface attached to the beginning of that Qur'an to be the work of Melanchthon, then it must be false when he says that Luther adorned the Qur'an with a preface. However, one could question whether Raymond meant what he said about Luther's preface for the Qur'an to refer to the *Premonition*, which was prefixed to the first edition of the Qur'an by Bibliander under the name of Luther, since nothing more foolish can be said than that "the Qur'an was adorned with that preface." Yet Raymond used those very words. If that preface adorns the Qur'an, let the Pontiffs cease to complain about Luther's very well-known Hymn, "Receive us, Lord, in your Word," as though the Roman Pontifex were treated most bitterly in it. Rather, they will need to recognize the statement with which the Pontiff is adorned. As an example, let me present some passages from that *Premonition* with which I am concerned, to leave to each man's judgment whether the Qur'an was adorned with the work either of Luther or Melanchthon. So, the abovementioned preface says:

> In the first place, the Christian reader should be advised against the ravings of Muhammad; he must maintain this righteous and protective bulwark. The Church of Christ proclaims a doctrine that was handed down by the first fathers, the prophets, the son of God, and the apostles. This is the first church, and the congruent church, and assured by the resurrection of the dead and by other extraordinary events which the Devil's power cannot replicate. Therefore, we recognize that the teaching of the Church has been handed down by God, the eternal Creator of all things, and that no other religions should be accepted. Muhammad openly declares that he rejects the writings of the prophets and the Epistles and replaces them with his own teachings. Therefore, these recent myths of Muhammad's can no more affect or disturb Christians than the ancient madness of the Egyptians, who worshipped cows, cats, and snakes as gods, and sought aid from them.

These words are a marvelous warning about the Qur'an and all Islam. Thus, it is obvious that no one who is not malicious can charge this work [the translated Qur'an] of conspiring with Islam. If one wishes to read more on this topic, the esteemed Acoluthus will provide further relevant excerpts.

How about the false equivalency that Anonymous draws between the Augsburg Confession and the Qur'an? Anonymous says that those who praise the Augsburg Confession congratulate themselves and their Confession because it spread so easily and quickly throughout the world and in various languages, and yet the same can be said about the Qur'an. I answer that this argument relies upon sophistry and can easily be refuted. Whenever our co-religionists, among their subordinate arguments, emphasize the swift dispersal of the Augsburg Confession as evidence of divine providence, they have not emphasized as keenly the fact that our confession was also spread among various languages and kingdoms. It has spread around and set before the hands and eyes of all very quickly, which cannot be said about the Qur'an and its translation into various languages. However, we grant that over the course of time the Qur'an has been translated into various Eastern and Western languages as well.

Finally, it is proper for us to set the authority of the more sincere and learned men in the Roman Church before the authority of those miserable men who slander the Augsburg Confession and Protestants. Above, in section 16, we mentioned a man who was great among his peers,

Marracci, to whom we owe the publication of an Arabic-Latin Qur'an in a folio, which was produced at Padua in 1698. But did this man also believe that the criticisms of the Protestant theologians and philologists, and the work that they expended in dealing with the Qur'an, were suspicious and poisonous? Of course not. Rather, that renowned man's humanity, and the fact that he gladly took the friendly criticisms, is proven by Master Acoluthus, in the cited *Specimen*; Acoluthus does not otherwise fawn upon Marracci whenever he made mistakes. The name of Marracci is more respectable in this sort of literature (among the fair-minded) than any thousands of others who know the art of slander better than Arabic literature and Turkish studies.

The third argument concerns placing stumbling blocks before the Turks regarding the publication of the Qur'an; and this can be taken in various senses. For one either thinks that the Turks will think that we admire their law if they hear that there was a Qur'an printed in Europe; or that they would have access to a new supply of copies of the Qur'an, which will strengthen their superstition; perhaps just as the publication of the Jewish book *Nizachon* made a target of its publisher [Theodor] Hackspan by twisting the editor's original intention to vilify him.

Yet in neither sense does this argument solve anything. If the above-mentioned first interpretation is preferred, certainly the Muslims will not rejoice because of the publication of their writings, especially the Qur'an, among Christians. Of course, the Muslims know well enough that these editors intend rather a refutation than the promulgation of their teachings. All such copies would be considered profane, or even be destroyed by fire, a practice not unknown among the Turks themselves. Also see the renowned Hottinger, in *Historia Orientalis* (published in 1651), as well as Ravius in *Spolio Orientis* (*Spoils of the East*), where he also bears witness to how much grief Muslim authors suffer when they leave their books in the hands of Christians. Why? Master Tenzelius explains it well enough, in the cited passage, where says that Muslim kings and princes are eager to pry Arabic books, especially the Qur'an, from the hands of Christians, no matter the means or the cost; they do not like it when their books are in Christian hands. Indeed, Raymond argues that "a certain Muslim man celebrated the gains that Islam made because of the publication of the Qur'an in Latin." But Master Acoluthus refutes Raymond, saying that "this is an unadulterated, plain lie," and that "it is clear that the Latin Qur'an contains no arguments in support of Islam—rather, it argues against it." This can be seen in Bibliander's edition. Indeed, Raymond persuaded no one of his claim, except for men who did not see the aforementioned book and are therefore simply ignorant of Turkish matters. Yet there are some who are free from this primitivism but still repeat Raymond's hateful lie (which is completely absurd) that Luther had told terrible lies about Pontifical affairs, and that he persuaded men with his abovementioned hymn, the *Schmalkaldic Articles*, and other books, which he uses to strongly criticize the Pontifical hierarchy. But I will pass those things over.

Whoever embraces the second interpretation of this third argument, which says that the copies of the Qur'an, especially the Arabic version, were rightly destroyed, let him beware lest he serve the superstition of the Turks. Apart from the fact that such copies were considered evil to Muslims rather than being a vindication of their religion, as we have said in the previous section, Master [Johann Christoph] Wagenseil answers this charge well enough in his preface to *Fiery Weapons*. Here, he includes his opinion when the question arises around a similar act by Ximenius, who also burnt copies of the Qur'an. He says,

> How much more valuable would it have been if Ximenius and those who followed him in their zeal were eager to purge errors from the minds of men rather than to destroy their book. This should be the task, this should be the work, to slander the foul teachings of the sycophant Muhammad, to lay bare his crafty arts, to mark out his most unclean habits (however much they may be masked by a certain feigned righteousness) and his burning lust, to point out the thefts he committed from the sacred literature of the Jews as well; for that is the only way to liberate a people from a poorly constructed religion.

There remains the fourth and last argument, which might trick the unwary. Indeed, a great many scholars have died in the past 150 years in the attempt to publish the Qur'an in Arabic. Various handwritten copies were for sale; explicit promises to undertake the printing of the Qur'an were made; but no Arabic Qur'an came forth until finally Hinckelmann produced his in 1694. This argument was outlined in the dissertation, *On the Copies, Various Attempts, and the Most Recent Successes of Learned Men in Publishing the Arabic Qur'an*. I refuse to concede that this is a worthy argument. Indeed, history will provide more examples of these attempts to argue that so many men of such stature were not hindered by pure mischance over such a long course of time. For whatever sort of superstition exists, I do not doubt that whoever looks with some care into the reasons for the failures to publish in the past will agree with me on the fallacy of this argument. Surely, some fellow or another was shackled by the shortness of life, so that he did not publish the Qur'an. It is certain that many other men were hindered by other things. Of course, insufficient preparation undermined the work of some, and for others, the preparation was too difficult; some lacked the necessary funds; while others who were engaged in still other tasks died before they could keep their word; decency could not compel some to undertake what they had promised—they were obviously afraid of excessively harsh criticisms for their efforts. But when there are so many hindrances, it is no wonder that even the attempts of countless great men could be thwarted for such a long time. But I will say more about that matter in its own time. This was the history of the first edition of the Arabic Qur'an.

Glory to God Alone.

Notes

1 Lange's biography was compiled from the following sources: Laurentio Reinhard, *Imitationes parallelae in Cornelium Nepotem, ex recentiori historia desuntae, in usum scholarum editae* (Leipzig, 1732), 117; Hugh James Rose (ed.), "Lang, or Lange, (John Michael)," in *A New General Biographical Dictionary*, vol. 9 (London, 1857), 183; Julius August Wagenmann, "Lang, Johann Michael," in *Allgemeine Deutsche Biographie*, vol. 17 (Leipzig: Duncker & Humblot, 1883), 601–2; John M'Clintock and James Strong (eds.), "Lange, Johann Michael," in *Cyclopædia of Biblical, Theological, and Ecclesiastical Literature*, vol. 5 (New York: Harper and Brothers Publishers, 1894), 230–1; and John L. Flood, *Poets Laureate in the Holy Roman Empire: A Bio-bibliographical Handbook* (Berlin: Walter De Gruyter, 2006), 1072–5.
2 [MK] On *Alcorano di Macometto*, see Tommasino, *The Venetian Qur'an*, 185–99.
3 [MK] On Andreas Acoluthus, see Alastair Hamilton, "Andreas Acoluthus," in *Christian-Muslim Relations: A Bibliographical History*, eds. David Thomas and John Chesworth, vol. 14 (Leiden: Brill, 2020), 437–44.

4 Turkish Muhammadan Theology

Johann Karl Valentin Bauer

Bauer was probably born around 1697 (or 1698 or 1699) and most likely lived in Rhetmar or Celle, based on the matriculation record in the University of Helmstedt and Jena as well as the dedication page for his *Conspectum theologiae Turcarum Mochammedica*. He initially studied at Helmstedt in 1718 before attending university at Jena in 1719, where he studied under philologist Heinrich Gottlieb Reime (d.1749). During his time at Jena, he studied Hebrew, Chaldean, Syriac, and Arabic. At Reime's suggestion, Bauer wrote this dissertation on the theology in the Qur'an, which was published in 1720. The text of this dissertation is followed by a laudatory message from Reime to Bauer in which he praises his student at length and describes the studies Bauer undertook. Other than this dissertation, no other information could be found on this author. Therefore, Bauer's biography is exclusively based on this dissertation, taken from his teacher Reime's encomium of Bauer at the end of this work as well as the Registries of University of Helmstedt and Jena. He most likely died in the eighteenth century.[1]

Variant Names: Johannes Carolus Valentinus Bauer, J.C.V. Bauer, Jo. Car. Val. Bauer, Io. Carol. Valentino Bauer, Jhn. Carl Valent., and Jhn. Carl Valent. Bauer

Summary and Analysis

Bauer's dissertation sets out to explain (Turkish) Islamic theology using the Qur'an as the sole source in the spirit of the Lutheran belief in *Sola Scriptura*. He organizes points of interest into thirty-three sections, liberally quoting from the Qur'an in Arabic and providing a Latin translation. In his dissertation, he portrays Muhammad as the deceptive fabricator of the Qur'an's contents, often dismissing as nonsense anything that does not agree with his own version of Christianity. Although he tends to portray Islam negatively, his dissertation is particularly worthy of study as he analyzes and compares Islamic and Christian theology articulated in the Qur'an and the Old and New Testaments, and as he examines intra-Christian differences between Catholics, Lutherans, and Calvinists (Reformed Church).

Bauer begins by saying that the foundation of Islam is a belief in one God and doing good works, unlike Lutheranism with its emphasis on *Sola Fide* as the means to salvation. This emphasis on good works as the means to salvation is closer to Catholicism than Lutheranism. Also, according to Bauer, Muhammad demanded to be recognized as God's envoy and considered those who follow a non-Islamic religion as damned. He notes that Muhammad thought of Islam as 'orthodox,' as a continuation from true Judaism and Christianity, recognizing the Apostles and prophets as far back as Abraham.

The second and third sections of Bauer's dissertation describe the Qur'an's divine origins, which he dismisses as fabrication. He is particularly critical of Muhammad's emphasis on his own importance as a religious authority by making himself second to God in the Qur'an and its co-author. Bauer would have found this particularly problematic as Protestants relied on scripture alone as religious authority, denying the need for a secondary interpreter such as the Pope or any other religious authority. The fourth section discusses Muhammad's recognition of the Old and New Testaments. He acknowledges that Muhammad was familiar with the Bible and discusses many passages from it, though, for Bauer, Muhammad intermingles much falsehood in his retelling. He highlights that the Qur'an is given in the Arabic language in Muhammad's "mother tongue" so that the individual Arabs could understand the text without intermediaries. This might have caught Bauer's attention as Luther translated the Catholic Greek and Hebrew Bible into the vernacular for the German speaking people so that they could understand God's words directly.

The fifth section acknowledges that Muslims (Turks) worship God. In the sixth section, Bauer criticizes Muhammad's understanding of the nature of God, a blasphemous description to a Lutheran reader. In section seven, he critiques the Muslim belief in one God as opposed to the Christian belief in a triune God. In sections eight through twelve, he describes the Creation, how man and animals were formed, the nature of angels, divine stewardship, and how they differ from the Christian view. The thirteenth through eighteenth sections describe Islamic views on death and the afterlife, which Bauer dismisses for the most part as "carnal, wrong, and absurd" as he is offended by Muhammad's hedonistic version of Paradise—men having multiple sexual partners, wealth, rich foods, finery, and so on. Sections nineteen and twenty cover eternal damnation. The following section outlines Islam's teachings on sin and the belief that men can only be saved through the grace of God and good works. Sections twenty-two and twenty-three state God's role on salvation and conversion. Section twenty-four outlines the importance of a true belief rather than an empty proclamation of faith (*shahāda*), while section twenty-five considers the scarcity of references to baptism in the Qur'an though there are a few. Section twenty-six lists the good works that Islam most values, such as alms and taking care of orphans, while twenty-seven describes the rules for how and when Muslims pray. Section twenty-eight considers dietary laws.

The last sections focus on areas that Islam and Christianity hold in common, in whole or in part. For example, section twenty-nine describes Islam's beliefs about Jesus: Muhammad denies the divinity of Christ and his ultimate crucifixion although he recognizes Jesus as a prophet and a righteous man who is immune from blasphemy. Bauer notes Muhammad's condemnation of those who worship Jesus (Christians) as being worse than infidels. Section thirty discusses the Islamic belief that God leads men into error, which Bauer judges to be compatible with the Reformed belief in predestination; however, he notes that Muhammad believes God can show sinners mercy. The thirty-first section outlines the importance in Islam of keeping oaths and lists the Ten Commandments, which appear in the Qur'an; Bauer says that Muhammad accepts commandments one through eight but does not mention the ninth and tenth commandments in the Qur'an. In section thirty-two, he discusses Muhammad's claim that the Qur'an is in harmony with and conforms to the Gospels, which came before it; and the final section briefly discusses marriage rules and sexual propriety for Muslims, including Muhammad's sanction of polygamy and beating a disobedient wife as long as it is done in private.

A Conspectus of Turkish Muhammadan Theology (Jena, 1720)

On Turkish Religion, Scripture, and Theology in General

بسم الله الرحمن الرحيم

Section 1

Concerning the theology of the Turks, you should note that Muhammad, that contemptible impostor, summarizes the business of his religion in the following few words: "faith in God and the Last Day so that men may do good works."[2] Besides that, he takes it very badly if someone does not acknowledge him as the Messenger of God, or rejects his instruction.[3] He calls his religion Islam.[4] Furthermore, he treats anyone who follows another religion like they are one of the damned.[5] He thinks that his religion is orthodox,[6] and that the Apostles were confessors [to his faith],[7] as was Abraham himself,[8] although Muhammad bitterly denies that Abraham was a Jew.[9] Muhammad did not want to be seen as someone whose intention was to forcibly compel everyone to accept the religion he invented,[10] but for now, let us note that he soon changed his mind.[11]

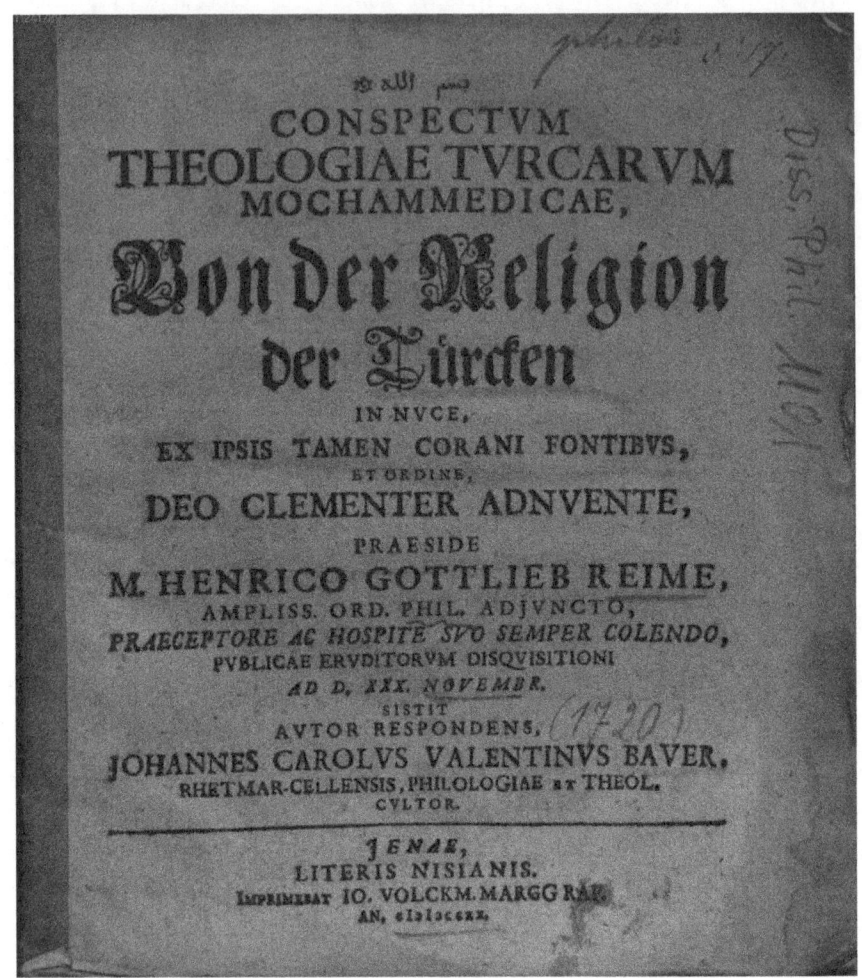

Figure 4.1 Johann Karl Valentin Bauer, *Conspectum theologiae Turcarum Mochammedicae, von der Religion der Türcken*, 1720 (Courtesy of the Bavarian State Library, Munich).

The following sections will contain an outline of certain aspects of this theology.

On the Foundation of Turkish Theology

Section 2

The Qur'an, which contains the dogmas of the Turks, is the foundation of Turkish theology. It is, if not unparalleled, at least interesting and remarkable.[12] I have put together a description of this book, which was born of Muhammad's imagination.[13] Muslims claim that God is the chief creator of the Qur'an,[14] and sent it down from heaven during the month of Ramadan[15] when followers should abstain from food and drink.[16]

The Qur'an declares that the path of salvation can be learned from Muhammad[17] and that all its contents are truthful.[18] Muhammad raves like a madman that "a book like this could not be composed by human powers";[19] he wants everyone to agree on the divine origin of his book.

Section 3

The secondary author of this book is none other than Muhammad, the Prophet of the worst quality.[20] In assuming this title for himself and boasting of other things, he exposes his great arrogance and remarkable lust for telling lies.

Under great compulsion, he boasts about the divine revelation that was granted to him.[21] He was sent alone "to teach the Qur'an,"[22] "proof of which he boasts about" repeatedly.[23] "God shall curse the man who scorns his teachings,"[24] and "whoever does not believe in him will be damned for eternity."[25] On the other hand, "his followers will enjoy eternal blessings."[26]

Therefore, no one should be surprised that Muhammad associates himself intimately with God,[27] and praises his own book.[28] But a clever man would be more careful and not claim the truth of his religion in this way.[29]

Section 4

The Holy Scripture, the foundation of our [Christian] theology, is not named once in the Qur'an. Despite this, Muhammad claims that the teachings of the Holy Scripture are in the Qur'an.[30] He discusses many Christian teachings, but intermingles them with random nonsense.[31]

Muhammad even recognizes both Testaments, for he recounts the history of the flood from the Old Testament (although corrupted by his added falsehoods),[32] and that of Moses[33] and the Pharaoh.[34] Although [Exodus] says that the Pharaoh drowned along with his soldiers,[35] Muhammad denies that the Pharaoh stayed under the sea.[36]

Muhammad also discusses the history of Lot,[37] Joseph, and so on.[38] He especially makes reference to the Pentateuch,[39] though the rest of the Books of Holy Scripture are hardly left out.[40] His Qur'an is at least their equal [the Old Testament],[41] such that all must believe in it.[42]

He also narrates many things from the New Testament.[43] He accepts that the Holy Scripture is inspired by God,[44] but he considers it much "inferior to the Qur'an,"[45] "which was revealed by God in the Arabic language," Muhammad's mother-tongue, "as a favor to the Arabs."[46]

Muhammad rails earnestly against the People of the Book,[47] by which he means nothing else than "those who exclusively follow the dogmas in the Holy Scriptures."[48] He sees the People of the Book as both good and evil.[49] Finally, Muhammad also declares that his teachings can and should be spread by force,[50] thus contradicting those things which we previously mentioned.[51] So, by his own admission, his book can hardly be divine.[52]

On God

Section 5

There is no people in the entire world so savage that they do not recognize God in some form; so too do the Turks embrace God with both hands,[53] and Him alone,[54] whom they worship. Thus, they believe that He is spirit,[55] self-governing,[56] immutable,[57] eternal,[58] omnipotent,[59] a miracle-worker,[60] omniscient,[61] merciful,[62] omnipresent,[63] alive,[64] just,[65] true,[66] and the only One deserving worship.[67]

Section 6

Nonetheless, Muhammad includes a great many things in the Qur'an which challenge the dignity of God to a tremendous degree. For instance, he makes himself almost equal to God,[68] attributes moral offense [misdemeanor] to Him,[69] and states that He swears by creations[70] and by the Qur'an.[71] He is also convinced that God needs the help of man.[72]

Section 7

The Turks do not accept the mystery of the Trinity.[73] They ardently deny that God the Father sired a son,[74] because He does not have a wife.[75] We have also discovered certain references to the Holy Spirit in the Qur'an,[76] but it is clear that these are to be understood as mere spiritual gifts.

Section 8

God created the heavens and the earth, and everything in them; this is emphasized throughout the entire Qur'an on almost every page.[77] Yet we find Muhammad talking about a great many things in his teachings on which there is not even the slightest mention in the Holy Books.[78] Among other things, he is hostile to divine glory when he claims that God conferred with his angels on the work of creation.[79]

On Creation

Section 9

The Qur'an discusses at length the time of creation, with a different account than the Holy Scripture, which declares that the earth was made on the first two days; on the other four days, the foodstuffs were produced that were necessary for the wild animals and man. This account is in opposition to Genesis.[80] Then the Qur'an declares outright that the task of creation was entirely completed within six days.[81]

Section 10

As for the formation of man, the description in the Qur'an is very similar to the one in the Holy Scripture.[82] For the Qur'an declares that man was shaped from mud,[83] and does not deny that a soul was divinely bestowed upon him.[84] It also grants that all subsequent men trace their origin from the first man.[85] As for the creation of wild animals, the Qur'an contains the fiction that all were fashioned from the water.[86] It places water above the heavens.[87]

On Angels

Section 11

The Turks accept the existence of angels,[88] both good and evil.[89] They also believe that God made angels from fire before man,[90] and that the good ones serve God[91] and men.[92] They say that the evil ones draw men to various sins.[93]

Concerning the fall of the angels, the Turks believe that God ordered the angels to worship man,[94] but some of them did not want to do this and for that reason they were expelled from heaven.[95] He also gave wings to the angels.[96] Finally, he accepts genies [*jinn*] as intermediaries between angels and men.[97]

Section 12

We also find in the Qur'an (and they are not to be scorned) traces of the divine Providence which began to make itself known immediately after the act of creation.[98] The Turks believe that divine Providence manifests itself in two activities, governance and stewardship. Concerning governance, they declare that God places limits on all things.[99] Likewise, they extend divine stewardship not only to men,[100] but to all other creations as well.[101]

On the Providence of God

Section 13

Muhammad teaches that death is the common lot of all men,[102] and that God established an end of life for men, which they neither forestall nor surpass.[103]

On Temporal Death

Section 14

The Qur'an declares that resurrection will follow death,[104] but it will not be equal for everyone.[105]

On the Resurrection of the Dead and the Last Judgment

Section 15

The Last Judgment will follow the resurrection;[106] it will be conducted by God Himself,[107] and nothing will help men, not an intervention, not a bribe, not friendship; but they will take their rewards and punishments according to their deeds.[108] "A trumpet will be heard at the same time,[109] and many other signs will precede it."[110]

On Eternal Blessing

Section 16

Muhammad believes in eternal blessing[111] and provides a description of it.[112] He is convinced that men can participate in whatever faith they wish,[113] if only they believe and do good works;[114] but that no one can receive eternal blessing without misfortune and strife—that is, suffering.[115] He identifies even the degrees of glory and rewards that will be bestowed upon the faithful.[116]

Section 17

There are a great many names by which he calls this blessed and ephemeral life. He calls it "Paradise,[117] the gardens of pleasure,[118] the gardens of Eden,[119] the place of good news,"[120] and other things of this sort, which I do not feel are necessary to deal with here.

Section 18

The conceptions which Muhammad fashions concerning eternal blessedness are, for the most part, carnal, wrong, and absurd, for he declares that chosen men will have wives,[121] and they will lie atop couches decked with gold and jewelry,[122] and they will eat there[123] and will wear valuable clothing, and so on.[124]

On Eternal Damnation

Section 19

But how will some men be absolved and others condemned in the Last Judgment?[125] Therefore, I am adding a section here on eternal damnation. The Turks believe in immediate damnation,[126] and it is not only a temporal thing, but also eternal;[127] moreover, they recognize that there will be degrees of punishment [in Hell].[128] Among other absurdities, Muhammad decreed that men condemned to eternal damnation will regenerate their skins [so that they burn continuously].[129]

Section 20

The names by which Muhammad calls eternal damnation are hot boiling water,[130] wretched resting place,[131] foul water,[132] and the destruction by fire.[133]

On Sin

Section 21

Muhammad does not deny that man is powerfully corrupted by sin. He also fully recognizes that man had a very fortunate lot [Garden of Eden] from the outset.[134]

He teaches that the creator of sin is the Devil;[135] but that God offers forgiveness.[136] For this reason, Muhammad compels his followers to repent,[137] although he denies that all sins are pardoned.[138]

On Grace, Conversion, and Justification

Section 22

Muhammad teaches that men are saved by the grace of God,[139] which no one should take for granted.[140]

Section 23

Muhammad asserts that man cannot convert himself [renewal of faith in God after sinning],[141] since it is God's role to convert men.[142] He describes how this is done.[143] He says that justification [salvation] is the task of God alone, from whom it freely flows, and that God acts justly toward whomever He wishes,[144] toward the one who does good deeds,[145] and the one who has faith.[146]

On Faith

Section 24

Muhammad commends faith as the primary means of salvation,[147] and thus he promotes it earnestly.[148] He says that it is insufficient for someone to say, "I believe,"[149] and that there are few who genuinely believe.

On Baptism and Good Works

Section 25

We cannot say there are no references to baptism in the Qur'an, but there are very few.[150]

Section 26

Muhammad includes good works among the means of salvation,[151] and says that through good works, men gain merit in the eyes of God.[152] In particular, he considers alms to be of great value;[153] but whoever gives alms without faith and for the sake of ostentation does so in vain.[154] He exhorts his followers to show pity for orphans,[155] whom it is a great sin to wrong.[156] Drunkenness, gambling,[157] and greed are also great sins according to him.[158]

On Prayers

Section 27

The Turks pray many times a day, however, it is not permitted for everyone to pray, such as drunkards and menstruating women.[159] As they pray, people turn their eyes toward the Temple at Mecca,[160] which they claim was created by God.[161] Also, they thoroughly wash their hands and face before prayers.[162] Moreover, they submit themselves totally in service,[163] and they state that [worshipping] God is the sole purpose of life.[164]

On Food

Section 28

They are extremely particular in their food choices. They do not eat everything indiscriminately. For example, they do not eat carrion, blood, pork, and strangled animals.[165] Nevertheless, it is permissible to eat these foods in times of necessity, or if someone does so unwittingly.[166]

On Christ

Section 29

Muhammad does not acknowledge our great Savior Christ as the true God,[167] nor as the son of God,[168] but as a pure and splendid man made of dust.[169] He thinks that Jesus is the son of Mary,[170] who bore him with pain.[171]

He also says that God, if he wished, could destroy Jesus.[172] Muhammad denies Christ's death and the sacrifice that he made for men. Instead, he asserts that Christ's likeness, a holy simulacrum of Him, not the Messiah himself, was crucified.[173]

At the same time, he states that Jesus reanimated not only men, but also birds. Jesus did this by the dispensation of God,[174] which he also used to perform miracles.[175] Muhammad calls Jesus a Messenger of God,[176] a righteous man,[177] immune from blasphemy, and says that those who worship Jesus are worse than infidels.[178]

Moreover, Muhammad calls him a prophet sent by God.[179] Yet Muhammad decrees that he himself is much greater than Jesus. This is quite evident, as Muhammad always mentions his own name next to that of God [in the Qur'an].[180]

On Predestination

Section 30

On the doctrine of predestination, Muhammad seems to stand on the side of the Reformed [i.e., the Calvinists]. I have noted a passage [in the Qur'an][181] which seems to prove this. He declares that God leads men into error and causes them to make mistakes.[182]

The rest of Muhammad's pronouncements on this matter seem compatible with the declarations of the Holy Scripture. For instance, Muhammad says that, "God grants His mercy on whom He wishes by special dispensation;[183] God spares and punishes whom He wishes,"[184] and other things of this nature. He also speaks at times in a reasonably orthodox way about this doctrine.[185]

On the Law

Section 31

Muhammad recognizes divine laws[186] as being necessary.[187] Hence, he stringently demands that agreements[188] and oaths[189] should be honored.

He wants anyone who has transgressed their oath to make up for it in a willing manner.[190]

He makes the Ten Commandments his own. Indeed, he approves of the first commandment,[191] the second,[192] the third,[193] the fourth,[194] the fifth,[195] the sixth,[196] on which he imposes a unique punishment,[197] the seventh,[198] and the eighth.[199] He says nothing about the ninth and tenth commandments.

On the Gospel

Section 32

Muhammad has his own interpretation of the Gospel,[200] and he says that the Qur'an is in harmony and in agreement with it.[201]

On Marriage

Section 33

Muhammad sanctions marriage[202] and polygamy,[203] but not with infidel women,[204] nor with those whom one's father has already married, nor with mothers, sisters.[205] It is not permitted to have sex with menstruating women.[206]

[The Qur'an] says, "Let men be dominant over women,"[207] and "it is permitted for them to give their wives a writ of divorce two times."[208] When a husband dies, a year's food and clothing is left as a gift for the spouse.[209] On the other hand, a wife should stay a widow for four months and ten days before she is married to another man.[210] If his wife refuses to obey, a man can set her in order with blows, but only in separate chambers and out of the sight of others.[211]

Notes

1 Bauer's biography was compiled from the following sources: Heinrich Gottlieb Reime, "Autori Respondenti, Io. Carol. Valentino Bauer, Theol. Stud." in *Conspectum theologia Turcarum Mochammedicae*, Augsburg Staats- und Stadtbibliothek, Diss. Phil. 1101 (Jena, 1720), 54–56; Wilhelm Haller, *Mochammads lehre von Gott aus dem Kor'aân gezogen*, Universitäts- und Landesbibliothek Sachsen-Anhalt, D Hb 775 (Altenburg, 1779), 146–7; Georg Mentz and Reinhold Jauernig, *Die Matrikel der Universität Jena* vol. 1 (Jena: G. Fischer, 1944), 31; and Herbert Mundhenke, *Die Matrikel der Universität Helmstedt 1685–1810*, vol. 3 (Hildesheim: Lax, 1979), 112.

2 This is sufficiently clear from Q. 2:62, according to the Marracci's edition, but also in Hinckelmann's translation in verse 59, where it has the following words: إن الذين آمنوا والذين هادوا والنص اري والصابئينَ مَن آمنَ باللهِ واليوم الآخِر وعمِلَ صالحًا فلهم أجرُهُم عند رِبهم ولا خوفٌ عليهم ولا هم يحزنون "Indeed, believers, whether

they are Jews, or Nazarenes (i.e., Christians), or Sabaeans, whosoever believes in God and the Last Day, and does good works; for such people will have their reward from their Lord, and fear will not fall upon them, and they will not be afflicted with sadness." [Hinckelmann, henceforth, Hinck.]

3 See Q. 2:90 (or Hinck. 84), where Muhammad names him "unfortunate, who sells his soul so that he does not believe in that which God has revealed" (in the Qur'an), "because of envy," and so forth. See also verses 91, 101, 122, 143 (Hinck. 95, 115, 137). But this is found in the last of these verses: "We placed you Muslims, the just people between Christians and Jews, to bear witness to the people, and for the Messenger to be an ambassador for you."

4 From the root سَلَمَ *salama* means "health," "peace," "greetings," "making peace," and, accordingly, in the fourth conjugation, أَسْلَمَ (*aslama*), "give oneself," "submit to mastery," and "entrust one's affairs to God." From this fourth conjugation comes the word إِسْلَام (*Islām*), which means "religion, whereby anyone assents to the will and revelation of God according to Muhammad's principles." Thus, no name pleases the Turks more than if we give them the title of the مُسْلِمُون (*muslimūn*), "men endowed with divine religion," in German, *Muselmänner*. This form of address was given by Muhammad himself, Q. 2:129, 132 (Hinck. 122, 125); see also 2:138 (Hinck. 130).

5 For example, Q. 3:85 says, وَمَنْ يَبْتَغِ غَيْرَ الإِسْلَام دِينًا فَلَنْ يُقْبَل مِنه وهو في الآخرة من الخَاسِرِين: "Whoever desires a religion other than Islam," that is, the religion of Muhammad, "this religious system of worship will certainly not be accepted by God and they will certainly be losers in the Hereafter," and see also verses 85 and 87 (Hinck. 78, 79, and 80): "Their punishment will be (he adds, in the final verse I cited) that the curse of God, the Angels, and all men will be upon them." Also, see Q. 3:19 (Hinck. 18) and likewise, Q. 5:4.

6 Muhammad calls "Abraham orthodox to that theology," which means that Abraham adhered to Muslim theology, as Muhammad prattles on in Q. 2:136 (Hinck. 129). See also Q. 3:67, *ḥanīf*, "worshipping the true religion," from حَنَفَ, "he followed the true religion, rejected idols," and so on.

7 This is demonstrated in Q. 3:52 (Hinck. 45–46). Muhammad says, "When Jesus felt disbelief among them (the Jews), he said, 'Who then are supporters of God?'" The Apostles answered, "We shall be the supporters to God, we believe in God, and He is the witness that we are indeed Muslims: "وأشهد بأنّا مسلمون"

8 Q. 3:67 (Hinck. 60) is relevant here, for it says: ما كان إبراهيم يهوديًّا ولا نصرانيًّا ولكن كان حنيفًا مسلمًا وما كان من المُشْرِكِين "Abraham was not a Jew, nor a Christian, but was in fact an orthodox true Muslim; he was not one of the polytheists."

9 This is agreed upon according to the verse already cited.

10 The passage from Q. 10:99 (Hinck. 99) is relevant here: "If Your Lord had wanted, surely all those men, who were all together on the earth, would have believed. Therefore, will you compel men by force to be believers?" [Q. 10:100]: "No soul may have belief except by the will of God."

11 See section 4, toward the end.

12 The Qur'an's name comes from the Arabic article أل and from the word قُرآن. This form occurs at Q. 72:1, but without *madda*, آ with a moveable قُرْأن, or even قُرَان from which it gets the common name 'Qur'an,' and which form exists in Sura 2 (verse 186 in the Marracci edition and 181 in Hinck.). That means "selection" or "collection," because the root قَرَأ means "selecting" or "collecting."

13　Q. 2:2 (Hinck. 2) says هُدًى لِلمُتَّقِينَ ذَلِكَ الكِتَابُ لا رَيْبَ فيه "There is nothing questionable in this book" (or anything scandalous), but "guidance for the righteous." Q. 3:138 describes the Qur'an in almost the same terms, هذا بيانٌ للناس وهُدِي وموعظةٌ للمُتَّقِينَ, "It is itself a clear explanation to men, and guidance and warning for the righteous."

14　This is clear from Q. 2:89 (Hinck. 83), for it says ولَمَّا جاءهُم كِتَابٌ مِنْ عند الله مصدِّقًا لِمَا مَعَهُم "After the Book, the Qur'an, came to them from God, confirming that which [was] among them," that is, containing the complement to those Biblical books which they previously had. See also the following verses Q. 2:90–91 (Hinck. 84 and 85) as well as Q. 3:2 (Hinck. 1), for he says:
الله لا إله الا هو الحيُّ القيّوم نزّل عَلَيْكَ الكِتابَ بالحقّ مُصَدِّقًا لما بين يديه وأنزَل التَّوْرَاةَ والإنجيل من قبل هُدًي للناس وأنزَل الفُرْقَان.
"God does not exist unless that God is living and enduring." [Q. 3:3]: "He sent to you the Book with truth, which confirms that which was in his hand," that is, which had been before him. "He sent the law of Moses and the Gospel previously as guidance for the righteous." Finally, He sent "individual Tomes of Prophets." See also Q. 4:82 (Hinck. 81), and following both editions, verse 136; likewise, Q. 5:7, 6:19, 7:196; Q. 9:111, Q. 10:15–16, and Q. 40:2.

15　Q. 2:185 (Hinck. 181).

16　Q. 2:185.

17　Q. 2:2; Q. 4:44 (Hinck. 50); 6:92 (Hinck. 92). These words are worthy to be mentioned here, from Q. 14:1, where Muhammad says about his Qur'an: كِتابٌ أَنْزَلْناهُ إِلَيْكَ لِتُخْرِجَ النَّاسَ من الظُّلماتِ إلى النُّور بإذنِ ربِّهم إلى صِراطِ العزيز الحَمِيد. "We sent a Book to you, in order that you might raise men from the depths of darkness into the light, according to the will of the Lord, upon the beloved and praiseworthy path."

18　He denies that anything perverse is found in the Qur'an in Q. 18:1, as well as the following. Among other things, he says about the Qur'an, in Q. 2:91 (Hinck. 85): وهو الحقُّ مصدِّقًا لما معهم "Certainly this Book confirms the [Books] that they had," meaning the Books that had been divinely granted to them previously.

19　In Q. 2:23–24 (Hinck. 21–22) he writes: وإن كُنتُم في رِيبٍ مما نزّلْنا على عبدِنا فأتُوا بسُورةٍ من مِثْله "[If you doubt] what we sent to our servant," meaning Muhammad, "then compose another sura," or chapter, "like this." In Q. 11:1, the Impostor boasts that "this Book is wisely laid out"; as well as other things.

20　Muhammad gave himself the title of Prophet: Q. 8:64, 65, and 70 (Hinck. 65, 66, 71), and elsewhere.

21　Q. 2:91 (Hinck. 85). He preaches in Q. 72:1: قُل أُوحِيَ إلَيَّ أنه اسْتَمَعَ نَفَرٌ مِنَ الجِنِّ فقالوا إنا سمِعْنا قُرْآنًا عَجَبًا "Say [to them], 'it has been revealed to me that a group of the *jinn* listened carefully and said: 'We have certainly heard a wonderful reading'." He speaks on this matter in Q. 53:5 with emphasis: عَلَّمَهُ شَدِيدُ القُوَى. In 53:2–4 "Your ally [Muhammad] has not gone astray" says God about him and "he [Muhammad] has not erred. He does not speak out of desire (or the itch), only through the revelation given to him" (ما ضلَّ صاحِبُكم). Likewise, in Q. 53:10–11, (و ما غوى * وما ينطِقُ عن الهَوى * إن هُو الا وحْيٌ يُوحَى). "The Lord of mighty power has فأُوْحَى إلى عبدِهِ ما أوحى * ما كَذَبَ الفُؤَادُ ما رأى : taught him. Indeed, He revealed to His servant what He meant to reveal. His heart and mind in no way made up what he saw."

22　See Q. 2:120 (Hinck. 113), and likewise 151 (Hinck. 146); Q. 3:164 (Hinck. 158). He says: لقد منَّ اللهُ على المُؤْمِنينَ إذ بعث فيهم رسولًا مِن أَنْفُسِهم يتلو عليهِم آياتِه ويُزكِّيهِم ويُعلِّمُهُم الكتابَ والحِكمة "Then God was favorable towards the faithful when He raised a Messenger among them from their midst to teach them the signs and purify them and to give His book," the Qur'an, "and His wisdom to them." Q. 11:2 says "that you do not do service except to God; indeed, I come to you from Him as a warner of punishments, and an evangelist."

23 Q. 2:159 (Hinck. 154). الذين يكتمون ما أنزلنا من البَيِّنَاتِ والهُدي "Those who conceal the clear signs we have sent down and the guidance." See also Q. 2:119 (Hinck. 112).

24 Q. 2:161.

25 Q. 4:52, 53, 115.

26 Q. 4:54; see also 2:25, 40:7, and 7:203.

27 Q. 8:1, 59:4 and the passages to be discussed in the next section.

28 Q. 2:78.

29 Q. 2:119 (Hinck. 113) says, إنّا أرسلناك بالحقّ بشيرًا و نذيرًا و لا تُسْأل عن أصحاب الجَحيم "Indeed, We have sent you [Muhammad] with the truth, as a bringer of good news (evangelist) and a warning, and you will not be questioned about the companions of Hellfire." See also Q. 2:76 and Q. 53:12, where he is asked the following: أَفَتُمَارُونَهُ على ما يري "Will you dispute with him about that which he saw?" Of course, this seems unbefitting to him.

30 See Q. 2:41 (Hinck. 38): آمِنُوا بما أنزلتُ مُصَدّقًا لما معكم "Believe in that which I sent, the Qur'an, in confirmation of the revelation (the Books of the Holy Scripture) which you have already had for a long time."

31 See Q. 2:29 (Hinck. 29), where he spouts off that God created the entirety of the earth, but also "seven heavens" (Q. 2:34); "that the Angels were compelled by God to worship Adam," the first man. And so, at the very least, he does not make up what he wants at every point according to his whims, such that he always assumes or mixes up some portion of truth from the Holy Books, as in the history of Abraham, Q. 6:75 (Hinck. 74 and 85; also Hinck. 84).

32 Q. 7:61 (Hinck. 57).

33 Sura 28.

34 Sura 28 and Q. 7:104 (Hinck. 101). They are trifles, to put it thusly, because in Q. 7:124, Muhammad tells the following tale: "Since the nobles of Egypt sincerely believed that they were under threat after Moses performed his miracles, the Pharaoh said that their hands and feet would be cut off and that they would be crucified." Whoever wishes will find many other things of that same nature here and in other verses.

35 Q. 7:136 (Hinck. 132).

36 Q. 10:90 (Hinck. 92).

37 Q. 11:70, 74, 77 (Hinck. 73).

38 Q. 12:4 (Hinck. 4).

39 Q. 2:87 (Hinck. 81), ولقد أَتَيْنا مُوسى الكِتاب وقَفَّيْنا من بعدِه بالرُسُل وآتينا عيسى ابن مرْيَمَ البيِّنات "We have already brought the Book to Moses, and We have made him obey the Messengers, and We have brought explanations to Jesus, the Son of Mariam."

40 Muhammad declares in Q. 2:4 (Hinck. 3) that his Qur'an will be useful to, among others, الذين يؤمنون بما أنزل إلَيْك وما أنزل من قبلِك "those who believe in that which has been revealed to you" (meaning Muhammad, since he lies that the Qur'an was divinely bestowed upon him); also, those who believe in the Holy books of the Bible, which have been divinely inspired long before Muhammad's time. See also Q. 5:53 (Hinck. 50).

41 Q. 2:40–41 (Hinck., toward the end of verses 38 and 39), where he says, "Believe in what I have revealed to you, in confirmation of that which is already with you." See also 2:91 (Hinck. 85).

42 See Q. 32:2; see also 32:23.

43 Q. 7:40 (Hinck. 38); it alludes to Christ's sermon (Matthew 19:24, Luke 18:25). See also Q. 5:46 (Hinck. 44); and also 5:52 (Hinck. 48), where he clearly draws his material from Luke 16:24. In Sura 19, it is repeated at length and likewise corrupted.

44 See Q. 2:53 and 3:3 (Hinck. 2) where it says: "God sent the law of Moses and the Gospel prior to the Qur'an." We have cited the passage above. Q. 5:77 is also relevant here, where He commands observation of the law and the Gospel. A verse dealing with Jesus, our blessed Savior, says likewise: Q. 19:30 (Hinck. 31), for He introduces him, speaking thus: قَالَ إِنِّي عَبْدُ الله آتانِيَ الكِتاب و جعلني نبيًّا و جعلني مباركًا "He (Jesus) said, 'I am of course the servant of God, who gave me the Book and sent me as His Prophet, and made me blessed'," and ذلك عيسى ابنُ مَرْيَمَ قَوْلُ الحَق "This is Jesus himself, the word of truth." See also Q. 5:87.

45 Q. 2:23, 24 (Hinck. 21, 22).

46 Q. 12:2 says, تِلكَ آياتُ الكِتابُ المُبِين إنَّا أنزلناهُ قرآنًا عربيًا لعلَّكُم تعقِلُون "Indeed, I sent the Qur'an to you in the Arabic language so that you might understand it." See also Q. 19:97.

47 They are called أهلُ الكِتاب, or "the people of the book, men of scripture" in Q. 3:70 (Hinck. 63), because they remain singularly committed to the Books of Holy Scriptures and reject the Qur'an, Talmud, and other books of this sort. See also Q. 4:153, 171.

48 This is clear from Q. 2:113 (Hinck. 107) and Q. 5:65, 68, 86 (Hinck. 81).

49 Q. 3:110 (Hinck. 109).

50 Q. 8:60 (Hinck. 62); also 65, 67 (Hinck. 67). There he says, و أعِدُّوا لهُم ما استطعتم من قُوَّة و من رباطِ الخيل تُرهِبون به عدو الله وعدوَّكُم و آخرين من دونهم لا تعلمونهم اللهُ يعلمهم وما تُنْفِقُوا من شيءٍ في سبيل الله يُوَفَّ إلَيْكُم وأنتم لا تُظْلَمون that is, "Take vengeance against the infidels as you can: with violence or chains or the reins of horses; that you may strike fear into these enemies of God, your own enemies, and all enemies of that stripe. You do not know them, but God knows them; and what you expend on this endeavor, along the path of God, will be repaid to you in whole, and you will not be oppressed."

51 Section 1 at the end.

52 This passage stands out in Q. 4:82, أفلا يتدبَّرون القُرآن و لو كان من عند غير الله لوجدوا فيه اختلافًا كثيرا "Will they not pay close attention to the Qur'an? If it were not from God, certainly they would find an abundance of discrepancies in it."

53 This can be proven at once, from the heading of the majority of Suras, which we have also put at the head of this treatise. But also, there are many passages in the Qur'an declaring the existing of a supreme divinity, and some assuming it. To be brief, Q. 2:1 says straightaway, الحمْدُ لله رب العالمين "Praise be to God, Lord of the Universe." See also Q. 2:7–8 (Hinck. 6, 7); likewise, Q. 2:19; and Q. 4:1.

54 Q. 40:3 says, لا اله الا هُوَ "There is no God but He." See too Q. 40:12. Also, see Q. 4:170 and 6:18.

55 A description of God is appropriate here, which is found in Q. 6:103: لا تُدرِكُه الأبصارُ و هو يدركُ الأبصار "Vision does not comprehend Him and He comprehends all vision."

56 Hence, Q. 6:14 says about God, هو يُطعِمُ و لا يُطْعَم "He Himself nourishes, but is not nourished."

57 Q. 6:34 (Hinck. 34) says, ولا مُبَدِّلَ لكلِمَات الله "none can change the words of God." See too Q. 6:115, 133; Q. 10:64 (Hinck. 64, 65).

58 Whence also Q. 6:102 recognizes Him as "the creator of everything that exists and the steward of all things."

59 "Omnipotent," قاهر is stated explicitly in Q. 6:18 (Hinck. 19), and verse 17 describes Him as such when it says, الله علي كل شيء قدير "God is powerful over everything." See also Q. 6:106 (Hinck. 100).

60 Thus Q. 3:113 (Hinck. 109) praises certain people who are dedicated to the Holy Scriptures, because "they are inspired by the marvelous signs of God," يَتْلُونَ آياتِ الله and he mentions here and there additional miracles performed by God. See Q. 7:107 (Hinck. 107, according to the Marracci's edition); likewise, Q. 7:117 and 118 (Hinck. 115); 28:31 (Hinck. 31).

61 See Q. 2:95 (Hinck. 89). Q. 8:43 neatly declares that عليمٌ بذاتِ الصدور "God knows what is in the heart," because He penetrates the secret depths even of one's breast. See also Q. 6:117, 124.

62 Q. 1:2 (Hinck. 1).

63 وللہ المشرق والمغرب فأينما تُولُّوا فثَمَّ وجُه الله إن الله واسعٌ عليم Q. 2:115 (Hinck. 109) says, "God is the East and the West. Therefore, wherever you turn is the face of God. Indeed, God is abundantly all-encompassing and knowledgeable." See also Q. 4:108 (Hinck. 108), and likewise 126.

64 Q. 3:2 (Hinck. 1) says, الله لا الَة الا هو الحيُّ القَيُّوم "God is not God unless He is alive and exists in and of Himself."

65 Q. 3:4 (Hinck. verse 3) ascribes to Him the power of taking vengeance and calls Him إنتقام. The description of God that exists in Q 3:56–57 is quite relevant here, وأما فأمَّا الذِين كفروا فأعذِّبُهُم عذابًا شديدًا في الدنيا والآخرة وما لهم من ناصرين * الذِين آمنوا وعملوا الصالحات فيوفِّيهِم أجورَهم واللهُ لا يحِب الظالمِين "And then, those who were infidels I shall certainly punish them terribly in this world and in the Hereafter, and no one will be able to help them. But those who believe and act rightly will be well compensated, for God does not love unfaithful."

66 Q. 3:95, صَدَقَ الله "God has spoken the truth" (Hinck. 58). See also Q. 4:87 (Hinck. 89).

67 Q. 41:37, و من آياتِهِ الليلُ والنهارُ والشمسُ والقمر لا تَسْجُدوا للشمس ولا للقمر واسجُدُوا للہ الذِي خلقهُن إن كنتم إياهُ تعبُدون "Among His signs are night and day, and likewise the sun and the moon; venerate not the sun nor the moon, but venerate God who created these things, if you wish to worship Him."

68 Q. 3:32 (Hinck. 29) declares: أطيعوا الله والرسولَ "Obey God and His Messenger." A similar message appears in 3:50 (Hinck. 44), فاتقوا الله و أطيعون "Therefore, fear God, and obey me."

69 Q. 3:54 (Hinck. 47) says, ومكروا ومكرالله واللہ خيرُالماكرِين "They, the Israelites, planned deception, but God schemed to deceive [them in turn] for God is the most outstanding of deceivers." See also Q. 8:30 (Hinck. 30).

70 See in addition to the others, the last Suras, particularly Sura 51, where the lie is told that He swore by sowers, by porters, by those who run easily, by the wind that scatter, and by all sorts of other nonsense.

71 Q. 44:2 swears, والكتاب المُبين "by the clear book."

72 Q. 47:7, يأيها الذِين آمنوا إن تنصُروا الله ينصُركم "O you who believe! If you help God, God will help you."

73 Q. 5:73 (Hinck. 77) makes a declaration on this matter: لقد كفر الذِين قالوا إن الله ثالِثُ ثلاثة و ما من إلٰه الا الٰه واحد الذِين كفروا منهم عذابٌ أليم "They are blasphemous who say, 'God is, of course, a third of three things'," a trinity. "But God is only a single God, and such infidels shall meet with a grievous torment." And Q. 5:75 (Hinck. 79) adds: ما المسيح ابن مريم الا رسول قَد خلت من قبلِه الرسل وأمه صدِّيق "The Messiah" (meaning Christ, may blasphemy be gone from the word!), "the son of Mary, is not, but a Messenger. Messengers came forth well before him, and his mother was a woman of truth." See also Q. 72:2–3.

74 Q. 112:2–4 says, الله الصمد لم يلد و لم يُولد* و لم يكن له كُفوًا أحد "God is everlasting. He does not beget; He was not begotten. And no other is His equal." See

also Sura 19, for after Muhammad had praised Jesus, our Savior, who can never be uplifted in praise enough, yet he holds backs his praises to deny that he is the son of God. Q. 19:35 (Hinck. 35, 36) says, ما كان لله أن يتخذ من ولدٍ سبحانه "It is not befitting for God to have a son; praise be to Him!"

75 Thus, Q. 72:3 charges earnestly, ما اتخذ صاحبةً ولا ولدًا "He did not take a wife, nor did He have a son."

76 Q. 2:87 (Hinck. 81) states, وآتينا عسى ابن مريم البيّنات وأيّدناهُ بروح القُدُس "We gave Jesus, the son of Mary, clear proofs and We strengthened him with the Holy Spirit." Muhammad says the same about him in 2:253, and about all people of faith—that is, such people who, in his judgment, oppose neither God nor Muhammad (Q. 58:22), whose praises could be witnessed by many.

77 Q. 2:21–22 proclaims, يأيها الناس أعبدوا ربكم الذي خلقكم و الذين من قبلكم لعلكم تتقون * الذي جعل لكم الأرض فراشا و السماء بناءً و أنزل من السماء ماءً فأخرجَ به من الثمراتِ رزقًا لكم فلا تجعلوا لله أندادًا و أنتم تعلمون "Men! Worship your God, who created you and those who were before you, that you may learn to worship Him who made for you the earth to spread across and the heavens to build in, and sends water from the sky and produces thereby crops for your nourishment. Therefore, do not make another equal to God knowingly." In Hinck., this is at the end of verse 19 and after.

78 Among such lies, I rightly mention here that "He creates seven heavens," سبع سماوات in Q. 2:29 (Hinck. 27). See also Q. 41:12 (Hinck. 11) and Q. 78:11.

79 Concerning these things, see Q. 2:30 (Hinck. 28). Also, see Q. 15:28–31, where Muhammad blathers on about God having wanted the angels to worship the created man, which the angels did, except the Devil.

80 Q. 41:9 (Hinck. 8) says, أئنكم لتكفرون بالذي خلق الأرض في يومين "Do you surely disbelieve Him who created the earth in two days?" Also, Q. 41:10 adds, وقَدَّر فيها أقواتها في أربعة أيام "He made them sustenance in four days." Muhammad offers up the rest of what is relevant here, in the cited verse and elsewhere, without any proper order and in quite a mixed-up fashion.

81 Q. 10:3 and Q. 11:7.

82 Q. 23:12 states فلقد خلقنا الانسان من سُلالةٍ من طين "We shaped man from pre-existing substance, from mud."

83 See also Q. 6:2.

84 In Q. 15:28, the lie is told that God said to the angels: إني خالقٌ بشرًا من صَلصالٍ من حمإٍ مسنون "I will indeed create a human being, fashioned carefully from pure and fine mud." Concerning the soul, however, it says the following in verse 29, فإذا سوَّيته و نفخت فيه من روحي فقعوا له ساجدين "Therefore, after I make him and breathe into him from My own Spirit, then bow down and worship him."

85 Q. 4:1 rightly claims, يأيها الناس اتقوا ربَّكم الذي خلقكم من نفسٍ واحدةٍ وخلق منها زوجها و بثَّ منهم رجالاً كثيرًا ونساء "Alas! Men, fear your Lord, who created you from one soul and fashioned from it his woman, and from these two spread abroad many men and women." See too Q. 6:99 (Hinck. 98), and Q. 7:189.

86 Q. 24:45, والله خلق كل دابةٍ من ماء "God created all the beasts from the waters."

87 Q. 23:18, وأنزلنا من السماء ماءً بقدر وأسكنّاه في الأرض "We sent water from the heavens (look upon it!) and We made it stay upon the earth." See also Q. 6:99 (Hinck. 99).

88 Muhammad mentions angels in Q. 3:18 and 39.

89 Q. 2:34 (Hinck. 32), وإذ قلنا للملائكة اسجدوا لآدم فسجدوا الا ابليس أبى واستكبر وكان من الكافرين "After We said to the angels, 'Worship Adam,' then they worshipped him; but the Devil refused and exulted in his arrogance and became an infidel."

90 Q. 15:27, و الجان خلقناه من قبل من نار السموم "But we have already made a de-
mon, a seething wind of fire" (a strong spirit).

91 Q. 4:172, لن يستنكف المسيح أن يكون عبدًا لله ولا الملائكةُ المقربون "The Messiah Jesus
Christ was not to be a servant to God, nor to the angels near to God."

92 In Q. 3:124 (Hinck. 120), he writes, إذ تقول للمؤمنين ألن يكفيكم أن يمدكم ربكم بثلاثة
آلاف من الملائكة منزلين "You shall say to the faithful, 'Does it not suffice for
you that your Lord gave you for help three thousand angels that were sent
to you?'."

93 Q. 2:268 (Hinck. 271) says, الشيطان يعدكم لفقر و يأمركم بالفحشاء "Satan rushes
upon you with poverty and will give you foul commands." See Q. 4:60
(Hinck. 63) and Q. 15:39–40.

94 Q. 17:61.

95 See Q. 15:31.

96 Two, three, or four each, Q. 35:1.

97 Q. 6:100 (Hinck. 100) says the following about them: و جعلوا لله شركاء الجن
و خلقهم و خرقوا له بنين و بنات "They made genies (*jinn*) associates with God,
although He created them. They falsely attributed to God sons and daughters." Q. 6:128 states that they were heavily involved with men, to whom
they were sent as Messengers from God and who fell in a similar manner as
men (Q. 6:130). See in its entirety Sura 72 as well as Q. 46:18.

98 Q. 10:3 (Hinck. 3) says, "Indeed! Your Lord is God, who created heaven
and earth in six days." It continues, ثم استوا على العرش يُدبّر الأمر "then He assumes His throne to manage affairs."

99 Q. 3:26 (Hinck. 25), قل اللهم ملك المُلك "Speak, Thou God, the keeper of the
kingdom! Thou shall give the kingdom to those whom Thou wish; and
Thou shall remove the kingdom from whom Thou wish. Thou shall make
him outstanding whom Thou wish, and humble whom Thou wish. For the
good is in Thine hand, for Thou are Almighty."

100 Q. 3:27 says, "Thou send night unto day, and Thou send day unto night;
Thou draw the living from the dead, and Thou draw the dead from the
living; and Thou draw boons to whom Thou wish, without reckoning." See
too Q. 10:31 (Hinck. 32), Q. 16:72 (Hinck. 74).

101 Q. 11:7, وما من دابة في الأرض الا على الله رزقُها "There is not an animal on earth,
but that its resources also come from God, and He himself knows its place
of rest." See too Q. 87:2–5.

102 Q. 3:185 (Hinck. 182), كلُّ نفس ذائقة الموت "Every person is going to taste
death." Q. 4:78 says, أينما تكُونوا يُدرككم الموت "Wherever you will be, death will
follow you, even if you are in lofty towers."

103 Q. 3:145 (Hinck. 139), وما كان لنفسٍ أن تموت إلا بإذن الله "No one dies except by
the will of God." What Muhammad says in the same verse is also noteworthy: "Whoever wants the wages of this world, We shall give it to him from
it; but whoever wants the wages of the future world, We shall give to him
from that, and then We shall count up those who give thanks." See also Q.
3:157–8 (Hinck. 50); Q. 7:34 (Hinck. 32), where it says, ولكل أُمّةٍ أجل فإذا جاء
أجلهم لا يستأخرون ساعةً ولا يستقدمون "An end has been set for every people, and if
their end comes, they shall not delay one hour, nor shall they forestall it."
See also Q. 23:43.

104 See Q. 2:85 (Hinck. 79) and 2:174 (Hinck. 169). Q. 3:9 says, ربنا انك جامع
الناس ليوم لا ريب فيه إنَّ الله لا يُخلفُ الميعاد "Our Lord! Indeed, Thou are going to
gather up men for the day (of the resurrection), there is no doubt about it:
God will not fail His promise." See also Q. 3:55, Q. 6:12, and 26:81.

105 A relevant passage in Q. 2:275 says, الذين يأكلون الربا لا يقومون إلا كما يقوم الذي
يتخبطه الشيطان من المس "Those who practice usury certainly shall not rise,
unless he rises as one who has been driven mad by Satan."

106   واتقوا يوما لا تجزي نفس عن نفس شيئا ولا يقبل منها شفاعة ولا يؤخذ (Hinckel. 45), 2:48 .Q
منها عدل ولا هم ينصرون "Thus, fear the day when any man will not be able to pay another's debts, nor will an intervention be accepted for him, nor will equivalent property be accepted for him, nor will they find any aid."

107   Hence, Q. 1:3 calls God, مالك يوم الدين "the Master, the King of the Day of Judgment." Q. 2:8 refers to الآخرة "the last and final day."

108   Q. 2:254 says the same. See also Q. 3:10 (Hinck. 8).

109   Q. 6:73.

110   They are described at length, particularly in Suras 81 and 82, from a translation of which I shall provide some examples to satisfy the curious reader: Muhammad speaks thus on these things: "When the sun becomes obscure; and when the stars fall; and when the mountains are made to walk about; and when pregnant camels lack in milk; and when wild beasts gather together; and when the seas are aflame." "And when books are revealed; and when the heavens are robbed of their covering; and when the netherworld burns more violently; when paradise draws nearer; will he know all things, and will man recall what he did?" He also says on the subject: "When the sky is split; when the stars are scattered; when the seas are mixed up; when graves are turned upside down; the soul will know what it accomplished and what it did not."

111   Q. 3:107 (Hinck. 103) says, وأما الذين ابيضت وجوههم ففي رحمة الله هم فيها خالدون "But as for those whose faces will turn white, they shall be in God's mercy. They will abide therein eternally."

112   He then describes the place [of eternal blessing] "as a garden, at the heart of which rivers flow, where there are also wives and the blessing from God," in the cited passage, 3:15 (Hinck. 13); likewise, Q. 3:133 (in Hinck., at the end of verse 126): He calls paradise the breadth of heaven and the earth. See also Q. 4:13 (Hinck. 17).

113   Q. 2:62 (Hinck. 59), إنَّ الذين آمنوا و الذين هادوا والنصاري والصابئين من آمن باالله واليوم
الآخر وعمل صالحًا فلهم أجرهم عند ربهم ولا خوفٌ عليْهم ولا هم يحزنون "Certainly, those who believe—the Jews, the Christians, the Sabaeans—whoever believes in God and in the final day and does good works, certainly their reward will be with the Lord, and fear will not hang over them, nor will they be stricken with sorrow."

114   See Q. 2:82 (Hinck. 76). But Q. 3:134 (Hinck. 128) requires specifically that those who wish to enjoy eternal blessing "give alms, both in times of plenty and times of hardship, control their anger, and pardon others."

115   Q. 2:214 (Hinck. 209), أم حسبتم أن تدخلوا الجنة ولما يأتكم مثل الذين خلوا من قبلكم
مستهم البأساء والضراء وزلزلوا "Do you think that you will enter Paradise, when nothing has yet happened to you similar to what others suffered before you? Disaster struck them, hardship befell them, they were afflicted with dread."

116   Q. 46:19, و لكلٍ درجاتٍ مما عملوا و ليُوفّيَهم أعمالَهم وهم لا يُظلَمون "Each man will have his rank, according to the things that he did, and He will repay him for his acts, and he will not be treated unjustly."

117   In Q. 2:25, Muhammad makes the pointless argument that rivers flow through it.

118   See Q. 22:56.

119   Q. 18:31 and 19:60.

120   Q. 78:2.

121   Muhammad often flatters his followers; see Q. 3:15, which says, "in the name of God," as he fashions it, قل أؤنبئكم بخيرٍ من ذالكم للذين اتّقوا عند ربهم جناتٌ
"Speak; تجري من تحتها الأنهار خالدين فيها و أزواجٌ مطهرة و رضوانٌ من الله والله بصيرٌ بالعباد
shall I tell you what is better than this? Those who kept faith with their

Lord dutifully, the gardens await; rivers flow by its seat. They will remain there. Likewise, pure wives will be there, and the blessing of God, for God gives rewards to His servants." See also Q. 4:54, 28:37, and 83:22.

122 Q. 56:15–16, where it says, "a few of the first men will lie upon the couch bedecked with gold and jewels"; and verse 18 continues, "with goblets, and cups with handles, and a chalice flowing perpetually with wine"; see also verse 17, "eternal youths will attend them."

123 Q. 13:35, in the middle, declares, أُكُلُها دائم و ظِلُها "His food is everlasting, as is His shade." See also Q. 19:61, Q. 80:24, and 78:32.

124 See Q. 18:31, and Q. 22:23.

125 Q. 26:82 says, يوم الدين أطمَعُ أن يَغفر لي خطيئتي "I wish for God to forgive my sins on the Day of Judgment," according to Muhammad himself, because it concerns himself and his persona. On the other hand, Q. 46:20 says, و يوم يُعرضُ الذين كفروا علي النار أذهبتم طَيباتِكم في حياتكم الدنيا واستمتعتم بها فاليوم تُجزوْن عذابَ الهُون بما كنتم تستكبرون في الأرضِ بغير الحق و بِم كنتم تفسُقون "On that day, those who rejected faith will be stood in fire. You have squandered your good deeds, the temporal affairs of life, and you have amused yourselves there. Today, though, shameful grief will be repaid to you. Thus, what you did in arrogance on the world, in injustice, and what you did duplicitously will be repaid to you!" See also Q. 20:56, 74 and 13:36.

126 See also Q. 2:24, 39, 81, 85 as well as Q. 3:10, 12, and 106.

127 Q. 2:162 says, "they will remain there constantly; their punishment will not be made any easier." See also Q. 3:87, 88, 90 as well as Q. 98:6.

128 See note f in Section 16 [footnote 113].

129 Q. 4.56 says on this: إنَّ الذين كفروا بآياتنا سوف نُصليهم نارًا كلما نضِجت جلودُهم بدَّلناهم جلودًا غيرَها لِيذوقوا العذاب "Indeed, We shall cast into the fire those who have disbelieved. As often as their skin becomes thoroughly burned, We will regenerate it with another so they may suffer eternally."

130 Q. 10:4.

131 Q. 13:18.

132 Q. 14:16.

133 Q. 18:53.

134 A memorable passage on this topic is found in Q. 7:19 (Hinck. 18). To avoid excessive wordiness, I will write out the translation here: He says, in the name of God, "Adam! Dwell, you and your wife, in Paradise; eat from whatever you wish; but do not approach this tree. And Satan whispered to them both, so that he made to appear before them what had been hidden from them concerning their genitals, and said, 'Your Lord has not kept this tree from you, except that you might not be two angels, or not be among those who live forever.' Then he swore to them, 'I am, of course, absolutely one of those who will offer you good counsel.' And he cast them down with deception. And after they had tasted the tree, their genitals were apparent to them and they began to sew garments for themselves from the leaves of Paradise. And their Lord cried out to them, 'Did I not keep this tree from you, and did I not say to you, 'Certainly Satan is a clear enemy to you?'.'"

135 See also Q. 2:36 (Hinck. 34), 168 (Hinck. 164).

136 Q. 3:135 (Hinck. 129), والذين إذا فعلوا فاحشةً أو ظلموا أنفسهم ذكروا الله فاستغفروا لذنوبِهم، ومن يغفرُ الذنوبَ الا الله ولم يصِّروا علي ما فعلوا وهم يعلَمون [They are] those who, after they have committed foul deeds and acted unjustly towards themselves, remember God and seek pardon for their sins—who forgives wrongdoing if not God?—and they did not knowingly commit constant sin." See also Q. 3:16 (Hinck. 14), likewise 31 (Hinck. 29).

137 See Q. 2:58.

138 Q. 4:136 is particularly relevant here, يا أيها الذين آمنوا آمنوا بالله ورسوله والكتاب الذي نزل على رسوله والكتاب الذي أنزل من قبل ومن يكفر بالله وملائكته وكتبه ورسله واليوم الآخر فقد ضل ضلالا بعيد "Then I say, O believers! Have faith in God and His Messenger, and the scripture which had been sent before. Whoever denies God, His angels, His scriptures, His messengers, and the final day has gone far astray." He adds in the following verse, إن الذين آمنوا ثم كفروا ثم آمنوا ثم كفروا ثم ازدادوا كفرا لم يكن الله ليغفر لهم ولا ليهديهم سبيلا "Indeed, those who believed then disbelieved; again, they believed, and then disbelieved again, then they increased their disbelief. God will never forgive them, nor will He guide them to the right path." More passages are relevant here. Whoever wishes may see Q. 3:89–90 (Hinck. 83, 84).

139 See Q. 3:103 (Hinck. 97), where he writes, واعتصموا بحبل الله جميعًا ولا تفرقوا واذكروا نعمة اللهِ عليكم إذ كنتم أعداءً فألَّف بين قلوبكم فأصبحتم بنعمته إخوانًا وكنتم على شفا حُفرةٍ من النار فأنقذكم منها كذلك يُبيِّن اللهُ لكم آياتِه لعلَّكم تهتدون "Therefore, hold firmly to God's covenant, and in no way separate yourselves from it. Rather, remember the divine favor shown to you: when you were enemies, yet He united your hearts so that you became brothers by His grace. You were at the edge of a fiery pit, but He freed you from it. In this way, God makes His signs clear to you that you may be led on the right path."

140 See Q. 2:211 (Hinck. 206).

141 Hence, Q. 2:18 (Hinck. 16) says, "He calls those who do not believe deaf, dumb, and blind." See also 2:20.

142 فتلقى آدمُ من ربِّه كلمات فتاب عليه إنه هو التوّاب الرحيم "Adam received the words of his Lord and He accepted his repentance; indeed, God is the merciful [of repentance]." See 2:64 (Hinck., at the end of verse 61).

143 In Q. 2:28 (Hinck. 26), Muhammad's statement is so fine that I could not fail to write it out. He says, كيف تكفرون بالله و كنتم أمواتًا فأحياكم ثم يُميتُكم ثم يحييكم ثم إليه تُرجعون "Why do you want to deny God, when you are mortal? Certainly, He can restore you to life. First, He will hand you over to death, then He will restore you to life, and then you will be brought down before Him."

144 Q. 4:49 (Hinck. 52), ألم تر الي الذين يُزكُّون أنفسهم بل الله يُزكي من يشاء ولا يُظلمون فتيلا "Have you seen those who want to justify themselves? Surely God justifies the one whom He wishes and not an ounce of injustice will be done to the one whom God justifies."

145 See Q. 3:92 (Hinck. 85) and see below on good works.

146 See 3:193 (Hinck. 190), for it says, ربنا إننا سمعنا مناديا ينادي للإيمان أن آمنوا بربكم فآمنا ربنا فاغفر لنا ذنوبنا وكفِّر عنا سيئاتنا وتوفنا مع الأبرار "O! Our Lord! Indeed, we heard a herald, who welcomed us to faith, saying 'Believe in your Lord!' Therefore, O! our Lord, we believed! So blot out our sins for us and cleanse us of our evils, and make us die with the righteous."

147 See Q. 2:25 (Hinck. 23); likewise, Q. 2:62 (Hinck. 59); Q. 29:9 (Hinck. 6) says, والذين آمنوا وعملوا الصالحات لنُدخلنهم في الصالحين "For We shall lead those who believed and acted rightly [into Paradise] together with the good." See also Q. 35:7.

148 Q. 3:179 (Hinck., at the end of verse 174); Q. 3:68 (Hinck., 63); 3:100 (Hinck. 94); and 102 (Hinck. 95).

149 Q. 2:8 (Hinck. 7), Q. 29:2 (Hinck. 1); for he writes, أحسب الناس أن يُتركوا أن يقولوا آمنًا وهم لا يُفتنون "Surely men will be unable to think that they will be left alone if they say, 'we believe'? and that they will not be put to the test?" Q. 4:46 (Hinck. 49) says, إلا قليلًا لا يُؤمنون "Not but a few believe." See also Q. 2:155.

150 No passage presented itself to us, except this single one, which is found in Q. 2:138 (Hinck. 132), where it says, صبغة الله ومن أحسن من الله صبغة ونحن له عابِدون.

"Baptism is divine. What is most outstanding than God? Baptism is or at least it is said to be. In fact, it is Him we worship."

151 He explains this in Q. 2:158 (Hinck. 153), إن الصفا والمروة من شعائر الله فمن حج
البيت أو اعتمر فلا جناح عليه أن يطوف بهما ومن تطوع خيرا فإن الله شاكرعليم "Indeed, the Ṣafā and Marwa are among the signs of God." These are two mountains located at Mecca. "Therefore, whoever sets out for the sake of pilgrimage to the temple of Mecca or goes there for an extended visit ['umrah], of course it will be no blame for him if he performs [pilgrimage] on either of those mountains. Whoever shows obedience, then God, indeed, will be gracious and all-knowing." See also Q. 4:114 (Hinck. 114) and 4:124.

152 Q. 9:103 (Hinck. 104), خذ من أموالهم صدقة تطهرهم وتزكيهم بها وصل عليهم إن صلاتك
سكن لهم والله سميع عليم "Take alms out of their property, that you might purify and cleanse them thereby. Pray for them; of course, your prayers will be a reprieve for them. For God Himself hears and knows."

153 See also: Q. 2:254, 267; Q. 3:134 (Hinck. 128); and Q. 4:36 (Hinck. 40).

154 Q. 2:264 (Hinck. 266), يأيها الذين آمنوا لا تُبطلوا صدقاتكم بالمَن والأذي كالذي يُنفق مالَه
رئاء النّاس ولا يؤمن بالله واليوم الآخر "O believers! Do not ruin your alms by giving in a spirit of resentment and injury, like the one who gives his wealth to men for appearances, yet does not believe in God, nor in the last day." See also Q. 4:38 (Hinck. 42).

155 See Q. 4:2.

156 See the cited passage and verse 2. See also verses 8 and 10.

157 See Q. 2:219 (Hinck. 215), يسألونك عن الخمر والميسر قل فيهما إثم كبيرٌ و منافع للناس
و إثمهما أكبر من نفعهما "They will ask you about wine and games; say, 'In both there is great injustice and usefulness for men; but the injustice is greater than the usefulness'." See also Q. 5:90 (Hinck. 92).

158 Q. 4:37 (Hinck. 41), الذين يبخلون ويأمرون الناس بالبخل ويكتمون ما آتاهم الله من فضله
وأعتدنا للكافرين عذابا مهينا "For those infidels who are greedy, and enjoin their greed on other men, and hide that which God gave to them in His generosity, we have indeed prepared a disgraceful punishment."

159 Q. 4:43 (Hinck. 46), يأيها الذين آمنوا لا تقربوا الصلاة و أنتم سكاري حتي تعلموا ما تقولون
ولا جُنُبًا الا عابري سبيل حتي تغتسلوا وإن كنتم مرضي أو علي سفر أو جاء أحدٌ منكم من الغائط أو
لامستم النساء فلم تجدوا ماءً فتيمموا صعيدًا طيّبًا فامسحوا بوجوهكم و أيديكم "O, those who believe, do not go to prayers while you are drunk, until you know what you are saying; neither should those who are ritually impure [junub], unless you are on a journey, until you have washed. If you are sick and are on a journey, or if you return from the bathroom, or if you have congress with women and do not wash with water; then you should take finer earth (that is, better earth, [tayammum]) and scrub your face and your hands with it."

160 See Q. 2:43 (Hinck. 139).

161 In the passage cited, 2:150 (Hinck. 145).

162 Q. 5:6 (Hinck. 8), Before prayers, He gives the order to wash one's hands up to the elbow. He also orders one to scrub one's head and feet.

163 He declares them to be fortunate, see Q. 23:1–2.

164 Muhammad strongly favors monasticism. Qur'an 57:27 says, و قفّينا بعيسي
ابن مريم و آتيناه الإنجيل و جعلنا في قلوب الذين اتّبعوه رأفةً و رحمة و رهبانية ابتدعوها ما كتبناها
عليهم إلا ابتغاء رضْوان الله "We made Jesus the son of Mary follow, and We gave him the Gospel, and We placed in the hearts of those who followed mercy, and pity, and the monastic life. They have recently established it although we did not command it to them, and only by a desire to please God."

165 Also forbidden are that which has been sacrificed for other than God, and which has been killed by chance, or has slipped and fallen and, thus, died; also, that which died by being gored, and other circumstances that he exempts. Q. 5:3, see also Q. 16:115 (Hinck. verse 116).

166 See the passages cited in the previous note.

167 Q. 5:17 says, كفر الذين قالوا إن الله هو المسيح ابن مريم "Whoever says that God is the Messiah, the son of Mary, is an infidel." See also 5:73 (Hinck. 76), where the Messiah himself is introduced speaking in the following manner: يابني إسرائيل اعبدوا الله ربي وربكم إنه من يشرك بالله فقد حرم الله عليه الجنة "O Son of Israel! Worship God, my Lord and your Lord. Indeed, whoever assigns a partner to God, He has already shut this man out of Paradise."

168 Q. 4:171 says, يا أهل الكتاب لا تغلوا في دينكم ولا تقولوا على الله غير الحق إنّما المسيح عيسى ابن مريم رسولُ اللهِ و كلمتُهُ ألقاها إلى مريم و روح منه فآمنوا بالله و رسله ولا تقولوا ثلاثة انتهوا خيرًا لكم إنّما الله الّة واحد سبحانه أن يكون له ولد له ما في السموات وما في الأرض و كفى بالله وكيلا "O people of the Scripture!," that is what he calls Christians, properly, those who stick to the letter of the Holy Scripture, "do not commit excess in your religion, and do not talk about God unless it is the truth. Indeed, the Messiah, Jesus, the son of Mary, is the Messenger of God and His word, which He sent to Mary. And the Spirit is from Him. Therefore, believe in God and His Messenger, but do not say [God is] three. Refrain (from such speech), it will be better for you. Indeed, God is one God, praise be unto Him. Surely, Jesus is not His son? Whatever is in the heavens and the earth is His, and God is sufficient for governing all affairs."

169 That is, entirely "in the likeness of Adam," in Q. 3:59 (Hinck. 52).

170 See, apart from the passages which have already been cited above, Q. 2:87 (Hinck. 81), 2:253, and Q. 3:45 (Hinck. 40).

171 Q. 19:19, the Angel Gabriel speaks to the Virgin Mary; "Indeed, I am the Messenger of the Lord, that I may give you a holy son." Mary answers him in Q. 19:20, "Where will my boy come from, since no man has not touched me, and I am not unchaste." According to verse 23, "Sorrow overwhelmed her by the trunk of a palm."

172 "No different than everything else in the world." See Q. 5:18.

173 Q. 4:157 says, و قولهم إنّا قتلنا المسيح عيسى ابن مريم رسول الله وما قتلوه وما صلبوه و لكن شبّه لهم و إنّ الذين اختلفوا فيه لفي شك منه ما لهم به من علم الا اتّباع الظنّ وما قتلوه يقينًا "Indeed, it is their speech," that is, the Jews' speech, "of course, we killed the Messiah, Jesus, the son of Mary, the Messenger of God. But they did not kill him, nor did they nail him to the cross. Rather, his likeness was put before them. Although there are those who disagree on that, let one ignore the doubt that arises in him. They do not possess knowledge about him, but a quest for conjecture; for they [Jews] surely did not kill him."

174 Q. 5:110 (Hinck. 109).

175 In the cited passage.

176 Q. 3:52; 4:157 and 170; 5:83; 19:30.

177 Q. 6:85.

178 Q. 3:55.

179 Q. 19:30.

180 I have already spoken about these things above.

181 Q. 7:179 (Hinck. 178), ولقد ذرأنا لجهنم كثيرًا من الجن والإنس لهم قلوبٌ لا يفقهون بها و لهم أعين لا يُبصرون بها و لهم آذانٌ لا يسمعون بها أولئك كالأنعام بل هم أضل أولئك هم الغافلون "We have created many men from genies and men for Hell. They have hearts they do not understand with, they have eyes they do not see with, and they have ears they do not hear with. These men are like animals. Or, rather, they are indeed worse than them. They act heedlessly."

182 Q. 4:88 (Hinck. 90), أن تهدوا مَن أضلّ الله و من يضلل اللهُ فلن تجدَ له سبيلا "Surely do you lead whomever God had led off onto the right path? Certainly, whosoever God has led off, you absolutely cannot find the path for them." See also 4:137 and Q. 16:37 (Hinck. 39).

183 Q. 3:74 (Hinck. 67), يختصُّ برحمتِّه مَن يشاء "God singles out His grace for whomever He wishes."

184 Q. 3:129 (Hinck. 124), و لله ما في السموات وما في الأرض يغفر لمن يشاء و يعذب من يشاء "Certainly, that is God's, whatever is in the heavens and on the earth. He will pardon whom He wishes and punish whom He wishes."

185 Q. 2:26 (Hinck. at the end of verse 24), وما يضل به إلا الفاسقين "God does not lead men into error, unless they are disgracefully corrupted."

186 Q. 4:113 (Hinck. 113) says, وأنزل الله عليك الكتاب والحكمة وعلمك ما لم تكن تعلم وكان فضل الله عليك عظيما "God sent you the Qur'an, and knowledge of divine law, and He taught you those things that you did not know; for the kindness of God towards you is great." See also Q. 6:89 and 45:16.

187 Q. 17:77 (Hinck. 79) says, لا تجد لسنتنا تحويلا "You will hardly find a change in our law."

188 Q. 5:1, يأيها الذين آمنوا أوفوا بالعقود "O those who believe, fulfill your promises." See also Q. 17:34 (Hinck. 36).

189 Q. 5:89 (Hinck. 91), لا يؤاخذكم الله باللغو في أيمانكم ولكن يؤاخذكم بما عقدتم الأيمان "God will not punish you for the thoughtless statement in your oath; but He will punish you for the oath you have sworn." See also Q. 16:91, 94 (Hinck. 93). There is also an elegant saying which should not be ignored in Q. 48:10, where it says, إنَّ الذين يبايعونك إنما يبايعون اللهَ يدُ الله فوق أيديهم فمن نكث فإنما ينكث على نفسه و من أوفى بما عاهد عليه الله فسيوتيه أجرًا عظيما "Indeed, those who struck a bargain with you struck the bargain with God too. The hand of God is over their hand. And whoever violates his oath, of course he will violate himself. But, God will certainly grant him a great reward for the one who keeps his promise."

190 Q. 5:89 (Hinck. 91), "There will be a satisfaction," that is, of the oath, "to feed ten paupers on modest food, which you feed your families with; or to clothe them; or to free slaves. But whoever cannot find the means," that is, whoever cannot do these things, "it will suffice for him to fast for three days."

191 Q. 11:123, ولله غيب السماوات والأرض وإليه يرجع الأمر كله فاعبده وتوكل عليه وما ربك بغافل عما تعملون "Certainly, the secret of the heavens and the earth is God's; everything will return to Him. Therefore, worship Him, and set Him as the trustee of your affairs; for your Lord will not be unaware of what you do." See also Q. 17:22–23 (Hinck. 23) and Q. 26:213 (Hinck. 213).

192 The words in Q. 18:15 are worthy of being cited here: فمن أظلم ممن افترى على الله كذبًا "Who is more unjust than him who invents a lie about God."

193 Q. 16:124 (Hinck. 125) says, إنَّما جُعِل السبت "Indeed, the Sabbath was established."

194 Q. 17:23 (Hinck. 24), و قضى ربُك ألا تعبُدوا الا إياه و بالوالدين إحسانًا إمَّا يبلغن عندك الكِبَرَ أحدهما أو كلاهما فلا تقل لهما أفٍّ ولا تنهرهما و قل لهما قولًا كريما "Your Lord has ordained that you should worship none but Him and be kind to your parents. If one of them reach a great old age, do not say to them ugh! nor should you rebuke them; speak to them rather with kind words." See also Q. 29:8 (Hinck. 7).

195 Q. 6:151, he says, لا تقتلوا أولادكم من إملاق "Therefore, do not kill your offspring out of poverty." He continues, "We have provided nourishment for you and them so that you do not kill your soul." See also Q. 17:31, 33.

196 Q. 17:32, ولا تقربوا الزنا إنه كان فاحشة وساء سبيلا "Do not indulge in whoring; of course, that road is very foul, and is very wicked." See also Q. 24:31.

197 Q. 24:2–3 commands, "For the fornicator, male and female, beat them each a hundred lashes, and do not let pity for them take hold of you in the judgment of God, and let there be some number of the faithful as witnesses

for their punishment. The fornicator is not to be married, unless to another fornicator. This sort of thing is forbidden to the faithful."

198 Muhammad orders the hands to be cut off thieves, male and female (Q. 5:38) and he prevents usury by force of this command: Q. 83:1.

199 Hence, he lays out a precept at Q. 24:4, "For those who accuse modest women and do not offer four witnesses, beat them eighty lashes, and do not allow them to be witnesses ever after." See also 24:19 and Q. 2:84.

200 Q. 3:3, نزّل عليك الكتاب بالحقّ مصدّقا لما بين يديه و أنزل التوراة والإنجيل من قبل هدي للناس و أنزل الفُرقان "God sent you the Scripture to confirm that which was before it, after He had already sent the Torah and the Gospel to men; He also sent the Qur'an." See also 3:65 (Hinck. 58) and Q. 9:113 (Hinck. 112).

201 See Q. 3:3, already cited.

202 Q. 2:187 (Hinck. 183).

203 Q. 4:3, فانكحوا ما طاب لكم من النساء مثنى وثلاث ورباع "Take for a wife those women who seem good to you: two, three, four."

204 Q. 2:221 (Hinck. 219) says, ولأمة مؤمنة خير من مشركة ولو أعجبتكم "Surely, a faithful slave girl is better than an unfaithful one, however pleasing [and attractive] she may be to you. And do not give faithful women to infidels for marriage, until these infidels believe."

205 Q. 4:23, where it also prevents "daughters, aunts on both sides."

206 Q. 2:222.

207 Q. 2:228 (Hinck. 228) and Q. 4:34 (Hinck. 38).

208 Q. 2:229–30 and Q. 4:20, 129.

209 Q. 2:240.

210 Q. 2:234 (Hinck. 234).

211 Q. 4:34 (Hinck. 38).

5 The Trifling Foundations and the Unwholesome Fruits of the Theology, or Rather, Prattlings of the Jews and Muslims or Turco-Persians

August Pfeiffer

August Pfeiffer was born in Lauenburg/Elbe in 1640. He was initially trained by a private tutor and then went on to study at the Hamburg Gymnasium, a humanist grammar school. As an adolescent, Pfeiffer was drawn to the mystical spiritualism of Christian Hoburg, but his professors influenced him away from this. Pfeiffer attended the University of Wittenberg in 1658 where he was fast-tracked in order to receive his Master's degree in 1659. At Wittenberg, he studied with two champions of Lutheran orthodoxy in the seventeenth century, Abraham Calov (d.1686) and Johann Deutschmann (d.1706). In 1665, Pfeiffer was appointed as an adjunct professor for the Faculty of Philosophy at Wittenberg, teaching oriental languages. In 1668, he was made extraordinary professor of oriental languages. In 1671, he was appointed as a pastor in the Duchy of Oels in Silesia, first in Medzibor and then in Stroppen near Breslau (Wroclaw). In 1678, he received his doctorate in theology at Wittenberg and in 1684 became an associate professor at the Theological Faculty of the University of Leipzig where he taught biblical Hebrew and was a full professor of oriental languages. In 1689, he was offered a post as the Superintendent by the Council of the imperial city of Lübeck. Pfeiffer's extensive scholarly publications include exegetical and philological works. In his works, he stressed the orthodoxy and the primacy of orthodox Lutheranism against Roman Catholicism as well as against all types of Pietism. He had a longstanding dispute with Philipp Jakob Spener, the 'Father of Pietism' and founder of the University of Halle. Pfeiffer is also considered to have strongly influenced the faith and thought of the famous composer Johann Sebastian Bach and some of his works can be found in Bach's theological library. He died in Lübeck in 1698.[1]

Variant Names: Augusto Pfeiffero, Augustus Pfeifferus, and Augusti Pfeifferi.

Summary and Analysis

Pfeiffer presents Islam as a corruption of Christianity. He begins by arguing that Islam is constructed out of a misguided amalgamation of Quraysh paganism, Judaism and Christianity. Then he points out the similarities in Jewish and Islamic discourses to demonstrate their teachings as analogous heresies. While there are similarities in Jewish and Islamic discourses, Pfeiffer notes that the Karaite Jews remained biblical literalists while the Rabbanites accepted both scriptural and subsequent rabbinical exegeses. Similarly, Persian Muslims accepted only the Qur'anic scripture as authoritative, while the Turks, Tatars, Arabs, Indians, and other Muslims embraced the *Sunna*, which is "oral law," according to Pfeiffer, in addition to the Qur'an for religious guidance and law. Pfeiffer likens the Jewish Talmudic writings to those of the *Sunna*, as supplementary texts to the central sources of scripture, and refers to them as contaminations of the sacred histories. Here, Pfeiffer interprets the Jewish and Islamic intellectual histories from his own Protestant commitment to *Sola Scriptura*, seeing religious history as a struggle between scripturalism and non-scriptualism.

Pfeiffer believes that since Jews and Muslims equally denounce the Holy Trinity, this deprives them of eternal life. Indeed, Jewish and Islamic teachings insult Christianity by refusing to accept the messianic concept of Jesus Christ, preferring conceptions of angels that are, to Pfeiffer, nonsensical. Both religions justify man before God by his actions as opposed to Christianity, which justifies man before God by accepting Jesus Christ as Savior. This critique of Judaism and Islam reflects Pfeiffer's Protestant belief in faith alone.

In the remaining part of his text, Pfeiffer provides his critique of Jewish and Islamic rituals and ceremonies. He maintains that Jewish and Islamic teachings are similarly steadfast on circumcision and sacrifice, with Jews restricting animal sacrifice to the Temple in Jerusalem. Although the sacrificial offerings of Muslims can occur anywhere, they distribute part of the sacrificial meat to the poor. Muslims, he says, worship their "false prophet" in the temples of Mecca and Medina, but both Muslims and Jews see Jerusalem as a holy city. According to Pfeiffer, Jews and Muslims have strict rules for prayer, including the precise time for prayer, as they focus on the quantity of prayers rather than on the quality of the believer's character. Pfeiffer criticizes Islamic and Jewish ritual oaths and fasting practices, seeing them as devoid of meaning and intention, and he rebukes both Jews and Muslims for their misguided dietary restrictions and superstitious washing rituals. With Jews and Muslims approving of divorce and legalized polygamy, he says that Jews believe happiness should be found within the joys of this life as opposed to the afterlife and that Muhammad believed in a sexually promiscuous Paradise. Both religions distinguish between Heaven and Hell in seven seats and locations and both believe in Purgatory as do Catholics.

Pfeiffer concludes that Jews and Muslims conspire against Christianity, hoping and believing that it will one day vanish. It is clear from this text that Pfeiffer presents Jewish and Islamic teachings as analogous to heresies of the Christian faith. Given the fact that Pfeiffer was

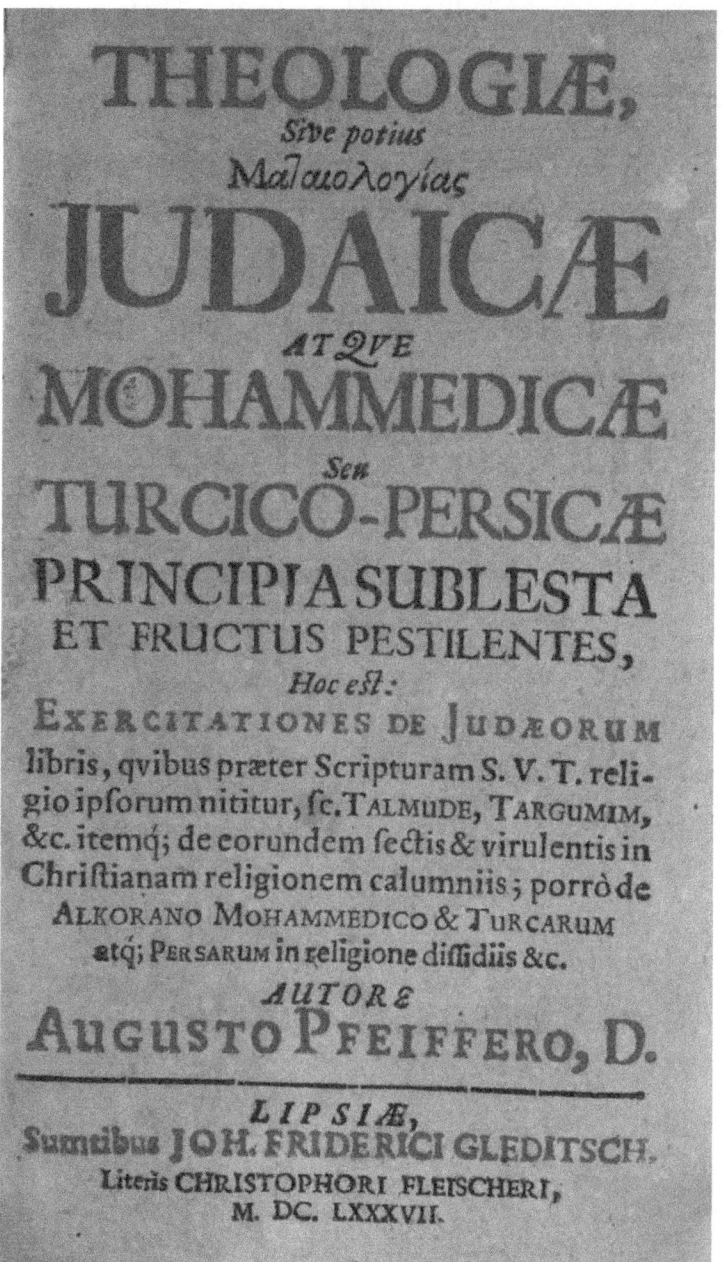

Figure 5.1 August Pfeiffer, *Theologiae, sive potius Ματαιολογίας Judaicae atque Mohammedicae seu Turcico-Persicae*, 1687 (Courtesy of the Bavarian State Library, Munich).

a zealous advocate for Lutheran orthodoxy, it is not surprising that he thinks Judaism and Islam, like Catholicism, are concerned with empty ceremonies and ritual displays rather than true faith. Both Orthodox Lutherans and Pietists criticize the Islamic focus on external rituals. However, while Pietists, such as Michaelis, argue that Islam is primarily concerned with religious observations rather than inner strength and morality, Orthodox Lutherans, such as Pfeiffer, criticized Islam for focusing on good works instead of faith alone. Pfeiffer also calls Islam as Syncretic religion as he believes it is a patchwork created from pieces of other religions. His use of the word "Syncretism" indicates he was not only criticizing Islam, but was also indirectly taking aim at the Syncretic Calixtinians.

The Trifling Foundations and the Unwholesome Fruits of the Theology, or Rather, Prattlings of the Jews and Muslims or Turco-Persians (Leipzig, 1687)

The Muslim religion is a poor patchwork made of the Qurayshite Paganism, Judaism, and Christianity. Nobody would doubt that, except someone totally unlearned in Muslim matters. It is easy to determine the cause of this foul Samaritanism or Syncretism. From the beginning, that impostor in Mecca [Muhammad] was nourished on the idolatry and impiety of the Qurayshites. Therefore, that Qurayshite Paganism leaves various traces here and there in his Qur'an.

Although Muhammad created his new religion, he did not borrow from just one religion because he was well aware of the Arab's intelligence [so the Arabs would not notice he was plagiarizing]. Muhammad was an unskilled man, but cunning and skillful for his [religious-political] revolution as he used both Jewish and Christian teachers. Indeed, from the Christians he cultivated a closer intimacy with some Nestorian monks, whose names can be found in this book of mine. Meanwhile, he also had secret meetings with a certain 'Abd al-Allāh b. Salām, although many others say Muhammad met with certain Jews.

For this reason, I wonder if one can detect any harmony in useless Jewish and Muslim or Turco-Persian prattlings. Demonstrating this throughout the whole system of theology would be more tedious than difficult; but I think I can prove my assertion if I show Muslim-Jewish harmony in the following.

Among the Jews, the Karaite writers—of whom a small group remains—are content with the scriptures only as they reject traditions. However, the Rabbanites, in addition to the scripture or the written law, venerate the traditions, the unwritten or oral law, which they embrace with a similar degree of piety. As for the Muslims, the Persians and several other smaller nations only accept the Qur'an for their religious rules. But the Turks, as well as the Tatars, Arabs, Indians, and other Muslims, accept a double foundation for their religion: besides the Qur'an, which is a written law, they also value the *Sunna* as the second tier [of religious traditions or authority]. These are the Muslim traditions of which Bukhari, who I will introduce shortly, has produced 5,275 traditions in a long volume, which is the oral law they call *Sunna*. It is worth noting here that the Arabic terms with which both laws are expressed, that is, Qur'an and *Sunna*, correspond to the Jewish terms Mikra and Mishnah, both in imitating their substance, as well as in their sound, origin, and meaning. This is to such an extent that for the Turks and other like-minded people among the Muslims, the Qur'an wholly mirrors the scriptures, and the *Sunna*, in turn, mirrors the Talmud. I set this matter before you in previous chapters clearly enough.

It is the custom of Jews and Muslims to contaminate their sacred histories with fables and nonsense. If I judge the matter correctly, the Impostor from Mecca does not solely owe all his fables to his Jewish teachers. We need to compare the following Jewish-Muslim stories: the angels that were ordered to worship Adam, who all obeyed with the exception of Satan, and the conversation between Cain and Abel; the angels who burned with lust for women; Abraham breaking the idols of his father Terah, and then being thrown into the fire and miraculously freed; Pharaoh violating the Israelites' wives and sacrificing their children; Mount Sinai being torn from its roots and hanging over the Israelites like a barrel, with a divine threat that here would be their grave unless they accept the law; assistance from spirits in building the temple of Solomon; and Solomon understanding and interpreting the noise and chatter of birds. In fact, the very phrasing of the Jewish and Muslim stories often agrees, suggesting that the Impostor received the gift of instruction from a certain Jew, Rabbi Yohanan ben Zakkai, a student [or disciple] of Hillel who boasted that "If all of heaven were parchment, and all trees were pens, and the whole sea were ink, and all men were scribes, it would still be impossible to record all the wisdom that he learned from his teachers," and so on. This is reflected in the Qur'an 31:27: "No matter how much wood and how many pens there are on the earth and how much ink is in the sea, which could then fill the seven seas, the words of God would not be exhausted."

The Jews most disgracefully slander the awe-inspiring mystery of the Trinity, as is very well-known: Muhammad calls the Christians *al-mushrikūn*, "polytheists" because of their belief in the Trinity, as if Christians place other gods beside the true God, for which reason Muhammad deprives Christians of eternal life in Q. 4:48. "God never forgives him who worships another God besides Him; but otherwise, He forgives whom He wishes."

The Jews spoil the divinity of the Messiah and insult our faith in Christ; [Johann Christoph] Wagenseil likens their faithlessness to "the fiery darts of Satan." Muhammad's opinion is no different, although he seems to show respect to Christians. Nevertheless, Muhammad asserts that what Christians say is a sin: "The Messiah is the son of God" (Q. 9:30).

Concerning angels, Muhammad talks nonsense and says they are made from fire (Q. 38:76) and that spirits [*jinn*] are made from poisonous fire (Q. 15:27). The Jews say something no saner. On the appearance of the angel of death, Muhammad insists on (Q. 16:28–32 and Q. 32:11) the same as the Hebrews.

The Jews ascribe the salvation of human beings before God to their good works as does Muhammad (Q. 99:6–8). Elsewhere (Q. 6:12–16 and 16:9), contradicting himself, Muhammad teaches that salvation is gained by grace.

The Jews are steadfast on circumcision; similarly, based on the teaching of their false prophet, Muslims defend circumcision although they no longer perform it on the eighth day.

The Jews make sacrifices (*korban olah*) because of a perpetual obligation, but they restrict them to the Temple of Jerusalem. Muslims offer their own sacrifices, not burning them entirely, but distributing them especially during the *Kudschuk Bairam* [*Küçük Bayram*] religious holiday, which is called the *Kurban*—that is, the holiday of offering.

Furthermore, Muslims worship not only at the temples of Mecca and Medina, dedicated to their false prophet, but also worship and visit the temple at Jerusalem daily with no less reverence than the Jews once did.

Jews perform prayers in the synagogue at fixed times out of superstition in addition to good works which are endorsed by the Savior Himself (Matthew 5:5). This, indeed, seems to have crossed over to the Muslims who also pray at fixed times in the *masjid* (that is to say, the Muslim synagogue), with quantity rather than quality and intention.

Christ once censured the Jews for heedless oaths made on creatures requiring animal sacrifice. Muslims also keep these oaths, reinstituted by Muhammad.

Strict Jewish fasts have been frequently observed, but no less rigorous is the fasting at least in the daytime in the month of Ramadan among the Muslims.

The Jews abstain from certain foods daily, and especially despise pork. In the same way, Muhammad strictly forbids his followers pork (Q. 6:145).

Jews are very superstitious about washing, and Muslims no less so.

Not only do the Jews approve of divorce even for cases other than adultery and malicious desertion, but so do the Muslims, with license given by Muhammad (Q. 4:130). Hence, they annul marriages for slight, even ridiculous reasons, as I have shown below.

The Jews argue that polygamy is lawful, although today they refrain from this. Following the example of their lascivious bull, Muhammad, Muslims do the same and polygamy thrives among them today.

The Jews, especially the ancient ones, place the happiness of eternal life among the joys of this life, although the more contemporary ones sometimes seem to speak more cautiously. As for Muhammad, it is quite obvious that he converts his Paradise into Peredesia and Perbibesia or rather a brothel.

The Jews divide Heaven and Hell into seven seats and locations, which is also observed in Muhammad's Qur'an and other Muslim writings.

The Jews believe in Purgatory and so does Muhammad.

Finally, it is not easy to tell who burns with greater hatred for Christians: Jews or Muslims? For the latter, I have adduced some words from Friar Ange de Saint Joseph's *Persian Medicine* in the margins of his book; for the former, *The Slanders of the Jews Against Christians* can furnish evidence. Indeed, experience testifies how the Turks are much more akin to Jews than to Christians; like two mules scratching each other's backs, the Jews, in turn, feel sympathetic toward the Turks.

From these, we can easily understand what sort of spiritual conspiracy exists among the Jews and Muslims against our religion; if God grants it, it is their intention that Christianity should completely fade away.

Greetings to the Kind Reader

If I take pains to understand the superstitious prattle of the Jews and the mad prattle of the Muslims, I sense a great, albeit blind, conspiracy of stubborn pride against the pre-eminent dogmas of Christianity. Indeed, it could seem strange to anyone, even if they do not examine it closely, that both peoples rely upon slippery and trivial foundations although they are not really at odds with each other. It seems worthwhile to consider these things somewhat more fully, and concurrently to expose the despicable delusions that propagate the lies that have arisen against Christianity. To that end, I have once again laid out preliminary observations, previously published at the University of Wittenberg, which aim exclusively at one target; laying clearly before your eyes both peoples' False Books of Prattle, Jewish and Muslim—that is, the Talmud and the Qur'an. Some men look to a revelation of Jewish religion and treachery concerning *Targumim*, the schools of the ancients, as well as the slander from both ancient and recent people against Christ, the Christian religion, and Christians. For a deeper knowledge of Islamic madness, there is an outstanding treatise on the principle disagreements existing between the Sunnis and Shi'ites (the Turks and Persians). From these works, one can easily understand the foundations and core beliefs of both peoples' nonsense. May you always enjoy good counsel, Kind Reader, and farewell.

Note

1 Pfeiffer's biography was compiled from the following sources: Johann Heinrich Zedler (ed.), "Pfeiffer, August," in *Grosses vollständiges Universal-Lexicon aller Wissenschafften und Künste*, vol. 27 (Leipzig, 1741), 1337–40; Adolf Schimmelpfennig, "Pfeiffer, August," in *Allgemeine Deutsche Biographie*, vol. 25 (Leipzig, 1887), 631–2; Robert Stevenson, "Bach's Religious Environment: The Well Springs of Religious Emotion That Nourished the Creative Life of Protestantism's Greatest Composer," *The Journal of Religion* 30/4 (1950): 246–55; Chafe, *Tears into Wine*, 64–75; David Yearsley, *Bach and the Meanings of Counterpoint* (Cambridge: Cambridge University Press, 2002), 7–27; Johannes Wallmann, "Pfeiffer, August," in *Religion in Geschichte und Gegenwart*, eds. Hans Dieter Betz et al., vol. 6 (Tübingen: Mohr Siebeck, 2003), 1231; Heike Krauter-Dierolf, *Die Eschatologie Philipp Jakob Speners: Der Streit mit der lutherischen Orthodoxie um die "Hoffnung besserer Zeiten"* (Tübingen: Mohr Siebeck, 2005), 173–85.

6 Concept of Fate among the Turks

Johann Friedrich Weitenkampf

Two years younger than Immanuel Kant, Johann Friedrich Weitenkampf was born in 1726 in Königsberg. Weitenkampf was the son of the
pastor of Alt-Rossgarten, but he was orphaned at eight and subsequently
educated at the Königsberg orphanage. In 1743, he matriculated at the
Alma Albertina in Königsberg and then attended the Lutheran institution
of higher education, the University of Königsberg, studying philosophy
and metaphysics under the eighteenth-century German Pietist philosopher Martin Knutzen (d.1751), an eclectic thinker who tried to strike a
balance between the rationalism of the German Enlightenment philosopher Christian Wolff (d.1754) and Pietism. In 1747, Weitenkampf studied
at the University of Leipzig, and in 1748, at Halle. In 1750, he attended
the University at Helmstedt, where he received his Master's in philosophy.
He then began to lecture in philosophy at Helmstedt. In 1754, he became
the pastor of the Magnuskirche in Brunswick. He died of a catarrhal
fever at the age of thirty-two in 1758, leaving a pregnant wife and his
son, born after his death, behind. Despite his early death, Weitenkampf's
influence lived on; one of Martin Knutzen's students, Immanuel Kant
referenced and engaged with Weitenkampf's essays on the question of
whether the universe is infinite, and this became part of Kant's thesis for
the first antinomy in his *Critique of Pure Reason*. Furthermore, Weitenkampf's influence went beyond the Atlantic Ocean and his book on fate,
Vernünftigte Trostgründe bey den traurigen Schicksalen der Menschen,
was published in Lancaster, Philadelphia in 1825 by Johann Bär. In the
early nineteenth century, Lancaster, along with other towns such as Al-
lentown, Reading, and Lebanon, was very prominent in German printing,
which served the Protestant immigrant diaspora in the United States.[1]

Variant Names: Johannes Fridericus Weitenkampf, Ioan. Fridericus
Weitenkampff, and J. F. Weitenkampf

Summary and Analysis

Weitenkampf sets out to explain and refute the Turkish concept of
fate, dividing his dissertation into two sections: the first outlining the
Turkish-Muslim view of fate; and the second seeking to prove the invalidity

of the Muslim concept of fate with philosophical argumentation. He begins with some brief notes on the historical origin of the Turks, turning then to the backstory of the Qur'an, which he claims can be divided into six sections or topics, the last of which concerns its teachings on fate. According to Weitenkampf, in mainstream Islamic thought, fate is predetermined and immutable. Weitenkampf categorizes most Turks as Jabrites who believe that God is the source of all evil and that men do not have free will. Therefore, men are compelled to do evil or good through God's omnipotence. He offers examples of how this belief is manifested in the actions and values of the Turks. According to Weitenkampf, since Turks believe in predestination, they do not flee plague-ridden cities or shun contact with those infected. They do not fear death. If they suffer, they believe fate decreed it. In battle, this makes them brave to the point of foolhardy. Weitenkampf also paraphrases an exhortation from the Qur'an in which Muslims are told not to avoid danger, as God has already determined their fate. He believes that the alleged lack of logic, physics, metaphysics, and mathematics in Turkish philosophy accounts for their belief in fate.

After detailing how revered the Qur'an is in Turkish society, Weitenkampf turns to a brief account of the schismatic differences between Sunni Turks and Shi'ite Persians. In his account, the Persians esteem 'Alī more than they do Muhammad, for which reason the Turks claim that they are corrupters of the religion. Although Weitenkampf classifies the seventeenth-century Ottoman Turks based on the ideas of early Islamic theological schools known as Qadarite and Jabrite, he still shows greater awareness of nuances in Muslim societies than early Reformation scholars. Therefore, he maintains that the Muslim Turks have theological differences, such as that of the Qadarites who reject the Jabrites' doctrine of predetermination. The Qadarites believe that humans have free will. Weitenkampf asserts that Turks predominately believe that fate is divinely ordered and immutable, but this view cannot be reconciled with rational principles.

In Weitenkampf's second section, his purpose is to disprove the Turkish view of fate through philosophical analysis. With a series of detailed logical arguments, he arrives at several conclusions, the most important of which is that all events in the world are mutable and contingent, therefore, not subject to a predetermined destiny. Weitenkampf states that the Turk's concept of fate can be described as 'gross' or 'subtle.' The former implies that a predetermined event must happen and not even God has the power to decree otherwise. Subtle fate, on the other hand, means that regardless of the outcome that natural forces would lead to, God can intervene to ensure that what he has decreed comes to pass (i.e., a miracle). Weitenkampf remarks that many Christians believe in a fate that accords with the subtle Turkish belief. He is dismissive of gross fate, as it is wholly incompatible with Lutheran teaching, using philosophical argumentation to refute it.

However, Weitenkampf also sees subtle fate as problematic. He begins by defining a miracle as anything that does not happen from natural causes, which would include an omnipotent God using His power to ensure that a predestined event happens, regardless of natural forces. The subtle view, therefore, implies a large number of miracles (for instance, preordained deaths would count as miracles, according to Weitenkampf's argument). With further arguments, he concludes that God does not cause many miracles, and therefore, the subtle view of fate is also incorrect. With this refutation of both the gross and subtle views on fate, he

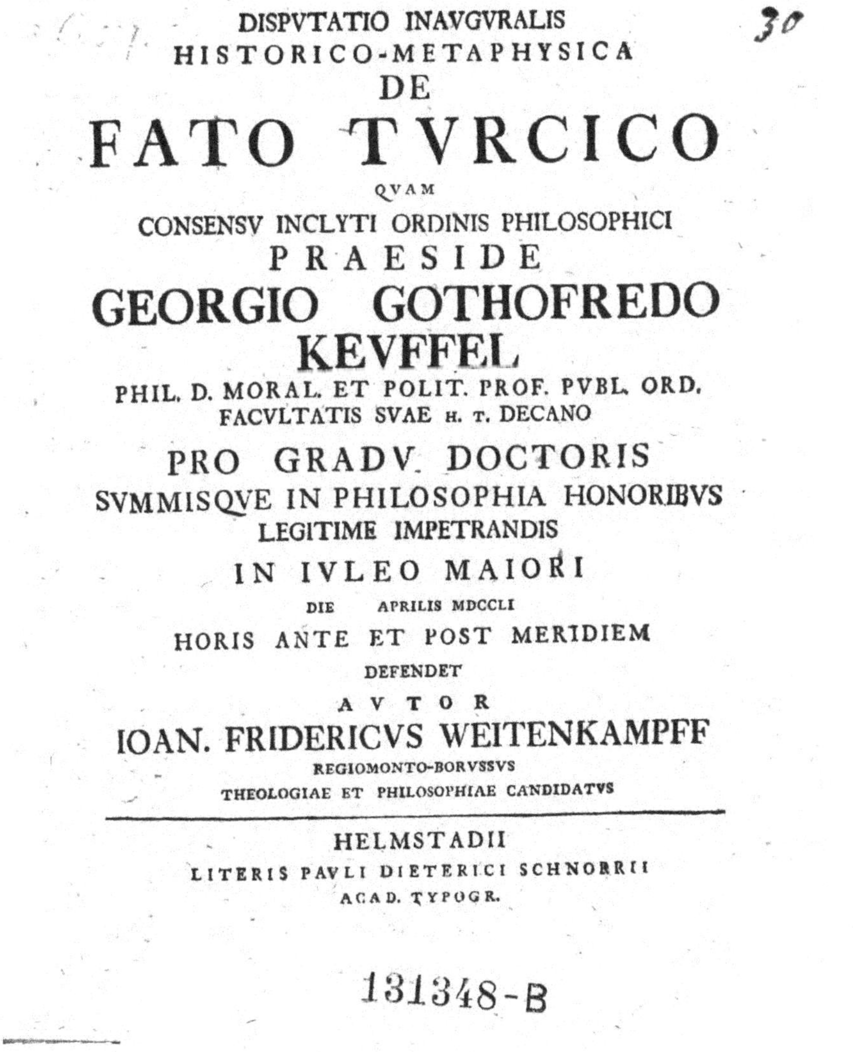

DISPVTATIO INAVGVRALIS

HISTORICO-METAPHYSICA

DE

FATO TVRCICO

QVAM

CONSENSV INCLYTI ORDINIS PHILOSOPHICI

PRAESIDE

GEORGIO GOTHOFREDO KEVFFEL

PHIL. D. MORAL. ET POLIT. PROF. PVBL. ORD.

FACVLTATIS SVAE H. T. DECANO

PRO GRADV DOCTORIS

SVMMISQVE IN PHILOSOPHIA HONORIBVS

LEGITIME IMPETRANDIS

IN IVLEO MAIORI

DIE   APRILIS MDCCLI

HORIS ANTE ET POST MERIDIEM

DEFENDET

AVTOR

IOAN. FRIDERICVS WEITENKAMPFF

REGIOMONTO-BORVSSVS

THEOLOGIAE ET PHILOSOPHIAE CANDIDATVS

HELMSTADII

LITERIS PAVLI DIETERICI SCHNORRII

ACAD. TYPOGR.

131348-B

Figure 6.1 Johann Friedrich Weitenkampf, *Disputatio historico-metaphysica de fato Turcico*, 1751 (Courtesy of the Österreichische Nationalbibliothek, Vienna).

ends his treatise with a wish that the Turks will recognize the absurdity of their religion and embrace Christianity. Weitenkampf's *dissertatio* is a symptom of the struggle between the weakened Lutheran orthodoxy and the rise of Pietism and rationalism in the wake of the Enlightenment in the eighteenth century. Unlike other Lutheran authors, he analyzes Islamic thought through systematic philosophical argumentation, deeply influenced by his logic and metaphysics teacher Knutzen, who tried to combine Wolffian Enlightenment rationalism with pietistic spirituality.

Historical-Metaphysical Dissertation on Turkish Fate (Helmstedt, 1751)

Section 1

On the History of the Concept of Fate Among the Turks and its Explanation

1 I am determined to speak publicly about the concept of fate among the Turks, and share my unique ideas about this subject. There are some who talk a lot about fate in daily life, and yet, if they were to speak publicly about this matter, they do not reveal their true opinion. In order to avoid this Scylla and Charybdis, I will focus on the history of the concept of fate among the Turks in the first section of my dissertation, using the works of the great writers; then in the second section I will clearly refute a most pernicious opinion on this subject.

2 The Turks are the subject of this dissertation on fate. It is not important to know the etymology of their name. This race lives in almost all parts of the world. [...].

3 The Turks, also called the Saracens or Muhammadans, recognize Muhammad as the originator and teacher of their religion. Muhammad's name means 'esteemed' to the Arabs and Turks. Muhammad was an Arab from Mecca who was born in the year 571. The life of this foulest impostor is so well known that it would be a waste of ink and effort to describe it. As a young man of thirteen or sixteen years he was a driver and fed camels in Medina. At that time, it is said that a black cloud appeared above him, leading his master to consult with augurs. The augurs made this prophecy: "that boy will draw a black cloud over Christendom," and immediately the chief augur begged Muhammad himself on his knees for his and his family's health. After this, the master sold Muhammad, whom he feared, to a merchant called Abdimoneples, who employed him in his business because of his intelligence and trustworthiness. When Abdimoneples died, Muhammad married his widow Khadīja, seeing this as an opportunity to realize his goal through her immense wealth.

This Muhammad made up a religion and a book, whose name is the Qur'an, and claimed that it came down from heaven. He asserted in his frequent sermons that God sent the angel Gabriel to reveal everything to him. However, it is as clear as day that Muhammad did not compose the whole book; soon after his death his son-in-law, Abū Bakr, assembled his notes and combined them into whole sections. The Turks worship this book, as if it were the most sacred, since it is the foundation of their religion.

4 This book, the Qur'an, the principal masterpiece of the Turks' religion, contains three sections. The whole of Muhammad's religion is described in six beliefs, according to Marracci's *In Refutation of the Qur'an*: first, belief in God and His Prophet Muhammad; second, belief in angels whom men imagine when they burn with desire for great pleasures; third, belief in the holy books, especially the Qur'an; fourth, belief in the prophets, the first of whom was Adam, and the last and best Muhammad; fifth, belief in the Last Day of Judgment; and last, belief in fate, which is relevant to my topic here. These six beliefs are the main points of the Turkish faith, which according to them should be explained like this: *Âmentü billâhi ve melâiketihi ve kutubihi ve rusulihi ve'l yevmi'l-âhiri ve bi'l-kaderi hayrihi ve şerrihi min Allâh* (I believe in God, angels, the holy books, prophets, the day of judgment, and that good and evil are from God).

5 The Turkish concept of fate originates from the foundations of Muhammad's religion above. In order to focus on the main point of this work, I will describe this concept of fate. The Turks believe that everything that happens to man is decreed by the Highest Godhead. They claim that all evils are decreed by God, but not in such a way that God shows benevolence to evil. Instead, He persecutes evil with hatred. They profess that God's decrees are immutable and they firmly believe that if this or that fate has been decided for man, then it is impossible to avoid it, either through natural causes or through any other means. So, it is pointless if a man struggles to avoid this or that event. Using a variety of sources, I will prove that this is the genuine Turkish understanding of fate.

6 Some Turks explain predestination or fate in a manner similar to that of the Manichean: that God is the originator of all evil, and that He introduced fate into the world. These men clearly believe that men are endowed with no ability or freedom to do anything, but that God is the one who compels us to all evil or good through His omnipotence. Those who believe this are called Jabrites and are the most persistent in this belief.

7 The Turks believe that all good and evil in the world happen according to decree and divine providence. Everything is predestined according to the Turks, past and future. The Turks imagine that there is a certain tablet guarded in heaven, on which all divine decrees

and the fates of men have been written since eternity. They name this tablet *Lawḥ al-Maḥfūẓ*. Whatever is written on this tablet will happen in the world, and it is quite impossible for it not to happen. The faith and good works of all faithful and pious men occur with the foreknowledge, will, predestination, and consent of God. Indeed, they believe that the bad deeds and sins of all unbelievers and impious men happen in the world with the foreknowledge, predestination, decree, and inscription on this tablet, but not with the consent and pleasure of God. The Turks hold this foulest opinion as an article of faith. If anyone asks the reason for these decrees or predestination, he hears that men are not permitted to inquire into the reason for these divine decrees, since these are mysteries known to God alone. Indeed, they say that the most grievous sin against God is to try to understand His immutable decrees and know the unknowable.

8   The Jabrites described in 6 above embrace the true doctrine of the Qur'an. For the Qur'an teaches that the Turks profess that there is one true God on whose will and approval all evil depends. Indeed, they ascribe evil's origin to God, who wants not only the faith of the faithful and the piety of the pious, but also the faithlessness and impiety of the unbelievers. As Jabrites agree, God introduces fate into the world to determine all actions, [good or evil]. They base it on this: according to the teachings of the Qur'an all good and evil depends on the will of God. Although evil men have the choice between good and evil, they will choose evil actions because it is fated (see 5). Therefore, according to the Turks, fate follows both the individual will and divine decree. If this is not so, then there is no enough reason why God would choose evil and compel us to evil and then punish our odious actions (see 5). Therefore, the Turkish concept of fate is absolute.

9   Experience, the finest teacher of all things, taught me what I described in the above paragraphs. For I have affirmed in 5 that the Turks believe that no event in the world can be avoided through natural causes or any other means, and that some of them profess a belief in absolute fate (see 8). Muslims also prove this with deeds and examples. Everyone who has visited this region testifies unanimously that the Turks do not withdraw from the cities when a plague rages. They live in the houses that are infected with plague, visit them, dine in them, and dress in them. Sick and healthy men sleep on one couch knowingly. They know that Christians preserve their lives by leaving cities infected with plague; they see that death keeps creeping up on them, but still do not leave their cities. People who write about the Turkish area unanimously declare that in one summer between 10,000 and 50,000 men succumbed to the plague or other contagious diseases in Constantinople. The reason is that,

according to doctors, Muslims rarely eat hot food, but prefer raw and uncooked food, and are infected and corrupted by the blood. The Turks do little about this, but say that it happened by fate and could not have been otherwise. They buy or sell clothes of those who died from the plague. They marry the wives of the men killed by the plague within three days, with the result that they seem immediately condemned by fate. They allow themselves to kill freely because they are persuaded that it is already demanded by fate, and that if they died in such a way they could die in no other way. In the historical account of the Embassy of the Count of Virmondt there is a story worth remembering. A certain Satrap of the Turkish region called Kara Mustafa claimed that he had been lifted to the highest degree of honor and the peak of happiness. He thought that there was nothing more in the world that could add to his glory and happiness. Yet one wish had not been fulfilled, namely that he could finish life with a fierce death that would bring the Sultan's honor and give him eternal glory as a martyr. Because of Kara Mustafa's supreme loyalty, the Sultan decided to satisfy his desire for glory by ordering him to be hanged by a silk rope. It is obvious from this account that the Turks do not fear death, but if they have to suffer from it they think that it has been decided by fate. If they wage war, they do not avoid the most pernicious dangers of death, but often think of the most desperate and dangerous plans. Many thousands subject themselves to death bravely and hurl themselves headlong into the greatest dangers, so that ditches and rivers might be full of their bodies and their friends might pass over them. If they take the palm first and gain victory, they take it as a most certain sign that their religion is true. For if their religion did not please God, it would hardly have been decreed by Him to grant victory. For this reason, the Turks persecute the Jews among all races with curses and the most hatred, since they have no fixed abode but live dispersed throughout the whole world. So, who does not see that the Turks' concept of fate affects all their beliefs and actions?

10   In the Qur'an, Muhammad clearly orders his followers not to avoid death because God has already counted our days [on Earth]; whatever happens to men flows from an eternal and immutable decree. The Turks believe that every event that happens to them is already written on their brow. They call this predestination and God decrees *nasib* and *takdir*, which can be explained as fate or chance or fortune. This *nasib* or fate is recorded in a certain heavenly book: this book contains all of man's events and misfortunes that cannot be avoided by any reason, any means, any foresight, or any cause. So, if death is decreed, it is avoided in vain, and only fools fear it. A determined time for life has been decided for all individuals, which cannot be shortened or lengthened in any way. If we reach the end of

our allotted time, death is inevitable and man cannot avert his fate
by any means.

11   Johann Andreas Bose in *Turkish Empire* thinks that this opinion on
the Turks is exemplified by their actions in war: they do everything
vigorously and do not care about the direst emergencies. It is no
wonder the liberal arts do not flourish in their region as the Turks
believe such absurd principles. The pinnacle of their studies consists
of the fact that they are skilled in Arabic, that they compose verses,
that they recite verses of the Qur'an, that they write concisely and
beautifully, and that they practice music. But philosophers, whom
they call *Talibul-'ilm* (seeker of knowledge), are rare birds in Turkish lands. Logic, Physics, Metaphysics, Mathematics are forms of
knowledge which they practice too little. Neither the flower of their
religion nor the state of their empire persuades me otherwise. For if
they were imbued with the principles of philosophy, I do not know
how they could embrace such an absurd religion. If the Turks recognized this, their whole empire would be ruined.

12   The Turks profess that their belief in fate was founded in the sacred
scripture. They cite [Romans 9] where it says: "How can anyone say
to the potter, why did you make me thus? I hardened Pharaoh's heart:
I loved Jacob, but Esau I hated." But anyone of sound mind must
question how they derive this belief from that source of sacred oracles. As Turks hold the Old Testament in the highest esteem and
their religion is glued together from the principles of Christianity
and Judaism, they respect the Old Testament as a holy book. But the
Turks pretend that the Qur'an, after falling from the sky, explained
God's will more closely and distinctly. Therefore, they worship this
book among others with the greatest respect to the extent that they
do not even touch it without ritual ablution. They take care that all
books and papers are not crushed underfoot or stained, since a verse
of the Qur'an or the name of God might be written on them. For
fear of capital punishment, no one dares sell the Qur'an or any other
sacred writings to a Christian or a man of any other faith, to ensure
they are not thrown down and trodden on by feet or touched by unclean hands. Often the Turks attach certain verses of the Qur'an to
their necks and arms, which act as charms against virulent plagues
or other diseases, to keep them safe from any danger to the body or
mind. When there is a storm, they place these verses on ships' masts
when it is tossed on the sea or tie them to the standards, if they want
to join hand in battle. It is considered a great sin among them to turn
one's back on this holiest book. They pay attention to the smallest
details of its punctuation, and revere those who have memorized this
book, since they conserve the Holy Law in the bookshelf of their
heart. From this it is obvious that the Turks worship this book greatly
and follow its teachings with the highest respect. Since the Qur'an

supplies them with this kind of pernicious opinion, it is no wonder that the Turks believe this doctrine of fate so strictly and firmly.

13   Schisms have arisen among all nations including the Turks. The Persians and Turks are divided into two sects. The Turks consider Muhammad as the last and greatest Prophet, the Persians, 'Alī. The latter believe that God ordered the angel Gabriel to give the Qur'an to 'Alī; however, Gabriel gave it to Muhammad out of negligence. Olearius and Hottinger unanimously agree that 'Alī was indeed a disciple of Muhammad, but with much greater inspiration. For this reason, they consider 'Alī a much better interpreter [of God's words] than Muhammad. The Turks say the Qur'an was corrupted by the Persians and call them those rejected by God and the slanderers of the Holiest Prophet. The Orthodox, or those who embrace the true teaching of the Qur'an, are called Muslims. The word 'Muslim' means 'the peaceful saved ones.' Heretics are called *Checidaei* after the prince of the Saracens Yazīd, who not only slandered and greatly insulted their prophet Muhammad, but even killed his grandchildren and the sons of 'Alī. The number of heretic sects is commonly given as seventy-two, but there seem to be even more.

14   Among these sects, we must refer to those whom the Turks usually call *Kaderiyye* [Qadarites]. This sect is opposed to the *Cebriyye* [Jabrites] and thinks their belief in fate that I spoke about in previous paragraphs is absurd. This sect, also known as Qadarites, denies predestination and believes that all good and evil that men do depends on their will and their freedom. They draw their name from the word *Kader*, which means *possible*, since the Qadarites say that all actions, good or evil, are in the power of man, and if they chose, they can do good works. They believe no malignancy and injustice originates from God. They often retreat from places infected with plague if they have a chance, and they avoid any obvious dangers, if it is in their power, but there are some who do not do this.

15   This belief in predestination, which the Jabrites mostly agree with, is known as Turkish fate. The vast majority of Muslims believe in this concept of fate. The proof is that the Turks agree that all events in the world are predetermined (5–6); and that this predetermination depends on no cause and cannot be avoided through any natural or ordinary means (5). The fact the Turks are completely convinced of this opinion has been proved over and over with their examples and deeds in 9.

16   From the above thirteen points, this definitive definition can be provided, namely, that the Turkish concept of fate is that the necessity of events depends on no natural causes or ordinary means. Therefore, let's ask ourselves what we should think about this fate, since we have already reviewed its history. The following section will clearly demonstrate that the Turks' concept of fate cannot be reconciled with any rational principle.

Section 2

*Demonstration of the [Logical] Impossibility of the Turks'
Concept of Fate*

17 It is impossible for the same thing to be and not be at the same time.

Note: This proposition is called the principle of contradiction, and this is so obvious that everyone agrees, it is the first absolute principle.

18 A positive notion is something that can be conceived of. That which is not a positive notion cannot be conceived of. A contradiction is the simultaneous affirmation and denial of the same thing. A reason is something through which something else is known, and that by which individual things are known to be true is called a sufficient reason.
19 There is nothing true without a sufficient reason.

Note: This proposition is called the principle of sufficient reason, and Archimedes is usually credited with its invention. But Leibniz, the Leader and Phoenix of Philosophers, revived this long-forgotten proposition and used it in his writings without proof. Leaving him aside, I provide no proof since one can find this proposition in abundance in books on metaphysics. These two principles, namely, of contradiction and sufficient reason, are the first foundations of all truth. Whatever legitimate consequences are deduced from these cannot be doubted.

20 A necessary consequence is a thing which has its own sufficient reason due to another thing. It is mutable if it can change. It is immutable if it cannot change.
21 The world [or universe] is a chain of all mutable things and mutually necessary consequences.
22 This world exists; this is established by our experience of it. All things in the world are mutable (21). Therefore, the world itself is mutable (20). All consequences have a cause and effect (21) whether it has its own sufficient reason in another or not (20).
23 If A is posited and B is denied, A and B are called opposites. That which involves contradiction is impossible. That which does not involve contradiction is possible. Whatever involves a contradiction when compared against itself is an absolute, and whatever contradicts with something else is a hypothetical impossibility. That which is possible is a contingent. The opposite of an impossible absolute is called a necessary absolute. The opposite of an impossible hypothetical is a necessary hypothetical.

24 Whatever is mutable is necessarily contingent. For whatever is mutable can be other than it is (20). Therefore, its opposite is possible. This possible opposite is called a contingent (23). Therefore, whatever is mutable is also contingent.

25 This world is not an absolute necessity, but contingent. For its opposite is either possible or impossible. It is not impossible since it is a mutable entity and can change (20, 22). So, its opposite is possible (24). The possible opposite of this is called contingent and its opposite absolute impossibility is an absolute necessity (23). Therefore, this world is not an absolute necessity, but a contingent.

26 A sufficient reason is an act of change. A cause is an entity that contains the sufficient reason of another existence [or existence of another thing] in itself. And an effect is an entity which has a sufficient reason for something that happened prior. A single act along with its effect is called an event.

27 If we posit a cause, we can also posit an effect. For a cause is an entity that contains a sufficient reason for another existence [or existence of another thing] in itself (26). Therefore, there is either something whose cause contains a reason in itself, or nothing (18). If the cause for something is nothing, then it is not a positive notion, and cannot be conceived of (18). Therefore, the sufficient reason for the existence of something is contained in a cause. But this is called an effect (26). Therefore, if we posit a cause, we also posit an effect.

28 Since a sufficient reason has been posited, a cause has also been posited, and if we take away the cause, we remove the sufficient reason. For a cause contains a sufficient reason of another existence in itself (26). Let us posit that if there is nothing that contains this cause in itself, then there is necessarily no sufficient reason. But this is impossible (19). Therefore, since a cause has been posited, a sufficient reason has been posited. But if we take away the cause we remove the sufficient reason. For a cause contains a sufficient reason for an effect to occur. If this cause is removed, it is necessary to remove the effect as well. Therefore, if the cause is taken away the sufficient reason is removed.

29 All events in the world are effects and causes. For all events in the world have a sufficient reason for their existence. If they were not to have one, they would be without a sufficient reason, which is impossible (19). Therefore, they have a sufficient reason for existence, either in themselves or in something else. They do not have this sufficient reason in themselves since then they would exist before they existed, which is absurd. Therefore, all entities in the world have a sufficient reason for existence in something else. An entity which has a sufficient reason for existence in something else is called an effect (26) and what contains the sufficient reason for its existence in itself is its cause (26). Therefore, all events in the world are effects and

have their own causes. *Note:* The truth of this theory is elucidated by experience. For if we closely examine the course of our lives, we will learn that all human affairs are concatenated, so that one always becomes the cause of another, and will produce an effect.

30 All events in this world are contingent. For all things in the world are mutable (21–22) and whatever is mutable is contingent (24). Therefore, all events in the world are contingent.

31 Nothing in the world becomes an absolute necessity, but its opposite is always possible (30), and whatever effect happens in the world has its own causes prior to it (29). Since everything in the world is a necessary consequence (22), a nexus of causes is given in a continuous chain.

32 An accident refers to an event in the world whose sufficient reason is unexplained. An accident is pure or absolutely random when its sufficient reason is not given at all.

33 A pure accident is not possible in this or any other world. For if a pure accident were possible then it would be something without a sufficient reason (32). But nothing is without a sufficient reason (19). Therefore, a pure accident is not possible in this or any other world.

34 When a thing's existence must be affirmed and not denied, it is said to be a determined truth.

35 Whatever happens in the world has its own determined truth. For whatever happens exists while it is happening; therefore, its existence must be affirmed and not denied. If this were not the case, it would follow that the same thing could be and not be, which is against [logic or reason] (17). A thing whose existence must be affirmed and not denied has a determined truth (34). Therefore, whatever happens in the world has its own determined truth.

36 God is given, whether He is an entity beyond the world [or universe] or not, because He takes all potential realities into account, and because He created this world. *Note:* I have established this truth without proof since this obvious thing is supported by almost all metaphysicians. Nor do the Turks deny it, with whom we are disputing. For they believe, following the first principle of the Qur'an (4), that there is one true God. But to avoid all digressions, I will save my paper.

37 We can define "the most convenient means" as when something contains the sufficient reason for all these things and this cause leads to the best affect [end]. An end means something that an intelligent entity acts to obtain. The height of wisdom is knowing how to apply the most convenient means to one's ends.

38 If God is the wisest entity, He possesses the highest wisdom. God possesses all potential realities (36). Therefore, He possesses the highest wisdom.

39 Omnipotence is the ability to bestow existence to all possible things. Therefore, if God possesses all potential realities, He is omnipotent (36).

40 The necessity of consequence is the absolute impossibility of being otherwise. Fate is the necessity of events in the world. Stoic fate is commonly called the necessity of the consequence of events in the world, which indeed depends on God's decree without necessity or an objective reason.

41 Turkish fate, described in 16, can be defined as a gross or subtle fate. It is called gross when it is the absolute necessity of events, not depending on natural causes. It is called subtle when it is the hypothetical necessity of events, under the condition of divine omnipotence, not depending on natural causes and ordinary means. *Note:* To understand this matter clearly, I will elaborate further. Some Turks are convinced of the absolute impossibility of being otherwise. They say that it is an absolute impossibility that this or that event should not happen in the world. Indeed, not only has God decreed it, but He is not able to decree otherwise [God cannot intervene]. These people believe in gross fate, and consequently are pessimists. But other Turks explain fate like this, that it is indeed not an absolute impossibility for something to happen, but that the opposite can happen through divine omnipotence. However, if this does not happen it is because God, who wrote this fate, impedes all natural causes so that their effect does not happen, and what He decrees happens [This is called subtle fate]. Therefore, all events should happen since God has decided on them, and He always acts through His omnipotence so that they happen with certainty. This is especially considered true concerning death. Of course, a determined end to life is fixed for each and every man by God, beyond which it is impossible to go, but if that end has already been passed, God impedes all means by which man can live longer. If the determined end to a man's life has not been passed, God impedes all natural causes of death through His immense strength. Many Christians often follow the Turkish concept of fate in their own daily lives, for if they have employed no effort in avoiding some fate, they decide that they deserved it, and that it could not be changed.

42 The gross Turkish fate is the Stoic fate. For this fate is the necessity of the consequence of events in the world (40–41) and it is a necessity, which depends on God's decree (5) and indeed is an absolute necessity without an objective cause (8). This kind of necessity of events is called Stoic (40). Therefore, the gross Turkish fate is the Stoic fate. *Note:* Everyone who writes about Turks states that innumerable Turks believe in the Stoic fate. The Stoics and Turks say that God Himself is subject to fate. For some Turks imagine God as the author of evil (6) and they affirm that evil is decreed by God by necessity; although He has no wish for these things, He must still decree these evils. This is the genuine opinion of the Jabrite Turks. See the first section of this dissertation.

43   The gross Turkish fate is impossible. For Turkish fate allows the necessity of the consequence of events in the world (40–41). But this is the absolute impossibility of earthly events being otherwise (40). Therefore, it is an absolute impossibility according to this fate for events in the world to be otherwise. If they cannot be otherwise, they are immutable (20) and their opposite is impossible, whether or not they are absolute necessities (23). But events in the world are mutable (22) and contingent (30) and do not become something else by absolute necessity (31). But since this involves a contradiction, and because it is impossible to have a contradiction (23), it follows that the gross Turkish fate is impossible [because it cannot be immutable and mutable at the same time].

44   The gross Turkish fate admits pure accident in the world for the gross Turkish fate has no sufficient reason. Let's suppose it has a sufficient reason: then this reason is either in the world, or is in an entity outside the world, whether or not it is in God. It is not in the world since Turkish fate depends on no natural causes (16, 41), and if we remove the cause, it is necessary to remove the sufficient reason (28). Therefore, it is not in the world nor is it in God. For in their judgment, God must decree all events by absolute necessity without reason (8). It is an absolute impossibility for events to be otherwise (40–41). Therefore, God is not the reason why events are as they are (18); and the sufficient reason is not in God, nor is it in the world. But if the sufficient reason of the gross Turkish fate is neither in the world nor in God, then gross Turkish fate necessarily has no sufficient reason. Whatever does not have a sufficient reason is called a pure accident (32). Therefore, gross Turkish fate allows pure accident in the world.

Note: I have affirmed in this section that the sufficient reason of the gross Turkish fate does not lie with God. Perhaps someone would interject that the sufficient reason for this fate is entirely in God, in His decree, of course. He would say that events happen in the world since God has decreed them. But he does not explain why God decrees these things. For if I ask why God decrees something according to the Turks' own reasoning, there is no sufficient or objective reason: for God persecutes evil with hatred according to the Turks' reasoning, and yet they believe that He decrees evil by necessity (5). Hence, according to the Turks, there is no sufficient reason for this fate in God, and it is not up to Him why this or that event happens in the world.

45   Therefore, gross Turkish fate is not possible in this or another world (33) since no pure accident can exist in any world. Behold a new proof, by which the impossibility of this fate has been demonstrated.

46 Now that the impossibility of gross Turkish fate has been demonstrated, let's look at what we should think about the subtle Turkish fate. To reach this goal, we must first know its sequence.

47 Whatever has a sufficient reason for its existence in things pertaining to the world is called entirely natural. Whatever does not have one is called supernatural. Supernatural events in the world that have a reason for their existence in an entity outside the world are called miracles.

48 God is that entity outside the world (36). Therefore, God is the cause of miracles, whether or not He contains a sufficient reason in Himself for why miracles exist (26).

49 Every event that does not depend on natural causes is a miracle. For every event that does not depend on natural causes does not have a sufficient reason for existence in things pertaining to the world, and is therefore supernatural (47). If it is supernatural, it either has no sufficient reason, but happens through pure accident [gross fate] or has a sufficient reason for its existence in an entity outside the world [subtle fate]. The first is impossible since nothing is without a sufficient reason (19), and pure accidents are impossible [thus disproving gross fate] (33). Therefore, it has a sufficient reason in an entity outside the world [God]. A supernatural event that has a sufficient reason for its existence in an entity outside the world is a miracle (47). Therefore, every event that does not depend on natural causes is a miracle.

50 The subtle Turkish fate supposes that there are events that do not depend on natural causes and means [of this world] ordained by God, but have a sufficient reason for their existence in divine omnipotence (39). Therefore, the subtle Turkish fate supposes miracles (49).

51 The subtle Turkish fate supposes that there are a huge number of miracles in the world. For this fate is the necessity of events not depending on natural causes (39), [but on God's decrees]. This belief particularly pertains to people's deaths (39). Therefore, the death of all men, according to their reasoning, is a miracle. Now I ask you to consider how many men in the world die in one year, one hour, even in this one moment. I ask you to consider further how many thousands have already lived and died from the beginning of the world, but their number is so great that we cannot comprehend it. Therefore, who will deny that the subtle Turkish fate supposes that there are a huge number of miracles in the world?

52 If God produces supernaturally what can happen naturally, He is using superfluous means. But since God possesses the highest wisdom (38), and always chooses the most convenient means (37), it is necessary that God uses no superfluous means.

53 The world is the chain of all mutual necessary consequences (21). Therefore, everything in the world is a necessary consequence (22).

Therefore, one thing has its own sufficient reason in another thing (20). Therefore, one thing causes another (26). But if the cause is posited, so is the effect (27). All events in the world are effects and their causes (29). Therefore, events in the world occur naturally, and will follow from their existent causes.

54   A miracle does not have a sufficient reason for its existence in worldly matters, but originates in God (47). Therefore, a miracle does not flow from previous causes and ordinary means; therefore, the ordinary nexus of events is impeded by the miracle's performance. If this is impeded, there should be a sufficient reason for why it is impeded (19). The sufficient reason is so that the nexus of events in the world either turns out better or not. If it does not turn out better, God would not be the wisest since He would prefer what is less good to what is better, and would not choose the most convenient means (37). But God is the wisest (38). Therefore, the nexus of events in the world should turn out better. Therefore, God should then perform the miracle, if the nexus of events in the world can turn out better.

55   God is omnipotent (39), and the world is contingent (25). Therefore, it is possible to perform miracles. Since God also possesses the highest wisdom (38). He always chooses the most convenient means in the nexus of the world; that is, He chooses such a nexus of the world which he should not keep impeding (37). Therefore, the nexus of the world, of what God chooses, cannot keep becoming better (45). Therefore, God is not able to make many miracles in the world, nor does He, and He impedes and should impede the nexus of causes and ordinary means very rarely [by miracles] (54).

56   The subtle Turkish fate is absurd. For this fate supposes a huge number of miracles in the world, which are performed by God every day, every hour, and every moment (51). But this contradicts God's highest wisdom. He is not able to make many miracles in the world with His wisdom unharmed, nor does He (55). Therefore, the subtle Turkish fate is absurd.

57   Events in the world have their own determined truth (35), and are placed naturally and follow from their existent causes (53). God impedes this nexus of causes and ordinary means in the world very rarely (55), and does not use superfluous means (52). But the Turkish fate, the subtle as well as the gross, is the necessity of events not depending on their own causes and ordinary means [but on miracles] (41–46). Therefore, either Turkish fate is impossible for this reason.

58   Gentle reader, I submit these points for public discussion, written with a hurrying pen through lack of time. May that Divinity who governs everything wisely fill our enemies [Turks] who believe in this fate with His light, so that they enlist with Christ, and at last recognize what a very absurd religion they embrace. Farewell and favor me, that is what I ask you most humbly. To the glory of the only God!

Note

1 Weitenkampf's biography was compiled from the following sources: Johann Gottlob Wilhelm Dunkel, *Historisch-Critische Nachrichten von verstorbenen Gelehrten und deren Schriften* (Cöthen/Dessau: Cörnerische Buchhandlung, 1757), 869; Johann Friedrich Weitenkampf, *Vernünftigte Trostgründe bey den traurigen Schicksalen der Menschen* (Lancaster: Johann Bär, 1825), 3–7; Oswald Seidensticker and Gerhard Friedrich (eds.), *The First Century of German Printing in America, 1728–1830* (Philadelphia: Schaefer & Koradi, 1893), 226; Pozzo, "Kant e Weitenkampf," 283–323; Kuehn, *Kant: A Biography*, 88–105; and Riccardo Pozzo, "Weitenkampf, Johann Friedrich," in *The Bloomsbury Dictionary of Eighteenth-Century German Philosophers*, eds. Heiner F. Klemme and Manfred Kuehn (London: Bloomsbury, 2010), 838.

Part III

Philosophy and Liberal Arts

7   History of Rational Philosophy among the Arabs and Turks

Johann Peter von Ludewig

Johann Peter von Ludewig was born in 1668 at Schwäbisch Hall in Honhardt and, at an early age, he attended Latin school in Crailsheim, a town in modern Baden-Württemberg. He studied theology and humanities at Tübingen in 1688; then at Wittenberg he studied theology and philosophy and received his Master's degree in 1690, before attending the University of Halle in 1693 to study law. After studying law and lecturing on the history of philosophy at Halle, Ludewig took up a professorship position there in theoretical philosophy in 1695. During his studies at Wittenberg and Halle, Ludewig was influenced by one of the most important figures in the evolution of German law, the jurist Samuel Stryk (d.1710). In this disputation written in 1699, Ludewig presents his ideas in a juristic systematic fashion by giving arguments and counterarguments before expressing his own judgment. Ludewig became the chair in history at Halle in 1703. A year later, he became the Court Historiographer and received his doctorate in law, and then in 1705 he took up the legal professorship position at Halle, which he held for the rest of his life. In 1722, he was appointed Chancellor of the University of Halle. Ludewig was also involved in politics, being appointed to the Privy Council in 1718 and becoming the Chancellor of the Duchy of Magdeburg in 1741. He died in Halle in 1743.[1]

Variant Names: Ioh. Petr. Ludovico, Johann Peter Ludewig, Joan. Petrus de Ludewig, Ioannes Petrus Ludewig, Johannes Petrus Ludewig, Johann Petrus Ludovic, and Johann Peter Ludovici

Summary and Analysis

In his *disputatio*, Ludewig provides a history of rational philosophy among the Arabs and sets out to contextualize the Turks' attitude to it. Like many Lutheran scholars of the time, Ludewig believed that Islam, as a religion, impeded the development of rational philosophy in the Arab world. However, unlike those philosophers, he examines external influences that may have fed the interest of Arab Muslims in rational philosophy, especially dialectic. He begins by suggesting that before Islam Arabs contributed to Greek philosophy and argues that the prevalent depiction of pre-Islamic Arabs (*jāhiliyya*) as barbarians fails to account for their being not only exposed to, but also contributing to, literature and philosophy.[2] Ludewig provides several arguments to support the claim that Arabs cultivated wisdom. For example, he argues that, during his journeys to the East, Pythagoras studied with teachers in Arabia descended from Abraham; they were exceptional teachers in divination and augury, and witnesses to Abraham's philosophy, contributing to its survival. Thus, Ludewig argues that the pre-Islamic Arabs practiced the art of disputation, even though they developed different modes of thought than the Greeks. He explains that the inhabitants of ancient Arabia were eager to learn their own language, the properties of speech, poetic arts, the composition of orations, and knowledge of the stars. These five focal points of study coincide with and, therefore, lend themselves to the development of an Arabic philosophical system based on five disciplines: grammar, dialectic, poetry, rhetoric, and astronomy.

Ludewig's focus, however, is on the dialectic, a form of rational inquiry based on a dialogue consisting of arguments and counter-arguments (advocating propositions and counter-propositions) in the quest for truth. According to the seventeenth-century travel writer Johannes Cotovicus (d.1629), who wrote an account of a journey to Jerusalem and Syria, the pre-Islamic Arabs placed considerable emphasis on practicing dialectic and rhetoric because it was rooted in ancestral customs. Ludewig uses the biblical story of Job as an example of dialectic from Arabic ancestry, arguing that the art of dialectics begins for the Arabs with the Jewish Holy Scripture. Rather than attribute the philosophical development of dialectics to the Jews, Ludewig makes the strenuous argument that Job was in fact of Arab descent. With this example of Job, who Ludewig claims is an Arab, it seems he is excluding Judaism from the creation of dialectic.

Ludewig argues that philosophy assumed a different form after Muhammad, who initially declared war on the liberal arts by issuing grave and serious exhortations to every follower who pursued these endeavors. He argues that Muhammad was illiterate and in order to remain in control, he ensured that all Muslims who studied the liberal arts would be criminally charged. According to Ludewig, for Muslims, the focus of study was the Qur'an, and no additional time was allotted to the blasphemous learning of liberal philosophy. Because of Muhammad's attempt to protect the authority of his religion, Arabs became unaccustomed to learning and the ancient Arabic philosophers were lost to them. Ludewig considers the time of Muhammad and the inception of Islam as a time of ignorance because Islam's doctrines and dogmas replaced the intellectual flexibility he associated with rational modes of thought.

Ludewig goes on to suggest that philosophy was reborn among the Arabs because of Christian influence, arguing that Christian and Arab

Muslim business relations re-exposed the Arab Muslims to Greek philosophy. In fact, Arab Muslims recognized the value of dialectic when they disputed with Christians. Ludewig explains that to keep his followers in harmony, Muhammad ordered them to refrain from disputations and to act in accordance with his sacred dogmas, not by reason but by faith. However, when this order was not fully observed, the result was the creation of a multitude of Islamic sects that sought to use rational philosophy to make their faith intelligible to others or to correct logic errors in Islamic theology.

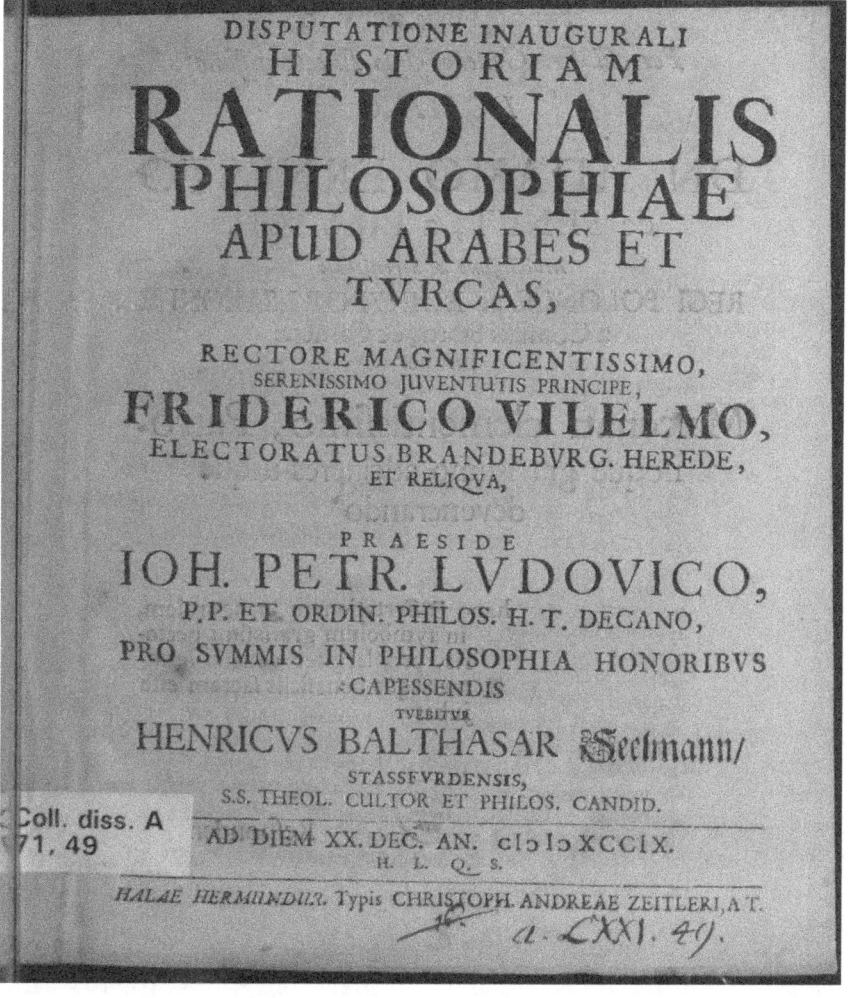

Figure 7.1 Johann Peter von Ludewig, *Disputatione inaugurali historiam rationalis philosophiae apud Arabes et Turcas*, 1699 (Courtesy of the Staats- und Universitätsbibliothek Dresden).

In short, Ludewig presents Islam as antithetical to modern philosophical developments and points to Muhammad's obsession with control over his populace as the reason behind the general reluctance of many Muslims to study liberal arts. In contrast, Ludewig presents rational philosophy as the natural conclusion of Christian thinking (referring to the Christian God as rational "logos") and claims that exposure to Christian intellectuals and ideas would lead to the re-emergence of rational philosophy among Muslims as he believed it had done before. Unlike Orthodox Lutherans, such as Pfeiffer and Kromayer, in his conclusion, Ludewig prays that Muslim philosophers cultivate reason to overcome the deceit of Muhammadanists toward rational worship. The use of the contentious and seemingly oxymoronic phrase "rational worship" (*logikē latreia*: λογικὴ λατρεία, from Rom. 12:1), combining "rationality" and "worship" together reflects, to a certain extent, the Enlightenment belief that reason could be used to understand the nature of God against any type of irrational religiosity. The idea of worshipping God rationally and equating God with reason shows the intellectual engagement of Protestant scholars with Enlightenment rationalism.[3]

Inaugural Disputation on the History of Rational Philosophy among the Arabs and Turks (Halle, 1699)

Every Discipline Needs a History

Although the history of geniuses [in rational philosophy] is synonymous with the name of [Gilles] Ménage, others such as [Lilius Gregorius] Gyraldus, [Peter] Criniti, Vergil, Renecci, Peirerius, Patritius, Crispus, Lipsius, Lavnoius, Adami, Heurnius, Vossius, Lambecius, Johnston, [Georg] Hornius, [Johannes] Schefferus, [Pierre] Gassendi, Stanley, Theophilus [Gale], and Thomasius pioneered annals of art and literature, dealing with the greatest minds of this and earlier ages. By periodically studying these annals closely, these geniuses compared them with the writings of ancient authors. After reading so many and such great names, one might ask oneself whether anything remains today that has not been influenced by the studious work of these men. Some have written on the general history of philosophy, others have shown what has been done in individual schools of philosophy; but none of them have focused on a specific discipline [of philosophy]; I should think this Sparta yet awaits a leader and a man. I want the history of logic—that is, its beginnings, its progress, its methods, its authors, its practice, and transformation—to be written fully and comprehensively. One could do the same with the other disciplines of philosophy; this would greatly benefit the Republic of Letters.[4] Indeed, I know that [Petrus] Ramus and [Bartholomäus] Keckermann attempted something in the history of rational philosophy; Gassendi was also successfully engaged in tracing out certain schools of dialectics. But no one has put each of these histories together, added in what was missing, or explained completely what one wished to know—no such person has yet appeared. Therefore, I determined that my hard work would contribute as well. I conceived of writing the *Polyhistor Logicus*, where I seek to present the history of logic and diligently follow up on it in chronological order, for I wanted to leave the glory to others, either to fulfill or increase the thousands of *Logica* that have already been published, with the thought that it would be better if I covered the full history of logic which began in rational philosophy. But whether the hardship at this time in my life (not to speak too gravely) hindered my discipline and very nearly extinguished it or a certain event drew my studies elsewhere, it so happened that my mind became a little disaccustomed to this practice, and my first efforts failed. Since I wanted most of the material that I had researched not to perish among the various authors of greater renown, I decided to break up these sections into individual topics and thus, to have a systematic rationale for this undertaking. [...]. Therefore, I do not offer here something fully fleshed out, but I give you only an outline of a dialectic of the Turks, which neither permits nor endures revision until I return to this study and create a more substantial body of work.

Division of the Work

As I am going to write the history of rational philosophy among the Turks, I shall divide up this work so that I may first delve into certain elements of the ancient dialectic of the Arabs; then I shall explain the current state of this discipline among the Turks with as much faith and diligence as I can.

On Rational Philosophy among the Ancient Arabs: Were the Arabs Aware of Literature? A Confirmation and Response to Initial Doubts

The fact that wisdom was not born in Greece is acknowledged among the Greeks themselves; it is no less certain that it was summoned from the East. Rather, the Arabs contributed to Greek philosophy, although philosophy was studied by a few, as it seems they had more of an interest. Those who consider the Arabs barbarians are guilty of the same fault as those who are ignorant of geography. For just as the latter consider unknown lands to be deserts, so the former find fault with those peoples whose customs are unknown to them, and do not consider them a people worthy of acquaintance. But even the Arabic writers themselves called the times in Arabia before Muhammad "ages of ignorance" [*jāhiliyya*], such that foreigners [non-Muslims] imposed letters on them in vain and indigenous witnesses called them ignorant in the arts.

They offer Gregory Abū al-Faraj of Malatya [as evidence], who said the following about ancient Arabia:

> As for the Arabs who remain, a double state is suitable for them: one of ignorance, the other of Islam. But the state of the Arabs in their times of ignorance is famous among the nations for its resiliency and might.

Many people cite these words, as though the study of letters was exiled from Arabia; but ignorance is not in opposition here with the arts, but with religion, for he writes that light drew near the divine culture with the dogmas of Muhammad, when previously the Arabs had been wrapped up in the shadows of idolatry. So, I think that the author is right, but that letters existed among the Arabs before. So why did Abū al-Faraj call them ignorant? He immediately declares that the Arabs are versed in rhetoric, logic, astronomy, and poetry. This raises a doubt that Abū al-Faraj considers the character of the Arabs to be unsuitable for the liberal arts. But he either does not say the same thing about the Arab nation as a whole, or he contradicts himself. For who would call men unfit for studies who were already considered skilled in the arts? Why? Because the opposite is rather agreed upon, based on the reasoning and character of that atmosphere. Edmund Castellus argues as follows:

> Has the East always been considered the most favorable to the Muses? Why not also its kingdoms? I will not have it. Look at Aristotle, Hippocrates, Galen, Ctesias, who assure us at every point with offered examples that everything is prettier, finer, and better in Asia [Castellus is talking about Arabia] than that which is found in Europe. Minerals and metals in the earth, plants and trees above, more pure and healthier air, a much clearer and calmer sky.

Thus Holdsworth, a man most skilled in philology, gave proof with examples that Asiatic authors always surpassed European ones. Additionally, among the feeble spirits of the Thebans one would find men like Epaminondas. Yet they say that he was buried in everlasting oblivion, although the Arabs know something of his arts. For thus Abū al-Faraj says about the ancient inhabitants of Arabia, "the nations have been destroyed, we are deprived of accurate historical memory of them, and their reasoning has utterly vanished (i.e., because their historical works have vanished), with which we could seek after traces of them." Yet this itself is what we shall now investigate.

Arguments for the Fact that Arabs Do Not Lack Literature/Philosophy

Since the Arabic [historical] writings did not survive, non-indigenous sources have had to be used, and when they themselves are insufficient we must use reasoning if we are to have any hope of pursuing this matter in our conjectures.

Argument 1: Many sources have shown that Pythagoras undertook journeys to the East for the sake of his studies, but Porphyry recalls that he also found teachers in Arabia. According to Diogenes: "Pythagoras reached both the Egyptians and the Arabs."

Argument 2: Schefferus argues that he learned divination [the augural art] while he was among the Arabs: divinations based on the flight and squawking of birds, and the knowledge of augury as Philostratus claims that the Arabs were outstanding in both. It is believed that Moses had the same experience, because when he was fleeing from Egypt he preferred to stay in Arabia more than anywhere else. Since he was a godly man, soundly trained in every wisdom, it is not likely that he would have wished to rot in idleness among barbarians and dimwits if all the inhabitants of Arabia had been illiterate.

Argument 3: The origin of that people does not allow us to question the literacy of the Arabs. With marvelous agreement, the Arabs say that they are the descendants of Abraham. Therefore, if they are plain witnesses of Abraham's philosophy, how shall we say that his descendants snuffed out his light once it was lit? Especially since we know, citing al-Shahrastanı, that the Arabs believe themselves to be descended from Abraham. In fact, they say that the writings of Abraham himself survive in Arabia.

Argument 4: There is also what the author of the *Book of Kings* says about Solomon, that his wisdom was greater "than everyone's in the Orient." We do not doubt this fact about the Arabs, as it is presented by men who were skilled in the Holy Tongue, with an indubitable argument again of Arabic learning.

Argument 5: Actually, it is the opinion of learned men that the Queen of Sheba came from Arabia for an audience with the wisest King, standing strong and not lacking in reasoning skills.

Argument 6: Why? Because the most outstanding men argue that the Magi from the East were themselves Arabs, such that, Pliny and Ptolemy, two very bright men, considered Arabia rightly and properly the home of the Magi. Although almost everyone considers them a stupid and wretched people, whoever reads this will grant that the ancient Arabs were in fact cultivators of wisdom.

The Arabs Proved to Be Rational and Zealous Philosophers

After examining the philosophy of the Arabs, I must ask if they were also trained in that part of philosophy that is engaged in argumentation. One may wonder whether the ancient Arabs valued dialectic. However, [by dialectic], I mean here not a *natural* but a *customary* ability, as I do not want the same art [dialectic] to be restricted solely to the pleasures of the Greeks, nor indeed to those of a single citizen of Stagira. Because if one asks about the Greeks' logic or about the Aristotelian *Organon*, it is obvious that the ancient Arabs knew nothing of his school. But there is not one road to truth, nor are all the lessons concerning the art of argumentation the same; for I agree here with a certain man's famous *bonmot*: "Men have argued before Aristotle, the God of syllogisms, was born." Yet it suffices only to prove this here: that the ancient Arabs, just like the rest, practiced the art of disputation. These are my arguments, which prove the matter.

Argument 1: Abū al-Faraj himself is a witness in this matter, for he writes about the ancient inhabitants of Arabia: "The learning of the Arabs, for which glory they were particularly eager, was as follows: knowledge of their language, property of speech, poetic arts, the composition of orations, and knowledge of the stars." Also, Arabic philosophy was formed of five disciplines; namely, grammar, dialectic, poetry, rhetoric, and astronomy. Only one of these concerns us here: dialectic. Others shall have to look into the rest. There are many reasons that suggest that this "property of speech" means the "dialectical art." Certainly this "property of speech" about which Abū al-Faraj speaks either pertains to grammar or is a part of oratory or of dialectic. But it can be called neither the first [grammar] nor the second [oratory], for the author wants it to be distinct from the others. Therefore, I must necessarily advocate this last one [dialectic].

Argument 2: Johannes Cotovicus writes that the Arabs of this age, who have not changed their old manner of living and teaching, while ignoring all other studies, practice dialectic and rhetoric, which, in my opinion, seems to be due to the ancient customs of their ancestors.

Argument 3: For the wisest of the ancient Arabs have an example of dialectic in Job, the first man who was clearly outstanding in the literate world in this skill. They make a good many convincing arguments that Job was an Arab, which the experts most skilled in Eastern philology also confirm. But they so far miss the mark that Job disputed, argued, answered, regressed, made exceptions, limited terms, which is clear chiefly in his speeches with his customary friends, such that we prefer to think he is right and is among the dialectical princes of his time. We have many men among the ancients who agree on this matter, among whom Jerome, Ambrose, and Cassiodorus suffice to mention at this point. Not to mention more recent figures who also reached the same conclusions by their own calculation. So, what if Job, the prince of dialecticians, was an Arab? Should we doubt that the study of dialectic flourished in Arabia? [...]. Leaving behind the rest of Arabia's ancient inhabitants, let us now examine more recent men to reveal the fate of rational philosophy among the Turks.

Arab Philosophy in the Post-Muhammad Era (From the Year 650) and the Decline of Ancient Philosophy

Indeed, philosophy after Muhammad took on quite a different appearance; for those people who think that the study of letters began among the Arabs are mistaken as has been shown, although it is beyond doubt that the philosophy of the Greeks first became known to the Asiatic people and the Arabs as well after these times [post-Muhammad era]. I pray that my perception in this matter may be keen, and that I may discern the cause of this change to letters that took place in Arabia. Muhammad had declared war on the *belles-lettres*, issuing grave and serious exhortations to every follower of his school against the culture of letters. Lest they should perhaps have free time to steep their minds in philosophy, after he wrote a book of his teachings, called the Qur'an, which they were to read, learn, understand, and resort to their strength and blood, he so engaged their better characters that no time would seem to be left to them for other sorts of studies. Then too, whatever was useful for his followers to know he kept in that book so they could be persuaded, but he considered the rest to be superfluous or useless. Either he did this to protect the authority of his religion, which was founded in fraud and from the bits and bobs of superstitious men (as he required faith from his followers, not knowledge), or he had another reason. Yet it came to pass that the Arabs became disaccustomed to letters, and those arts of Abraham, Job, the Sabean woman [the Queen of Sheba], and the Magi, were lost to them, although they had been cultivated by their ancestors with such great zeal, as we have shown. Therefore, as all men do, I consider the times immediately after Muhammad to be times not of knowledge, but of ignorance.

Birth of a New Philosophy among the Arabs

Once Muhammad's doctrine made the Arabs disaccustomed to good letters, like some sort of couch of ignorance, by some kindness of fate they were at last roused again to their culture and natural skills. This did not occur all at once; there were many factors that led them to better understanding.

Reason 1: Christians often conducted business among the Arab Muslims. When the Arabs saw that the Christians were trained in Greek philosophy, they came to understand how much honor lay in letters.

Reason 2: When Muslims ever came into conflict with Christians—which happened often—then they understood the use dialectic provided in disputes.

Reason 3: Then Muslims turned their minds toward the other sciences, for understanding and explaining—and more so, for defending—the Qur'an.

Reason 4: They also recognized the value of the art of dialectics further when differences of opinion arose among themselves concerning the head of the Muslim religion.

Reason 5: When one considers that, after so many peoples were conquered, they frequently found libraries and other books of letters they wanted (as tends to happen) to be trained in the use of dialectics. So, at

last I believe the Arabs also acquired Greek philosophy, which had long
ruled in the world.

Dialecticians

Moreover, it is agreed that dialectic was among the first arts that the
Arabs cultivated. Whether because they believed that, without dialectic, there were no means to convince the others [non-believers]; or because the individual reasons I have stated above seemed to commend it
to them. Now I will investigate the success the Arabs enjoyed in learning
and cultivating this art of debate.

History of the Birth and Progress of Rational Philosophy among the Muhammadans

I have found three authors, who have mentioned Turkish philosophy
in our day. Baptista Donatus, the Venetian Senator; Samuel Schelwig,
the overseer of the people of Danzig; and Abraham Hinckelmann; the
overseer of the people of Hamburg. But perhaps their works had another
aim. I know that their work did not help me in any way at all in my
little work: there was nothing about the literature of the ancient Arabs,
nothing about the cause, time, or history of Greek philosophy being
brought to Arabia. There is so much missing concerning the history of
logic among the Arabs though one of these authors makes some mention
of it in order to deny that the study of dialectic flourished among the
Turks.[5] Therefore, as I am the first to write on this subject, I shall endeavor to make up for the deficiencies of these authors in my own work.

I have read that for roughly a hundred years and more after the death
of Muhammad, the Arabs were in ignorance, being disaccustomed to
the ancient discipline that we Christians have restored for them for the
most part. But afterwards, I think that they began to struggle out of this
shameful laziness. I will now demonstrate how this was done. Indeed, I
have shown above that the Christian Arabs had studied Greek literature,
but the Muslim Arabs had many obstacles preventing them from taking part. First, the caliphs avoided Greek philosophy, partially so that
the Arab Muslims would not become familiar with these works, and
partially so they would not be associated with Christians, and second,
because of the foreignness of the Greek language in which these works
were taught. The Arab Muslims had to labor to remove both obstacles. I have shown in paragraph 7 how they overcame the first obstacle.
For the second obstacle, there was no better solution than to translate the writers from Greek to Arabic. After this I read in Abū al-Faraj
that caliph Walid ordered the Christians, in about the year 710, to use
Arabic instead of Greek. Fifty years or so after this, there were also clear
signs that caliph al-Manṣūr wanted to translate the works of the Greek

philosophers into Arabic. We know that under his successor al-Mahdī, the works of Homer were translated from Greek to Syriac. But under Hārūn al-Rashīd's rule (810 AD), who succeeded this caliph, not only were schools in Greek philosophy founded among the Muslims, but he also had the chief practitioners of every kind of learning with him in his entourage at home and abroad. But whatever remnants of Greek philosophy had sometimes been welcomed among the Muslims up to this point was soon dismissed again. Under caliph al-Ma'mūn, Greek philosophy had finally so insinuated itself into the Arab court that it seemed it had flown from Greece across the sea into Arabia for this caliph was most praiseworthy, and he himself was learned. Al-Ma'mūn drew scholars who knew Greek philosophy and provided them with large earnings; he eagerly searched for books from all places, especially Greece, and paid great remunerations, and he ordered the most excellent to be translated from Greek to Arabic. Finally, he commended the philosophers to his subjects because of their excellent maxims, so that *belles-lettres* could be nurtured in Arabia in the schools that had opened far and wide. This ought to be a source of immortal glory to the great caliph.

The Progress of Philosophy among the Muslims and their Studies, Especially of Dialectic

This finally brought about that true age of Greek philosophy to Muslim Arabia, in a fortunate and blessed beginning. Philosophy sunk such deep roots after those times that it could not be torn up by the tyranny of one man or another. [...]. I will now consider the chief philosophers among the Muslims and Arabs, but especially those who had a regard for the art of dialectic. In the time of caliph al-Mutawakkil (850 AD), a school of Greek philosophy flourished among the Muslims, which Yūḥannā ibn Māsawayh had opened. We even read that there was a renowned philosopher among them called Isḥāq ibn Ḥunayn. The foremost dialectician among the Muslims, Ya'qūb al-Kindī, and also Qusṭā ibn Lūqā, not much his junior, lived not long after Isḥāq ibn Ḥunayn. In the early tenth century, many were celebrated with praise for their philosophy, so that there was a mention of the Muslim Academy in history (940 AD). Thābit ibn Qurrah, a writer of dialectic, also lived in this time. About ten years after him, there was the celebrated Mattā b. Yūnus, who was called a dialectician because of his brilliance in logic. Afterwards al-Fārābī revealed the secrets of the art of analytics to the Muslims. Afrihi ibn 'Adī, close to him in age, was just as highly praised. Not long afterwards, they prevailed over the Islamic scholars, who confessed that theology was mixed with error, which could not be corrected, except through logic. Muḥammad al-Būzjānī, a renowned dialectician, lived at the same time, and in this art, there was no less praise for al-Fārābī, Abū Bakr al-Rāzī, and al-Bāqillānī. Abū 'Abd Allāh would have been unknown

if he had not acted as the logic teacher for the great Avicenna. Everyone knows what Avicenna's reputation for medicine was like. Avicenna,
writing about himself, says that though he had an incompetent teacher,
God himself made the art of dialectic clear to him in dreams. So, what
do they know—who claimed he was philosophically blind? Abū al-Faraj
'Abd Allāh ibn al-Ṭayyib was near him in age, and he himself was an
eminent dialectician.

In the following century (1150 AD), the distinguished men were
Abul-Chais, al-Ghazālī, al-Ṭughrāī, al-Sharīf, Saighus, Abū al-Barakāt
al-Baghdādī, Ibn al-Ḥusayn, Abu'l Helmus, al-Maghrībī, Ibn Ṭufayl, Ibn
al-Bayṭār, and others; some in medicine; some in astrology; and some
in math; but all the most celebrated among their own people in the art
of dialectic. Also, the thirteenth century was not barren in wise men
either. For we read that Averroes, the philosopher, theologian, jurist,
doctor and astrologer, who was the most skilled in all these disciplines,
was attended by great fame and renowned for his writings and teachings, not only among his own people but among any learned nation.
So much so that though the others I have mentioned were translated
among Muslims alone, many, though obviously in error, gave credit to
this man for translating Greek philosophy into Arabic. Near contemporaries or successors to him were 'Abd al-Salām, Yaḥyā ibn Saʿīd, Saʿīd
b. Hibatullāh, Muḥammad, Maimonides, al-Rāzī, al-Masīḥī, al-Yūsuf,
al-Ḥasan, Yaʿqūb, Fakhr al-Dīn al-Rāzī, and Najm al-Dīn al-Qazwīnī,
who was not only skilled in logic like the others, but also made a great
addition to this discipline with new tenets he had devised. The fourteenth century produced men no less praiseworthy in this same discipline. Among them, since I now pass over those from lesser nations,
Naṣīr al-Dīn al-Ṭūsī and Najm al-Dīn al-Qazwīnī deserve special mention, but of these two, and certainly of all the rest, al-Ṭūsī deserves first
place, if not for his teachings then for his fame and kindnesses, for he
was a man of stupendous learning and the most translated writer in all
fields of knowledge. Also, al-Ṭūsī was considered the best prefect and the
universal head teacher of all the schools and universities in the kingdom
of the Mongols, though there were so many. He is now in the vanguard
of Arabic philosophy. Thus, it followed, with literary studies ordered so
well and wisely, that the Muslims easily transmitted them to posterity
and entrusted them to the centuries to come, so that we now know that
the Muslims are not without these councilors of wisdom.

Muslim Universities

We have considered the main practitioners and teachers of the art of
dialectic. I will now touch upon the teachings of the academies among
Muslims. From the beginning, experts in these skills were free to discover stores of wisdom wherever they wanted; their literary education

was not fixed to one location. There were more cities that sustained men who taught youth. I have given examples to prove this. Indeed, among those cities, Baghdad had a literary school built at the prerogative of the universities. At that time, professors of all orders were celebrated and each had their own rank and office, their own wages, and six thousand young students of *belles-lettres*. It seemed that the university lacked no perfection or fame in the literate world.

The Enemies of Philosophy among the Muslims

Although wiser men would have understood that it was a gift of God that *belles-lettres* came to Arabia from Greece, madness and insanity drove some of them the other way. Under a false pretense of peace, some scholars and teachers defended their old laziness, so that they filled the lazy minds of the dreaming and sleepy youth with superstition, under the guise of religion, while men with acute intelligence roused their minds and spirits. They did not allow themselves to be led by the well-ordered authority of the magistrates, to be enveloped in too much religion, and to be bewitched and ensnared by the charms of the *Muftī*, but rather sighed in the depths of their hearts so that they could worship God, who is in truth the *Christian God*, with logic, that is to say *logical worship*. So, the sum of my prayers is that they [Arab/Muslim rational philosophers] finally uncover and recognize the deceit of the Muhammadanists toward *rational worship* (*logikē latreia*) by cultivating reason with the assistance of God.

Notes

1 Ludewig's biography was compiled from the following sources: Johann Heinrich Zedler (ed.), "Ludewig, Joh. Peter von," *Grosses vollständiges Universal-Lexicon aller Wissenschafften und Künste*, vol. 18 (Leipzig, 1738), 954–9; Reinhold Koser, "Ludewig, Johann Peter von," in *Allgemeine Deutsche Biographie*, vol. 19 (Leipzig, 1884), 379–81; Notker Hammerstein, *Jus und Historie. Ein Beitrag zur Geschichte des historischen Denkens an deutschen Universitäten im späten 17. und 18. Jahrhundert* (Göttingen: Vandenhoeck & Ruprecht, 1972), 169–204; and Bernd Roeck, "Ludewig, Johann Peter von" in *Neue Deutsche Biographie*, vol. 15 (Berlin: Bürklein-Ditmar, 1987), 293–5; Flood, *Poets Laureate in the Holy Roman Empire*, 1208–10.

2 [MK] On the pre-Islamic period as Islam's past, see Michael Cook and Carol Bakhos (eds.), *Islam and Its Past: Jahiliyya, Late Antiquity and the Qur'an* (Oxford: Oxford University Press, 2017).

3 [MK] The idea of worship that comes from knowledge or of a rational service to God (*logikē latreia*) was an important concept among Reformed and Anglican scholars in the seventeenth and eighteenth centuries. See two examples, Reformed and Anglican works respectively; Wilhelmus à Brakel, *Logikē latreia, dat is Redelyke godtsdienst, in welke de goddelyke waerheden des genaden-verbondts worden verklaert, tegen partyen beschermt,*

en tot de practyke aengedrongen (Rotterdam: Hendrik vanden Aak, 1715) and Ireneus Freeman, *Logike Latreia: The Reasonablenesse of Divine Service: Or Non-conformity to Common-prayer, Proved, Not Comfortable to Common Reason* (London: Thomas Basset, 1661).

4 [MK] On the Republic of Letters, see Marc Fumaroli, *The Republic of Letters*, trans. Lara Vergnaud (New Haven: Yale University Press, 2018).

5 Among the Lutheran authors, Ludewig is the one who noticed the importance of the study of dialectic among the Turks. Dialectic was not only significant for the study of law or as a theory, it permeated in all fields of knowledge, including the Ottoman divan poetry, and even up until the early twentieth century. See Mehmet Karabela, "Lovers in the Age of the Beloveds: The Classical Ottoman Divan Literature and the Dialectical Tradition," in *Beloved: Love and Languishing in Middle Eastern Literatures and Cultures*, eds. Alireza Korangy, Hanadi al-Samman and Michael Beard (London: I.B. Tauris, 2018), 285–99; idem, "The Dialectical Discourse in Classical Ottoman Literature: The Beloved between Lover and Rival in the Game of Love," *The Journal of Turkish Literature* 10 (2013): 7–19; and "Beşir Fuad and His Opponents: The Form of a Debate over Literature and Truth in Nineteenth-Century Istanbul," *The Journal of Turkish Literature* 8 (2011): 96–106.

8 Development of Logic among the Arabs

Johann Georg Walch

Johann Georg Walch, born in Meiningen in 1693, was a German Lutheran theologian, a historian of logic and an eclectic philosopher. After studying at Leipzig and Jena, Walch married the only daughter of his Pietist teacher Johann Franz Buddeus (d.1729), considered to be the most accomplished German theologian of his time, an *ordinarius* professor. Walch's reading of the history of logic reflects the influence of his teacher's historical approach to the study of philosophy. In 1716, he published *Historia critica Latinae linguae*, which was widely circulated and used as a textbook. In 1718, he became a visiting professor of philosophy at Jena and, in 1719, was appointed as full lecturer in rhetoric. In 1721, he was cross-appointed full professor in poetry and, in 1724, became a visiting professor of theology. In 1728, he was appointed full professor in theology and theology became his primary discipline in 1730. He espoused a moderate theology influenced by philosophical eclecticism and Pietism during this period. Walch's university lectures and published works cover a wide range of church history and its various branches, with specific attention to the literature and controversies of the church, ethics, and pastoral theology. Apart from numerous works on theology, Walch also edited Luther's complete works. He died in Jena in 1775 at the age of eighty-one.[1]

Variant Names: Io. Georgius Walchius, Ioannes Georgius Walchius, and Johannes Georg Walch.

Summary and Analysis

Walch's chapter in his book, *Parerga Academica*, presents a history of Scholastic logic in the Middle Ages. However, by "logic" Walch means dialectic. Before delving into the development of Scholastic dialectic, he sets out in sections one to eight the main achievements of philosophy up until that point. Walch singles out John of Damascus, Michael Psellus the Younger, and George Pachymeres as early Christian Aristotelian dialecticians, but notes that there was a simultaneous upsurge in philosophical study and thought among Arab Muslims. Walch cites the prominent Arab Aristotelian logicians of the time: al-Kindī, Thābit ibn Qurrah, Mattā b. Yūnus, al-Fārābī; Avicenna, and Averroes. He argues that dialectic emerged as a discipline among Arabs when Christians skilled in Greek philosophy began living among Muslims. The Christian presence that made these texts accessible worked in tandem with the appointment of the liberal-minded caliph al-Ma'mūn, who encouraged and created a favorable environment for Greek philosophy. According to Walch, the Arab Muslims took great pains to understand, explain and apply Aristotelian logic, but, for him, the Arabs had an understanding neither of the content of philosophy nor of the Greek language, and corrupted Aristotle's ideas. However, Walch argues that even though the fate of logic was doomed among the Arabs as they barely understood Aristotle, this Arabic-Aristotelian quasi-philosophy proved useful to the Jews in Africa and Spain, who had similarly set their minds to cultivate philosophy.

According to Walch, Jewish scholars used Arabic primary and secondary sources to produce commentaries on Aristotelian philosophy that suggest an interdisciplinary learning process among Arab Muslims and Jews. Walch concludes that the Jews similarly corrupted true Aristotelian logic, as both religious groups were incapable of disentangling the highest truths of reason from the lowest judgments of their scriptural dogmatism. The Jews and the Muslims were thus incapable of grasping the fundamental Aristotelian truths in their attempts to join peripatetic philosophy with divine oracles. When the Arabs seized a large part of Africa and passed into Spain, they brought Arabic-Aristotelian philosophy to Europe and this laid the foundation for Scholasticism. According to Walch, Christian Aristotelian dialecticians proved to be the only scholars capable of preserving Aristotelian truths within their system of theology, although this line of logic presents a conundrum to the modern reader.

Walch's argument about the corruption of Aristotelian logic by Arabic and Jewish scholars, each trying to interpolate it within the bounds of their respective scriptural truths, serves to situate Arabs as the bad influence, because they laid out the shaky foundation for Scholastic philosophy, which the prominent Lutheran theologians and historians of philosophy, such as Buddeus and Brucker, also associate with Catholicism. Therefore, Walch credits Scholasticism as the system of theology and philosophy that dominated almost "the entirety of the empire of philosophy" in medieval European universities from the eleventh century until the Reformation. His overall analysis depends on two unstated assumptions. First, that Aristotelian philosophy is the highest truth; and second, that the "true" Aristotle can be preserved only within a Protestant (rational) theological framework. Given the context that Walch was himself a Lutheran theologian and philosopher, whose own mode of thinking rested on the reconciliation of 'true Aristotelian logic' with Lutheran theology, he readily associates Arabic and, by extension, Jewish philosophy with Scholasticism.

Development and Fate of Logic (Leipzig, 1721)

On the Development and Fate of Logic
  Chapter 2: Middle Ages
  Synopsis
  Section 1: Summary. Section 2: On John of Damascus, Michael Psellus, George Pachymeres, and their Logical Writings. Sections 3–4: On the Dialectic of the Arabs. Sections 5–7: That of the Jews. Sections 8–12: That of the Scholastics.[2] Sections 13–14: That of Raymond Lullius.

[In previous chapters] I have discussed the development and fate of logic in ancient times from Plato up to the sixth century. Now, let us turn to the Middle Ages, when those learned men, the Scholastics, first appeared and almost completely dominated the empire of philosophy.

But before moving on to the history of the Scholastics' logic, I think I should touch briefly upon the works that have been done in this discipline before them. [For example], John of Damascus wrote a book on dialectic in which he showed his debt to the philosophy of Aristotle. The art of logic itself, however, he hardly progressed, and did not expand upon it with his new approaches to reasoning. [...]

I would like to say a few words on the reason for the flourishing of dialectic because at this time philosophical studies appear to have been on the rise among the Arabs. Johann Peter von Ludewig sheds a very bright light on this for us. He observes that the Arabs cultivated the Greek language and that philosophy transferred from Greece to Arabia. He also mentions various men who are outstanding in their praise of dialectic. Ludewig mentions the Prince of Dialecticians, Yaʻqūb al-Kindī, about whom Abū al-Farāj says:

> Yaʻqūb, in fact, was skilled in medicine, philosophy, arithmetic, dialectic, music, geometry, and astronomy, and he composed famed books and long treatises on most of these fields. He did not spend time [solely] among the Muslims; he was a man so noted for his study of philosophy that he was named 'philosopher,' apart from the name Yaʻqūb.

He also references the slightly lesser known al-Thābit, a writer of dialectic; Matthew, the son of Yūnus, called 'the Dialectician' because of his outstanding knowledge of this art, al-Fārābī; and, not to mention the many others whom he cites, there is also Avicenna and Averroes, extremely well-known authors.

The first is Avicenna, whose name is properly written as Abū ʿAlī al-Ḥusayn ibn ʿAbd Allāh ibn Sīnā. He believed that the science of logic had been bestowed upon him divinely. Abū al-Faraj quotes him as saying:

> I spent a full year and a half diligently reading books. Every time I became confused on some question or could not find the middle term of a syllogism, I went to the mosque and poured out my prayers to the Creator of All as a suppliant until that which had been murky and hidden was revealed. Returning to my home at night, a lantern placed before me, I spent time reading and writing, and whenever sleep came upon me or I felt some weakness, I drank a proffered cup of wine until my strength came back; then I returned to reading. But if even the slightest sleep overtook me, I dreamt about those very questions, until the solutions to many of them were made known in my dreams. I did not cease from such activity until I had acquired a firm understanding of dialectics and physics.

Concerning Avicenna's writings, including his book on logic, we can read Leo Africanus, Johann Heinrich Hottinger, Pierre Daniel Huet, as well as others, whom the most famous Johann Christoph Wolf compiled.

Averroes, more properly called Ibn al-Rushd of Cordoba, was a famous philosopher and physician, who, as he was exceedingly dedicated to Aristotle, composed commentaries on his philosophical writings: *On Categories, On Interpretation, On Prior Analytics, On Posterior Analytics, Topics,* and likewise *Introduction to Porphyry.* He also wrote an introduction to Aristotle's logic, about which we can read more in Nicholas Antonius, Peter Bayle, Bartholomew Merbelotus, and Johann Heinrich Hottinger. Aside from those two, there is a reputable man, Abū Aḥmad al-Ghazālī, who also wrote on logic, which was translated into Hebrew. He also wrote *Destruction of Philosophers,* which Averroes opposed with his *Destruction of the Destruction.*

In order to clarify the development of logic among the Arabs, we must briefly discuss their philosophy. Initially, among the Arab Muslims there were Christians skilled in Greek philosophy. Over time, the obstacles that separated Muslim Arabs from this philosophy and the Greek language were overcome and they immersed themselves gladly in this literature. This first occurred under the caliph al-Ma'mūn, who was himself versed in literature, as evidenced by George Elmacin: "al-Ma'mūn learned astronomy wonderfully, as well as the stations of the winds. Even today, astronomers refer to 'the wind of al-Ma'mūn'." He treated men who were passionate about Greek philosophy with great kindness, as Johann Gravius writes:

> The caliph al-Ma'mūn, the seventh in the family of the Abbasids, was rightly renowned among the greatest princes due to his learning and his remarkable generosity to learned men. After summoning

men noteworthy for their learning from all corners of the world and buying up the most outstanding books from Greek libraries, al-Ma'mūn had them translated into Arabic. This quickly brought the liberal arts to their peak among the Arabs, who were previously more committed to arms than to literature. Because of al-Ma'mūn's vision the knowledge of ancient Greek philosophers, renown among the Greeks themselves, still survive among the Arabs.

He also ensured a great supply of books were obtained from the Greeks, and many were translated into Arabic. Thus, Leo Africanus says:

> Since there was no science written down at that time in Arabic, al-Ma'mūn, with his undying desire to understand the knowledge of the ancients, gathered together a great number of men versed in languages. From these men, he sought the names of authors and their books on the arts in Greek, Persian, Chaldean, and Egyptian. They provided him the names of many volumes. He then sent many of his closest associates to Syria, Armenia, and Egypt to buy these books. Then the good and useful ones were separated out, such as writings on medicine, physics, astronomy, music, cosmography, and annals. He placed John, the son of Mesuah, along with a great many other men, in charge of translating from the Greek, since at that time Christians studied Greek literature. He also placed Mahan and Mesuah in charge of Persian translation, including Galen's book on medicine. Afterwards, they, along with many other masters, translated all the works of Aristotle into Arabic.

So we know from Leo Africanus' account that these works of Aristotle were translated into Arabic in the time of al-Ma'mūn (820 AD).

Avicenna and Averroes, however, flourished after 1000 AD; thus, we can also gather that the glory of Greek philosophy, translated into the Arabic, was slightly diminished for these men. Even so, the Arabs were committed to the philosophy of Aristotle. They took great pains to understand, explain, and illustrate it, a fact which shows us at the same time how much they valued logic. They, of course, struggled to follow the teachings of Aristotle, especially Avicenna and Averroes, who were in fact drawn by their studies toward this philosopher—if only they had been able to follow the actual words of Aristotle! For they had an understanding neither of the content of philosophy nor of the Greek language. Because of this ignorance, they could hardly make good progress in their interpretations, which is why they corrupted the true teaching of Aristotle terribly. Caelius Rhodigius writes about Averroes:

> As to why the commentator (Averroes) so often went astray from Aristotle's own opinion, they think it is because he was born in Spain and was raised in the Arabic language. He never read the books

of Aristotle in the original Greek, but translated into a barbarian tongue, butchered, mutilated, and perverted. Therefore, he was less able to follow the author on things pertaining to higher knowledge and more complex meaning, as Aristotle was a man supremely renowned for his passion for brevity. Struggling philosophers have often failed to make sense of his terse style.

Luis Vives dolefully complained about these studies in which the Arabs followed Aristotle and brought literary philosophy to a critical point. As they chose Aristotle as their leader, they spent special effort on that aspect of philosophy which is called "logic." They were extremely careful about his words, although they struggled to understand Aristotle's real meaning. Therefore, they are called "skilled," or rather, "masters of the words of wisdom," by Johann Heinrich Hottinger and Pococke. Adam Tribbechovius, however, when he showed the major turning points in Arab philosophy, adds this:

> Based on this account of practicing philosophy, three things in particular followed: (a) that all things were engaged in their terms and fixed notions; (b) that they demonstrated everything by these definite consequences and principles; and (c) in fact weighed the things themselves on both sides with this scale of reasoning.

As they barely understood Aristotle, whose doctrine they endeavored to follow, logic fared less well in the Arabic philosophy, and they added many misleading and useless things. However, this Arabic-Aristotelian sort of philosophy did prove useful to many Jews in need in Africa and Spain, who were roused by this and set their minds to cultivating literary philosophy.

Some men wrote commentaries on divine scriptures; others gave themselves to study of the Talmud; others examined the secretive art of Kabbalah; still others put their efforts into Aristotelian philosophy (see Johann Franz Buddeus). Many documents show how diligently they were engaged in Aristotle's philosophy, since they not only translated his and the Arabs' books of philosophy into the Hebrew language, focusing on studies of his wisdom, but also expanded upon them with commentaries and glosses.

We can learn about these authors from Julius Bartoloccius, Johann Heinrich Hottinger, Johannes Buxtorf, Johann Julius Struve, Johann Franz Buddeus, and Johann Christoph Wolf, in order to touch upon these inflection points; illustrate the fate of logic among the Jews at this time; and examine them with appropriate brevity while consulting these books and authors.

Indeed, they were the first Jews who translated the logical writings of Aristotle; thus, Bartoloccius attests that these manuscripts exist: *Book* of *Categories*, translator unknown, in the Vatican Library 4; *On Inter-pretation*, anonymous translator, in the Urbinata Library 4; *Book of Analytics*, anonymous translator, in the Vatican Library 4; and *Book of Topics*, anonymous translator, in the Vatican Library 4.

As is clear from his hand-written catalog of his books, Erpenius had a four-volume *Logic of Aristotle with the introduction of Porphyry and with certain Arabic commentators, in the Hebrew language*. [Peter] Lambeck, moreover, reviewed [Sebastian] Tengnagel's book, which contains the treatise on logic by Maimonides; Porphyry's introduction to the five predicables, with Averroes' commentary; the categories of Aristotle, with Averroes' comments; the book by Abū Naṣr al-Fārābī, an Arab philosopher, on demonstrative syllogism, books 1 and 2, with Averroes' comments; all of which have been translated by Rabbi Jacob, the Spanish son of Simson of Anatolia, who lived in the thirteenth century. Maimonides does not fail to testify, in a letter to Rabbi Yehuda Aben Tibbon, that Rabbi Isaac, the son of Chonaim, translated the writings of Aristotle, although it is unknown whether or not he applied the same dedication to logical works as well.

The actual writings of Aristotle as well as Arab commentaries on Aristotle and their books on logic were translated by the Jews into their language. Maimonides translated the works of Avicenna, including his logic, into Hebrew as evidenced by the title. This appeared at Bologne as Bernard de Montfaucon bears witness. The logical writings of Averroes translated into Hebrew aim at shedding light on Aristotle, as Johann Christoph Wolf diligently records. Abū Aḥmad al-Ghazālī, the Arab philosopher, wrote a book on logic which, together with the commentaries of Rabbi Moses Narbonensis, exists as a manuscript in the Bodleian Library. The famed Wolf thinks that this work is identical with *On the Use of Logic*, a treatise for which master Vitalis Tolosanus wrote commentaries that were translated into Hebrew by Rabbi Moses ben Joshua Narbonensis. This exists in manuscript, together with scholia, in the Vatican library. Abū Naṣr al-Fārābī, considered a great philosopher among the Arabs and first championed by Maimonides, wrote a book on sophistic arguments, consisting of three parts: the first, an introduction; the second, fallacies in speech; and the third, fallacies beyond speech. This work also exists in a Hebrew manuscript in the Vatican library, as well as other libraries.

The Jews also applied their efforts to writing books on logic, which they call, *contemplating*, because they consider this activity to be contemplative. Rabbi Abraham ben Meir Ibn Ezra, who lived in the twelfth century after the birth of Christ, gained great authority not only among the Jews, but even among other people, since they name him "*par excellence*." Bartoloccius calls him "an excellent philosopher, astronomer, physician, poet, grammarian, kabbalist, and renowned translator of the Holy Scripture." His *Book of Logic* is found in manuscript form in the Vatican Library. At the end of the fifteenth century, Elias Beschitz, known as Karaeus, the son of Moses, lived in Constantinople, so he was named "the Byzantine." Wolf thinks that the *Book of Logic*, which is included in the catalog of the library of Leiden, belongs to Beschitz. Hottinger mentions that Rabbi Joseph, famous in the thirteenth century, wrote a manuscript on logic. Wolf also states that there is a commentary on ten categories of Aristotle. Rabbi Levi, the son of Gershom, who was dedicated to the philosophy of Aristotle, made various mistakes on the eternity of the world and on the natural gift of divination. Buxtorf mentions that his logic was published in Venice, and Johann Julius Struve agrees with him. Wolf states that he wrote a brief exposition on Averroes' logic, or rather, ten categories of Aristotle, books on interpretation, analytics and syllogism, which exists as a manuscript in the Urbinata Library. Buxtorf undoubtedly means by "logic published at Venice," his gloss on Averroes' commentary on Aristotle, published in four volumes at Venice in 1552.

Rabbi Moses Maimonides, who was born in Cordoba, Spain in the year 1131, accrued great praise for his genius and teachings, especially since he was studiously engaged in literary philosophy as well. Certainly, in his documents, he makes mention of Aristotle, Plato, Galen, Themistius, and others; he himself bears witness in his preface to the Mishnah that "he read through all the philosophical books." Thus, in the book which carries the inscription "by a teacher of ambiguities," he touches upon many philosophical arguments, and his book contains traces of Aristotle and the Arabs. He even teaches, in the manner of Aristotelians, that a return to the sublime knowledge of divine matters is open to no one, unless they properly train their spirit and genius in logic and metaphysics. Richard Simon makes this assertion on this teacher's philosophy:

> Rabbi Moses, with the surname 'Maimonides' or 'son of Maimon,' accrued great esteem, not only among Jews but even among Christians, who often cite in their own works one of his books, titled *Guide for the Perplexed* (*Moreh Neuochim*). The aim of this author is to clarify challenges inherent in the scriptures and to eliminate all ambiguities that occur in them. A great many Jews rebelled against his method and condemned this book, because he seemed to thwart the tradition of his people with this manner of reasoning. Indeed, Rabbi Moses was extremely eager to be considered a philosopher, and he prepared a certain selection from the writings of Aristotle and the scriptures, which is not satisfactory to every palate. His metaphysics is far too subtle, and in his exploration of the true meaning of a great many Hebrew words, he does not seem to be a skilled grammarian. Moreover, he almost always answered questions according to his own biases, which are in accordance at every

point with the lessons of the religion which he professes. But he was also often influenced by the opinion of the Arab philosophers, whose books he had read.

Among other things, he also wrote a book on *Logic*, which is divided into fourteen chapters and exists in manuscript form in the Vatican library. His compendium, *A Work of Logic*, was also found there by Rabbi Moses ben Tibbon, who lived in 1270, as Bartoloccius attests. This logical compendium is also included in the library of Vienna, as we have learned from Nesselius. There also exists a work titled *On Logical Distinctions*, which is attributed to Maimonides, including two commentaries, both anonymous, published at Venice in 1550, and Cremona in 1550 and 1564.

Bartoloccius distinguishes this last book, *On Logical Distinctions*, from that *Logic* and *Compendium of Logic*. But Wolf rightly suspects that it is one and the same book, because that was also separated into fourteen chapters, from which that *Logic* is said to be drawn. Buxtorf, Hottinger, and Struve mention the *Logic* of Rabbi Schimeon, which was translated into Latin and expanded with vocalic points by [Sebastian] Münster, and printed at Basel by Frobenius in 1527. But Richard Simon proves that this *Logic* belongs to Maimonides, which Wolf also notes.

This should be sufficient proof that everything here indicates that Aristotle enjoyed great authority among the Jewish people. But the fate of Aristotelian logic was less fortunate because they followed the Arabs who had a poor understanding of him and mixed reason with their holy texts and traditions—the highest with the lowest. Indeed, the Jews were also influenced by the Arabs' corrupt dispositions, which produced vile judgments. Maimonides demonstrates with his own example how unfavorably at times they joined Peripatetic philosophy with their divine oracles. In Exodus 24:10, Moses says: "Indeed, it was under His feet, like a work of the whiteness of a stone of sapphire." Maimonides interprets these words based on the Aristotelian concept of the first substance:

> Therefore, I say that 'under His feet' is the same as 'on His account, that is, by Him and because of Him,' as we explained. What they understood was the first substance itself, which is a blessing from God, and for which He is the efficient cause. We must observe what Moses says, 'like a work of the whiteness of a stone of sapphire.' If he had wanted to indicate the color or external appearance, he would have simply said, 'like the whiteness of sapphire.' But he adds 'like a work,' because a substance, as you know, always takes its form from its nature and bears it; but it never acts unless by accident, just as the form always acts through itself; and it never bears it unless by accident, in the manner in which they are explained in the books of physics.

According to this method of applying philosophy, we can easily determine the outcome of their logic, which relies upon the use of human reason, a firm and singular foundation. There is no reason to discuss here what the Jews call 'Talmudic logic,' which would have led to a truer assessment of these books had they used it. But we can reference Johann Heinrich Hottinger and Johann Julius Struve, whose *Basics of Jewish Logic* lay out a method of debating the Talmud, primarily from the book, *Halichos Olam*.

Because the Saracens, an Arab people, had seized a large part of Africa and had moved into Spain, they introduced Arabic-Aristotelian philosophy to Europe and laid out the foundation of Scholastic philosophy. There are three divisions of Scholastics. The first originated with Rucelinus, or as others think, with Peter Lombard, and extends up to the time of Albert the Great, whose floruit was around the middle of the thirteenth century. The second age goes from Albert the Great to Durand de St. Pourçain, that is, the beginning of the fourteenth century. In the second [age of Scholastics], Thomas Aquinas and John Duns Scotus, in particular, gained fame. The third age, which lasted up until the Reformation of Christian doctrine, produced the philosophy of William of Ockham and Gabriel Biel. Daneau first established these ages, which Alsted and Jakob Thomasius followed. Alsted observes that, if we trace the history of the Scholastics from Rucelinus, from 1094 to the Reformation, this Scholastic doctrine encompasses almost four and a quarter centuries. However, this must be dated differently for those who mark the origin of Scholastic theology from Lanfranc—a man who preceded Abelard, the student of Rucelinus, by a full century. Nor is there any agreement on the ages of Scholastics and especially not on the origin of Scholastic philosophy and theology or its creator. Some men grant this glory to Lanfranc; others, including Adam Tribbechovius, attribute it to Peter Lombard; others to Abelard, and still others to Rucelinus. Jakob Thomasius thinks that Rucelinus is the founder of Scholastic philosophy, but that Abelard is the founder of Scholastic theology, although his student, Peter Lombard, became more famous than his teacher Abelard. It is challenging to lay out this controversy and to form a definitive opinion, since the question which they argue about can be considered from different angles. If we examine the title and the word 'scholastic,' it was already frequently used in the Middle Ages. Scholastic used to refer to many who excelled in *belles-lettres* and arts; later, it was used to refer to a man who performed the duties of a teacher and professor. This sort of person was considered to be a light to the learned world at that time, as Christoph August Heumann observes. But let us focus entirely on the debate between the philosophy and the theology of the Scholastics. Regarding the philosophy [of the Scholastics], we should look at how it was nurtured by the Arabs. When it comes to theology [of the Scholastics], however, we should look at the first studies in which Arabs publicly professed Scholasticism and more importantly, how the Arabs connected a weak, dry, useless, even wicked philosophy to it. The first to do so cannot be easily determined due to the lack of historical documents. But who was the first to treat this genre of literature, specifically, that of theology, with such singular zeal and success that he gave it his own famous name? It seems that Lombard deserves that glory, as he was easily able to snatch fame from his teacher Abelard, who had been under suspicion of holding "heretical opinions."

In order to understand the dialectics of Scholastics, we must first mention and describe the authors who engaged in this discipline, and then provide a proper account of Scholastic dialectic. Therefore, the following were engaged in philosophy, including in dialectics. [First, let's look at] Rucelinus, who other authors call Roscelinus, and Henry of Ghent calls Ruzcelmus, which Jakob Thomasius thinks to be more correct. He is the founder of the nominal doctrine in Aristotelian logic. Hence Otto of Freising says: "Abelard had a certain teacher Rozelini who was the first in our times to establish an opinion on terms in logic." By "an opinion on terms," he means the doctrine of nominals; there are also verses known on Rucelinus' doctrine, which can be found in Aventinus:

> Quas Ruceline doces, non vult dialectica voces,
> Iamque, docens de se, non vult in vocibus esse,
> Res amat, in rebus cunctis vult esse diebus.

Peter Abelard, the student of Rucelinus, was famous for his philosophy. Thus, John of Salisbury constantly calls him "The Peripatetic of the Palatine," since he followed Aristotle and taught on Mont-Ste.-Genevieve (Mt. Genovefa), where there was a noteworthy palace. Abelard also cultivated dialectic, for which he was called "the Dialectician," as Hornius states. The aforementioned Thomasius wrote Abelard's biography.

Albert the Great had been extremely devoted to Aristotelian philosophy, such that he was called "Aristotle's Monkey." Thus, Langius says: "Because of the quantity of his polymath doctrine, he was called the Great; he was extremely skilled in the entirety of Peripatetic philosophy. However, a great many called him Aristotle's Monkey, as he was a man who, being too drunk on the wine of secular science, dared to couple human wisdom with divine letters. He was not afraid to mix argumentative, thorny, and talkative dialectic with the most sacred and pure theology, providing new and philosophical ways of teaching and explaining sacred letters to his followers. He was an outstanding general and monarch for the school of theologians, who are called 'Albertists' in his honor." This Albert wrote commentaries on all the books, which encompass Aristotle's *Organon*, "in which he demonstrates a great skill in logic," according to Bartholomew Keckermann.

Thomas Aquinas is bestowed with great, almost divine praises from those who practice philosophy and theology. He is called "the angelic doctor, more than Solomon, an interpreter of divine will, the morning light, like a full moon in his wisdom and customs, and like a rising sun to the world." He wrote commentaries on the entire *Organon* of Aristotle, as well as a logical summation on four opposites, demonstration, fallacies, modals, the nature of classification, the nature of accident, and the nature of syllogism. Keckermann says that men who read the fiery genius of Aquinas with discernment will know how much his commentaries contributed to the art of logic. Furthermore, according to René Rapin, Aquinas was the first to create a method of studying Arabic philosophy.

Notes

1 Walch's biography was compiled from the following sources: Johann Heinrich Zedler (ed.), "Walch (Johann Georg)," in *Grosses vollständiges Universal-Lexicon aller Wissenschafften und Künste*, vol. 52 (Leipzig, 1747), 1108–25; Paul Tschackert, "Walch, Johann Georg," in *Allgemeine Deutsche Biographie*, vol. 40 (Leipzig, 1896), 650–2; Christoph Schmitt, "Johann Georg Walch," in *Biographisch-Bibliographisches Kirchenlexikon*, vol. 13, ed. Friedrich W. Bautz (Herzberg: Traugott Bautz, 1998), 183–6; Gerald MacDonald, "Die Religion derer Reformierten. Das Bild der reformierten Kirche in der lutherischen Spätorthodoxie am Beispiel Johann Georg Walchs (1693–1775)," in *Reformierter Protestantismus vor den Herausforderungen der Neuzeit*, eds. Thomas K. Kuhn and Hans-Georg Ulrichs (Wuppertal: Foedus, 2008), 197–207; and Manfred Kuehn, "Walch, Johann Georg," in *The Bloomsbury Dictionary of Eighteenth-Century German Philosophers*, eds. Heiner F. Klemme and Manfred Kuehn (London: Bloomsbury, 2010), 829–30.
2 [MK] Please note that the translation ends with the Section 9.

9   Inaugural Speech on Turkish Philosophy

Samuel Schelwig

Samuel Schelwig was born in 1643 in Lissa, now Leszno in western Poland. He was the son of a preacher man and studied at Breslau and Wittenberg. In 1663, he earned a Master of Philosophy and became a preacher at Wittenberg Castle Church (All Saints' Church). In 1667, he served as an adjunct professor in the Faculty of Philosophy at Wittenberg. In 1673, he was appointed a professor of philosophy at Danzig (modern Gdansk, Poland), where he taught classes on philosophy, logic, metaphysics, ethics, and economics. In 1675, he became a professor of theology, and in 1681, Schelwig ceased to give lectures on philosophy and concentrated solely on theology. After receiving his doctorate degree in theology in 1685 from the University of Wittenberg, he was appointed rector of the prestigious Danzig Academy, where he held the position until 1715. As a proponent of Lutheran orthodoxy, Schelwig prevented a more Pietist influence in the curriculum at Danzig Academy. Also, in 1693, he began a dispute with a colleague, Konstantin Schütz, accusing him of speaking in favor of Pietism. This controversy resulted in several polemical writings being published back and forth, and continued for years, drawing the intervention of the town council. Schelwig also engaged in conflict with the well-known leader of Pietists, Philipp Jacob Spener, and made a journey across northern Germany to defend orthodox Lutheranism against Pietism. Schelwig's experiences with Pietists resulted in three influential works: *Itinerarium Antipietisticum* (1695), followed by his most comprehensive anti-pietistic tract, *Die sektiererische Pietisterei* (1696–97), and then *Synopsis controversariarum sub pietatis praetextu motarum* (1701–2). He married twice and had a total of twelve children, three of whom reached maturity. He died in Danzig in 1715.[1]

Variant Names: Samuel Schelwigius, Samuel Schelgvig, Samuel Schelwigen, Samuel Schelguigius, Sam. Schelgvigius, and Samuele Schelguigio

Summary and Analysis

Schelwig begins his *oratio* by celebrating the recent Ottoman defeat at Vienna, saying that he intends to contribute to the fight against the "Turkish Hannibal" by attacking the Turks using his own field of expertise—philosophy. After a short and unfavorable assessment of the Turkish attitude toward philosophy compared to that of other major civilizations, Schelwig outlines the Turkish system of higher learning, beginning with grammar and continuing through rhetoric, dialectic, and philosophy, and ending with theology and jurisprudence. He asserts that the Turks are deficient in areas like music and history-writing and suggests that their alleged deficiency in logic goes back to a ban by Muhammad, who did not want his doctrine to be undermined. He then gives a cursory and dismissive assessment of Turkish metaphysics, pneumatics, and physics, citing many bizarre assertions on the nature of the universe and supernatural beings from the Qur'an, and suggesting that anything that seems philosophically sound is borrowed from Christian or Greek philosophy. Schelwig claims that the Turks were discouraged from learning mathematics by the teachings of Muhammad, their only knowledge of the discipline being borrowed from the Christians for sailing and torture, or for fortifying their cities and fortresses. He does, however, concede that the Turks achieved some things in practical philosophy, yet are not capable of theoretical philosophy. That is why, for Schelwig, the Turks are interested more in the table and cup that they see than the tableness and cupness that they do not see. He perceived Turks as people who can point out the concrete features present in reality, yet lack the theoretical mind to consider the abstract ideas that relate to reality in the way that Lutheran philosophers can.

Schelwig thinks that Turks' inability to understand theoretical philosophy is reflected in their sensuous view of heaven. He acknowledges that some of the 'finer minds' dismiss these tales as allegory, but thinks the majority of Turks believes these tales to be literally true. He then describes the five daily prayers of Islam, after which he enumerates the many things that Muslims swear oaths by to avoid swearing by the name of God. Schelwig is far more admiring of Islamic ethical practices relating to judicial testimony, business dealings, and charity. He does, however, condemn the apparent Turkish tolerance of sodomy. A description of Islamic hygienic practices follows, but Schelwig dismisses a common fable about alcohol's prohibition as too foolish to recount. He describes the Turks' kindness to animals and their refusal to kill even insects and lice while on the pilgrimage to Mecca and Medina, but claims that they do not extend this kindness to humankind, especially Christians.

Schelwig turns then to a discussion of Turkish practical philosophy which he divides into political and economic philosophy. On Turkish political philosophy, Schelwig attributes the Turks' submission to their rulers—even tyrannical ones—to the Qur'an's injunction about obedience. He also claims that the Turks view wars against the infidel as an obligation and outlines the teachings and policies of Muhammad that led to a highly militarized Islamic society. A description of how the spoils of war are divided gives way to an outline of the rules of inheritance and power dynamics in Islamic society. He notes that the Ottoman sultan tends to ignore these customs to appropriate the riches of the wealthy, and he describes the traditional punishments for murder, adultery, theft, false accusations and drunkenness. Schelwig then discusses Turkish economics (i.e., household management), outlining the Islamic rules concerning marriage, including the number of spouses allowed to a man, modest dress, proper sexual behavior, divorce, remarriage, and the duties of parents and children toward one another. He also touches on Islamic property laws as they relate to familial relations and explains that the goal among the Turks is to increase the family fortune.

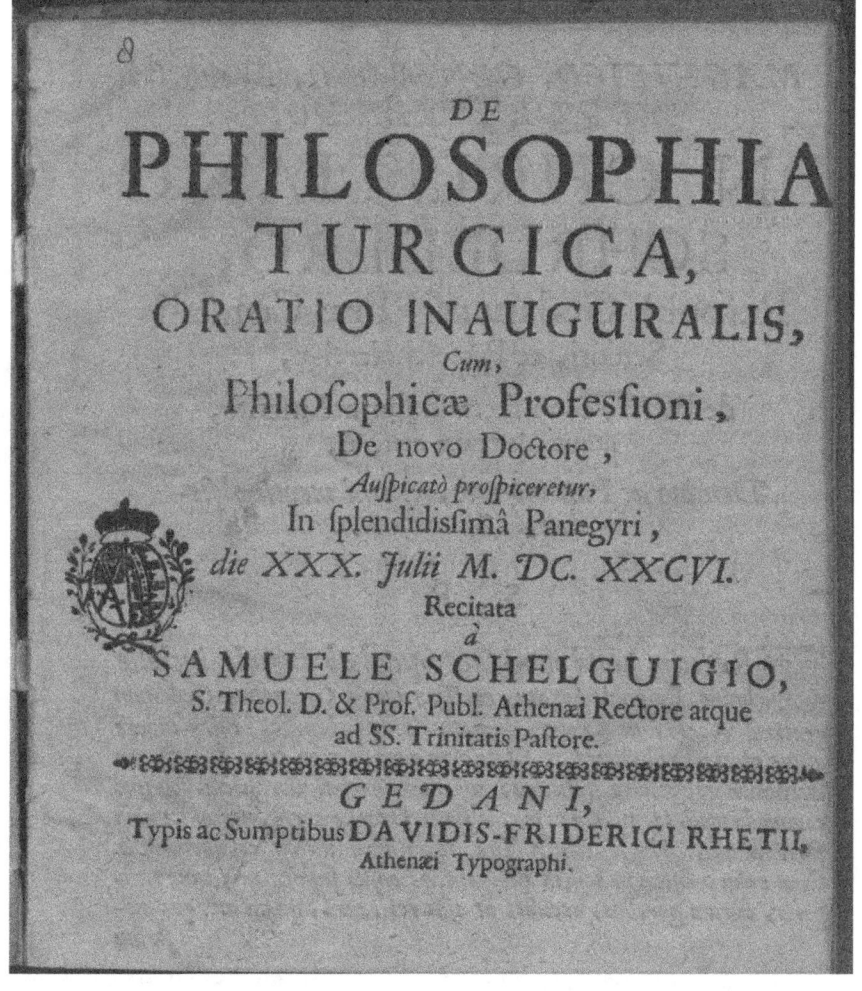

Figure 9.1 Samuel Schelwig, *De philosophia Turcica, oratio inauguralis*, 1686 (Courtesy of the Staats- und Universitätsbibliothek Dresden).

It is significant to note that despite Schelwig's negative portrayal of Turkish philosophy he still shows awareness of early modern Islamic philosophy and acknowledges that the Turks made important contributions to grammar, rhetoric, and dialectic. Paradoxically, he finds this surprising given Muhammad's discrediting of logic as it lends itself to argumentation and critique of the religion. Although Schelwig sets out to present an account of Turkish philosophical developments, he only does so with the intent of discrediting Islamic practices and teachings to differentiate Protestant Europe from its Islamic counterparts.

Another significant point Schelwig makes is about Sufism as he positions himself against mysticism by comparing Muslim Sufi dervish groups to Catholic Jesuits. He condemns both Muslim mystics and Jesuits as being involved in politics where they do not belong because, for Lutherans, religion and politics cannot mix. By comparing Sufis to Jesuits, Schelwig kills two birds with one stone: extending his negative appraisal to Pietism as well as Catholicism. He also compares theological and legal Islamic schools to Scholastic/Catholic philosophical theology movements by calling Ash'arite and Shafi'ite schools Realists, while calling the Mu'tazilite school Nominalists. Schelwig uses the Ottoman Turks as a foil to construct his own identity through his criticism of Islamic philosophy and mysticism.

Inaugural Speech on Turkish Philosophy (Danzig, 1686)

In the Name of Jesus,

S.R. Majestatis, the most outstanding Burggrab, the glorious, most noble, most insightful, most wonderful, quite worshipful, most excellent, most famous, most notable, most humane men, the masters, patrons, sponsors, colleagues, hosts, and friends, who should be honored and cherished with due observance, and you, the future of the country, the most flourishing crown of the citizens of this Athenaeum:

The Turkish Hannibal is no longer before the gates of Christendom. By a twist of fate, he [the Ottoman Sultan] was stricken by a terrible defeat near Vienna thanks to the virtue of our most invincible King and Lord, John III, and the allied Princes, especially the Elector of Saxony. The Turkish Grand Vizier sought aid from his weakened infantry, as he was being pressed by the conquering troops—Germans on one side, Venetians on the other. The Sarmatians and Roxolani joined with us in a most favorable treaty and armed alliance against the common defiler of the Christian world. We beseech God Almighty with worshipful entreaties and prayers that they may make the Turks' victory doubtful in the battles to come. That insatiable plunderer of all nations is finally vomiting forth what he has unjustly devoured over the course of so many centuries. Let him belch forth his half-eaten provinces. However, many have submitted to the yoke of the treacherous Muhammad; since they were forced to do so against their will, let them become subject instead to our God and Savior. Let our most merciful King, surrounded by an angelic guard, increase the glory of his name, long ago established by daring deeds and the wise administration of affairs in peace and war. Let him go after Camenecius (Kamianets-Podilskyi) has been recovered, after the Tatars have been bested and overturned, after the Moldavians and Wallachians have been freed from slavery, after the Danube has been made secure, after Constantinople has been cowed, let him return, victorious and triumphant. What shall we do in the meantime? Or how shall we explain the division of our labor? Once, when King Philip of Macedon was said to be setting out with his army, all the Corinthians were hard at work: some furnished weapons, others built up walls, each worked on his own task, which was intended to hold back the enemy. When Diogenes the Cynic saw this, as no one would make use of his counsel, he girded himself in his cloak and rolled the barrel in which he lived up and down through the Craneus (this was the name of the gymnasium in Corinth) with great dedication. When he was asked by one of his friends why he was doing that, he said, "I keep working with my barrel so that, with so many people engaged in work, I will not be the only one caught doing nothing."

Therefore, it is certainly not permitted for us to be lazy when our most merciful King and so many other heroes among Christians are engaged in this single mission: that the Turk be sought out, attacked, and wiped out. But truly, you should mind well this warning, which many a man offered wisely: "Whatever skill someone knows, he must practice it." I shall not hurl wood with catapults, nor rocks with ballistae; I shall neither strike walls by driving a ram, nor shall I drive a scythed chariot, nor shall I equip my head with a helmet. Let those things which the divine will has purposed for others be alien to me. I will also abstain from those other weapons, creations of modern times, which were unknown to our ancestors. Because I do not know their names precisely when I describe wartime matters, I must be satisfied with the terminology that I learned from reading Vegetius, Frontinus, Aelian, and other authors of martial affairs. Nevertheless, I shall attempt to achieve greater and more useful things than Diogenes. It is my intention to attack those Turks clad in togas [the philosophers], using my pen as a spear. Therefore, I make for the battlefield—unarmed against the unarmed. I have delved into Turkish Philosophy over the span of a few days, so that I may praise virtue in the enemy wherever possible, but also critique their foolish and pointless doctrines, which are most widespread although they are easily refuted. While I strive to do this, I seek no more effort from you, my patrons, sponsors, friends, most honored and cherished men of all orders, than I hope—nay, than I promise to myself.

Among the barbarians, philosophy once thrived and historians say that they first endowed the Greeks with wisdom. Tatian the Assyrian, a Christian of gentile origins, speaks boldly: "O Greeks, it does not befit you to pursue the barbarians with hatred and to begrudge their principles. For did not your scholarship start with the barbarians?" The Assyrian and Babylonian astrologers, known as Chaldaeans, ought to be mentioned alongside Egyptian priests, Persian magi, Indian gymnosophists, Celtic druids and bards, and Bactrian śramaṇas; many Greeks went to these people to benefit from their learning. Even now, various schools of philosophers in the expansive Chinese Empire teach wisdom. The foremost follows Confucius, "the Socrates of China" as he is called by Christians, because he was believed to flourish at the same time as Socrates and because, like Socrates, Confucius first cultivated a doctrine of morality. Certainly, the authority of that man is no less among his followers in the East than that of Plato and Aristotle in the West. Likewise, among the Muslims, philosophy finds many students, and some have met with great success. The Moors of Africa brought Averroes into Spain. He deserves to be hailed as the Commentator of Aristotle for the books he published, which adroitly illuminated the mind of Aristotle. Arabia has produced many wise mystics, who are known as the loquacious speakers (*mutakallim*, theologians), since they argue with 'great subtlety.' Ibn Furak and al-Shahrastānī stood out above the rest. Even now, the Persians incorporate astronomy into their poetry, and the observers of the stars, the *minatzim* [*munajjim*], are held in high regard by their King and Princes.

Perhaps what I have said about Turkish philosophy will be thought blasphemous. Who are those men and what sort are they? If we look at their name, 'Turk' or 'Turkish' indicates a crude and rustic person. Thus, they are so ashamed of this name that they prefer 'Muslim,' or 'Musulman,' meaning 'saved' or 'believing.' Nevertheless, their nature and customs, which trace their beginnings back to the ancient Turks, do not depart even a finger's breadth from their crude and rustic origins. Since the Turks are thought unfit for conducting affairs, apostates and the children of apostates, those born of Christian ancestors, are entrusted with most important offices. Therefore, why should we think nothing useful can be created from such base material? The Turkish hatred of literature has its origins with the birth of Islam. Under the influence of the caliph 'Umar, the Turks only valued the Qur'an. The caliph sought out all manner of books and sent everything he acquired to the baths to be burnt; they provided heat for half a year. Lest anyone believe that the Turks' attitude has changed since that time, let us pay heed to the observations that Wenceslaus Baro of Budowa made during his many years of travel. He found kindlier fates among the barbarians than he did at home among his own people. As an eyewitness, it would be wrong to question his trustworthiness. He left this testament to his children: "I myself have heard from others that Turks cannot understand what is in the Qur'an since it is prohibited to translate it into Turkish, except for a few compilations, which contain some of their prayers and rituals." And in another passage, he continues: "The Turks learn nothing except to read and write, but only a few of them, for they mock scholarship and all books, both those of their countrymen and of others." Hence, the Turks who wish to apply themselves to scholarship 'occur seldom, swimming in a great void,' compared to all the others who, like cattle who follow their bellies, spend their lives in silence. Nevertheless, even in Turkey itself, schools are fostered, even good ones, which Solomon Schweigger in his *Itinerary* has not hesitated to call 'academies.' Lest someone think that Schweigger misapplied that word, he accurately describes the advances that the Turks make in their studies. For if, as is fair, we trust Schweigger's account, a Turkish student who is skilled in reading and writing is called *suhte* or *softa* in their own language. If the student is capable, he is placed in the higher College and learns Persian, Arabic, and Turkish grammar. They divide this curriculum, over twenty volumes, into etymology and syntax, of which the first is called *ṣarf*, the latter *naḥw*. Dialectic, or *manṭiq*, follows grammar, so that it is possible for us to have [philosophical] discourse with them. After this, they study six books on *kalām*, by which they mean rhetoric and philosophy. After this course of study is completed, whoever has excelled is called a *Talisman*—that is, a Master of Arts. Then, if the student has loftier ambitions, he advances to the high college of theology and jurisprudence, which is called *medrese*. The only thing missing is medicine, which the Turks tend to relegate from the schools to barbershops and apothecaries to their detriment. Georg Christoph of Neitzschiz, who spent seven full years on an Eastern journey, agrees with Schweigger's testimony. Christoph counted five schools of this sort at Constantinople, in which each teacher has his own quarters. In the first year, two garments and two small loaves of bread are provided for everyone, with barley-water for drinking. In the second year, there is a daily allowance of one *asper*, which is a type of coin, and it increases to two in the third year. If anyone wants to live more lavishly, he must provide it himself, or earn it with the scribe's pen. According to Stephan Gerlach, there were five *müderris*, or professors, teaching at the school in Constantinople, near the Temple of Suleyman. In another school, which Sultan Bayezid had founded, the *Muftī*, the highest priest in Turkey, taught. But he also says that the payment of professors does not exceed seventy *aspri* per day, and many receive less. Michael Heberer observed a school at Pera, or Galata, which is a suburb of Constantinople across the Bosphorus, in which around 500 youths were trained under various masters, dressed in silken clothing. Therefore, it is quite clear that Apollo is not entirely exiled from Constantinople. We have been able to find few things about the academies of other cities. Johann Boehme, author of *The Customs of Peoples*, says that he visited many grand gymnasia among the Turks, but he does not provide much detail. Yet we learn from him that some gymnasia may be found [outside Constantinople], because Lazarus Soranzius writes that when Mehmed III, tyrant of the Turks, was still a youth and had surrendered Manisa at the order of his father, he slaughtered 2,000 students for a trifling cause.

Since it is clear that at least some men in the massive empire of the Turks apply themselves to scholarship, let us consider what sorts of disciplines or to what end they commit themselves. Certainly, their false Prophet ordered them to stay away from poetry, just as Plato once cast the poets out of his *Republic*. In the Qur'an, it is utterly forbidden to compose poems with such ferocity that poets are condemned to the kingdom and power of devils until they cease lying or practicing their art. Nevertheless, I recall, last year, when I was at Leipzig studying daily with the most learned men with which that famous Academy abounds by the grace of God, that I saw a small Turkish book filled with erotic poems in the library of my old friend, August Pfeiffer, a man most gifted in Eastern languages. Thus, it is evident that some men, through poetic license, as they call it, broke the laws of their own religion and followed their hearts rather than the Qur'an. A passion for annalistic history and chronicles is almost nonexistent among the Turks. To quote Ogier Ghiselin de Busbecq:

> The Turks have no sense of time or age, and they mix up and confuse all their histories in a strange way. For instance, they will not hesitate to declare that Job was the head of court for King Solomon, that Alexander the Great was in charge of his army, or things even more ridiculous than these.

There are other examples, and many more appear in the Qur'an, which we would discuss here if there was not a danger that it would soon become unbearable.

Therefore, we now move to the 'instrumental disciplines' of philosophy: grammar, rhetoric, and logic, which are offered to students in Turkey, but not to an advanced level, as we have proven with absolutely trustworthy evidence. The Turks study logic despite the fact that Muhammad wanted the practice of logic, which is particularly useful in argumentation, to be alien to his followers. For hardly anything is attacked more frequently in the Qur'an than logic. In the first place is that lovely law: "If anyone wants to argue, order him to hold his tongue until the day of final judgment, when God will settle all scores." Guillaume Postel offers the reason for the ban, saying that the Impostor "frightens his followers so that they do not look into his doctrine and his deceit does not reveal itself." According to Postel,

> Muhammad says, 'Do not confuse true with false, cover up and hide what is true and you will be wise.' Muhammad reveals himself

plainly here when he enjoins them to hide from what is true, which is what he did, casting forth all the most untrue things.

I cannot pass over a few cunning remarks which Muhammad included in his Qur'an. Unless I am mistaken, Muhammad seemed to be a logician—that is, to argue with himself. The question was: "What flame eats and drinks, and if it is snuffed out once, cannot be kindled and restored until the Day of Judgment?" The answer is the natural fire in the human body—of course, it is maintained by eating and drinking but is not restored after death, unless a chain is fashioned between body and soul in the resurrection of the dead. Another laughable question was: "what two things are such that one of them is always large and the other is always small?" The answer is that pebbles are never not small, and mountains are never not large. Another question was: "what moisture takes its origin neither from the sky nor from the land?" The answer is the sweat of animals worn out by effort. Another question: "how large is the universe?" The answer is that the universe does not surpass one-day's journey, for from the sunrise in the morning until the sun sets in the evening, the sun goes around that far every day. I have chosen these examples out of many to illustrate the skill in argumentation with which the Turks would attack us if the opportunity presented itself to them. I purposely exclude the remaining question, which cannot pique our longing unless for those born in the land of wethers and under the thick air.

So, with mouths open and hindrances banished, we can now examine the heart of Turkish philosophy. To begin, we will keep the order that is customary in our schools; we will examine theoretical philosophy first, including metaphysics, pneumatics, physics, and mathematics, and then practical philosophy. As for metaphysics, the Turks are more often considered to have the table and cup that they see concretely than the 'tableness' and 'cupness' that they do not see. Diogenes once used this example to mock Plato and his concept of ideas; but Plato offered a response, which fits the Turks no less than the Cynic: he has eyes, with which the table and cup are seen but he does not have a mind, with which the 'tableness' and 'cupness' are seen. Nevertheless, traces of metaphysics are evident in the excerpt from the small Turkish book of 'Azīz Nasafī the Tatar, which Andreas Müller, the steward of Eastern Obscurities, particularly Chinese, published by the Library of the Elector of Brandenburg; and they are obvious to someone who is researching a little more carefully. Otherwise, how would we know what they say about essence and attributes?

Some think that essence and attribute more properly belong to pneumatics, which our contemporaries consider to be its own discipline, different from metaphysics. In fact, the essence and attribute are connected to God insofar as He is the chief object of pneumatics, which

'Azīz Nasafī proposes in his praiseworthy little work, using these words: "The attributes of God are the essence of God, in their own way; and His works are His life, in their own way; His names are His appearance, in their own way." A little later, Nasafī writes: "The attributes, indications, and comparisons of God are in fact His essence, because there is no existence without essence." In his *Commentary* on this question, Müller states that Muslims pose the following question: "Do the attributes of God differ from His essence?" The Ash'arite and Shafi'ite affirm this, but the Mutazilite deny this. So, the same sects that have risen in the West among the Scholastics have also risen in the East. For those Scholastics who share the former [Ash'arite and Shafi'ite] opinion are called *Realists*, while those who share the latter [Mu'tazilite] opinion are called *Nominalists*. Moreover, we approve of what is in the Qur'an concerning God's omnipotence, omniscience, justice, the creation of the universe, and that God is recognized from the creation and preservation of the things that He made. On the other hand, we disapprove of anything that describes God as finite and limited in place, or, what we despise above all else, "as the Creator of sin." The False Prophet speaks appropriately at times about Providence; but he errs because he pulls Stoic Fate from the pits of Hell. The reason is because this belief [i.e., belief in fate] bolsters martial resilience, when those who go to war think of the end of life as prescribed, to the year, month, day, hour, instance, such that it cannot be avoided, nor adjusted, nor changed for any reason. God is followed by the angels, whose division into good and evil the Turks recognize as we do. But in other matters, they prattle about trivialities, ridiculously and childishly, arguing that angels are corporeal and that they engage in forbidden congress with women; that they surpass the world a thousand times in size, and have 70,000 heads, and 70,000 tongues in each mouth; and that they die before the final judgment. The argument that the angels are divided into 70,000 armies and that each army consists of 5,000 angels is nothing but the product of Muhammad's imagination. As for the soul, they think that if it is separated in infancy from the body it is polluted with sin; then it becomes a spirit, which they call a *jinn*.

Now we move onto a discussion of physics. The Muslims have few reasonable men among their ranks, and come up with the most horrendous opinions. Muslims count up seven heavens, the first of which is of green water, the second of pure water, the third of emerald, the fourth of gold, the fifth of hyacinth, the sixth of extremely calm clouds, the seventh of lightning bolts. The Muslims also tell lies about heavens of smoke; they say that this smoke traces its origins to sea-mist and is enclosed in golden gates. They likewise teach nonsense about the stars, saying that they are bound to heaven by shackles and meddle in earthly affairs; devils lie in wait to interfere with heavenly matters; the sun and moon have souls and are faithful to God; and the moon shines more dully than the Sun because the angel Gabriel struck it with his wings as he was flying past. Nasafī rightly establishes that man is the micro-cosm, but it seems that he took that from Christian books, unless he took it from Pythagoras, who spoke in a similar fashion. Nasafī recog-nizes three souls in man: the vegetative; the sensitive; and the animal, by which, if he means "rational," he agrees with Christians in this regard completely. Gerlach says that, according to the Turks, Man is more pow-erful than angel, such that angel served Man and is only of spirit, while Man shares in both a bodily and spiritual nature at the same time. Con-cerning the origin and qualities of Man, the Qur'an says the following: the embryo awaits the seed for forty days, assumes the color of blood for forty days, gains flesh over another forty days, and finally is completed over the remaining forty days, and is endowed with life by an angel breathing a soul into it.

The variation in face and skin color comes from the fact that God first fashioned man out of dust of various colors that were chosen deliberately; women are weaker than men because God fashioned Eve from a rib on the left side; for if it had been otherwise, because of the perfection of the right side, there would have been no lapse in willpower from Adam; children sometimes are more like their father, other times more like their mother, according to how one or the other engaged in the conjugal acts with greater desire and pleasure. If we turn to the same pandect of van-ity concerning the origins and nature of beasts, we shall hear that the pig and the mouse came from elephant dung, and the cat from the sneeze of a lion, a completely Ovidian metamorphosis. The donkey bent its knee out of respect toward a young Muhammad, and spoke in a human voice like the donkey of Balaam; an elephant had done the same thing previously before Muhammad's grandfather, 'Abd al-Muṭṭalib. Strange that the elephant did not also dance in this tale! Among the birds, the hoopoe assumed the duty of an ambassadorship, from Solomon to the Queen of Sheba, and executed it faithfully; and ants warned each other to flee, lest they be trampled by Solomon, who understood the languages of all beasts. "In saying such things, who/of the Myrmidons or Dolopes, or a soldier under tough Ulysses/would refrain from laughing?" There remain a great many fever dreams: the world rests upon a fish; another world may be found under this world; that within the seventh sphere of the world, there is a bull armed with forty horns, whose head extends to the East and its tail to the West, and from one horn to another there is a distance of a thousand-day's journey; and Death will finally be changed into a goat and killed for its arrogance. We have taken these things from the part of the Qur'an which the Turks treat with the greatest honor of all. Since the Turks consider truth irrelevant, preferring instead the most tasteless myths, they prove that saying of Martial's: "it has not been granted to everyone to have a nose."

Let us examine a few little blossoms from other authors. It is, of course, delightful that, just as the pagans once argued that the rose came from the blood of Venus, the Turks say that it came from the sweat of Muhammad, and thus they do not allow a single one of its petals to lie on the earth. They absurdly claim that the motion of the world arises because it rests upon columns which are turned about by a cow. They nonsensically describe the ascent to heavenly paradise as one hundred steps, the first of which is of silver, the second of gold, the third of hyacinth, coal, pearl, and so on. They also believe that certain women become pregnant after long speeches and constant bodily action; and they bear children whom they call *Nefes oğlu*, that is, "the offspring of the Spirit." Unlike Christians, Muslims keep dogs out of the house, considering them foul and unclean animals, and adopt cats instead, as they are thought to be much cleaner and are treated with a certain reverence. Muhammad held cats in such esteem that, when one had fallen asleep on his shirtsleeves and he had to attend to a pressing holy matter, he preferred to cut off his sleeve than to disturb the sleep of his most beloved animal. We pass over other trifles with a dry foot, as they say, lest a lack of time forces us to leave the other parts of philosophy untouched, particularly those in which the Turks are somewhat more skilled.

Therefore, we must speak now about mathematics. Few among the Turks have knowledge of this, except for certain Apostates who rely upon knowledge taken from Christians for sailing and siegecraft, or for fortifying their fortresses and cities. Muhammad has frightened the rest of them away from this discipline that otherwise delights humanity with such great joy and usefulness. Muhammad equated mathematicians to morons, just as the Roman emperors once equated them to witches.

But in practical philosophy, to which our discussion now turns, we admit that the Turks are not altogether blind. One must hope that one always lives according to the precepts of philosophy. But oh! This is the thing; many tears arise from here, because the advice of the Poet [Persius] is also ignored among Christians at every turn: "It is trivial to talk about virtue; to live according to virtue, that is work, that is effort!"

Let us now talk about Turkish political and economic ethics. They philosophize on the Highest Good, which exists beyond the slime commonly attributed to Epicurus. By acting in accordance with the Qur'an, they aim for paradise, which abounds with all sorts of pleasures more appropriate for Sardanapalus or Elagabalus rather than blessed minds. They believe that they will occupy houses roofed in silver; lie on couches of gold; lie on sofas and carpets fashioned from silk; walk clad in the most costly clothing and jewelry; abound in wealth and various trappings of pleasure; refresh themselves with supremely sweet springs and waters that run year round; feast upon the liver of the fine fish, Albehut or Alimpeput; lie under shady trees and eat their fill of fruit; drink from cups of silver and crystal and myrtle, in such a way, though, that they never become drunk, nor vomit up again the food and drink once it has digested in their bellies. The most beautiful maidens will also attend upon them, with round and heaving breasts and large and striking eyes—such eyes, I say, to catch the attention of those who look upon them, by the glamour of their pupils and the blackness of their brows, "invitations to love," so to speak. The Turks look down on prostitutes; and yet, Postel proves that the Qur'an places prostitutes in Paradise. He says the Turks anticipate "sexual acts with both delicate boys and women, each of which will last for fifty years without pause." What trumpery! What madness! What wickedness! Muslims of finer taste, such as Aḥmad of Persia [probably the brother of al-Ghazālī], repent of these cradle-songs; and thus, they consider all these things as allegorical. But most people take everything literally, according to Brother Richard of the Order of Preachers, who published *Refutation of the Qur'an*. Literal interpretation was deemed necessary by al-Ghazālī, an authority among the Arabs; he labeled those who interpreted these [verses in the Qur'an] as allegorical as heretics. In order to reach the Elysian Fields, the Turks believe that mankind has various duties toward God, toward other men, toward oneself, and finally toward animals. So that "the song begins with God" as Virgil advises, the Qur'an stridently requires prayers to God, to the point that it is forbidden to forego them even in a military campaign. Muhammad enjoins Muslims to set themselves before God twice, at the beginning and end of the day. Today, however, those who are more devoted set aside five periods for prayer: the first before sunrise, which they call *Salah* [*Sabah*]; the second at noon, *Vhile* [*Öğle*]; the third around evening, *Chnidi* [*İkindi*]; the fourth at sunset, *Acsa* [*Akşam*]; and the fifth at midnight, which is called *Jastna* [*Yatsı*]. In the first one, they bend their face to the ground four times; the second one ten times; the third one thirteen times; the fourth one eight times; the fifth one five times. Before doing anything, they address their Divinity in the following manner: "Lead me, and do not let me be led without you, Lord Almighty; For I die when I am the leader, I will be saved with you as the Leader."

The Turks forbid and punish blasphemy [i.e., swearing], which you will not readily hear from any Turk, unless he has converted from Christianity. They discourage hasty oaths, but if serious testimony is required, they are ordered to swear not by God, out of reverence for Him, but by worldly things. Muhammad himself established the truth of his dogmas by swearing by the winds, rain, ships on the sea, angels, Mount Sinai, a book inscribed with a very fine map, a lofty house, the setting of stars, night and the dawn, the heavens, the Morning Star, and springtime, so that he could lie so much more brazenly. Among the obligations that people have, these stand out: not to enter anyone's house without permission; to greet people they meet on the road and answer those who greet them with kindness; to honor contracts and other deals, especially treaties; not to refuse to give testimony for anyone if they are able to give it; to be on guard against false testimony; not to accept payment for testimony; to show favor to everyone equally; not to charge interest; to return deposits; to aid the impoverished with alms, or with whatever can be done; to take studious care of widows and wards, and not harm them in any way; not to make slanders or spew out foul words. These and other obligations deserve respect. Perhaps also this one: not to have business with the blind, the deaf, or the lame; for the Qur'an, following the example of Pythagoras, seems to speak symbolically and recognize failures of character through defects of the body.[2] If this is taken literally, however, we see that Turks recognized what our men recommend: "We must beware of those whom nature has made note of [i.e., deformed people]." On the other hand, we absolutely deplore and curse in terrible terms that they allow the crimes of the Sodomites; in fact, they do not even reckon them in the tally of sins, by which detestable filth the majority of the wealthy and powerful are polluted. These are their most important obligations: to get up, and to wash their face and hands (up to the elbow) and their feet up to heel before prayers, unless bodily ailment prevents it, or if there is not enough water, to scrub them with pure earth; to wash their members after sex; to patiently endure insults against the faith by family members and entrust them to God; and to refrain from gambling; and most of all, from drinking parties, as though they were created by the Devil. I would explain the reason that wine is banned by the Turks; but since the tale of the angels, Haroth and Maroth, tricked by a woman who had mixed wine with their food, is terribly stupid, and the lack of time implores me to move on, I will stay away from it, and I will add only this single thing, that the Turks struggle against this prohibition no less than others, and they always desire what is denied. Ogier Ghiselin de Busbecq is insightful on this topic:

> I saw a certain old man in Constantinople who, after he had taken
> a goblet in his hand to drink, first let out great cries. When we
> asked his friends why he was acting that way, they answered that
> he wanted to remind his soul with those cries that it was going to
> another corner of his body or was leaving altogether. That way, it
> would not be convicted of that failure which he himself was going
> to allow, and it would not be polluted by wine which he was going
> to consume.

Ah, well done! Who can purify himself of sin merely by shouting? We said before that the Turks are careful even with regards to animals. During the four months when they make a journey to Medina and Mecca, or send a proxy in their place, they completely abstain from any hunting at all, such that even lice, bugs, and fleas enjoy a reprieve. Besides that, they take it as a point of righteousness to set free small birds that they capture and bring back. It is also considered righteous if anyone feeds dogs and cats that they meet on the street, especially pregnant ones; if anyone feeds them organs, bones, porridge, or leftovers of other side-dishes, in their house or on the street. Sometimes, for this reason, Turks are reproached by men of our faith because they do those things for wild animals which they refuse to humans, especially Christians. They justify this in the following way:

> God has gifted man with reason, which is a wonderful tool for everything. Yet, man misuses reason, so that nothing unfortunate happens to him which he did not earn from his own faults; therefore, he is worthy of less pity. But nothing has been given to animals by God apart from their natural movements and appetites, which they cannot fail to follow; thus, they must be lifted up by human power and kindness.

Moving on to politics, with which our discussion will end, we find no family nobility among the Turks—among whom, of course, that satiric line holds: "Nobility is the one and only virtue." The Qur'an commands obedience of subjects toward their masters, even wicked and tyrannical ones. They are ordered to sacrifice their lives, and the Turks submit to this command as Achille Tarducci wrote: "There is such great obedience that greater could not be imagined; and its like could not be replicated," that is, among the Christians. Turkish monks [Sufi dervishes] are accused of the same thing that we accuse the Jesuits of doing—namely, that they set various traps against the lives of their Princes. Among others, Bayezid I learned this lesson to his misfortune when he was almost killed on a public road by such a knave who was begging for alms. The Turks consider war, particularly against those whom they call infidels, to be not only permitted, but even commanded by God. In order that war be waged bravely and with greater force, Muhammad exempted no one from performing military service except for the blind, the lame, and others who suffered from a serious ailment. Muhammad persuaded his followers that soldiers are loved by God more than other mortals, even those who perform the holy undertaking of a pilgrimage, and thus soldiers would have the finest rewards in the next life. Nevertheless, they are required to fight bravely; for those who would do otherwise receive temporal and eternal punishments. After victory has been achieved, however, a fifth part of the spoils, according to the Qur'an's commands, are to be given to Muhammad or his companions, or to other impoverished persons. As for divvying up inheritances, the same Lawgiver decreed that a son should take as much from his father upon his death as two daughters; but if there are more than two daughters, that two-thirds should be passed down to them. If there is only a single daughter, she should have half. In the absence of children, the inheritance passes to kinsmen, with only a third reserved for the mother. When a wife dies, if she passed without children, the husband becomes heir to half the dowry; if she left children, then only a fourth. After the death of the husband, if there are no children, a fourth is left to the surviving wife; if there are children, she is due only an eighth. Today, however, hardly any of these commands are honored, because the Emperor of the Turks makes himself heir to those of abundant wealth, and leaves to his wives and children only as much as he wishes.

We should also discuss punishments. After Muhammad had ordered wicked men to be condemned and noticed that this was ineffective at motivating his followers to obey him, he decided that other forms of punishment would also have to be inflicted by the leadership. Thus, in the Qur'an, whoever commits intentional homicide should be cast into fire; whoever does it unintentionally should fast for two months, or he should ransom some prisoner of war and repay the kinsmen of the slain. An adulterer, if caught in the act, is given a hundred lashes; thieves have their hands cut off; whoever charges his wife with adultery and loses his case is cleansed of his impudence with eighty lashes; a like number of lashes purifies drunkenness; whoever is unaware of the severity of a sin when he engaged in it will have his punishment lightened.

Turkish economics is engaged with the three simple associations and with enlarging the family fortune. Thus, there are three rules in the Qur'an for those planning to enter the association of marriage. It is permitted for one man to have four wives—and in fact, however many he can support. No man may marry his mother, daughter, sister, daughter-in-law, or the mother and sister of the daughter-in-law. One may not take a wife from another religion, nor marry a prostitute. It is proper for wives to go about with their faces uncovered before their husbands, children, kin, and family; before others, they must remain covered, unless they are unwell. It is considered wrong to have intercourse in the mosque or with a menstruating woman. Husbands should live at peace with their wives and not weigh them down with suspicions or false accusations. Wives should obey their husbands, live modestly, and keep their husband's secrets. It is permitted to leave a wife by divorcing her. A wife whose husband leaves may be married to another man after waiting four months and with the permission of her former husband. No one may turn out a pregnant wife; he should wait for the time of childbirth, after which the offspring should stay with the father. It is proper for a widow to enter into a new marriage four months after the death of her husband. The father is governed by fewer rules, for the Qur'an commands nothing except that parents should nurture their children, and no one should ruin his own family by concealing poverty. In turn, children should love their parents, honor them, and willingly support them in old age. Association with a master needs no rules, although it is not right for the Turks to have a Muslim slave, and all things are permissible against a Christian, without exception. Finally, there is a custom that whatever profit is derived, by whatever means, a fifth part of it should be given to the false Prophet Muhammad.

Where shall we go now? Certainly, more time has been spent on Turkish philosophy than we had intended... [the author goes on to give his best wishes to Master M. Johann Christoph Rosteuscher of Danzig, who will succeed him in the professorship of Logic, Metaphysics, and Ethics] [...]. I beg God Almighty to save our most peaceful King, the Curia, the Church; and protect this office of the Holy Spirit against the designs of Satan. Amen.

Notes

1 Schelwig's biography was compiled from the following sources: Johann Georg Walch, *Historische und theologische Einleitung in die Religions Streitigkeiten der Evangelisch-Lutherischen Kirchen*, vol. 1 (Jena, 1733), 740–5; Johann Heinrich Zedler (ed.), "Schelwig oder Schelgvig, Samuel," in *Grosses vollständiges Universal-Lexicon aller Wissenschafften und Künste*, vol. 34 (Leipzig, 1742), 1204–15; Johann Horkel, *Der Holzkämmerer Theodor Gehr und die Anfänge des Königl. Friedrichs-Collegiums zu Königsberg* (Königsberg 1855), 15–62; Heinrich Schmid, *Die Geschichte des Pietismus* (Nördlingen, 1863), 227–342; Eduard Schnaase, *Geschichte der evangelischen Kirche Danzigs aktenmäßig Dargestellt* (Danzig, 1863), 80–183; Christian Friedrich David Erdmann, "Schelwig, Samuel," *Allgemeine Deutsche Biographie*, vol. 31 (Leipzig, 1890), 30–36.

2 [MK] Here, Schelwig does not present the correct understanding of the Qur'an although he is careful about his interpretation concerning the blind, deaf, and lame (being a symbolic character defect rather than a physical defect).

10 History of Arabic Logic

Johannes Steuchius

Johannes Steuchius was a prominent Swedish Lutheran theologian and academic, a descendant of celebrated Lutheran bishops and academics. Born in 1676 in Härnösand in northern Sweden, Steuchius moved with his family to Lund in 1694 when his father, Matthias Steuchius, the renowned academic and theologian, was appointed Bishop of Lund. After completing his studies in logic and metaphysics at Uppsala University, Steuchius was given the opportunity to attend some of Europe's foremost Protestant academic institutions, a luxury afforded to few. He continued his theological and philosophical studies as a visiting student at the universities of Rostock, Hamburg, Wolfenbüttel, Helmstedt, Wittenberg, Altdorf, London, Oxford, Amsterdam, Haarlem, and Leiden. During this period, he studied under many prominent Lutheran academics, such as Professor Johann Fecht, one of Germany's leading representatives of Lutheran orthodoxy. He also met Gottfried Wilhelm Leibniz and visited the famous library in Wolfenbüttel during this time. In 1701, Steuchius was appointed as a lecturer and associate professor in the Faculty of Philosophy at Uppsala University. In 1702, he returned to Lund and was appointed a librarian and professor at the University of Lund. By 1707, he became a full professor of logic and metaphysics as well as extraordinary professor of theology. He returned with his family to Uppsala University in 1710 and became its archbishop and prosecutor in 1714.

Steuchius had tremendous influence in the University because of his relationship with the executives. He presided over nearly one hundred dissertations at Uppsala University, drafted a new school order that was ultimately adopted at the parliamentary level in 1723, and was appointed superintendent in Karlstad that same year. He believed religion was fundamentally important to society and that there needed to be unity between religion and society. He had a strict Orthodox Lutheran view and in 1735 introduced a law, the Charter of Religions, to intervene on suspicion of any religion other than the Church of Sweden being practiced to combat radical Pietism. As superintendent, he was also responsible for visiting parishes, prescribing priests, and participating in priesthood meetings. After serving as bishop of Linköping, Steuchius succeeded his father as Archbishop of the Church of Sweden in 1730 and held this position until his death in 1742.[1]

Variant Names: Johann Steuch, Jöns Steuch, Joanne Steuchio, and Iohannes Steuchius Suecus

Summary and Analysis

Steuchius' *disputatio* uses Arabic logic to present an historical account of the development of philosophical thought in Arabia before and after the emergence of Islam. In doing so, he argues that philosophical thought was hindered in Arabia because of Islam. His argument can be divided into four propositions.

Steuchius first proposes that philosophy drew its origins from the East. His evidence for this claim is that many of the Greek philosophers, considered the forefathers of European philosophy, began cultivating their philosophical thinking as a result of exposure to ancient Eastern philosophy.

Second, he argues that Arabs living in pre-Islamic Arabia were among the Easterners who cultivated philosophy. His evidence for this is based on the scholarship of historians, such as Thomas Stanleius and Georg Hornius, who described the ancient Arabs as skillful logicians and astronomers with advanced systems of speech composition and poetic structures. Steuchius claims that the Chaldeans and Egyptians are two of these cultivators of philosophy and that Arabs and Persians learned from them. He also cites the biblical narrative of Job as demonstrating the natural capacity of pre-Islamic Arabs for argumentation and dialectics.

Third, like many Lutherans, Steuchius asserts that the development of philosophical thought halted among the Arabs with the arrival of Muhammad. His evidence for this is that once Muhammad gained power and was recognized as a great prophet, he declared war on philosophy, prohibiting his followers from cultivating any literary culture, an offense punishable by death. Steuchius supports his claim by saying that Muhammad feared that philosophical studies would call into doubt his superior status among his followers and he wanted to protect his Qur'an as the principal source of truth. As a result, all philosophical developments outside the Qur'an were superfluous and the Arabs grew unaccustomed to philosophy.

Steuchius' fourth and final proposition is that philosophy ultimately re-emerged among the Arabs when Christians began translating Greek literature into the Arabic vernacular. His evidence for this is that from the time Christian academics re-introduced philosophy to Arabia, Arabs started to visit Greece to study philosophy. He cites a series of caliphs who allowed Greek philosophy to flourish in Arabia by supporting Arab

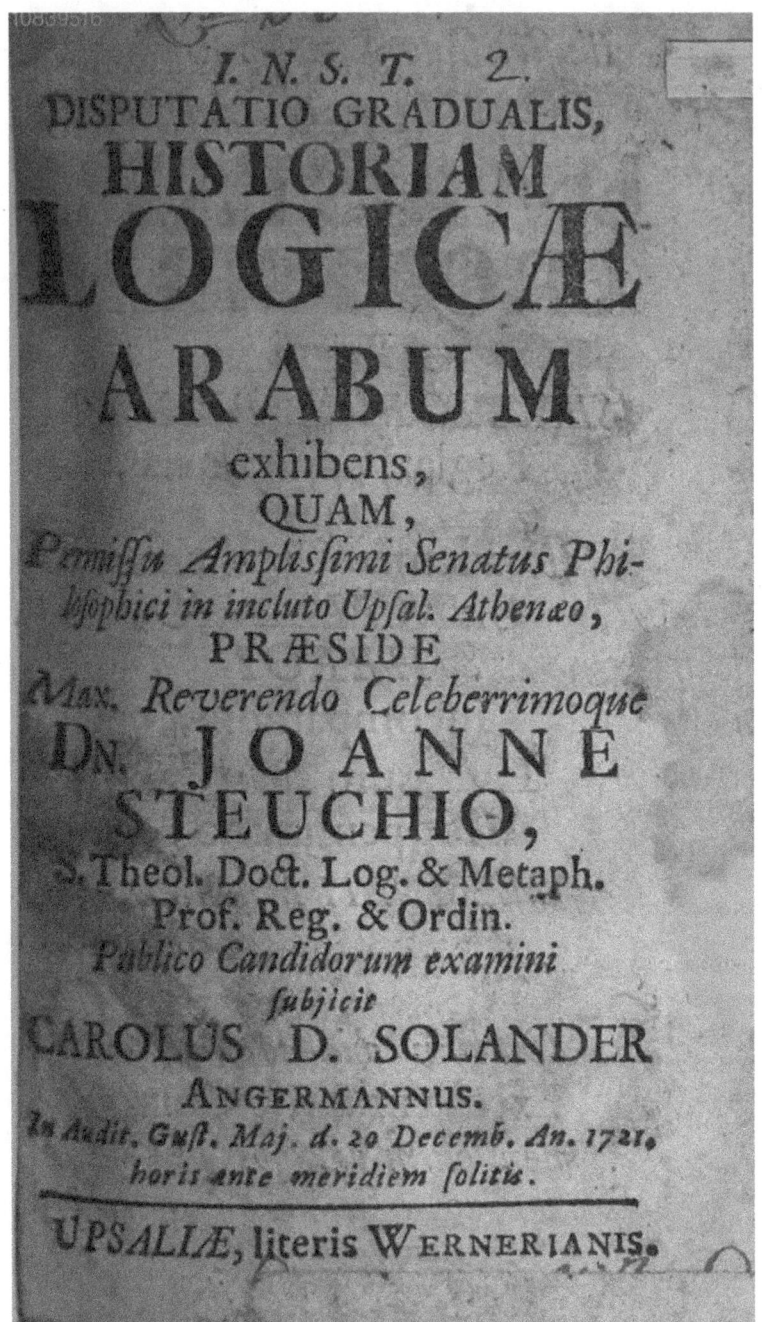

Figure 10.1 Johannes Steuchius, *Disputatio gradualis historiam logicae Arabum*, 1721.

liberal arts academies and funding philosophy in schools. Steuchius also lists a series of eminent Arabic philosophers from the tenth to fourteenth centuries, arguing that many learned Muslims considered their own theology to contain various errors that could not be reconciled with philosophy. Accordingly, a state of perfection was only possible once a marriage occurred between Greek philosophy and Islam.

In sum, Steuchius argues that these philosophical studies once again began to languish among the Arabs under the Turks' "barbarous arms." According to him, the Arabs as a race are capable of captivatingly novel and insightful philosophical developments, but were prevented from doing so when Islam appeared. Steuchius likens Turks' appearance on the world scene as a military power to a kind of reappearance of Muhammad: an excuse for the decline in Arabic philosophy. His disputation is a reflection of the political context when the Ottoman Empire lost power in Europe, resulting in a Lutheran interest in Arabia in the post-failed Turkish 1683 Siege of Vienna. Steuchius believes Christian academics saved the day by introducing Muslims, who had no other avenue to restore their loss of learning, to Greek philosophy. This suggests that as a true representative of Greek philosophy, Protestant Europe can now save Arabic philosophy from the hands of the 'barbaric Turks.'

Disputation on the History of Arabic Logic (Uppsala, 1721)

I think I can claim without any risk of being mistaken that philosophy draws its origins from the East. This is supported by the testimony of the most distinguished men [such as Plato, Manetho, Georg Hornius, Thomas Stanleius and others]. However, I am aware that the Greeks worked hard in this field, spreading philosophy not just to the Romans but to almost the whole world. They were the first to write about philosophy, and the origin of all wisdom is owed to them. Even the Romans believe this as Cicero and Seneca clearly hint. But this masquerade, with which the Greeks claim glory for themselves, should be removed according to Hornius. There are also some Greeks who argue the same. A certain Laertius will be sufficient as an authority; he began his work thus: "There are some who say that the study of philosophy began among the barbarians." Who does not know that Homer, Solon, Lycurgus, Pythagoras, Plato, Eudoxus, Democritus, and a great number of other Greeks recorded in history took long journeys to the East? Because of this Hornius says,

> There is no doubt that when cities were built and states founded, a seat for literature and wisdom was also founded, and just as the East was the first place to have a more humane culture, so it was the first to stand out in its praise of wisdom. From this it came about

that eminent ancient Greek philosophers set out there as if to buy wisdom.

Porphyry, on the authority of Diogenes, says that Pythagoras went to Arabia, among other regions, and lived there with its king. Hence, Eusebius rightly says: "the Greeks sought out teachings in other places like merchants."

Before I elaborate on this point, I think it is relevant to say a few words to shed light on the question of whether the Arabs paid attention to philosophy first, as did the other Easterners. Indeed, I am aware of various scholars who consider the Arabs barbarians, including [Zacharias] Ursinus, Hottinger, and others. Also, many geographers, displaying a lack of skill, portray these regions as unknown deserts. All these scholars, except the greatest ones, are guilty of this line of thought (according to Ludewig, who is harsher than is fair). But they reveal to us that the native writers of this nation call the era before the Arab Empire and Muhammad, who compiled the Qur'an, the "Age of Ignorance." Gregory Abū al-Faraj, the keenest investigator into Arab affairs, said this about old Arabia: "The fact that some [old Arabs] survive to these times springs from that double lineage, namely Kathan and Adnan, and a double condition fits for the Arabs, one of ignorance, the other of Islam." What about Islam? Pococke, the most learned commentator on Eastern matters, gives an excellent description of this state by Mustafa Ebn or his son Kassai in the book *Ta'rifāt*: "Islam is when someone heeds and submits himself to the things handed down by Muhammad." Hence, they call their sect *al-Eslam* or Islamism, and themselves Muslims or Islamists; and of course, if we rearrange the letters it derives from Ishmael, the son of Abraham, whom he produced from the slave Hagar. Certain investigators into his genealogy say that this cunning soldier [Muhammad] originated from this seed and lineage. To this end, Muhammad claims Abraham to be a Muslim, and he wants the laws in his Qur'an, which he imagines was sent down from heaven, to be known as Islam.

To return to the main point, following Pococke's lead, I interpret the words of Abū al-Faraj given above not to mean the ignorance of *philosophy*, but of *religion*. Here we must listen to the Arab Ibn al-Athīr (through Pococke's translation), who describes 'ignorance' as the condition of the Arabs before Islam, since they were ignorant of God and His messenger. Therefore, Jacob Golius' [Arabic-Latin] *Lexicon* [mostly based on al-Jawharī] defines the state of ignorance as the Arabs' paganism, or the time before Muhammad, and Ibn Kathīr al-Farghānī, or more commonly Alfraganus, comments on the elements of astronomy: "... in the age of ignorance, which is what Muslims called this time that preceded their religion." Abū al-Faraj would not have agreed with Ibn al-Athīr if he had felt differently. For the Arabs were certainly not ignorant, and Abū al-Faraj had an excellent understanding beyond "the skill of his own tongue, correct speech, poetic structures, the composition of speeches, or the cause of the stars' rising and setting." If indeed Abū al-Faraj called the ancient Arabs unphilosophical, I think that he meant that they lacked proper philosophy or Greek Aristotelianism, which they were ignorant of until the eighth century. But Abū al-Faraj's words seem to imply at first glance that the Arabs were completely incompetent in learning philosophy. Thus, he says: "Truly God had not allowed anything much of the knowledge of philosophy to them, nor had He made them suited to these studies." But the lack of [philosophical studies] has an explanation, since Abū al-Faraj informs us elsewhere that he understood philosophy as 'theology' (i.e., the exploration of the origin of the universe), about which he writes that the ancient Arabs were ignorant. If this was not really Abū al-Faraj's opinion, then he was contradicting himself, as [Herman] Conring says.

I have limited access to ancient Arab authors, so I will consult non-Arab writers, from whom I will seek aid and assistance to advance my thesis further. For example, the first one is Porphyry, who quotes Diogenes: "Pythagoras went to the Egyptians and Arabs." [Johannes] Schefferus also argues convincingly that the Greeks learned divination and the art of augury from them. The Arabs take pride that they are the children of Abraham, and that many of them have absorbed something of Abrahamic philosophy. On this matter, I rely on the authority of al-Shahrastānī, whose words Pococke translates like this: "the light which went from Adam to Abraham was divided; it was dispersed from him to his children in two parts. One of them stayed with the sons of Israel, the other with the sons of Ishmael, and so on." The most distinguished men concur with this point of view. Ludewig, whom I have praised above, says that the ancient Arabs were skilled in astronomy, geometry, physics, and other disciplines. Hornius, following Eusebius, claims that their brilliance shone like a star. Some even argue that Solomon's wisdom was being favorably compared to that of the Arab philosophers in 1 Kings 4:30. Tacitus notes that Judaea is bordered on the East by Arabia; and Johannes Wandalinus says the same. It is clear from this that Arabia was considered part of the East by the Hebrews themselves. For this reason, the anonymous Jew who translated the *Book of Kings* into Arabic understands the "sons of the East" in the passage cited above as being the Arabs. This is also Conring's opinion. Let us also hear Stanleius, who says that among the ancient Arabs there were learned men, skilled in natural philosophy, astronomy, and other disciplines. If this is true, then it is likely that the ancient Arabs and Persians received philosophy from the Chaldeans and Egyptians, who were among its earliest cultivators. Therefore, whoever examines the matter a little more closely and dispassionately will easily discern that the ancient Arabs, among other nations, cultivated philosophy.

Many have thought deeply about logic, but too little has been said on this subject by historians of philosophy. Everyone knows that logic can be divided into two main areas: natural logic, which is the innate ability of the mind to receive, decide, and reason; and artificial logic, or dialectic. Natural logic goes back to the beginnings of humankind. The history of dialectic can also easily be outlined, for it developed gradually. But I digress, and will continue with the Arabs, demonstrating that they had skill in the art of logic as well.

Even if we concede that Aristotelian logic was unknown to the ancient Arabs until the eighth century, it may not be inferred from this that they all lacked the art of reasoning, since reasoning is not solely bound to the maxims of a certain Stagirite [Aristotle]. For there is not just one path to the truth, nor does everyone reason in the same way. Thus, it was rightly said by someone: "men made arguments before Aristotle, the god of syllogizers, was born." These are the words of Abū al-Faraj, which I will illustrate with a brief commentary: "But the learning of the Arabs, who were especially eager for glory, was this: skill in their own tongue, correctness of speech, the structure of their poetry, and their composition of speeches." By "correctness of speech," we understand grammar or oratory or dialectic. But he distinguishes "correctness of speech" from "skill in their tongue" and "composition of speeches." Therefore, by "composition of speeches" he undoubtedly meant dialectic. Indeed, Pococke hints this in his notes to that book of Abū al-Faraj. Johannes Cotovicus also confirms this conjecture and says that "modern Arabs, preserving the old way of living and teaching, ignore other subjects and occupy themselves with dialectic and rhetoric." We must listen to his words: "Arabs do not pay any attention to philosophy, but a few at least occupy themselves with dialectic and rhetoric." The nationality of Job, who was from the land of Uz in Arabia, also supports this argument. The vast majority of the learned, whose works I do not have time or space to quote, affirm that Job was a true Arab. When Job engaged in dialogue with his friends, he disputed with them in such a way that he deserves to be called the best of the dialectician of his time. For in his life story we find that he not only made arguments against his friends, and made correct responses, but also made objections and used limitations in his argumentation. The Church Fathers recognized him as the best logician. Jerome said about Job that "he determined all the laws of dialectic, with propositions, assumptions and conclusions. In fact, he even showed up specious arguments for solving problems." Cassiodorus thought the same: "Where are those who say that the art of dialectic did not begin from the holiest scriptures? The pages in Job are full of allegory, propositions and holy questions." Ambrosius affirms that Job was the first to discover dialectic: "Job, who discovered these things, was much more ancient [than the Greek dialecticians]." Among more recent men, we must listen to Volaterranus, who shows that four kinds of disputation

occur in the book of Job, and that the first is dialectic: "The first disputation is dialectic, which proceeds from provables. This happens with
Job and his three friends, when he proves his thesis that God sometimes
afflicts a just and innocent man. But his friends argue to the contrary;
that God strikes no one beyond their deserts." [Theophilus] Gale says,
"It is clear that Job was a profound and perceptive philosopher, for he
speaks very keenly." From this [Andreas] Rivetus rightly observes: "Anyone who is not skilled in dialectic will oppose Job to no effect."

What should we think about Job's friends? Surely, they are also dialecticians? Some deduce this from the conversations they have with Job.
For this reason, Hornius affirms that their conversations were imbued
with philosophy—he understands this to be dialectic, which is clear
from the context—and that they came from Job's school and engaged
in disputation with him. But when Job is spoken of as a dialectician,
this should not be understood as if the art of argumentation were restricted to the rules and precepts outlined in Aristotle's *Organon*. Indeed, the natural ability of speaking in various manners and forms has
manifested itself in a variety of nations and philosophers. Furthermore,
according to the very distinguished Hornius, since Job was the greatest
philosopher, he did not want to hide his wisdom in private. Accordingly,
he opened a school and taught logic to the public. This, according to
Eliphas Themanites, is proven in the book of Job. For this reason, there
must have been more dialecticians in Arabia, for the Arabs had a teacher
"compared to whom there was no one more ancient, more learned, or
more sublime in all of antiquity." [...]. The Arab, Aḥmad ibn Yūsuf, says
that among the ancient Arab kings there was a certain al-Ḥārith, who
was called a philosopher. Pococke says that this man was not a philosopher; and Johann Ludewig, following Ibn Yūsuf, thinks that al-Ḥārith
was called a philosopher because of his wonderful speaking abilities.
Ludewig wishes to attribute the study of literature to the Arabs before
the time of Muhammad, and he does not wish to attribute it to al-Ḥārith.

When Muhammad, that monster who burst from a dark corner into
the middle of the theater of the weakening world, had obtained power,
he became so conceited that many treated him as the greatest prophet
and worshipped him, and philosophy vanished among the Arabs for a
time. For this most evil illiterate man feared that the students would be
superior to the master if they continued to pursue philosophy. He called
philosophical studies delusions, fallacies, and trifles, and declared war
on them. Not only did he discourage his followers from cultivating literature, but he also prohibited it with the threat of punishment. Hornius
cites this law: "no Muslim, no matter his status or level of learning, may
learn any of the seven liberal arts, otherwise he will be punished with
death." Indeed, Muhammad attracted everyone to him as if he were a
teacher, and portrayed the Qur'an as if it were a treasury of the highest
wisdom, declaring everything else to be superfluous and useless. Thus,

the Arabs grew unaccustomed to literature at last, and all their philosophy, cultivated by their elders with care and effort, disappeared. I think this fact should be attributed neither to their laziness nor the dullness of their spirits, but to that false prophet and the Umayyad Caliphate's administrators, who put no effort into promoting study. Therefore, I think that the time of Muhammad was clearly not a time of knowledge, as some argue, but rather ignorance.

I will now briefly explain how the Arabs began to practice philosophy again. Since Greece shone throughout the whole world, especially in its cultivation of the liberal arts and literature, the Arabs believed that the only way for them to restore their loss of learning was to translate Greek books into Arabic. The Christians in Arabia gave examples of Greek learning in the Arabic language. From this time onwards, the Arabs routinely visited Greece, and returned home having been enriched with much learning. The first of the caliphs who worked on introducing Greek philosophy was Abū Ja'far al-Manṣūr, who began to sit on the throne in the year 754, and the second was the caliph of the Hashemites. Under Hārūn al-Rashīd, not only were men of any kind of learning held in high honor, but schools were also founded where Greek philosophy was taught. He finally opened the way for the caliph al-Ma'mūn, whose deeds almost all writers praise and extol. He was kind and favorable to the Muses and proved himself in these arts. Thus, Greek philosophy flourished brilliantly among the Arabs under his rule. This prince summoned men thoroughly learned in philosophy from every place; he sought books everywhere, especially from Greece, which he ordered to be translated into Arabic at great expense. When these studies took deeper root, he particularly encouraged them among his subjects. Finally, he founded schools and supported them with his generous patronage, and these schools were so successful that they rivaled those of the Greeks. Greece has produced many exceptional works; in addition to borrowing these from the Greeks, the Arabs produced many exceptional works of their own. Due to this, many works of wise Greek men that have been lost among the Greeks themselves survive among the Arabs.

After the introduction of Greek philosophy, it is agreed that dialectic was among the first of the arts the Arabs practiced. Abū Zakarīyā Yūḥannā ibn Māsawayh taught dialectic in Baghdad in the eighth century. Abū al-Faraj speaks of him thus: "Johannes was considered a great man in Baghdad. He composed elegant books. He founded a school for the sake of debating, where he talked about every kind of ancient discipline. He even lectured, and as many students as possible were gathered to him." Abū Ya'qūb ibn Ḥunayn was another eminent philosopher, who was active in about the year 850. After returning to Arabia from Greece, he practiced philosophy using Greek principles to the praise of his countrymen. He was succeeded by Ya'qūb al-Kindī, a superb dialectician, who also knew the other parts of philosophy and wrote various books about them. Qusṭā ibn Lūqā, roughly contemporary to al-Kindī, was by no means inferior to him. In the beginning of the tenth century, these philosophical studies flourished to the point that many new universities were founded. Thābit ibn Qurrah was also active during this time; it is said that his *Logica* is still unparalleled. In about 940, Abū Bishr Mattā b. Yūnus was also very valuable and useful to the Muslims. He was called 'the dialectician' because of his exceptional ability to reason. Abū al-Faraj says that "the dialectician Abū Bishr Mattā was skilled in the art of logic; while teaching, he would often go over the same speech to make it understandable." Here I can also mention al-Fārābī, who taught his students analytics, and who "brought the art of logic out of the depths, uncovering its secrets, and making them easy to grasp. He outlined all that he knew about logic in clearly organized books. In these books, he covered aspects of the art of analytics and methods of speaking which had been overlooked by al-Kindī and others. His books on logic, physics, metaphysics, and politics fulfilled their purpose satisfactorily." Al-Fārābī's contemporary Afrihi ibn 'Adī was a notable logician of this age, who, Leo Africanus says, died in Arabia Felix.

Abū al-Faraj says that some learned Muslims thought that their theology—if it can be called that—was mixed with various errors and could be cleansed with the help of logic. They said that if Greek philosophy were joined to Arab religion, it would at last achieve a state of perfection. Now let us skip over al-Būzjānī, al-Fārābī, al-Rāzī, al-Bāqillānī, and Abū 'Abd Allāh, the teacher of Avicenna, all of whom Abū al-Faraj, Leo Africanus and others write were dialecticians. In about the year 1050, the celebrated Avicenna was active. He was no less a dialectician than he was a doctor. For he himself asserts that God would make the art of dialectic clear to him, if only he had faith in Him. There is a certain lengthy passage of Avicenna, which is worth citing here in full:

> For about 18 months I lay down to read books carefully. Whenever I was confused on some point, or could not find the middle term of a syllogism, I went to the mosque and poured out prayers as a suppliant to the Creator of all things, until that which was obscure and hidden was opened to me. At night I went home and worked on reading and writing by lamplight. Whenever sleep or some other weakness in the senses troubled me, I drank some much-needed wine until my strength came back. Then I turned back to my reading. Even if some light sleep overtook me, I dreamt about those problems, with the result that many solutions became known to me through lack of sleep. Nor did I stop, until I had acquired a solid understanding of dialectic and physics.

This is not the time to discuss the claim that Avicenna had one eye closed when it came to medicine and was blind when it came to philosophy. But a certain man exaggerates when he says that "[Avicenna] labored with such great efforts that he alone wins the medal among the interpreters of Aristotle, nor did anyone understand the mind of that philosopher so well." Abū al-Faraj ʿAbd Allāh ibn al-Ṭayyib was active in the same century; he was not only a dialectician but also practiced metaphysics for twenty years. Ibn al-Rāwandī was also a dialectician.[2] Important dialecticians from the following century include Abul Chais, who founded a school of logic and metaphysics; al-Ghazālī who taught 6,000 students logic and other subjects in the university at Baghdad; and al-Ṭughrāʾī, al-Sharīf, and Saighus. Abū al-Barakāt al-Baghdādī wrote a book called *Kitāb al-Muʿtabar*, in which he described many things that pertained to dialectic (according to Ludewig). There was also Osanius, Abul Helmus, Mogrebinus, Thosactus, the teacher of Averroes, who he praises in his writings, and many others, who I do not have the space to list. But all of them are considered famous among their own people in the art of dialectic.

Averroes lived in the twelfth and thirteenth centuries, and his followers are called Averroists, just like the Thomists and Scotists among the Scholastics. His commentaries on Aristotle are still extant. Although Averroes was known as 'the interpreter' and as a commentator, Ludewig thinks that Averroes was responsible for corrupting the arts, for he constantly erred in explaining Aristotle's books due to his ignorance of Greek, Latin, and the history of philosophy. All that he absorbed from Aristotle he owed to Arabic translations, which were inaccurate on many points. The noble Hornius claims that Averroes was a contemporary of Avicenna, though I do not know how, as Avicenna lived a whole century before! Leaving aside this anachronism, we continue to list the other philosophers of this century. They include ʿAbd al-Salām, whose books were burned due to the envy of some malevolent men, "most of which were about all kinds of philosophy" meaning that he too was a dialectician; Saed, who is said to have been perfectly skilled in the art of medicine and dialectic; Muhammad, who commentated on certain works of Avicenna; Abū Bakr al-Rāzī, Abū Sahl Yaḥyā al-Masīhī, Yuseph, Hasnus, Jakub, and Al Enanus, who also contributed to logic; and Noimoddis Nachjaranensis, who ends my list of philosophers of this age, which Averroes began, and is no less praiseworthy, though he was much inclined to the sect of metempsychists [*tanāsukh*].

In the fourteenth century, al-Ṭūsī stood out among his peers for his exemplary work on Fakhr al-Dīn al-Rāzī's logic and Avicenna's metaphysics. They record his saying: "Some pens can accomplish more than a hundred thousand armored horses." Najm al-Dīn al-Qazwīnī, the author of *Ḥikmat al-ʿAyn*, was also a distinguished logician. One of the last notable Arabic philosophers was Naṣīr al-Dīn al-Ṭūsī, a man of wondrous learning, whose teaching and reputation shone so brightly that he became the prefect of all the schools and universities of the Mongols.

He was a wise man, distinguished in all kinds of philosophy. Under his command all the schools that were under the Mongols' power were returned to their former glory. He composed many books on logic, physics, metaphysics, and so on. But after the fourteenth century, I cannot say for certain that there were dialecticians among the Arabs, because their intellectual poverty since that time has left few traces of philosophical activity. When the Turkish Empire arose among the Muslims, I am compelled to agree with the much-praised Pococke that these nations did not retain their previous study of literature: "These studies finally began to languish among the Arabs under the Turks' barbarous arms, and along with their former honor they also banished their former vigor." But Dr. Olaus Celsius verbosely demonstrates that the Arabs' studies were not completely extinguished by Turks, and some remains of their former learning endured.

Dear reader! This is what I have been able to say at present about Arabic dialectic. I know that a more talented man could have written about this better than I; but, in writing about these complex matters, I am content to obtain pardon from good men, even if I do not receive praise.

Notes

1 Steuchius' biography was compiled from the following sources: Martin Weibull, *Lunds universitets historia: 1668–1863*, Vol. 1 (Lund, 1868), 272–3; Adolph Hofmeister, *Die Matrikel der Universität Rostock*, vol. 4 (Rostock, 1891–1895), 21; John Wordsworth, *The National Church of Sweden* (London: A. R. Mowbray, 1911), 331; C. V. Jacobowsky, "Svenska studenter i Oxford c. 1620–1740," *Personhistorisk Tidskrift* 28 (1927): 128; Jan Olof Rudén, "Ensemble Music Copied by the Swedish Student Nils Tiliander in Greifswald, Rostock and Wittenberg 1698–1699," in *The Dissemination of Music in Seventeenth-Century Europe*, ed. Erik Kjellberg (Bern: Peter Lang, 2010), 279–304; Patrik Winton, "Johannes (Jöns) Steuchius (Steuch)," in *Svenskt biografiskt lexicon*, vol. 33 (Stockholm: Albert Bonnier, 2011), 413; Kay Zenker, *Denkfreiheit: Libertas philosophandi in der deutschen Aufklärung* (Hamburg: Felix Meiner Verlag, 2012), 230.

2 [MK] On the significance of Ibn al-Rāwandī in Islamic intellectual history, see Mehmet Karabela, "Ibn al-Rāwandī," in *Oxford Encyclopaedia of Islam, Philosophy, Science and Technology*, ed. İbrahim Kalın (Oxford: Oxford University Press, 2014), 352–4; Sarah Stroumsa, *Freethinkers of Medieval Islam: Ibn al-Rāwandī, Abū Bakr al-Rāzī, and Their Impact on Islamic Thought* (Brill: Leiden, 1999); and Josef van Ess, "Ibn ar-Rewandī, or the Making of an Image," *Al-Abḥāth* 27 (1978–79): 5–26.

11 Turkish Philosophy

Christian Friedrich Rudolph Vetterlein

Vetterlein was born in 1758 in Warmsdorf, a village in Anhalt-Köthen, but moved to the small town of Sandersleben in Anhalt-Dessau as a child. In 1775, he attended the Reformed Gymnasium in Halle and later studied *schöne Wissenschaften* (*belles-lettres*), philosophy, and theology at Halle until 1781. In the same year, he was unanimously elected by the city council (*Magistrat*) in Köthen to be the new Rector of the Reformed Town School (*Stadtschule*). Immediately after his arrival, he turned his attention to the elimination of the *Stocksystem* method (hitting students with a stick to punish them), which had been tolerated up until that point. In 1802, Duke August Christian Friedrich commissioned him to prepare a plan for the modernization of this school. He received approval to implement his plan and was also given the directorship of the school. Between 1802 and 1804, Vetterlein's translation of Jean Gagnier's *La vie de Mahomet* (*The Life of Muhammad*) was published in German, *Leben Mohammeds des Propheten*, in two volumes in Köthen. In 1811, Vetterlein received an order to plan to combine and improve the municipal schools. He presented the necessity for the establishment of three educational institutions for the city of Köthen, a *Bürger- und Gelehrtenschule* (municipal school for boys), a *Mädchenschule* (school for girls), and an *Armenschule* (school for the poor) for children of both sexes, as well as the educational requirements for the schools.

Soon afterwards, Duke August appointed him a member of the state committee for school issues of the duchy. In this role, he was engaged in conceiving a total school reform of the country until the Duke died in 1812 and the committee for school issues was abolished. He was the director until 1821, when he was removed from his position due to his perceived lack of authority, although he remained a teacher in the upper classes. Vetterlein knew the requirements of the school system and had the great skill to conceive school plans according to the respective local requirements. Unfortunately, he did not have enough energy or funds from the state to implement his new vision for the vital flourishing of the institution. He did, however, possess great scholarly knowledge and showed his taste and dexterity in explaining ancient poets, especially Homer and Horace.

In the earlier years, according to Vetterlein's biography in *Neuer Nekrolog der Deutschen*, he only left his study room for teaching and exams. Despite his reclusiveness, he was neither clumsy nor pedantic. He was known for his witty conversation and good humor. As a writer, he was excellent and gave generously from his wealth of knowledge. He advanced the understanding of German poets, such as Friedrich Gottlieb Klopstock (d.1803), through his teachings and writings. As a member of the Reformed Church, Vetterlein did not emphasize church authority or sacraments. He believed that the Redeemer (*Erlöser*) would be of Germanic descent and that this could be proven historically.

In 1836, he was retired upon his own request, with continued payment of his full salary, and bought a small property in the nearby village of Geuz, where he engaged in horticulture in addition to his scholarly studies. Toward the end of his life, he returned to Köthen, where he died of old age (eighty-four) in 1842. The post-structuralist philosopher Friedrich A. Kittler considers Vetterlein an important figure in the transformative period of the German Protestant education system.[1]

Variant Names: C. F. R. Vetterlein and Chrs. Fred. Rud. Vetterlein

Summary and Analysis

Vetterlein begins his treatise with a justification of why he is writing about Turkish philosophy since popular opinion is that the Turks have nothing comparable to European philosophy. However, according to Vetterlein, the Turks have progressed to the first basics of philosophy, so that the little they have achieved is worthy of inquiry. He says that the Turks have ignored philosophy for the most part because of their despotic regime and their "savage and intolerant" religion. He finds it remarkable that, despite this inhospitable environment, some philosophies bearing similarities to Greek philosophy have arisen nonetheless. He seeks to explain how this occurred.

He begins by outlining the Turkish educational system; its public schools are connected to mosques. The schools teach Arabic and Persian, together with Ottoman history, and the students read literature "written foolishly in an effeminate style." The Turks do not study geography, Greek, Latin, or "any other science or liberal art with reason or good methods." Although they value medicine, the Turks are hampered by little knowledge of chemistry and anatomy. Some Turks read philosophers, such as Averroes and Avicenna, but "more for show than use," and although Aristotle has been translated into Arabic, the translation is poor. The Ottomans waste their time studying alchemy, astrology, magic, and prophecy. Overall, Vetterlein describes a people who favor superstition and magic over reason and philosophy.

He argues that some sects of Islam have ways of thinking which are similar to the Greek philosophical schools. There are the Calendery (*Kalenderî*), who are similar to the Epicureans, and the Maelumitae (*Melâmetî*), who believe that self-knowledge is a prerequisite for knowledge of the divine. The Munachistae are similar in doctrine to the Pythagoreans, and he likens the highly skeptical Haeretitae to the Academics in ancient Greece. The Jabrite and Qadarite hold opposite views on free will and predestination, and the Ishrāqiyya school rejects parts of the Qur'an they find absurd. According to Vetterlein, atheists exist among the Turks and some are Ottoman sultans. The Charavidschitae deny that any man can receive divine revelations, whereas the Musserini deny the existence of God. Vetterlein's treatise ends rather abruptly, with no conclusion about the philosophy of the Turks. He finds Turkish philosophy a primitive curiosity, valuable, and interesting, not in its own right, but only insofar as it relates to Greek philosophy. However, Vetterlein shows great awareness of the Sufi groups, and different religious sects, including atheists, in the Ottoman Empire. As a member of the Reformed Church, Vetterlein's criticism of Christian sects that are foreign to philosophy as well as full of mystics and fanatics with no theological education is a veiled critique of Pietism and orthodox Lutheranism.

Turkish Philosophy (Köthen, 1790)

My readers will perhaps wonder why I have written this little book about Turkish philosophy, since it is commonly agreed that the Turks have neither philosophy, as we understand it, nor any books on philosophy. But I think that the human genius and intellect has progressed among the Turks to something that resembles the first basics of philosophy. They have begun to exercise their reason in a way that we can speak of as philosophizing. For philosophy is nothing other than reason and the human mind seeking natural causes and the laws of nature. I truly believe that any effort spent on philosophy is not at all useless, whether one reaches a higher understanding of things through the powers of a civilized or barbarian mind. What then might cause the Turks to ignore philosophy? For philosophy helps us to understand history, which is very useful for human and divine knowledge. The reason the Turks never undertook a deliberate study of rational philosophy is because they never wanted to apply themselves to it. Their despotic and irrational empire opposes the refinement of the mind; and their religion is not only devoid of reason, but savage and intolerant. This intolerance, backed by civil law, represses all attempts at free thought and free speech. A third reason for this lack of philosophy is the slowness of the Tatar genius, although they exercise their judgement rationally enough in everyday affairs. But this nation lacks the mental strength and passionate force of mind necessary to discover and understand the deepest and greatest science of all: philosophy. They seem fonder of leisure and frivolous matters than is appropriate to cultivators of the most difficult and honorable discipline. But these barbarians have progressed to some semblance of philosophy, which can also be observed in the histories of other uncivilized nations in the process of laying aside their barbarousness. For us who are led by the Supreme Deity, reason seems of secondary importance, yet it too can lead us to the truth. Thus, there are certain means by which some nations are led to a deeper philosophical understanding of things. The first of these is religion, even one that is superstitious and foolish. The second is an understanding of history and foreign languages. With these means, the more talented intellects of a barbarous age can reach a deeper knowledge of nature and begin to philosophize.

The possessor of a sophisticated mind craves knowledge of the truth and understanding of the obscure when he has been freed from work and can enjoy leisure time. Thus, he explores things that he usually fears due to religious superstition; he cannot help seeking explanations for the unknown, and this, on its own, is philosophizing. For every organized religion pronounces on almost all matters, and dares to respond to all serious questions: the origin and end of man and the universe, the causes of both, God, and the good life. This is why even Christians who do philosophy mostly start with inquiring into their paternal religion and the opinions formed in childhood before anything else, as if they could not step out into the light of philosophy without throwing down these chains. These chains and impediments need to be removed in order to make the love for truth and justice stronger and more enduring.

Religion alone does not lead to truth for the majority of people. This is demonstrated by the existence of many heretical sects arising within any given religion. Many think that religion combined with sound reason is far superior. Many opinions and doctrines, some of which are absurd, have arisen from a mixture of religion and reason. These opinions and doctrines bear a marvelous resemblance to those of the Greek philosophers. This is what I want to demonstrate with examples drawn from the Turkish nation, although I could easily do the same with the Indians, the Jews, other barbarians, or even Christian sects that are foreign to true philosophy. Mystics and other fanatics who lack theological teaching often reach judgements in a way that is similar to the keenest discoveries of the free mind and the metaphysical inquiries of philosophers, although they are expressed in unpolished and impure words, and corrupted by other ineptitudes. This is how religious sects arose among the Turks, expressing varied opinions in a manner reminiscent of different schools of philosophy. But first we must speak a few words about their education and intellectual history, which will elucidate their understanding of nature and the universe. For other disciplines tend to precede philosophical study. For the following, I have consulted the works of Busbeck, Ricaut, Businello, Büsching, Lüdecke, and Volney.

[In the Ottoman] *medrese*, the public school attached to the mosque, [students] learn Arabic and Persian. Arabic is taught so the Turks could read and recite the Qur'an; Persian is studied for reasons of style and ornamentation in writing. Besides this, they study the native history of the Ottomans. I doubt that this [initial education] prepares their minds for philosophy. In the Persian language, they read the fiction that we call Romance. This genre is written foolishly in an effeminate style, telling tales of lovers and monsters, which is the genius of the East. The works that [Pierre de] Marivaux and [Henry] Fielding composed based on these Romance stories are almost philosophical, but the Persian source material could not be acknowledged as such. Other literary studies were unknown to the Ottomans, except for knowledge of the law and sacred matters, which were based on the impure Qur'an. For they cared neither for history or geography, nor Greek or Latin, nor any other science or liberal art with reason or sound methods. They were drawn to medicine, but they were unsophisticated, and were ignorant of chemistry and anatomy. Some Turks read books in Arabic about medicine and philosophy by Avicenna and Averroes. But this was more for show than for use, so they could engage in mere sophistry and subtleties instead of divine abundance and Aristotelian acuteness. These barbarians also translated Aristotle to their own language very poorly. That is why they were unskilled and unteachable in physics. Many princes of this nation were fruitlessly engaged in and enthusiastic about alchemy, astrology, magic, and prophecy. The court employed an astrologer at public expense, who was consulted for advice. They had no sophisticated moral teachings, but they had brief aphorisms which were allegorical in the Eastern manner.

The Muslim religion is divided into many sects. These sects have opinions which resemble those of the Greek philosophical schools, which were founded by the pioneers of philosophy. [For example], the ideas of the Calendery [Kalenderî] resemble those of the Epicureans: they wickedly opine that all abstinence is futile; and all sadness is roused by black bile, which is natural to the superstitious; and every day should be lived to the fullest; and they think men should enjoy themselves in order to live a good life. The heretics called Maelumitae [Melâmetî] uphold a certain dogma which is wiser than the teachings of other philosophers: they believe that men can reach a perfect knowledge of God over the course of their own lives if they first know themselves fully. According to them, divine nature can only be understood through human nature. Those who are called Munachistae [Bektaşi?] believe in metempsychosis [*tanāsukh*]² just like the Pythagoreans, and refrain from all use of animals. Another sect, the Haeretitae [Cerrahi?], doubts everything, affirms nothing, and denies knowledge of truth to men, attributing it to God alone. This makes them unargumentative, dutiful, and compliant. But they are very pious and diligent in worshipping and performing rites on their paternal sacred days. Behold! These Tatar barbarians are like Academics!

Just as the question of free will and fate is important to philosophers, it is also a matter of importance to Muslims. Hence arose the Jabrite sect, which believes that everything, including men, are ruled by a supreme deity; and that all our actions depend on divine will. They believe that we would not even think of doing anything against God's will; and that whatever we do, it comes from a natural and determined beginning. They also think that the whole mind is controlled by physical laws, as is water flowing down from a height, and heavy objects which are carried downwards. However, the Qadarites believe the opposite. For they do not believe in fate and an immutable nexus of human events; they attribute free will to men, otherwise God would be the cause of evil and the author of sin.

The majority of those skilled in law and those who function as royal priests in mosques constitute the order of the Ischrakitae [Ishrāqiyya], who espouse liberal doctrines. According to their beliefs, it is most important that we be loved by God, which is impossible unless we love humans. Hence, they show great generosity to the poor, and great companionship and constancy in friendship. Besides this, they show great freedom and wisdom in religious matters. They do not praise the Qur'an completely, but only those parts that contain goodness; the rest they despise as absurd and stupid. They treat the followers of foreign religions humanely and bear themselves with equanimity. When they debate with Christians, they do not wholly reject their mysteries, but challenge certain aspects of their reasoning and dogma. They define goodness as contemplation. They use well-considered judgement in sacred matters and exercise laudable caution toward the masses, whose religious opinions no wise man would ever impugn openly. Thus, I can justly claim that the source of wisdom, the Academic school, has transferred from old Greece to these masters of new Greece. [...].

For just as a shadow of a man gave rise to the art of statuary, so thought, with some religion as its foundation, gives the opportunity to investigate everything about nature. And thus, we come to true and false judgements. The Charavidschitae [Kharijites?] deny all religious revelations given by a man. They do not think that there is any man divinely instructed and sent down from heaven for the sake of founding a religion, for every man can be deceived and make mistakes. If God had wanted to help humankind by revealing religion, it is extremely unlikely that He used one man or one nation. Either none or all organized religions in the world should rest on the authority of God, since He is the kind of being who cares for the whole race of mortals. Therefore, the Charavidschitaes reject the Muslims who think more of domination and empire than of virtue.

But the Musserini are bolder and they deny that there is a God. They say that nature is inward and that the force of things, "in which the cause of each thing is situated," lies in the individual.

This is what produced everything that we see of its own accord and what maintains it in its nexus; this is what gave forth the sun, moon, and stars and what forces them to stay on their course; this is where man gets strength to stand and move himself, where he is born and grows and gains strength like a plant; this is that force and wonderful nature which stands out so clearly that the mind comprehends it as if it were visible.

They think that this inward force is the cause of the marvels of nature and they say that we feel the divine without seeing it. They use the [dialectical] question of whether or not there is a god. If there is, He is not wise, since prophets imagine Him for us. For He would not have created atheists, who deny His strength and nature, and persistent thinking that He does not exist. Many of these atheists preside over the laws and are princes of the Ottoman Empire, boasting of the sophisticated elegance of their ways. Indeed, these atheists tend to hide their own beliefs, and for that reason they are called Musserini, that is, "those who have the mystery."[3] These men pay much more attention to [secular] morality, hospitality, and companionship; they freely pursue their studies, cultivate friendship, and dispute among themselves with great freedom on public and religious matters. Therefore, good and civil ways are not always foreign to atheists, if they must be called thus, for they do not reject the concept of a divine power, but rather the concept of an anthropomorphic god. Indeed, Strato, Spinoza, and others philosophized on this matter. The opposite viewpoint comes from those who attribute the idea of personhood to the divine power, which is something extraordinary and therefore not subject to human understanding.

Notes

1 Vetterlein's biography was compiled from the following sources: Andreas Gottfried Schmidt, *Anhaltisches Schriftsteller-Lexikon, oder historisch-literarische Nachrichten über Schriftsteller, welche in Anhalt geboren sind oder gewirkt haben* (Bernburg, 1830), 432–4; Christian F. R. Vetterlein, *Klopstocks Oden und Elegieen mit erklärenden Anmerkungen* (Leipzig, 1833); Friedrich A. Schmidt and Bernhard F. Voigt, *Neuer Nekrolog der Deutschen*, vols. 20–21 (Weimar, 1844), 127–31; Friedrich A. Kittler, *Aufschreibesysteme 1800/1900* (Munich: Wilhelm Fink, 1985), 155; Ingrid Tomkowiak, *Lesebuchgeschichten: Erzählstoffe in Schullesebüchern, 1770–1920* (Berlin: Walter de Gruyter, 1993), 36–42; and Hole Rößler, "Polyhistorie und Polymathie," in *Neue Diskurse der Gelehrtenkultur in der Frühen Neuzeit: Ein Handbuch*, eds. Herbert Jaumann and Gideon Stiening (Berlin: Walter de Gruyter, 2016), 635–76.
2 [MK] On the believers of metempsychosis in the Safavid context, see Kathryn Babayan. *Mystics, Monarchs, and Messiahs: Cultural Landscapes of Early Modern Iran* (Cambridge: Harvard University Press, 2002), 3–8 and 484.
3 [MK] On the Musserini sect (spelled also *Muserin* or *Muserim*), see Alan Charles Kors, *Atheism in France, 1650–1729, Volume I: The Orthodox Sources of Disbelief* (Princeton: Princeton University Press, 1990), 151–2.

12 Politics of the Turkish Republic

Michael Wendeler

Wendeler was born in Schlettau in 1610. In 1628, he began his studies at Wittenberg, becoming a Magister in 1632. He initially studied philology with Erasmus Schmidt and mathematics and astronomy with Ambrosius Rhodius. Wendeler obtained his Master of Philosophy from the University of Wittenberg in 1633. He then advanced his study of theology with prominent Lutheran scholars, such as Jakob Martini, Paul Röber, Wilhelm Leyser, and Johann Hülsemann. Around 1637, he was an adjunct professor in the Faculty of Philosophy at Wittenberg. After a short training at the University of Helmstedt, he became professor of ethics at Wittenberg in 1640. He was also a visiting professor at the University of Helmstedt. In the same year, he became a professor of moral philosophy at Wittenberg. In 1650, he was a professor of theology, and in 1666, he became an assessor in the Faculty of Theology. During his tenure at Wittenberg, Wendeler also participated in administrative tasks. He was Dean of the Faculty of Philosophy and Rector of the Alma Mater in several winter and summer semesters from 1645 to 1669. He was also the director of the University's library. As a Lutheran philosopher and theologian, Wendeler was a prolific writer, publishing many disputations on topics such as political philosophy, theology, moral philosophy, and Jewish political thought. He also wrote a manual on how to conduct an academic disputation, *Breves observationes genuini disputandi processus*, a handbook influential among Lutheran academic circles. He died in Wittenberg in 1671.[1]

Variant Names: Michael Wendler, Michael Wendelerus, Michaele Wendelero, Michael Wendlerus, Michaeli Wendelero, and Michaelis Wendeleri.

Summary and Analysis

Wendeler's disputation on the Turkish republic is a discussion of Turkish history, political philosophy, and the concept of monarchy and tyranny. Half of his disputation concerns the identification of the Turks with the little horn which arises on the head of the fourth beast in the prophet's vision described in the Book of Daniel 7:1–28 (This section was not included to improve readability). Giving copious historical references, Wendeler explains that this little horn cannot be referring to Christ as the Jews believe, nor to the Seleucid monarch Antiochos Epiphanes as the Calvinists believe. Nor can it be identified with the Antichrist as the Catholics believe. Wendeler puts forth a detailed argument that the little horn on the fourth beast in the prophecy of Daniel can only be identified with the Turkish monarch (Sultan).

Concluding his lengthy discussion on the identity of the little horn, Wendeler then turns to a discussion of the Turkish monarchy. He outlines Aristotle's description of three types of monarchic rule: kingship, domination, and tyranny. Kingship is the ideal, in which the ruler is concerned with the welfare of his subjects; domination is when the ruler controls his subjects like a master controls his slaves; and tyranny is the worst form of all, wherein the ruler disregards the public good for his own selfish reasons.

According to Wendeler, the Turkish ruler can properly be called a monarch, but not a king; he is instead a master of slaves or a tyrant. Wendeler's reasoning is that the Turkish monarchs respect neither the property rights nor the personal freedom of their subjects. They also do not allow the rulers of defeated states to keep their titles and kingdoms, as the Romans did on some occasions, which Wendeler selectively recounts from history. How then, asks Wendeler, has such a violent and unjust monarchy maintained its rule over the empire for so many centuries? The answer has more to do with divine punishment than any virtue or worthiness on the part of the Turkish monarchs.

Wendeler then gives an account of the history of the Ottoman state, from its foundation to the reign of Selim II. A constant theme in this account is that the Ottoman Empire did not rise to its great extent through the virtue or worthiness of its rulers, but through the infighting and mistakes of its Christian neighbors. The Ottoman monarchs are regularly described as savage, brutal, cunning, and given to committing acts of fratricide and patricide in order to rise to the top. Wendeler's tone in describing the deeds and policies of these monarchs is clearly condemnatory; these ruthless acts are not the ideal methods by which a good monarch should maintain his rule. He concludes his account of the reigns of the Turkish monarchs by reiterating his statement that the Ottoman Empire was only able to rise to the heights of power through the divisions of its Christian neighbors and the wrath of God.

He then states that those Christian scholars who advocate this tyrannical way of governing are in error. He condemns the writings of Niccolò Machiavelli as immoral and satanic. He is especially disgusted that an unnamed Protestant German scholar educated at his own University of Wittenberg has publicly defended these pro-tyrannical doctrines of Machiavelli. Wendeler cites the names and writings of several scholars who, he says, refute the teachings of Machiavelli quite handily. However, he disagrees with them on whether or not the Turkish monarchy can properly be termed a republic. According to Adam Contzen and Johannes Casus, a republic requires consensus among its subjects to be ruled, and cannot exist without trust, justice, and Christ. Wendeler, on the other hand, claims that consensus is not required for every civil community and that a republic can still be called a republic without Christ, as the great pagan republics of ancient times existed without Christianity.

Wendeler then turns back to the subject of the Turks, saying that their judicial system is corrupt and unjust, and that they are untrustworthy

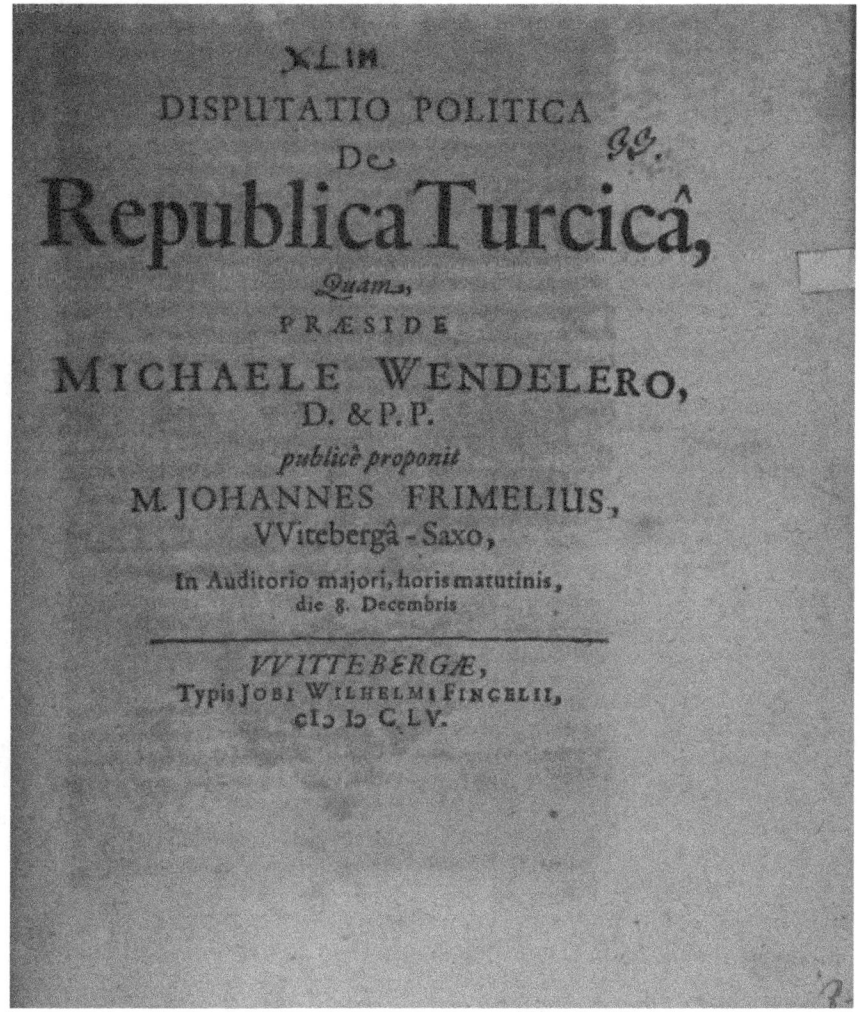

Figure 12.1 Michael Wendeler, *Disputatio politica de republica Turcica*, 1655 (Courtesy of the Bavarian State Library, Munich).

in their foreign relations. However, according to Wendeler, they are still more trustworthy than the Pope. With this remark about the untrustworthiness of the Pope, the disputation ends. In conclusion, Wendeler draws a parallel between the monstrous 'little horn'—the tyrannical Turkish monarchy—and the tyranny of the Catholic Church, exemplified by the untrustworthy Pope and the satanic writings of the Catholic Machiavelli.

Politics of the Turkish Republic (Wittenberg, 1655)

The preceding disputation provided an opportunity to talk about the Turkish State (*republica*). In this, I made a comment when quoting the Book of Daniel about the horn, that is, the horn of the Turkish kingdom, the birth of which, according to historians, occurred in the year of Christ 622. At this time Muhammad, more commonly known as Mahomed, after gaining power, founded the kingdom of the Saracens, or Arabs, which was ruled by twenty-six kings until the year of Christ 1545. In the same year, Muhammad began the Caliphate, that is, the vicariate, in Baghdad and Damascus. There were thirty caliphs from then on until the year of Christ 868. A year later, the Caliphate was divided into the Caliphate of Syria and Egypt. The Caliphate of Egypt flourished until the year 1245, when the Mamluks gained control. The Caliphate of Syria endured until the year of Christ 1297, after which it was named the Ottoman Empire for Osman I. Anyone can record the succession of the remaining emperors from Turkish history. In the present disputation, I will talk about Chapter 7 of Daniel's prophecy, as the "little horn" is a reference to the Turkish kingdom. Thus, I will explain the Ottoman regime: its duration, judiciary, laws, treaties with outsiders, and more.

[MK: The sections from one to forty associating the "little horn" of Daniel 7:8 with the Ottoman Empire are omitted. In sum, Wendeler thinks that the little horn is the last sign before the last judgement, and the last sign was the then current Turkish Sultan.]

So much for the explanation of the little horn. Now, let's see the other limbs of this disputation. I will explain the structure and history of the Turkish regime in the following paragraphs. After Aristotle speaks about republics in general, he describes five types of monarchy with the last type denoting the true king. In that passage, he describes monarchy as the rule of one man.

Along with Aristotle, let me enumerate the types of monarchy, beginning with the typical form of monarchy: the kingdom. A kingdom is a monarchy in which the subjects' welfare is placed above all. This happens when the monarch, refraining from the possessions of his subjects, rules his subjects justly and fairly, according to the established laws of God, nature, and his kingdom. This type of monarch is a king, distinguished from the rest by his virtues.

A *dominium* is a form of monarchy between a kingdom and a tyranny. The word *dominus* (master) derives from *dominium*, which the *dominus* exercises over his slaves. The *dominus* controls all the fortunes of his slaves, whether they were made slaves by the law of war or made subject by agreement. Aristotle distinguishes a *dominus* from a king and a prince, though Plutarch testifies that Aristotle used to warn Alexander to rule the Greeks in his office with fatherly devotion and to rule foreigners as a *dominus*.

Tyranny, the worst of all states, is farthest from a kingdom; since it is opposed to the highest good. Along with Aristotle, I judge a tyrant by how much he contributes to the public good. A tyrant is the opposite of a king. It is the duty of a king to give his full attention to the state; a tyrant is one who neglects and subverts the public good for the sake of his own convenience. The resulting vices follow from this inversion of the public good. For the tyrant cannot transfer the state to himself if the laws or wise and judicious men oppose him, so he removes them.

The Turkish Sultan is properly called a monarch: not a king however, but rather a *dominus* or a tyrant, for these two terms are easily interchangeable. I would say that the Turk is a *dominus*; Jean Bodin says that according to their laws only the caliph, the High Priest, can openly lay claim to domination, or call himself the *dominus* of any household.

Indeed, Menavinus also ascribes dominion over the household to the emperor, saying that the third son from any family throughout all of Greece, Bosnia, and Wallachia can be conscripted into the army of the Janissaries. When Constantinople was struck by an earthquake, Bayezid II imposed a tribute on every subject, and called together every tenth craftsman under the [threat of] capital punishment to restore the city.

It is evident that the Sultan dominates conquered enemies harshly. The Romans gave defeated enemies peace without immediately depriving them of their former dignity. Hence Virgil says: "[the Romans] spare the subdued and conquer the arrogant." After the first Punic War, Florus says: "Peace was given to the Carthaginians, nothing besides that." Florus also says that the consul gave peace to Philip of Macedon and granted him his kingdom. Indeed, according to Florus, the Roman people never reproached his victory over his conquered enemies.

But would the Turks have left dignity and possession to either the prince or the city or the conquered king? Although Johannes Castriotes, King of Epirus, had freely gone to surrender to Murad II, his children were still deprived of his kingdom. Süleyman was not willing to make peace with Ferdinand unless he withdrew from all of Hungary and made Austria tributary to the Turks.

Such an empire should not be long-lasting: it is violent, and everyone hates it, even those who live in the highest honor. Therefore, I will try to explain why it has endured so long. That tyranny has now persevered for 355 years. It was founded by the hard work and fraud of Osman in 1300. This empire is long-lasting and savage; I do not attribute its strength to the domination of an unjust barbarian, but to the punishment of a divine godhead, mutual hatred and wars with their neighbors.

Anyone can agree that the endurance of this empire has many causes, such as the very lucky successions, the mutual slaughter of brothers, military tumult, and many other things. To understand it correctly, it is my intention to examine the whole matter in depth. In the year 1300, Osman, a man of great counsel and good courage, defeated the weak Turkish princelings in various battles because of their disunity. He became a great Sultan from their spoils and ruled the empire for twenty-seven years.

Orhan, the son of Osman, began his rule after the murder of his two older brothers; this rule was more successful than its inauspicious beginning would suggest. For he added most of the empire of Constantinople to his kingdom, not through his virtue, but through the long dissensions and civil wars of the grandfathers and grandsons of the Andronici, Kantakouzenos, and Palaeologus. Fighting them with wickedness, treachery, and mutual slaughter, Orhan easily occupied these regions, which lacked outside assistance. While helping the Greek factions, which was the custom of leading Turkish men, he turned his neighbors' calamities into an opportunity for expansion.

Murad succeeded Orhan and was superior to all the Turkish leaders in ambition, tolerance for hard work, shrewdness, military discipline, strength, fairness, kindness, temperance, and charm. He was approachable, kind, and humane in distributing honors and rebuking people. The Turkish empire was different at that time; under the growing monarchy, although the subjects were not free, they were at least secure from danger. He weakened the empire of Constantinople, not on his own initiative, but because he was summoned by [John V] Palaeologus, who was under assault by the leading men of Greece and the Bulgars. Murad easily won a victory over the Greeks after being transported to Europe by this greedy Christian emperor.

Bayezid, the son of Murad, and the killer of his brother Süleyman, had the greatest ferocity. He defeated Sigismund, the king of Hungary. In this fight, the Christians erred greatly. Without a plan, the French rushed forward against their leaders' wishes, were surrounded by the Turkish cavalry, and destroyed. Bayezid was conquered by Tamerlane in the year 1394 and shut in prison with ignominy and misery. The Turkish Empire sustained their greatest disaster at that time; besides the 140,000 who fell in the battle, 120,000 were crushed by the cavalry while retreating [at the battle of Ankara].

Having been assisted by the Greek princes, Çelebi, the son of Bayezid, restored his deeply fallen fortunes with his veteran soldiers. After a short time, he engaged in battle against Sigismund, the king of Hungary, and was victorious. In this fight, having boldly attacked the enemy before their infantry could assist them, the Christian knights were driven into an ignoble retreat. They allowed the infantry lines, which were in disarray, to be finished off with arrows.

Musa ambushed and killed Orhan, the son of Çelebi. Mehmed then killed Musa; he also made the Turkish kingdom—thus far good in part—harsher and crueler in many ways. For he despoiled the princelings and princes of the Turkish state, suspected them for the most insignificant reasons, and oppressed them partially by force and partially by fraud. Mehmed's harsh policies were extended for so long and so widely that after a short while there were no princes anywhere, but mere slaves. Mehmed died in the year 1419; up until his time, the Turkish monarchy was most temperate.

Murad II followed, whom Johannes Hunniades defeated in five battles, and whom Scanderbeg forced to die during the unsuccessful siege of Krujë. Murad II brought disaster to the Greeks, who resisted weakly. After Murad died, the Turkish soldiers did not choose a leader from the clan of the dead man to command their army, but chose Mustafa, Murad's uncle. Under him, they defeated another Mustafa, Murad's brother, an adolescent of thirteen years. Therefore, no one should wonder that Murad thrived, with some Christians being idle, and others even surrendering, and the Greeks offering the fortune of their kingdom to a contemptible boy.

Under Mehmed II, this empire degenerated into an absolute tyranny. Mehmed II occupied Constantinople in 1453 or, as Alstedius says, 1457, not through the virtue of his Turks, but with the worst sort of help: treachery from the Illyrians, Wallachians, Dardanians, and Serbians. These people came to fight for Mehmed II in the hope of booty. He was a savage man to them, a despiser of all laws, oaths, and nobleness. With his death in 1487, it became clear how badly he had governed the kingdom.

Bayezid II, who brought remarkable military defeats to the Venetians, succeeded him. Soon he was pushed back by them and forced to make peace. Then, he was harassed by the Persians, so that he was not far from losing all North Asia in one expedition. While these conflicts were going badly for their father, his sons, Selim, Ahmed, and Korkut, fought among themselves for control of the empire at home. At last, Selim obtained the throne with help from the Janissaries, having killed his father with poison. He killed not only his brothers, but also their sons, and destroyed the Persians, losing 100,000 men. Süleyman I succeeded Selim I and Selim II succeeded Süleyman I. Historians agree that these men far exceeded their elders in savagery and rapacity. It is not necessary to recount more about these sultans as it is almost the same story with only the protagonists changing.

After careful consideration, we find that the Turkish Empire lasted 200 years, and that it began to be very absolute, tyrannical, and

250 Philosophy and Liberal Arts

wretched. There were many perpetual evils in this kingdom. For since there were many princes, they all hoped to rule, either by their father's favor, or the charms of some concubine, or an uprising of the pretorian soldiers. This desire to rule was fueled by a perpetual fear of death. Hence these princes, who otherwise would have to die, tried everything, on the grounds that there was nothing between the throne and the grave, between the crown and the noose.

Furthermore, the fear of death and hope of domination made the princes suspicious and dangerous in their father's eyes. For as soon as they learned whom their father preferred among his sons, they at once judged themselves to be condemned to death. Furthermore, since the whole empire was ruled by one person, anybody, even a fool or a boy, could become the kingdom's successor. There were innumerable calamities for the subjects, which arose from incompetent rule. Fertile fields far and wide turned into forests, and everything headed toward ruin because of the rulers' injustice. None of the farmers could look forward to success. Hence, the regions were so despoiled that there were hardly any of the necessities of life left.

From all these things that I have recounted, it is certain how unlucky and weak the Turkish Empire was. It lasted so long not because of their rulers' counsel, but because of God's anger and their neighbors' discord. If these two means of preserving the longevity of the Turkish state did not exist, it would most certainly have been weak, short, and defenseless against all invaders.

Therefore, politicians who recommend this way of ruling to German princes err enormously. What the inauspicious Niccolò Machiavelli advocated in the previous century is well known to all learned men. In particular, the way this monstrous man advocates for a hypocritical prince can be seen from Chapter 8 onward. Indeed, throughout *The Prince*, Machiavelli seems to concern himself with opportunistically attributing to the good prince everything that Aristotle said about the Sophist's way of preserving tyranny. In *Introduction to Aristotle's Politics*, Hermann Conring agrees with this.

I wish this monstrous dogma had either been extinguished in its first flowering in the region in which it was born, or that no German had learned any knowledge of it. In truth, everyday experience together with public writings teaches us this dogma, exceedingly pestilential and clearly of the devil, has set deep roots in the minds of many Germans. I will not speak of what others described long ago, but I will only mention what happened recently at Frankfurt an der Oder. There, a certain P.P. and J. U. Doctor, educated in our University of Wittenberg, wrote a certain disputation for the public about the good prince. In it, the dogmas of Machiavelli are summoned from hell and publicly defended. When I saw that disputation, which was already in the hands of many, I shrank from it wholeheartedly, and greatly detested it, along with all good and wise men.

The dogmas in it are so horrible that they need no refutation. Anyone who has been steeped in their first letters and any sort of piety can refute this new and absurd doctrine. But anyone who does not know how to oppose these dogmas should read *A Defense of Liberty against Tyrants: Or, Concerning the Legitimate Power of a Prince over the People, and of the People over a Prince*, published by Stephanus Junius [Brutus] at Hanover in 1595. He disputes Machiavelli's evil arts, depraved advice, and false and pestiferous doctrine.

I, in turn, opposed the author of these theses in another work using the criticism of Machiavelli by Johannes Casus of Oxford, a man of Reformed religion. On the first page of *The Sphere of State*, he says:

> I wrote these things, so that those devoted to studying politics might understand that I flee from and detest Machiavelli, hateful to God and man, as if he were a dog and a snake. For although much of his work has the appearance of wisdom, he sets before you more poison than honey, more wickedness than virtue. I warn that it must not be read or heard. For what Paracelsus does for medicine, Machiavelli does for government. The former peddles his medicine as something beautiful, valuable, remarkable in essence and quality, but resulting in the body's ruin. The latter sells his teachings, seemingly learned at first appearance, and unique on the first hearing, but utterly disastrous to the state. Therefore, just as the former must be evaded, lest he cause men to perish, so the latter is to be removed, lest he is accepted and ruin the state. Therefore, I oppose Machiavelli, and detest his axioms on founding a republic and a state as anathema to my soul.

This ingenious judgement of Johannes Casus on Machiavelli has pleased all Calvinists. I am very certain that it still pleases them, and that the evil undertakings of the disputator from Frankfurt deeply displease them. Indeed, I have no doubt that good princes turn their studies to Casus and many other counselors of his type and are never detested.

Although the Turkish Empire became an absolute tyranny in all degrees, it is properly called a republic, since my definition of a republic agrees with Aristotle's description, which does not distinguish between a good republic and a bad one. If we consider war, laws, and offices in general, we define them as neither good nor bad, lest we confuse quality with essence. In the same way, a praetor is not only said to administer the law, but to judge fairly or unfairly. This way of defining is used in Aristotle's *Logic*, *Rhetoric*, and *Politics*. It is commonly used by politicians and jurists, especially [Herennius] Modestinus, who define laws, marriage, war, and so on, from essences alone.

On this issue [definition based on essences alone], I am opposed to Adam Contzen and Johannes Casus. For Contzen clearly denies it, "the form," he says in the cited passage, referring to the republic, is the reason for law, on which the people agree, that is, the order of the rulers and the rule of subjects, from which form the triple republic rises. From this, it is obvious that when there is no consensus there is no republic, but rather a gathering of slaves living under the power of a master. Therefore, the Turkish emperor does not have a proper republic. For he has the absolute right over life and death of his subjects, even his supreme war leaders. Everyone dedicates themselves and all their abilities, as the property of the great emperor, in a manner greater and more potent than that between slaves and masters. This is a despotic regime, in no way civil, for although he has cities, he does not rule them by the law of citizens, but with the absolute power of a master. So, their great cities are nothing other than more spacious workhouses and their great Pashas and Beylerbeyis are like slave overseers to die at the nod of their master without the defense of laws or rights.

Casus, in *The Sphere of State*, agrees with Contzen. "Truly," he says,

I am making an assertion against Machiavelli, that a city does not stand, that there is no state without trust, without justice, and without Christ; since without these arms one is not called a king, but a tyrant, not a city, but a raging crowd, not an ordered republic, but fearful confusion.

Both Contzen and Casus distinguish between the virtuous and wicked conditions of a republic, and affirm that the former constitutes a proper republic, and denies that the latter can be called a republic. As I have said, I strongly deny this distinction. I have mentioned above the reasons for my assertion. I disagree with Adam Contzen, that the form of a republic is the rule of law, on which the people agree. I know that consensus is required for marriage, but not for any civil community. I also deny Casus' words, that where there is no trust, justice, and Christ, there is no republic. If it were so, then it would follow that no pagan republic, however virtuous, was a proper republic for they were all without Christ.

Finally I must say a few words about the Turks' judicial system and treaties. The handing down of judgements among the Turks is quick, but not just. For their highest judge, knowledgeable in law, and of a grand old age, judges cases on the spot. Appeals can be made to a *kadı* [judge], who in dubious cases seeks the opinion of a *Muftī* [jurist]. But since the Turks still have few written laws, the judges have great influence on sentencing. Hence, the Turkish judges never judge promptly without bribes, and they have hands in the pockets of the litigants on both sides. This causes the calamitous oppression of the poor and the whole republic. For those who afflict the poor are so powerful, especially if they are eminent, that they cannot be punished without damage to the empire.

Almost all treaties are measured by their usefulness. For this reason, no one is an ally to the Turks. They do not comply with treaties, except when it pleases them, on the grounds that they believe it sacred to destroy their enemies in any way. [...]. Although the Turks' malice in their agreements is obvious, Murad brought Vladislav, the king of Hungary, whom he had caused to break a treaty, as a defendant in front of God's tribunal.

Our political officials and writers are not the only ones who desire treaties with heretics, but the Turks do as well during times of great necessity. Georg Schönborner was in a great uproar, constantly urging that such treaties should be completely forbidden. On top of that, political elites point out that we could enter a treaty less safely with the Pope than with a Turk. This is because Papists equivocate, and their oaths are vain, due to the ready acquittal of the Jesuits, and also because of the difficulty of the Successor [Pope], who denies that the law can constrain him. If the number of pages permitted, I would say more about this tyrannical republic. I will expound further, if God grants it, at a more convenient time.

Note

1 Wendeler's biography was compiled from the following sources: Johann Heinrich Zedler (ed.), "Wendler oder Wendeler, (Michael)," in *Grosses vollständiges Universal-Lexicon aller Wissenschafften und Künste*, vol. 54 (Leipzig, 1747), 2067–9; Walter Friedensburg, *Geschichte der Universität Wittenberg* (Halle: Max Niemeyer, 1917), 507–8; Heinz Kathe, *Die Wittenberger Philosophische Fakultät 1502–1817* (Köln: Böhlau, 2002), 223–32; and Kenneth G. Appold, *Orthodoxie als Konsensbildung: das theologische Disputationswesen an der Universität Wittenberg zwischen 1570 und 1710* (Tübingen: Mohr Siebeck, 2004), 102–25.

13 Fate of Learning among the Arabs

Cornelius Dietrich Koch

Koch was born in 1676 in Quakenbrück, Lower Saxony. He first attended a school run by his father, in which he acquired knowledge of Latin, Greek, French, philosophy, and mathematics, before enrolling in the municipal school of Helmstedt. Afterwards, he studied theology at the University of Helmstedt, a Lutheran institution. He won a scholarship to study oriental languages for two years in Hamburg under the prominent Lutheran theologian Esdras Edzard. He acquired the degree of Magister in 1700 in Helmstedt and took an academic journey to Holland when he failed to be considered for the chair in poetry despite the recommendation of Leibniz, the well-known seventeenth-century German Enlightenment philosopher. In 1711, he obtained his doctorate in theology under the supervision of the Lutheran theologian Johann Andreas Schmidt. Koch then became a professor of philosophy at Helmstedt, teaching logic, metaphysics, theological dogmatic, and morality. Although he is neglected in the modern scholarship, Koch is considered a forerunner of the early Enlightenment in Halle. He was an influential figure as he established the basis of studying the history of logic. His contribution was recognized by a letter sent to him by Leibniz. He died in Helmstedt in 1724.[1]

Variant Names: C. D. Koch, Corn. Diet. Koch, Cornelius Didericus Koch, Cornelius Dietericus Koch, Cornelius Dietericus Kochius, and Corneille Theodore Koch

Summary and Analysis

At the beginning of his dissertation, Koch remarks that throughout history learning has originated, flourished, and declined in various parts of the world. Intending to trace the history of learning among the Arabs, he begins by listing the categories of knowledge valued by the pre-Islamic Arabs, namely poetry, rhetoric, astronomy, genealogy, dream interpretation, and medicine. However, he thinks that the advent of Islam and their wars of expansion distracted the Arabs from their literary studies. According to him, fifty years or so after Muhammad's death, learning resumed, this time with a considerable interest in a new category: Islamic law.

Despite this renewed attention to learning, Koch claims that the Arabs had no knowledge of philosophy and, indeed, were discouraged from its study by religious prohibition. Arabs did not hesitate to burn philosophical books in the lands they conquered; Koch recounts the tale of the caliph 'Umar ordering books from the library of Alexandria to be burned to heat the baths. However, Abū Ja'far al-Manṣūr, the twenty-second caliph after Muhammad (and second Abbasid caliph), became a patron of philosophical learning, and the Arabs began to take up the study of philosophy in earnest. After al-Manṣūr, their interest in philosophy continued. The caliph Hārūn al-Rashīd traveled in the company of a hundred learned men, scholars sought books written by the Greek philosophers and translated them into Arabic, and many universities and libraries were founded throughout the Arab world. Koch compares this favorably with the situation in the West, which "seemed to threaten ruin and destruction for the best letters when barbarousness slowly crept into our minds." Koch particularly emphasizes the Arab contribution to mathematics, whose notation was used in Europe in his day. Inspired by the works of Aristotle, the Muslims also produced accomplished philosophers of their own, whose names Koch lists from the early Islamic period, unlike Ludewig and Steuchius who also mention later Islamic philosophers, such as Naṣīr al-Dīn al-Ṭūsī (d. 1274) as well as Najm al-Dīn al-Qazwīnī (d. 1276), the author of popular work *Ḥikmat al-'Ayn*.

Koch goes on to name some famous Arab patrons of philosophy and learning, including many Abbasid caliphs, to show that philosophy did not lack for official patronage in the Arab world. He attributes the decline of their learning to the general war and chaos which engulfed the Islamic world during the time of Tamerlane, but, strangely, he does not mention the earlier destruction of Baghdad by the Mongols. He says that the various disciplines of learning, such as poetry and history, saw a resurgence among the Persians. Therefore, he presents Persian and Turkish scholars' preference for writing in Persian instead of Arabic as proof of the decline of learning among Arabs. He ends his dissertation with a statement that it was his original intention to go into detail about the life and doctrine of the Arab philosopher al-Kindī, but that he will leave that task for someone else. Thus, by using the Arabs as an example, Koch's dissertation leaves the reader with the impression that the state of civilized learning is cyclical, flourishing, and declining according to internal factors, such as religion and official patronage, and external factors, such as war and empire building.

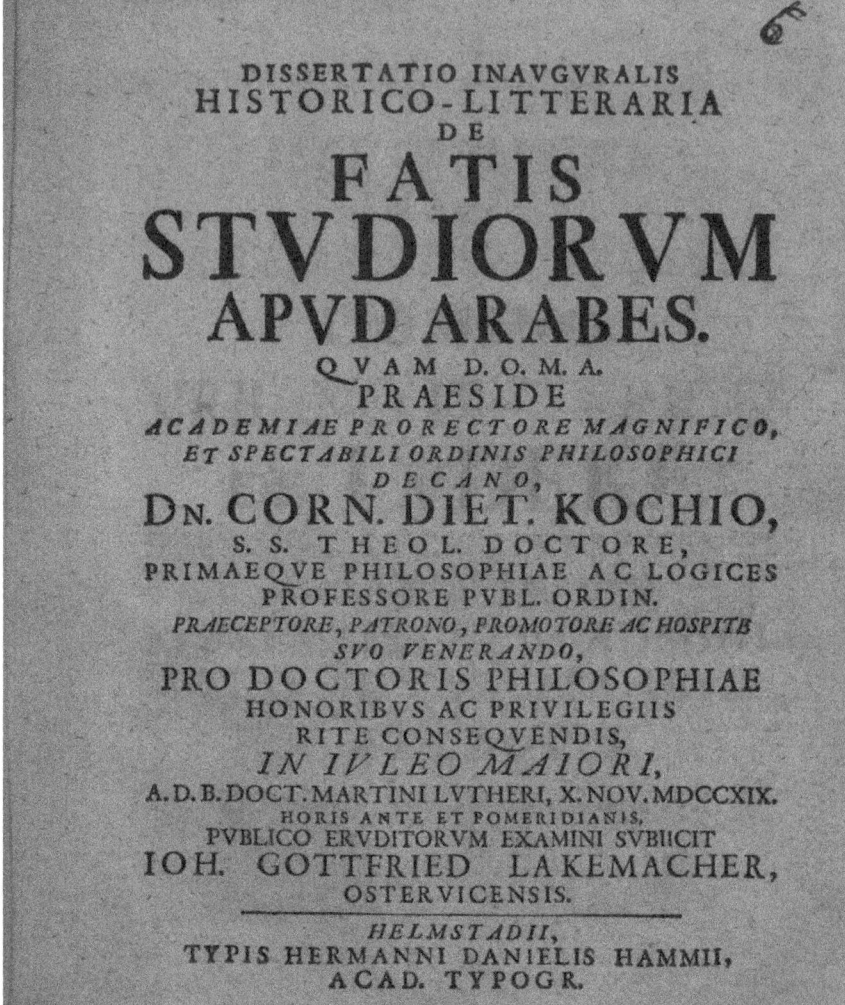

DISSERTATIO INAVGVRALIS
HISTORICO-LITTERARIA
DE
FATIS
STVDIORVM
APVD ARABES.
QVAM D. O. M. A.
PRAESIDE
ACADEMIAE PRORECTORE MAGNIFICO,
ET SPECTABILI ORDINIS PHILOSOPHICI
DECANO,
DN. CORN. DIET. KOCHIO,
S. S. THEOL. DOCTORE,
PRIMAEQVE PHILOSOPHIAE AC LOGICES
PROFESSORE PVBL. ORDIN.
PRAECEPTORE, PATRONO, PROMOTORE AC HOSPITE
SVO VENERANDO,
PRO DOCTORIS PHILOSOPHIAE
HONORIBVS AC PRIVILEGIIS
RITE CONSEQVENDIS,
IN IVLEO MAIORI,
A. D. B. DOCT. MARTINI LVTHERI, X. NOV. MDCCXIX.
HORIS ANTE ET POMERIDIANIS,
PVBLICO ERVDITORVM EXAMINI SVBIICIT
IOH. GOTTFRIED LAKEMACHER,
OSTERVICENSIS.
HELMSTADII,
TYPIS HERMANNI DANIELIS HAMMII,
ACAD. TYPOGR.

Figure 13.1 Cornelius Dietrich Koch, *Dissertatio inauguralis historico-litteraria de fatis studiorum apud Arabes*, 1719 (Courtesy of the Bavarian State Library, Munich).

Dissertation on the Fate of Learning among the Arabs (Helmstedt, 1719)

The nature of human affairs is so fluid that it is no wonder I frequently discover varying transformations in the history of letters. Literature flourished for long intervals of time, so that one would have thought it had risen to perfection. But in a short period, it withered so much that it seemed to disappear altogether and be buried with hardly any trace. Once Greece won great praise for its wisdom; its fame fed many men who were conspicuous in their erudition and cultivated the most efficacious disciplines, so that they were a miracle to the whole world. People from outside gathered there, where they became immersed in the precepts of these men. But the happiness of this region, although it cheered its inhabitants over the course of many centuries, could by no means be perpetual and endure until our age. Instead of the old splendor of their *belles-lettres*, we see now in that same place a certain barbarousness and an ignorance of the best studies.

In turn, the peoples who had once been ignorant of letters, and were not concerned with learning anything from them, became polished in all the delights of the better literature. We Germans are ourselves an example. Indeed, our ancestors are still distinguished in the study of military tactics; but they have left the literary disciplines untouched. As Tacitus' *Germania* said "they loved laziness," which does not lend itself to the literary disciplines. In fact, those poems, whose authors Germans celebrate as their heroes, were without a doubt primitive, and not endowed with native polish. The state of the ancient Germans was so primitive and barbarous that they either did not study letters or treated them with disregard. Therefore, they struggled in any type of learning compared to other people.

We can now examine the vicissitudes that letters underwent among the Arabs as literature moved from the West to the East. Although there is no way that everything I have mentioned can be discussed, I will still touch on the notable moments in the history of letters. Now, if we look back at more ancient times [pre-Islamic Arabia], we must certainly think about how that race fell in love with literature, which we consider the most elegant; astronomy, which is the most undeveloped; and the art of medicine, which they cultivated with the highest care. Abū al-Faraj in *History of the Dynasties*, which Edward Pococke published in Arabic and Latin, recounts their strongest areas of learning:

> The erudition of the (ancient) Arabs, for which they were especially enthusiastic, was this: skill in their own language, propriety in speech, composing poetry, and writing speeches. The rising of the stars was also known to them, and their setting, and likewise how the stars are so positioned so that as one sets the other rises, and what influence the stars have in producing rain. Indeed, they pursued these things with the highest attentiveness and daily experimentation, with which true knowledge is acquired, since their way of life produced practical knowledge of these things.

But in this passage, however notable it is, Abū al-Faraj did not explain the extent of the erudition of the ancient Arabs. Otherwise, he should have also recalled their study of genealogy and history; the art of interpreting dreams (if indeed this deserves to be called an art, and not instead a cunning and fraudulent semblance); and certainly medicine. It is clear from the testimony of al-Shahrastānī, which Edward Pococke mentions in the preface to the commentary on the poem of al-Ṭughrā'ī, where there is a concise mention of "a knowledge of genealogies, histories, and interpreting dreams," which Arabs studied. In *Life of Pythagoras*, Porphyry, after the introduction, says that Pythagoras had also gone to Arabia, "where he became acquainted with the knowledge and interpretation of dreams." Furthermore, the most celebrated al-Ḥārith ibn Kalada, already famous before Muhammad, whose life he influences, proves that medicine had some value among the Arabs. After Ibn Kalada set off to Persia to learn the art of medicine, he made so much progress that he came back to his homeland with such excellent skills in curing diseases that Muhammad himself recommended him to the sick. Therefore, he was held in such high esteem that he was called "the doctor of the Arabs" [*ṭabīb al-'Arab*]. His general rule that he prescribed to anyone wanting a long life is wonderful: "If anyone wants to live for a long time, eat in the morning, wear light clothes, and have sex sparingly." By "light clothes," Abū al-Faraj thinks that Ibn Kalada is hinting that one should not burden oneself with debt. The Arabs valued poetry most of all and they cultivated it with a fervent enthusiasm. Like the Greeks who enclosed all their wisdom in poetry, the Arabs also expressed every kind of learning in verses, which displayed the splendor of their language. There is a memorable saying of Muḥammad ibn Salām: "During the age of ignorance, poems were encyclopedic pandects, the repository of wisdom, from which they drew what was useful to them and where they deposited everything." Hence, when a unique poet arose among them, he was a common joy to all, a common source of applause, who would keep the nation's erudition in good shape; indeed, he would increase it, and defend their deeds from oblivion. Thus, we have the old Arab grammarians, poets, orators, astronomers, historians, interpreters of dreams, and doctors.

Through Muhammad's skills, another religion, or rather superstition, entered the lands of the Arabs; circumstances suddenly changed, and minds were turned away from literary studies. Then, they were clearly obsessed with an insatiable desire to propagate the new religion and to extend the boundaries of their rule. When they were able to achieve this using violence, as usually happens, by constantly restraining the neighboring peoples and also their own countrymen, the Arabs diminished their own power with their all-encompassing religion. For this reason, everyone was converted to the study of arms, which suffocated letters, and destroyed it for a time. With this, the whole nation was at war, some on Muhammad's side, and some opposing him. And the Muses were drowned out among the din of arms. After about fifty years, these conflicts quietened down a bit. Then the ancient studies were resumed, with an additional one added, namely Muhammadan law. This is the time that al-Qāḍī Ṣā'id ibn Aḥmad al-Andalusī talks about:

> In the beginning of Islam, the Arabs cared about no other disciplines than skill in their own language, and knowledge of the constitutions of their law, with the exception of medicine, which some were familiar with, and most did not prohibit because it was universally necessary for men. This was the state of the Arabs under the rule of the Umayyads.

The Umayyads had fourteen caliphs, who succeeded each other in power in an almost unbroken line. Their dynasty was founded by the seventh caliph after Muhammad, called Mu'āwiya, the son of Abū Sufyān, in the year 41/661. But the era of the Umayyads ended with Marwān, the twenty-first caliph, in the year 131/748.

However, the Arabs had not yet applied their minds to the philosophical sciences. Of those who came before Muhammad, Abū al-Faraj says: "God had still granted nothing of philosophy to them, nor had He made them suitable for this study." Although the author observes that the ancient Arabs were indeed lacking in philosophy, the reason that he proposes is weak. So, did they, who were capable in other disciplines and arts, persuade themselves that their minds were unsuitable for philosophy? Rather, they neglected philosophical studies because they lacked philosophy teachers to reveal the secrets of these sciences to them. Therefore, they dedicated their lives to other occupations and studies. Afterwards, when the laws of Muhammad were so strong in this nation, religion stood in the way of philosophy as he banned them from immersing themselves in this. This is what Ibn Ṭufayl openly states in his novel *Ḥayy bin Yaqẓān*, which Pococke published in Arabic and Latin in 1671 at Oxford. When Ibn Ṭufayl contemplates philosophy, he says that "there were several men among the Arabs who were adept in philosophy, especially of the more sublime kind, but they never dared to profess it openly." Then, he immediately adds: "The Ḥanifite school and Muhammadan law forbade men to study philosophy and warned them to beware of it."[2] Perhaps this was in case their minds became more observant through cultivation, and philosophy laid bare the absurdity of Islam and the deceit of Muhammad, and caused men to slowly cease to follow the religion. We also see that the caliphs of the Muslim Arabs observed this ban of Muhammad with such superstitious rigor that they had no fear in destroying with fire and flames the most outstanding philosophical books. Abū al-Faraj tells an illuminating example of this concerning 'Amr ibn al-'Āṣ, the leader of the Arab army. When he seized Alexandria, the noblest city of Egypt, he was asked by the grammarian Yaḥyā al-Naḥwī, whom he otherwise favored, to give him the many philosophical books that were found in the royal library. But 'Amr ibn al-'Āṣ did not dare to decide on this matter himself, and deferred it to the caliph 'Umar ibn al-Khaṭṭāb looking for his judgement. 'Umar pronounced thus:

> Either those books agree with the Qur'an, or they contain doctrines against it. If the former, we will easily get on without them, since one Qur'an is enough, and is equal to all of them. If the latter, they are undoubtedly not to be tolerated, but rather are to be destroyed.

Accepting this response, 'Amr ibn al-'Āṣ ordered them to be distributed immediately throughout all the baths in Alexandria (of which there were 4000 then in the city) to be burned to heat the baths. In this way they were destroyed in the space of six months. So much did the Arabs despise the eminent sciences of the time, submerged in a deep abyss of ignorance.

But the darkness has its own limits, so that the light can emerge when it was dispelled; and the sciences once oppressed were highly regarded in another time. This indeed happened, when a prince favored the best letters. The Arabs had already caused enough injury and calamities to philosophy, so that it was impossible to succumb to them any longer. So, it was a necessity for some Maecenas [patrons] to rise to redeem philosophy from further contempt and oppression to bring it to the light and treat it with due respect. This man was Abū Ja'far al-Manṣūr, the twenty-second caliph after Muhammad, from the family of the Abbasids, a most prudent prince and of the best nature. He was endowed with an admirable spirit and stood out as a great lover of the sciences. Without a doubt, he took pains so that his subjects were roused from their previous stupor, in which they had completely neglected philosophical doctrines, and were inspired to study as much as him. Abū al-Faraj, already deservedly praised so many times, says about this eminent prince:

> After God founded the dynasty of the Hashemites, and passed the kingdom to them, their minds were turned from their previous lack of care, and their intellects were awoken from their delinquency. But the first of them, who cared about the sciences, was the caliph Abū Ja'far al-Manṣūr, who excelled in law, and also fostered an enthusiasm for studying philosophy and, especially astronomy.

Indeed, it should be noted in this passage that to Abū al-Faraj, the Hashemites were the same people who George Elmacin called the Abbasids. One of their ancestors called Hashem, and all the Saracen princes who descend from him are known as Hashemites. But we should hardly believe that the studies of philosophy were propagated so widely by the auspices of this excellent prince, so that they immediately fully occupied their minds with it. Circumstances were such that this would demand not the lifetime of one man, but whole centuries. But the Arabs slowly began to cleanse themselves of their indolence, especially since after Abū Ja'far al-Manṣūr, they also enjoyed several caliphs who incited them to seek greater wisdom with their illustrious examples. Among these, the most praiseworthy of all is the fifth caliph of the Abbasids, Hārūn al-Rashīd, who George Elmacin says was the most humane and liberal caliph toward the erudite. He was so captivated with love for the erudite that he never went on a journey without the company of one hundred learned men. Hence, there was a great conflux of them in his court. Elmacin writes: "In no caliph's court did as many learned men (philosophers), erudite men, and poets meet as in Hārūn al-Rashīd's court." [...].

The son of Hārūn al-Rashīd, his father's sole heir, is given the seventh place among the Abbasids. Known as Abū 'Abbās al-Ma'mun or Abū Ja'far 'Abdāllah, he was a prince worthy of eternal remembrance because of his distinguished merits in letters. According to Abū al-Faraj:

> His grandfather al-Manṣūr arose and began to seek knowledge. When corresponding with the Greek kings, al-Ma'mun asked them to send him books on philosophy. When they sent him the books they had, he gathered translators to translate them accurately. When they translated them to the best of their ability, he encouraged men to read them, and expressed his wish that they learn. Al-Ma'mun also had time for learned men and was interested in their disputations. He delighted in their disputations, since he knew that 'those whom God chose from His creatures were learned and protected his own men from his slaves'.

George Elmacin praises al-Ma'mun "His nature was excellent in every way, liberal, very merciful, and a good ruler."

Neither was there anyone more erudite, nor more outstanding than him among the Abbasids. He had especially become learned in astronomy and the positions of the winds. Hence, 'the wind of al-Ma'mun' is known among those skilled in this science. R. Abraham Sachut also remembers him with a similar eulogy: "Ma'mun bin Rashīd loved wisdom (sciences) and wise men (philosophers and mathematicians) and celebrated them." Also, "In his time, many books were translated from Greek to Arabic." But a certain Takiddinus fearlessly pronounced thus: "It is possible that God punished al-Ma'mun because he has hindered the Muslims' piety by introducing the philosophical sciences." Meanwhile, these testimonies prove that the Arabs had shaken off all their sleepiness in the illustrious disciplines and had begun to compensate for it with a certain dogged industry. Edward Pococke says: "The slower the study of philosophy burst forth, the deeper its roots dug, and at last it reached maturity in happy increments."

At this time in the West, barbarousness slowly crept into our minds and threatened the ruin and destruction of the best letters (literature). Hence, exhausted with our contempt, literature looked for a home elsewhere in the East, with good success. For there, as we just saw, it straightaway found favor, especially among the Arabs, who welcomed it most humanely and treated it most kindly. They showed literature such honor that in time it gained pleasant dwelling, magnificent mosques, and innumerable worshippers among them. Famous universities were founded in Baghdad, Kufa, and Basra, in which the most learned men gathered. They built well-stocked libraries and the youth competed marvelously over their studies. Once the study of literature was established, their attention turned to other types of letters they had previously overlooked. They studied ornate writing, which we usually call calligraphy, especially after Abū 'Alī ibn 'Alī ibn Muqla transformed their old, primitive Kufan characters into something much more elegant. "For he was a famous author of (modern) writing, and he was the first to translate the foreign Kufan writing into something useful to the Arabs." Following the example of their elders, they excessively loved the humanities. The fertile crop of their most genius poets, such as al-Mutanabbī, and Abū al-'Alā' al-Ma'arrī, and their most subtle grammarians, such as Abū al-'Abbās Aḥmad ibn Yaḥyā and Mālek, and their most eloquent orators, such as Hariri of Basra, and finally their most accurate geographers, such as Abū al-Fidā' and their historians, such as 'Alī ibn al-Athīr al-Jazarī and Abū Ja'far al-Ṭabarī, proves this sufficiently. Arabs also cultivated the more sublime disciplines with accurate diligence and also demonstrated how sharp their minds were in these as well.

> Nor are the Arabs enemies of the sciences, but for seventy whole years have been most studious not only in war, but in art as well, throughout almost the whole of Africa and Asia, and also a kingdom of Europe, Spain, which they then held sway in, darlings of Mars and Minerva. Indeed, although we were very barbarous, they themselves were very studious and instructed in prestigious universities in each of their most noble cities, Morocco, Fez, Istanbul, Tunis, Tripoli, Alexandria, Cairo, and others. Nor were they names without substance. One could hardly speak of any science that their most distinguished professors, of which there were many in any university, had not produced the most accomplished works.

Although we know that the Arabs began to pursue the sciences in the time of al-Ma'mūn, there is still no agreement on the extent of their contributions. Philosophy and mathematics especially flourished in Arab schools. Indeed, no one will doubt this if one bears in mind that the best Greek writers were translated from Greek into Arabic, among whom were Euclid, Plato, Ptolemy. Pococke says that "it was barely one hundred years ago before we read any Greek philosopher, mathematician, or doctor that had not been translated from Arabic." But what use would these translations have been, if we did not learn the mathematical disciplines? No one denies that there were mathematicians among us, and it is certain that mathematical sciences, especially astronomy and algebra, were transmitted to us by the Arabs. Are there not enough examples of Arab contributions, which still today are frequently cited in the school of mathematics? According to Johann Gravius, Arab works on mathematics were translated into Latin for the first time when Alfonso X, King of Castile and Leon, sponsored the Alfonsine Tables by Hebrews, Moors, and Arabs, whom he had gathered together. This occurred in about the middle of the thirteenth century. There was a reward for explaining certain foreign words since it mattered to the Republic of Letters to know the origins of these words. The word "zenith" is the most overused among astronomers, although it is used wrongly, because it denotes "the point of the sky lying opposite to our pole." This word is derived from Arabic *samt*, which properly signifies a "way" or a "course" in general. If *samt* is joined to the word *ar-ra's*, so that it reads Arabic *samt ar-ra's* (i.e., "the course of the pole"), then it indicates the point just defined, which the Arabs assigned to the circle of the horizon as if it were the pole. The same word joined with the Arabic article *al*, placed before nouns, denotes the same as the Greek *ho, he, to*, giving a new word to mathematicians: Arabic *as-samt*, i.e., "the way," corrupted to *Azimut*, with a very different meaning than before. For that word usually denotes "the arc of the horizon, which is between the vertical circle, in which the sun or another star turns, and in which the meridian of another location is contained." Jacob Golius explains it otherwise, because he thinks it is "a region or point on the horizon, and a circle pertaining to it from a pole in the sky." A *nadir*, on the other hand, denotes "the zenith (i.e. *samt*), a course, or point in the sky lying opposite to our feet." But there is an Arabic word *Nadzīr* or *Naẓīr*, which properly signifies "the thing that looks to the other, and lies opposite to the same," from the word *naẓar*, "looked back at, positioned from a region." Another noun, with the same sense, is called *samt al-qadam*, a "course of a foot." Algebra, the name for the most outstanding mathematical discipline, equally owes its origin to the Arabs. They have the word *jabr*, which means "the broken whole restored." Hence, *jabr* or with the article *al-jabr*, from which Algebra is formed: "a restoration of the broken to wholeness, a mathematical analysis." This is its special function "to reduce the terms for comparison to a desired form of equation; and especially to restore the parts of the same to a whole."

Hieronymus Cardanus [Gerolamo Cardano] says that a certain Arab, called Muḥammad ibn Mūsā al-Khwārizmī, was the author of the science of Algebra, and took the name Algebraicus. The name *Almagesti*, which denotes Ptolemy's great work, is also known to mathematicians, especially astronomers. But this word does not get its origin from Arabic, but rather Greek. For it seems to be corrupted in the Arabs' schools from *megale syntaxis megiste*; to which they add the article and say *Almagest*. We should note that this work was also translated with other Greek writings in the time of al-Ma'mūn. If anyone wants to know why these foreign words were not translated into Latin, I think that it was because they could not be easily expressed with one Latin word.

Now, I turn from the mathematical sciences to philosophy, in which the Arabs excelled as well. This is demonstrated by the many great philosophers that arose among them. For anyone who wishes to know about them in detail, I recommend Hottinger's *Bibliotheca Orientalis*, as he recounts histories of a great many of them. They had so much enthusiasm for the precepts of Aristotle's philosophy that they had all of his works translated into Arabic. They also translated several commentaries on Aristotle's works; however, I do not believe that translations reflected the "true Aristotle." This man, Aristotle, of course, influenced some Arabic philosophers whose names are renowned. Such men (to leave aside al-Kindī, who I will expand on later) were: al-Fārābī, the miracle of the third and fourth centuries after hijra; Abū al-Qāsim al-Junayd ibn Muḥammad ibn al-Junayd, who lived in the third century of hijra; Avicenna, famous in the fourth and fifth centuries after hijra; Abū Ḥāmid Muḥammad al-Ghazālī, who they honor by calling "the proof of religion and the ornament of Islam," the ornament of the fifth century after hijra; Ebno'l Sajeg or Abu Bakr Mohammed Ebn Johja Ebno-Sajeg, a most intelligent man, who was the honor of the sixth century; Averroes, or Ibn Rushd, who illuminated the shore of Africa with his light also in the sixth century of hijra. Among them, Avicenna and Averroes especially are so famous that anyone who dabbles even lightly in the history of philosophy knows their names. They say that Emperor Frederick II invited Averroes to Europe and took pains to have Avicenna's books and those by many other Arab writers on every science brought by him. But I think that this was Frederick I, Barbarossa, since Aegidius Romanus [Giles of Rome] testifies that he saw Averroes' two sons in his court. Besides this coincides better with the time period, since historians say that Frederick I died in the year 1190, though Averroes died in the year of hijra 595, which corresponds to 1198. From this, it is clear that they were the same age.

Arabs also had notable doctors that they could boast of, Avicenna and Averroes, who I just now presented among the philosophers. Their works are still to this day esteemed by many doctors. Guerner Rolfinck, a doctor in Jena, wrote marginal notes found in the book *Institutiones medicas* on Avicenna. In these, Rolfinck demonstrated his high regard for Arab doctors as he wrote that there was much to learn from them. I am silent about the Arabs' jurisprudence and theology, neither of which they neglected, but inquiry and disputation were not encouraged by Muhammad's doctrines and laws. From these, I think it is evident that the Arabs were consistently zealous in mathematics, philosophy, and other disciplines after al-Ma'mūn, and they were not content with elegant literature alone.

Thus, from the previous evidence, it seems that literary study had a kind fate among the Arabs. Now I especially want to point out some favorers, patrons, and incubators, who were particularly celebrated after al-Mamun. The first is the ninth caliph of the Abbasids, Hārūn al-Wāthiq Bi'llāh Abū Ja'far, in the year 227/841, who held power and "loved poetry, and rewarded it, and imitated al-Ma'mūn in most of his ways." Under him, al-Ḥasan, a celebrated astrologer, wrote a book *Kitāb al-Anwār* (*The Book of Lights*). Al-Wāthiq's brother, Ja'far Mutawakkil succeeded him from 231/845 on. [...]. Under his rule, the Christian doctor, Ḥunayn ibn Isḥāq, found fame.

Later, 'Abd Allāh Muqtadir Billāh became caliph in 296/908. He "was an outstanding poet, and the eloquent author of the *Similitudes*, which was of a unique nature, as nobody had published anything like it before." The most praiseworthy is the twentieth caliph of the Abbasids, Aḥmad Abū al-'Abbās al-Rāḍī Billāh, who took the reins of empire in 322/933, and is particularly praised by Elmacin as "munificent, liberal, erudite, and a poet of great eloquence, rejoicing in the presence and conversation of erudite men, and endowed with many virtues." Under him, the Christian dialectician Mattā b. Yūnus, very skilled in the art of logic, flourished. In around the middle of the century, the emperor Sayf al-Dawla also held erudite men in high honor, since he himself was learned. His house was "a synagogue of learned men," and his court "a refuge for the erudite and the poets." He loved Mutanabbī above others, a most elegant poet, who sang his praises in seven poems. Nor did he cherish al-Fārābī any less, a renowned philosopher, often praised by Maimonides, who came to the court in the year of hijra 343. At the same time, Kafur Akshidi, a ruler of Egypt, proved himself as a great patron to the erudite, who "invited all learned and distinguished men to his court including poets, such Mutanabbī," by whom he was no less praised in a special poem than Sayf al-Dawla. In almost the end of the fifth century of hijra (in the eleventh century after Christ), the twenty-seventh caliph of the Abbasids, 'Abd Allāh Abū al-Qāsim al-Muqtadī Billāh, "the most studious of learned men," himself an excellent poet, nurtured good letters. His successor, Aḥmad Abū al-'Abbās al-Mustaḍhir Billāh, followed his example, and showed that he was no less "a lover of the erudite." He died in 512/1118. These individual examples confirm that the Arabs did not lack the best caliphs, who wondrously promoted the study of letters with their favor, munificence and rewards, and produced so many diligent practitioners.

Thus, the Arabs' progress in the sciences was continuous until the age of Timur, commonly known as Tamerlane, which covered the eighth and ninth centuries of hijra (Timur came to power in the year hijra 771 and died in 807, the fourteenth and fifteenth centuries of Christ). There were still some distinguished erudite men among the Arabs when Timur was ravaging the East as he pleased, and flooding everything like a tidal wave. Slowly their minds began to detach from their former passion for letters, as they were concerned whether they could hold back the invader's attack with their force of arms and be safe from his injustices and tyranny. Although I do not want to imply that no trace of their studies remained among the Arabs, it is certain that the center of scientific learning was removed to the land of Tartars. The Persians now applied themselves to literature as they had before, as well as poetry and history; astronomy was not completely neglected either.

Hence, we see a resurgence of the most elegant poets; Ḥāfez, who sang about divine love, deserves the most praise. His handwritten poetic work is kept in the library of Orphanotropheus Halensis. Emir Shah, commonly known as Khondemir, famous in the beginning of the tenth century of hijra, stands out among their historians as the most effusive writer of global history. If his work had been known it would have poured out the distinguished light of Eastern history, a small part of which I am still ignorant of. According to the astronomical writing of Persian Maḥmūd Shāh Khuljī, published by Johann Gravius, the Persians were strong in astronomy. Also, the Tartars applied themselves to mathematics and astronomy in particular. Astronomers still gratefully celebrate to this day the works of Ulugh Beg, prince of the Tartars, grandson of Tamerlane. His geographical tables, in which he assigns his measurements of latitude and longitude to more noble cities, were published by Johann Gravius in London in 1652. [In the future], I will expound on the condition of literature in today's Turkish Empire, and then in Tartary, since there is much information available [on this subject].

Indeed, my intention in this treatise was to show some examples of Arabic erudition, especially of the philosopher al-Kindī, explaining his life and philosophy at length; but it seems best to leave that exercise to another man, to be undertaken soon, God willing. That is all.

Notes

1 Koch's biography was compiled from the following sources: Johann Heinrich Zedler (ed.), "Koch, Cornelius Dietrich," in *Grosses vollständiges Universal-Lexicon aller Wissenschafften und Künste*, vol. 15 (Leipzig, 1737), 1186; Christian Gottlieb Jöcher, *Allgemeines Gelehrten-Lexicon*, vol. 2 (Leipzig, 1750), 2131–2; and Julia Hauser, "Koch, Cornelius Dietrich," in *The Bloomsbury Dictionary of Eighteenth-Century German Philosophers*, 430.

2 [MK] On the significance of Ibn Ṭufayl's Ḥayy b. Yaqẓān in the post-classical Islamic intellectual history, see Mehmet Karabela, "Cedel ile Burhān arasında: İbn Ṭufeyl'in Ḥayy b. Yakẓān adlı eseri üzerinden klasik dönem sonrası İslam düşünce tarihini okumak," *Ankara Üniversitesi İlahiyat Fakültesi Dergisi* 54/2 (2013): 77–93.

14 Turkish Schools and Colleges

Matthias Norberg

Matthias Norberg was born in Nätra, the Ångermanland province of north Sweden in 1747. In 1768, he enrolled at Uppsala University and obtained his Master of Arts in 1773. In 1774, he was awarded a Doctorate in Greek. After being educated at Uppsala, he traveled to Göttingen in 1777, where he met the biblical scholar Johan David Michaelis, the son of Christian Benedikt Michaelis, a prominent Lutheran theologian. Michaelis encouraged Norberg to study the pre-Islamic Mandaean religion and language. These studies laid the foundations of Mandaean textual study and began the theological discussion about the relation between the Mandaean religion and the Johannine writings of the New Testament. As Norberg was from a wealthy family, he was able to pursue Oriental and classical studies during extensive overseas trips to Denmark, Germany, the Netherlands, England, France, Italy, and Turkey. In 1779, he arrived in Constantinople and studied Turkish, Arabic, and Persian with native speakers, an experience he shared with few Protestant scholars of Western Europe at that time.

In 1780, Norberg was appointed professor of Greek and Eastern languages at the University of Lund in Sweden. He subsequently published over 150 dissertations on various subjects from Arabic astronomy to Turkish warfare, from Arabic language and medicine to the concept of *trimūrti* in Hinduism. He also translated the seventeenth-century Ottoman scholar Kâtip Çelebi's well-known geographical work, *Cihannümâ*, from Ottoman Turkish to Latin under the title *Gihan Numa, geographia orientalis, ex turcico in latinum versa* in 1818. In 1821, he was appointed a member of the Royal Swedish Academy of Sciences. In 1822, his book *Turkiska Rikets Annaler* was published: the first European translation of the major Ottoman historical works by Gelibolulu Mustafa Âlî Efendi (d.1600), Mustafa Naima (d.1716), Mehmed Râşid (d.1735), Çelebizâde İsmail Asım (d. 1760), and Ahmed Vâsıf Efendi (d.1806). As an academic, Norberg enjoyed European fame along with other Swedish Lutheran theologians and scholars, such as Henric Benzelius, Johan Engeström, and Jakob Jonas Björnståhl. He died in Uppsala in 1826.[1]

Variant Names: Matthew Norberg, Matthias Nordberg, Matthias Norbergus, Matth. Norberg, and Matthiae Norbergi

Summary and Analysis

In the opening of his dissertation, Norberg dismisses the popular notion that the Turks are savage barbarians. He concedes that the Ottomans engage in brutality and plunder, but he admires their love of learning and education, which he thinks his Western contemporaries underestimate. Although he believes that the state of learning and education in the West is superior, it might be surpassed one day by the East.

Norberg begins his account of education in the Islamic world with the colleges of the early Caliphate. In these schools, students were taught about religion and law, rendering them superstitious and hostile to the humanities. This changed, however, when Arabs were introduced to the literature of ancient Greece and Rome, which "established virtue" among them, brought "great prudence in their counsel, and speed and clarity in their deeds." Thus, for Norberg, Eastern or Islamic education was inferior until it incorporated Western education.

He says that exposure to material wealth from conquering the Arabs caused the Turks to degenerate into luxury and idleness. Consequently, the state of literature in the Turkish-dominated Islamic world also declined. He believes there is a difference in the physiology of the two races: the heat and sunlight of the Arab homeland stimulated the Arab mind, whereas the Turks came from a "middling climate" and, as a result, had a "middling genius." The Arabs are independent and freedom-loving by nature, which spurred them toward studying the humanities, whereas the Turks, subjugated by a tyrannical sultan, had been conditioned to unimaginativeness. However, after the Ottoman sultans assumed the mantle of caliph, the Turks began valuing literature more highly, restoring ruined and abandoned Arab schools, and patronizing the humanities. Norberg quotes a speech by Osman I in which he exhorts his son to value learning above all else. He then outlines various contributions made to education by successive Ottoman sultans, including the establishment of schools and the financial support of scholars.

Norberg describes the two types of educational institutions in the Ottoman Empire: the *mekteb* (school) and the *medrese* (college). The former provides a basic education and the latter advanced studies. Education is free: the students and teachers are supported by the generosity of those who have left a bequest in their will. Teachers differ in their teaching styles and their level of commitment; the higher a teacher's rank, the lazier and more unwilling to teach he is likely to be. Students in these schools learn Arabic grammar, dialectic and rhetoric, which is followed by a variety of subjects, including philosophy, religion, the natural sciences, and the art of reading and writing. Norberg criticizes the excessively practical orientation of Turkish attitudes toward education: many students, especially rich ones, focus on the study of law, which is quite lucrative, while scorning the natural sciences and philosophy as impractical and excessively difficult.

He claims that the state of education in the Ottoman Empire had declined from former times. He blames the decline on the Ottoman practice of imprisoning royal princes and denying them access to knowledge and books to prevent them from posing a threat to the reigning sultan. Later released, the princes were often sent to govern a province, where their ignorance and lack of learning defined their governing skills. Although the tyranny of the sultans and the decline of Turkish society into materialism lead educated people to hide their learning for fear of causing offence or arousing suspicion, Norberg ends his dissertation on a hopeful note, saying that if freedom and emphasis on education are reintroduced to Turkish society and openness to the outside world (presumably Western) prevails, then learning will flourish among the Turks and they will produce intelligent works again.

Significantly, Norberg's *dissertatio* illuminates the importance of the Ottoman ruler (*sultân*), as he sets the tone for the level of engagement in education and liberal arts, and his policies influence the public engagement with education and liberal arts. Therefore, Norberg understands that knowledge is not an independent enterprise of scholars (*'ulemâ*) separate from the state. Another interesting observation he makes is that as having a legal education in *medrese* became a lucrative source of income for students, the Ottoman Empire used positions in Islamic law to solidify power in the Empire. As noted by Norberg, many students, especially rich ones, focused on the study of law to the detriment of philosophy and liberal arts as they were more difficult career choices. Norberg's dissertation also displays an intimate and in-depth knowledge of the Ottoman educational system. He is familiar with the Ottoman educational structure and *medrese* curriculum as he cites the disciplines the students studied in the Turkish colleges, such as grammar, rhetoric, and dialectic (*ādāb al-baḥth*).[2]

Turkish Schools and Colleges (Lund, 1792)

When I turned my attention to writing, I promised myself to find something that seemed worthy of the paper, the reader's leisure, and the interest of learned men. I think that the present material is of great value, being long sought for and aptly unique. It is pleasing to know the geniuses, education and the types of literature the Turks have as unskilled men believe the Turks are hardly men, and the learned call them barbarians. My book focuses on this people's humanities. Driving provinces into slavery, nations into defeat, and extracting wealth from their tribute is not the only virtue of the Ottomans; they also embrace academic disciplines, welcome wise men, and found schools. Indeed, our world does not treat their learning and genius as equal, as I will discuss below. It is characteristic of a superior people to overlook the merits of its inferiors. The judgement that the Turkish race is unlearned and uncultured stands in the memories of our ancestors. Things go in circles, and the star that now illuminates the West will cross around the world to the East.

Since the birth of Muhammad's religion, there has been no failure in its defense and expansion. Mosques consecrated to their new sacred relic were founded and the caliphs generously paid for the adjoining colleges (*medrese*). Just as God was worshipped through priests and ceremonies in the mosques, so were the youth taught divine and human law, the foundation of religion and power, in the colleges. Muslims did not include other disciplines [into the curriculum]: the more faithful they were to the superstition of their origins, the more intolerant they were of the humanities. However, abundance slowly brought satisfaction, and time and reason measured and tempered their insane error. Muslim study of the liberal arts resulted in the establishment of virtue among the Arabs during antiquity and the Middle Ages. The more they learned from the Greek and Roman literatures that relate to the glory of the republic in peace and its defense in war, the more time they devoted to the teachings of the ancients and their history. Therefore, there is great prudence in their counsel, and speed and clarity in their deeds. Coming from a martial origin, the Turks quickly conquered the Arabs. But material wealth produces vices: they descended from industry to idleness, from temperance to decadence, from good arts to shameful vows and wicked crimes. Therefore, their fortune waned, and the name of the Turks became famous not so much for their virtue as for the indolence of the Arabs. With the establishment of the Eastern Empire, Turks acquired the knowledge of Eastern doctrine. The Ottomans were equal to the Arabs in the greatness of their deeds, but inferior in the glory of their literature. I would like to understand the reasons and causes for this disparity. Let us consider both the environment and their differing ways of life. The position of the sun and its heat did much to stimulate the mental vigor and quickness of the Arabs. Not in fear of any threat of domination, the eternal freedom of the Arabs living in the fields and forests greatly nourished and roused their genius. Indeed, the beginnings of Islam were cruel and harmful to this unique and free race; they expended time and effort on wars caused by the orders of the Caliphate. Overcoming the oppression the ideology of the accursed Muhammadans had placed on their upright spirits and feeble minds, the Arabs turned more and more toward a good intellect, judgement and study of the ideal conduct/ethics [*adab*]. Consequently, the Arabs cared more about being sufficiently skilled men than seeming very religious. The Turks, on the other hand, acquired a middling genius from their middling climate, long formed in their ancient homeland, Tatarstan. They have strong bodies, serious faces, and weak minds. They walk, think, and talk slowly; they are the product of a colder sky, more invigorating air, and harder land. Long domination increased their indolence, weakening their judgment in action and their speed in thinking. The Sultan had a double persona: one civil, that of a prince, which was obtained by the glory of his lineage and the law of heredity, and the other holy and of a caliph, which was acquired by the virtue of his ancestors and by the custom of Muhammad's race. He steadfastly held on to both for many centuries. Nothing existed at home or abroad that could challenge that two-sided man from taking the empire and usurping the Caliphate. The conquered races were weak and the neighboring peoples in disarray: due to this powerlessness and envy, this Caesar ruled not only his subjects' lives and resources, but even their minds and thoughts. Indeed, his power was so great and so above any laws that it became an enemy to true reason, which should be the queen and mistress of all things.

However, the closer the Ottomans began to associate themselves with the Caliphate, the prouder of their literature they became. They were still intact, sincere, and not exhausted by the pleasures of the East, and it was the nature of their strong race to bear physical labors with composure. Nor had the Ottomans' love of speaking fallen into oblivion as it had among the Arabs. They worked hard in private for the sake of the public. The Ottoman sultans spared no expense in restoring and renovating anything in the Arabs' schools that had collapsed through time, been wrecked by violence and the sword, or lay forgotten through barbarousness and neglect. The Sultan's virtue and doctrine, not his nobility or money, brought him authority among the men of power, and learning to the populace. Consider the following examples. Osman I, after whom the Ottoman Empire is named, highly valued literature; but despite the effort he spent on it, he was impeded by his ambitions and the cares of founding a new kingdom. This excellent speech to his son will show how much he valued the liberal arts:

> Son! Hold back your tears: grief is empty, which this fatal necessity makes for you. It is the law to obey the divine plan, for which men are born. The fatal breath of the west wind savages every age and condition equally: young, old, citizens, kings. I concede my fate happily and make my brow calm, when I see the heir of my fortune and the successor to my power in you. But it will be pious and obedient of you to apply your ear to your most beloved father's words, your mind to his advice, and effort to your vows. Take this scepter, so that you may hold power with a strong mind and temper it with justice. Let justice illuminate your throne with its rays, and may its splendor not be defined by narrow limits, but by the limits of the whole kingdom. Remember to hate violence and injustice, guard

the divinity of the Qur'an, spread the faith of the holy ancestor, nurture the noble arts, and be beneficent to men of proven religion and doctrine. As much as you become known to them for wisdom and probity, you will be stronger in yourself in respect and authority. May you always and everywhere walk the path that leads to fame, strength, and victory; and you will not stray in this if you prefer to follow my footsteps and imitate my arts. Material prosperity, resources, wealth, riches, armies and fleets are vanity. Study so that however much majesty and power you have, it will be subject to the sign of religion, and set up under the foundation of the Holy Law. May you always bear God, alone and eternal, before your eyes, who has ordered our arms not to increase our magnificence, but to protect the worship of His name and His worshippers. Let this be your concern and what you think about, which the health of your people, which the Divinity handed over to you to guard, demands from you. Finally, I would like to convince you that you were not born a prince and made an emperor, except to bring and show deference to the religious, fear to the enemy, love to the citizens, and justice, generosity, and mercy to everyone.

Succeeding to his father's established state and paternal wealth, Orhan I had more leisure and time for the works of peace, quiet reflection, and the good arts. This is evidenced by the large gymnasium he built after he conquered Nicomedia; and that he allowed the defeated to use the literary works he had seized, which were glories for the victor. Mehmed II, after the siege of Constantinople, founded eight renowned schools in that city. He also funded quarters, wages, rooms, and assistants for the teachers and students to further the study of literature, which is an expensive art. However, these rulers alone do not deserve all the credit for the genius of this nation. Recently, other Turkish sultans have also patronized the literary arts. When in doubt, Murad and Bâyezid sought the counsel of learned men, followed their best advice, and honored them in public. The Vizier of Mustafa III, Koca Mehmet Ragıp Pasha, was a man of great genius and learning. Abdülhamid bestowed wealth and honors on poets that made their theme the power of his empire in poems and thanksgivings. These examples of generosity and patronage from the court excited much love and emulation. It is a virtue or a vice of servile men to align themselves to their Sultan's habits, good or bad; fawning is an honor which the Ottomans also apply to their Caesars. These servile men flatter their princes whether they are just or unjust; they call theft power; they call charity and giving largesse and humanity. This humanity is very widespread. The rulers established quarters for learned men throughout the towns and countryside, providing a place for literature in the cities and villages.

These institutions bequeathed to the pious for the mind's improvement have become widespread, making wisdom freely available. There is a great number of them in the large cities of two types: one is called a *mekteb*, which is a 'school,' and the other *medrese*, which means 'college.' The *mekteb* gives a less advanced education but is more generous to the students. Not only can they learn for free, but they can even live there free, making them open to the children of the poor. The teachers receive money and the students receive food from the goods left to them in wills. Although it is illegal for those who teach to charge money for their work, it is perfectly appropriate for a grateful mind to leave a legacy for the studious. These schools of literature are more concerned that boys become good men rather than distinguished citizens. While they learn the art of reading and writing, they learn the principles of religion and the elements of their native tongue, and each transforms himself from literate idleness to productive business. The students of the colleges (*medrese*) receive extensive praise due to the holiness of the place, the dignity of their studies, the vast extent of their learning. They are connected to mosques in the ancient way, so that the youths have reverence for the divinity, modesty toward their teachers, and act honorably and diligently. In this way, the colleges can better withstand the ravages of time and are less susceptible to fire. Each college has rooms in which the boys live separately to instruct them better in morals. But when there is not enough space because of their large numbers, a compromise must be made and two or three share one bedroom. Each gymnasium has its own teacher, whose role is to temper the leisure activities of the students with reason so that it is safer and their work with discipline so that it is more profitable. Their teachers' title is *Hoca*, which means 'old man'—a suitable name, and an apt description for the obedience which the students are expected to show to their elders. Their learning is mediocre and does not go beyond the basics: faith, works, virtue, auspices. However, those who have greater prestige are called 'professors' (*müderris*), a title which begets indolence. The law orders that these men put effort into educating their students. But they go unpunished and judge themselves to have done enough if they come to their schools once or twice a month! These days, their laziness is equaled by that of the High Priest (*Muftī*), who once considered it a sacred duty to dedicate himself to study and apply his mind in the gymnasium. The manner of instruction in the schools differs according to the inclinations of the teachers: some teach pedantically and dogmatically, whereas others teach liberally and philosophically. A teacher instructs students either individually, in small groups, or in large crowds.

Let us now consider the curriculum taught in these schools of wisdom. First, students learn the basics of Arabic and syntax. After this, they study dialectic [*ādāb al-baḥth*], followed by rhetoric. Then the skill of explaining obscure points concisely is taught; afterwards, students learn the order and selection of words in a speech. Then the two types of theology are taught: scholastic and moral. Aside from this, students learn philosophy, astronomy, geometry, the Qur'an, the traditions of the prophet, ethics, chronology, medicine, the interpretation of dreams, astrology, the art of writing, and finally, poetry. But few students are willing or able to finish this whole course of study. In the old days, as is the case today, it was the tendency to focus on religious teachings and the elements of civil law. The material prosperity resulting from these studies makes them popular among the youth. In the other disciplines, there is little or no hope for titles and prestige, honors and opportunities, since these disciplines are difficult to study at an advanced level. The native languages also demand a lot of time and study. Turkish recalls an image of old simplicity; Arabic serves for majesty and abundance; and Persian adds beauty and elegance. Turkish is the common language learned in infancy even to those who are unwilling and has few foreign words from the other two languages. However, Arabic and Persian, more elegant scripts, are mixed with Turkish for the sake of magnificence and grace. Indeed, the more difficult a work is, the more Arabic and Persian words it has and the more intricate are its constructions, in such a way so that although someone may be born and raised with this speech, he cannot fully encompass its meaning and depth. Some obscurity always slows his reading speed, and he must interpret its ambiguous meaning. Obscurity is something barbarians think is beautiful; the less prolix the writing is, the more care is placed in the choice of words, so that while they do not speak with variety, they still seem to have spoken copiously and ornately.

When the minds of the youth have been sufficiently softened in the colleges by the rigor of discipline, they are transferred into the sacred and civil offices of the Empire, as if from a nursery. Sometimes those from poorer backgrounds pursue a higher rank of dignity, while those born rich demand this for themselves. For the children of the rich tend not to be educated in a school, where praise or blame for their hard work is particularly strong, but at home, where the mind luxuriates or grows torpid in front of a negligent parent and away from their unknowing instructor. Nor do they learn the necessities as much as they can follow their pleasures. They consider it too laborious to pursue more obscure studies, but they are eager to embrace more practical ones. They seem clever enough and fit for the administration of the state if they have learned certain life lessons from moral philosophy and examples of prudence from Eastern history. The sublimity of astronomy and geometry, the subtleties of dialectic [*ādāb al-baḥth*], and learning the secrets of their own and of the outside world does not please rich children in their idleness or the slave class in its servitude. However, this race of men is not so barren of virtues that they have not given eminent examples of themselves. There are many who either excelled in the erudition of their own race, or benefited from foreign learning. Those familiar with them will praise their resources and hard work, and those who read them will not berate their art and prose.

The study of wisdom among the Ottomans used to be more wide-spread than it is in these times. There are many causes for this present inactivity and ignorance; the origin of this problem lies with the court. The first crime of a new Sultan is to throw a son or a brother into prison. In order that the prisoner's mind may not perceive such a great injustice clearly and look around eagerly for a chance of escape, he is shut away not only from light and contact with men, but he is also denied the use of books. In this loneliness, in these silent places, living like a caged beast, he forgets virtue. When he is later freed and brought into daylight out of darkness and chains, the light blinds him as he limps into office. Thus, the evils of ignorance are born in court and slowly spread to the provinces. Out of imitation of the Sultan, the negligence of parents, the idleness of youths, and the neglect of old disciplines are now common vices in the cities. Self-love and contempt for strangers have developed. The example of their ancestors seems pious and honorable to them, and they are content not to be exposed to new ideas in literature or the arts. They care only for their own property and their present circumstances; there is no desire for anything deeper, no deep thought. It is not easy to persuade them to advance their studies beyond the threshold, to follow the reputation of the greatest men, to seek out monuments of literature, and to be mindful of their subjects. They think that they are rulers over mortals in their strength and virtue, law and religion, judgement, and speech. Those who value intelligence and virtue do not have the ability to remedy the evils that the state labors against. They prefer to keep up the old ways rather than try something new out of fear of causing offence, arousing the envy of their superiors, and public unpopularity. But, let this be granted to this superstitious and unskilled race. I think that, if education and conformity with doctrine replace their distinguished indolence; if freedom, which nature imparts to every living thing, and virtue, which is man's peculiar benefit, is regained so that everyone may say what they feel; if besides this, contact with the outside world is re-established—if all these things occur, just as their genius is not inherently deficient, so too the works of Turks' genius will not be deficient.

Notes

1 Norberg's short biography was compiled through the following sources: Matthias Norberg, *Selecta opuscula academica*, ed. J. Normann, 3 vols. (Lund, 1817–19); Christian Callmer, *In Orientem: svenskars färder och forskningar i den europeiska och asiatiska Orienten under 1700-talet* (Stockholm: Almqvist & Wiksell International, 1985), 82–90; Christer Westerdahl, *Från Norrtjärn till Konstantinopel: Matthias Norberg* (Stockholm: Örnsköldsviks Museum, 1990); Jerker Blomqvist, "Matthias Norberg and the Modern Greek Language," in *Filia: Studies in Honour of Bo-Lennart Eklund*, eds. V. Sabatakakis and P. Vejleskov (Lund: Wallin & Dalholm Boktryckeri, 2005), 41–74; Karin Berner, "Communities, Limits and the Ability to Cross Borders: Two Swedes' Experiences in Constantinople During the Eighteenth

276 Philosophy and Liberal Arts

Century," in *Traces of Transnational Relations in the Eighteenth Century*, eds. Tim Berndtsson, Annie Mattsson, Mathias Persson, Vera Sundin, and Marie-Christine Skuncke (Uppsala: Uppsala University Library, 2015), 53–73; and Bernd Roling, "Arabia in the Light of the Midnight Sun: Arabic Studies in Sweden between Gustaf Peringer Lillieblad and Jonas Hallenberg," in *The Teaching and Learning of Arabic in Early Modern Europe*, eds. Jan Loop et al. (Leiden: Brill, 2017), 93–132.

2 On *ādāb al-baḥth* and its significance in the Ottoman educational system, see Mehmet Karabela, *The Development of Dialectic and Argumentation Theory in Post-Classical Islamic Intellectual History*, Ph.D. dissertation (Montreal: McGill University, 2010), 118–39 and 177–89.

Part IV
Muslim Sects
Sunni and Shi'a

15 Persian Discourse

Sebastian Kirchmaier

Sebastian Kirchmaier was born in Uffenheim in 1641. He enrolled at the University of Altdorf in 1660 and at Wittenberg in 1661, where he earned a *Magister der Philosophie* in 1662. He became an adjunct professor of theology at the University of Wittenberg in 1665. Kirchmaier's school remembrance book (*Stammbuch*) written between 1660 and 1667 reveals his significant Lutheran network at Wittenberg. Most prominent figures of seventeenth-century orthodox Lutheranism, such as Abraham Calov, Johannes Musaeus, August Pfeiffer, and Hieronymous Kromayer, wrote entries in Kirchmaier's *Stammbuch*. Later, in 1668, he became professor at the college in Regensburg. Some of his most important works were on ancient German paganism and ancient papyri. In 1681, he became the superintendent of St. Jacob Church in Rothenburg ob der Tauber. As is clear from his *Persian Discourse*, Kirchmaier valued arts and poetry. He also wrote the foreword to Lutheran pastor Georg Falck's *Idea boni cantoris*, a Lutheran singing treatise of 1688. In 1692, as the chief ecclesiastical official in the city of Rothenburg, Kirchmaier visited a woman, Barbara Ehness, awaiting execution for attempted murder by poisoning, where, according to her, he coerced her into confessing to being a witch. Luckily his attempt to start a witch-hunt failed, due to a lack of support from the city councilors. He died in Rothenburg in 1700. The year after Kirchmaier's death, Johann Andreas Planer (d.1714), Professor of Philosophy and Mathematics at the University of Wittenberg, wrote *Panegyricus, Memoria Celeberrimi Theologi, Sebastiani Kirchmaieri* (Honoring the Memory of the Celebrated Theologian, Sebastian Kirchmaier), and eulogized Kirchmaier to posterity.[1]

Variant Names: Sebastian Kirchmayer, Sebastiano Kirchmaiero, Sebastiani Kirchmayeri, Sebastianus Kirchmaier, Sebastian Kirchmaierus, Sebastian Kirchmair, Sebastianus Kirchmaierus, Sebastianus Kirchmajerus, Sebast. Kirchmaierus, and Sebastian Kirchmajerus

Summary and Analysis

Kirchmaier's speech was originally written in Persian before being trans-lated into Latin.[2] The Rector of Wittenberg, Johann Erich Ostermann, whose preface introduces the speech, explains that it outlines the re-ligious hostility between the Persians (praised as 'a quite ancient and exceedingly noble nation') and the Turks ('foul and four-day-old swill'). The Persians' more favorable characterization by Ostermann, along with Kirchmaier's speech being written in Persian, reflects an authorial bias for a civilization with roots in classical antiquity. Furthermore, being geographically more distant from Europe than the Ottoman Empire, Persians had not recently clashed militarily with German-speaking cen-tral Europe.

Kirchmaier begins his speech by noting that most Europeans are un-aware of Muslim sectarian violence or their differences. He states that these differences result from various interpretations of the Qur'an, dif-ferences in the understanding of sainthood, articles of faith, religious authorities (i.e., *imām*s), and miracles. After some brief invective against Muhammad and an account of the spread of Islam, Kirchmaier outlines the origin of sectarian differences and the problem of the succession of Muhammad in Islam. Thus, the succession story of the first three caliphs, 'Alī, and the fate of his sons are discussed. Then, Kirchmaier discusses the Sofians (referring to the Safavid dynasty), a contemporary Persian sect that rejected the three caliphs who came before 'Alī in the succession line—Ṣafī al-Dīn Ardabīlī being one of 'Alī's descendants. According to Kirchmaier, this influential sect among the Persians believed that the Qur'an had come to Muhammad by mistake—it was meant for 'Alī—and this led to a violent disagreement between the Sunnis and Shi'ites.

Kirchmaier discusses several interpreters of the Qur'an, now consid-ered saints, whose teachings are followed in different parts of the Islamic world. Many of these were descendants of 'Alī and were "high priests and prophets of their religion." The Turks, however, are contemptuous of them, venerating the three caliphs (who reigned before 'Alī) as equal to gods. It is clear from his account that Kirchmaier's impression of Is-lam is of an idolatrous religion while, to his Protestant audience, the Persian (Shi'ite) veneration of saints was reminiscent of the prominence of saints in Catholicism. Islam is thus likened to Catholicism, the major Christian sect, which conflicted with Kirchmaier's Protestantism.

Kirchmaier concludes by describing the main prayers of Islam, some of which (though not all) are shared by the two principal sects—not unlike Christianity. He says that Muslims are indifferent to the Bible, believing it to be a Greek and Jewish fabrication. The Persians believe that the story of Adam, the Last Judgement, and eternal life are marvel-ous tales, which the Turks ridicule. Of the two sects, Kirchmaier sees the Shi'ites as less hostile to Christianity, which might account for the

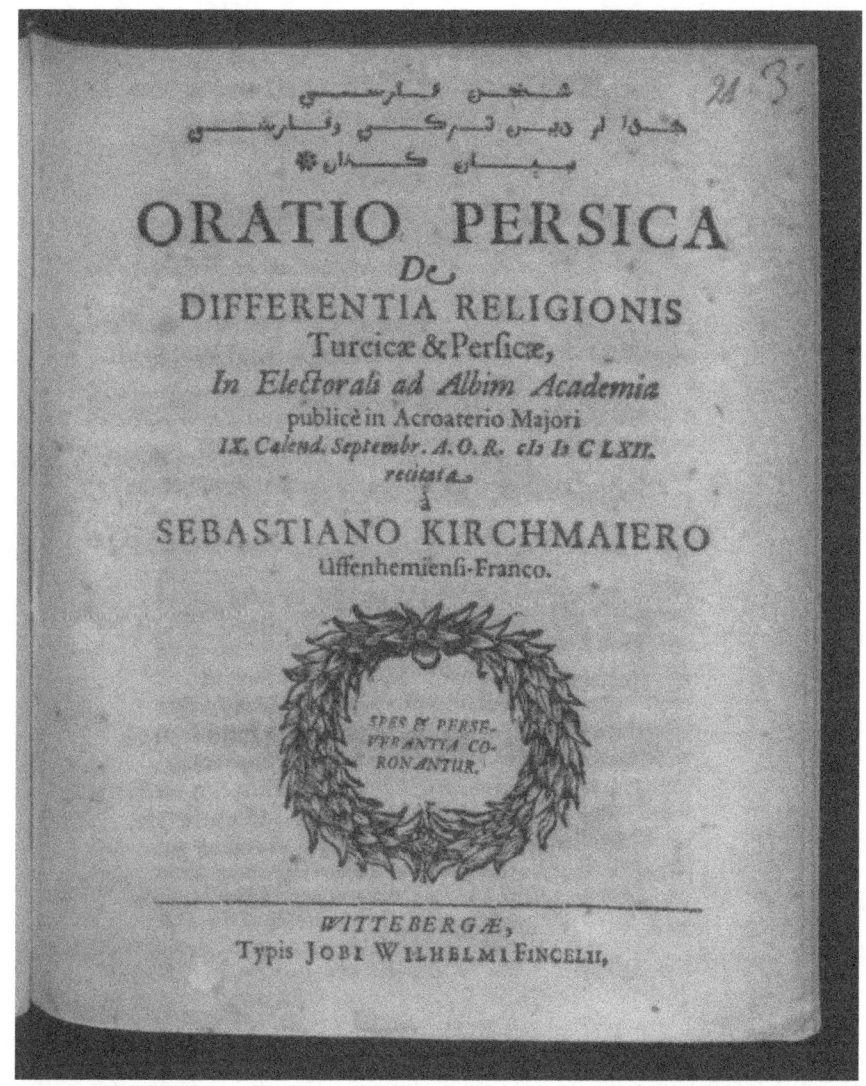

Figure 15.1 Sebastian Kirchmaier, *Oratio Persica de differentia religionis Turcicae & Persicae*, 1662 (Courtesy of the Staatsbibliothek zu Berlin, Preußischer Kulturbesitz).

Rector of Wittenberg University's favoring the Persians in his opening comments. Kirchmaier's speech ends with a prayer that God himself will convert both Turks and Persians to the path of salvation, so that they all may live in peace.

Persian Discourse (Wittenberg, 1662)

[Opening Remarks] by the Rector of the Academy of Wittenberg
    Johann Erich Ostermann, Public Professor of Greek Letters
    To the Members of the Academy:
    Greetings,

After the second hour of the afternoon and the religious rites have been conducted, Sebastian Kirchmaier, the most learned youth and a noble man of Uffenheim, is going to give a speech in Persian, which he recently wrote at his house. Whether or not we respect his reason for writing it or deem it a praiseworthy endeavor in less common languages, we cannot but support the effort. As for its contents, he will explore and at the same time explain the causes of the disagreement between Persians and Turks and the hyper-Vatinian hatred between them, the tremendous difference in both of their fabricated superstitions, and a scarcely feasible process for reuniting Persians with the Turks.

Kirchmaier thought that this was his business, especially at this time when some men are contemplating the bonds of religion and wish to rejoin religions into peaceful unity. As things stand now, they are neither willing nor able to be united. The Persian and Turkish races are akin to each other and intermingled. When they received the mad teachings of the impostor Muhammad long ago, it seemed that they would more easily join in the bonds of shared friendship. Yet they are divided in tremendous wrath, and they quarrel over their myths as though the salvation of their souls depended on it. How many thousands of soldiers have been cut down and destroyed just since the times of Sofi Shah Esmā'īl? What has brought Muslims to infighting is not the desire for more possessions, but their divergent adherence to their superstition to Muhammad, 'Umar, 'Uthmān, and others with similarly barbaric names.

Religion, indeed, is the apple of strife, and you can easily find wars for which religion was either the mother or at least the midwife. The annals of all ages and peoples bear witness; the monuments of history, both sacred and profane, attest to it. Even today this holds true. Who would be surprised at the fatal hostilities of the Persians, a quite ancient and exceedingly noble nation, against the foul and four-day-old swill of the Turks? When Kirchmaier spent significant time on these issues, he despaired of finding any means of reuniting the two sects. But we do not wish to speak further on this matter, since the man himself is shortly going to address us on this subject. Attend then, Members of the Academy, attend, in a great thronging crowd! Beyond the love that is due to the Eastern Muses, come together in greater numbers despite the unfavorable time, because of the rarity of this endeavor. *They always enjoy novelty. If it is good, they gain envious emulation.* And you are the best, with such abilities that your pious fellow colleagues will join you readily.

Sunday, the 13th day after the Trinity, in the year of received grace 1662.

Latin Version [Kirchmaier's Persian Speech][3]

Magnificent rector, the most reverend man of all, the wisest, most experienced, most excellent, most generous, most distinguished, most learned, and you, my friends in faith! [...] Most honored men of all ranks! I am motivated to say a few words about the present theme to this most splendid audience. I think that the mutual animosity between Turks and Persians is well-known; but the more intimate reasons for this hostility are not clear to everyone.

Both Turks and Persians follow Muhammad's religion and the Qur'an, but most Europeans lack knowledge of the foundations of this faith. Turks and Persians persecute each other with the fiercest hatred; however, Europeans do not know how the religions of Turks and Persians differ. Therefore, I wanted to speak about this to the best of my modest abilities, and, have also decided to use others' written works to explain why the Turks curse Persians. When I speak, I wish that I had the persuasive elegance and rhetoric power of Sa'dī [Shīrāzī]: a certain style of speech that the Persians cultivate and value. Such a skill would have made a huge impact. Although my wish has not been granted, I long for your benevolence, listeners, and most earnestly beseech your patience.

O listening friends! One would generally assume that both nations [Turks and Persians] have a common faith and, thus, would maintain a sincere friendship. However, one should now be able to trace from whence that deadly dissent between these two races arose. Where does that highest bitterness of spirit and jealousy come from? Those insults and horrible wars with which they persecute each other more than they do Christians? I will speak briefly on where all of this arises from. It is born from different interpretations of the Qur'an, the differences in their *imām*s, articles of faith, rites, religious authority, and finally miracles done by their prophets. While I enumerate these one by one, I will not speak of the evolution of their lineage, morals, state, and kingdoms, as these are variously treated by other writers. So, here I will not introduce the old religion of the ancient Persians, who venerated the sun, fire, moon, the planets Venus and Jupiter, earth, water, winds, and rivers instead of gods, and sacrificed their own wives and children. Here I will treat one thing alone; I will illustrate the reasons why these two nations commit mutual savageries against each other.

Everyone knows that there are three main religions in the world, namely, Judaism, Christianity, and Islam. Leaving aside the first two, Muslims boast that their religion is the first and best of all, although it was invented most recently by that most foul serpent Muhammad. Not many centuries have passed since their religion came into existence, and yet they still do not blush from selling it as the best. At that time, we did not refute this stupid opinion of theirs more rigorously. For what were you wretched races able to recognize that was healthful or good, illuminated by no splendor from the divine word? These are errors, these are

tricks, and more than diabolic falsehoods, which you believed so easily
through persuasion, wretched heathens! For what did you good men
expect from a sinful man, a heretic, a pimp, a tyrant, a word, a portent?
What is that kind of man, teaching a religion without piety and justice,
other than a wanderer without knowledge, a bird without wings, a wise
man without good works, a tree without fruit, a teacher without a teaching, a building without doors? Therefore, it is no wonder that heathens
fell into such error with such a leader that they soon loved their religion
devotedly and embraced it fiercely.

Henceforth Muhammad's very pestilent dogmas were spread throughout almost the entire East; so many nations adopted the Qur'an and
its author that they worshipped him as a god among mortals. He soon
obtained formidable followers, and the most noble peoples of the East,
namely the Turks, Persians, Indians, Moors, Tartars, and, if it is to be
believed, more than seventy nations. No one can wonder that when one
religion was divided among so many nations, their doctrines soon became dissimilar from one another and hostility arose because of this
disparity.

To return to my own thesis, I will start explaining the whole thing
"from the first egg" as they say. The reason that Muslims persecute each
other as enemies started originally when Muhammad named a certain
man as his successor (his nephew and son-in-law, 'Alī by name), founding a throne at once sacred and profane [the Caliphate]. However, 'Alī's
inheritance was snatched away from him, beyond all law and morality,
by Muhammad's father-in-law, Abū Bakr, and 'Umar and 'Uthmān as
they were more powerful and richer. Soon all the populace burned in
anger and preferred to hail 'Alī as King in their presence. For that reason, they became more and more divided, so that afterwards there was
no way they could return to their old favor and friendship. If 'Alī had
opposed the first three caliphs from the beginning they would not have
set such deep roots of hostility, as the wise Persian [Sa'dī Shīrāzī] said:

> A tree that has just set root is uprooted from its place by the strength
> of one man; if you leave it for any amount of time, you cannot even
> tear it out from its roots with a chariot. The beginning of a spring
> can be blocked by a covering, but when it swells with the waves, it
> cannot even be crossed by an elephant.

Persians always belittled Abū Bakr, who was said to have entered into
a contract with the devil. They venerated 'Alī like a man of heaven who
was wise, a just ruler on the royal throne, victorious over his enemies,
a refuge to the poor, a haven for wanderers, an upholder and judge of
learned men, a lover of pious men, the pride of nation and faith, and
helper of Islam and Muslims. But the Turks believed the opposite and
were enflamed to a greater hatred of that superior man and his sons,
which further fueled the enmity between the Turks and Persians.

Because of all these reasons, an unworthy exile and banishment came to 'Alī and his sons. This situation greatly increased the fury of the populace as well as their pity, and they longed for 'Alī alone, and everyone wanted to see him, above all others, appointed to the highest pinnacle of merit. When the populace heard that the first three caliphs [Abū Bakr, 'Umar, and 'Uthmān] had died, how much, immortal God, they rejoiced. Indeed, they praised him wishing 'Alī's life would be fulfilling:

> An intercessor, a reverend man, a prophet, a generous man, a powerful man, a smiling man, and a standard bearer. What sorrow can befall the wall of the nation when you are its supporter? What fear would one have if his ship's captain is Noah? God wanted to have mercy on this world, so He appointed you as the King of this world.

O my listeners! Friends and enemies in a nation may love or despise their rulers or treat them as something important. It was for this reason that the Safavid Persians unanimously execrated the three previous caliphs as if they were unjust and illegitimate usurpers; none of the Persian Muslims were dubious about comparing 'Alī to them to their detriment and venerating him excessively. Meanwhile, in later years, a certain wise and holy man, Ṣafī al-Dīn al-Ardabīlī, who was of 'Alī's lineage, appeared in Ardabīl and extolled the immortality of 'Alī's fame. This man led his impoverished life in uncultivated places in order to impose himself more easily on the populace, and thus, influenced them without difficulty. For he [al-Ardabīlī] taught that the succession of 'Alī was usurped illegally, grievously angering God when the Turks suppressed his greatest miracles so evilly. Therefore, the Persians believed in him [al-Ardabīlī] as a reformer and this caused disunity between Turks and Persians. Those bloody wars that they waged against each other can testify as to how much dissent and tumult were soon roused by this diversity of religion.

Human nature is such that whatever is imposed on it, it thereafter serves continually. Indeed, a sapling changes its form if you bend it, but an oak does not change form if you try to bend it; so, the Persians formed their opinion about 'Alī so deeply as soon as it was conceived that they were never able to forget it afterwards. It is for this reason that they ascribed 'Alī a certain prerogative, almost ahead of Muhammad himself, claiming that the Qur'an had come by the archangel Gabriel's mistake into Muhammad's hands though it was truly owed to 'Alī.

The Persians also professed that if 'Alī did not approach God's divinity, he at least came close to it. Hence their common prayer came about: "praise to no one other than God alone, the prophet Muhammad, and 'Alī, the prefect and helper of God." So, as much as they worshiped 'Alī most religiously, they execrated his predecessors as unjust and impure, indeed with poisonous witticisms. Among their insults, this one is by no means the least: "May dogs' testicles be upon their faces!" Whenever their *imām* calls a sacred congregation [five daily prayers], he must rant against the reputation of those men like a dog. This irritates the Turks so much that they are all angered. This is the first root and spring of this fierce hostility.

Furthermore, I will illuminate the differences between the Persian and Turkish interpretations of their religion; particularly, the different interpretations of the Qur'an. For example, the Persians respect and praise the wisest men, 'Alī and Ja'far al-Ṣādiq, who had been endowed with a talent for interpreting the scripture and whom Muslims still call saints; the Turks respect and praise the Ḥanafī; the Indians respect and praise Ḥanbalī and Mālikī; the Uzbek Tatars respect and praise al-Shāfi'ī. Since the Qur'an is obscure in many passages with meandering and vague sentences, so that barely one in a hundred can understand what Muhammad meant, therefore, the more learned Arabs commented on it and yet they filled it with greater lies. This situation soon made the Qur'an distorted [the meanings] and altered in such a way that it was up to each one's interpreter [*imām*] as an authority to determine what to believe and what to reject. As a result, *imām*s provided interpretations which caused new disputes and enmities among Muslims. As the Safavid Persians treated Abū Ḥanīfa's interpretations as trivial and himself as a fraud, yet the Persians exclaimed that he was a disciple of Imām Ja'far al-Ṣādiq who made miracles in the service of the Turks.

The Persians also claim that Shah Tahmasp turned the grave of this infamous man [Abū Ḥanīfa] in Baghdad into a stable, and, what is worse, a latrine to belittle him. They see each other with their sharp words, so it is no surprise that these people could not resume their previous bond of friendship. Add to this 'the infinite miracles of 'Alī, his horse and his marvelous sword,' which the Persians believe are holy; and the Turks ridicule and look down on as false. Think how much fuel all this adds to their hatred!

Today, all Persians venerate their saints equally. Just as the Persians attribute great prerogatives to 'Alī, they seem to worship and venerate his sons and successors no less. 'Alī had two sons from his wife Fāṭima, Ḥasan and Ḥusayn. They were succeeded by Zaynal 'Ābidīn, Muḥammad al-Bāqir, Ja'far al-Ṣādiq, Mūsā Kaẓim, 'Alī Mūsā al-Riḍā, Muḥammad al-Taqī, Ḥasan al-Askarī, and Muḥammad al-Mahdī. The Persians say they are all high priests [*imām*s] and prophets of their religion, and they most solemnly attend their tombs annually. On the contrary, Turks show hostility toward the Persian veneration of *imām*s and consider them contemptuous; they venerate their own men, Abū Bakr, 'Umar, and 'Uthmān, like gods.

There is more to say on this topic, which supports me in this last claim. If I am not mistaken, other authors refer to "27 particular articles of belief" Turks and Persians wrote; according to these doctrines they judge and damn each other to hell. I could explain these articles, however, it is not my intention to write a long and detailed text. Therefore, it is enough for us to know the number of those articles of belief. As the others have already discussed them, I will explain [a further difference] which is no less important. When I turn to it, I see obvious traces of this hatred between these two nations. Indeed, I will discuss this enmity. Isn't it obvious how different the 'appearance of Church rites' of the Persians and the Turks is to us? If I wanted to discuss their differences in detail, I could go on forever. However, I will give one example: how they differ in performing prayers at the mosque. The Persians have some prayers and ceremonies, Turks others. One recites their prayers, the other hates them. That is why they always strive in opposite directions. This is the main prayer for all of them:

> Glory to God the Father, Lord of things created, King of the Last Judgement, we worship you, we call on your aid, lead us into the true path of salvation, into the true path of those you have blessed, but not into the path of those on whom you have poured your wrath, nor indeed into the path of those who stray! Amen.

After this, they finish with *al-ḥamdu li'l-lāh*, then *subḥana rabbī*, and *Allāhu akbar*, and finally *salāmun alaykum*. They treat our most Holy Bible indiffcrently, as if it were written by Jews and Greeks, as they think. Therefore, they praise their Qur'an, as if it was directly given by God Himself as an uncontaminated scripture from the sky.

The Persians think that the creation of Adam and other sacred histories, the Last Judgement, and eternal life are marvelous tales; the Turks, however, ridicule them. If I now intended to recount all the differences between them in a longwinded rambling style, it would take a whole volume to write. Finally, I should mention the two sects' differing celebrations of religious holidays, historical memories, and miracles of the prophets. As they have different *imām*s and celebrate different religious holidays in their mosques, there is great hostility between them.

This is the end of my speech on the different interpretations of religion between these races, Turks and Persians. This may sound a retreat, but I will repeat my wish again and again, that the Supreme God Himself is willing to convert these idol worshippers along with all other unbelievers, so having followed the straight path of salvation, they may live in tranquility with us now and forever!

I have spoken.

[Kirchmaier's Note]: The reader should be aware that I was not able to write [my Persian text] using the four letters which the Persians use but Arabs do not, except through cognate letters, because of a lack of appropriate typescript. Those with more than a rudimentary knowledge of Persian will not be offended. And those who have not gathered the rudiments of the language will not cast judgment in this matter. As for my translation, it is translated to the sense, not to the word. Since a word by word translation stuffed with foreign loan words would exasperate the reader, I thought that it would be better to translate sense for sense. Finally, if certain errors have crept into the typesetter despite my care, let the prudent reader restore them easily in his candor.

To the Glory of the only God.

Notes

1 Kirchmaier's biography was compiled from the following sources: Sebastian Kirchmaier, *Stammbuch Sebasian Kirchmaier*, Herzogin Anna Amalia Bibliothek, Klassik Stiftung Weimar, MS Stb 155 (Wittenberg, 1660–67); Johann Andreas Planer, *Panegyricus, memoriae celeberrimi theologi, Sebastiani Kirchmaieri, antistitis, consistorialis, et scholarchae Rotenburgensis ad tubarim optime meriti, dictus Vitembergae*, Bayerische StaatsBibliothek MS 4 Diss. 43 (Wittenberg, 1701); Christian Gottlieb Jöcher, *Allgemeines Gelehrten-Lexicon*, vol. 2 (Leipzig, 1750), 2099–100; Nicolas Maria Serrano, *Diccionario Universal*, vol. 15 (Madrid, 1881), 5471; Paul Schattenmann, "Neues zum Briefwechsel des Rothenburger Superintendenten Dr. Johann Ludwig Hartmann (1640–80) mit Philipp Jakob Spener in Frankfurt am Main: Ein Beitrag zur Geschichte des Frühpietismus in Franken," *Zeitschrift für bayerische Kirchengeschichte* 7 (1932): 36–44; John Butt, "Germany-education and Apprenticeship," in *The Cambridge Companion to Handel*, ed. Donald Burrows (Cambridge: Cambridge University Press, 1997), 15; Horst Weigelt, *Geschichte des Pietismus in Bayern: Anfänge, Entwicklung, Beudeutung* (Göttingen: Vandenhoeck & Ruprecht, 2001), 50–57; Alison Rowlands, "Father Confessors and Clerical Intervention in Witch-Trials in Seventeenth-Century Lutheran Germany: The Case of Rothenburg, 1692," *The English Historical Review* 552/1 (2016): 1010–42.
2 [MK] Although the Latin version was taken as the main text for translation, the Persian text was also used for clarification and flow. Some paragraphs were joined together to improve the readability of the text.
3 Kirchmaier's note: "Translated more to the sense than the word."

16 Investigation of Religions
On Turkish and Persian Muhammadanism

Hieronymus Kromayer

Hieronymus Kromayer was born in 1610 in Zeitz in Saxony-Anhalt. Coming from a noble family of important Protestant theologians settled in Silesia, Kromayer was originally educated by private tutors and later attended a Lutheran school (*Stiftsschule*) in Zeitz. In 1628, he attended the University of Leipzig where he received his bachelor's degree in 1629. Subsequently, he attended the University of Wittenberg and the University of Jena, and received his master's degree from the Faculty of Philosophy in 1632 upon his return to Leipzig. He was driven out of Leipzig as a result of the Thirty Years' War, but upon his return in 1633 became a lecturer in Logic, Physics, and Astronomy. In 1640, Kromayer received his Bachelor of Theology and in 1643, he was a professor of history. In 1645, he was awarded his Licentiate of Theology and became a professor of rhetoric in 1648. Two years after the Thirty Years' War ended, Kromayer gave a speech in the presence of the ruler, Elector Johann Georg I, in Leipzig to celebrate the restoration of peace in Saxony and the Holy Roman Empire. A year after, in 1651, Kromayer received his doctorate in theology, and served as the rector of Leipzig University in 1653. He wrote the *Consensus repetitus fidei vere Lutheranae (Recurrent Consensus of the True Lutheran Faith)* in 1655 along with Daniel Heinrici, an important Lutheran figure at Leipzig University after the Thirty Years' War. This book was designed as an Orthodox Lutheran theological platform in the Syncretistic Controversy. Kromayer received his full professorship in 1657. In 1661, he succeeded Johann Hülsemann, an opponent of Georg Calixt during the Syncretic Controversy, by taking over the canon of Meissen and in 1666 began his first theological professorship as successor to Daniel Heinrici. Kromayer was appointed Dean of the Theological Faculty in Leipzig for five consecutive years until 1670. He wrote a series of books that have been frequently reprinted on exegetical, theological, and ethical subjects. These texts were often quite divisive in nature. In his later years, Kromayer produced *Ecclesia in politia (Political History of the Church)* and *Theologia positivo-polemica*, which attempts to deal in objective order with the controversies the Lutheran Church had with the Catholics, Calvinists,

Romanstrants, Socinians, Anabaptists, Weigelians, and Jews. In his work, *Scrutinium religionum tum falsarum*, Kromayer presents each religion and subsequently refutes their authenticity, including Paganism, Judaism, Islam, and various non-Lutheran Christian sects, such as Anabaptism, Quakerism, Calvinism, Socinianism, and Catholicism, in order to prove that orthodox Lutheranism is the only true religion (*tum unice verae & orthodoxae Lutheranismi*). He died in Leipzig in 1670.[1]

Variant Names: Hieronymi Kromayeri, Hieronymus Kronmayerus, Hieronymus Kromayerus, Hieronymus Kromaier, and Hieronymus Kromeyer

Summary and Analysis

In his *disputatio*, Kromayer tries to construct a position about what is 'true' in religion, based on its relationship to Christianity. In so doing, rather than providing an analysis of Islam as a single entity, he presents it in relation to its Abrahamic predecessors, with a focus on Qur'anic conceptions of Christ. Islam, therefore, represents a 'true' religion, according to Kromayer, because, unlike paganism, it consists of conceptions of divinity that are reflected in Christian doctrine. Thus, his text examines Islam according to scriptural dogmas. He begins by outlining the story of Muhammad having been born to a Gentile mother and Jewish father and argues that Muhammad began Islam by spreading the dogmas of a monk named Sergius with whom he had established a new religion. These dogmas, he says, were codified into what is now called the Qur'an. Kromayer suggests that Muhammad's wealth, which came from his late wife, was used to create an Arab army that extended across Palestine, Persia, Egypt, and most of the African shoreline, as well as the Aegean islands. Therefore, Kromayer saw Islam as political and militaristic, more than religious. He argues that Islam changed from a religion comprised of nomadic Arabs to a major religion after the Turks embraced it, leading to the spread of Islam across the Persian Empire. He hopes that this "tyrannical empire" will be destroyed.

Kromayer argues that the principal dogma of Islam is the Qur'an, a doctrine full of many false stories, contradictions, and riddles without any order. He maintains that Muhammad claimed the law was handed down to Moses, the gospel to Christ, and the "*al-furqān*," the "pleasing and welcome book," to himself. As a result, the Qur'an retains certain ceremonial laws, such as washing and circumcision as well as public laws like alms-giving and mandated times for fasting that are prescribed in the laws of Moses. Kromayer explains some of the Qur'an's regulations, such as restrictions and restraints on gambling, pork, and alcohol consumption. He argues that these laws spring from Muhammad being unaware that the individual might be freed in liberty through Christ and, because of this, the Jewish covenant between God and man had been superseded.

Kromayer says that, although Muhammad commends the gospel handed down by Christ, he does not accept it as a form of salvation. Muhammad believed that Abraham is the father of all believers and all the prophets of the Abrahamic tradition share the same law, which culminated in the reception of the Qur'an as the highest good. Christians and Jews should not judge Muslims and a Muslim cannot take a non-Muslim wife. To show how Islam differs from and is, therefore, lesser than Christianity, Kromayer discusses Islamic views on divorce, polygamy and purgatory, explaining how Islam is comprised of certain Judeo-Christian tenets. He adds that when Christianity began to decline

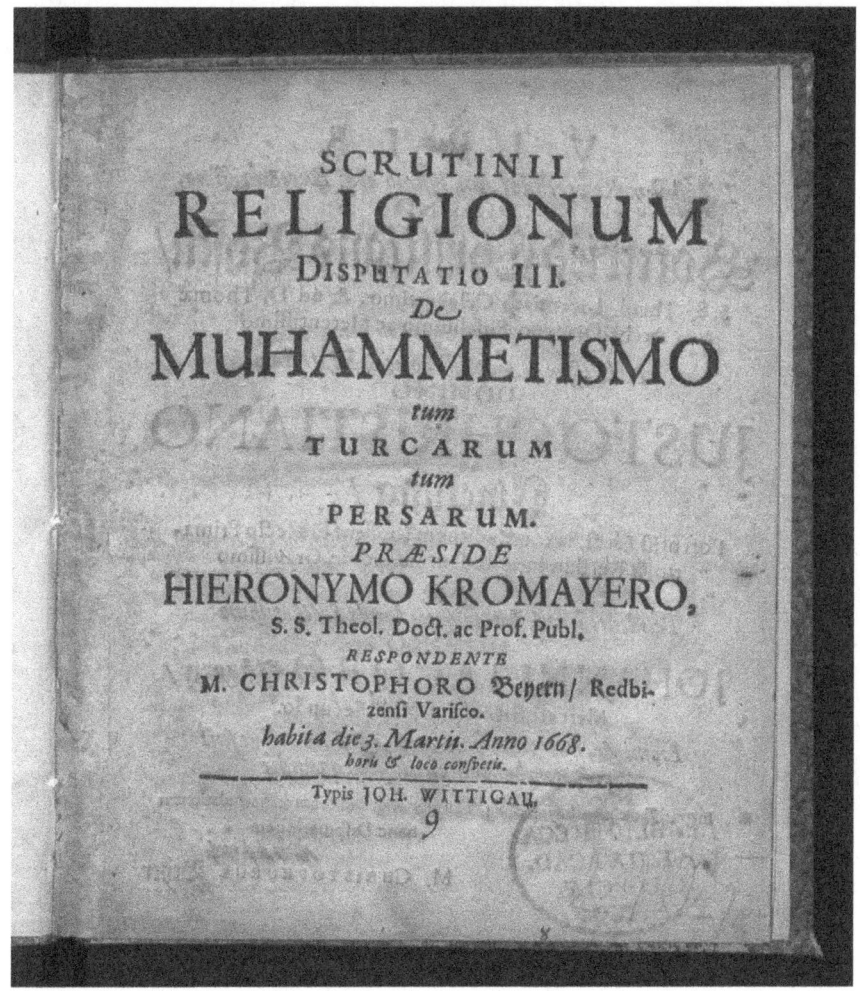

Figure 16.1 Hieronymus Kromayer, *Scrutinii religionum disputatio III, de Muhammetismo tum Turcarum tum Persarum*, 1668 (Courtesy of the Niedersächsische Staats- und Universitätsbibliothek Göttingen).

in Arabia only a shadow of the knowledge of Christ remained. He concludes by noting key differences between Persian and Turkish Islam: the interpreter and interpretation of the Qur'an; certain sacred matters, ceremonies, and rites; and miracles. Over these, the Turks and Persians persecute each other.

Although Kromayer's title refers to Turkish and Persian Muhammadanism, his disputation focuses on comparing Islam to various heresies. However, Kromayer's title, *Turkish and Persian Muhammadanism*, implies that the two main Islamic sects and their theological dispute were restricted to the Ottoman-Safavid political tension. In contrast, Pfeiffer's use of *Alishiis* and *Sunnitis* in his title indicates, to a certain extent, a familiarity with the Sunni and Shi'a schools of thought. In other words, for Kromayer, Muslim denominations are ethnic and political as much as theological.

Disputation III on the Investigation of Religions: On Turkish and Persian Muhammadanism (Leipzig, 1668)[2]

Introduction

In the preceding disputation, we examined Paganism, first in general, and then the form it took among the noble Roman race. Now let us consider to Muhammadanism. I have defined Paganism as a received religion, suitable for those who live outside the Church, unaware of God. [By this definition], I mean to distinguish true religion from heresy, that is to say, to distinguish Paganism from Muhammadanism. As Pagan awareness of God is very remote indeed, Paganism differs to a certain extent from Muhammadanism and Judaism. Muhammadanism acknowledges Christ, the son of Mary, and Judaism retains a part of the principal theology, namely the Old Testament. Muhammadanism should, therefore, be associated with both Christianity and Judaism. As Paganism denotes all religion outside the Church, who will go as far as to include Muhammadanism and Judaism in its ambit? Indeed, could anyone doubt that Judaism and Muhammadanism are close to Christianity when Muhammadanism accepts Jesus of Nazareth as a remarkable prophet? Judaism rejects this; although the Jews maintain the principal part of theology in good repair in the Masora and tenaciously cling to divine law; yet they still discuss the Messiah as one who is to come. However, I will connect Muhammadanism to Paganism based on evidence. I will undertake this labor, first describing the dogmas of that faith, and then examining its scripture to the Lydian stone. God grant that this succeed!

Part 1: Describing the Dogmas of Muhammadanism

Muhammadanism gets its name from Muhammad, an Arab who lived in the seventh century after the birth of Christ. Muhammadanism easily drew many races into its fellowship, integrating components from Sergius the Nestorian monk, heretics, Judaism, Christianity, and Paganism, just as a cake is made from many ingredients.

Some claim that Muhammadanism mixes Judaism with Paganism because Muhammad was born of a gentile [Pagan] father and a Jewish mother. However, the explanation I have given above seems to be correct, unless perhaps they are both correct.

I will now briefly expound upon Muhammad's life. He was an Arab, born in the late sixth century after the birth of Christ to obscure and poor parents, endowed with a keen spirit, eloquence, and a noble appearance. When Muhammad traveled to Spain, Saint Isidore of Seville recognized that he would do great injury to both Church and State, and advised that he be imprisoned. Muhammad was sold to a rich merchant to oversee camel caravans. Because he was handsome, he was given nice clothes and put in charge of sales. The young man excelled in seeking profit for his master, and for this reason he was treated well and came to know many Christians and Jews through business. When Muhammad's master died childless, he married his fifty-year-old widow, winning her affections either through his good looks and industry or through the magic arts. She made him the heir to all of her possessions. Muhammad's wife often suffered from epilepsy. As an explanation [for her seizures], Muhammad told her to say that an angel of God appeared to her, and that her whole body was shaking because she could not endure the sight of it. Therefore, when his wife died, he was treated as God's prophet.

Around the time when this impostor lived, a certain monk called Sergius was expelled from Byzantium, because of the Nestorian heresy (some say Arian), and he came to Arabia. After he became friends with Muhammad, Sergius suggested a plan to forge a new kind of religion, that was neither Christian nor Jewish nor Ethnic [Pagan], but was harmonious with all of them for these three religions were then stretching their threads far and wide throughout Europe, Asia and Africa. After a while, Muhammad spread this monk's teachings in his Qur'an, just as he spread teachings from the works of Jews and other heretics.

Muhammad's riches furnished the means to recruit a gang of robbers into a huge force. He also enlisted Arab soldiers defecting from the Emperor Heraclius because the Quaestors paid Roman and Greek soldiers more and treated the Arabs like a pack of dogs.

Fortune favored the enterprise of this robber and his successors wherever they went in the following century. Not only did they make Palestine, Persia, Egypt and most of the African shoreline their own, but they also attacked the Aegean Islands with their ships and laid siege to Constantinople, the Imperial seat; however, they were repulsed after their ships had been burned by Greek fire.

Nevertheless, Muhammadanism found followers easily among so many races because various [Christian] heretics, especially Arius and his parasites, had already spread the seeds of [heterodoxy]. As the saying goes: Arianism strew the path in the East for Muhammadanism. I will have more to say on this after evaluating the erroneous dogmas of the Muhammadan sects.

Muhammad's followers are called *Hagarian*. It is doubtless that they trace their descent from Ishmael, an inhabitant of Arabia. Then there are the Saracens: they are not named after Sarah, the free wife of Abraham, nor does their name mean "inheritors of the world," as *Carion's Chronicle* says. Rather, their name comes from the Arabic *al-sārik*, which means "thieves" and "nomads." The Saracens are the same sort of men as the Cossacks and Tartars are to the Turks, and as the Martolos are, and as the Bandoliers are in the Pyrenees, etc. For the old proverb teaches, and experience confirms, that these wandering and nomadic men rejoice in rapine (Jeremiah 3:2 and Ezekiel 38:13). Arabs haunted the Holy Land in the time of the Church Fathers, and provoked public animosity, as described by Nicolaus Radzvil, Jakob Breuning, Salomon Schweigger, and Johann Helffrich.

Indeed, the Arabs themselves (Hagarians and Saracens) take their name from the [Hebrew] root word *arav*, that is to say, "mix" (from which they trace; *erev*, that is to say, "dusk," because light would then be mixed with darkness; and, *orev*, that is to say, "crow" from its dusky color) on the grounds that they are a random horde or mixture of various peoples (Jeremiah 25:20–24). When Kimchi writes "wandering and mixed Arabs," they are to be understood as living in tents; Pliny therefore called them Scenitae, and they did not own the best pastures. Hence, they were named Nomads from *nemos*, that is, "pasture." For when the grasses exhausted in one place, the Arabs did not keep their tents there, but rather they moved their possessions elsewhere in wagons in order to feed their flocks, as is attested in Isaiah 13:20.

About one thousand years after Christ's birth, the Turks, having spread from the womb of the races in the north through the Caspian mountains into Persia, embraced Muhammad's religion. After that, the people who professed the religion of this seducer were called Turks, especially after the Sultans of the Ottoman house took over the state and crushed the other leaders. Johannes Leunclavius in his *History of the Turks* discusses the various rulers of these races.

The name Turk, which they pronounce in their own whispering language as Turk or even *Jurk*, perhaps as it is written and pronounced differently in France, means "wandering herder." They owe their lineage to the Scythians, who are called "people living in wagons" in Greek. In the Scriptures (Ezekiel 38–39 and Revelation 20:8), they are called Magog, and in abbreviated form Gog (from the word roof, as if they were roof men, *dachmänner* in German, for the same reason), because they derive their lineage from their first father, from Magog, the son of Japheth, grandson of Noah.

Perhaps on this point Psalms gives some evidence, when it introduces the lamenting church (Psalm 120:5) wandering among the Mesech camps and Kedar huts. For the Turks are clearly understood as northerners descended from Mesech (from Mesech, the son of Japheth, Gen. 10:2); the Arabs descended from Kedar (from Kedar, the son of Ishmael, Genesis 25:13). This passage applies to the situation of the Eastern Churches spread far and wide throughout Europe, Asia, and Africa.

The Turkish Empire, in which the doctrine of the impostor Muhammad flourishes, is represented by the image of a crescent. In this empire there are three horns, i.e., kingdoms: Greece, Asia, and Egypt (in Hebrew, kingdoms are called "horns" because of their power and strength). These were once part of the Roman Empire. These "horns" have eyes looking about them for their self-preservation and propagation, and a mouth spreading whisperings of portents and expounding blasphemies against the only begotten son of God, as prophesied by Daniel (Dan. 7:1–28).

The deceiver himself predicted the longevity of his empire. Near death, he was asked for the duration of his empire, and, unable to speak, extended ten fingers to signify ten centuries. As it will have been a thousand years this very century, I beg God, Threefold, Best and Greatest, either to place His supreme hand upon this tyrannical empire at His final coming, or to destroy its power so that it cannot harm the Church anymore.

I have seen a lot of the dangers to Christians from this poisoned religion. Christians are taken captive almost every day partially through hostile incursions from lower Pannonia, Croatia, Dalmatia and other neighboring places, partially because the boundaries of the Turkish Empire are still being extended. I will give examples of their dogmas, especially from the Qur'an itself, as translated by Salomon Schweigger, preacher of Noricum, once preacher of the legate to the Sublime Porte, the Imperial Baron from Sintzendorff, published in three books (Noriberg, 1623), a distinct impression translated from Arabic to Italian, and from Italian to German.

Their main dogma is al-Qur'an, or, leaving out the [Arabic] article 'al,' the Qur'an, which was written based on the books of the Bible, and stuffed with many added false stories, contradictions, riddles without order; a horrible chaos. In the Qur'an, accounts and histories stick together like the dreams of a sick man, so as to drive away any reader with the slightest bit of intelligence at the first impression. The Sacred Scriptures present a temporal succession through several thousand years: the origin of human beings, the rise of empires and nations; its passages are joined together with the most beautiful harmony. In fact, the word Qur'an comes from the Hebrew word *Kara*, which means either reading, narrating, or summarizing.

If one wants to see some specimen of the fables and contradictions, one should read the story of Joseph in the Qur'an. The Qur'an says that

Joseph wanted to tempt the wife of the King of Egypt into bed at one time, and another time Mezzara's wife, in addition to many other things. It also says that Adam was circumcised by the angel Gabriel and that Moses' breath was extracted through his nose by the angel of death. Muhammad describes Paradise as *"als ein Schlaraffenland,"* a land of fairytales or the Land of Cockaigne, because rivers of milk and honey flow through it. [Moreover], the Qur'an says that the pig was born out of elephant's dung on Noah's Ark. It also says that the people who asked Moses to show God to them were destroyed by lightning, plus many other examples, which I will mention as I proceed.

The Qur'an says that the book that contains the word of God was handed down to Muhammad from God, no different than how the law of Moses and the Gospel was handed down from Christ. That book [Qur'an] is called *al-furqān*, which means pleasing and gratifying. Muhammad says the angel Gabriel brought many revelations to him. Muhammad, no less, handed over the Qur'an to be arranged by the wisest and most eloquent men, undoubtedly, Sergius and his collaborators, Bahira the Jacobite, and the two Jews, Phineas and Aurias.

There was confusion in the Qur'an because the impostor's successors received many dogmas written on paper. As these scriptures came into their hands, they were compiled together, and organized into separate sections.

Muhammad decrees that the one and only creator, God, can be known from His divine work in heaven and earth, from the cycle of day and night, from the rain nourishing the earth, from the design of animals and so on. God's works are evident through the study of nature.

Muhammad teaches that God is eternal, knows what the heart holds, and all things, and has the key to all secrets. He alone can make miracles although they also ascribe this to Christ. He is all-powerful, the creator of the world, and can be worshipped in any place.

Muhammad says that there is only one person in his godhead. Therefore, he denies that God has a son or allies. He says that there are not three Gods, but one God who does not have a son, and whom Christ is subject to no less than the angels are. He mocks the Christians for believing in three persons in the godhead. He calls those who believe that God has a son "outstandingly stupid."

It seems that Muhammad believes the Holy Spirit is an angel; the Qur'an says that the same angel appeared to Mary, and informed her of the conception of her son. This is attributed to the angel Gabriel in the Gospel of Luke 1:26.

Muhammad calls Christ not the son of God, but of the Word (perhaps recalling the word 'logos' in John 1:1), and indeed a prophet to whom God sent the gospel for him to teach.

Muhammad says that Christ is the son of Mary and uses this to prove he was not the son of God, since his mother ate and drank no differently than other human beings. As further evidence, he points out that Jesus called God his Lord and many before him were prophets. Muhammad calls Mary the purest of them all and a virgin greeted by angels, the daughter of Joachim raised by Zachariah.

However, Muhammad says that God gave His breath (perhaps because it is called the Word) and more of His power to Christ, the son of Mary, than any other man.

Muhammad says that Christ, like Adam, made miracles the elders called childish; forming birds from the ground and giving them life with his breath, giving back sight to the blind, hearing to the deaf, and curing leprosy. Christ confirmed the Old Testament, but relaxed certain precepts.

Muhammad says that it was not Christ, the son of the Virgin Mary, sent by God, but another very similar man who was crucified. Christ was taken away by God, and will testify to this in the next life. Hence the cross of Christ became a stumbling block to Muslims, when the Turks proclaimed in the siege of Buda that a thief had been crucified and hailed as the God of the Christians. While others add that as Christ sits at the right hand of God, so Muhammad sits at the left hand. The reason for this might be that the left place is the more honored among the Turks.

Muhammad says that God created the world. The Qur'an also admits its destruction, but confuses the order of creation, saying that: first, the wings; second, man; third, God's throne; and then, Paradise were created.

Muhammad asserts that the first man was formed from a fistful of variously colored dust. That is why there is such a variety of faces and so many colors on this earth. He says that there were sixty colors in the earth, without which variety one man could not be distinguished from another.

Muhammad says that Eve was created from Adam's left side, not his right. Otherwise, if she had been from the right, she would actually have had as much strength as Adam. He says that Eve drew her origin from Adam alone, and Christ from the Virgin Mary alone.

He says that everything was created within seven days, and indeed that seven heavens were formed.

The angels Gabriel, Michael, and Raphael are the three secretary angels of God. There are sixteen legions of cherubs standing before God and ministering to Him. Also, Muhammad teaches that there are legions of seventy thousand angels praising God and five thousand where you will.

Muhammad says that the world was subjected by God to the rule of the first man, and all the angels showed reverence to Adam, except Beelzebub, for the sake of which he was cast down by God.

Muhammad teaches that God rules everything according to His good will. God defines certain limits on all things and times. He hardens the hearts of men so that they can be cast down into Hell. The deaf and mute are hated by God. The devils cannot do anything more than what God allows to them.

The Qur'an decrees that some men are predestined for the fire and that God wills the impious to proceed in their erroneous ways. He keeps two books of the impious and the pious. Some compare this doctrine to the doctrine of predestination and the Stoic doctrine on fate.

Concerning the fall of the first-formed, Muhammad says that the forbidden tree produced seven thorns, filled with five seeds, one of which Adam plucked. He nonsensically says that Adam ate two seeds, gave two to Eve, and stole the fifth for himself, which was divided into six hundred parts. This is why there is a variety of seeds. Muhammad says that Adam hid himself in the leaves of Paradise, and Eve hid herself in her hair. They were ejected from Paradise. They became the first parents by the Devil's encouragement. After the Fall, they sought forgiveness for their sins. All men will die.

In another place in the Qur'an, talking about Adam and Eve's quest for forgiveness, Muhammad describes their penitence through remorse and abstention from further sin. Muhammad seems to approve of the errors of the followers of Novationus, because he believes that one will perish if one falls back into sin after forgiveness. Like Novationus, [Muhammad says] God can only forgive light sins and not mortal ones. It should be noted that Muhammad considers certain sins venial, according to their nature.

The Impostor says that the law was handed to Moses, the gospel to Christ, and *al-furqān*, the pleasing and welcome book, to himself. He retains certain ceremonial and public laws from the law of Moses. From these laws, he especially commends charity and fasting. If anyone raises his face to the East in prayer, or if he sets it to the West, he is not a faithful man. Muhammad argues that one is praying to God if one distributes money among friends, relatives, widows, orphans, and the poor begging from door to door; and likewise, if one redeems captives, keeps faith in agreements, and endures every kind of injustice. He seems to describe faith as obedience to divine orders. He decrees that these things conform to the will of the Creator of heaven and earth.

Furthermore, Muhammad says that everyone born on Earth must give alms. Possessions must not be given conspicuously; more should be given in secret than in the open. He suggests that the dispossessed, orphans, and widows receive alms and that they should be considered brothers and sisters.

Muhammad designates certain times and certain days for fasting. But he makes exceptions for the ill and for pilgrims. He decrees that the rich can give to charity instead of fasting. He specifies the times of fasting from early morning to the evening. The phases of the moon indicate pilgrimages and fasting.

From the ceremonial laws, he retains washing and circumcision to such a degree that he says Adam himself was circumcised. From the civil laws, he retains the separation of food, polygamy, divorce, and many other things. He is too little informed about the liberty into which Christ freed us, and the abolition of the old covenant.

Muhammad says that the face, feet, and arms must be washed before prayer, because God delights in cleanliness. One must wash after knowing one's wife, but if a supply of water is not on hand, one must wash with simple dust. One must not eat from carrion, suffocated animals or ones attacked by wolves, or from any forbidden parts of animals; however, pilgrims are excepted from this law. He especially hates pork. Anyone who can sustain two, three, four, or however many wives may do so. Congress with [household] slaves is allowed. Women, if they are no longer pleasing, can be changed. He forbids the enjoyment of wine, the game of dice and gambling, and usury, as if they were invented by Satan.

Muhammad commends the Gospel handed down to Christ, because it is a light, a confirmation of the Testament and the true way of fulfilling the Law. But he has nothing [in his book] about the free forgiveness of sins through Christ's sacrifice. In his law, he decrees that the axis of salvation is turned by the Gospel and the Qur'an. The Qur'an confirms the Old Testament and the Gospel.

Muhammad teaches that man is saved through good works. One should strive to win merit from God. He often says that the sins of a generous person who does not expect a reward will be forgiven. If a man feeds ten paupers, or clothes them, or redeems captives, he can obtain forgiveness from his sins. He says that hypocrites, who call on God as a witness of their hearts in public, but do evil to men, have a place prepared in Hell. He also says God rewards good intentions. He says that outside of God nothing [done] by man endures. He says only God requires perfection. He says men's deeds are balanced in the scales. He says Saracens are saved through faith (i.e., in one God) and through works, especially fasting, alms, prayers, and pilgrimages, as I have said above. If someone is a Christian, faith is enough, or if he is a Jew, to embrace the Saracen faith and do good works before he dies. Abraham is considered the father of all believers. Muhammad teaches in the Qur'an that Abraham, Ishmael (from whom the Saracens were descended), Jacob, the twelve tribes, Christ and other prophets are a common means to salvation as they believed the same thing.

Muhammad says that one can pray anywhere on foot or on horseback, and that God must be invoked in the morning and evening. Without washing, one cannot enter the temple of Mecca. He says that those offering prayers should turn their faces southwards to the temple of Mecca. But Muslims consider these ceremonies secondary, according to their moral system. (See above). In war, some soldiers are committed to prayer (perhaps from the example of Moses in Exodus 17:11), and some to fight against the enemy. Before prayer they must wash their faces, feet, and arms. Muhammad mocks the Jews because they worship Uzair and Christians because they worship Jesus. He says the former worship the priests, the latter the son of Mary, but God alone must be worshipped.

On the sacraments instituted by Christ, baptism and communion, nothing appears in these patchworks [i.e., Muhammadanism is a cento, pieced together from other works, the Old Testament and New Testament]. Nor were any of these sacraments observed in practice, according to the writers of Turkish history. But if a man wants to be a Muslim, he must be circumcised.

In the matters of faith, elders must not be followed. Muhammad favors Puccianism, since he thinks that anyone who lives uprightly, whether Christian or Jew, can be saved. God does not want to force anyone into faith. Hence, it is certain that the Turks tolerate religions of all kinds. Muhammad made no miracles since God alone makes miracles. But though he concedes that miracles were done by Christ (as a separate instrument) and by the prophets, he thinks that they were treated as illusions by unbelievers. [He says that] Jerusalem is the center of the terrestrial world, and is called a blessed home, because God spoke there with the patriarchs and the prophets. On the last day there will be strife among the two sects, Jews and Christians. God can be found wherever he is worshipped. Nothing in the Qur'an must be changed.

Muhammad says that the prophets had one and the same law, but that it was multifaceted. Muhammad boasts that his doctrine will lead to the highest good, the joys of Paradise. Abraham and Ishmael accepted God's order to build a temple. The proper observation of fasting, pilgrimages, and religious holiday is commended. The Sabbath must be observed, but the day is controversial since the Turks differ from the Jews and Christians as they fix divine worship on Fridays every week. They turn away from arguments about how the last day will happen because this can lead to error; but if they are forced into an argument, they should speak with kind words. They say that the law has been corrupted by the Jews when it differs from the Qur'an.

Muhammad says that wars must be carried out against unbelievers, yet soldiers are not to be summoned to Mecca. The Turks' victories are considered proof that they have pleased God. Those following other doctrines cannot be victorious, as victory only comes from God. Cowardly soldiers are not saved. It is a sin to flee in war. One must be persuaded to go to war [not conscripted]. In war, soldiers must alternate between prayer and fighting against the enemy. Unbelievers who are neither Jews nor Christians must be killed. Muhammad considers being a pilgrim to Mecca inferior to being a brave soldier. He says that the highest rank of glory in the afterlife is destined for soldiers. Since the year is divided into twelve months, four months should be spent as a soldier fighting against unbelievers. There is no nobler way to lose one's life than in a war for the glory of God. There must be no oaths, because God pays attention to perjury, and one who swears falsely is odious to Him. But one must not refuse to give testimony. Usury is prohibited even to merchants. He says that the punishment for adultery is life imprisonment. Involuntary homicide must be redeemed by the ransom of a prisoner of war or a fast of two months, and voluntary homicide is punished by fire. The punishment for theft is either restitution or the amputation of a hand. Christians and Jews should not be judges over Muslims. In times of pilgrimage, hunting is forbidden. One must abstain from the enjoyment of wine, dice, and gambling, as if they were invented by the devil.

One must not take a wife from another religion. One must abstain from congress [intercourse] during menstruation because God delights in purity. Polygamy and congress with slaves are permitted. Divorce is allowed. A divorced woman cannot enter a marriage with another man without the consent of her previous husband. The time of widowhood is set at four months. A woman who has divorced three times cannot enter into marriage with another man, except with a man who previously divorced her. Daughters cannot be given in marriage unless they consent and are fit for a husband. Changing a wife, if she no longer pleases, is permitted. Incest is prohibited in marriage, because a man cannot marry his mother, sister, niece, daughter-in-law, his nurse, nor her mother, nor her sister. A whore cannot be taken as a wife.

When someone is dying there should be a minimum of two or three persons present. All men will die. There is an intermediate place between Paradise and Hell, where those who lived in the hope and expectation of Paradise go. The day of judgement must always be contemplated. The last judgement will endure for a thousand years. God himself together with His angels will come down from the clouds for the day of judgement. It seems that Muhammad does not recognize Christ will come as a judge. Everyone must congregate at Jerusalem (perhaps he alludes to the valley of Josaphat), where the scales will be set, on which all men are to be weighed. On the last day, the faces of the pious will appear white, and the impious black. The judgement must be given according to the Qur'an. He describes Paradise as a place abounding in pleasures of the flesh: rivers of milk and honey flow through the same; a thousand days are equal to a thousand years; all the inhabitants will have the stature of Adam and the face of Christ; they will be without pain, suffering, and cares; anything from fish liver (perhaps the Leviathan from Jewish tales) to the sweetest fruits must be prepared for them; they will not cook food; sweat will smell like the fragrance of balsam; and meat of every kind, except pork, may be eaten. Hell will be full of pitch, sulfur, humans, and devils.

Since Muhammadanism is a mix of Judaism, Christianity (or rather heretical Christianity) and Gentilism [Paganism], when these three religions prevail in three parts of the world at the end of time, Muhammadanism will be appealing to everyone.

Many Christian heretics have opened the way for Muhammadanism by promoting false dogma that later found its way into the Qur'an.

The Severian heresy forbade drinking wine before Muhammad, as did the Manichean heresy, which called wine "the bile of the serpent." But I should point out that the Turkish emperors dispense wine so freely it is as if they are drunk [every day].

The authors of the Qur'an learned from the Arians to pursue the enemies of their religion with the sword. Not to mention Aristobulus, priest of the Jews, and Emperor Heraclius, who also tried to drag men to his religion with violence. Why? Because of the statement falsely attributed to Abraham that he wanted to propagate his faith by the sword after Lot had been arrested, persecuted, and tortured by four kings.

In common with Messalians (on whom Epiphanius writes a lot), Pepuzians and Manicheans, Muslims treat sacraments instituted from heaven as nothing. But they allow circumcision along with the Jews as the sacrament of initiation. Muslims do this not on the eighth day, but on about the ninth.

It seems that taking many wives relies on the example of the [Israelite] Patriarchs, because although God tolerated it, he did not order it. They must look back to the first institute, and Christ's explanation (Matthew 19:l-10). The Nazarenes, who insisted not only on circumcision, but the observation of the whole law, followed Christ [on marriage].

Origenians also taught what the secondhand cloth dealer teaches about washing. But the Impostor asserts that Paradise is full of pleasures of the flesh following the heresy of the Chiliasm, which was founded by Cerinthus and Papias of Hierapolis.

Along with Cerdo and Marcion, Muhammad claims that Christ did not die, but after evading the Jews was carried to heaven. Saturninus, Basilides, and Manicheans allege that Simon of Cyrene was crucified in his [Christ's] place.

Along with the Audians, also called Anthropomorphitae, Muhammad attributes the form of a human body to God, analyzing the scripture in an over-literal manner.

Also, along with the Noetians and Sabellians, who are called Patripassiani in the sacred scriptures, Muhammad denies the Trinity. In denying the divinity of Christ, he has many predecessors: Nicolaites, Simon Magus, Menander, Ebion, Cerinthus, Marcion, Alogiani, Theodotiani, Artemon, Paulus Samosatenus, the Arians, and the Photians.

God judges men who do not value the truth revealed to them; they will not be saved. The Arabs stand out as people of this type. Paul the Apostle preached to the Arabs (Galatians 1:17). The light of the Gospel shone on them, but after Arian's controversy began to divide the Eastern

Church, Christianity began to decline in Arabia, so that the Arabs retained only a shadow of the knowledge of Christ.

Muslims practice these doctrines: they fix divine worship on Friday (in which they differ from Jews and Christians); they have the *Muftī* as their Supreme Chief of sacred affairs; they do not tolerate bells and striking clocks, as if they were instruments of sedition; they do not allow women a place in public temples to avoid vagrant lust; they do not have images in their sacred shrines, but they decorate their temples with the eggs of ostriches. Muslims use rosaries and their preachers armed with swords ascend a loftier position to preach. They celebrate their religious holidays according to the phases of the moon. The beginning of their lunar year varies, unlike [our solar] calendar. Every year, they pay out alms [*zakāt*] to the paupers they meet. They do not approach sacred shrines unless they wash. They publicly humiliate the violators of sacred places by draping them in animal intestines and guts.

The Persians follow the above doctrines, as they follow Muhammad and the Qur'an. They are circumcised and called Muslims. But after they split from the Turks and began to establish their own kingdom, they started to diverge in the business of religion.

According to Adam Olearius of the Faculty of Philosophy in this university, the differences [between the Turks and the Persians] consist of the following: first, the interpreter and interpretation of the Qur'an; second, various sacred matters; third, ceremonies and rituals; and fourth, various miracles.

Persians accept 'Alī as the interpreter of the Qur'an, son-in-law of Muhammad, to whom they attribute many miracles, and nearly extol above Muhammad himself. For they say that the law put in the Qur'an was to be handed to 'Alī, but through error it came to Muhammad.

They seem to accept 'Alī as the interpreter of the Qur'an because of Ṣafī al-Dīn Ardabīlī, who derived his origin from 'Alī through his son Hossain and shook off the Turkish yoke about 300 years ago (in the year 1363 after Christ's birth). Although 'Alī changed nothing in the Qur'an, he disagreed on some points, as did his predecessor caliphs, Abū Bakr, the father-in-law of Muhammad, 'Umar and 'Uthmān. The Persians detest these predecessors, who are greatly esteemed by the Turks, because they believe those caliphs unlawfully and immorally stole the key of government from the hands of the nearest heir [to Muhammad].

Concerning the sacred men (interpreters of the Qur'an from the early Muslim communities), the Persians venerate 'Alī and Ja'far al-Ṣādiq; the Turks revere Abū Ḥanīfa; the Tartars highly esteem Imām Shāfi'ī. I am ashamed to recall the stories and fables, which they use to illuminate the obscurity of the Qur'an [commentaries on the Qur'an], or which they wish to add to the scripture that had been handed down to them quite concisely.

Persians and Turks differ on ceremonies, prayers, ablutions, religious holidays, the use of images, calling for prayers, creeds, and other things. Salomon Schweigger in his *Ein newe Reiss Beschreibung auss Teutschland nach Constantinopel und Jerusalem* says that, unlike the Turks, the Persians weave images into their clothes. The Persian envoy to the Sublime Porte is dressed in clothes decorated in this way. But the Turks do not tolerate images, not even on their gold coins. Through their opposition to icon worship, the Turks are said to have influenced the Greek emperors, who tolerated images in their temples, to become iconoclasts.

The miracles, which the Persians ascribe to their saints (although Muhammad performed no miracles), are obviously fiction rather than fact; indeed, they are so incongruous and ridiculous that anyone who believes in them should himself be considered a miracle.

Turks and Persians persecute each other with a more than Vatinian hatred. The Turks use white cloths for their heads just as the Christians use blue, and Jews yellow. They mockingly call the Persians "redhead" [*kızılbaş*] in their language because of their red headgear. The Persians tend to wear green leggings to cover their feet. These are also worn among the Turks, who claim that Muhammad wore them.

Notes

1 Kromayer's biography was compiled from the following sources: Hieronymus Kromayer, *Loci Anti-Syncretistici, sive Sententiae diversarum Religionum Conciliatriculae visae* (Leipzig, 1668); Johann Heinrich Zedler (ed.), "Kromayer, Hieronymus," in *Grosses vollständiges Universal-Lexicon aller Wissenschafften und Künste*, vol. 15 (Leipzig, 1737), 1959–62; Günther Wartenberg, "Kromayer, Hieronymus," in *Neue Deutsche Biographie*, vol. 13 (Berlin: Bürklein-Ditmar, 1982), 74; Otto Kirn, *Die Leipziger Theologische Fakultät in fünf Jahrhunderten: 1409–1909* (Leipzig: Hirzel, 1909), 124–6; Claudia Tietz, *Johann Winckler (1642–1705): Anfänge eines lutherischen Pietisten* (Göttingen: Vandenhoeck & Ruprecht, 2008), 59–62; and Hans Medick, "The Thirty Years' War as Experience and Memory: Contemporary Perceptions of a Macro-Historical Event," in *Enduring Loss in Early Modern Germany: Cross Disciplinary Perspectives*, ed. Lynne Tatlock (Leiden: Brill, 2010), 25–50.

2 [MK] For this text, I did not include all the Qur'anic numerations in order to improve readability. Kromayer uses Salomon Schweigger's German translation of the Qur'an in his references in his original Latin text; see Salomon Schweigger, *Alcoranus Mahometicus, Das ist: der Türcken Alcoran, Religion und Aberglauben*, Bayerische Staatsbibliothek München, 422 A (Nuremberg, 1616). Also, I eliminated the second part of this disputation as Kromayer focused on the Trinity as part of an intra-Christian discussion rather than a critique of Sunni and Shi'ite division.

17 Shi'ites and Sunnis or the Critical Disagreements between Persians and Turks Concerning Religion

August Pfeiffer

The biography of Pfeiffer is provided in part II, Religion and Theology (Chapter 5).

Summary and Analysis

Pfeiffer sets out to describe the religious differences between the Persians and the Turks, the two major powers in the seventeenth-century Islamic Middle East. He begins his dissertation with the proverb, "Truth is singular, falsehood is multifaceted," implying that Islam is the latter. He says that Islam is divided into 73 sects, the most famous of which are the Sunni and Shi'ite sects. Pfeiffer then states his intention to adumbrate the religious differences of the Shi'ite Persians and Sunni Turks, using Muslim writings along with firsthand accounts of European observers. His work is divided into three chapters: the first contains background information on the ethnic origins of the Persians and the Turks and their pre-Islamic religions; the second outlines the articles of faith that both hold in common; and the third focuses on their religious differences, which Pfeiffer claims are the cause of their division and enmity.

In the first chapter, Pfeiffer gives several potential etymologies of Persian, compiled from European sources, mostly based on biblical evidence and Hebrew derivations. The origin of the Persian people is then discussed before he gives a similar account of the Turks. He explains that, although both peoples take the name Muslim, the Persians are called Shi'ites and the Turks Sunnis due to doctrinal differences. Thus, Pfeiffer outlines two Muslim groups, divided along ethnic and religious lines, which he compares throughout the rest of the dissertation. Pfeiffer then turns to a discussion of pre-Islamic religions. According to his account, drawn chiefly from European sources, the Persians worshipped first the sun, then Venus, and then fire. He discusses whether fire-worshippers still exist in Persia and their relation to the Magi, whose name is the subject of a lengthy etymological digression. Pfeiffer describes how Turks were steeped in the most savage idolatry, worshipping many gods and goddesses before Islam. This religious heterogeneity in the pre-Islamic Middle East, along with a description of Muhammad's teachings being a mix of Christianity, Judaism, and ancient Saracenism, portrays a region riven by religious doctrine, much like Christian Europe at that time. Since I did not think this chapter would be of general interest I omitted it. Sentences that are omitted in the text are indicated by [...].

In his second chapter, where the translated text starts, Pfeiffer focuses on the religious agreements between the Persians and the Turks; he claims that an understanding of the Turks' and Persians' religious agreements will underscore their religious differences. Both groups agree on the divinely inspired nature of Muhammad. They place a high value on the Qur'an, with the Turks, in particular, taking pains to see that no copy is sullied by Christian contact. Both recognize the Qur'an as the word of God, and there is no disagreement about dogmas originating in the Qur'an itself. Both sides have a religious leader analogous to a president or pontiff. Both have holy men, similar to Catholic saints and monks, who practice asceticism and chastity, and both keep Friday as a holy day. Both practice circumcision, engage in five obligatory daily prayers, and observe Ramadan as the holy month of fasting. For dietary restrictions, both prohibit alcohol in theory, but find ways of circumventing it in practice, obeying a shared prohibition of pork more strictly. Both observe the religious holiday in honor of Abraham known as *Bayram* or *Kurban*, practice polygamy, and allow divorce. They honor saints and make the pilgrimage to Mecca. Finally, both groups have mosques of various sizes and names in which they congregate to worship. Thus, in this chapter, Pfeiffer acknowledges Islam's two major sects and their similarities that transcend ethnic and sectarian bounds.

Pfeiffer begins his third chapter with a question: since the two groups do not differ significantly about the fundamentals of their faith, why do they "attack one another with such implacable hatred"? He gives no geopolitical reasons for this, but rather uses a religious lens, describing how both Persians and Turks show little compunction about killing each another, despite their being coreligionists. He traces their enmity to sectarian differences between the Shi'a (Persians) and the "rest of the Muslims" (the Sunni). According to Pfeiffer, the two differ in the foundation of their faith, the designation of Muhammad's legitimate successor, their explanation of the Qur'an, and in certain religious holidays and rites. The Persians take the Qur'an alone as the canon of their faith, while the Turks give legitimacy to the *Sunna* as well. The Shi'ite Persians believe that 'Alī should have succeeded Muhammad immediately following his death, while the Sunni Turks acknowledge the legitimacy of the three caliphs who came before 'Alī. Much of this chapter is taken up with a description of the exalted place that 'Alī and his descendants hold in Persian Islam. The two sects also differ on their interpretation of the Qur'an, with the Turks favoring that of Abū Ḥanīfa and the Persians favoring that of 'Alī. Pfeiffer then outlines some differences in religious rituals celebrated by the Persians and centered primarily on 'Alī and his family, before ending the dissertation somewhat abruptly. Unlike Pietist Lutherans or Calixtinians, Pfeiffer is not concerned with conversion of Muslims or the unity of religions as his interest lies with religious differences rather than similarities as he believes in Lutheran orthodoxy.

Shi'ites and Sunnis or the Critical Disagreements between Persians and Turks Concerning Religion (Wittenberg, 1670)

The oft-repeated phrase "Truth is singular; falsehood is multifaceted" is proved by the division of the Muslims into so many branches. Under the category of "Islam," one counts 73 branches that disagree with each other to a greater or lesser extent. The most famous of them is the heresy of the 'Alites, or rather, the followers of 'Alī, who are themselves divided into 70 branches, occupying Persia today. As the Persians disagree the most with the Turks, it seems useful to look at some writings from Eastern peoples and the accounts of eyewitnesses concerning their differences. I will briefly survey the most important reasons for which these nations curse one another so terribly. Let God make it turn out successfully!

[...]

On the Agreement between the Persians and Turks

I will not tarry further examining the superstitions of Persians and Turks, but I shall explain the differences between them in modern times with regard to Islam. In order to reach a better understanding of their disagreement, and to further illuminate the points of distinction between them, it is best to use a thorough methodology. First, I will explain the points on which they have heartfelt agreement and which they defend with equal passion.

The Turks and Persians treat Muhammad, who is also called Aḥmad, Abū al-Qāsim, Ṣābi'īn, and Muṣṭafā, as a true and universal Apostle, a most outstanding Prophet, and a divinely inspired Author. The Turks have no doubt about this. They say that "the angels knew Muhammad and his excellence before they knew Adam." Two sayings of Muhammad are in circulation: "I was the Prophet, when Adam was still among the water and mud." And: "What God created first was my light." In his *Travel to the East*, Jean Jacques Breuning declares that it was a capital offense in Turkish lands for anyone, whether Christian or otherwise, to call the Prophecy of Muhammad false; such a person can be spared at no price, unless he becomes a Muslim or *mamlūk*. From the Persians, let us cite here Muṣliḥ al-Dīn Ṣa'dī Shīrāzī, their most famous author, whose *Gulistan* was translated into Latin by the famous George Gentius, and into German by Olearius, who attributes these honorific titles to him and calls him: "Intervener, Reverend, Sage, Generous, Steward, Mighty, Delightful, Sign-bearer." Ṣaʿdī Shīrāzī calls him "sign-bearer" because the Muslims say that Bahira the Monk graciously received the young Muhammad as he was coming to Damascus with his uncle Abū Ṭālib. After he had seen all the signs of a future sage in him, Baḥīrā asked Muhammad to lay bare his shoulders; when Muhammad did this, Baḥīrā is said to have found the sign of the Prophecy, as if it were burned into him by a brand, and gave him his full approval. The noble Olearius adds that the Persians claim the name ʿAlī was written in that mark, and so it was indicated in Muhammad himself that ʿAlī would be his true successor.

Both Turks and Persians follow the Qur'an with equal adoration, and they praise it as a God-given gift. Indeed, Leunclavius says that the Turks will worshipfully kiss the Qur'an; and Busbecq states that a Christian who is disrespectful to it is punished by death. It is also a capital offense for the Turks to sell a Qur'an to a Christian, if we believe Georgiewitz's depiction in his *On the Customs of the Turks*. Indeed, Hottinger, using his own experience and that of F. Barton, confirms this, for the Turks deem it unworthy for such a marvelous gift from God to be polluted by the filthy hands of Christians.

As for the Holy Scripture, both people recognize it as the Word of God, because Muhammad himself conceded it. Thus, in the orthodox understanding of Islam, the phrase of al-Ghazālī is repeated: "The Qur'an, the law, the Gospels, and the Psalms are books handed down by God to his Apostles." In fact, they seek legitimacy for Muhammad and for the prophecies of his arrival in the Holy Scriptures. [...].

There is no disagreement between the Persians and Turks on Qur'anic theology or those dogmas which can be deduced from the Qur'an precisely. [...]. In what follows I will demonstrate the similarities between the Persians and Turks in their Ecclesiastical rites and their holy practices.

Both recognize that the high leader in religious matters is the leader or Pontiff. The Persians call him a *Sadr*, from whom the King and others seek answers—like from the Oak of Dodona—in disputes concerning religion and justice. Olearius says: "The *Sadr* is the spiritual High Priest, just as in the Catholic Church the Pope is." The *Sadr* can also conduct political affairs by public authority. He also oversees all the *madrasa*, or "Academies" in Persian, nine of which are those outstandingly famous ones: at Isfahan, Shiraz, Ardabil, Mashhad, Tabriz, Qazvin, Qum, Yazd, and Shamakhi. The Turks, on the other hand, have a *Muftī*, the supreme and highest authority. Earlier caliphs, the first successors to Muhammad, engaged in political and ecclesiastical business. Afterwards, once the Arab Empire gave way to the Turks, their Emperors, when they were engaged in public business, either could not or would not deal further with sacred matters, therefore, they chose High Priests [*Muftī*] and judges for all disputes concerning religion. They are generally compared with the Roman Pontiff: "Among the Turks, the *Muftī* is the chief of Priests, just as the Roman Pontiff is with us." George Dousa says: "The *Muftī* holds that authority among the Turks as the Pope does among the Latins." To demonstrate the *Muftī*'s unique position, we shall recount here the order of Turkish officials outside of the Saray, or "the Sultan's Court," which is as follows: 1. *Muftī*; 2. Three supreme *Kadılar*, commonly known as the *Kazasker*, "Military Judges," special judges whom Breuning compares with Cardinals; 3. *Vezir Başı*, the chief and highest of whom is *Vezîr-i Âzam*, commonly called the Grand Vizier or Chief Vizier; 4. Three *Beylerbeyi*, overseeing Romania-Greece, Anatolia-Asia, and the Sea; 5. Three *Defterdâr*, or Prefects of the Treasury; 6. *Reisü'l-Küttâb*, Vice-Chancellor; 7. *Ağalar*, that is, tribunes of the Agha; 8. *Emîr-i Alem*, or Supreme Standard-bearer, who carries the standards for all *Beylerbeyi* and *Sancakbeyi*, when they are appointed; 9. *Çavuşbaşı*, or the Prefect of the *Çavuş*, who come with noble courtiers.

Among the Turks, the less educated priests are called *Talismanlar*. They differ very little or not at all from the commoners. Busbecq says that they can be found in great numbers in their mosques or *masjid* and that they need to be called from their tasks to prayer. The literate priests are called *hoca*, whose particular role is to interpret the Qur'an and teach boys. The Persians, apart from their *mullahs* or priests, who are also pedagogues, have their own Monks, who are called *dervishes*. The monks of the Turks are divided into three classes, according to Georgiewitz:

> The Monks, called *dervishler*, are of varying and, most importantly, a tripartite ranking. The first rank is such that has nothing of its own; they go forth nearly nude, apart from a sheepskin covering for their genitals, and in times of cold, they likewise use the skin for covering their back. Their side, hands, feet, and head they cover in absolutely no clothing, begging alms, asking both Christians and Turks, *Allah için*, which means 'For Allah.' They consume the herb called *maslach* and are driven into a fury, so that they make a crosswise wound across their entire chest and likewise across their arm, pretending never to be in pain, and once they place a burning mushroom from the trees on their head, breast, or hand, they do not remove it until it has turned to ash. I have seen another sort, who have their member, or their penis pierced, prevented from having sex with a small bronze ring put in, to maintain chastity. A third sort seldom goes about, but stays in temples day and night, keeping little huts in the corners of the temples; no shoes, no clothing, their heads uncovered, wearing nothing but a single linen shirt, fasting

and praying for many days at a time that God will reveal the future to them, the very people that the king of the Turks, when he plans to wage wars, tends to consult.

They differ in their clothing, and each one carries a mark of his profession, according to Georgiewitz:

> If you see someone carrying feathers on their head, it indicates that he is dedicated to meditations and revelations. If he wears clothing interwoven with scraps of various colors, it indicates poverty. Those who wear earrings show themselves obedient in spirit. Wearing chains on the neck or the arms indicates the violence or passion that they have in their ecstasy.

He also has various passages on certain people's marvelous abstention from food and drink, their constant silence, their unsound dancing, and the twirling of their bodies. Among the Persians, chief in fame is 'Abdāl, whom they call Qalandar because of his avoidance of luxury and worldly pleasures [...].[1] The Persians also have their own *dervishes* and their various orders; for some men are described as eremites in Sa'dī Shīrāzī. Some men are chiefly praised for their abstinence from food and drink, like the man who would eat only on every other day, and another man who lived off the leaves of trees; and although some men are celibate, still others are said to have a wife. Sa'dī Shīrāzī has more passages on these topics throughout, especially in *On the Customs of Dervishes or Monks*.

Both peoples hold Friday holy, and they both call it the day of *jum'a*, or of the congregation, for which Muhammad also intended his Q. 62:9. They both extol it with great praises and call it the "prince of days." Al-Ghazālī says that this day "was granted to Islam by God, as a token of honor, and was made special for Muslims." A commentator on the Qur'an writes: "God elevated Mecca among the cities, Ramadan among the months (the month of fasting), and Friday among the days." In fact, they think that Friday will be the Day of Judgment; so the same commentator says: "Why did God choose Friday? Because the Sun first rose then, Adam was made then, was put in Paradise then, was cast out onto the land then, and the judgment day will occur then." Yet they do not spend the whole of Friday in worship, but once they complete their prayers and rites, they return to work. [...]. They keep many things out of superstition up to this day, and they argue, among other things, that one's nails must be trimmed on that day, "if one cuts his nails on Friday, God will free him from illness and restore him to health."

Turks and Persians practice circumcision religiously, but they do not perform it on the eighth day like the Jews, but delay it for some years. Flavius Josephus says that the Saracens before Muhammad were circumcised at age 13, because they read that Ismael was circumcised then, in Genesis 17:24. Ibn al-Athīr the Arab seems to agree with Josephus, writing that the Arabs in the days before Muhammad "tended to be circumcised at a certain time, between ten and fifteen years of age." But today that age is not observed by the Turks or the Persians. [...] Georgiewitz describes the rite of circumcision at length in *On the Customs of the Turks*:

> First, they invite friends to a banquet, and platters are prepared of every sort of meat, which they feast upon, and among the wealthier families a cow is slaughtered, and inside of it they close up a sheep, skinned and gutted, in which they place a chicken, and they put an egg in that, all of which are designed for the glory of that day. Then, between the banquets and dinnertime, they bring forward the boy who is going to be circumcised. The doctor of this skill reveals the glans and seizes the folded-back skin with small tongs. Next, to ease the boy's fear, he says that he will perform the circumcision on the next day, and so he departs; then, pretending as though he had lost something which he needs for the task, suddenly he cuts off the foreskin and applies a small amount of salt and bombazine to the wound. Now he will be called a Muslim, meaning 'circumcised' (or 'orthodox' or 'faithful'). Boys are not given names on their day of circumcision, but on their actual birthday.

[...]

The Turks and Persians are compelled to pray five times a day in the public temple, or *mescid* (which they distinguish, being a smaller temple, from a larger one, which they call *cuma*), unless they are legitimately prevented (in which case, they can pray anywhere). The Turks are summoned to prayer by the *Hoca* and the Persians by their *muazzin*. According to Cotovicius, the Turks call these five prayers: *Ascher, Zuhr, 'Asr, Maghrib, Alescher*; but according to others, they call them: *Sabba-Namas* [*Sabah Namazı*], *Ulli-Namas* [*Öğle Namazı*], *Scinti-Namas* [*İkindi Namazı*], *Aschtsam-Namas* [*Akşam Namazı*], *Jasci-Namas* [*Yatsı Namazı*]. Cotovicius writes that they hold their first prayers before sunrise, and that it contains four *erket* [*rekat*] and two *chalamath; rekat* means a double prostration, *chamalath* is said after prostration; the second prayers, around noon, contain ten prostrations and five *chalamath*; the third, in the afternoon, eight prostrations and three *chalamath*; the fourth, at sunset, five prostrations and three *chalamath*; the last around midnight (or, as some say, when they usually go to sleep), fifteen prostrations and eight *chalamath*. Olearius says that the Persians observe the same hours of prayer [...]. Although in certain prayer ceremonies the Persians may differ from the Turks, yet they collude in their hypocritical devotion and outright madness. Fabricius, based on eye-witnesses, says in his *Specimen Arabicum*,

Not only with their heart and spirit, but also with the entire body and all one's strength they think that the divine name must be praised and worshipped. Thus, some people repeat *Lā ilāha illā Allāh*, etc., 'There is not God but Allah,' with such haste (they have contests on it among themselves) and such passion that they cannot utter those words further (ending their utterances with the word *Hū, Hū*, as Cotovicius says). Some men extend this cry to such an extent that, whenever they are worn out by this great outcry, some of them emit spittle from their mouths, others grow black in the face because of the force expended by their cries, and they fall to the ground as though they are half-dead; for they think that God is greatly soothed by their bodily suffering. In fact, the greater the force someone inflicts upon themselves, the more pleasing he thinks he will be to God.

[…].

Both Turks and Persians strictly observe the month-long fasting of Ramadan, although in other instances they will also hold certain fasts. They fast throughout the entire month of Ramadan because the Qur'an was brought to Muhammad in that month in a Night of Power, as they call it. Therefore, Muslims excessively praise this month, for in it they say the gates of Paradise were opened and the gates of Hell closed. The stench of the mouth in that month of fasting is supposed to be more pleasing to God than the scent of musk. The Turks call that month-long fasting *oruç*, and they begin it during the new moon in the month of Ramadan. "When they fast," Georgiewitz says, "they eat nothing for the entire day, not even bread or water. Then, once a star has been seen, they are allowed to eat everything except for something strangled and pork." […]. Moreover, once their fast during the day has been completed, they frequently carouse for the entirety of the nights, and although they refrain from wine, they indulge most abundantly in drinking coffee.

Both Turk and Persians abstain (or at least, should abstain, under penalty of law) from wine, the use of which Muhammad famously forbids in Q. 2:219 in the following words: "They shall ask you about wine and gambling; answer them, in both cases, that it is a terrible sin." Concerning the Turks, see Georgiewitz and Busbecq, who also cite a particular example of an old man who would cry out every time he drank wine, as though he were in this way trying to warn his soul to retreat to some safer part of the body for a time. But if wine goes down one's throat just one time, the same author says that they make a compromise with this religion of theirs. This is also the case with the Persians; Olearius relates that they are compelled to refrain from wine by law, but he says that, since they are seized by an insatiable desire for wine, although they are busy with the fulfillment of their law at the same time, everywhere, both in the cities and the countryside, they allow Armenian Christians to grow grape vines and then buy wine from them, as though the law were satisfied if they did not prepare the wine themselves. Both sides allow grapes to be eaten, however.

Both Turks and Persians abstain entirely from pork blood and meat. In Q. 6:145, Muhammad prevented these two things in the following words:

> I do not find in what has been revealed to me that a prohibition has been issued against anyone eating anything, unless it is carrion, or the blood has been poured out, or the accursed flesh of pig, or if something were offered in honor of an idol.

Concerning the Persians, Olearius' *Itinerary* speaks at length, and he tells an utterly revolting tale from the Qur'an, how the pig on Noah's ark was born from the dung of an elephant and thus must be deplored.

Both Turks and Persians fastidiously observe *Bayram*, or the religious holiday of *Kurban*, in honor of Abraham. Following the example of their Impostor, they declare with the foulest mendacity that he wanted to offer Ismael as a sacrifice to God. As soon as their month-long fast ends, the Turks celebrate their *Ulu Bayram* (i.e., a great religious holiday corresponding to our Easter) on the new moon of the following month (*shawwāl*). Ulugh Beg the Tatar says in *On Eastern Ages*, "on the new moon of *shawwāl* is the holiday of Muslim Easter." They continue for three days, taking some time in the mornings for their divine worship and spending the rest of the day in banquets, dancing, and merriment. After two months, they celebrate their *Küçük Bayram*, wherein, amidst other rites, they offer sacrifices, but they do not burn them; rather, they distribute them among the poor. [...]

Both Turks and Persians permit and practice simultaneous polygamy. Strabo testifies that it has been practiced by the Persians for many ages, and that they did it for the sake of increasing their offspring. But today, Olearius argues that multiple wives are taken rather to satisfy one's lust, to which those people are devoted. He states that the Persian compares a wife to a calendar, whose use can only extend for a single year. [...] At the same time, Busbecq in his *Epistles* says that Turks take multiple wives (four at one time, according to Cotovicius and Breuning), but they may take as many mistresses or concubines (which are only distinguished from proper wives by a dowry) as each man can support with his wealth. How much strife and annoyance this polygamy begets among them, however, a certain Turkish saying, from a famous poet, proves: "Two asses, one caravan. Two wives, one forum." Or—as the meaning is somewhat unclear because of the succinct Turkish phrase—to say it more clearly: Two asses create as much annoyance as an entire train; and where there are two wives, there is a constant forum because of quarrels. Both, on this account as well, follow the instruction or allowance of their Pseudoprophet Muhammad, a most lustful man, in Sura 8; they even follow his example, since he had, besides his concubines, seventeen wives as Abū al-Faraj says. According to Abū al-Fidā' and others, it was fifteen; according to some, it was more than twenty wives.

Divorce is practiced among both Turks and Persians, although not as frequently among the Persians as the Turks, because with the Persians, husbands without a pregnant wife are divorced under certain circumstances, but his case is first heard by a judge or *kadı* or *qāḍī*. Although divorce may take place, it is not possible to take a second set of vows right away [...]. Among the Turks, though, divorces are more frequent, and can be obtained for trivial, or more often absurd reasons. In the first place, though, that foul custom of theirs must be mentioned here, whereby it is sometimes permitted to take in cohabitation a woman who has been rejected three times. [...] But the Persians detest this practice.

Both Turks and Persians rigorously visit the tombs of their saints, whose power and guardianship they beseech in certain cases, although they do not worship those saints in either place. Apart from the more ancient saints (for they visit the tombs of Abraham and other Patriarchs, according to Leunclavius), the Turks also worship some new and fraudulent saints and apotheosized miracle-workers, over whose tombs they perform their vows and prayers. Seyyid Gazi was just such a miracle-worker—or rather, an Impostor, who is greatly esteemed throughout Turkey, according to the Transylvanian monk, in the work cited. According to the same witness, they call another man Harschi Pettesch, that is, "the travelling assistant," who is honored by travelers. Another is Aşık Paşa, that is, "the guardian of love," who is said to bring aid to married persons, those laboring in childbirth, those who desire offspring, or others who are pressed by needs in their marriage. Ali van Paşa is said to sooth contrary souls and bring them to harmony. Şeyh Paşa is called upon as the guardian of the disturbed and sorrowful. Gotvelmirtschim and Bartschin Paşa are believed to take care of the flock. Hıdırellez is said to be an aid to travelers pressed by need. The Persians studiously visit the tombs of their saints as well—first the tomb of Sheikh Sofi, their first reformer; then the twelve tombs of the *imām*s, or rather, the sons and grandsons of their High Priests, the Sofi, about whom we shall talk later, as well as the monuments to other saints. Thus, they travel to the tomb of Seyyid İbrahim, in the region of Pyrmaraas, for whom there is a nearby monument to another saint, whose name was Tiribabba [Piri Baba?]. The Persians also seem to owe some of their saints to the Christians, for they visit the tomb of the seven sleepers, or rather, the cave saints of which there is also mention in the Qur'an. [...]

The Turks and Persians both make compulsory pilgrimages to the Temples of Mecca, of Jerusalem, of Medina, and others. For Muhammad demanded this in his Qur'an, and he wanted it to be an important part of his religion, to the extent that, as al-Ghazālī relates it, according to Muhammad's judgment, if anyone were to die before he undertook such a journey, he would not die as a Muslim, but as a Jew or Christian. Both Turks and Persians visit the Ka'ba, that is, the Temple of Mecca, because that is the homeland of the Impostor Muhammad. Concerning the Turks and Persians, the authors say that they encamp at Mecca amid various troubles and great dangers. Whenever they are on a three-day journey away from the city, they approach it almost completely naked, covered only around their genitals; and preparing themselves with various lotions, they enter the temple of Mecca, and they perform their rites with a great many particular observances. Every year, a troop of a thousand men under a certain Duke (who is called *amīr al-ḥajj*) visit it. Concerning the Persians, there is similar agreement, according to Sa'dī Shīrāzī, that many thousands from the most remote provinces come to Mecca and pray, often on foot, laying their heads on the temple threshold. Every year, that temple is covered with a shroud, which is called *Kiswat al-Ka'ba*, "Holy Mantle of the Temple, Temple's Dress or Garment," and that is sent by the Ottoman family at Constantinople to Mecca by land journey through Damascus, full of pomp. Every year a new shroud is produced, and the old one is carried away, made a revered treasure by its contact with the majesty of that most sacred place. It is divided by priests into pieces and is sold at a high price to those making the pilgrimage for the sake of religion. Mecca is held in such great esteem because it is renowned for the birth of Muhammad, and they believe that Abraham laid the foundations of the temple there. Likewise, Muslims make the journey to the temple at Medina, with great earnestness, regularity, and amidst the various trials of the road, where one may find the tomb of the Impostor. The Sunnis say that Muhammad encouraged them to visit it: "Whoever comes to Medina to visit my tomb, I will intervene on his behalf on the Day of Resurrection. If anyone dies in either holy place," that is, Mecca or Medina, "he will certainly be revived and saved." Likewise: "Whoever visits my tomb, it is as if he were visiting me while I was alive." Thus, they also establish travels to the temple at Jerusalem, which the Turks call *Kudüs-ü Mübarek*.

The Turks and Persians have temples in a great number of places. There are the smaller ones, or *masjid*, which they commonly call *Moskeas*; they differentiate them from *Jum'a* (which you might call Synagogues), or the Cathedral Temples, being the greater ones. In those *masjid* of theirs, they gather not only on Friday for their holy practice, but every day as well for their sacred prayers, after washing, which we shall discuss below. They do not permit their women to enter the mosque, but they place them at the doorway. If they are noblewomen of a higher status, they have a spot separate from their men, and so secret that no one can peer in, which they occupy every Friday. Men remove their shoes and leave them in front of the Temple door. The floors of the Temple, strewn with mats, they do not touch with their shoes. They grant entrance to

Christians with great reluctance unless it is granted to someone as a special favor. Going before the *Hoca* or the *Molla*, they enter and perform their prayers and other sacred rites. Speeches to the people, however, are more seldom. Concerning the Turks, Cotovicius says in his *Journey through Jerusalem and Syria* that when a new Pasha enters his position, a summoner calls out to the people, holding a straight sabre in his hands. Otherwise, both the Turks and the Persians (who do sometimes have Ecclesiastical orations) are generally satisfied with a reading from the Qur'an, illustrated with a brief explanation, which takes place in certain cathedrals [greater mosques]. Neither people tend to summon their fellows to holy rites with bells, but both use heralds instead. The Persians call them *muazzin*, the Turks *talismanlar*, who call men to prayer at established times with extremely piercing voices from small towers built near the temples. Concerning the Turks, Georgiewitz says

> around the temple is a tower of wonderful height. Their priest climbs it at the time for his call. With a high voice and his fingers in his ears, he repeats the following words: *Allah hak bir*, that is, 'God is true and singular'.

Concerning the Persians, in the well-known words of Sa'dī Shīrāzī: "A holy herald, or, *muazzin*, has cried at the wrong time," notes the famous Gentius.

> Because Muslims refuse to use bells out of their intractable hatred of Christians, every day they summon their fellows to perform their prayers and holy rites with the living voice of heralds (following the example of Muhammad); five times each from the top of small towers, which they have built beside their holy buildings.

Yet they do not reject clocks in their private buildings. But that is enough about this.

Concerning the Disagreement between the Persians and Turks

We have so far seen agreement and harmony between the Persians and Turks. Now, we must dig into the matter and explain in what ways they differ. As can be seen from what was said so far, these cannot be too numerous. One might therefore wonder why they attack one another with such implacable hatred. The Persians condemn the religion of the Turks and attack them in their prayers, and the Persians hardly consider murdering Turks a sin. Thus, a certain highly esteemed Persian author declares: "The Turk, although he is highest in learning; Still it is acceptable to kill him." The most famous author among the Persians, Sa'dī Shīrāzī, left a good indication of how he felt toward them in his preface to *Rose*

Garden—that is, he compares them to bloody wolves, savage lions, and tigers, and in contrast to them, he likens his Persian people to the angels. Nor do they hold themselves from slanderous names, and they regularly call them *Sag Sünnis*, or dog Sunnis. On the other hand, the Turks hate the Persians no less, and as a jeer they call them *Kızılbaş*, or Redheads, because those who celebrate their descent from the family of 'Alī or Sophi wear red turbans, which they usually call *Tatsch* or *Takye*. [...] Busbecq, says that the Turk Rüstem Pasha said to him: "We abhor the Persians more and treat them as more sacrilegious than Christians." Leunclavius says that Turks who had crossed over to the Persians were killed by other Turks. Based on this, then, there is sufficiently clear evidence of the agreement that exists among Turks concerning the Persians.

We should explore the cause of such great hatred, which it seems few people have properly explained. They say this hatred is caused by a difference in religion; but they have not thoroughly laid out what constitutes that disagreement. Petrus Bizarus in *History of Persian Affairs*, Giovanni Tommaso Minadoi in *On the Turkish-Persian War* and others discussed several things. However, they do not touch upon the differences between the Persians and Turks, or only do so lightly. Recently, the noblest Olearius has pursued the core of the matter with a marvelous attempt in *Itinerary*. Therefore, we shall briefly and clearly outline this topic.

To relate everything "from the egg," as they say, the chaotic nature of that Monster of Mecca immediately dragged Muslims into different camps. According to al-Shahrastānī, Arabs say that disunity emerged and finally produced 73 sects in Islam, for so this prattler says: "the Magi are divided into 70 sects; the Jews into 71; Christians into 72; Muslims into 73. Among the sects, however, one always has to be correct." The same author, however, counts four primary sects: al-Qadariyya, al-Ṣifāṭiyya, Khārijites, and al-Shī'a; some count six, others eight, Mu'tazilites, Shi'ites, Khārijites, Murji'ites, al-Najjāriyya, Jabrites, al-Mushabbiha, al-Nājiyya, and the Ash'arites, which most of the Arabs follow and treat as orthodox. Others identify more primary sects, from which the rest have emerged. Our current project does not allow us to treat each one individually but let us guide the good reader to Abū al-Faraj and his commentator, Pococke. Here, we will only examine how the Persians differ from the rest of the Muslims, who are called Sunnis. Although even these people [Sunnis] have various disputes and arguments (especially scholarly ones among themselves in different regions), they share common cause against the Shi'ite Persians; I will illustrate those issues they have in common against the Persians. Also, the Persians do not follow the same custom in all places, but in times of abundance and in times of want they sin against their own principles. The Persians oppose the Sunnis with the same passion that we do. Therefore, among the disagreements between the Persians and Turks, the most learned gentleman Joachim Camerarius and others, cite certain scholarly debates on the origin of evil, on the eternity of law, and similar things. But in doing so, they do not seem to explain sufficiently the cause of such disharmony, since debates of this sort are not dealt with among the Sunnis themselves. As for the Turks, who are called either Sunnis or Ash'arīs, we believe that they differ from the Shi'ites or Rāfiḍī, whose sect is called Imāmiyya by some, in the following ways: first, the foundation of their faith; second, the designation of Muhammad's legitimate successor; third, their explanation of the Qur'an; and, fourth, certain religious holidays and rites.

As for the first, both accept the Qur'an as the canon of their faith; but the Persians accept it alone, while the Turks have the *Sunna*, or tradition, in addition. Thus, the Turks are called Sunni, that is, traditionists. For this disagreement, we could compare the Persians with the Sadducees, insofar as they rejected unwritten traditions, satisfied with the letter of the law alone. Thus, some people called them scripturalists, but the Turks are compared to the Pharisees, who followed not only the written divine law, but also the "unwritten law," or rather, a variety of ancestral traditions. Therefore, because the Turks see that their traditions are shunned by the Persians, they hate the Persians. As we also see today, the remaining Karaites are crushed under a hatred worse than Vatinius' because they rejected the Talmudic traditions. Still, we must talk briefly about the *Sunna*. There were seven men who compiled all Muhammad's words and deeds outside the Qur'an with the greatest diligence, and they passed it down to their descendants. Among them was Abū Hurayra, named by Muhammad for the kitten that he held very delicately and would constantly carry about with him in public assemblies. He had the most remarkable memory and, outliving the other six traditionists; he alone kept alive in later days the traditions [*ḥadīth*] that he had heard from Muhammad, keeping them in his wonderful memory until they were finally put in the literary record.

A second, no less worthy question on the successor to Muhammad is passionately debated among the Persians and Turks. The foundation of their disagreement is: "Did Abū Bakr, 'Umar, and 'Uthmān lawfully succeed Muhammad in his ecclesiastical and political governance after his death? Or was injury done to 'Alī on this account?" The Sunnis, or Turks, assert the first; but the Shi'ites, or Persians, endorse the latter; for just as the Turks are called Sunnis because of the previous debate, so too are the Persians called Shi'ites because of this one. Therefore, the origin of this debate must be shown at some length. After Muhammad died, the Muslims were troubled concerning the *Imām*, or rather, the leader or caliph—that is, Muhammad's successor, who would be supreme over the whole Muslim people, in matters relating to the world as well as to religion; or rather, who would take the place of Muhammad in all matters. The Turks count four such caliphs, the sole successors of Muhammad, in a rather strict sense (although all Muslim Emperors in

Saracen history are otherwise called caliph). They succeeded each other in order: Abū Bakr, 'Umar, 'Uthmān (whom they start from in counting Muslim Emperors, and who are thus called *Osmanli*, and their family "Ottoman," and their court the "Ottoman Porte"), and 'Alī. For so it is said in al-Ghazālī's confession of faith, which is commonly treated as orthodox among the Turks:

> It is likewise necessary for a Muslim to confess the virtue of Muhammad's companions and their positions; and that, after Muhammad, the most outstanding man was Abū Bakr, then 'Umar, then 'Uthmān, then 'Alī, and he ought to have good feelings about all the companions and celebrate them, just as God and His Envoy celebrated them all.

In fact, so far from the Turks accusing 'Alī of being the Persians' High Priest, they rather extol him with the highest praise. The Turks argue that 'Alī should not be put ahead of the first three, but that he should be subordinate. The Persians think that the first three caliphs did a terrible injury to 'Alī, and that they stole the Caliphate and position of High Priest, against what is right and fair, since 'Alī took the daughter of Muhammad, Fāṭima, in marriage, and he completely outshone the first ones, because of his learning, his virtue, his righteousness, and his other gifts as the High Priest and caliph.

This controversy arose in 1363 AD, because of a certain man name *Sefi* or *Sofi* (whom some men call "wool" in Arabic, because he only used woolen clothes). He said that he was a descendant of 'Alī and carried himself with an appearance of great learning and holiness. Then at Ardabil and other places in Persia, he publicly argued that the right of the first Stewardship and Caliphate, dating back to Muhammad—that is, the right of succession in political and religious matters, lay in the hands of 'Alī, whom Muhammad called his cousin and his own son-in-law for purposes of inheritance and succession. Abū Bakr, 'Umar, and 'Uthmān, however, because they were greater in might, wickedly took his due from him, and assumed for themselves the things that were his. Finally, Sofi [al-Ardabīlī] said that 'Alī alone deserved the name of High Priest, because he had plainly performed so many wondrous things. Many were immediately opposed to his opinion and things began to move in the direction of war. In fact, from the great authority this revolutionary Reformer [al-Ardabīlī] held, one can surmise that he gave his name to Kings (of course, those who call themselves *Sefi* or *Sofi* do so for that reason, not from the Greek word for "wise," or for some other reason, a fact which Ismael was the first to use, for they call him *Ismael Sophinus* [Shah Esmā'īl] for this reason), and to all Persians generally (those who are called the *Sofiani* [Ṣafaviyya]). The Persians make much of his various miracles. Among other things, when Temürleng, or Tamerlane, the King of the Tatars, wanted to determine whether or not

Sofi's religion was genuine and they say that he thought of three signs that, if Tamerlane beheld these signs in the presence of Sofi, he would convert to Sofi's sect—that is, if Sofi did not rise up for Tamerlane as he approached, if he prepared rice with wild goat milk, and if he survived poison that he had to drink as a toast—all of which signs they say were fulfilled by Sofi.

Over time, the argument concerning 'Alī's succession was carried on by the descendants of Sofi [al-Ardabīlī], Sadredin and Tsinid (who is called Junayd in other sources), as well as Ḥaydar and others. This issue grew so much that it created tensions between the Persians and Turks, although this dispute does not seem to be of much importance. In fact, some men were not afraid to say (according to al-Shahrastānī) that "religion lay in the knowledge of the High Priest alone." Indeed, it can scarcely be stated how much strife both sides fight with on behalf of their High Priests. The Persians, following their own 'Alī, make him semi-divine; the Turks do not accuse him, but rather they praise him, and when they are going to mount a horse, they usually say "O 'Alī, i.e., Aly" (i.e., a famed knight and High Priest). They dismiss the Persians' boasting with mockery and slander. The Turks, however, honor Abū Bakr, 'Umar, and 'Uthmān as the successors to Muhammad. The Persians, however, condemn them and curse them savagely; indeed, they even speak foully in their hatred for them: *Kir-i sag dar dahan-i Abubekir, Omar, Hanife baad*, that is, "May the penis of dog be in the mouth of Abū Bakr, 'Umar, and Abū Ḥanīfa."

We must show further how much the Persians honor 'Alī. On one hand, they compare him with Muhammad; on the other, they in fact prefer 'Alī to Muhammad. They say that Muhammad, at some point while he was still alive, said to 'Alī: "Is it not enough for you if you are by my side, in the same position Aaron occupied beside Moses?" In fact, some people say that the Qur'an came into the hands of Muhammad because of a mistake by Gabriel when it ought to have been given to 'Alī. But they also consider 'Alī a symbol of their faith, which they use as grounds to distinguish themselves from the Turks, that is, "There is no God but the true God, Muhammad the Apostle of God, 'Alī the prefect of God." The Turks leave out the final words. In fact, some people support the praises of 'Alī that come from the Persians so indecently that they do not hesitate to ascribe divinity to him. That blasphemous utterance from the Persians is well known: "I do not acknowledge 'Alī as God, but I know that he is not far from God." This one is not much better: "Whoever is not like dust, when he stands before the doors of 'Alī, even if he is an angel, dust will cover his head." These words, attested by Olearius, have a place too in their royal standards. Al-Shahrastānī also says that there were some men among the Shi'ites, whom he calls Nuṣayrī, who say that 'Alī was the one "in whose form God appeared, and by whose hands He made the world, and by whose tongue He gave his teachings, and so they said that 'Alī existed before the creation of the heavens and earth." Thus, it can hardly be overstated how great were the miracles attributed to 'Alī. They worship his sword no less than the one which the Turks once dreaded as belonging to George Castriot (who is called by the Turks Scanderbeg [Iskender Beg], that is, Master Alexander, for *Beg* means Master in Turkish, and Alexander is abbreviated among the Turks as Scender, just as Constantinople is shortened to Stamboli), which Marinus Marletius wrote about. According to Olearius, the Persians say that 'Alī was in fact able to split rocks with his sword. They call that sword *zulfiqār*, and they tell tales about it being given to Muhammad by Gabriel on the condition that he give it to his cousin 'Alī. Thus, they say that 'Alī at some point carried the city gates to a place in Khaybar, and they say "the evidence is clear that there was in him a divine spark and heavenly might." When he could not find water on a certain island to relieve his thirst, he is said to have brought forth a spring on the spot, as Olearius says; he also adds that, today, this island is called *Alybarluch* because of this myth. 'Alī is also said to have miraculously produced grapes in Iran in the wintertime, whence the Persians say that grapes are still cultivated, which they call *Enkuri aly deresi*. Finally, they tell the story that, when Muhammad was taken up to heaven, 'Alī followed him and found Muhammad sitting with the angels and refreshing himself with heavenly nectar. But because the angels refused to allow 'Alī entrance, they say that 'Alī said that he was "the Lion of God," and that after they heard it, the angels brought to him a vial of the exact same sort of nectar. Let us leave his horse *duldul* in silence.

As the Persians worship their native 'Alī for this reason, they perform almost all their official acts, both political and ecclesiastical, in his name. Thus, when a new King is crowned, the crown is brought to him, to be kissed in the name of God, Muhammad, and 'Alī. The Persians swear by God and 'Alī alike. When they forge brotherhood among themselves, they are given three strikes by the caliph, who says at the first stroke Allah, at the second Muhammad, at the third, 'Alī. Finally, they also celebrate unique religious holidays in memory of him and his descendants, as we shall discuss shortly.

Just as the Persians worship 'Alī, they also glorify his descendants, as though his virtue were grafted upon them by a cutting. Chiefly, they worship 'Alī's two sons, Ḥasan and Ḥusayn, whom he begat from Muhammad's daughter Fāṭima; likewise his nine grandsons, Zayn al-'Ābidīn, Muḥammad Bāqir, Ja'far al-Ṣādiq, Mūsā al-Kāẓim, 'Alī ibn Mūsā (al-Riḍā), Muḥammad al-Taqī, 'Alī al-Naqī, Ḥasan al-'Askarī, and Muḥammad ibn al-Ḥasan (al-Mahdī); and they call these twelve *Imām*s, their High Priests, and they give them deep devotion, together with 'Alī and Shaykh Sofi, the reformer of their religion; and people make pilgrimages to their tombs, especially people who cannot visit the Temple of Mecca because of the distance. Even today, those of their descendants who remain are marked by special signs, and they enjoy various privileges.

Third, the Persians and Turks have various authors whom they follow in their interpretation of the Qur'an. The Turks, although they otherwise have few scholars and are satisfied with almost a bare explanation of the words (so says Georgiewitz), nevertheless they follow Abū Ḥanīfa in difficult passages of the Qur'an. They endow Abū Ḥanīfa with the special instinct of God, and they put him at the side of Abū Bakr, 'Umar, and 'Uthmān. The Persians, however, consider him an impostor and a heretic, and they follow 'Alī in their explanation of the Qur'an, and his grandson Ja'far al-Ṣādiq. There would obviously be cause for some difference, if what Hottinger relates were true, based on the evidence of F. Bartoni, that the Persians translated the Qur'an into their own language (although Muṣliḥ al-Dīn Sa'dī Shīrāzī, in his *Rose Garden*, constantly cites passages from the Qur'an in Arabic), something which is not done by the Turks.

Finally, the Persians differ from the Turks in certain ceremonies and rites, especially their religious holidays, prayers, and ablutions. To the annoyance of the Turks, the Persians celebrate various religious holidays in honor of 'Alī and his descendants. On the fourteenth day of the month *Shawwāl*, they celebrate the event of *Ghadīr Khumm*, in memory of 'Alī, who is said to have succeeded Muhammad on the very day that 'Uthmān died. They conduct this holiday with many entertainments and trivialities. On the twenty-second day of Ramadan, they perform funeral rites for 'Alī, who is said to have been killed on the twenty-first day of the month in the Great Mosque of Kūfa while praying by his slave 'Abd al-Raḥmān ibn Muljam. They also celebrate his memory with many solemn rites and tears. Persians perform their *'āshūrā'* for ten days, to commemorate Hussein, the younger son of 'Alī, who was wounded with 72 spears, stabbed by a certain Sinān ibn Anas, and finally killed by Shamr ibn Dhū al-Jawshan. In remembrance of this, some men shed their blood in various ways and perform other rites.

As for their prayers, there is a difference in some of their ceremonies [...]. There are differences in ablutions which they always perform before they enter mosque [...]. It is certain that Persians also separate themselves from the Turks in their clothing, wearing green stockings, something that the Turks despise, because the turban of Muhammad was green. Let what has currently been said on the disagreements between the Persians and Turks suffice.

Note

1 [MK] On the term 'Abdāl, see Matti Moosa, *Extremist Shiites: The Ghulat Sects* (Syracuse: Syracuse University Press, 1988), 110–19. For Qalandar, see Katherine Pratt Ewing and Ilona Gerbakher, "The Qalandariyya: From the Mosque to the Ruin in Poetry, Place, and Practice," in *Routledge Handbook on Sufism*, ed. Lloyd Ridgeon (New York: Routledge, 2020), 233–68.

Selected Post-Reformation
Works on Islamic Thought

This selected Latin bibliography should not be taken as a comprehensive list; however, it does show how much research could still be done on post-Reformation perceptions of Islamic thought and Muslim culture (1650–1840), which corresponds from the end of the Thirty Years' War to the establishment of Oriental Institutes in Europe. Some of the Lutheran and Calvinist works on Islam between these periods have been studied primarily by Alastair Hamilton, Martin Mulsow, Asaph Ben-Tov, Gregory Miller, Jan Loop, and Pier Mattia Tommasino. However, there are literally hundreds of unstudied *dissertationes*, *disputationes*, *orationes*, and *exercitationes* in Lutheran and Calvinist universities.

In determining the authors of these Latin texts, I have followed this rule: when an *auctor* has not been explicitly identified on the title page of a work the authorship has been attributed to the *praeses*. Also, a word of caution about the religious affiliations of the authors: although the majority of the scholars are Lutherans, or Evangelical as they called themselves, the Calixtinian Syncretic controversy in the seventeenth century, the rise of Pietism, and the radical Enlightenment ideas in the eighteenth century contributed to loosen the bonds of conservative orthodox Lutheranism. Therefore, some scholars adopted a more eclectic or latitudinarian perspective on Biblical and theological studies. This list is prepared chronologically with the publication year, followed by the name of the author, the title of his work, place of publication, the dates and locations of his birth and death, and his affiliation.

1653 Hoornbeek, Johannes. *Summa controversiarum religionis, cum infidelibus, haereticis, schismaticis: id est, Gentilibus, Judaeis, Muhammedanis; Papistis, Anabaptistis, Enthusiastis et Libertinis, Socinianis; Remonstrantibus, Lutheranis, Brownistis, Graecis (Summary of Religious Controversies with Infidels, Heretics, Schismatics: Pagans, Jews, Muhammadans; Catholics, Anabaptists, Enthusiasts and Libertines, Socinians; Remonstrants, Lutherans, Brownists)*, published in Utrecht. Born in 1617 in Haarlem, died in 1666 in Leiden; Calvinist Theologian of Dutch Reformed Church and Professor of Theology at Utrecht and Leiden.

1660 Dannhauer, Johann C. *Muhammedismus, breviter delineates* (*Muhammadanism, Briefly Outlined*), published in Strasbourg. Born in 1603 in Köndringen (Breisgau), died in Strasbourg in 1666; Lutheran theologian.

1661 Rentsch, Johann Wolfgang. *Disputatio de Turcis* (*Disputation on the Turks*), published in Wittenberg. Born in 1637 in Bayreuth, died in 1690 in Bayreuth; Lutheran.

1661 Strauchius, Aegidius. *Dissertatio chronologica de computo Turcico-Arabico, excidii Constantinopolitani anno* (*Chronological Dissertation on Turkish-Arabic Calendar, and the Year of the Destruction of Constantinople*), published in Wittenberg. Born in 1632 in Wittenberg, died in 1682 in Danzig; Lutheran theologian.

1661 Dürr, Johann Konrad. *Disputatio theologica qua evincitur quod coram judicio divino sint Muhammedani inexcusabiles* (*Theological Disputation Proving the Inexcusability of Muslims in the Face of Divine Judgement*), published in Altdorf. Born in 1625 in Nuremberg, died in 1677 in Altdorf; Lutheran theologian.

1663 Kortholt (der Ältere), Christian. *De religione Muhammedana disquisitio* (*An Investigation on the Muhammadan Religion*), published in Rostock. Born in 1633 in Burg auf Fehmarn, died in 1694 in Kiel; Lutheran Pietist theologian.

1664 Rosa, Christianus. *Discursus politico-theologicus de turcismi fuga, et graecae (sub Turca exsulantis) linguae apud Christianos, incremento* (*Political-Theological Discourse on the Avoidance of Turkism, and the Rise of the Greek Language – Banned under the Turks – Among Christians*), published in Berlin. Born in 1609 in Mittenwalde, died in 1667 Neuruppin; Lutheran.

1664 Bebel, Balthasar. *Dissertatio historico theologica de Saracenorum initiatione ex fragmento libri xx. Thesauri Nicetae* (*Historical-Theological Dissertation on [Religious] Initiation of the Arabs [the Beginning of Islam] from a Fragment of Book 20 of the Thesaurus of Niketas Choniates*), published in Strasbourg. Born in 1632 in Strasbourg, died in 1686 in Wittenberg; Lutheran theologian.

1664 Dannhauer, Johann C. *Dissertatio theologica de fato flagelli Turcici fatique luce divinae irae, Ottomanica tela in Christianos suos hactenus vibrantis, caussas limitesque perpendens* (*Theological Dissertation on the Fate of the Turkish Scourge and the Light of Fate (Divine Wrath), Ottoman Missiles Brandished against their Christians Hitherto, Assessing Origins and Limits*), published in Strasbourg.

1664 Raith, Balthasar. *Arbaʿīna ḥadītan hoc est Pandecta dictorum factorumque Muhammed* (*Arbaʿīna ḥadīthan: Collection of the Words and Deeds of Muhammad*), published in Tübingen. Born in 1616 in Schorndorf, died in 1683 in Tübingen; Lutheran theologian and Professor at Tübingen.

1665 Müller, Andreas. *Excerpta manuscripti cujusdam turcici, quod de cognitione Dei et hominis ipsius a quodam Azizo Nesephaeo, Tataro, scriptum est* (*Excerpts from a Turkish Manuscript, which was Written by Tatar 'Azīz Nasafī, Concerning the Understanding of God and Man*), published in Berlin. Born in 1630 in Greifenhagen, died in 1694 in Stettin; Lutheran theologian and sinologist.

1665 Pfeiffer, August. *Dissertatio philologica quarta de Muhammedis impostoris Alkorano* (*Fourth Philological Dissertation on the Qur'an of the Impostor Muhammad*), published in Wittenberg. Born in 1640 in Lauenburg/Elbe, died in 1698 in Lübeck; Lutheran theologian.

1666 Kortholt (der Ältere), Christian. *De religione ethnica, muhammedana et iudaica, dissertatio tripartite* (*Three-Part Dissertation on Heathen Religion: Islam and Judaism*), published in Kiel.

1666 Henningsen, Henning. *Muhammedanus precans, id est Liber precationum Muhammedicarum arabicus manuscriptus* (*The Praying Muslim: An Arabic Manuscript Book of Islamic Prayers*), published in Schleswig.

1668 Dannhauer, Johann Conrad. *Ecclesia Muhammedana* (*The Muhammadan Church*), published in Strasbourg.

1670 Kromayer, Hieronymus. *Scrutinium religionum tum falsarum, Paganismi, Muhammetismi, Iudaismi, Catabaptismi & Quakerismi, Weigelianismi & Rosae-Crucianismi, Secinianismi, Arminianismi, Calvinismi, Abyssinismi, Anatolicismi, Papismi, Tum unice verae & orthodoxae, Lutheranismi* (*An Examination, first, of the False Religions: Paganism, Muhammadanism, Judaism, Catabaptism and Quakerism, Weigelianism and Rosicrucianism, Socinianism, Arminianism, Calvinism, Abbyssinism, Anatolicism, Catholicism and then of the One True and Orthodox Religion, Lutheranism*), published in Leipzig. Born in 1610 in Zeitz, died in 1670 in Leipzig; Lutheran theologian and Professor at the University of Leipzig.

1673 Dürr, Johann Konrad. *Publici Triga Disputationum Theologicarum quibus occasione oraculi Paulini Rom. I, 20. evincitur, quod coram iudicio divino sint ethnici, Iudaei, Muhammedani inexcusabiles* (*Three Public Theological Disputations, in which by the Explanation of Romans 20 of the Oracle Paul it is Proven, That Before Divine Judgement the Heathens, Jews, and Muslims are Inexcusable*), published in Jena.

1683 Capel (Capellus), Rudolf. *Dissertatio publica de Alcorano sive Alfurcano, Muhamedis et Muhamedanorum* (*Public Dissertation on the Qur'an or al-Furqān, of Muhammad and the Muslims*), published in Hamburg. Born in 1635 in Hamburg and died in 1684 in Hamburg; Protestant philologist and Professor at Hamburg.

1683 Wasmuth, Matthias. *Disputatio inauguralis Hodomoriam Muhammedanam breviter exhibens* (*Inaugural Disputation Briefly*

Presenting Islamic Heresy), published in Kiel. Born in 1625 in Kiel, died in 1688 in Kiel; Lutheran theologian and Professor.

1684 Zentgraf, Johann Joachim. *De parricidio gentis Ottomanicae, quo Imperium Turcicum niti dicitur* (*Concerning the Parricide of the Ottoman Clan, on which the Turkish Empire is Said to Depend*), published in Strasbourg. Born in 1643 in Strasbourg, died in 1707 in Strasbourg; Lutheran theologian.

1684 Möbius, Georg. *Disquisitio theologica de causis & mediis, quae Mahomedisticam religionem partim introduxerunt, partim adhuc conservant* (*Theological Discussion on Origins and Means, Some of which have Given Rise to the Muhammadan Religion, Some of which Still Preserve it*), published in Leipzig. Born in 1616 in Laucha an der Unstrut, died in 1697 in Leipzig; Lutheran theologian, Professor and biblical exegete.

1685 Frischmuth, Johann. *Exercitium academicum, ad loca quaedam Scripturae illustranda, quibus Turcarum Persarumque doctores Muhammedem veri nominis, et a Deo promissum fuisse prophetam probare satagunt* (*Academic Exercise, to Elucidate Certain Passages of Scripture, by which the Learned Men of the Turks and Persians Trouble Themselves to Prove that Muhammad Was a True Prophet, and That He Was Sent Forth by God*), published in Jena. Born in 1619 in Wertheim am Main, died in 1687 in Wertheim am Main; Lutheran theologian and Professor.

1685 Falck, Nathanael. *Arcana status in religione Muhammedana, disputatione historico-theologica* (*Arcane Beliefs in the Muslim Religion: An Historical-Theological Disputation*), published in Rostock. Born in 1663 in Danzig, died in 1693 in Stettin; Lutheran theologian.

1685 Carolus, Andreas David. *De religione Lutherana* (*The Lutheran Religion*), published in Wittenberg. Born in 1658 in Calw, died in 1707 in Kirchheim unter Teck; Lutheran theologian.

1687 Calixt, Friedrich Ulrich. *Ad dissertationem de idolatrica religione auctarium primum de Judaeorum et Muhammedanorum idolatria* (*First Supplement to the Dissertation on Idolatrous Religion Concerning the Idolatry of the Jews and Muslims*), published in Helmstedt. Born in 1622 in Helmstedt, died in 1701 in Helmstedt; Lutheran theologian.

1688 Schwimmer, Johann Michael. *Exercitatio politica de republica Turcica* (*Academic Exercise on the Politics of the Turkish Republic*), published in Rudolstadt. Born in 1638 in Rudolstadt, died in 1704 in Rudolstadt; Lutheran philosopher and Professor.

1688 Beck, Matthias Friedrich. *Specimen Arabicum, hoc est, Bina Capitula Alcorani XXX. de Roma et XLIIX. de Victoria, e IV. Codicibus MSS Arabice descripta, Latine versa, et Notis Animadversionibusque locupletata. His nostris Temporibus, Quibus Imperium Romano-Germanicum Victorias contra Muhammedanos prosequitur, accomodatum Argumentum* (*Arabic Specimen on Two Chapters of the*

Qur'an: 30, Concerning Rome [al-Rūm], and 48, Concerning Victory [al-Fatḥ], from Four Manuscript Books, Written Out in Arabic, Translated to Latin, and Enriched with Notes and Observations: the Topic [is] Suitable for These Our Times, in which the Roman-German Empire Pursues Victories Against the Muslims), published in Augsburg. Born in 1649 in Kaufbeuren, died in 1701 in Augsburg; Lutheran theologian.

1694 Celsius, Olaus. *Historia lingua et eruditionis Arabum (History of Arabic Language and Learning*), published in Uppsala. Born in 1670 in Uppsala, died in 1756 in Uppsala; Lutheran theologian and philologist.

1696 Reland, Adriaan. *Exercitatio philologico-theologica de symbolo Mohammedico (non est Deus nisi unus) adversus quod S. S. Trinitas defenditur* (Philological-Theological Exercise on the Muslim Shahāda– There is no god but the One God–Against Which the Holy Trinity is Defended), published in Utrecht. Born in 1676 in de Rijp, died in 1718 in Utrecht; Calvinist theologian, philologist and Professor.

1697 Lange, Johann Michael. *De fabulis Mohhamaedicis circa SS. Trinitatis mysterium et generationem in divinis* (On the Muslim Fables Around the Holy Spirit, the Mystery of the Holy Trinity, and Divine Creation), published in Nuremberg. Born in 1664 in Etzelwang, died in 1731 in Prenzlau; Lutheran theologian.

1700 Stürmer, Reinhold. *Dissertatio historico-politica de fratricidio a quo Turcarum monarchae non raro imperii initium facere consveverunt* (*Historical-Political Dissertation Concerning the Fratricide with which the Monarchs of the Turks Have Not Infrequently Become Accustomed to Make a Beginning of Their Rule*), published in Königsberg. Born in 1677 in Königsberg, died in 1708 in Königsberg; Lutheran Lecturer in Philosophy.

1701 Mantzel, Joachim. *Spicilegium historico-philologicum, historiam litarariam Alcorani sistens (Historical-Philological Gleaning Consisting of the Literary History of the Qur'an*), published in Rostock. Born in 1678 in Rostock, died in 1712 in Parchim; Lutheran theologian.

1701 Acoluthus, Andreas. *Tetrapla Alcoranica, Sive Specimen Alcorani quadrilinguis, arabici, persici, turcici, latini (Quadruple Qur'an or Selections from the Qur'an in Four Languages: Arabic, Persian, Turkish, and Latin*), published in Berlin. Born in Bernstadt in 1654 in Lower Silesia and died in 1704 in Breslau (Wrocław); Lutheran theologian and Professor of Theology.

1704 Lange, Johann Michael. *Dissertatio historico-philologico-theologica de speciminibus, conatibus variis atque novissimis successibus doctorum quorundam virorum in edendo Alcorano arabico* (*Historical-Philological-Theological Dissertation on the Varied Examples and Efforts and Extraordinary Successes of Certain Learned Men in Publishing the Arabic Qur'an*), published in Altdorf. Born in 1664 in Etzelwang, died in 1731 in Prenzlau; Lutheran theologian.

1705 Upmarck, Johann. *Dissertatio historico-politica de statu Persarum hodierno in Oriente* (*Historical-Political Dissertation on the Present State of the Persians in the East*), published in Uppsala. Born in 1664 in Uppsala, died in 1743 in Stockholm; Lutheran philologist and classicist.

1706 Jacobi, Christian Ferdinand and Johann Heinrich Martius. *De lotionibus Mohammedanorum exercitatio prima* (*First Exercise on the Ablution of the Muslims*), published in Leipzig. It seems that both worked on the paper and presented it jointly; neither is identified as a *praeses* or *respondent*; Jacobi was born in Wrocław, lived in the seventeenth century; Lutheran philologist. Martius was born in 1677 in Mittweida, died in 1756 in Wittenberg; Lutheran and Professor at Wittenberg.

1706 Schultens, Albert. *Disputatio theologico philologica de utilitate linguae arabicae in interpretanda scriptura* (*Theological-Philological Disputation on the Utility of the Arabic Language in Interpreting Scripture*), published in Groningen. Born in 1686 in Groningen, died in 1750 in Leiden; Dutch Calvinist theologian and philologist, and Professor at Leiden.

1707 Von Sanden, Bernhard. *Disputatio theologica de Mohammede Pseudo-Propheta prima* (*First Theological Disputation on the False Prophet Muhammad*), published in Königsberg. Born in 1666 in Königsberg, died in 1721 in Königsberg; Lutheran theologian and Professor at Königsberg.

1708 Doederlein, Johann Michael. *Dissertationem philologicam de fundamentis et partibus theologiae Muslimannorum* (*Philological Dissertation on the Fundamentals and Particulars of the Theology of the Muslims*), published in Altdorf. Born in 1687, died in 1735 in Weissenburg am Mordgau; Lutheran theologian and pastor.

1717 Silberrad, Elias. *Dissertatio moralis de Turcis ex Europa pellendis* (*Moral Dissertation on Driving the Turks Out of Europe*), published in Strasbourg. Born in Lampertheim in 1688 and died in Strasbourg in 1731; Lutheran Professor of Theology and Pastor in Temple Neuf in Strasbourg.

1718 Schroeder, Matthias Georg. *Muḥammad shāhid al-ḥaqq ʿalā nafsihi. Muhammed testis veritatis contra se ipsum, Turcis verax, qui mendacia admittat, christianis mendax, qui veritatem dicat, utrinque ex locis Alcorani utrisque demonstratus* (*Muhammad [is] a Witness of the Truth Against Himself, Truthful to the Turks, Though He Admits Lies, [and] a Liar to the Christians, Though He Speaks the Truth; Both Demonstrated from Passages of the Qur'an to Both [Groups]*), published in Leipzig. Born in 1695 and died in 1719; Lutheran theologian.

1719 Lakemacher, Johann Gottfried. *Ex historia philosophica orientali, de Alkendi, Arabum philosopho celeberrimo* (*From Eastern Philosophical History, Concerning al-Kindī, a Most Renowned Philosopher of the Arabs*), published in Helmstedt. Born in 1695 in Osterwieck, died in 1736 in Helmstedt; Lutheran philologist and Hellenist.

1720 Pater, Paulus (Pater Pál). *Insignia Turcica: ex variis superstitionum tenebris, orientalium maxime populorum, disquisitione academica* (*Turkish Signs: from Varied Shadows of Superstition, Especially of the Eastern Peoples: An Academic Investigation*), published in Jena. Born in 1656 in Ménhárd, died in 1724 in Danzig; Hungarian Lutheran mathematician and astronomer. Apparently religious persecution led many Hungarian Lutherans to resettle in Prussia in the late seventeenth and early eighteenth centuries.

1723 Kehr, Georgius Jacobus. *Saraceni, Hagareni et Mauri, quinam sint? et, undenam dicti?* (*Saracens, Hagarenes and Moors, Just Who Are They? And, Just What Are They Named After?*), published in Leipzig. Born in 1692 in Schleusingen, died in 1760 in Saint Petersburg; Pietist.

1729 Callenberg, Johann Heinrich. *Iuris circa Christianos Muhammedici particulae* (*Particulars of the Muslim Law on Christians*), published in Halle an der Saale. Born in 1694 in Molschleben, died in 1760 in Halle; Studied philology and theology at Halle; Pietist Professor of Theology and missionary who focused on conversion of Jews and Muslims.

1731 Michaelis, Johann Heinrich. *Dissertationem philologicam de historia linguae Arabica* (Philological Dissertation on the History of the Arabic Language), published in Hale. Born in 1668 in Klettenberg, died in 1738 in Halle; Pietist theologian, philologist and Hebraist.

1732 Neubauer, Ernst Friedrich. *Dissertatio philologico-hermeneutica de angelo mortis ex mente Ebraeorum ac Muhammedanorum* (*Philological-Hermeneutic Dissertation on the Angel of Death According to the Mind of the Jews and Muslims*), published in Halle an der Saale. Born in 1705 in Magdeburg, died in 1748 in Giessen; Lutheran theologian and Pietist.

1739 Michaelis, Christian Benedikt. *Dissertatio philologica, ritualia quaedam Codicis Sacri ex Alcorano illustrans* (*Philological Dissertation Illustrating Certain Rituals of the Sacred Book from the Qur'an*), published in Halle an der Saale. Born in 1680 in Ellrich, died in 1764 in Halle (Saale); Lutheran Professor of Theology, Pietist.

1743 Mill, David. *De Mohammedismo ante Mohammedem* (*Muhammadanism before Muhammad*), published in Leiden. Born in 1692 in Königsberg, died in 1756 in Utrecht; Reformed theologian and Professor.

1745 Kortholt (der Jüngere), Christian. *Disputatio theologica inauguralis de enthusiasmo Mohammedis* (*Inaugural Theological Disputation on the Enthusiasm of Muhammad*), published in Göttingen. Born in 1709 in Kiel, died in 1751 in Göttingen; Lutheran theologian and Professor of Divinity.

1747 Aurivillius, Carl. *Disputatio philologica de usu dialecti Arabicae in indaganda vocum Ebraicarum significatione propria et originaria*

(*Philological Disputation on the Use of the Arabic Language in Examining the Proper and Original Meanings of Hebrew Words*), published in Uppsala. Born in 1717 in Uppsala, died in 1786 in Stockholm; Swedish Lutheran theologian and philologist.

1761 Avellan, Michael. *Dissertatio historico-philologica de caussis puritatis ac floris perennis linguae Arabica* (*Historical-Philological Dissertation on the Causes of the Purity and Perpetual Bloom of the Arabic Language*), published in Åbo, Finland. Born in 1736 in Tammela, died in 1807 in Tammela; Finnish Lutheran theologian, philologist and Professor.

1761 Cotta, Johann Friedrich. *Exercitatio de religione Muhammedica* (*Exercise on the Muhammadan Religion*), published in Tübingen. Born in 1701 Tübingen, died in 1779 in Tübingen; Lutheran theologian and Professor of Theology.

1772 Hommel, Carl Ferdinand. *Über Belohnung und Strafe nach Türkischen Gesezen* (*On Reward and Punishment According to Turkish Law*), published in Bayreuth and Leipzig. Born in 1722 in Leipzig, died in 1781 in Leipzig; Lutheran jurist and legal theorist.

1775 Storr, Gottlob Christian. *Dissertatio inauguralis critica de Evangeliis Arabicis* (*Inaugural Critical Dissertation on the Arabic Gospels*), published in Tübingen. Born in 1746 in Stuttgart, died in 1805 in Stuttgart; Lutheran theologian.

1793 Norberg, Matthias. *Dissertatio de ingenio Muhammedis* (*Dissertation on Ingenuity of Muhammad*), published in Lund. Born in 1747 in Nätra in Sweden, died in 1826 in Uppsala; Swedish Lutheran historian of religion and linguist.

1821 Tholuck, Friedrich August. *Sufismus sive Theosophia Persarum Pantheistica* (*Sufism, or, the Pantheistic Theosophy of the Persians*), published in Berlin. Born in 1799 in Breslau, died in 1877 in Halle (Saale); Pietist theologian.

1823 Peiper, Carl Rudolf Samuel. *De Moallaka Lebidi, celeberrimi veterum arabum poëtae carmine laudatissimo dissertationem* (*Dissertation on the Muʿallaqa, the Most Praised Poem of the Most Celebrated Poet of the Ancient Arabs, Labīd*), published in Jordanimola ad Nimitium. Born in 1798 in Striegau, died in 1879 in Hirschberg; Lutheran pastor and philologist.

1829 Lindgren, Henrik Gerhard. *De lingua neo-Arabica disquisitio* (*Investigation on the Neo-Arabic Language*), published in Uppsala. Born in 1801 in Stockholm, died in 1879 in Tierp; Swedish Lutheran pastor and philologist.

1834 Bergmann, Frédéric-Guillaume. *De religione Arabum anteislamica dissertatio historico-theologica* (*Historical-Theological Dissertation on the Pre-Islamic Religion of the Arabs*), published in Strasbourg. Born in 1812 in Strasbourg, died in 1887 in Strasbourg; Alsatian (Reformed Church) Calvinist theologian, philologist, and Professor.

Glossary of Terms

'Abdāl This term refers to the wandering Muslim saints who occupy a higher rank in the Sufi hierarchical order as they are believed to possess the power to change from physical to spiritual form. The men of *'abdāl* are also called the men of the unseen spiritual realm (*rijāl al-ghayb*) in Sufi literature.

Adab (*ādāb*, plural) This popular Arabic term means refinement and good manners. Historically, it refers to Arabic literary culture (*belles-lettres*) in the early centuries of Islamic civilization, but the concept came to denote a code of conduct for the more professional and elite classes: administrative secretaries, governors, supervisors of bazaars, judges, jurists, and even Sufis.

Ādāb al-Baḥth Referring to the genre of Islamic dialectics and the theory of argumentation, this was one of the popular subjects in the Ottoman *medrese* curriculum from the fifteenth century up until the early twentieth century. It was also studied in Eastern Europe, Egypt, Iran, Central Asia, and India.

'Āshūrā' The commemoration of the martyrdom of Ḥusayn, the son of Ali and the third *imām* of the Shi'as at Kerbela in Iraq, in a battle against the 'Umayyad caliph Yazīd in 680 AD. This is remembered on the tenth day of the month of Muharram to honor the suffering and oppression the Shi'ites endured throughout history. Religious rituals are performed on this day, including self-flagellation, singing tragic songs, and lamentations.

Augsburg Confession A summation of the Lutheran faith, known as *Confessio Augustana* in Latin, was written by Melanchton and Luther in 1530 and presented to the Emperor Charles V at the Diet of Augsburg. It was denounced by the Roman Catholic Church, but served as a model for later Protestant Churches' confessions of faith.

Bayram This means holiday in Turkish, which includes two Ottoman religious holidays called *Ramazan* and *Kurban bayramı*. The former followed the month-long fast (*oruç*) at the end of Ramadan and the latter followed the end of the annual pilgrimage to Ka'ba in Mecca (*Ḥajj*) in which believers sacrifice animals. According to the seventeenth-century Lutheran authors, Turks celebrate *Ramazan* as an important sacred holiday (*ulu bayram*) and *Kurban* as a lesser one (*küçük bayram*).

Chederle   Called *hıdırellez* by the Turks, it is the festival of celebration for the beginning of Spring. Derived from the combination of two names of Islamic saints, Hızır (Khiḍr) and İlyas (Ilyās), there is also a religious connation as *hıdırellez* is a celebration of the day the twin brothers Khiḍr and Ilyās meet once a year. On *hıdırellez* night, some Muslims utter up a prayer believing that it will magically come true due to their faith in these saints.

Dervish   This Persian word, spelled as *derviş* in Turkish, refers to an individual who is a fully initiated member of a Muslim Sufi mystic order and has gone through training in a *tekke* (Sufi lodge) to become a full adherent. This could be considered the equivalent of a Christian monk and both Sunni and Shi'a Muslims have their own Sufi orders.

Dominus   The lord or the king, who is master by the right of property or the ownership of slaves in ancient Rome. Each *dominus* has a *dominium* that may include ownership of land, property, or slaves. Therefore, *dominium* naturally brought the question of the relationship between a *dominus* and a subject. In this context, Luther asserted that God is the real *dominus*, and not the rulers or kings, and all other creatures in the world are His *dominium* and the Lord governs everything.

Duldul   A symbolic creature in Shi'a iconography, it is believed to be the female mule owned by the Prophet Muhammad. This mule was given to 'Alī by Muhammad and ridden by him and his sons, Ḥasan and Ḥusayn, according to tradition. From the fifteenth century onward, 'Alī's depiction in Shi'ite art has standardized details; in paintings he is drawn, veiled and red-haired, to stand out from the crowd with his sword *zulfiqār* and his mule *duldul*. Therefore, 'Alī's successors, the Shi'a *imām*s, are said to bear these important spiritual attributes of 'Alī's within themselves.

Elysian Fields   This paradise is reserved for heroes, virtuous people, and relatives of the gods as a reward in ancient Greece. Described as the happy land where the blessed souls live in tranquility in the hereafter, Lutheran authors use this term to refer to the idea of Muslim heaven. After a period of probation and suffering in Hell, which corresponds to the Roman Catholic idea of purgatory, all believers reach the Elysian Fields.

Furqān   This is one of the names of the Qur'an which God identifies as the final holy writ (Q. 3:4 and 25:1). Called *furqān* or criterion, Allāh clarifies once and for all the difference between truth and falsehood for the believers. Qur'an (21:48) also refers to the Torah as the *furqān*: "Certainly, we had already given Moses and Aaron the criterion (*furqān*)."

Ghadīr Khumm   It is the name of a place between Mecca and Medina, which acquired its importance in religious narrative due to the alleged conversation between Muhammad and 'Alī when they were returning from the Prophet's last pilgrimage. Muhammad said: "Whoever is my friend, 'Alī is his friend too; my enemies are his enemies." There are different versions of this event; however, the significance of this for Shi'a Muslims is the clear indication of Muhammad's designation of 'Alī as his successor, as opposed to the first three caliphs that Sunnis accept.

Ḥadīth With the definite article *al-ḥadīth*, this means Prophetic tradition, believed by Sunnis to be an account of what Prophet Muhammad said or did, or of his tacit approval of something said or done in his presence. The study of tradition is called *'ulūm al-ḥadīth* or the sciences of tradition, and the traditionists are called *ahl al-ḥadīth*.

Ḥanifite It is one of the schools of Islamic law, founded by Abū Ḥanīfa (d.767 AD). It was first adopted by the Abbasid caliphs (751–1258) and later became the legal school used by the Ottoman Turks. It was incorporated into the Empire and the Ḥanafite school (*madhhab*) became the official legal system since it gave the ruler more powers in financial and legal matters than did the Shafi'ī *madhhab* or any other Islamic legal school. This school is also popular in the Indian Subcontinent, Central Asia, and Western China.

Jāhiliyya It means the age of ignorance. Historically, it referred to the era before the advent of Islam in the Arabian Peninsula during which time pre-Islamic Arabs were considered ignorant of God and the monotheistic religion. However, ignorance did not mean that pre-Islamic Arabs were uncultured or uneducated people. Conceptually, the notion of *jāhiliyya* signified a new Muslim identity as it marked the conversion from the non-Muslim past (*jāhiliyya*) to the Muslim present. Therefore, this new identity through conversion represented a state of alterity and a belief in the uniqueness of Islam, rather than a historical event as a sharp distinction between pre-Islamic and Islamic periods. During the modern period, the Muslim thinker Sayyid Quṭb (d.1966) used *jāhiliyya* as a typology for any un-Islamic culture or lifestyle.

Jinn In the Qur'an, the *jinn* is part of Creation as God created two separate species living in parallel realms, man and the *jinn*, the former from clay and the latter from fire. The Qur'an addresses the *jinn* as nations (*umam*) like humans, and the idea of the *jinn* being among us, living and interacting with us, although they are mostly invisible to us, is integral to Muslim culture and religion.

Kızılbaş Also spelled as *qizilbash*, this means "red heads" in Turkish for the red caps these individuals wore. Historically, it refers to the Shi'ite Turkomans and the Sufi groups who supported and helped found the Safavid Empire in Persia. In the Ottoman Sunni discourse, *kızılbaş* has the pejorative meaning of heretic and rebel.

Korban Olah This is an ancient Jewish animal offering where the meat is entirely burnt on the altar as a tribute to God; none is kept for the owner of the animal to distribute or to eat.

Lawḥ al-Maḥfūẓ   Mentioned in the Qur'an (85:22), this term means the preserved tablet. Qur'anic commentators and theologians generally agree that God's word as a divine revelation was transferred onto this preserved tablet (*Lawḥ al-Maḥfūẓ*) and later into the written Qur'an.

Lutheran Jubilee-Year   Every century, there is a Protestant celebration to commemorate the Reformation. The Lutherans appointed the first Jubilee in 1617, a century after Luther's publication of the ninety-five thesis. The last Reformation Jubilee was celebrated in 2017.

Mikra   This Hebrew term is used, along with Tanakh, to refer to the entire canonical collection of Hebrew Scriptures, also called the Old Testament.

Mishnah   This is the ancient codification of Jewish rabbinic law (oral Torah), the Talmud is the later rabbinic commentaries on it.

Nahiv   The study of Arabic grammar, a mandatory course in the Ottoman colleges, is known as *nahw* in Arabic.

Nasib   This Turkish Muslim belief in fate decrees that every man's fortune is written in the Book of Heaven and no man's fate can be avoided.

Nefes oğlu   It literally means the son of the breath; it is also known as *nefes evladı*, which means the children of breath. This term is usually associated with the Turkish Bektaşi Muslim Sufi tradition. In this context, a *nefes oğlu* is a blessing from the leader of the Bektaşi Sufi order, known as *baba*, for a woman to have a child. This blessing to have a child comes through the intercessory prayer or breath of a *baba*. The Bektaşi belief that God created Jesus by impregnating Mary with His breath was the origin of the blessing of *nefes oğlu*.

Peredesia and Perbibesia   These are fictious names originally used by the Roman playwright Plautus; *Peredia* (hungry land) and *Bibesia* (thirsty land). Lutherans used the Latin version of these names to refer to the sensuous Muslim vision of paradise.

Puccianism   This is a doctrine of the universal salvation of mankind, including people who had never heard of Christ, based on the ideas of Francesco Pucci, a Florentine religious exile burnt for heresy in 1597. Pucci's radical doctrine of God's universal mercy became well-known through his manifesto *De Christi servatoris efficacitate* (*On the Efficacy of Christ the Savior*) in the seventeenth and eighteenth centuries. Puccianism was unanimously considered a heresy by the Catholics, Lutherans, and Calvinists as his ideas challenged the authority of their religions. Lutherans used it further as a swear word to solidify their orthodoxy. Significantly, Orthodox Lutheran theologian Kromayer likened Islam to Puccianism as Muhammad claimed that anyone who lived uprightly, whether Christian or Jew could be saved.

Qalandar   This Persian term refers to persons who are free from all cares of this and the next world. These are Muslim Sufis and saints, who have reached a high level of spirituality, essentially the state of spiritual ecstasy, to become perfect human beings (*insān-i kāmil*). In Persian Sufi poetry, *qalandar* is depicted as someone living outside the worldly domain and free from the taint of religious rites and rituals, beyond the dictates of Islamic law (*Sharī'a*). The term is also generally associated with the Qalandariyya, wandering ascetic Sufi dervishes, found in Iran, Central Asia, India, Pakistan, Nepal, and South Asia.

Republic of Letters This refers to the highly literary culture of the seventeenth and eighteenth centuries. It denotes an imagined territory that existed on no European map; long-distance intellectual communities during the age of Enlightenment created transnational networks in Europe and the Americas where philosophers and thinkers could exchange ideas. French Protestants in diaspora played an important role as exporters of the ideas of Parisian *philosophes*. The Republic of Letters is historically significant because this literary movement was not only transregional but also multi-religious, consisting of French Protestants, Lutherans, Calvinists, Catholics, Anglicans, and some Jews.

Ṣarf It is the part of Arabic grammar which deals with words in their different contexts and the conjugation of the verbs.

Schlaraffenland This fictional place mentioned in European fairy tales, either as *Schlaraffenland* or the Land of Cockaigne, alludes to an imaginary place like the Elysian Fields, in which blessed souls live happily ever after and enjoy sensual delights forever. Luther and Lutherans used this term to describe the Muslim paradise (*jannat*). Based on his understanding of the relationship between religion and work ethics, Luther's references to *Schlaraffenland* were a critique of clerical lifestyle that fostered laziness. Luther rejected the mediaeval ecclesial dichotomy between the active life and the contemplative life, and the Catholic devaluation of the laity's work while presenting the monastic life as ideal.

Schmalkaldic Articles It is one of the confessions of Lutheran faith, written by Luther in 1536 at the behest of Johann Friedrich, Elector of Saxony. The Schmalkaldic Articles discussed theological subjects, such as the unity of God, the Trinity, Christ, justification by faith, sin, the Law, repentance, confession, and the ministry. After Luther's death, these articles, which were incorporated into the *Book of Concord*, became the official confession of faith for most Lutheran churches.

Schwärmer Usually translated as enthusiasts and sometimes as fanatics, *schwärmer* is a derogatory term invented by Luther to castigate the theologies of the peasant revolt and radical Christian groups, involving Andreas Carlstadt, Thomas Müntzer, and the Zwickau prophets. *Schwärmer* (enthusiasts) and *Schwärmerei* (enthusiasm) are both highly loaded terms in the post-Reformation Lutheran and German Enlightenment discourse. However, the relevancy of these terms for us here is that Lutheran theologians used them to describe

Islam as an enthusiastic religion, which involves irrational tendencies and excessive imagination in religion and Muhammad as an enthusiast, who was obsessively convinced of his divine mission to spread his religion throughout the world.

Scylla and Charybdis They are the two sea monsters of Greek mythology placed on opposite sides of the ocean; sailors must choose between these two monsters. It means having to choose between two evils.

Sunna This refers to the second source of Sunni Islamic law, which is based on the custom and habit, particularly the words and deeds, of the Prophet Muhammad as collected in the *ḥadīth*.

Takdir This Turkish word means predestination and refers to the Ottoman Turk's belief that every human being's destiny is written on their forehead.

Tanāsukh This is the transmigration of souls from one body to another, known as metempsychosis. The extremist Shiʻite sects (*ghulat*) believed that *imām* ʻAlī's and his sons' souls transmigrated into the body of chosen *imām*, thereby establishing the spiritual authority of the Shiʻite *imām*. Unlike other Shiʻite groups, ʻAlawites and *ghulat* sects also believe that ʻAlī was the incarnation of God due to their belief in the *ḥulūl* doctrine, which maintains that God could pass into human form.

Targumim These are ancient translations and paraphrases of the Bible in Aramaic, the ancient *lingua franca* of the Middle East.

Ummī Muhammad was referred to as the *ummī* Prophet (*al-nabī al-ummī*) in the Qur'an (7:157–8); this term has generally been translated as "illiterate," making Muhammad the unlettered Prophet. As Muhammad was active in the caravan trade in the Arabian Peninsula, some scholars questioned whether Muhammad could neither read nor write. Some Qur'anic commentators also suggested that being *ummī* meant that Muhammad was a man who did not have a formal education; however, they believe he might have been able to read and write. Others suggested that *ummī* refers to the Arab nation; therefore, *ummī* should be more properly understood as "the Prophet for the unlettered people," denoting people without a scripture (Qur'an). This idea of Muhammad being illiterate was significant for Lutheran scholars as it reinforced their interpretation of Islam as anti-intellectual and anti-*belles lettres*.

Zulfiqār It is the name of ʻAlī's sword, also written as *dhū'l-fiqār* and *dhū'l-faqār*. The Shiʻites believe that the Prophet Muhammad gave ʻAlī *zulfiqār* to replace his broken sword on a battlefield; therefore, it is considered to have miraculous powers. The popular saying *Lā fatā illā ʻAlī lā sayf illā dhū'l-faqār* in Shiʻite culture means "There is no hero but ʻAlī; there is no sword but *dhū'l-faqār*."

Bibliography

Primary Sources

Libraries

Augsburg

Bauer, Johann Karl Valentin. *Conspectum theologia Turcarum Mochammedicae, von der Religion der Türcken.* Augsburg Staats- und Stadtbibliothek, Diss. Phil. 1101. Jena, 1720.

Berlin

Wendeler, Michael. *Disputatio politica de republica Turcica.* Staatsbibliothek zu Berlin—Preußischer Kulturbesitz, Bibl. Diez Qu. 2537. Wittenberg, 1655.

Dresden

Ludewig, Johann Peter von. *Disputatione inaugurali historiam rationalis philosophiae apud Arabes et Turcas.* Sächsische Landesbibliothek—Staats- und Universitätsbibliothek Dresden, Coll. Diss. A 71/49. Halle, 1699.

Planer, Johann Andreas. *Panegyricus, memoriae celeberrimi theologi, Sebastiani Kirchmaieri, antistitis, consistorialis, et scholarchae Rotenburgensis ad tubarim optime meriti, dictus Vitembergae.* Sächsische Landesbibliothek—Staats- und Universitätsbibliothek Dresden, Biogr. erud. D. 1599. Wittenberg, 1701.

Schelwig, Samuel. *De philosophia Turcica, oratio inauguralis.* Sächsische Landesbibliothek—Staats- und Universitätsbibliothek Dresden, Hist. Turc. 495. Danzig, 1686.

Göttingen

Clasen, Daniel. *De religione politica liber unus.* Niedersächsische Staats- und Universitätsbibliothek Göttingen, 8 Pol IV, 9359-b. Magdeburg, 1681.

Kromayer, Hieronymus. *Scrutinii religionum disputatio III, de Muhammetismo tum Turcarum tum Persarum.* Niedersächsische Staats- und Universitätsbibliothek Göttingen, Th. Polem. 124/3. Leipzig, 1668.

Halle (Saale)

Haller, Wilhelm. *Mochammads lehre von Gott aus dem Kor'aân gezogen.* Universitäts- und Landesbibliothek Sachsen-Anhalt, D Hb 775. Altenburg, 1779.

Kortholt, Christian. *Disputatio theologica inauguralis de enthusiasmo Mohammedis.* Universitäts- und Landesbibliothek Sachsen-Anhalt, D Hb 815. Göttingen, 1745.

Michaelis, Christian Benedikt. *Disputatio academica de Muhammedismi laxitate morali.* Universitäts- und Landesbibliothek Sachsen-Anhalt, D Hb 870. Halle, 1708.

Pfeiffer, August. *Dissertatio philologica quinta de Alishiis et Sunnitis, sive de praecipuis Persarum et Turcarum circa religionem dissidiis.* Universitäts- und Landesbibliothek Sachsen-Anhalt, Bb 282. Wittenberg, 1670.

Vetterlein, Christian Friedrich Rudolph. *De philosophia Turcarum.* Universitäts- und Landesbibliothek Sachsen-Anhalt, AB 155562/8. Köthen, 1790.

Walch, Johann Georg. "Libri II: De progressu ac fatis logicae," in *Parerga Academica.* Universitäts- und Landesbibliothek Sachsen-Anhalt, TM0848. Leipzig, 1721.

Jena

Koch, Cornelius Dietrich. *Dissertatio inauguralis historico-litteraria de fatis studiorum apud Arabes.* Thüringer Universitäts- und Landesbibliothek Jena, 4 Bud. Hist. Lit. 6/18. Helmstedt, 1719.

Munich

Calixt, Friedrich Ulrich. *De religione muhammedana dissertatio.* Bayerische Staatsbibliothek München, 4 Diss. 632/9. Helmstedt, 1687.

Luther, Martin. *De captivitate babylonica ecclesiae praeludium Martini Lutheri.* Bayerische Staatsbibliothek München, 4 A. gr. b. 969. Wittenberg, 1520.

Pfeiffer, August. *Theologiae, sive potius Ματαιολογίας Judaicae atque Mohammedicae seu Turcico-Persicae Principia Sublesta et Fructus Pestilentes.* Bayerische Staatsbibliothek München, Exeg. 856. Leipzig, 1687.

Schweigger, Salomon. *Alcoranus Mahometicus, Das ist: der Türcken Alcoran, Religion und Aberglauben,* Bayerische Staatsbibliothek München, 422 A. Nuremberg, 1616.

Steuchius, Johannes. *Disputatio gradualis historiam logicae Arabum.* Bayerische Staatsbibliothek München, Diss. 55/2. Uppsala, 1721.

Wallich, Johann Ulrich. *Religio Turcica, Mahometis vita, et orientalis cum occidentali antichristo comparatio.* Bayerische Staatsbibliothek München, 4 Turc. 73u. Stade, 1659.

Paris

Lange, Johann Michael. *Dissertatio historico-philologico-theologica de Alcorani prima inter Europaeos editione Arabica.* Bibliothèque nationale de France, BNF Gallica 4 O2G 195. Altdorf, 1703.

Regensburg

Kirchmaier, Sebastian. *Oratio Persica de differentia religionis Turcicae & Persicae.* Persian title: (سخن فارسی جدا از دین ترکی و فارسی بیان کنان), Staatliche Bibliothek Regensburg, 999/4 Theol. syst. 284 angeb. 17. Wittenberg, 1662.

Saint Petersburg, Russia

Norberg, Matthias. *Dissertatio de scholis et collegiis Turcarum.* Российская национальная библиотека, Шифры: ФБ Осн. хран. Приплет. к: W 71/171. Lund, 1792.

Vienna

Weitenkampf, Johann Friedrich Weitenkampf, *Disputatio historico-metaphysica de fato Turcico.* Österreichische Nationalbibliothek, 131348-B. Helmstedt, 1751.

Weimar

Kirchmaier, Sebastian. *Stammbuch Sebastian Kirchmaier.* Herzogin Anna Amalia Bibliothek, Klassik Stiftung Weimar, MS Stb 155. Wittenberg, 1660–1667.

Secondary Sources

Abisaab, Rula Jurdi. "The Ulama of Jabal 'Amil in Safavid Iran, 1501–1736: Marginality, Migration and Social Change," *Iranian Studies* 27 (1994): 103–22.

———. *Converting Persia: Religion and Power in the Safavid Empire.* London: I. B. Tauris, 2004.

Abou-El-Haj, Rifa'at 'Ali. *Formation of the Modern State: The Ottoman Empire, Sixteenth to Eighteenth Centuries.* Albany: SUNY Press, 1991.

Abu Zayd, Nasr. *Reformation of Islamic Thought: A Critical Historical Analysis.* Amsterdam: Amsterdam University Press, 2006.

Adelman, Howard Tzvi. "A Rabbi Reads the Qur'an in the Venetian Ghetto," *Jewish History* 26 (2012): 125–37.

Ágoston, Gábor. "Information, Ideology, and Limits of Imperial Policy: Ottoman Grand Strategy in the Context of Ottoman-Habsburg Rivalry," in *The Early Modern Ottomans: Remapping the Empire.* Eds. Virginia H. Aksan and Daniel Goffman. Cambridge: Cambridge University Press, 2007.

Ahmad, Nazir. *Qur'anic and Non-Qur'anic Islam.* Lahore: Vanguard, 1997.

Akbari, Suzanne. *Idols in the East: European Representations of Islam and the Orient, 1100–1450.* Ithaca: Cornell University Press, 2009.

Alatas, Syed Farid. "Contemporary Muslim Revival: The Case of "Protestant Islam," *The Muslim World* 97 (2007): 508–20.

Ali, Abdullah Yusuf. *The Holy Qur'an.* London: Wordsworth, 2000.

Ali, Kecia. *The Lives of Muhammad.* Cambridge: Harvard University Press, 2014.

Allen, Michael. "Disputation for Scholastic Theology: Engaging Luther's 97 Theses," *Themelios* 44/1 (2019): 105–19.

Almond, Ian. *History of Islam in German Thought: From Leibniz to Nietzsche.* London: Routledge, 2009.

An-Na'im, Abdullahi Ahmed. *Toward an Islamic Reformation: Civil Liberties, Human Rights, and International Law.* Syracuse: Syracuse University Press, 1990.

Antognazza, Maria Rosa. *Leibniz on the Trinity and the Incarnation: Reason and Revelation in the Seventeenth Century.* Trans. Gerald Parks. New Haven: Yale University Press, 2007.

———. "Ecclesiology, Ecumenism, and Toleration," in *The Oxford Handbook of Leibniz.* Ed. Maria Rosa Antognazza. Oxford: Oxford University Press, 2018.

Appold, Kenneth G. "Academic Life and Teaching in Post-Reformation Lutheranism," in *Lutheran Ecclesiastical Culture: 1550–1675.* Ed. Robert Kolb. Leiden: Brill, 2008.

Armstrong, Brian. *Calvinism and the Amyraut Heresy: Protestant Scholasticism and Humanism in Seventeenth-Century France.* Eugene: Wipf & Stock, 2004.

Asselt, Willem J. "Protestant Scholasticism: Some Methodological Considerations in the Study of its Development," *Dutch Review of Church History* 81/3 (2001): 265–74.

Aue-Ben David, Irene, Aya Elyada, Moshe Sluhovsky and Christian Wiese (Eds.). *Jews and Protestants: From the Reformation to the Present.* Berlin: De Gruyter, 2020.

Austin, Kenneth. *The Jews and the Reformation.* New Haven: Yale University Press, 2020.

Babayan, Kathryn. "The Safavid Synthesis: From Qizilbash Islam to Imamite Shi'ism," *Iranian Studies* 27 (1994): 135–61.

———. *Mystics, Monarchs, and Messiahs: Cultural Landscapes of Early Modern Iran.* Cambridge: Harvard University Press, 2002.

Backus, Irena. "G.W. Leibniz and Protestant Scholasticism in the Years 1698–1704," in *Church and School in Early Modern Protestantism: Studies in Honor of Richard A. Muller on the Maturation of a Theological Tradition.* Eds. Jordan J. Ballor, David Sytsma, and Jason Zuidema. Leiden: Brill, 2013.

———. *Leibniz: Protestant Theologian.* Oxford: Oxford University Press, 2016.

Baer, Marc David. *Honored by the Glory of Islam: Conversion and Conquest in Ottoman Europe.* Oxford: Oxford University Press, 2007.

———. "Protestant Islam in Weimar Germany: Hugo Marcus and "The Message of the Holy Prophet Muhammad to Europe," *New German Critique* 44/2 (2017): 163–200.

Barkey, Karen. *Empire of Difference: The Ottomans in Comparative Perspective.* New York: Cambridge University Press, 2008.

Bartolucci, Guido. "Jewish Thought vs. Lutheran Aristotelism: Johann Frischmuth (1619–1687) and Jewish Scepticism," in *Yearbook of the Maimonides Centre for Advanced Studies 2.* Ed. Bill Rebiger. Berlin: Walter de Gruyter, 2017.

Bayraklı, Bayraktar. *Kuran Müslümanlığı.* Istanbul: Düşün Yayıncılık, 2019.

Beiser, Frederick C. *The Sovereignty of Reason: The Defense of Rationality in the Early English Enlightenment*. Princeton: Princeton University Press, 1996.

Bell, Dean Phillip and Stephen G. Burnett (Eds.). *Jews, Judaism and the Reformation in Sixteenth-Century Germany*. Leiden: Brill, 2006.

Ben-Tov, Asaph. *Lutheran Humanists and Greek Antiquity: Melanchthonian Scholarship between Universal History and Pedagogy*. Leiden: Brill, 2009.

———. "Hellenism in the Context of Oriental Studies: The Case of Johann Gottfried Lakemacher (1695–1736)," *International Journal of the Classical Tradition* 25 (2018): 297–314.

———. "Historia Literaria Alcorani: Two Lutheran Scholars Chronicling Oriental Scholarship at the Turn of the Eighteenth Century," in *Scholarship between Europe and the Levant: Essays in Honour of Alastair Hamilton*. Eds. Jan Loop and Jill Kraye. Leiden: Brill, 2020.

Benzine, Rachid. *Les nouveaux penseurs de l'islam*. Paris: Albin Michel, 2004.

Berg, Johannes van den. *Religious Currents and Cross-Currents: Essays on Early Modern Protestantism and the Protestant Enlightenment*. Leiden: Brill, 1999.

Berman, Harold J. *Law and Revolution, II: The Impact of the Protestant Reformations on the Western Legal Tradition*. Cambridge: Harvard University Press, 2003.

Berman, Nina. *German Literature on the Middle East. Discourses and Practices, 1000–1989*. Ann Arbor: The University of Michigan Press, 2011.

Bevilacqua, Alexander. *The Republic of Arabic Letters: Islam and the European Enlightenment*. Cambridge: Harvard University Press, 2018.

——— with Jan Loop. "The Qur'an in Comparison and the Birth of 'scriptures'," *Journal of Qur'anic Studies* 20/3 (2018): 149–74.

——— with Frederic Clark. *Thinking in the Past Tense: Eight Conversations*. Chicago: The University of Chicago Press, 2019.

Biagioni, Mario. *The Radical Reformation and the Making of Modern Europe: A Lasting Heritage*. Leiden: Brill, 2016.

Bisaha, Nancy. *Creating East and West: Renaissance Humanists and the Ottoman Turks*. Philadelphia: University of Pennsylvania Press, 2004.

Blackwell, Constance. "The Case of Honoré Fabri and the Historiography of Sixteenth and Seventeenth Century Jesuit Aristotelianism in the Protestant History of Philosophy: Sturm, Morhof and Brucker," *Nouvelles de la Republique des Letters* 15 (1995): 49–77.

Bochinger, Christoph. *Abenteuer Islam: Zur Wahrnehmung fremder Religion im Hallenser Pietismus des 18. Jahrhunderts*, Habilitationsschrift. Munich: LMU, 1996.

Bohnert, Daniel. *Wittenberger Universitätstheologie im frühen 17. Jahrhundert*. Tübingen: Mohr Siebeck, 2017.

Bohnstedt, John W. *The Infidel Scourge of God: The Turkish Menace As Seen by German Pamphleteers of the Reformation Era*. Philadelphia: American Philosophical Society, 1968.

Bonacina, Giovanni. *The Wahhabis Seen through European Eyes (1772–1830): Deists and Puritans of Islam*. Leiden: Brill, 2015.

Boogert, Maurits H. van den. "Learning Oriental Languages in the Ottoman Empire: Johannes Heyman (1667–1737) between Izmir and Damascus," in

Teaching and Learning of Arabic in Early Modern Europe. Eds. Jan Loop, Alastair Hamilton, and Charles Burnett. Leiden: Brill, 2017.

Bossy, John. *Christianity in the West 1400–1700.* Oxford: Oxford University Press, 1985.

Brucker, Johann Jakob. *Historia critica philosophiae,* 5 vols. Leipzig: C. Breitkopf, 1742–44.

Bruening, Michael W. *A Reformation Sourcebook: Documents from an Age of Debate.* Toronto: University of Toronto Press, 2017.

Buddeus, Johann Franz. *Elementa philosophiae instrumentalis, seu institutionum philosophiae eclecticae.* Halle: Typis Orphanotrophii, 1722.

Bulliet, Richard W. "Islamic Reformation or "Big Crunch"? A Review Essay," *Harvard Middle Eastern and Islamic Review* 8 (2009): 7–18.

Burman, Thomas. *Reading the Qur'an in Latin Christendom 1140–1560.* Philadelphia: University of Pennsylvania Press, 2007.

Burnett, Amy Nelson. "The Educational Roots of Reformed Scholasticism: Dialectic and Scriptural Exegesis in the Sixteenth Century," *Dutch Review of Church History* 84 (2004): 299–317.

———. "Luther and the *Schwärmer*," in *The Oxford Handbook of Martin Luther's Theology.* Eds. Robert Kolb, Irene Dingel, and L'ubomír Batka. Oxford: Oxford University Press, 2014.

Burnett, Stephen G. *Christian Hebraism in the Reformation Era (1500–1660): Authors, Books, and the Transmission of Jewish Learning.* Leiden: Brill, 2012.

Cameron, Euan. *The European Reformation.* Oxford: Oxford University Press, 1991.

Campi, Emidio. "Early Reformed Attitudes towards Islam," *Theological Review of the Near East School of Theology* 31 (2010): 131–51.

Catana, Leo. *The Historiographical Concept 'System of Philosophy': Its Origin, Nature, Influence and Legitimacy.* Leiden: Brill, 2008.

Chadwick, Owen. *The Early Reformation on the Continent.* Oxford: Oxford University Press, 2001.

Chafe, Eric. *Tears into Wine: J. S. Bach's Cantata 21 in its Musical and Theological Contexts.* Oxford: Oxford University Press, 2015.

Chakrabarty, Dipesh. *Provincializing Europe: Postcolonial Thought and Historical Difference.* Princeton: Princeton University Press, 2000.

Champion, Justin. *The Pillars of Priestcraft Shaken: The Church of England and Its Enemies, 1660–1730.* Cambridge: Cambridge University Press, 1992.

Chang, Kevin . "From Oral Disputation to Written Text: Transformation of the Dissertation in Early Modern Europe," *History of Universities* 19/2 (2004): 129–87.

———. "Kant's Disputation of 1770: The Dissertation and the Communication of Knowledge in Early Modern Europe," *Endeavour* 31/2 (2007): 45–49.

Clark, Timothy. *The Theory of Inspiration.* Manchester: Manchester University Press, 1997.

Colombo, Emanuele. "Western Theologies and Islam," in *The Oxford Handbook of Early Modern Theology, 1600–1800.* Eds. Ulrich L. Lehner, Richard A. Muller, and A. G. Roeber. Oxford: Oxford University Press, 2016.

Conrad, Sebastian. "Enlightenment in Global History: A Historiographical Critique," *American Historical Review* 117/4 (2012): 997–1027.

———. *What Is Global History?* Princeton: Princeton University Press, 2016.

Cook, Michael and Carol Bakhos (Eds). *Islam and Its Past: Jahiliyya, Late Antiquity, and the Qur'an.* Oxford: Oxford University Press, 2017.

Curry, John. *Transformation of Muslim Mystical Thought in the Ottoman Empire: The Rise of the Halveti Order, 1350–1650.* Edinburgh: Edinburgh University Press, 2010.

Cyranka, Daniel. *Mahomet: Repräsentationen des Propheten in deutschsprachigen Texten des 18. Jahrhunderts.* Göttingen: Vandenhoeck & Ruprecht, 2018.

Daniel, Norman. *Islam and the West: The Making of an Image.* Edinburgh: The Edinburgh University Press, 1960.

Darling, Linda. "Ottoman Politics through British Eyes: Paul Rycaut's *The Present State of the Ottoman Empire,*" *Journal of World History* 5/1 (1994): 71–97.

Dascal, Marcelo. *Gottfried Wilhelm Leibniz: The Art of Controversies.* Dordrecht: Springer, 2008.

Decot, Rolf. *Geschichte der Reformation in Deutschland.* Freiburg: Herder, 2015.

Deutsch, Yaacov. *Judaism in Christian Eyes: Ethnographic Description of Jews and Judaism in Early Modern Europe.* Oxford: Oxford University Press, 2012.

Dickens, A. G. and John M. Tonkin. *The Reformation in Historical Thought.* Cambridge: Harvard University Press, 1985.

Diemling, Maria. "Jewish-Christian Relations in Early Modern Germany," *European Association for Jewish Studies Newsletter* 17 (2005): 34–47.

Dieter, Theodor. "Luther as Late Medieval Theologian: His Positive and Negative use of Nominalism and Realism," in *The Oxford Handbook of Martin Luther's Theology.* Eds. Robert Kolb, Irene Dingel, and L'ubomír Batka. Oxford: Oxford University Press, 2014.

Dimmock, Matthew. "'Machomet dyd before as Luther doth nowe': Islam, the Ottomans, and the English Reformation." *Reformation* 9 (2004): 99–130.

Dixon, C. Scott. *The Reformation in Germany.* Oxford: Blackwell, 2002.

———. *Contesting the Reformation.* Oxford: Wiley-Blackwell, 2012.

Donnelly, John Patrick. *Calvinism and Scholasticism in Vermigli's Doctrine of Man and Grace.* Leiden: Brill, 1976.

Duffy, Eamon. *Reformation Divided: Catholics, Protestants and the Conversion of England.* London: Bloomsbury, 2017.

Ehmann, Johannes. *Luther, Türken und Islam: Eine Untersuchung zum Türken- und Islambild Martin Luthers (1515–1546).* Gütersloh: Gütersloher Verlagshaus, 2008.

Eickelman, Dale. "Inside the Islamic Reformation," *The Wilson Quarterly* 22 (1998): 80–89.

Elton, Geoffrey R. *Reformation Europe: 1517–1559.* Oxford: Blackwell, 1985.

Elyada, Aya. "Protestant Scholars and Yiddish Studies in Early Modern Europe," *Past & Present* 203 (2009): 69–98.

El-Zein, Amira. *Islam, Arabs, and the Intelligent World of the Jinn.* Syracuse: Syracuse University Press, 2009.

Emilsen, William. "Calvin on Islam," *Uniting Church Studies* 17/1 (2011): 69–85.

Enfield, William. *The History of Philosophy from the Earliest Period: Drawn up from Brucker's Historia Critica Philosophiae.* London, 1791.

Erginbaş, Vefa (Ed.). *Ottoman Sunnism: New Perspectives.* Edinburgh: Edinburgh University Press, 2019.

Ess, Josef van. "Ibn ar-Rewandī, or the Making of an Image," *Al-Abḥāth* 27 (1978–79): 5–26.

———. "Fatum Mahumetanum. Schicksal und Freiheit im Islam," in *Kleine Schriften by Josef van Ess.* Ed. Hinrich Biesterfeldt, vol. 3. Leiden: Brill, 2018.

Estakhr, Mehdi. *The Place of Zoroaster in History: Using the Cult Personality as a Literary Source of Authority in the Western Tradition.* Queenston: Edwin Mellen Press, 2012.

Ewing, Katherine Pratt and Ilona Gerbakher. "The Qalandariyya: From the Mosque to the Ruin in Poetry, Place, and Practice," in *Routledge Handbook on Sufism.* Ed. Lloyd Ridgeon. New York: Routledge, 2020.

Facca, Danilo. *Early Modern Aristotelianism and the Making of Philosophical Disciplines.* London: Bloomsbury, 2020.

Fischer-Galati, Stephen. *Ottoman Imperialism and German Protestantism, 1521–1555.* Cambridge: Harvard University Press, 1972.

Francisco, Adam S. *Martin Luther and Islam: A Study in Sixteenth-Century Polemics and Apologetics.* Leiden: Brill, 2007.

Frazee, Charles A. *Catholic and Sultans: The Church and the Ottoman Empire, 1453–1923.* Cambridge: Cambridge University Press, 1983.

Frymire, John M. *The Primacy of the Postils: Catholics, Protestants, and the Dissemination of Ideas in Early Modern Germany.* Leiden: Brill, 2010.

Fumaroli, Marc. *The Republic of Letters.* Trans. Lara Vergnaud. New Haven: Yale University Press, 2018.

Garcia, Humberto. *Islam and the English Enlightenment, 1670–1840.* Baltimore: Johns Hopkins University Press, 2012.

Gawthrop, Richard L. *Pietism and the Making of Eighteenth-Century Prussia.* Cambridge: Cambridge University Press, 1993.

Gerdmar, Anders. *Roots of Theological Anti-Semitism: German Biblical Interpretation and the Jews, from Herder and Semler to Kittel and Bultmann.* Leiden: Brill, 2009.

Gindhart, Marion and Ursula Kundert (Eds). *Disputatio 1200–1800: Form, Funktion und Wirkung eines Leitmediums Universitärer Wissenskultur.* Berlin: De Gruyter, 2010.

Glei, Reinhold F. and Roberto Tottoli. *Ludovico Marracci at Work: The Evolution of His Latin Translation of the Qur'an in the Light of His Newly Discovered Manuscripts.* Wiesbaden: Harrassowitz Verlag, 2016.

Goffman, Daniel. *The Ottoman Empire and Early Modern Europe.* Cambridge: Cambridge University Press, 2002.

Goldenbaum, Ursula. "Leibniz as a Lutheran," in *Leibniz, Mysticism, and Religion.* Eds. Allison Courdert, Richard H. Popkin, and Gordon M. Weiner. Dordrecht: Kluwer, 1998.

Goldfeld, Isaiah. "The Illiterate Prophet (*nabī al-ummī*): An Inquiry into the Development of a Dogma in Islamic Tradition," *Der Islam* 57 (1980): 58–67.

Gow, Andrew Colin. *The Red Jews: Antisemitism in an Apocalyptic Age 1200–1600.* Leiden: Brill, 1995.

———— with Jeremy Fradkin. "Protestantism and Non-Christian Religions," in *The Oxford Handbook of the Protestant Reformations*. Ed. Ulinka Rublack. Oxford: Oxford University Press, 2016.

Graetz, Heinrich. *Influence of Judaism on the Protestant Reformation*. Trans. Simon Tuska. Cincinnati: Bloch & Co, 1867.

Grafton, David. *Piety, Politics, and Power: Lutherans Encountering Islam in the Middle East*. Eugene: Pickwick Publications, 2009.

————. "Martin Luther's Sources on the Turk and Islam in the Midst of the Fear of Ottoman Imperialism," *The Muslim World* 107/4 (2017): 665–83.

Gran, Peter. *Islamic Roots of Capitalism: Egypt, 1760–1840*. Texas: University of Texas Press, 1979.

Greengrass, Mark. *The European Reformation c.1500–1618*. London: Longman, 1998.

————. *Christendom Destroyed: Europe 1517–1648*. New York: Penguin, 2015.

Gregory, Brad S. *The Unintended Reformation: How a Religious Revolution Secularized Society*. Cambridge: Harvard University Press, 2015.

Grimmsmann, Damaris. *Krieg mit dem Wort: Türkenpredigten des 16. Jahrhunderts im Alten Reich*. Berlin: De Gruyter, 2016.

Gritsch, E. W. *A History of Lutheranism*. Minneapolis: Fortress Press, 2010.

Guggisberg, Hans R. and Gottfried G. Krodel (Eds.). *Die Reformation in Deutschland und Europa: Interpretationen und Debatten*. Gütersloh: Gütersloher Verlagshaus, 1993.

Guibbory, Achsah A. *Christian Identity, Jews, and Israel in Seventeenth-Century England*. Oxford: Oxford University Press, 2010.

Gutas, Dimitri. *Greek Thought, Arabic Culture: The Graeco-Arabic Translation Movement in Baghdad and Early 'Abbāsid Society (2th–4th/8th–10th centuries)*. London: Routledge, 1999.

Hamilton, Alastair. "The Study of Islam in Early Modern Europe," *Archiv für Religionsgeschichte* 3/1 (2001): 169–82.

————. "A Lutheran Translator for the Qur'an. A Late Seventeenth-Century Quest," in *The Republic of Letters and the Levant*. Eds. Alastair Hamilton, Maurits H. Van Den Boogert, and Bart Westerweel. Leiden: Brill, 2005.

————. "'To Rescue the Honour of the Germans': Qur'an Translations by Eighteenth-and Early Nineteenth-Century German Protestants," *Journal of the Warburg and Courtauld Institutes* 77 (2014): 173–209.

————. "Lutheran Islamophiles in Eighteenth-century Germany," in *For the Sake of Learning*. Eds. Ann Blairs and Anja-Silvia Goeing. Leiden: Brill, 2016.

————. "After Marracci: The Reception of Ludovico Marracci's Edition of the Qur'an in Northern Europe from the Late Seventeenth to the Early Nineteenth Centuries," *Journal of Qur'anic Studies* 20/3 (2018): 175–92.

————. "Andreas Acoluthus," in *Christian-Muslim Relations: A Bibliographical History*. Eds. David Thomas and John Chesworth, vol. 14. Leiden: Brill, 2020.

Hampson, Daphne. *Christian Contradictions: The Structures of Lutheran and Catholic Thought*. Cambridge: Cambridge University Press, 2001.

Hanna, Nelly. *Ottoman Egypt and the Emergence of the Modern World 1500–1800*. Cairo: The American University in Cairo Press, 2014.

Heumann, Christoph August. *Acta philosophorum, das ist: Gründliche Nachrichten aus der Historia philosophica.* Halle: Rengerischen Buchhandl, 1715.

Heyd, Michael. *"Be Sober and Reasonable": The Critique of Enthusiasm in the Seventeenth and Early Eighteenth Centuries.* Leiden: Brill, 1995.

Hicks, Rosemary R. "Comparative Religion and the Cold War Transformation of Indo-Persian "Mysticism" into Liberal Islamic Modernity," in *Secularism and Religion-Making.* Eds. Markus Dressler and Arvind-Pal S. Mandair. Oxford: Oxford University Press, 2011.

Hinlicky, Paul R. "A Leibnizian Transformation? Reclaiming the Theodicy of Faith," in *Transformations in Luther's Reformation Theology: Historical and Contemporary Reflections.* Eds. C. Helmer and B. K. Holm. Leipzig: Evangelische Verlagsanstalt, 2011.

Höfert, Almut. *Den Feind beschreiben: "Türkengefahr" und europäisches Wissen über das Osmanische Reich 1450–1600.* Frankfurt: Campus Verlag, 2003.

Husain, Adnan and Katherine Elizabeth Fleming (Eds.). *A Faithful Sea: The Religious Cultures of the Mediterranean, 1200–1700.* Oxford: Oneworld, 2007.

İnalcık, Halil. "Dervish and Sultan: An Analysis of the Otman Baba Vilayet-namesi," in *The Middle East and the Balkans under the Ottoman Empire: Essays on Economy and Society.* Ed. Halil İnalcık. Bloomington: Indiana University Turkish Studies, 1999.

Isom-Verhaaren, Christine. "An Ottoman Report about Martin Luther and the Emperor: New Evidence of the Ottoman Interest in the Protestant Challenge to the Power of Charles V," *Turcica* 28 (1996): 299–317.

Israel, Jonathan. *Enlightenment Contested: Philosophy, Modernity, and the Emancipation of Man 1670–1752.* Oxford: Oxford University Press, 2006.

Iyigun, Murat. "Luther and Suleyman," *The Quarterly Journal of Economics* 123/4 (2008): 1465–94.

Johnson, Gregory R. "The Tree of Melancholy: Kant on Philosophy and Enthusiasm," in *Kant and the New Philosophy of Religion.* Eds. Chris L. Firestone and Stephen Palmquist. Bloomington: Indiana University Press, 2006.

Jung, Dietrich. "Islamic Studies and Religious Reform: Ignaz Goldziher—A Crossroads of Judaism, Christianity, and Islam," *Der Islam* 90/1 (2013): 106–26.

Jung, Martin H. *Reformation und Konfessionelles Zeitalter, 1517–1648.* Göttingen: Vandenhoeck & Ruprecht, 2012.

Kalmar, Ian. *Early Orientalism: Imagined Islam and the Notion of Sublime Power.* New York: Routledge, 2011.

Karabela, Mehmet. *The Development of Dialectic and Argumentation Theory in Post-Classical Islamic Intellectual History*, PhD dissertation. Montreal: McGill University, 2010.

———. "Beşir Fuad and His Opponents: The Form of a Debate over Literature and Truth in Nineteenth-Century Istanbul," *The Journal of Turkish Literature* 8 (2011): 96–106.

———. "Review of Rémi Brague, The Legend of the Middle Ages: Philosophical Explorations of Medieval Christianity, Judaism, and Islam," *Philosophy East and West* 62/4 (2012): 605–08.

——. "Cedel ile Burhān arasında: İbn Ṭufeyl'in Ḥayy b. Yaḳẓān adlı eseri üzerinden klasik dönem sonrası İslam düşünce tarihini okumak," *Ankara Üniversitesi İlahiyat Fakültesi Dergisi* 54/2 (2013): 77–93.

——. "The Dialectical Discourse in Classical Ottoman Literature: The Beloved between Lover and Rival in the Game of Love," *The Journal of Turkish Literature* 10 (2013): 7–19.

——. "Ibn al-Rāwandī," in *Oxford Encyclopaedia of Islam, Philosophy, Science and Technology*. Ed. İbrahim Kalın. Oxford: Oxford University Press, 2014.

——. "Review of the Art of Dialectic between Dialogue and Rhetoric," *Journal of the History of Philosophy* 52/4 (2014): 841–42.

——. "Lovers in the Age of the Beloveds: The Classical Ottoman Divan Literature and the Dialectical Tradition," in *Beloved: Love and Languishing in Middle Eastern Literatures and Cultures*. Eds. Alireza Korangy, Hanadi al-Samman and Michael Beard. London: I.B. Tauris, 2018.

Karamustafa, Ahmet. *God's Unruly Friends: Dervish Groups in the Islamic Middle Period 1200–1550*. Salt Lake City: University of Utah Press, 1994.

Kármán, Gábor. "Johann Ulrich Wallich," in *Christian-Muslim Relations: A Bibliographical History. Volume 9, Western and Southern Europe (1600–1700)*. Eds. David Thomas and John A. Chesworth. Leiden: Brill, 2017.

Karpuk, Susan. "Cataloging Seventeenth- and Eighteenth-Century German Dissertations: Guidelines and Observations," *Cataloguing and Classification Quarterly* 48/4 (2010): 303–14.

Kaufmann, Thomas. *Luther's Jews: A Journey into Anti-Semitism*. Trans. Lesley Sharpe and Jeremy Noakes. Oxford: Oxford University Press, 2017.

——. "Luthers Sicht auf Judentum und Islam," in *Der Reformator Martin Luther 2017: Eine wissenschaftliche und gedenkpolitische Bestandsaufnahme*. Ed. Heinz Schilling. Munich: De Gruyter, 2015.

——. *Geschichte der Reformation*. Frankfurt: Suhrkamp, 2009.

Keller, Marcus and Javier Irigoyen-García (Eds.). *The Dialectics of Orientalism in Early Modern Europe*. London: Palgrave Macmillan, 2018.

Kittler, Friedrich A. *Aufschreibesysteme 1800/1900*. Munich: Wilhelm Fink, 1985.

Klein, Dietrich. "Hugo Grotius' Position on Islam as Described in *De veritate religionis Christianae, Liber VI*," in *Socinianism and Arminianism: Antitrinitarians, Calvinists and Cultural Exchange in Seventeenth-Century Europe*. Eds. Martin Mulsow and Jan Rohls. Leiden: Brill, 2005.

Klein, Lawrence Eliot and Anthony J. La Vopa (Eds.). *Enthusiasm and Enlightenment Europe, 1650–1850*. San Marino: Huntington Library, 1998.

Kling, David William. *A History of Christian Conversion*. Oxford: Oxford University Press, 2020.

Knox, Ronald Arbuthnott. *Enthusiasm: A Chapter in the History of Religion, with Special Reference to the XVII and XVIII Centuries*. Oxford: Oxford University Press, 1950.

Koch, Ernst. *Das konfessionelle Zeitalter-Katholizismus, Luthertum, Calvinismus (1563–1675)*. Leipzig: Evangelische Verlagsanstalt, 2000.

Kolb, Robert. *For All the Saints: Changing Perceptions of Martyrdom and Sainthood in the Lutheran Reformation*. Macon: Mercer University Press, 1987.

Komorowski, Manfred. "Research on Early German Dissertations: A Report on Work in Progress," in *The German Book 1450–1750: Studies Presented to David L. Paisey in His Retirement*. Eds. John L. Flood and William A. Kelly. London: British Library, 1995.

Kors, Alan Charles. *Atheism in France, 1650–1729, Volume I: The Orthodox Sources of Disbelief*. Princeton: Princeton University Press, 1990.

Krstić, Tijana. *Contested Conversions to Islam Narratives of Religious Change in the Early Modern Ottoman Empire*. Stanford: Stanford University Press, 2011.

Kruse, Jens-Martin. *Universitätstheologie und Kirchenreform: Die Anfänge der Reformation in Wittenberg, 1516–1522*. Mainz-am-Rhein: Philipp von Zabern, 2002.

Kuehn, Manfred. *Kant: A Biography*. Cambridge: Cambridge University Press, 2001.

———. "Kant's Teachers in the Exact Sciences," in *Kant and the Sciences*. Ed. Eric Watkins. Oxford: Oxford University Press, 2001.

Kurzman, Charles and Michaelle Browers (Eds.). *An Islamic Reformation?* Lanham: Lexington, 2004.

Landolt, Hermann. "Azīz-i Nasafī and the Essence-Existence Debate," in *Consciousness and Reality: Studies in Memory of Toshihiko Izutsu*. Eds. Sayyid Jalāl al-Dīn Āshtiyānī, Hideichi Matsubara, Takashi Iwami, and Akiro Matsumoto. Leiden: Brill, 2000.

Leaver, Robin A. *Bachs Theologische Bibliothek: Eine kritische Bibliographie*. Stuttgart: Hänssler, 1983.

———. "Johann Sebastian Bach and the Lutheran Understanding of Music," *Lutheran Quarterly* 16/1 (2002): 21–47.

———. "Bach's Mass: 'Catholic' or 'Lutheran'?" in *Exploring Bach's B-minor Mass*. Eds. Yo Tomita, Robin A. Leaver, and Jan Smaczny. Cambridge: Cambridge University Press, 2013.

———. "Churches," in *The Routledge Research Companion to Johann Sebastian Bach*. Ed. Robin A. Leaver. New York: Routledge, 2017.

Leibniz, Gottfried Wilhelm. *Sämtliche Schriften und Briefe*. Berlin: Akademie Verlag, 2005.

Leopold, A. M. and J. S. Jensen (Eds.). *Syncretism in Religion: A Reader*. New York: Routledge, 2004.

Leppin, Volker. *Antichrist und Jüngster Tag: Das Profil apokalyptischer Flugschriftenpublizistik im deutschen Luthertum 1548–1618*. Gütersloh: Gütersloher Verlagshaus, 1999.

Lindberg, Carter. *The European Reformations*. Oxford: Blackwell, 1996.

Lisy-Wagner, Laura. *Islam, Christianity and the Making of Czech Identity, 1453–1683*. Burlington: Ashgate, 2013.

Loimeier, Roman. "Is There Something like 'Protestant Islam'?" *Die Welt des Islams* 45/2 (2005): 216–54.

Loop, Jan. *Johann Heinrich Hottinger: Arabic and Islamic Studies in the Seventeenth Century*. Oxford: Oxford University Press, 2013.

———. "Introduction: The Qur'an in Europe—The European Qur'an," *Journal of Qur'anic Studies* 20/3 (2018): 1–20.

———. "Islam and European Enlightenment," in *Christian-Muslim Relations: A Bibliographical History*. Eds. David Thomas and John Chesworth with al., vol. 13. Leiden: Brill, 2019.

———— with Alastair Hamilton and Charles Burnett (Eds.). *The Teaching and Learning of Arabic in Early Modern Europe*. Leiden: Brill, 2017.

Lovejoy, David S. *Religious Enthusiasm in the New World: Heresy to Revolution*. Cambridge: Harvard University Press, 1985.

MacCulloch, Diarmaid. *Reformation: Europe's House Divided 1490–1700*. London: Penguin, 2003.

————. *All Things Made New: The Reformation and Its Legacy*. Oxford: Oxford University Press, 2016.

Mahmood, Saba. "Secularism, Hermeneutics and Empire: The Politics of Islamic Reformation," *Public Culture* 18/2 (2006): 323–47.

Mäkinen, Virpi (Ed.). *Lutheran Reformation and the Law*. Leiden: Brill, 2006.

Malcolm, Noel. "The Study of Islam in Early Modern Europe: Obstacles and Missed Opportunities," in *Antiquarianism and Intellectual Life in Europe and China, 1500–1800*. Eds. Peter N. Miller and Francois Louis. Ann Arbor: The University of Michigan Press, 2012.

————. *Useful Enemies: Islam and the Ottoman Empire in Western Political Thought 1450–1750*. Oxford: Oxford University Press, 2019.

————. "Islam as a 'Rational' Religion: Early Modern European Views," in *Scholarship between Europe and the Levant: Essays in Honour of Alastair Hamilton*. Eds. Jan Loop and Jill Kraye. Leiden: Brill, 2020.

Manuel, Frank E. *The Broken Staff: Judaism through Christian Eyes*. Cambridge: Harvard University Press, 1992.

Marchand, Suzanne L. *German Orientalism in the Age of Empire: Religion, Race, and Scholarship*. Cambridge: Cambridge University Press, 2009.

Marshall, Peter. *1517: Martin Luther and the Invention of the Reformation*. Oxford: Oxford University Press, 2017.

Marti, Hanspeter. *Philosophische Dissertationen deutscher Universitäten, 1660–1750: Eine Auswahlbibliographie*. Munich: K.G. Saur, 1982.

Matar, Nabil. *Islam in Britain, 1558–1685*. Cambridge: Cambridge University Press, 1998.

————. *Europe through Arab Eyes, 1578–1727*. New York: Columbia University Press, 2008.

————. *Henry Stubbe and the Beginnings of Islam*. New York: Columbia University Press, 2014.

————. "The 2018 Josephine Waters Bennett Lecture: The Protestant Reformation through Arab Eyes, 1517–1698," *Renaissance Quarterly* 72 (2019): 771–815.

Matthee, Rudi. "Safavid Iran and the "Turkish Question" or How to Avoid a War on Multiple Fronts," *Iranian Studies* 52/3–4 (2019): 513–42.

Matthias, Markus. "Pietism and Protestant Orthodoxy," in *A Companion to German Pietism, 1660–1800*. Ed. Douglas Shantz. Leiden: Brill, 2014.

Mayer, Thomas F. (Ed.). *Reforming Reformation: Catholic Christendom, 1300–1700*. Burlington: Ashgate, 2012.

McGrath, Alister E. *The Intellectual Origins of the European Reformation*. Oxford: Blackwell, 1987.

Mee, Jon. *Dangerous Enthusiasm: William Blake and the Culture of Radicalism in the 1790s*. Oxford: Clarendon Press, 1992.

Meggitt, Justin J. *Early Quakers and Islam: Slavery, Apocalyptic and Christian-Muslim Encounters in the Seventeenth Century*. Eugene: Wipf & Stock, 2016.

Meserve, Margaret. *Empires of Islam in Renaissance Historical Thought.* Cambridge: Harvard University Press, 2008.

———. Miller, Gregory J. "Islam," in *The Dictionary of Luther and the Lutheran Traditions.* Ed. Timothy J. Wengert. Grand Rapids: Baker Academic, 2017.

———. *The Turks and Islam in Reformation Germany.* New York: Routledge, 2017.

———. "The Turks," in *Martin Luther in Context.* Ed. David M. Whitford. Cambridge: Cambridge University Press, 2018.

Mills, Simon. *A Commerce of Knowledge: Trade, Religion, and Scholarship between England and the Ottoman Empire, 1600–1760.* Oxford: Oxford University Press, 2020.

Minkov, Anton. *Conversion to Islam in the Balkans: Kisve bahası Petitions and Ottoman Social Life: 1670–1730.* Leiden: Brill, 2004.

Moeller, Bernd. *Deutschland im Zeitalter der Reformation.* Göttingen: Vandenhoeck & Ruprecht, 1981.

Moeller, Bernd and Bruno Jahn. *Deutsche Biographische Enzyklopädie der Theologie und der Kirchen.* Munich: K. G. Saur, 2005.

Moosa, Matti. *Extremist Shiites: The Ghulat Sects.* Syracuse: Syracuse University Press, 1988.

Mortimer, Sarah. "Early Modern Socinianism and Unitarianism," in *The Oxford Handbook of Early Modern Theology, 1600–1800.* Eds. Ulrich L. Lehner, Richard A. Muller, and A. G. Roeber. Oxford: Oxford University Press, 2016.

Mugnai, Massimo, Han van Ruler, and Martin Wilson (Eds.). *Leibniz: Dissertation on Combinatorial Art.* Oxford: Oxford University Press, 2020.

Muller, Richard A. "J. J. Rambach and the Dogmatics of Scholastic Pietism," *Consensus* 16/2 (1990): 7–27.

———. "The Problem of Protestant Scholasticism: A Review and Definition," in *Reformation and Scholasticism: An Ecumenical Enterprise.* Eds. W. J. van Asselt and Eef Dekker. Grand Rapids: Baker Academic, 2001.

———. "Reformation, Orthodoxy, "Christian Aristotelianism," and the Eclecticism of Early Modern Philosophy," *Dutch Review of Church History* 81/3 (2001): 306–25.

———. *Post-Reformation Reformed Dogmatics: The Rise and Development of Reformed Orthodoxy, ca. 1520–1725.* Grand Rapids: Baker Academic, 2003.

Mullett, Michael A. *Martin Luther.* London: Routledge, 2004.

Mulsow, Martin. "Socinianism, Islam and the Radical Uses of Arabic Scholarship," *Al-Qanṭara* 31/2 (2010): 549–86.

———. "Socinianism, Islam, and the Origins of Radical Enlightenment," in *Religious Obedience and Political Resistance in the Early Modern World: Jewish, Christian and Islamic Philosophers Addressing the Bible.* Ed. Luisa Simonutti. Turnhout: Brepols, 2014.

———. *Enlightenment Underground: Radical Germany, 1680–1720.* Charlottesville: University of Virginia Press, 2015.

———. "Antitrinitarians and Conversion to Islam: Adam Neuser Reads Murad b. Abdullah in Ottoman Istanbul," in *Conversion and Islam in the Early*

Modern Mediterranean: The Lure of the Other. Ed. Claire Norton. New York: Routledge, 2017.

———. *Radikale Frühaufklärung in Deutschland 1680–1720.* Göttingen: Wallstein Verlag, 2018.

——— with Jan Rohls (Eds.). *Socinianism and Arminianism: Antitrinitarians, Calvinists and Cultural Exchange in Seventeenth-Century Europe.* Leiden: Brill, 2005.

Musa, Aisha Y. *Ḥadīth as Scripture: Discussions on the Authority of Prophetic Traditions in Islam.* New York: Palgrave Macmillan, 2008.

———. "The Qur'anists," *Religion Compass* 4/1 (2010): 12–21.

Nüssel, Friederike. *Bund und Versöhnung: zur Begründung der Dogmatik bei Johann Franz Buddeus.* Göttingen: Vandenhoeck & Ruprecht: 1996.

Oberman, Heiko A. "Simul Gemitus et Raptus: Luther and Mysticism," in *The Reformation in Medieval Perspective.* Ed. Steven Ozment. Chicago: Quadrangle Books, 1971.

———. *The Two Reformations.* New Haven: Yale University Press, 2003.

Ocak, Ahmet Yaşar. "Kalenderi Dervishes and Ottoman Administration from the Fourteenth to the Sixteenth Centuries," in *Manifestations of Sainthood in Islam.* Eds. Grace M. Smith and Carl Ernst. Istanbul: Isis Press, 1993.

Ocker, Christopher. *Luther, Conflict, and Christendom: Reformation Europe and Christianity in the West.* Cambridge: Cambridge University Press, 2018.

Ormsby, Eric. *Theodicy in Islamic Thought: The Dispute Over Al-Ghazālī's Best of All Possible Worlds.* Princeton: Princeton University Press, 1984.

Osella, Filippo and Caroline Osella (Eds.). *Islamic Reform in South Asia.* Cambridge: Cambridge University Press, 2013.

Ozment, Steven. *Mysticism and Dissent: Religious Ideology and Social Protest in the Sixteenth Century.* New Haven: Yale University Press, 1973.

Öztürk, Yaşar Nuri. *Kur'andaki İslam.* Istanbul: Yeni Boyut, 1999.

Packull, Werner O. "Luther and Medieval Mysticism in the Context of Recent Historiography," *Renaissance and Reformation* 6/2 (1982): 79–93.

Pailin, David A. *Attitudes to Other Religions: Comparative Religion in Seventeenth- and Eighteenth-Century Britain.* Manchester: Manchester University Press, 1984.

Pangritz, Andreas. "Martin Luthers Stellung zu Judentum und Islam," in *Arbeitsbuch Religion und Geschichte: Das Christentum im interkulturellen Gedächtnis.* Ed. Harry Noormann. Stuttgart: Verlag, 2013.

Pannier, Jacques. "Calvin et les Turcs," *Revue historique* 180 (1937): 268–86.

Parker, Charles H. *Global Interactions in the Early Modern Age, 1400–1800.* Cambridge: Cambridge University Press, 2010.

Pearce, Joseph. *Through Shakespeare's Eyes: Seeing the Catholic Presence in the Plays.* San Francisco: Ignatius Press, 2010.

Pettegree, Andrew. *The Early Reformation in Europe.* Cambridge: Cambridge University Press, 1992.

———. *Brand Luther: 1517, Printing, and the Making of the Reformation.* New York: Penguin, 2015.

Platt, John. *Reformed Thought and Scholasticism: The Arguments for the Existence of God in Dutch Theology, 1575–1650.* Leiden: Brill, 1982.

Pocock, J. G. A. "Enthusiasm: The Anti-Self of Enlightenment," *Huntington Library Quarterly* 60/1–2 (1998): 7–28.

Poma, Andrea. *The Impossibility and Necessity of Theodicy: The "Essais" of Leibniz.* Trans. Alice Spencer. Dordrecht: Springer, 2013.

Pozzo, Riccardo. "Kant e Weitenkampf: Una fonte ignorata della Allgemeine Naturgeschichte und Theorie des Himmels e della Prima Antinomia della ragion pura," *Rivista Di Storia Della Filosofia* 48/2 (1993): 283–323.

Preus, Robert. *The Inspiration of Scripture: A Study of the Theology of the 17th Century Lutheran Dogmatics.* St. Louis: Concordia Publishing House, 1955.

———. *The Theology of Post-Reformation Lutheranism: A Study of Theological Prolegomena.* St. Louis: Concordia Publishing House, 1970.

Quinn, Frederick. *The Sum of All Heresies: The Image of Islam in Western Thought.* Oxford: Oxford University Press, 2008.

Raffe, Alasdair. *The Culture of Controversy: Religious Arguments in Scotland, 1660–1714.* Woodbridge: Boydell Press, 2012.

Ragni, Alice. "Johannes Clauberg and the Search for the Initium Philosophiae: The Recovery of (Cartesian) Metaphysics," in *The Oxford Handbook of Descartes and Cartesianism.* Eds. Steven Nadler, Tad M. Schmaltz, and Delphine Antoine-Mahut. Oxford: Oxford University Press, 2019.

Rehlinghaus, Franziska. "Der Grenzbereich zwischen Wissen und Glauben: Zur Geschichte des deutschen Schicksalsbegriffs," *Archiv für Begriffsgeschichte* 55 (2013): 111–43.

Ridgeon, Llyod. *Persian Metaphysics and Mysticism: Selected Works of ʿAzīz Nasafī.* Richmond: Curzon Press, 2002.

Ringer, Monica. *Pious Citizens: Reforming Zoroastrianism in India and Iran.* Syracuse: University of Syracuse Press, 2011.

Rittgers, Ronald K. *The Reformation of the Keys: Confession, Conscience, and Authority in Sixteenth-Century Germany.* Cambridge: Harvard University Press, 2004.

Rittgers, Ronald K. and Vincent Evener (Eds.). *Protestants and Mysticism in Reformation Europe.* Leiden: Brill, 2019.

Roberson, B. A. (Ed.). *Shaping the Current Islamic Reformation.* London: Frank Cass, 2003.

Rorem, Paul. "Martin Luther's Christocentric Critique of Pseudo-Dionysian Spirituality," *Lutheran Quarterly* 11 (1997): 291–307.

Rowland, Christopher. "Scripture," in *The Cambridge Companion to Christian Political Theology.* Eds. Craig Hovey and Elizabeth Phillips. Cambridge: Cambridge University Press, 2015.

Rublack, Ulinka. *Reformation Europe.* Cambridge: Cambridge University Press, 2005.

Rummel, Erika. *The Humanist-Scholastic Debate in the Renaissance and Reformation.* Cambridge: Harvard University Press, 1995.

Said, Edward. *Orientalism.* New York: Vintage Book, 1978.

Salzmann, Ariel. *Tocqueville in the Ottoman Empire: Rival Paths to the Modern State.* Leiden: Brill, 2004.

Scaer, David P. "Johann Sebastian Bach as Lutheran Theologian," *Concordia Theological Quarterly* 68 (2004): 319–40.

Schilling, Heinz. *Martin Luther: Rebell in einer Zeit des Umbruchs.* Munich: C. H. Beck, 2012.

———. *1517: Weltgeschichte eines Jahres.* Munich: C. H. Beck, 2017.

——— with Silvana Siedel Menchi (Eds.). *The Protestant Reformation in a Context of Global History: Religious Reforms and World Civilizations.* Bologna: Società editrice il Mulino/Berlin: Duncker & Humblot, 2017.

Schmitt, Carl. *Römischer Katholizismus und Politische Form.* Munich: Theatiner-Verlag, 1925.

Schnabel-Schüle, Helga. *Die Reformation 1495–1555: Politik mit Theologie und Religion.* Stuttgart: Reclam, 2006.

Schneider, Hans. *German Radical Pietism.* Translated by Gerald T. MacDonald. Lanham and Toronto: The Scarecrow Press, 2007.

Schorn-Schütte, Luise. *Die Reformation: Vorgeschichte, Verlauf, Wirkung.* Munich: Verlag, 1996.

Schönfeld, Martin. "Kant's Early Dynamics," in *A Companion to Kant.* Ed. Graham Bird. Oxford: Wiley-Blackwell, 2006.

Schramm, Brooks and Kirsi I. Stjerna (Eds.). *Martin Luther, The Bible, and The Jewish People: A Reader.* Minneapolis: Fortress Press, 2012.

Seidel, Robert. "Debating the Use of Academic Travel: Early Modern Disputations *De arte peregrinandi*," in *Artes Apodemicae and Early Modern Travel Culture, 1550–1700.* Eds. Karl A. E. Enenkel and Jan de Jon. Leiden: Brill, 2019.

Sezgin, Fuat. *Geschichte Des Arabischen Schrifttums: Qur'ānwissenschaften, Ḥadīṯ Geschichte, Fiqh, Dogmatik, Mystik. Bis ca. 430 H.* Leiden: Brill, 1967.

Shantz, Douglas (Ed.). *An Introduction to German Pietism: Protestant Renewal at the Dawn of Modern Europe.* Baltimore: The Johns Hopkins University Press, 2013.

———. *A Companion to German Pietism, 1660–1800.* Leiden: Brill, 2014.

Slomp, Jan. "Calvin and the Turks," *Studies in Interreligious Dialogue* 19/1 (2009): 50–65.

Smith, Charlotte Colding. *Images of Islam, 1453–1600: Turks in Germany and Central Europe.* London: Pickering and Chatto, 2014.

Soergel, Philip M. *Wondrous in His Saints: Counter-Reformation Propaganda in Bavaria.* Berkeley: University of California Press, 1993.

———. "Miracle, Magic, and Disenchantment in Early Modern Germany," in *Envisioning Magic: Princeton Seminar and Symposium.* Eds. Peter Schäfer and Hans Kippenberg. Leiden: Brill, 1997.

Sorkin, David Jan. *The Religious Enlightenment: Protestants, Jews, and Catholics from London to Vienna.* Princeton: Princeton University Press, 2008.

Spener, Philip Jacob. *Pia Desideria.* Trans. and Ed. Theodore G. Tappert. Minneapolis: Fortress Press, 1964.

Spitta, Philipp. *Johann Sebastian Bach: His Work and Influence on the Music of Germany, 1685–1750.* 2 vols. London, 1899.

Steinmetz, David. *Luther and Staupitz: An Essay in the Intellectual Origins of the Protestant Reformation.* Durham: Duke University Press, 1980.

Stewart, Quentin D. *Lutheran Patristic Catholicity: The Vincentian Canon and the Consensus Patrum in Lutheran Orthodoxy.* Verlag: Münster, 2015.

Stoeffler, Fred. Ernest *German Pietism During the Eighteenth Century*. Leiden: Brill, 1973.

Strom, Jonathan. *German Pietism and the Problem of Conversion*. Pennsylvania: The Pennsylvania State University Press, 2018.

Stroumsa, Sarah. *Freethinkers of Medieval Islam: Ibn al-Rāwandī, Abū Bakr al-Rāzī, and Their Impact on Islamic Thought*. Brill: Leiden, 1999.

Subrahmanyam, Sanjay. *Empires between Islam and Christianity, 1500–1800*. New York: SUNY Press, 2019.

Sukidi. "Max Weber's Remarks on Islam: The Protestant Ethics among Muslim Puritans," *Islam and Christian-Muslim Relations* 17/2 (2006): 195–205.

Taji-Farouki, Suha (Ed.). *Modern Muslim Intellectuals and the Qur'an*. Oxford: Oxford University Press, 2004.

Tamburello, Dennis E. *Union with Christ: John Calvin and the Mysticism of St. Bernard*. Louisville: Westminster John Knox, 1994.

———. "The Protestant Reformers on Mysticism," in *The Wiley-Blackwell Companion to Christian Mysticism*. Ed. Julia Lamm. Malden: Wiley-Blackwell, 2013.

Terpstra, Nicholas (Ed.). *Global Reformations: Transforming Early Modern Religions, Societies, and Cultures*. New York: Routledge, 2019.

"The Traveling Idea of Islamic Protestantism: A Study of Iranian Luthers," *Islam and Christian-Muslim Relations* 16/4 (2005): 401–12.

Thomas, David and John A. Chesworth (Eds.). *Christian-Muslim Relations: A Bibliographical History*. Leiden: Brill, 2009–present.

Tolan, John. *Saracens: Islam in the Medieval European Imagination*. Columbia: Columbia University Press, 2002.

———. *Faces of Muhammad: Western Perceptions of the Prophet of Islam from the Middle Ages to Today*. Princeton: Princeton University Press, 2019.

Tommasi, Francesco Valerio. "Zwischen radikalem Aristotelismus und lutherischer Orthodoxie: Die These der doppelten Wahrheit in der Altdorfer Schule," *Archiv für Begriffsgeschichte* 55 (2013): 61–74.

Tommasino, Pier Mattia. *The Venetian Qur'an: A Renaissance Companion to Islam*. Trans. Sylvia Notini. Pennsylvania: University of Pennsylvania Press, 2018.

Toomer, G. J. *Eastern Wisedome and Learning: The Study of Arabic in Seventeenth-Century England*. Oxford: Clarendon Press, 1996.

Toscano, Alberto. *Fanaticism: On the Uses of an Idea*. London: Verso, 2017.

Tracy, James D. *Europe's Reformations, 1450–1650: Doctrine, Politics, and Community*. Oxford: Rowman and Littlefield, 1999.

Tramontana, Felicita. "An Unusual Setting: Interaction between Protestants and Catholics in the Ottoman Empire," in *Protestant Majorities and Minorities in Early Modern Europe: Confessional Boundaries and Contested Identities*. Eds. Simon J. G. Burton, Michal Choptiany, and Piotr Wilczek. Göttingen: Vandenhoeck & Ruprecht, 2019.

Trueman, Carl R. and R. Scott Clark (Eds.). *Protestant Scholasticism: Essays in Reassessment*. Eugene: Wipf & Stock, 2006.

Tucker, Susie I. *Enthusiasm: A Study in Semantic Change*. Cambridge: Cambridge University Press, 1972.

Truxillo, Charles A. *By the Sword and the Cross: The Historical Evolution of the Catholic World Monarchy in Spain and the New World 1492–1825.* Connecticut: Greenwood Press, 2001.

Velde, Dolf te. "Reformed Theology and Scholasticism," in *The Cambridge Companion to Reformed Theology.* Eds. Paul T. Nimmo and David A. S. Fergusson. Cambridge: Cambridge University Press, 2016.

Veltri, Giuseppe. "Academic Debates on the Jews in Wittenberg: The Protestant Literature on Rituals, the *Dissertationes* and the Writings of the Hebraists Theodor Dassow and Andreas Sennert," *European Journal of Jewish Studies* 6/1 (2012): 123–46.

Vitkus, Daniel J. "Early Modern Orientalism: Representations of Islam in Sixteenth- and Seventeenth-Century Europe," in *Western Views of Islam in Medieval and Early Modern Europe.* Eds. David Blanks and Michael Frassetto. New York: St. Martin's Press, 1999.

Vrolijk, Arnoud and Richard van Leeuwen. *Arabic Studies in the Netherlands: A Short History in Portraits, 1580–1950.* Trans. Alastair Hamilton. Leiden: Brill, 2014.

Waite, Gary. "Menno and Muhammad: Anabaptists and Mennonites Reconsider Islam, 1570–1650," *Sixteenth Century Journal* 41 (2010): 995–1016.

———. *Jews and Muslims in Seventeenth-Century Discourse: From Religious Enemies to Allies and Friends.* New York: Routledge, 2018.

———. "'Turning Turke the Anabaptist Way': Muslims, Jews, Christian Spiritualists, and Polemical Discourse in the Dutch Republic, c. 1570 to c. 1630," in *Global Reformations: Transforming Early Modern Religions, Societies, and Cultures.* Ed. Nicholas Terpstra. New York: Routledge, 2019.

Walker, D. P. "The Cessation of Miracles," in *Hermeticism and the Renaissance: Intellectual History and the Occult in Early Modern Europe.* Eds. Ingrid Merkel and Allen G. Debus. London: Associated University Press, 1988.

Walsham, Alexandra. "Miracles in Post-Reformation England," *Studies in Church History* 41 (2005): 273–306.

Weber, Hans Emil. *Der Einfluss der protestantischen Schulphilosophie auf die orthodox-lutherische Dogmatik.* Darmstadt: W. Buchgesellschaft, 1969.

Weber, Max. *Die protestantische Ethik und der Geist des Kapitalismus.* 3rd ed. Munich: Verlag, 2010.

Weigelt, Horst. *Spiritualistische Tradition im Protestantismus.* Berlin: Walter de Gruyter, 1973.

Wiesenfeldt, Gerhard. "Academic Writings and the Rituals of Early Modern Universities," *Intellectual History Review* 26:4 (2016): 447–60.

Wilbur, Earl Morse. *A History of Unitarianism: Socinianism and its Antecedents.* Cambridge: Harvard University Press, 1945.

Williams, Peter. *Bach: A Musical Biography.* Cambridge: Cambridge University Press, 2016.

Witte, John Jr. *Law and Protestantism: The Legal Teachings of the Lutheran Reformation.* Cambridge: Cambridge University Press, 2002.

———. "'The Law Written on the Heart': Natural Law and Equity in Early Lutheran Thought," in *Law and Religion: The Legal Teachings of the Protestant and Catholic.* Eds. Wim Decock, Jordan J. Ballor, Michael Germann, and Laurent Waelkens. Göttingen: Vandenhoeck & Ruprecht, 2014.

Wolff, Christian. *Philosophia rationalis sive logica, methodo scientifica.* Leipzig: Rengeriana, 1740.

Wriedt, Markus. "Mystik und Protestantismus—ein Widerspruch?" in *Mystik: Religion der Zukunft—Zukunft der Religion?* Ed. Johannes Schilling. Leipzig: Evangelische Verlagsanstalt, 2003.

Yıldırım, Rıza. "The Safavid-Qizilbash Ecumene and the Formation of the Qizilbash-Alevi Community in the Ottoman Empire, c. 1500–c. 1700," *Iranian Studies* 52 (2019): 449–83.

Zellentin, Holger M. *The Qur'an's Reformation of Judaism and Christianity: Return to the Origins.* New York: Routledge, 2019.

Index

Note: Page numbers followed by "n" denote endnotes.